PUCCINI

GIACOMO PUCCINI
(about 1920)

PUCCINI

A CRITICAL BIOGRAPHY

by

MOSCO CARNER

SECOND EDITION

HM

HOLMES & MEIER

NEW YORK

Published in the United States of America by
Holmes & Meier Publishers, Inc.
30 Irving Place
New York, NY 10003

This book has been printed on acid-free paper.

Library of Congress Cataloging in Publication Data

Carner, Mosco.
  Puccini: a critical biography.

  Bibliography: p.
  Includes indexes.
    1. Puccini, Giacomo, 1858–1924. 2. Composers—
Italy—Biography.
[ML410.P89C3 1977]   782.1′092′4[B]   76-30456
ISBN 0-8419-0302-6 (cl) (alk. pa.)
ISBN 0-8419-1172-X (pbk) (alk. pa.)

Manufactured in the United States of America

TO THE
MEMORY OF
HELEN

Contents

vii

Preface

To the critical biographer Puccini presents a fascinating subject for study—an artist who bore the authentic stamp of genius but who for some reason failed to cross the boundary into the realm of absolute greatness. If there was ever a 'border-line case', it is Puccini. Here was an operatic composer, endowed with a sense of the theatre that may rightly claim the epithet 'stupendous'; equipped with a technical *savoir faire* that with growing maturity attained sovereign mastery; born with a most original gift for lyrical melody that, bursting forth in his very first stage work, scarcely ever deserted him during his entire career and made his finest inspirations common musical property; dominating the opera houses of the world, great and small, with five out of the total of twelve works he wrote and thus qualifying for inclusion in the company of Mozart, Wagner, Verdi and Strauss. Puccini, it would appear, possessed all the prerequisites for a supreme musical dramatist—why was it not given to him to achieve this stature? Did his limitations reside in a restricted range in sheer creative imagination, or did they largely spring from peculiar twists in his mental make-up? These are some of the major questions which will occupy us in this book.

No less interesting are the curious vicissitudes his work suffered in the opinion of the musical world. For two-thirds of his career rapturous praise and fierce denunciation held the scales of judgment in a precarious balance. While large majority audiences of five continents have been acclaiming him ever since his early *Manon Lescaut*, critical opinion has been singularly reluctant to extend to him the recognition he deserves. Indeed, time was when in serious musical circles the subject of Puccini was held to be no less than taboo. Surprisingly enough, the most articulate anti-Puccinian phalanx was active, during the first decade or so of this century, in the composer's native country; but condemnation of his art and its ethos, or lack of it, was widespread. I myself still have vivid memories of the unmitigated hostility to his operas shown in the Vienna of my youth. Though the accidents of geography and history made the Austrian capital an ideal musical clearing-house between north and south, with a large opera-loving public that could scarcely be accused of a bias against Italian opera in general or Puccini in particular, there were factions to whom Puccini's name was a synonym for meretriciousness, false sentiment and brazen exploitation of the lower instincts. His art was dismissed as *kitsch*. No responsible critic would deny the element of truth contained in such gross exaggerations and enough will be said about it in this book. The first appreciable change in this negative attitude was brought about in the 1920s, by *Gianni Schicchi* and, notably, *Turandot*. Were these works from the same pen which had written the 'tear-jerkers' *La Bohème* and *Madam Butterfly*, and 'that brutal assault on our nerves', *Tosca*? This question was on the lips of every observant musician and intensive searchings of the heart started. Puccini began to appear to us in a new light. Symptomatic of this process was the appearance, in 1932, of a book by Richard Specht, an eminent Viennese critic, who devoted to Puccini, man and artist, what must be accounted the first study to claim comprehensive treatment allied to a critically sympathetic and highly perceptive approach. Significantly, Specht opened with the declaration that his book represented 'an admission of error' on his part and 'an act of atonement and expiation', words testifying to this author's intellectual honesty. However, writing a generation after Specht, I feel no cause to echo the sentiments expressed in his preamble. For in the intervening period our opinions of Puccini have travelled a long distance farther in his favour; partly, perhaps, because modern operatic aesthetics are no longer exclusively dominated—as during the early decades of this century, particularly in Central Europe and the Anglo-Saxon countries—by the Wagnerian concept of the mission of opera. The lyrical theatre as a moral institution, a vehicle for *Weltanschauungen* and meta-physical thought—these were the tenets to which traditional Italian opera could and would never subscribe. For all his so-called 'internationalism', the thorn in the flesh of his quondam Italian critics, Puccini never deserted the ground in which that tradition had grown; indeed, it is part of his strength that his roots are so deeply embedded in it. It was the young George Bernard Shaw who was one of the first to recognize this outside Italy: after the first London production of *Manon Lescaut* in 1894 he gave it as his opinion that 'Puccini looks to me more like the heir of Verdi than any of his rivals'. These were prophetic words. For in the period since Verdi's death, who is it who towers above a host of Italian opera composers and who in a sense is the only one to claim the *proxime accessit*? Puccini. In addition to those misapplied Wagnerian concepts, it was, I hazard the suggestion, the inability or the refusal of the majority of his critics to perceive him in this light which so long delayed recognition of his full stature. After the lapse of more than a century since Puccini's birth, and exactly fifty years since his death, we should at last be in a position to see him in historical perspective and assess his achievements with a measure of dis-passionate detachment denied to his contemporaries.

This book represents an attempt in that direction. It is the result of both practical experience and a close study of the 'problem' Puccini. My years as an operatic conductor brought me into almost daily, living contact with his operas and permitted me an insight into his stagecraft such as I should never have obtained from poring over his scores in my study or as a passive spectator in the opera house. After settling in England, I began to occupy myself more systematically with the man and his music but for a variety of reasons it was not until much later that circumstances became favourable for writing the kind of book I wished to write. There was one great difficulty I encountered, especially in the case of the three operas on which Puccini's world-wide fame largely rests: to erase from my mind the sediment left from innumerable performances heard, and to undertake my assignment in the spirit of an entirely fresh adventure.

My purpose in this critical biography is threefold: to present an account of Puccini's life as complete and accurate as lies within my ability on the basis of all the material accessible to me; to study the artist and his style against the background of his time, to subject the individual operas to an examination of their dramaturgy and music. Hence the division of this book into three parts: The Man—The Artist—The Work. Admittedly, such a scheme entails some overlapping and repetition but it perhaps presents the reader with a picture of the composer drawn in depth.

Part One is largely concerned with biographical facts. There are, it is true, small gaps to be filled in by fresh information that is bound to come to light but it is safe to say that it is unlikely to add intrinsically to what we already know of Puccini's external circumstances. With the exception of some stormy episodes, his life affords the biographer scant material of a sensational order; but the genesis of his operas, attended by perennial battles with his publisher and his various librettists, are punctuated by dramatic incidents. I have aspired to completeness, but trust I shall not be judged too ardent an adherent to the 'what porridge ate John Keats?' school of biography. In my reliance on previous writers I have been guided by Herodotus, who wrote that whereas it was his 'duty to record what I hear from other people, it is not my duty to believe them'. I applied this splendid maxim in particular to some Italian biographers who knew Puccini from close personal acquaintance over a number of years. Hero-worship allied to an understandable regard for the susceptibilities of people still living at the time resulted in highly coloured accounts and the suppression of important details. These sources had to be consulted with great circumspection though they contain a large amount of authentic information. I have also had personal interviews with people who were in touch with the composer either privately or in a professional capacity. My chief source material, however, has been the large collections of published letters by Puccini and a considerable number of letters reproduced in other publications; their sources are given in Appendix D. A great many letters of this second group appear here for the first time in any English book. They include letters by Ponchielli, Catalani, Puccini to Tamagno. Toscanini, Simoni and Magrini. Of special interest for the genesis of *La Bohème*, *Tosca* and *Madam Butterfly* are recently published letters from the correspondence between Puccini, Giacosa and Illica which enables us for the first time to obtain a direct view of the opposite camp in the ferocious tug-of-war fought between the composer and his two foremost poets. On many occasions I have allowed large excerpts from these and other letters to supplant my own narrative; a characteristic turn of phrase, a striking metaphor, an unusual simile, to say nothing of the shafts of wit and caustic irony aimed at one another by Puccini, Giulio Ricordi and Giacosa—all this makes lively reading and puts a point far more tellingly than I could ever have done in a paraphrase. (Of all letters that were available to me in the Italian original I have made my own translations.) Nor could I resist the temptation to sketch the personalities of some persons who played roles of variable importance in Puccini's career: the good-natured but obstinate Giacosa, the shrewdly diplomatic Ricordi, the choleric and irrepressible 'know-all' Sardou, the flamboyant Belasco and others. Equally new to the English reader will be the account given in the opening chapter of the musical dynasty of the Puccinis which counted five generations. For this I am greatly indebted to Signor Alfredo Bonaccorsi, whose detailed researches into Lucca's musical and social history, published in *Giacomo Puccini e i suoi antenati musicali* (Edizioni Curci, Milan, 1950), and whose personal communications to me, spared me the long hours I should have otherwise had to spend in Lucca's State Archives and the Conservatorio Luigi Boccherini. I am none the less indebted to Mr. Frank Walker, who during his intensive researches for his Verdi biography has come across valuable new information regarding Puccini; at no little inconvenience to himself he generously placed this material at my disposal and also gave me his kind permission to reproduce an unpublished letter by Teresa Stolz to Verdi, discovered by him in the archives of Sant' Agata.

Part Two attempts a general assessment of Puccini the musical dramatist in the context of his native operatic tradition and as the product of the general artistic climate of his period—the *fin de siècle*. I have also endeavoured to throw some fresh light on the personality of the artist and the mainspring of his creative processes. It is my conviction that no modern biographer can afford to ignore the results of 'depth psychology'. I have hence availed myself of its heuristic method in trying to elucidate the unconscious motives that in my opinion largely dictated Puccini's choice of subjects and that were responsible for a recurrent compulsive pattern displayed in his dramatic imagery. A close study of the kind of subjects he favoured and the kind he rejected, of the kind of treatment he gave to the first, and of certain biographical facts, suggested to me a line of thought developed in the middle chapter of Part Two. Needless to say, the reader is free to accept or refute what is intended as no more than a *working hypothesis*; other explanations are possible, for in studying an artist's unconscious drives and fantasies and their 'enactment' in his work, conjecture must frequently take the place of certainty. In order to clarify my ideas I discussed them at length with Dr. Max Josef Mannheim, the distinguished London psychiatrist, who also made a graphological examination of Puccini's handwriting. His findings not only confirmed my own views but also revealed hidden traits in the composer's personality which tallied with the general picture I had formed of it independently. I wish to express my profound debt of gratitude to Dr. Mannheim for the time he gave me and for many invaluable suggestions.

Part Three is designed to combine a practical, if somewhat unorthodox, guide through each opera and the more important non-operatic works with a critical examination of them. I have paid special—some reader may feel, excessive—attention to the libretti and their sources, comparing the two in an endeavour to illuminate Puccini's musico-dramatic technique by discussing the modifications, some radical and striking, which a given subject underwent in its translation from the original novel or play to the operatic 'book'. I have also devoted space (Part One) to a brief analysis of certain subjects which the composer contemplated at length, and even started work on, but which he eventually discarded. His reasons for rejection seemed to me as revelatory of the way his mind worked as his reasons for acceptance. For Puccini the shaping of a libretto formed part of his creative work and he set about it as though he envisaged a spoken play. In my discussion of the libretti I have therefore applied the methods of dramatic criticism, the individual targets being characters, plot, action, situation, text and atmosphere. The last was for the composer an aspect of paramount importance; in fact the musical characterization of atmosphere —documentary, poetic and psychological—constitutes one of the most fascinating features of his general style. His full response, in each new opera, to the specific tone and temper of its subject defines the extent of his flexibility and empathy. My study of the music is made from two principal angles: its dramatic relevance and its quality as music *per se*. These represent two different values and it is one of my chief concerns to show where in my view they merge and where they remain apart. It is perhaps the supreme criterion by which to judge the powers of a musical dramatist.

In addition to the aforementioned persons and institutions, my grateful thanks are due to:

The House of G. Ricordi & Co., Milan, and its present head, Dr. Eugenio Clausetti, for permission to quote from books, libretti and scores published by them, and for generous help in other matters, including the provision of photographic material. I treasure the memory of the days spent in their library perusing Puccini's autograph scores, and I wish to express my debt of gratitude to Maestro Raffaele Tenaglia, who drew my attention to points I would otherwise have missed;

Mills Music Ltd., London, for permission to quote from *Messa di Gloria*;

Universal Edition, Vienna, and Casa Musicale Sonzogno, Milan, for permission to quote from *La Rondine*.

The following Authors and their Publishers, for permission to quote from letters reproduced in their publications:

The legal heirs of Giuseppe Adami, and Arnoldo Mondadori Editore, Milan;

Mario Corsi, and Ceschina Editore, Milan;

Dante Del Fiorentino, Victor Gollancz Ltd., London, and Prentice-Hall, Inc., New York;

Carlo Gatti, and Aldo Garzanti Editore, Milan;

George R. Marek, and Cassell & Co. Ltd., London;

Mario Morini, and the Editor of *La Scala*, Milan;

Piero Nardi, and Arnoldo Mondadori Editore, Milan;

The legal heirs of Pietro Panichelli, and Nistri-Lischi Editori, Pisa;

The legal heirs of Vincent Seligman, and Macmillan & Co. Ltd., London.

The Authorities of the Conservatorio Giuseppe Verdi, Milan, for permission to inspect musical autographs and other documents;

The Istituto Italiano di Cultura, London, and Signora Marcella Barzetti, for assistance in certain enquiries;
The Italian State Tourist Department (ENIT), London, for photographs of Lucca.
The BBC Music Library and Mr. J. H. Davies for the loan of scores.

The following individual persons:

Dr. Eric Blom, C.B.E., for translating the poems and doggerels reproduced in this book, for reading the proofs and making many valuable suggestions.
Signora Rita Puccini, Milan, the composer's daughter-in-law and legal heir, for permission to reproduce copyrighted illustrations, published in *Puccini nelle imagini*, ed. Leopoldo Marchetti (Garzanti, Milan, 1949);
Mr. Jacques Samuel, London, for the loan of an unpublished letter by Puccini;
Mrs. Violet Schiff, London, for information on her sister, the late Sybil Seligman, and for the provision of a photographed portrait of her;

For ready assistance in various details:

Mr. Martin Cooper	Mr. Philip Hope-Wallace
Mr. Alan Frank	Mr. A. Hyatt King
Mr. Miron Grindea	Mr. Edward Lockspeiser

My Publishers for their inexhaustible patience with a dilatory author and for taking the keenest interest in the writing and production of this book.
Mrs. Rosemary Cahn, Mrs. Sylvia Carvell and Miss Hazel Sebag-Montefiore, for heroic typing. Mrs. Carvell also compiled the Index.

The book is dedicated to the memory of my dearly loved wife. Without her encouragement during the planning stages it might never have come into being.

London, September, 1958.   M. C.

Preface to the Second Edition

Simultaneously with the first edition of this book (1958) there appeared in Italy two important publications—Claudio Sartori's *Puccini* and *Carteggi pucciniani* (ed. Eugenio Gara), which is a large collection of letters by and to Puccini as well as correspondence about him. This second edition has afforded me the welcome opportunity to incorporate in it a great deal of this Italian material and also to take into account Cecil Hopkinson's exemplary *A Bibliography of the Works of Giacomo Puccini 1858–1924* (1968). Some of this new material will be found in footnotes, but more important information is worked into the main text. In addition, I have corrected errors and rectified inaccurate statements some of them pointed out to me by critics of the Italian edition of the book. While this new material does not alter essentially the composer's physiognomy, it sheds fresh light on his life and character and on the literary background of his music. This enlarged and, I hope, improved edition supersedes the original version of my book.

London, January, 1974   M.C.

List of Illustrations

LIST OF ILLUSTRATIONS

FIRST PART

The Man

I have always carried with me a large bundle of melancholy. I have no reason for it, but so I am made.—*Puccini*.

The serial numbers in the text refer to entries in Appendix D giving the source-material.

The italicized capitals in brackets, after quotations (mostly from letters), indicate the following sources:

(E)   *Epistolario di Giacomo Puccini* (ed. Adami).
(C.P.) *Carteggi Pucciniani* (ed. Gara).
(L)   *La Scala* (Periodical)
(M)   Marek (*Puccini*).
(N)   Nardi (*Giacosa*).
(S)   Seligman (*Puccini Among Friends*).
        (See Bibliography).

I

Preludio in Modo Antico

I

HIGH UP IN THE APUAN ALPS—that rolling chain of green, wooded hills and mountains which forms one of the peculiar beauties of the Tuscan landscape —there lies ensconced in the remote Val di Roggio a village called Celle. It is no more than a conglomeration of perhaps three score houses, and the entire Commune to which it belongs—Pescaglia—numbers just a little over 6,000 souls. From this tiny village, one day in the early 1700s, a man rode on his mule in an easterly direction, down to the narrow valley of the Serchio and, following the river's winding course southwards, proceeded to the ancient city of Lucca. There he settled, took a wife and founded a family. His name was Puccini. We do not know what manner of man he was or what trade he plied—all we know is that he was the forebear of five generations of musicians, of whom Giacomo Puccini was the last and the greatest.

What drove this early ancestor to forsake his mountains and seek his fortune among the people of Lucca was, no doubt, the lure of wealth and prosperity. Lucca was a famous city, with a long and chequered history to its name. Mentioned by Livy and Pliny, it had played an important part in the war against Hannibal when the Carthaginian general, after his daring crossing of the Alps, marched through Tuscany in 217 B.C. It is said that his troops endured great hardships from the unwholesome, treacherous swamps in the neighbourhood of Lucca, the very name of which is a pointer to the one-time character of this region; for it is presumed to derive from the Celto-Ligurian word *Luk*, signifying a 'place with swamps'—'*luogo con paludi*'. Lying at the junction of strategic roads, Lucca was subsequently turned into a Roman fortress, remains of which are still to be seen in the town. During the Middle Ages it rose to become the capital of Tuscany under the rule of an oligarchy, which from the twelfth century onwards jealously guarded the political independence of the *Serenissima Repubblica di Lucca*. Although it later lost its hegemony in fierce internecine wars with its sister republics Florence and Pisa, Lucca still retained its position as one of the great city-states of central Italy and as an important centre of commerce. Its silks, its leather and woollen wares could be seen at fairs in France and Germany, and as far afield as England.

For the visitor to present-day Lucca, the living testimony to its past splendour and glory lies in its magnificent ancient buildings: its *palazzi*— some forty of them—and its churches. There is the lovely Church of San Michele where young Giacomo was a choirboy; there is the austere Basilica

San Frediano founded in the sixth century; and most impressive of all is the Cathedral of San Martino, where four Puccinis occupied the post of organist and choir-master throughout their lives. With its three-arched façade built in the austere Tuscan Romanesque style and fascinating in its irregularity; with its rich interior adorned with paintings by the hands of Tintoretto, Ghirlandaio and Fra Bartolomeo; with the marble sacrophagus of Ilaria del Carretto filling the eyes with wonder at the superb realism with which Jacopo della Quercia invested his celebrated sculpture; and with two resplendent organs dating from the seventeenth century, a joy to the ear as well as the eye—with all this and more, San Martino must have lent dignity, pride and fame to the long line of musicians who discharged their duty there.

Lucca still is the compact, cramped town it was when the first Puccini settled there. It was built in a haphazard style to suit the requirements of the moment, and you may easily lose your way in its dark *vicoli*, its narrow, tortuous lanes and streets which criss-cross the city in all directions. Looking out over it from the elegant Tuscan tower of the famous Palazzo Guinigi, where oak trees grow on the platform, you receive the impression of a circular chess-board, its edges formed by the magnificent medieval *mura*, perhaps the finest city walls in all Italy. It is as though the builders had anticipated the nervous haste of modern times in planning these walls broad enough for the construction of a carriage-way, along which motor traffic now hurries in both directions. You step on to one of the eleven *baluardi* or bastions, which jut out from the walls like gigantic spurs—they still are a favourite children's playground, just as they were when Puccini was a boy— and an enchanting vista opens up, as far as the green band of the Serchio, leisurely wending its way to the distant, invisible sea, with the surrounding hills covered by pines, cypresses and olive trees, through whose foliage beckon hamlets, villages and the ruins of ancient castles. Puccini's native town has remained an entrancing place, as yet scarcely touched by the international tourist traffic; to the foreign visitor it still conveys something of the pastoral image evoked by the fourteenth-century poet Fazio degli Uberti:

Andando noi vedemmo in piccol cerchio	Walking, we see, within a little circle,
Torreggiar Lucca a guisa di boschetto	Where Lucca towers in a bosky frame

2

Lucca, it is true, lay outside the main stream of Italian music, and was unable in this field to rival such illustrious cities as Rome, Florence, Naples and Bologna. Yet up to the end of the eighteenth century it enjoyed a considerable reputation for its church music, the fruit of a long tradition. As early as the tenth century the Canons of San Martino had founded a *cantoria* or music school, which was attached to the seminary; and its fame must have spread far afield in the following centuries. For some time between 1468 and 1486 the eminent John Hotby, '*ex Anglia in arte musicae expertus et magister*', taught at this school as Giovanni Ottobi, making Lucca his town of adoption. Other such *cantorie* were founded at San Michele and San

CATHEDRAL OF SAN MARTINO, LUCCA

SAN MICHELE,
LUCCA

VIEW OF THE MEDIEVAL WALLS, LUCCA

Giovanni. For the performance of secular music the Republic maintained an orchestra and choir in the *Cappella della Signoria*, which in the eighteenth century became known as the *Cappella Palatina* and counted among its string players Francesco Geminiani, Leopoldo Boccherini and his celebrated son, Luigi—all natives of Lucca.

Lucca also boasted an important form of musical entertainment, peculiar to the town and found nowhere else in Italy. This was the so-called *tasche*; these owed both their origin and curious name to a festivity which was held at first every three years, and later every two years and a half, in celebration of the election of a new government, and was known as the *Festa delle Tasche*—Feast of the Pockets, from the shape of the receptacles into which the voting slips were placed. It is uncertain whether these *tasche* were intended for stage representation or performed in the form of an oratorio.* They consisted of three dramatic parts or *giornate*, one for each of the three days which the festival lasted. As with Italian opera of that period, the subjects were largely drawn from Greek and Roman antiquity glorifying heroism and the struggle for liberty. Initially, the three parts of a *tasca* were unconnected, but from about 1680 these were replaced by a single work in three linked sections, like the three acts of an opera. It resembled the *pasticcio* still in vogue in Mozart's time, in that each section was written by a different composer, who, like the author of the text, had to be a native or at any rate a citizen of Lucca. The long list of composers, most of them of merely local reputation, included Luigi Boccherini and three of Puccini's ancestors, with whom the writing of *tasche* became almost a family concern: between them, the Puccinis composed thirty-two works of this description, in several of which father and son collaborated. With the abolition, however, of the Republic of Lucca by Napoleon in 1799, this small but prolific branch on the tree of Italian music was abruptly lopped, and an attempt to revive the *tasche* in 1803 proved abortive.[1]

Beside the 'Feast of the Pockets', there were two other festivals of great importance for Lucca's music. The first was of a popular religious character, the *Festa del Volto Santo* or *della Santa Croce*. This feast takes its name from a striking, almost El Grecoesque, wood-carving of Christ on the Cross adorning the little marble chapel in the Cathedral of San Martino, which for centuries had been the object of holy pilgrimages from all parts of Europe; its effigy was imprinted on Lucca seals and coins. This annual feast, which goes back to the Middle Ages, is held to this day on 14 September. On the day before the feast the wood-carving is taken from the Cathedral on the south side of the city to the Basilica San Frediano on the north side and is carried back again in the evening in a solemn procession across the town, the holy ceremony being attended by the whole clergy, led by the Bishop of Lucca, and by the military and civil authorities. The next day a Solemn Mass is celebrated in the Cathedral, for which since about the middle of the seventeenth century it has been the custom to compose special music. Heinrich Heine, who visited Lucca and its neighbourhood, gives a most vivid

* The first recorded performance of a *tasca* took place in 1636.

5

description of the colourful and picturesque sight of the procession and of the ceremony in San Martino; this was in 1829, and he thus missed by a few years hearing Puccini's father conduct a composition of his own there, a so-called *mottettone*.

This was the set-piece required for the *Festa del Volto Santo*. It was not, as the title might suggest, a large motet, nor was it written in the strict contrapuntal style of the medieval form; it was a big cantata for soli, mixed chorus and orchestra in which upwards of two hundred executants took part. And as San Martino boasted, like San Marco in Venice, two organs facing each other across the nave, the *mottetone* was invariably composed for double chorus and double orchestra, the first group consisting of vocal and instrumental soloists and the second of *tutti*, so that the form resembled that of a *concerto grosso*. All four of Puccini's ancestors contributed such cantatas. Yet the general trend in Italian church music of the nineteenth century toward the secular and operatic also affected Lucca's church composers and it was this increasingly profane character that eventually prompted Pope Pius X to interdict the *mottetone* in his *Motu Proprio* of 1904. Though strong protests were raised and attempts made to reverse this interdiction, this is the last we hear of a form of composition which, like the *tasche*, was a characteristic product of Lucca's music.

Another feast which demanded music as a matter of course and which is still held at Lucca is that in honour of St. Cecilia, the patron saint of music. In 1864 there was founded the *Compagnia de' Musici Santa Cecilia*, a kind of musicians' guild, of which, in their days, all five Puccinis were members. This society arranges concerts in various churches on the festival of the saint (22 November), with special works composed for the occasion. Notable among these during the eighteenth century were the *Sacre Veglie* or *Sacred Vigils*, religious cantatas, some of them from the pen of Puccini's ancestors. It is worth mentioning that, faithful to the democratic tradition of the one-time Republic of Lucca, the society elects the members who are to contribute music for each feast by secret ballot.

3

The prominent part which music played in Lucca suffered a temporary eclipse during the Napoleonic Wars. In 1799 the Republic lost its political independence, being occupied first by the French and later by the Austrians, who, incidentally, removed the beautiful ancient cannons—124 in all—which used to stand on the bastions of the city walls. When in 1805, however, Napoleon raised Lucca to a principality and installed his sister Marianne Élise and her husband Felice Baciocchi as rulers of Tuscany, with the court at Lucca, musical life revived again.* It is true that one of the Princess's first acts after her installation was to dissolve the ancient *Cappella Palatina*,

* The court was established in what is now the Palazzo Provinciale, the seat of the provincial government, a large and impressive edifice erected on the site on which some five hundred years before Giotto had built a castle for one of Lucca's noble families. The big square in front of the palace was built under Élise's régime and was suitably named Piazza Napoleone, as it is still called.

then directed by Puccini's great-grandfather Antonio, also the seminaries of San Michele and San Giovanni, with their music schools. Yet, as though wishing to make amends for her precipitate action, she founded her private orchestra, the *Cappella da Camera*, placing it under the charge of Puccini's grandfather Domenico. She also invited Paganini to Lucca to conduct this orchestra and also operas at court.*

The reign of the Baciocchis came to an end in March 1814 when the Congress of Vienna handed Tuscany over to the Parma branch of the Bourbons. Though the new government was autocratic and bigoted, it did much to encourage music at Lucca. Marie Louise decreed in 1818 the formation of the *Cappella di San Romano*, which was to serve the musical requirements of both the court and the town; and her son Carlo Ludovico, who succeeded her, amalgamated this orchestra with a municipal music school and thus laid the foundation for the Conservatoire, in which in 1842 all public and private music schools were merged. In 1867 this became known as the *Istituto Musicale Pacini*, after its first director Giovanni Pacini, a reputable opera composer and eminent teacher. One of the later directors of the *Istituto* was Puccini's father, Michele, and it counted among its later students our composer and his fellow-Lucchese, Alfredo Catalani. In 1943 the Conservatoire was re-named *Istituto Musicale Luigi Boccherini*, to mark the bicentenary of the birth of this famous son of Lucca. The Conservatoire, which is now a state school, is housed together with a medical school (!) in what was once a monastery of considerable size, with a lovely eleventh-century cloister still standing. The library contains a large collection of music by Lucca composers of several centuries, including Puccini's ancestors; also the autographs of some of Puccini's youthful compositions.

If I have dwelt on what seems no more than a backwater of Italian music, it is because it forms the background to the lives and activities of four musical members of the Puccini family. They played so eminent a part in it that it is scarcely an exaggeration to say that Lucca's musical history during the eighteenth and the best part of the nineteenth centuries is almost identical with the history of the Puccinis.

4

If we were to draw up a statistical list of the great families in which a creative gift for music was hereditary, it would show that the Puccinis,† with their five generations, rank immediately after the Bachs, who, with seven generations, represent the record. The Puccini family thus beats the

---

* The house where Paganini stayed in 1809, in 4 Via San Frediano, opposite the Basilica, still stands and bears a plaque with the proud inscription *'Amore e Povertà ne tormentavano il Suo genio ma la città dava al Suo arcano violino le ali della gloria'*—'Love and Poverty tormented his genius but the city rendered the wings of glory to his mysterious violin'. The favours which the Princess showered on Paganini would seem to suggest a sentimental attachment. According to him, it was a remark of hers that inspired in him the idea of writing 'my military Sonata for the G string entitled *Napoleon* which I performed before a numerous and brilliant audience' (quoted in *Grove's Dictionary of Music and Musicians*, 5th ed., ed. by Eric Blom. London, 1954).

† See family tree, Appendix A.

Couperins by one generation, the Vienna Strausses by two and the Gabrielis, Scarlattis and Mozarts by three generations.

The founder of the musical branch was Giacomo Puccini, the son of the man who had come down from the mountains in Pescaglia, and the great-great-grandfather of our composer, who bears his Christian name. This first Giacomo, born at Lucca on 26 January 1712, went to study at Bologna, then a city at the height of its musical renown, on account of the celebrated Padre Martini who lived and taught there and attracted musicians from all parts of Europe for study and enlightenment. Students of Mozart's life remember him well. It is uncertain whether Giacomo Puccini actually studied under Padre Martini or his colleague Giovanni Caretti, but he knew Martini personally, and after his return to Lucca engaged in friendly correspondence with the eminent Padre, sending him some compositions of his, with a request for his advice and testimonial. A recommendation from Padre Martini acted like an Open Sesame for a young composer trying to get his music performed or to obtain a post.* Giacomo Puccini's letters to Martini reveal him as an artist of great seriousness and integrity, and Martini's replies show that the latter held him in great esteem.[2] In 1739, at the age of twenty-seven, Puccini was appointed—it would appear that Padre Martini brought some influence to bear—conductor of the *Cappella Palatina*, at seven *scudi* (21s.) a month, and organist and choir-master at San Martino. It was at this church that Puccini established a reputation which was not only maintained but increased by his progeny, to reach international fame in the last Giacomo, albeit in a sphere poles apart from that of his ancestor.

The first Puccini must have been a man of pride and fully conscious of the leading position he occupied in Lucca's musical life. Thus he resented the fact that his modest emolument should be no greater than that of Lucca's hangman, and demanded from the city that the difference in their respective positions be marked by a corresponding difference in their salaries. These being fixed, however, by statute, Puccini was granted monthly a small loaf of bread, worth a *soldo*, as a token of his superior status!

Giacomo Puccini left three large volumes of diaries, *Libri delle musiche annue*, covering the years from 1748 to 1777, which are preserved in the State Archives of Lucca. These give us a vivid and detailed picture of the city's musical and general life, and contain entries on a great variety of topics: on the services in the various churches, on important musical and social events—one entry, for example, referring to a concert held on 17 April 1764 'in honour of the Duke of York, brother of the reigning King of England' (George III)—and on incidents from Puccini's travels. He rarely records his impressions of the music of other composers, but there are frequent entries on the conduct of the musicians under his charge, among

---

* Leopold Mozart sent Martini compositions by his young son; and when in 1777 Mozart endeavoured to secure a post at the court of the Elector of Bavaria, the father wrote to Martini asking him to intervene with the Elector on behalf of his son 'as two words from you are worth more than the warmest recommendation from a king'. (22 December 1777. *The Letters of Mozart and his Family*, translated by Emily Anderson. London, 1938.)

whom we find the Boccherinis, father and son, Leopoldo playing the double-bass and Luigi the cello. Puccini is a severe critic of his performers, notably of 'those braggarts of eunuchs!'—'*spacconata di castrati!*'—who take the greatest liberties with the music for the sake of showy effects and who ignore words and expression. Elsewhere he writes on the necessity for opera singers to read the words of the libretto so as to know the whole drama and render their recitatives expressive.

Puccini's duties included the composition and the direction of music for the services at San Martino and also for all official occasions; hence his large output which includes Masses, oratorios, cantatas, instrumental works and *tasche*. He was a composer of great versatility and technical skill, notably as a contrapuntist, as this excerpt from a *Vesper* (1740) illustrates:

Giacomo died at Lucca on 3 February 1781, aged sixty-nine. His son Antonio Benedetto Maria, born at Lucca on 31 July 1747, laid the general pattern that was to be followed by the three succeeding members of the Puccini family. After lessons with his father and the Abbate Lucchesi, Antonio too went to Bologna for further studies. For this purpose his father was compelled to apply to the government for the grant of a loan of 200 *scudi* (about £130), repayable at the rate of two *scudi* a month. From Bologna Antonio brought home his future wife, Caterina Tesei, sister of his fellow-student, Valerio Tesei, and herself a composer and organist of some repute. This fact is important, for through this marriage the musical gift in the male

Ex.1 (contd.)

line of the Puccini family was now reinforced by that of the female line; and the same, as we shall see, was to occur again when Puccini's father married Albina Magi.

In 1771 Antonio was received into the illustrious *Accademia dei Filarmonici* of Bologna, a much coveted honour and one that could only be achieved after the most gruelling examination in the art of counterpoint. Antonio was still at Bologna when the fourteen-year-old Mozart visited the town with his father, and he may have been present at the solemn ceremony at which the same honour was conferred on Mozart. In the following year (1772) we find Antonio installed as his father's assistant and, later, as his successor, at San

Ex.1 (contd.)

Martino and the *Cappella Palatina*. Like his father he composed a large number of religious and secular works; a Requiem Mass on the death of the Emperor Joseph II (1790) and several *tasche* are specially praised in the records. On one occasion Antonio collaborated with his father in a *tasca* entitled *Marco Manlio Capitolino* (1777), Antonio writing the first part and Giacomo the second. The following example from the overture will give the reader an idea of Antonio's instrumental style:

Ex.2

Antonio was a 'modern' who exchanged the 'learned' or contrapuntal style of his father for the suave and graceful manner of the *style galant* which flourished in Europe in the middle of the eighteenth century; if the above example recalls Mozart it is because Antonio belonged to that group of Italian composers whose symphonies exercised a formative influence on the young Salzburg master;* Antonio was also the first of the Puccinis to display a gift for opera. The reputation of Antonio and his father was sufficiently

* The most notable members of this group were Sammartini, Sarti, Anfossi, Galuppi and also Bach's son, Johann Christian, the 'Milan' or 'London' Bach.

GIACOMO PUCCINI (1712–81)
The Founder of the Musical Dynasty

ANTONIO PUCCINI
(1747-1832)

DOMENICO PUCCINI
(1771-1815)

widespread for both to be mentioned in several musical dictionaries of the nineteenth century, including Fétis's great *Biographie Universelle des Musiciens*. Antonio's portrait already shows certain features characteristic of the last Puccini: the oval shape of the face, the sensitive mouth, the melancholy gaze of the eyes. He died at Lucca on 3 February 1832, aged eighty-five.

An element of drama is introduced into the family chronicle by Antonio's son, Domenico Vincenzo. Born at Lucca in 1771, he died suddenly on 25 May 1815, at the age of forty-four. Rumour had it that he was given a cup of poisoned sherbet at a nobleman's party; Lucca was just then under Austrian occupation, and Domenico was suspected of harbouring liberal ideas which were regarded as the mark of a dangerous rebel. (Did Puccini remember the fate of his grandfather when he composed *Tosca*?) Whether the actual cause of his untimely death was murder and, if so, whether the motive was a political one or professional jealousy, was never established.

Like his father and grandfather, Domenico studied at Bologna and became a member of the *Accademia*; he also went to Naples where he had lessons from Paisiello. At the age of twenty-five he became his father's assistant at San Martino, and in 1805 was appointed director of Princess Élise's court orchestra. When this was dissolved three years later, Domenico, with a family of four children, appears to have fallen on hard days; we gather as much from a submission he made to the Princess in which he calls her attention to 'the most unhappy situation in which your most humble servant finds himself, being deprived of the income he received as Maestro di Cappella di Camera of your Imperial Highness. This deprivation is not only the cause of extreme anxiety for himself and his poor family but it also prevents him from exercising his ability, small though it be, in the service of your Imperial Highness, which is the principal aim of all his desires'.[3] The submission seems to have been successful, for in the following year Domenico was made director of the municipal orchestra.

But for his premature death, Domenico might have achieved great eminence. A precocious youth, he was twenty-two when he collaborated with his father in *Spartaco*, a *tasca* written in 1793. In addition to a great deal of church music, he composed a large number of instrumental works, among them a fine harpsichord concerto which suggests that he was an accomplished player on this instrument. Here is a solo passage from the Adagio:

Ex.3

Domenico's style was marked by a captivating melodic charm and great technical fluency, both of which stood him in excellent stead in his operas, with which he achieved an almost international reputation. An album published in 1850 by the German firm of Breitkopf and Härtel contains his portrait along with those of Bach, Handel and Beethoven! His bent was for *opera buffa*—not perhaps surprising in this one-time pupil of Paisiello—three of his five known operas being of that genre, but the work which earned him most acclaim was the *opera seria*, *Quinto Fabio*, produced at Leghorn in 1810. The writer of the notice in the *Corriere del Mediterraneo* refers to 'magnificent results' and expresses the hope that Domenico Puccini may 'one day fill the void left by the death of Cimarosa'; and from Paisiello he received a highly congratulatory letter in which, incidentally, Napoleon's protégé did not omit to request Domenico to convey to Princess Élise the message that 'I throw myself at her feet with the assurance of my constant esteem and friendship'. Paisiello knew how to play his cards.

Domenico left at his death a widow and four young children. Of these, Michele, born at Lucca on 27 November 1813, became Puccini's father. After lessons with his surviving grandfather and other Lucca musicians, Michele too studied at Bologna, transferring thence to Naples, where his two teachers were Donizetti and Mercadante, Verdi's early and most serious rival. On his return to Lucca, Michele became organist and choirmaster at San Martino and composed religious and secular music; two operas of his, *Antonio Foscarini* and *Giambattista Cattani*, are said to have achieved success. Michele was a composer of academic respectability who excelled in the strict contrapuntal style of an earlier period and in the use of all scholastic devices. Thus he wrote an *Ecce Sacerdos* in the form of a canon with as many as thirty-two 'real' parts, a contrapuntal *tour de force* composed for and dedicated to Pope Pius IX on the occasion of his visit to Lucca on 15 August 1857—the first visit paid by a pope to the city for more than three hundred years.

Michele's chief reputation was, however, as a theorist and teacher. He was the author of two textbooks on harmony and counterpoint and for a great many years occupied the post of director of the Conservatoire and inspector of Lucca's school music.*

Michele married Albina Magi, the sister of Fortunato Magi, a former pupil of his, who on Michele's death was to succeed him as director of the Conservatoire; Magi later became director of the famous Liceo Benedetto Marcello at Venice. (We shall meet him in connection with Puccini's early studies at Lucca.) This marriage thus caused the second musical 'blood transfusion' from the female line into the veins of the Puccini family. Michele's portrait shows a countenance to which the beard lends a masculine, almost Verdi-like appearance; at the same time there is about it an air of feminine softness and tender melancholy such as we have already encountered in his grandfather Antonio, and shall encounter again in his son Giacomo.

* Some biographers state that one of his pupils was Alberto Franchetti, who later made a name in opera. If so, Franchetti would present a unique case of an infant prodigy: he was *four* years old when Michele died!

II

Early Years at Lucca

I

MICHELE PUCCINI WAS FIFTY-ONE when he died at Lucca on 23 January 1864, leaving Albina—who was eighteen years younger than her husband and then aged only thirty-three—with a family of seven children. Of these, five were girls bearing the euphonious names Odilia, Tomaide or Dide, Iginia, Nitteti and Ramelde, and two boys—Giacomo and Michele, the latter being born three months after his father's death. Another girl, Macrina, died in early infancy. Giacomo,* the fifth child, was born at Lucca on 22 December 1858, the date shown on his birth certificate, though he himself insisted on the date of 23 December. The family lived then at 30 Via di Poggio, which is in one of the oldest parts of the city and takes its name from an ancient noble family who played an important role in the chequered history of Lucca. One of their several palaces, the Palazzo Citadella, still stands in the little square facing the entrance to Puccini's house.† It is an ungainly looking, three-storeyed house in which the Puccini family occupied the whole of the first floor; but the rooms are spacious, with high ceilings. A plaque, affixed to an outside wall of the house shortly after Puccini's death, bears the inscription:

Da lunga progenie di musici
Degni della viva tradizione patria
Qui nacque il 22 Dicembre 1858

GIACOMO PUCCINI

Che alle nuove voci di vita
Accordò note argute di verità e leggiadria
Riaffermando con le schiette agili forme
La nazionalità dell' arte
Nel suo primato di gloria nel mondo

———

La città orgogliosa di lui
Nel trigesimo della morte
29 Dicembre 1924

(Descending of a long line of musicians worthy of the living tradition of the fatherland, Giacomo Puccini was born here on 22 December 1858, who blended with the new voices of life sounds inspired by truth and charm,

---

* His full name was Giacomo Antonio Domenico Michele Secondo Maria.

† The whole district lies within the narrow precinct which in Roman times was girt by fortifications, the first of Lucca's three walls.

reaffirming, in pure and lively forms, the glorious primacy of our national art in the world.—The proud city, on the thirtieth day of his death, 29 December 1924.)

Via di Poggio, a dark, narrow street, leads to the charming piazza in which stands the church of San Michele. Many were the times when the young Giacomo crossed this square on his way to discharge his organist's duties at San Martino, reflecting perhaps on the striking contrast—if he possessed an eye for it—between the austere exterior of his cathedral and the marbled façade of San Michele, with the winged effigy of the archangel greeting him from the gable. As he proceeded, he would pass the spacious Piazza Napoleone, flanked by the large Palazzo Provinciale where his grandfather Domenico used to conduct Princess Élise's court orchestra; and turning the corner of the present Albergo Universo, a one-time monastery, he would face the Teatro del Giglio where he made his first acquaintance with opera.

Giacomo was little over five years old when his father died. He hardly remembered him, though his first contact with music in the most literal sense of the word was through his father, who used to play a game with him on the organ. Michele would place small coins on the keyboard, and the child, trying to grasp them, could not help pressing the keys down and thus producing sounds. Despite such blandishments, Puccini never became a celebrated organist; he even developed an aversion to the instrument of his ancestors. Yet the tradition of the son succeeding the father was firmly established in the Puccini family; and Lucca took it for granted that Giacomo was to become an organist and choir-master, ready at the appointed time to fill Michele's post. Thus, Pacini, in his oration delivered at Michele's funeral, referred to Giacomo as 'the sole survivor of and heir to that glory which his ancestors have earned in the harmonious Art and which perhaps one day it will be in his power to revive'.[4] Moreover, the decree by which on 18 February 1864 the Lucca authorities installed Fortunato Magi as Michele's successor contains the clause that Magi 'should and must hand over the post of Organist and *Maestro di Cappella* to Signor (*sic*) Giacomo, son of the aforementioned defunct master, as soon as the said Signor Giacomo be able to discharge such duties'.[5] That a six-year-old child should thus be assured of his father's posts must be unique in musical history; it certainly betokened great optimism on the part of the Lucchese authorities. Yet from the little we know of Puccini's early years—and that little is almost completely undocumented—he gave at first small ground for such expectations. By all accounts, the boy was conspicuously lazy; his school reports were bad;* work was little to his liking and most of the day he could be found with his young playmates either on the ancient walls of Lucca or in the fields near the banks of the Serchio indulging his passion for bird-catching. As for composing, far from showing any precocity, there was little indeed to suggest more than the possession of average gifts.

* Puccini, like Hugo Wolf, displayed a particular aversion to mathematics—a fact which Fausto Torrefranca uses to account for the alleged inferiority of Puccini's music. (G. *Puccini et l'opera internazionale*. Turin, 1912.)

Puccini's first teacher was his uncle Magi, himself a one-time pupil of Michele Puccini and at that time director of the Pacini Institute. Magi, who taught the boy singing and the organ, was a martinet blessed with the short temper that usually goes with such disciplinarians. He was tempted to resort to a rather drastic device in order to keep his indolent pupil up to the mark, kicking Giacomo on the shin when he sang a wrong or untrue note—a method which is said to have had its effect, since in later years Puccini would nervously jerk his leg whenever he heard a singer sing out of tune. These lessons, as was to be expected with a boy of Puccini's temperament, bore little fruit and in the end led Magi to declare to his sister Albina Puccini that her son was a 'falento'—a 'go-slow'—and in fact had no talent at all. This was reckoning without the mother's unshakable confidence in her son's outstanding gifts; she was determined to give the boy the best schooling available at Lucca—not only in music, but also in general education. Had not her husband's motto been: 'puro musico, puro asino!' Albina, to judge from various accounts, must have been a woman of signal energy and perseverance, endowed with a large dose of horse-sense, and quite capable of managing her affairs. If the lessons with Magi were a failure, then a change of teacher was indicated. So her 'Giacomino' was handed over to Carlo Angeloni, another of her husband's former pupils and teacher at the Pacini Institute. Angeloni proved far more successful than Magi; he instructed the boy in all musical subjects of the curriculum, conscientiously preparing him for the duties Puccini was expected to perform as his father's successor.

2

The first steps in Puccini's career were modest enough. At the age of ten he became a choirboy at San Martino and San Michele and at fourteen began to play the organ at the service, extending this activity also to churches in Lucca's neighbourhood, such as at Mutigliano, Pescaglia and Celle, whence his family had originally come. These engagements and others as a pianist in Lucca's taverns and places of entertainment—even, it was said, in a house of ill-repute in Via della Dogana*—as well as at the once fashionable resorts of Bagni di Lucca and Lerici, helped to eke out the meagre pension of seventy-five lire per month (£3) on which his widowed mother had to maintain her large family. Puccini began smoking as a young boy and later became a chain-smoker—a fact worth mentioning in view of the disease of which he died; he told his friend Don Pietro Panichelli[6] that in order to obtain money for cigarettes and his beloved *Toscanos* (a local brand of short cigar) he would keep part of these earnings himself. With the same end in view, his younger brother Michele and some friends, often acting as his blowers at the organ, were ordered to steal organ pipes and sell them. In order to prevent a discovery of the theft, Puccini made appropriate changes in the harmony avoiding the notes of the missing pipes, with the result that

* We are here reminded of the young Brahms who earned his living in Hamburg in similar ways and places.

3—P

the 'crime' remained unnoticed for a long time. Like other anecdotes related about his early years, this too we are tempted to acknowledge with the old Italian adage 'se non è vera, è ben trovata'. Another source of income was Carlo Della Nina, the only pupil Puccini ever had. Teacher and pupil were both sixteen when the weekly lessons began which were continued for four years (1874–8), Puccini receiving the handsome fee of sixty centesimi per lesson. Nina, a tailor by profession and a musician by vocation, seems to have been as proficient at composing and organ-playing as he was at his needles. Puccini's teaching must have fallen on fruitful soil, for, according to Bonaccorsi who saw the autographs, Della Nina's compositions show ability and fluency, and he was much in demand as an organist. It was for this pupil that Puccini wrote some of his earliest compositions, consisting largely of short organ pieces.

He began composing in all earnest between the ages of sixteen and seventeen, chiefly organ music for the service. Some of these compositions originated in improvisations which he subsequently put down on paper. The art of improvising was then still alive, and it is recorded that Puccini often startled priests and congregation by introducing into his fantasies snatches from Tuscan folk-songs and from popular operas of the time;* especially in the so-called *marcia*, a piece comparable to the English voluntary, with which according to an old custom at Lucca the organist played the congregation out of church. This gave cause for much adverse comment, and the young composer was severely reprimanded by his elder sister Iginia, who was then preparing to take the veil as an Augustinian nun. Puccini's reply was that while grave music was certainly appropriate during the service, he saw no reason why the recessional should not be in a joyous strain. 'But you are trying to outdo the theatre' was Iginia's retort— exaggerated, no doubt, but significant as a pointer to the gradual emergence in Puccini of a bent for opera, a bent which is clearly shown in some surviving compositions of that period.

Puccini's first contact with opera was through his teacher Angeloni, who introduced him to the scores of *Rigoletto*, *Traviata* and *Trovatore*, Verdi representing for the young Italian composers of the time an unsurpassable idol, even as Wagner did for their German contemporaries. The experience which was to have a decisive influence on Puccini's career was a performance of *Aida*. Hearsay had aroused in the eighteen-year-old composer an irrepressible desire to hear that masterpiece, and the opportunity came when *Aida* was given at Pisa for the first time on 11 March 1876. Some time during the spring or summer of that year Puccini and two of his friends decided, money being short, to travel the twenty miles from Lucca to Pisa and back on foot.† From what we know of his reaction in later years to the

* The same story is told of the young Mascagni and of Johann Strauss, who in his early years was for a time organist at the Church of Mariahilf in Vienna.

† One of his two companions was the musician Carlo Carignani, who later arranged the vocal scores of some Puccini operas; the other was the young Lucca painter and sculptor Zizzania, Puccini's boon companion in many a prank played on Lucca's citizens. In one

operas of other composers, *Aida* seems to have made on him the profoundest impression of all. As though in a flash, it revealed to him the direction in which his own talent was subconsciously driving him. 'When I heard *Aida* at Pisa', he later stated, 'I felt that a musical window had opened for me.' It may be that in that moment the idea was born in him to break away from the family tradition and launch out into opera and opera only. It was an adolescent's dream for the realization of which Puccini had hardly the necessary technical equipment, nor was Lucca the place for a budding operatic talent. Operatic craft could be learned only in Milan, the new Mecca of Italian opera, its holy shrines being the famous Teatro alla Scala and the Conservatorio Reale (now the Conservatorio Giuseppe Verdi), Italy's most progressive music school. Four years were to pass before Puccini achieved the realization of his most ardent wish. Yet the immediate result of the Pisa visit was to spur the young composer on to more intensive work in order to acquire the theoretical knowledge necessary for the entrance examination at the Milan Conservatoire. It is significant, too, that Puccini now began to turn from the composition of organ music to that of more ambitious works. A large-scale *Preludio Sinfonico* dates from 1876; and in the following year Puccini took part in a musical prize competition held in connection with an exhibition at Lucca—'Treasures of Sacred Art'. The prize was to be awarded to the best setting of a patriotic text *I Figli d'Italia Bella—The Sons of Fair Italy*. Puccini's cantata not only failed to win the prize, but its manuscript was returned by the jury with the advice to study harder and acquire a more legible handwriting. The first he took to heart; but he never succeeded in the second—to the great discomfiture of his various copyists to whom in particularly flagrant cases he would address a pacifying '*scusi!*'—'please forgive!'—written on the margin of the score. His bad handwriting was soon to play him a similar trick in another competition of far greater importance.

From his failure with the cantata Puccini rehabilitated himself in the following year with a *Motet* and *Credo* (1878), written for the annual Feast of San Paolino, Lucca's first bishop and its patron saint. Legend has it that San Paolino was the inventor of the church bells, and so on the saint's day which falls on 12 July the bells of all Lucca churches were rung and religious works by pupils of the Pacini Conservatoire were played in his honour. The performance of Puccini's two pieces was his first public success. Two years later he incorporated them in a Mass (1880), written as his 'leaving exercise' from the Conservatoire and also first performed on San Paolino's day. The Mass was much acclaimed, and even Angeloni, his highly critical teacher, was greatly pleased with it, though he found it 'a little theatrical'. As we shall see, the *Agnus Dei* was used later as a madrigal in *Manon Lescaut*. This is one of several instances of Puccini's self-plagiarism from early works; but to

---

instance the two set the town agog by a sensational hoax in which the painter feigned suicide, having hung a dummy in his exact likeness in the cellar of a house near the Piazza Napoleone. The hoax led to a court case in which Zizzania was charged with faking suicide and Puccini with aiding and abetting him.

attach to it the stigma of creative poverty, as some critics have done, is fatuous. One might as well accuse Schubert of lack of invention when, to cite merely a single example, he uses the same theme in the incidental music to *Rosamunde*, in the A minor String Quartet and in a set of piano variations. Before the advent of romanticism, with its axiom of 'original' art, composers 'borrowed' from their own works and those of others without compunction. It was an accepted practice with such masters as Bach, Handel and the Viennese classics, not to mention Rossini, the most unconcerned of self-plagiarists.

Puccini's Mass is a considerable piece running to some two hundred pages of full score and well deserving to be heard, for in addition to its splendid choruses it represents the most important and inspired of his early work and the summing-up of his style as a church composer.* To the Lucca period also belong a *Salve Regina* for soprano and harmonium, and short choral pieces.

* The Mass was published in 1951 under the title *Messa di Gloria* but its authentic title is *Mass for Four Voices and Orchestra*. It was first revived in a concert at Naples in 1952 and has been recorded. According to a note in the published score, the autograph was discovered by Dante del Fiorentino at Lucca after the Second World War. Yet the fact is that long before this 'discovery', the existence of this Mass was not only well known, but several of Puccini's biographers had inspected the autograph and commented upon it. This is, of course, not to detract from Father Dante's merit in instigating its publication and revival.

MICHELE PUCCINI
(1813–64)

ALBINA MAGI-PUCCINI
(1831–84)

PUCCINI'S BIRTHPLACE IN LUCCA, 30 Via di Poggio

III

Milan

I

WITH THE APPROACHING END of Puccini's studies at the Pacini Institute—
he was now in his twenty-second year—the question of his entering the Milan
Conservatoire began to loom large. Yet there were difficulties to surmount
first. In the straitened circumstances in which Albina and her family lived
Giacomo's earnings, small though they were, represented a source of
income which could not be readily dispensed with; moreover the means
had to be found to support Giacomo during his three years' term at the Milan
Conservatoire. Again it was Albina who, with her wonted single-minded-
ness of purpose and energy, cleared every obstacle from her son's path.
She first approached her bachelor uncle Nicolao Cerù, a well-known doctor
in Lucca and in his spare time a gossip writer for the local paper *Il Moccolino—
The Little Candle*. Dr. Cerù had been most favourably impressed by his
great-nephew's Mass; he had concluded his notice of the performance with
the proverb *I figli dei gatti prendono i topi*—meaning Puccini was 'a chip off
the old block'. Not only was he in favour of Giacomo continuing his studies
in Milan, but he was prepared to contribute to his support. There existed
also a royal scholarship, awarded by Queen Margherita to talented music
students of indigent families. At the instigation of a Duchess Caraffa 'who
knows me well', Albina addressed a petition to the Queen, 'the mother of all
poor', in which, after duly reminding her that 'for five generations the
Puccinis have founded a dynasty of musicians' and adding hopefully that 'if
the opportunity should present itself, Giacomo will continue the glorious
tradition', she appealed to the Queen's 'immense generosity to come to the
help of a poor mother and an ambitious boy'.[7] Influence was also brought
to bear on the Queen through a Marchesa Pallavacini, a lady-in-waiting and
an acquaintance of Albina's from former years. After some delay, the
scholarship was granted for a year, with monthly instalments of 100 lire
(about £4 at that period), while Dr. Cerù stood guarantor for the remaining two years of Puccini's term at the Conservatoire.* It is puzzling, however,
why the town of Lucca, which had granted financial help to his ancestors
during their studies, should not have done the same in the case of the last
Puccini or why the resourceful Albina should not have approached the
authorities in the first place. Reading between the lines of del Fiorentino's

---

* The parallel with Verdi is noteworthy. Verdi also lived during his early studies on a
subsidy provided by his future father-in-law Barezzi, who sent him to Milan at the age of
eighteen; but unlike Puccini, Verdi failed at the entrance examination.

eulogistic account we gain the impression that a possible reason may have been Puccini's reputation as a scallywag which he had earned by the pranks and escapades which had set the respectable city fathers against him. A yet more plausible ground for refusing him a subsidy may have been Puccini's known intention to devote himself to opera, which meant farewell to the traditional career as organist and choir-master of Lucca Cathedral. Why support from public money a musician from whom the town would later derive no benefit?

Albina approached the Town Council at least twice after Puccini's first year in Milan, by which time the Queen's scholarship had terminated, but without success. In her first application she stated she was 'in dire need', her monthly allowance of sixty-seven lire being insufficient to support her family, as she was now deprived of the help of her married daughter (Romelde) and had to keep her son Giacomo at the Milan Conservatoire. A second application was rejected by six votes to one; and when, in 1882, at the end of his second year in Milan, Puccini himself applied to the Mayor of Lucca for a grant, referring to an honourable mention of his name in the Conservatoire's report during the first year and to an extraordinary mention in the second, and also reminding the Mayor of the 'many benefits bestowed on my family by the Council of this City' and of how his father Michele had been 'held in high esteem by the honourable Council', the result was equally negative; his application was not even acknowledged.[8] In later years Puccini became a very rich man, but in matters of money he was often ungenerous to the point of meanness. It may be that the poverty he experienced in his youth and the exaggerated value which money must thus have acquired in his eyes were largely responsible for this unattractive trait in the mature man.

It was in the late autumn of 1880 that Puccini, with the diploma of the Pacini Institute and the Queen Margherita scholarship safely in his pocket, arrived in Milan and applied for admission to the Conservatoire. Founded in 1807 by Napoleon, it was modelled on the pattern of the ancient Naples Conservatoire, the prototype of all similar institutions in Italy. The original rules of the Milan Conservatoire had been laid down by Simon Mayr (1763–1845), a Bavarian composer who had settled at Bergamo and played a significant part in the history of Italian opera of the early nineteenth century. According to these regulations, a candidate had to pass a preliminary examination which, if successful, admitted him 'on probation' for a year; not until he had passed a second examination at the end of this period was he accepted as a student proper. A minimum of three years was compulsory for students of composition, and the syllabus included courses in aesthetics, drama and literature.

In November Puccini submitted himself to the preliminary examination informing his 'cara Mamma' a few days later that 'so far, I know nothing about my admission to the Conservatoire. On Saturday the Council will meet to discuss the candidates and decide whom to admit; there are only very few vacant places. But I have good hope of being admitted because I received most marks. Tell Carignani that the examination was ridiculously simple. I was given to harmonize a bass unfigured and very easy* and then they made me develop a melody in D major which was very succesful. Enough, it all went almost too well!' (E). Puccini passed the examination successfully; in fact he came out top. The lessons began on 16 December and three days later the faithful son reports home: 'Yesterday I already had my second lesson with Bazzini which went very well. So far these have been my only lessons, but on Friday I begin the course in aesthetics', a subject which, like literature, was to bore him 'to tears'.

Puccini's chief teachers at the Milan Conservatoire were Bazzini and Ponchielli. Antonio Bazzini (1818–97) had begun his career as a violin virtuoso touring various European countries, particularly Germany, where he settled for a time at Leipzig. In 1873 he was appointed professor of composition at the Milan Conservatoire and became its director in 1882, while Puccini was still a student there. As a composer Bazzini belonged to that small group of Verdi's contemporaries—Arrigo Boito was another of its members—who were well acquainted with German music of both the classical and romantic periods and were influenced by it in their own works. It is significant that Bazzini was especially active in the field of instrumental music. His solitary opera *Turanda* (after Gozzi's fable), produced at La Scala in 1867 with little success, is a forerunner of Puccini's last opera *Turandot*; it is probable that the pupil knew his master's work, and thus made his first acquaintance with a subject which some forty years later he was to use himself. As a teacher Bazzini laid stress on neat craftsmanship and technical perfection—qualities that characterize his own rather anaemic music; and for a musician of Puccini's temperament the strict academic training under Bazzini could only be beneficial. It was for Bazzini that he wrote the fugues and the string quartet mentioned in one of his early letters to his mother.

Puccini's second teacher, Amilcare Ponchielli (1834–86), took a paternal interest in his young pupil; unlike Bazzini, he was an operatic composer in the first place and therefore exercised a more direct influence on Puccini. His first opera, *I Promessi Sposi* (1856), after Alessandro Manzoni's masterpiece, is significant for the choice of a subject dear to the hearts of the Italian patriots of the period of the *risorgimento*.† Of Ponchielli's remaining four operas, all of which were given with great success during his lifetime, only *La Gioconda* (1876) survives. The libretto, incidentally, is by one 'Tobia Gorrio'—none other than Arrigo Boito, Verdi's later librettist, who used to sign many of his literary works with this anagram. Based on Victor Hugo's drama *Angelo, Tyrant of Padua*, the action shows a close resemblance to that of Sardou's subsequent *Tosca*, and it is not without irony that Ponchielli's *chef d'œuvre*, once a great favourite with operatic audiences, should now be

---

* Puccini gave this bass in alto-clef notation which suggests that his mother had had some musical training.

† In 1882 Ponchielli wrote a hymn in memory of Garibaldi which achieved immense popularity.

so completely overshadowed by the far more effective opera of his one-time pupil. Together with Verdi and most musicians of his generation, Ponchielli championed the tradition of vocal supremacy in Italian opera against the 'symphonism' of the Wagnerian music-drama,* the influence of which was soon to become manifest in the music of his own pupil and that of other young Italian composers.

What kind of a student was Puccini? Self-confident he certainly was, and fully convinced he could make his way on his own merits without the aid of the usual introductions and recommendations by influential persons which seemed so important to his family at Lucca. When Dr. Cerù once volunteered to put in a good word for him with his two eminent teachers, Puccini's angry reply was: 'You people at Lucca, you always believe in recommendations! Cursed be he who invented them! One can see that Carlo Ludovico† has filled your heads with nonsense. You none of you know what sort of people Ponchielli and Bazzini are' (*E*). Throughout his life Puccini was to preserve, if not always self-confidence, yet an independence of mind and an aversion to the 'string-pulling' which in the artistic life of Latin countries (and not only there) represents a favourite and generally recognized method of self-advancement. As to his studies, it is true that at Lucca Puccini had been anything but an exemplary pupil; but he greatly changed once he had entered the Milan Conservatoire, which, he felt, constituted the first important step in the realization of his most ardent ambition; it set the course for his future career in precisely the direction he had for years intended it to develop. Admittedly, with opera as his ultimate goal, his interest in counterpoint and purely theoretical disciplines was luke-warm and on his own admission he resorted to a useful labour-saving device, as the following lines from a letter to his mother show: 'My teacher [Ponchielli] is so absent-minded that I bring him the same home-work I prepared for Maestro Bazzini. I even submitted to him the same fugue three or four times over with only the slightest changes.'[9] Some further light on his work as a student is thrown by a letter, recently published,[10] which Ponchielli addressed to Puccini's mother in reply to what had evidently been a request to him to exert his influence on behalf of his pupil to procure him, after the completion of his studies, a post at the Conservatoire. Puccini was then at the end of his three-year term. Ponchielli writes:

Milan
8 January 1883

Honoured Lady,
    You will excuse me if, owing to much work, I am a little late in replying to your kind letter.
    Your son is one of the best pupils of my class, and I am well satisfied with him. Indeed I should be extremely satisfied if he applied himself to his work

* This, however, did not prevent him from conducting the first Rome production of *Lohengrin* in 1878.

† I was unable to establish the identity of this person; he may have been a friend of the Puccinis.

with a little more assiduity, for if he wants to, he can do it very well. It is necessary that, beside the work he has to do for my class, he should steep himself in his Art by studying the great masters for himself and write as much as possible—really plunge himself into composing.

As to the Diploma, he is sure to obtain it at the end of the scholastic year although I tell him firmly that another year at the Conservatoire would do him no harm.

However, since he wishes to obtain the Diploma, counsel your son not to miss the other courses, for in this way he will obtain a full Certificate. So far as I am concerned, rest assured that I shall do everything in my power to help him and also procure him a post when one becomes vacant. But this will not be possible until he has finished his studies. In any case I shall omit nothing to assist him as soon as the opportunity presents itself to me.

I reciprocate your very sincere wishes most cordially and remain with respectful greetings,

your humble servant

A. Ponchielli.

An inspection of Puccini's student exercises, deposited at the Library of the Milan Conservatoire, proves them to have been numerous and to contain a number of pieces written in strict counterpoint as well as in free style. They include the romanza *Melancolia* for voice and string accompaniment (1881), to words by Ghislanzoni, the librettist of Verdi's *Aida*—which is worth mentioning because its melody strikingly anticipates a characteristic pentatonic phrase in *Madam Butterfly*, to say nothing of the fact that Puccini used it literally in the love-duet of his first opera, *Le Villi*.

There is also an *Adagietto* for orchestra dating from his last year at the Conservatoire (1883) the theme of which recurs in an aria of his second opera, *Edgar*.

2

We have little first-hand information on the impressions which the artistic and social life of Italy's most prosperous city left on the young provincial from Lucca. In later years Puccini came to detest Milan, but during his student days he appeared to relish life there, despite his hand-to-mouth existence, and with the adaptability of youth he soon adjusted himself to the new and bewildering atmosphere. From the few published letters to his mother we are able, however, to form a fairly detailed picture of how he spent his days:

'I have made myself', he writes 18 December 1880, 'a time-table: in the morning I get up at half-past eight. If I have lessons, I go to them. If not, I practise the piano a little. Not that I need do much, but I must study it a bit. I'm going to buy a "Method" by Angeleri which is excellent. It's the sort of method from which you can very well teach yourself. I carry on till half past ten, then I have my breakfast and go out. At one I come home and do some work for Bazzini for a couple of hours. From three to about five I study some classical music at the piano. I would also like to take out a subscription for scores but I haven't got the money. At the moment I'm going through

25

Mefistofele by Boito. A friend of mine, a certain Favara★ from Palermo [a Sicilian composer], has lent me a copy. At five I go to have my frugal (my very frugal!) meal—*minestrone alla Milanese*, which, to tell you the truth, is very good. I have three plates of that, then some other things to fill up with, a small piece of Gorgonzola cheese and half a litre of wine. Then I light a cigar and go for my usual stroll up and down the *Galleria*. I stay there till nine and come home dead tired. I do a little counterpoint but don't play: I'm not allowed to play at night. Then I go to bed and read seven or eight pages of a novel. And that's how I live, (*E*).'

Every one of these early letters home contains a reference to his frugal existence. After telling his mother that a season ticket for a reserved seat at La Scala costs 330 lire, he exclaims, almost in the same breath: 'How rich is Milan!' and 'Cursed be misery!'. 'While I spent a few *soldi* to hear *La Stella del Nord*† in "the gods", *Fra Diavolo* cost me nothing because I was given a ticket by Francesconi, who used to be an impresario at Lucca.' Again, 'the evenings when I happen to have a few centesimi, I go to the café, but there are very many evenings when I don't go because a glass of punch costs forty centesimi! So I go to bed early.' 'I'm not starving, but I wouldn't say I'm eating well. I fill up with minestrone, thin broth—and still thinner broth. My tummy is satisfied.' The satisfaction derived from such meals could not have been very lasting, for a little later he writes: 'There's one thing I need, but I'm afraid to tell you about it because I know too well that you have no money to spend. But listen, it's not very much!' The request so timidly made was for nothing more than a can of fresh olive oil to be used for cooking beans—a favourite dish of his.

Puccini occupied a single room in a narrow little street, Vicolo San Carlo —'a rather pretty room and everything clean and tidy in it, with a writing-table of polished walnut which is a real beauty'. In his second year he had to share the room with a cousin and his younger brother Michele, then seventeen, who had also come to Milan to study singing. Another of Puccini's fellow-lodgers for a time was the future composer of *Cavalleria Rusticana*.

Mascagni came, like Puccini, of a poor family. His father was a baker who wanted him to study law, but the son was determined on a musical career and secretly entered the Cherubini Institute at his native town, Leghorn. The father's discovery of this deception led to a fierce quarrel which had, however, the good result that young Mascagni was adopted by an uncle of his who, like Puccini's Dr. Cerù, supported him in his musical studies. After several compositions which proved his outstanding talent, Mascagni set, in youthful challenge to Beethoven, Schiller's *Ode to Joy* to music which was so successful that it won him the patronage of Count Florestano de Laderel, a wealthy amateur, who enabled him to continue his musical education at the Milan Conservatoire. There he became a pupil of Michele Saladino and thus

★ Alberto Favara (1863–1923), whose large collection of native folksongs, edited by Ottavio Tiby, was published in 1957.
† One of Meyerbeer's operas popular at that period.

met Puccini, his senior by five years. Yet temperamentally unfit to stay the course of regular studies (a fact that shows in his technique), Mascagni left the Conservatoire after a year or so and joined a touring opera company as a conductor. His early friendship with Puccini cooled off in later years when they became rivals, but a letter from Puccini to his wife Elvira written from Naples in 1906 suggests that the real cause for their estrangement may have been Mascagni's wife: 'Mascagni left today . . . speaking all manner of good of me and recalling the time when we were friends. But whose fault it is we no longer know—certainly not mine: everybody says that it is she who did all the harm and that if he had been alone he would have become a different man' (M).

A number of amusing anecdotes are related to illustrate Puccini's penurious life as a student. Some sound too good to be true and others seem embellished by the addition of fanciful details. Thus Puccini's landlord, a post office official, evinced little trust in his lodger's financial bona fides; in order to make sure of his monthly rent of thirty lire he would open the letters which regularly arrived for Puccini from Rome containing the monthly instalments from the Queen Margherita scholarship, and pay himself what was due to him. This somewhat drastic method appears to have worked, for in 1910, in an interview given to a journalist of *Vita Nazionale*, an Italian newspaper published in New York, Puccini recalled this early episode, adding that he never enjoyed 'the supreme consolation of cheating my landlord'. But he did succeed in cheating his Milan creditors. When one of these tiresome people called—it was at the time of his *ménage à deux* with Mascagni—he would be told by Mascagni that Puccini had just gone out, whereas he was concealed in a wardrobe; the same game was played when creditors came and asked to see Mascagni. Again, their lack of funds would often compel them to cook their meal in their room, against their landlord's strict prohibition; so in order to drown any noise caused by the clatter of plates, Puccini would improvise on the piano *con tutta forza*. And when we read that Puccini once pawned his only coat in order to have the wherewithal to entertain a young ballet dancer from La Scala, or that in his diary entries (which contain little more than expense accounts) herring figured as a prominent item, do we not feel as though we were in the very atmosphere of Mürger's novel *Scènes de la Vie de Bohème* and of Puccini's evergreen opera? Even as the four Bohemians and their *petites amies* betake themselves to the Café Momus for a merry evening, so Puccini, Mascagni and their female encumbrances would frequent the cafés of Milan's famous Galleria Vittorio Emanuele and the *Osteria Aida* where the obliging proprietor kept an account for them which required many months of repeated reminders before it was settled. Puccini's personal experiences during those years of gay poverty in Milan no doubt coloured his opera; but to assert, as more than one of his biographers has done, that the excellence of the Bohemian scenes in it was due to those experiences is to take a somewhat naïve view of the mysterious relationship between an artist's physical life and the life of his creative imagination.

As might be expected, most of the music which Puccini went to hear in those early Milan days was operatic. About the only non-operatic work to which he refers in the letters to his mother is Gounod's oratorio *La Rédemption*, which 'bored me to distraction' (a reaction not unknown among present-day listeners to that work). *Carmen*, on the other hand, into a performance of which at La Scala 'I sneaked in for nothing, is a most beautiful work'. He also saw there the production of a new opera, *Dejanice*, by his fellow-Lucchese Catalani. 'People in general', he writes home, 'don't go into ecstasies about it, but I think, artistically speaking, it is a fine work, and if they repeat it, I shall go to hear it again.' (*E*)

Alfredo Catalani (1854–93) was then the great hope of Italian opera, yet with the advent of *verismo*, the Italian brand of operatic realism, his works, with their strong influence from German romanticism, began to lose their attraction. Of Catalani's five operas, *Loreley* (1890) and *La Wally* (1892), the best of them, can still be heard in Italy. One of Catalani's most ardent admirers and devoted interpreters was Toscanini, who in fact made his Italian début in 1886 with Catalani's third opera, *Edmea*. There was a close spiritual kinship between these two musicians, both being men of ideals and high artistic principles; and an intimate friendship sprang up between them which was only severed by Catalani's premature death in 1893. In later years Toscanini would often extoll his friend's noble yet rather anaemic music at the expense of Puccini's.[11]

While Puccini was still a student at the Milan Conservatoire he often visited Catalani, his senior by four years; Catalani 'is most kind to me', he wrote home. But this friendly relationship subsequently deteriorated into an ill-concealed hostility on the part of the older composer when Puccini, as we shall see, was taken up by Giulio Ricordi, then head of the great firm of Milan music publishers, and when Catalani's own operas were beginning to be overshadowed by those of his fellow-Lucchese. There is every reason to suspect that Ricordi, who first had encouraged Catalani, dropped him in favour of Puccini's rising star. Catalani was a sick man—he suffered from tuberculosis and died at the age of thirty-nine—who grew embittered and morbidly jealous of the successes of others, notably Puccini, whom he accused of intrigues against him and of plagiarism from his operas. There are in existence a number of highly interesting letters by Catalani on this subject, which also throw a revealing light on what was going on behind the scenes of the Milan operatic world of that period. They were addressed to the Turin critic Giuseppe Depanis, an intimate friend of his, to whom Catalani unburdened his heart without restraint.[12] In order to appreciate what Catalani has to say, the reader must be asked to take a jump forward in time, to the period between 1889 and 1893 when Puccini's *Edgar* and *Manon Lescaut* had already been composed.

In April 1889 the first production of *Edgar* had taken place at La Scala and in the following summer Puccini was sent by Ricordi to Bayreuth whence he was

PUCCINI
IN BOYHOOD

AT THE TIME OF *LE VILLI*

THREE OF PUCCINI'S SISTERS
(In the middle: Iginia)

to report on a production of *Die Meistersinger*. These two events prompted Catalani to write the following to Depanis:

Casate Nuovo,
nr. Monteregio
20 August 1889

Lucky you to be there now [Bayreuth] to enjoy the most elevated enjoyment that the soul of an artist could ever desire! Not everyone has the luck to travel at his publisher's expense like Puccini, who, provided with a good pair of scissors, has been charged by the publishers to make the necessary cuts in the *Die Meistersinger* so as to adjust them, like clothes, to the shoulders of the good Milanese. But the Milanese are growing rebellious, they now want the clothes just as they have been worn until now by the Germans, and the papers are beginning to protest. It is therefore not surprising if (between ourselves) the same pair of scissors which served to cut Wagner, will, instead, serve to cut that 'web of publicity' which the publisher has woven round his favourite composer, or if the tailor himself will become a laughing-stock. But joking apart, I believe that Puccini, with a levity that is unheard of, undertook a task which might cause him serious damage. What do you say? To me it seems unbelievable, like a dream.

I am telling you these things in confidence because you are my intimate friend; but to you, my friend, I can't conceal the bitterness in my heart when I see what succeeds; and I am frightened at the thought of what my future will be, now that there is only one publisher and this publisher won't hear mention of anybody else but Puccini. Do you know that Verdi himself—I was told this by Pantaleoni*—intervened so that *Edgar* should be given again this year at La Scala and that Verdi himself begged Pantaleoni to sing again the part of Tigrana in it? All this seems absurd to me... But it is only right that it should be like that, because these days 'dynasties' reign also in the realm of art and I know that Puccini 'must' be the successor of Verdi ... who, like a good king, often invites the 'Crown Prince' to dinner! Oh! what a comedy the world is, and what ugly comedy! And how sick I am of it all!

As to the cuts which Puccini made in *Die Meistersinger* at Ricordi's bidding, and which roused Catalani to justifiable indignation, it has to be explained that performances of cut versions of the Wagner operas were, with the sole exceptions of the Bayreuth productions, the rule rather than the exception well into the 1900s, not only in Italy but elsewhere too, including Germany. Yet what, one wonders, would Catalani's reaction have been had he ever had an inkling of the proposal which in 1880 Giovannina Lucca, the enterprising wife of a well-known Milan music publisher, made to Wagner in all seriousness? Of this she informed Catalani's friend Depanis in a letter which must be read to be believed:

17 November 1880

I have so far abstained from publishing the *Ring* because I want to persuade Wagner to reduce the tetralogy, if possible, and while preserving its grandiose character, shorten it so that it will last one single evening [*sic!*]. At the moment he does not yet seem to me disposed to it, and when I discussed this matter

* Romilda Pantaleoni was a celebrated soprano and Verdi's first Desdemona, though not to his satisfaction.

with him, he said he didn't know how to do it but that I should do it myself if I thought I could succeed. It is therefore a serious matter about which I would have to think a lot, and perhaps I shall do it myself. When I go to Bayreuth again I shall be able to form a better idea of how the drama could be cut.[13]

There is no record whether Giovannina's fantastic proposal was ever put into effect.

As to Catalani's caustic remarks about 'dynasties' and Puccini being 'the successor of Verdi', there is no evidence at all that Verdi himself regarded him in this light, though he may conceivably have considered him the most gifted of the young school of Italian opera composers. It was, very possibly, Ricordi who encouraged rumours of Verdi 'like a good king often inviting the Crown Prince to dinner' and who kept bringing up Puccini's name in the presence of the old master. Had not Ricordi, according to Catalani, described *Manon Lescaut* as 'the most beautiful opera so far written by a composer who is not Verdi'? Verdi's own attitude to the *'giovane scuola'* was one of paternal benevolence and, in Puccini's case, of critical interest, though it may be doubted whether this interest went at all far. His general relation to the young composers of his time, especially to Catalani, would appear in a far less benign light if we were to give credence to three letters, included in the *Carteggi Verdiani* but whose authenticity is very doubtful.[14] They are supposed to have been written to his friend Perosio, from Genoa in the autumn of 1892. I quote the following extracts:

> . . . I do not believe that those gentlemen [the directors of the Genoa Opera] will expect that on the pretext of giving my *Otello* or because they wish to honour the Great Discoverer of Genoa, I shall show myself in the theatre; still less, in order to hear the new German opera of that little master of Lucca [*maestrino lucchese*] of which they tell me, however, that it had a success at La Scala.* Ricordi spoke to me about it; he obstinately insists on publishing his operas but I do not think this will be to his advantage. The public wants Italian music and not imitations or travesties of German music. We need other stuff than 'the Music of the Future'! You can tell everyone that I am not in Genoa and that I will not come to hear any new opera, not even my own. Write to me about these events but I don't believe that the opera will survive, in spite of the Milan production, because no vital music can be written without heart and inspiration. These young composers who want reforms and to pursue new paths, seem to me a little ill-advised, and by placing too much trust in the future will end by losing the present.

This was followed by a second letter to Perosio:

> It is being said that I am making war on Catalani and that I am exerting pressure on Signor Giulio [Ricordi] so that he should not publish his operas or obstruct their sale and hire. Fairy-tales! I have other things to bother my head about than the little master from Lucca; Catalani won't cause me sleepless nights. These Lucchese are very obstinate and headstrong people. Tell him that I can't be bothered with him or the others. At this rate he will not

* *La Wally* by Catalani, produced there on 20 January 1892. Yet Verdi had heard a performance of it in March of that year!

make his way by himself. But if he fails to get on, he should not accuse me of not being interested in him.

'These Lucchese' would seem to include Puccini, too.

To return to Catalani's feud with Puccini. On 1 February 1893 the latter's *Manon Lescaut* was to be produced at Turin. Catalani writes to Depanis:

Milan, 26 January 1893

I know that *Manon* is to be given at Turin on Wednesday, but unfortunately I can't come. I certainly don't wish Puccini what he wished me for the first production of my *Edmea* at La Scala [1886], any more than I wish that Ricordi's prophecy should come true, namely that *Manon* will cast into oblivion all the other modern operas; that would be a little too much! The whole Milan Press will be there . . . and I know that the critics are inspired by benevolence and enthusiasm for Puccini to compensate him for the excessive attacks they had made on his *Edgar*. But the truth I shall find, as usual, in your notice.

I now want to tell you something concerning myself, which Noseda [a Milan critic] told me and which, in all modesty, pleased me. At the dinner which Franchetti gave in Milan, they talked about Tuscan composers— some extolling Puccini and others Mascagni, trying to make the one or the other into the leader of a school, when Franchetti joined in and said: 'Since it seems indeed that a Tuscan school is in the making, it is neither Puccini nor Mascagni who deserves the credit for it but Catalani. At Hamburg when *Cavalleria* was produced there, they found that it derived from *Le Villi* [Puccini's first opera]. But let them give *Loreley* there—*La Wally* is too recent—and you will see what they will say. Puccini derives from the old *Elda* from which he took, amongst other things, the theme of the Funeral March, and from *Dejanice* [another of Catalani's operas].

This is what Franchetti said and it pleases me that it should have been he who said it, because I myself, though thinking the same, did not have the courage to say it. I assure you, I believe in nothing more than in that truth expressed by Franchetti, and I could wish that one day when an opportunity offers itself, you would affirm it. Noseda has promised to do the same. By God! for twelve long years have I been working and fighting: should I now sit still and watch the ground being taken away from under my feet? Indeed, no! But excuse this chatter!

Franchetti's assertion about the great artistic debt owed by Puccini to Catalani, which pleased Catalani so much, is a fantastic exaggeration; such influence as Catalani exercised on him was, as we shall see later, of a slight and episodic nature.

Poor Catalani experienced the most bitter stabs of jealousy when Puccini's *Manon Lescaut* began its triumphant round in Italy while his own operas were being increasingly neglected. He wrote to Depanis:

Milan, 28 February 1893

I found the air here fully saturated with an extraordinary Puccini enthusiasm [*Puccinianismo*]. All the papers are in his favour and so are all the theatres. Lucky Puccini who knew how to plant his feet firmly on the ground. I haven't managed yet to do that. *La Wally* should have been given at Brescia this year but instead . . . I swear to you I would not complain but for the partiality shown by the House Ricordi. There ought to be room for everybody in this world but that is not the view there—in that House!

Catalani, who looked upon the success of the veristic school with an ill-concealed mixture of jealousy and ironic contempt, commented to Depanis:

Milan, 20 May 1893

Yesterday I read in the *Corriere della Sera* a report from Berlin which states that Wagner has been completely abandoned by the German opera houses and been replaced by Mascagni, Leoncavallo, Puccini and Franchetti! I am glad not to have been mentioned among those for whom it is reserved to bear such artistic responsibility! They will be lucky if they possess shoulders strong enough to carry Wagner's heritage. Ah, decadence, decadence!

Seven weeks after this letter, Catalani was dead.

4

We have anticipated in our chronicle and must now return to the year 1883. In mid-July, Puccini's studies at the Milan Conservatoire came to an end, and according to the regulations he had to pass his final examination by way of a 'leaving exercise'. This was, surprisingly enough, not a vocal but an orchestral composition, the *Capriccio Sinfonico*, the only independent orchestral piece of his that possesses more than a merely biographical importance. It was composed in bits and pieces. As Puccini told his biographer Fraccaroli: 'I felt inspired and composed it at home, in the street, in class, at the *Osteria Aida* or at the *Excelsior* of good old Sgr Gigi where one ate without the silly pretence of being able to pay for it; I wrote on odd sheets, bits of paper and the margin of newspapers. . .' No wonder that his teacher Ponchielli found it impossible to make head or tail of the composition; but the miracle is that Puccini himself contrived to write out a full and legible score from those sketches and, still more, that, despite such an erratic method of composing, the *Capriccio* makes musical sense and good sense at that. The work was played by the students' orchestra on 14 July under the direction of Franco Faccio, the outstanding Italian conductor of the time. (Verdi held him in the highest esteem, entrusting him with the first European performance of *Aida*.) The success of the *Capriccio* must have been considerable, for the next day Filippo Filippi, Italy's most influential critic, devoted in *La Perseveranza* a highly favourable and fairly detailed notice to the work.* He speaks of Puccini showing 'a decisive and

* Filippi was a staunch supporter of Verdi but at the same time an ardent Wagnerian who fought hard for the acceptance by his compatriots of the German composer's music. His *Riccardo Wagner* (1876) was translated into German. Verdi exchanged some correspondence with him and to Filippi was addressed the famous letter of 1869 in which the great man discusses his own attitude to the music of other musicians, declaring himself 'the least learned of composers, past and present'. In later years, Verdi seems to have resented Filippi's advocacy of more frequent performances of orchestral and chamber music (which meant a great deal of German music) as 'the Great Art', as Filippi called it (see Verdi's ironic letter to Arrivabene of 1879). Filippi was the editor of the *Gazzetta Musicale*, founded by Tito Ricordi in 1852 and later renamed *Musica d'Oggi*, a most useful source for the musical history of that period.

very rare musical temperament, one that is specifically symphonic' and singles out 'unity of style, personality and character. In the *Capriccio Sinfonico* there is so much of these things, such as few composers of greater experience have given proof of in their orchestral works. I speak, of course, only of the living'. Filippi was certainly justified in his praise, for the *Capriccio* is genuinely inspired, fresh and engaging music; yet in describing Puccini's temperament as 'specifically symphonic' he was wide of the mark. Filippi's strong bias for orchestral music made him no doubt miss the structural weakness of a work whose chief claim to symphonic stature may be said to lie in its title. However, a notice by so eminent a critic appearing in one of Italy's great national papers was enough to render the twenty-five-year-old composer famous literally overnight. After the performance at the Conservatoire, Faccio, who was conductor at La Scala, offered to include the *Capriccio Sinfonico* in one of the regular orchestral concerts there, but nothing appears to have come of it. It was played, though, on two more occasions, also under Faccio, during an exhibition at Turin in the following year, but this is the last we hear of that work. For in later years, Puccini could not be persuaded to consent to publication or even a performance, presumably because he thought very little of this youthful excursion into the symphonic field. Did he not declare on more than one occasion that he lacked the symphonic gift? But an equally potent reason for this refusal may be found in the fact that having freely lifted from the *Capriccio* for two operas, *Edgar* and *La Bohème*, he did not wish these barefaced 'borrowings' to be discovered by the Italian public, a public notoriously sensitive to and quick in nosing out 'reminiscences'; as the composer was to experience to his cost at the first performances of *La Bohème* and *Madam Butterfly*. To make assurance doubly sure, he later went to the length of loaning the autograph score from the Library of the Milan Conservatoire, where according to the regulations it had been deposited after that students' performance in 1883, and never returned it! (It may now be inspected again at the Conservatoire.) Yet Puccini appears to have forgotten the arrangement for piano duet, made by Giuseppe Frugatta, which *was* published.

The publisher of this version was Francesco Lucca, whose wife Giovannina we have already met in connection with her famous proposal to Wagner. Up to 1887, the year in which this firm was bought up by Ricordi, Lucca was Ricordi's most serious rival. Ironically enough, he had learned his trade with Giovanni Ricordi, the founder of that firm and grandfather of Giulio, but in 1825 he had made himself independent and founded his own publishing house. Lucca brought out two of Verdi's early operas, *I Masnadieri* (1847) and *Il Corsaro* (1848), and might have continued as Verdi's publisher but for a contretemps he had over some contractual matter to do with the last-named opera, as a result of which Verdi broke with 'this most exacting and indelicate Lucca'—and went over to his rival Tito Ricordi. Yet when in November 1866 *Un Ballo in Maschera* was given at Venice, and owing to a bad production proved a disastrous failure, Verdi blamed Ricordi for it, accusing him of negligence in the supervision of the rehearsals and making a veiled threat of leaving the firm: 'I would not feel disconsolate', he wrote to Tito in December 1866, 'if my operas were in the hands of someone who took greater trouble over their success. The affair of *Un Ballo in Maschera* at Venice was a scandal !'[15] That 'someone' was Francesco Lucca, who, according to Verdi, always saw to it that the operas published by his firm (*L'Africaine*, *La Juive*, *Faust*) were staged with proper care. 'But the damage', Verdi concludes his letter, 'has been done. If I permit myself to give you an advice in order to repair some of it, I should say: combine your interests with those of Lucca at the first favourable opportunity and establish one large firm. It is good and useful advice. Do with it what you like!' Verdi's advice, tendered to his father, remained in young Giulio Ricordi's mind; and twenty-one years later he carried it into effect when, as already mentioned, he bought up the firm of Lucca and merged it with his own into G. Ricordi & Co., a limited company, consisting of a number of shareholders with himself as managing director. By this transaction Ricordi acquired the Italian rights of the Wagner operas as well as those of other non-Italian works; for Lucca's special line of business had been foreign operas, while Ricordi, more conservative and nationalistic in outlook, confined himself largely to the publication of native operas.

The driving spirit in the firm of Lucca was Giovannina, a woman of great enterprise and of advanced artistic tastes, who was inspired by a genuine interest in the 'new music' of her time, especially Wagner's. At her instigation Lucca became his first Italian publisher and this at a period when Wagner was known in Italy only from hearsay and when in Germany also he was still encountering strong opposition in many quarters. She it was who visited him at Lucerne in July 1868 and negotiated with him about the publication and first Italian production of *Rienzi*, which on account of its subject seemed the most suitable opera with which to introduce Wagner to the Italian public. In the event it was not *Rienzi* but *Lohengrin* which was first published by Lucca; it was also the first Wagner opera to be produced in Italy (Bologna, 1871), an event that gave rise to all those heated controversies and polemics of which we shall hear later in connection with Puccini's first opera.

Giovannina also instituted a travelling scholarship to be awarded annually to the most gifted student composer on leaving the Milan Conservatoire, including publication of his 'master' composition—hence her publication of Puccini's *Capriccio Sinfonico*. The old lady's ardent patronage of youth was made the subject of an amusing cartoon, published in 1879 by the *Gazzetta dei Teatri*, showing Giovannina as a grandmother, with crinoline, bonnet and all, dangling a grandchild of hers by his legs, upside down, and lifting him high up. The grandchild wears a beard and pince-nez, with a score in his hand bearing the title '*Preziosa*. Opera Seria del Maestro A. Smareglia. F. Lucca. Editore'.*

* Smareglia, a contemporary of Puccini's and a Wagnerian, later made his name with *Cornelius Schutt* (1893) and, especially, *Nozze Istriane* (1895). The cartoon is reproduced in *La Vita di Arrigo Boito*, by Piero Nardi. 2nd ed. Milan, 1944.

IV

First Steps in Opera

I

AT THE TIME OF LEAVING the Conservatoire Maestro Puccini, as he now
had to be addressed by virtue of his diploma, was faced with a serious
dilemma. Dr. Cerù's subsidy had ceased, nor could any substantial help be
expected from his mother, who was beginning to ail. The choice was
between remaining in Milan and fending for himself as best he could or—a
far less inviting prospect—returning to Lucca, where probably he could have
obtained the post of organist at the Cathedral for the mere asking. An offer
to teach at his former Conservatoire, the Pacini Institute, he declined with
the words 'class-rooms give me claustrophobia'. Puccini thus showed early
in life his characteristic aversion to occupying a teaching or any other
official post, such as most musicians in his precarious circumstances would
have accepted with alacrity. Neither then nor later was he prepared to
sacrifice the freedom of a creative artist to a secure but humdrum career as a
teacher of composition, for which he was in any case temperamentally
unfitted. To return to Lucca was out of the question—after all, had he not
left it and gone to Milan because opera was the be-all and end-all of his
ambition?

While still at the Milan Conservatoire he was already 'biting my fingers
with rage' because 'here they all write operas at full steam, but for me,
nothing!' as he wrote to his mother (undated, E). True, the *Capriccio* had
revealed an outstanding talent and its success had made Puccini's name known
in influential Milanese circles, but as an operatic composer he was a completely unknown quantity; it was not likely that any librettist of experience
and repute would be prepared to associate himself with a fledgling, nor had
Puccini the means to commission a libretto. It was here that his fatherly
friend and teacher Ponchielli came to the rescue. He sought to engage Giulio
Ricordi's interest in his former pupil, though, as he pointed out to the
impatient Puccini, the great publisher was not likely to extend his patronage
to one who had not yet given tangible proofs of his operatic talent, and the
first step to that was finding a suitable libretto and setting it to music. A
happy coincidence set things into swift motion. On 1 April, shortly before
Puccini was to leave the Conservatoire, there appeared in the *Teatro Illustrato*
the announcement of a competition for the best one-act opera. Operas of
such short duration were comparatively rare before this period; that the
competition was expressly for one-act works shows the growing influence
exercised by short realistic stories and plays upon the operatic stage. This

35

vogue was to reach its peak, in the following decades, in the veristic operas of Mascagni and Leoncavallo, and the two one-act operas by Richard Strauss; and a last echo of its was heard some thirty years later in the three short operas of Puccini's *Trittico*.

The competition of 1883, the first of several, was sponsored by Edoardo Sonzogno, the scion of a wealthy family of Milan industrialists. A writer himself and the proprietor of the newspaper *Il Secolo*, Sonzogno also owned a theatre in Milan, the Teatro Lirico, and had recently founded a music publishing firm. Combining business acumen with genuine enthusiasm for music, he sought to discover and attract to his firm new talents, with which end in view he instituted a prize competition for one-act operas—the *Concorso Sonzogno*. At first no outstanding work was discovered in these *concorsi*—until in 1889 *Cavalleria Rusticana* was brought to light in this way. It is interesting to mention that, before Mascagni entered the work for this competition, Puccini had shown the score to Giulio Ricordi, who rejected it because 'I don't believe in this opera'—one of the very few miscalculations ever made by this shrewdest of operatic judges. After the tremendous success of *Cavalleria*, however, Ricordi attempted to redress his error by publishing Mascagni's opera *Iris* (1898) on a Japanese subject, a work far more refined yet far less successful than *Cavalleria*; *Cavalleria* was the only one to survive of the operas that at one time or another won the Sonzogno Prize, which ceased to be awarded after 1904.*

To return to Puccini. No sooner had the announcement of the competition been published than he decided to take part in it—'but the thing is most uncertain', he writes to his mother in July, 'imagine, the contest is open to all Italy, not restricted and local as I had thought. Besides, time is short' (*E*). Indeed there were no more than nine months between the date of Sonzogno's announcement and the closing date for the submission of entries, 31 December 1883.

Of the ten rules governing the competition the last deserves special mention:

> The music must be inspired by the best traditions of Italian opera but must not ignore contemporary achievements in our own and foreign music. Moreover, the apt choice of a libretto considered from the point of view of both *subject* and *versification* will speak in favour of a candidate. For we think it desirable in a work for the theatre that there shall be no discrepancy between the values of the music and those of the libretto.

Hence the most urgent problem for Puccini was to find a librettist who would be able to meet this intelligent requirement. It was his erstwhile teacher and fatherly friend Ponchielli who came to the rescue. Ponchielli happened to know a young writer and journalist, Ferdinando Fontana, who appears to have been busy just then on a libretto for some composer

* In 1902 Delius wrote for it his unpublished opera *Margot-la-Rouge* of which his biographer Peter Warlock wrote that 'there is hardly a trace of the familiar Delius from beginning to end and it seems as if he had deliberately "written down" to the well-known competition level in this opera'. (*Frederick Delius*. 3rd ed. London, 1953.)

or other. As it happened, Ponchielli and Fontana were both invited, about the middle of July, to stay with Ghislanzoni, the librettist of Verdi's *Aida*, at Caprino Bergamasco, near Milan, where he ran a kind of family hotel called *Il Barco;* the majority of guests were poets, writers and musicians to whom their generous and slightly eccentric host would rarely present a bill—no wonder that Ghislanzoni's *pensione* was filled to capacity almost all the year round. It was there that Ponchielli, taking advantage of the opportunity of meeting Fontana, broached the subject of a libretto for his young protégé. Fontana was willing enough to oblige but made difficulties over the fee. The matter was eventually settled, chiefly owing to Ponchielli's entreaties; in a letter (25 July 1883) he told Fontana it was 'useless to repeat that Puccini has no means and that therefore he appeals to your well-known generosity'.* Fontana's reply is worth quoting in full for the vanity and amusing tortuosities of its writer:

> I should be very happy to be of use to Maestro Puccini, but you know how I am always sailing in shallow water. I have managed to keep the wolf from my door even without resorting to the boring task of writing librettos, and if I write one now I expect to make a profit at least. Therefore I shall write no more librettos for less than 300 lire per act.
>
> However, since I consider myself an intelligent and not unattractive young man, and you know that I am not intransigent and the fee I am quoting is the minimum within reason, and much less than I would earn at some other task though it might be one less glamorous than that of librettist, yet writing a libretto is an appealing occupation and very amusing and more in keeping with my intellectual tastes: I propose therefore to follow your suggestion, and I ask 100 lire to be paid on the completion of the libretto with an additional 200 lire to be paid if Puccini wins the contest. Surely this is sufficiently reasonable!†

The bargain was finally struck in August when also the question of the subject was settled, a supernatural one based on a legend about ghost-maidens and said to be of Slavonic origin though its setting is the Black Forest. It remains a mystery why Fontana should have thought that 'with the *Capriccio Sinfonico* still vivid in my memory, a fantastic subject seemed to me what the young composer needed'.[16]

After that meeting Puccini wrote home:

Milan, July 1883

Dear Mother,

I went to stay four days at Ponchielli's [at the latter's summer-villa at Maggianico]. I spoke to Fontana, the poet, who was spending his holiday in the neighbourhood and we have almost settled the matter of a libretto. He also told me that he liked my music. Ponchielli then intervened and

---

* The full letter is reproduced in Fraccaroli, op. cit.

† Reproduced in del Fiorentino, op. cit., without indication of source and date. Fontana provided the libretti, in addition to those for Puccini's first two operas, for *Asrael* by Franchetti and for a number of other composers, and was later responsible for the Italian translation of d'Albert's *Tiefland* and Lehár's *Die lustige Witwe*.

recommended me warmly. It would be a good subject. Somebody had been considering it, but Fontana would like to give it to me instead, all the more so since I like it very much. It will give me ample scope for music of the symphonic descriptive kind which rather appeals to me because I think I ought to make a good job of it.

He concluded his letter with his customary refrain, a request for money:

I have here two weeks' board and lodging to pay and if I return to Lucca, I shall need twenty lire in order to redeem my watch and tie-pin which at the moment breathe the air of the mountain* (E).

In early September Puccini returned to Lucca—it is uncertain whether with or without his two precious effects—but with Fontana's completed libretto in his pocket. He at once plunged head over heels into the composition of his first opera, which was at first called *Le Willis* but was subsequently Italianized into *Le Villi*. He worked at immense pressure, yet even so he all but missed the closing date of the competition, dispatching the manuscript on the last day of December, without having had the time to make a fair copy. This fact appears to have been his undoing. When the result of the contest was announced in early 1884, Puccini's opera received not even an honourable mention. There is a strong suspicion that the jury scarcely troubled to examine Puccini's work, the score of which had been written in such haste that, according to his own description, it was all but illegible. The prize of 2,000 lire (£80) was divided between two composers neither of whom was to achieve eminence thereafter: Guglielmo Zuelli for his *Fata del Nord* (based, like Puccini's opera, on a legend) and Luigi Mapelli for his *Anna e Gualberto*; both operas were produced at the Teatro Manzoni in May 1884. Zuelli, a fellow-student of Puccini's at the Milan Conservatoire and later director of the Parma Conservatoire, frankly admitted in an interview given after Puccini's death that *Le Villi* was far superior to his own prize-winning opera. Writing to Puccini in 1913 to request his support in some musical project or other, Zuelli reminded him of that competition in this amusing doggerel:

> Sebben di Sonzogno vincessi il concorso
> Il pelo rimisi qual fossi un grand'orso;
> E tu che perdesti il Concorso Sonzogno
> Vincesti la gloria e a me restò il sogno!†

2

Puccini's setback in failing to win the competition was soon to be redressed, however. Fontana, being as anxious as the composer to see the child of their

* This is a pun on *monte di pietà*, an Italian euphemism for a pawnshop.

† Reproduced in Fraccaroli, op. cit. It is impossible to render this doggerel in English since it makes play with untranslatable puns on *Sonzogno—sogno* (dream) and *Concorso—orso* (bear). Zuelli says, in effect, that although he won the Sonzogno Prize and Puccini lost it, *he* remained with only vain hopes and dreams while Puccini achieved fame.

united efforts come to life on the stage, now began, with the active help of Ponchielli, to canvas *Le Villi* among a wide circle of influential persons. And the most expedient way in which to bring Puccini himself to the direct attention of such circles was to get him invited to those elegant *salons* of which Milan, like Paris, boasted a number during the nineteenth century, and which were the meeting-place for Milan's social and artistic *élite*. In Verdi's time two of the most celebrated *salons* were those of his friend and confidante, the Contessa Clara Maffei, and of the Contessa Eugenia Litta; in Puccini's early years it was the house of Marco Sala, a wealthy and somewhat eccentric member of Milan society, who was himself a gifted amateur composer, violinist and the author of light verse.

Early in 1884 Puccini was invited to Sala's, with a view to playing excerpts from his opera before a select gathering. Among the guests was Boito, a fact not without irony. In his capacity as writer and composer Boito was frequently asked to sit on various juries for the adjudication of dramatic as well as musical works, and it is almost certain that he sat on the very jury which had rejected Puccini's opera. That Boito served on one of Sonzogno's juries is attested by a photograph which shows him sitting *in camera* with other judges and examining libretti.[17] Boito's presence at that party was of paramount importance to Puccini. Boito, who at that time was occupied with the libretto for Verdi's *Otello*, represented the foremost arbiter of Milan's intellectual and artistic taste. Poet, writer, critic and composer in one person and the leader of Italy's *avant-garde*, his influence was immense.* To become his protégé signified for the tyro that his first battle had been won. Yet Boito was a man of unimpeachable integrity and penetrating judgement who would give his support only where his artistic conscience and convictions permitted him. He lent a helping hand to Catalani, Zandonai and Puccini during their early struggles, and he it was who, after the successful première of *Le Villi*, introduced its young composer to Verdi. Yet Boito was out of sympathy with Puccini's later development and altogether rejected the general movement toward realistic opera. Steeped as he was in the great literature of the past, in Dante, Shakespeare and Goethe, and pursuing in his own poetry and music the path of a romantic idealism (*Mefistofele*, 1875), Boito was unable to reconcile himself to the new tendencies which increasingly invaded Western art after the 1870s. Boito was a striking illustration of a well-known phenomenon: the man who in his young days had fought an unceasing battle against his country's conservative taste and who by his polemical and critical writings had urged his countrymen to active participation in a movement towards a new European art—not for nothing had he been dubbed by his enemies '*un avvenirista*'—'a futurist'— in his middle age deliberately shut himself off from the ideals of a younger generation. When Puccini was considering the subject of *La Bohème*, Boito

* The nickname given by the Milanese to these young iconoclasts was '*La Scapigliatura*'— 'The Dissolute Ones'. Their habits strikingly recalled those of Mürger's Bohemians in his celebrated novel. The musical members included Puccini, Leoncavallo, Mascagni and Franchetti.

tried his utmost to dissuade him from it, his fundamental argument against the use of a realistic subject in opera being that 'music is written to bring to life episodes worthy of being remembered ... music is the essence distilled from history, legend, the heart of man and the mysteries of Nature'. The subsequent success of *La Bohème* was so unexpected to him that henceforward he declined to pronounce judgment on any libretto submitted to him. Nevertheless, with *La Bohème* his interest in his one-time protégé waned and in later years he lumped Puccini together with the representatives of unadulterated realism whom he held in utter contempt. Thus in his frequent correspondence with Camille Bellaigue, one of Verdi's early French biographers, he referred on one occasion to Leoncavallo's *Pagliacci* as 'that vile spectacle' and on another declared that 'the *charivari* entitled *Salome* [Strauss's opera] is nothing but a clatter of pots and pans which lasts for an hour and fifty minutes'.[18]

We must retrace our steps to that evening at Marco Sala's. The excerpts from *Le Villi*, sung and played by Puccini at the piano, made so favourable an impression that it was decided there and then to collect funds in order to get the opera produced. Fontana took charge of this operation and was soon able to inform the composer—in the meantime Puccini had returned home as his mother was beginning to show serious signs of ill health—that the appeal had been so successful that only twenty more lire were needed to reach the sum of 450 lire, which was the estimated cost for costumes and for copying the orchestral material. In addition, Giulio Ricordi volunteered to print copies of the libretto *gratis*. This too was probably due to Fontana's persuasive advocacy, for he writes to Puccini in April 1884: 'I'm putting the finishing touches to the libretto and will send it tomorrow to Ricordi with a flowery letter'—Ricordi, in his anti-Wagnerian attitude, having first inquired of Fontana whether there was not in Puccini 'a bit of a Wagnerian'.[19] It may well be that the publisher had suggested certain alterations and improvements in the text, as he was to do with Puccini's subsequent libretti. Also the music was revised. Boito was instrumental in getting Steffanoni, the manager of the Teatro dal Verme (now a cinema), to agree to a production at his theatre which was fixed for the end of May. Puccini arrived back in Milan and reported on 13 May to his mother:

> As you will have heard, my little opera is to be given at the dal Verme. I did not mention it before because the thing was not certain. Many people in society and also persons of importance like A. Boito, Marco Sala and others have helped to make the production possible by each guaranteeing a certain sum. I wrote to our relatives and to Cerù to ask them to help me with the expenses for copying which may amount to 200 lire and more; but at the moment I'm not sure, it may be more... How are you? I know you're always the same, poor Mother! Michele is well and sends you much love. Later I'll write you a longer letter. I have so much to do that I have no time to write to my dear, good Mother.
>
> Be gay. A Kiss.
Giacomo (E).

The première of *Le Villi* on 31 May was announced in this unorthodox manner: 'Tonight at the Teatro dal Verme will be given the first performance of another of the operas submitted to the competition of the *Teatro Illustrato*, one of the works that received neither a prize nor an honourable mention.' No doubt curiosity to hear an opera rejected by the jury yet championed by such musicians as Boito and Ponchielli was largely responsible for filling the theatre to capacity. The principal roles were taken by Caporetti (Anna) and Antonio d'Andrade (Roberto), (the brother of the more celebrated baritone), and the conductor was Achille Panizza; one of the double-bass players was—Mascagni.

Le Villi, styled '*opera-ballo*' on account of a witches' dance in it, and given in a triple bill with two other works,* achieved a sensational success. The symphonic *Intermezzo*† had to be played three times and two other numbers were encored—the love duet and the tenor's *Romanza*. On the next day, Albina Puccini received the following telegram: 'Clamorous success. Hopes surpassed. Eighteen calls. First finale repeated three times. Am happy. Giacomo.' The critics appeared to vie with one another in bestowing the highest praise on Puccini's first-born, Gramola of the *Corriere della Sera* committing himself to the hyperbole: 'Here is craftsmanship so elegant and finished that from time to time we seem to have before us not a young student but a Bizet or Massenet.' Reference is made to the freshness of Puccini's invention, the moving appeal of his phrases and a singular gift for melody. What pleased in particular was the blend of 'symphonic' writing with operatic melody or, as Gramola put it more generally, Puccini's acceptance of 'those new theories which favour an [orchestral] comment, yet without disdaining the artistic criteria of the great old master'. Gramola concludes his long notice with the prophetic sentence: 'We sincerely believe that Puccini may be the composer for whom Italy has been waiting a long time.' Needless to say, scorn and derision were poured out over the '*povera commissione*'—'that wretched jury which accorded Puccini not even an honourable mention . . . and threw him into a corner like a piece of rag' (Filippi in *La Perseveranza*).

The success of *Le Villi* was immediately reported (possibly by Ricordi) to Verdi, who in a letter to Arrivabene, dated 10 June, made the following characteristic comment:

> . . . I have seen a letter speaking very highly of the composer Puccini. He follows modern tendencies, of course, but sticks to melody which is neither ancient nor modern. It seems, however, that the symphonic element predominates in him—though there's no harm in that. Only, it is necessary to go warily in that direction; opera is opera and symphony, symphony; and I don't believe in introducing symphonic passages just for the sake of giving the orchestra a chance to let fly. . .[20]

It is uncertain whether Verdi ever saw *Le Villi* in the flesh, or, for that matter, any of Puccini's three subsequent operas; but while in Genoa in

---

* The opera *Jone* by Petrella and a ballet *La Contessa d'Egmont*.

† In the first, one-act version of the opera it formed the conclusion of the first finale.

1899 he expressed admiration for his 'theatrical intuition', which suggests that he may have attended an actual production.

The most immediate result which the success of Le Villi brought to Puccini is seen from an announcement in the Gazzetta Musicale of 8 June: 'The House of Ricordi herewith notifies that they have acquired the absolute rights of Le Villi for all countries. . . In addition they have commissioned Maestro Puccini to compose a new opera to a libretto by Ferdinando Fontana. The new work is to be given at La Scala.'* Puccini's youthful dream had come true. His ship was now launched on the waters on which he had so much wanted to sail. Many years later when he had amassed a huge fortune from royalties accruing in every corner of the globe, he remembered Le Villi and the sudden change of fortune it had brought him: 'I arrived with forty centesimi in my pocket', he told Adami. 'That was all the capital I had when, dressed in the only maroon-coloured suit I possessed, I stepped amidst acclamations before the footlights. But four days later Giulio Ricordi bought the opera and handed me the first thousand-lire note of my life.'[21] Thus began Puccini's lifelong association with the House of Ricordi which was to suffer only a brief interruption at the time of La Rondine. Moreover, in the head of the firm he was to find not only a publisher who early recognized that Puccini carried a field-marshal's baton in his knapsack, but also a paternal friend and shrewd counsellor.

On Ricordi's advice Puccini recast Le Villi into a full-length opera of two acts, in which form, as the publisher rightly guessed, it proved more acceptable to the larger theatres. The new version, completed on 28 October, was first given at the Teatro Regio, Turin, on 26 December, when it repeated the success of the Milan première, though the performance itself was an inferior one—'the singers are a lot of crocks. The orchestra is weak and lifeless . . . the chorus is lamentably weak . . . the less said about the ballet the better', as Puccini reported to Ricordi (E). This report is the first example to illustrate that highly critical attitude toward his artists which, coupled with his insistence on the strictest observation of his demands, musical no less than scenic, later discomfited producers, singers and conductors alike. Verdi's example had not been wasted on Puccini.

On 24 January 1885, five weeks after the Turin production, Le Villi reached Italy's teatro massimo, La Scala. This was no mean distinction for a young beginner, but the reception was cool. It appears that the same features which Verdi had criticized—the symphonic-descriptive orchestra and its conspicuous role in vocal numbers—troubled the conservative Scala audience too. This we gather from a letter of the famous singer Teresa Stolz, Verdi's intimate, which she wrote him a day after the Scala performance:

> . . . Last night I attended the première of Le Villi by Puccini. The public was not greatly excited about it. . .

* Here again the parallel with Verdi is noteworthy. Verdi, too, had his first opera produced when he was only twenty-six; and, like the success of Le Villi, that of Oberto (Milan, 1839) resulted in a commission to write an opera for La Scala.

The second act begins with a descriptive orchestral piece, in the middle of which one sees, behind a veil, the funeral of the young girl. . .

These dances [the ballet of the ghost-maidens] reveal nothing new and also remind one of the music of Bizet.

Then the tenor appears to sing in a long dramatic scene; the orchestra, which is very elaborate, entirely covers the tenor's voice. One sees him open his mouth and gesticulate but it's only every now and again that one hears some shouts on the high notes, and that is all.

This piece made no effect, either—all descriptive music in which the singer appears to do little more than mime. . .[22]

The extent to which conservative circles in Italy considered Puccini a follower and imitator of Wagner is also seen from a letter of the celebrated English soprano, Clara Novello. In later life, Clara had married Conte Gigliucci and had settled at the small town of Fermo whence she wrote to some friends in 1886:

. . . Our pretty little theatre here . . . opened last night with a small opera, Le Villi, by a young beginner, Puccini, who has imitated Wagner; a sequence of intricate harmonies without a trace of melody [sic!] or inspiration, which might never end . . . and never begin! This substitution for music is now the mode and consoles me for being old. When I was young, music was still then music. . .[23]

It was, however, at Naples, in the spring of 1885, some four months after the Scala production, that Le Villi suffered a truly resounding fiasco, the performance being punctuated by hisses and catcalls from the auditorium. Whether the public of the San Carlo Theatre actually found fault with the work or whether it was prompted by the notorious antagonism which southern Italians nurture toward the more sophisticated northerners, or both, the fact remains that at Naples Puccini was given, as Verdi had been before him, a potent taste of the southerners' uninhibited way of expressing their disapproval. Puccini later told Fraccaroli that at a banquet given for him at Lucca to celebrate the forthcoming Naples première all bottles—fiaschi, a pun on the ambiguous word fiasco—were removed from the table!

For an immature work, Le Villi boasted a remarkable number of productions outside Italy: Buenos Aires (1886); Hamburg (1892), where the conductor was Gustav Mahler; New York (1908); and more recently Vienna (1938) and Mannheim (1940). An English version, under the title The Witch-Dancers, was given by the Carl Rosa Company at Manchester on 24 September 1897.

V

Predicaments

I

FIVE YEARS WERE TO ELAPSE between *Le Villi* and Puccini's next opera *Edgar*, a period of severe tribulations in both his private and professional life. On 17 July 1884 Puccini's mother died at Lucca; she had been in poor health for some time, and though he had been prepared for it her death affected him very deeply—more than so natural an event would normally affect a son. Puccini had been her favourite child and the bond between them had been remarkably close and affectionate. Various persons who knew the composer in later years stress the great tenderness with which he used to speak of her.* Puccini's relationship with his mother is a point to which we shall return when discussing his psychology as an artist.

The death of his mother appears to have precipitated an event that might have otherwise occurred at a later date. This was Puccini's elopement with Elvira Gemignani, the wife of a former school friend. It is not certain when Puccini met her for the first time; according to del Fiorentino,[24] he knew her already before her marriage to Narciso Gemignani, a wholesale grocer. Elvira, whose maiden name was Bonturi, was by all accounts a woman of striking beauty, tall and full in figure, with dignified carriage, a face of classical proportions, dark shining eyes and rich, dark-blond hair which in the fashion of the day she wore in plaits piled up on top of her head. Elvira was, in short, a woman of impressive appearance. Yet she possessed little gaiety of spirit to temper the rather severe beauty of her features and to respond to the boyish exuberance of her young lover. With advancing years she grew increasingly morose and bitter and was given to gloomy moods. Her union with Puccini was not a happy one; but during the spring of their love the storm clouds, which were to overhang their lifelong association and often burst upon it with lightning and thunder, were still beyond the horizon.

When Giacomo and Elvira decided to set up home together, he was twenty-six and she twenty-four. He was a handsome youth—tall, long-legged and slim; on firm shoulders sat a well-formed head with a high fore-head; a certain lack of symmetry in his sensitive features lent his face a character of its own; its expression was very changeable, but in his grey eyes, with a slight droop of the left eyelid, there often was a dreamy, melancholy look. The prominent nose had been hereditary in his family since his great-grandfather Antonio. On small sensitive lips the youth sported a long flowing

* To her memory was dedicated a new organ which Puccini had had built at San Nicola at Lucca, where his sister Iginia was a nun.

44

moustache; his hair was the colour of chestnut, thick and curly. He spoke in a soft, somewhat husky baritone voice—*una voce bruna*—which fell on the ear with a melodious ring;* but he sang tenor, and at rehearsals would indicate the part of a female character in a light falsetto. With growing wealth he dressed with studied elegance. Except with his intimates, his manner was reserved, his bearing dignified and aristocratic—not for nothing had Ricordi nicknamed him 'Doge'. The fascination which this handsome and world-famous man exercised on women was irresistible; to what extremes this fascination was apt to drive his female admirers on occasion is illustrated by the episode of the fair nymph of Vienna, which his two painter friends relate in their book.[25] Puccini's conquests were easy and numerous.

Elvira's marriage with Gemignani was by all accounts at first a happy one —it was said to have been a love match. She bore him two children, a daughter named Fosca and a son Renato, three years younger than his sister. Elvira sang, and it appears that it was at her husband's request that she began to take lessons with Puccini in singing and piano. Teacher and pupil fell passionately in love with one another and, shortly after the death of Puccini's mother, Elvira left her husband and joined her lover in Milan, taking Fosca with her. Puccini's son Antonio was born two years later (1886); he remained an illegitimate child until the age of eighteen, that is, until the death of Elvira's first husband when the union of his parents was legalized in 1904; Elvira's Catholic marriage could not be dissolved while Gemignani was alive.

Puccini's elopement with Elvira, with whom he was now 'living in sin', created, as was to be expected, a scandal of the first order in provincial Lucca. His relatives were up in arms against him, accusing him of having brought shame and disgrace on the honourable name of the Puccinis. His great-uncle Dr. Cerù now demanded the repayment with interest of the sum of money he had lent him during his studies at the Milan Conservatoire, using the somewhat curious argument that if the young composer could afford a mistress he could also afford to repay his debts, and that the money should be sent to the unfortunate Michele, who had meanwhile emigrated to South America where he was finding it hard to eke out a living as a singing-teacher.

2

Puccini was extremely sensitive and vulnerable to criticism and altogether easily affected by adversities; they would plunge him into despondent moods that seriously interfered with his creative work. There is, hence, little doubt that one of the reasons why his work on *Edgar* made such halting progress is to be sought in the emotional upheavals of that period. Another reason was Fontana's libretto. More will be said about it at the appropriate time, but we may note here that rarely had a librettist chosen a subject less suited to the particular genius of a composer than had Fontana with his choice of *Edgar*. Based on Alfred de Musset's verse-play *La Coupe et les Lèvres*, the theme of the opera much resembles that of *Carmen*, with a Moorish adventuress

* A recording of a short speech made by him in New York in February 1907 confirms this.

called Tigrana seducing the weak Edgar away from his chaste bride Fidelia. Was it the expectation that Puccini might produce a second *Carmen* that induced Fontana and Ricordi—who accorded his full *imprimatur* to Fontana's choice—to foist this subject on him and made them turn a deaf ear to his timid remonstrances about weaknesses in its dramatic treatment? And how striking the contrast between the Puccini who in his inexperience would meekly accept an impossible libretto and the Puccini who, a few years later, began to worry the life out of his librettists!

The toil with *Edgar*—'a work of such importance and difficulty', as Puccini described it to Ricordi (*E*)—began in the summer of 1884 and lasted till the autumn of 1888. In order to free the composer from material worries, Ricordi added to his small earnings from the royalties of *Le Villi* by granting him a monthly advance of 300 lire which started in July 1884 and was to run for a year; but already six months before this period elapsed, Puccini begged the publisher to prolong what he jestingly called '*la mia pensione*'— diffidently, pointing out that he had no other means of subsistence and that, in addition, he had to support his brother Michele in South America. Ricordi acceded to this request and in fact continued paying him a 'pension' well into the time when Puccini was already working on his next opera, *Manon Lescaut*. Living on a pittance with a wife and two children—his stepdaughter Fosca and Antonio, who had meanwhile been born—was little calculated to create an atmosphere conducive to sustained work. No wonder that *Edgar* proceeded at a snail's pace, despite Puccini's assertions to the contrary. Nor did Fontana prove helpful. Conceited as he was and con- vinced of the excellence of his libretto, he obstinately refused to accept Puccini's various suggestions. Still more disagreeable, there were scenes with the publisher, who was growing impatient and even threatened to drop him, while at home Elvira kept nagging him with the constant reminder that Verdi had written *three* operas in as few years.* Puccini, it has to be admitted, was never a quick worker. Yet, whereas with his mature operas he would devote the greater part of time to work on the libretto, with *Edgar*, of which he had had the complete libretto in his possession since July 1884, it was the actual composition which was the cause of all this delay. There is a telltale look about the autograph which in parts recalls a typical Beethoven sketch: a great many pages are crossed out and defaced by ink blotches; staves belonging to instruments not playing at the moment are filled with cor- rections referring to passages on other instruments; different colours of ink are used—black, red and green; the handwriting varies from legible to just legible and to completely illegible, though this was to remain a permanent feature of Puccini's manuscript scores.

3

The first night of *Edgar* was to take place at La Scala on Easter Sunday, 21 April 1889. It was with profound apprehension that the composer looked

* *Rigoletto, Il Trovatore* and *La Traviata*.

to this important event, largely because he feared intrigues against him on the part of the many enemies he had made with the successful *Le Villi*. Writing to Michele, who in the previous year had settled in the Argentine, he says: 'I have terrible fears for the opera because I am furiously attacked on all sides. If you can find work for me after *Edgar*, I shall come. But not to Buenos Aires, to the interior amongst the redskins!' (6 February 1890, *E*); but in an undated letter to his sister Dide he expresses the hope that he would make his enemies 'burst with envy and rage if God grants me a long enough life' (*E*).

Puccini had pinned his hope on Francesco Tamagno (Verdi's first Othello) singing the part of Edgar. During his Milan student days he had struck up a friendship with the great tenor, his senior by eight years, and he now sought to persuade him into an acceptance of this role. 'Since I've heard my music sung by you', he wrote to Tamagno on 31 December 1888, 'I know no more peace! . . . It is in your power, if you are willing, to see to it that my work should be worthily appreciated.'[26] And on 21 February 1889, only two months before the date of the première of *Edgar*, he positively prostrated himself before Tamagno:

> . . . To live in hope is already something, at least it's better than a certainty that is lousy.* There comes in the life of every man a decisive moment, and that is for me the good success of *Edgar*. I cling to him who can save me, as one who has suffered shipwreck clings to the last plank. And that plank is you! . . .

Tamagno, however, was not free, having just then contracted for a long tour in America.

Puccini's foreboding as to the reception of the opera proved true. Despite an excellent cast that included Romilda Pantaleoni (Tigrana), Aurelia Cattaneo (Fidelia), Gregorio Gabrielesco (Edgar) and Franco Faccio at the conductor's desk, the opera achieved little more than a *succès d'estime* and was given only two more performances at La Scala. Faccio, reporting afterwards to Verdi, exaggerates (he was in love with Pantaleoni!) when he writes that *Edgar* 'was received by the public with much warmth'; though he adds that 'as happens regularly—but quite often the other way, too—the robed (*togata*) critics displayed great severity. Pantaleoni achieved magnificent effects in the dramatic scene of the fourth act [now the third] and although she did not fully bring out the harshness in Tigrana's character, she powerfully contributed to the happy result'. When after the performance Giacosa and Boito went behind the scene to offer their congratulations to Pantaleoni, she would not accept their compliments, declaring that Tigrana's was 'a cruel part which I don't feel'. She also told them the following anecdote; during one of the rehearsals Puccini, admiring with covetous eyes the rich fur coat worn by the bass Lecherie, said to her: 'Signora Romilda! When shall I have a similar coat, too?' She smiled and encouraged him in his hope but thought to herself that he would find it difficult to buy such a garment with the royalties from *Edgar*.[27]

* Puccini's expression was '*puzza di canile*'—'it smells of dog'.

The critics, it is true, recognized the technical advances Puccini had made in *Edgar* since his first opera and found praise for some numbers, yet essentially they declared it a failure. The most favourable notice came from Gramola in the *Corriere della Sera*; he drew special attention to the effective orchestration, described Edgar's aria 'O soave vision' as 'impassioned and limpid' and found the most successful music in the last act, including the Requiem music for Edgar and Fidelia's two arias, of which the second, a lament, had to be encored. In retrospect Gramola's judgment proves to have been singularly sound, for a critical study of the score reveals that the music he singled out for praise indeed represents the most inspired portions of the work.

Neither the composer nor his publisher entertained any illusion about the general reception of the work. Ricordi admitted as much publicly when he summed up the events of the evening in a notice in the *Gazzetta Musicale*, not without aiming a shaft at the critics 'who are sometimes so kind to mediocrities'. Six days after the first performance—two more performances were given during that season—Ricordi convened a meeting between himself, Puccini and Fontana to hold a post-mortem or, rather, to discuss the kind of surgical operation by which the life of the newborn might possibly be saved. From a long letter,[28] sent by Ricordi to Puccini the following day, we gather that the meeting was a stormy one and lasted well into the night. The crucial question that had to be decided was whether there was time enough left to make the necessary alteration so that the opera 'might again be given in May on two or three evenings'. Ricordi stressed that he was not in agreement 'with the systematic belittlers of the libretto. There are two effective acts and that is something. But it also contains much obscurity, many fallacies which derive from the theories of Fontana, who assumes that everybody thinks with his head'. Ricordi speaking 'as a practical man who has known people and business for many years' and stating the facts 'with that frankness which I derive from the affection and esteem in which I hold you', begs Puccini to remember that he was 'in one of the critical and difficult moments' of his artistic career. He asked him whether the 'rapid and feverish labour' to be undertaken in order to rescue the opera could be done in the short time available, and reminded him that 'after all, it is the imagination and the personality of the musician who colours the work, who presents it to the public. Without him it is a zero'. 'I', Ricordi affirms, 'who am neither a writer nor an artist nor an opera composer, yet sense the worth of *Edgar*. I read in it clearly all your gifts, all the hopes for the future. But to realize these hopes it is necessary to follow our motto: *Excelsior!*' (M).

What Ricordi was insinuating to Puccini was to wash his hands of the pig-headed Fontana—who remained adamant in his refusal to consider any changes—let the moribund opera die its natural death and cast about for a subject for a new opera. Yet *Edgar*, as we shall see, was not abandoned, though Fontana was; he vanished for good from Puccini's horizon, except for a momentary reappearance some eighteen years later when he offered to adapt Oscar Wilde's *A Florentine Tragedy* for him.

GIULIO RICORDI
(1840–1912)

ALFREDO CATALANI
(1854–93)

GIUSEPPE GIACOSA
(1847–1906)

CARTOONS OF PUCCINI

WITH MADAM
BUTTERFLY

AS SEEN BY
CAPPIELLO

MASCAGNI, LEONCAVALLO, PUCCINI, FRANCHETTI
(The four musical members of the Milan '*Scapigliatura*')

The failure of *Edgar* might have easily lost Puccini his connection with the House of Ricordi had not the publisher himself intervened with determination. At a meeting of the shareholders, convened shortly after the première, the motion was put forward that Puccini be dropped by the firm. Had he not proved a liability? The advances so far paid to him had reached the considerable sum of 18,000 lire, a debt which in the composer's own words weighed upon him like an 'incubus'. This investment had not produced the expected yield. Why then continue to burden the firm with such a useless load? Giulio Ricordi, however, opposed this motion with all the energy and conviction at his command; after all, it had been he who had persuaded Puccini to compose *Edgar* and, most probably, felt guilty about this whole venture. At one moment he even threatened his own resignation—a hollow threat, presumably, since he owned the majority of the shares—if Puccini were to be sent packing. The upshot was that not only was Puccini retained on the firm's books, but that Ricordi continued his grant of a monthly allowance, binding himself in the event of another failure to reimburse the firm, out of his own pocket, for the total sum of money advanced to Puccini. Needless to say, this contingency never arose.

4

Let us pause here in our narrative to take a closer look at the man to whose support and encouragement Puccini owed so much and who in fact may be said to have been the architect of his career. Giulio Ricordi (1840–1912) represented the third generation of a family of Spanish descent, which by industry, enterprise and business acumen had succeeded in building up one of the great music publishing houses of the world. Giulio, who had inherited these qualities from his grandfather Giovanni and his father Tito, both trained musicians, was in addition a man of culture and versatility. His knowledge of world literature was wide, he spoke fluent French, knew English and German, and combined in his person the several gifts of composer, poet, writer and critic. Under the pseudonym J. Burgmein* he had published a great number of charming drawing-room pieces for piano, some orchestral music, a ballet, and an opera *La Secchia Rapita*, produced at Turin in 1910.† Even so stern a critic as Verdi had found praise for his publisher's creative efforts and so, later, did Puccini, who specially mentions in one of his letters a Hungarian Fantasy which he had heard at Lucca in 1898 and had liked very much. Not that Ricordi ever achieved eminence with any of his diverse talents; but added to his long experience of the theatre, to which he was devoted, they rendered him a shrewd judge of opera and enabled him to offer invaluable practical advice to his composers and librettists.

* The choice of this German-sounding pseudonym is indicative of the growing popularity which German music was beginning to enjoy in the 1870s.

† It is interesting to note that the text was by Renato Simoni, who later collaborated in the libretto of Puccini's *Turandot*. Ricordi also contemplated a second opera, *Tappeto Rosa*, after a French subject, which was versified in Italian by another of Puccini's librettists—Giuseppe Adami. It was through his work for Ricordi that Adami met Puccini.

Immaculately dressed in a formal, rather severe style, a black tie neatly tied round a high stiff collar, the short beard carefully trimmed, the corners of his moustache slightly turned up, and invariably with a slightly quizzical, ironic expression on his countenance, Giulio suggested a diplomat rather than a hardboiled publisher. Indeed, diplomacy was one of his great assets. Skill in handling his artists, notably so temperamental and moody a composer as Puccini, and an instinctive knowledge of human foibles on which he played to achieve his ends—these were qualities worthy of a Machiavelli. It was not easy to be accepted as one of Ricordi's composers; and to have one's works published by him represented a distinction in itself. Yet once convinced of an artist's worth, he promoted his interests (and his own) with all the authority at his command. Ricordi was a real power in Italian music during the last third of the nineteenth century—a king-maker in that realm and its *éminence grise*. The fact that he was the publisher of works which dominated the repertory of the world's opera houses, great and small, and that he owned the exclusive rights of these works, placed him in a unique position, from which he was able to exert pressure on managements in favour of this or that young protégé of his. The practice established by his grandfather whereby the House of Ricordi could refuse permission for the production of operas owned by them was applied by Giulio both covertly and openly.* For all his culture, artistic insight and urbanity, this *faux bonhomme* was ultimately guided by a cold, calculating brain; to further the interests of his large concern was Giulio's first article of faith. The degree of a composer's success was the sole criterion as to whether to support him or discard him. He dropped the gifted Catalani in favour of the more gifted Puccini;† he resorted, as we shall see, to questionable methods in persuading Franchetti to release the *Tosca* libretto for Puccini, and although he possessed an extraordinary flair for backing the winner, he yet committed some grave errors of judgment, as when he refused to publish works by Bizet, Leoncavallo and Mascagni. For Giulio there existed only one god and that god was Verdi —Verdi whose associations with his firm dated back to the time of Giulio's

* Thus, for some reason or other, he refused in 1907 to permit *Tosca* to be given at La Scala and only yielded to Puccini's persuasion.

Similarly, when in 1901, following Verdi's death, Toscanini intended to present *Trovatore* at La Scala, Ricordi declared that he would not allow the opera to be given if Toscanini was the conductor. The reason for his antagonism was both personal and professional. During the Turin celebration of 1898 Toscanini had refused to perform an orchestral composition by J. Burgmein, *alias* Ricordi, and this the vindictive Ricordi would neither forgive nor forget. Moreover, Ricordi disliked Toscanini's style of interpretation and as editor of the house magazine *Gazzetta Musicale* he would scarcely let an opportunity pass without attacking the conductor for rigidity of execution, mathematical accuracy and lack of poetry, which he considered essential to Italian music. Thus he once likened a performance under Toscanini of *Falstaff* to a 'mastodontic mechanical piano'. (See *The Magic Baton. Toscanini's Life for Music*, by Filippo Sacchi. London, 1957.)

In later years, though—seeing Toscanini's incomparable successes, notably in Verdi and Puccini—Ricordi relented and even permitted himself to laud him.

† Admittedly, he had been compelled to take over Catalani from the publisher Lucca when that firm was bought up by him.

grandfather Giovanni. Giulio himself had come into personal contact with Verdi about the mid-1860s, and later became Verdi's confidant. Giulio saw in Verdi not only the greatest Italian musician of his age but the embodiment of Italy's national aspirations, the essence of *italianità*. It was, hence, no wonder that in the fierce aesthetic battles fought in Italy over the question Verdi versus Wagner, Giulio was one of the flagbearers of the nationalist party, expressing his hostility to the 'northern colossus' in fervent polemical articles in his *Gazzetta Musicale*. The amusing paradox was that even after Wagner had become one of his own composers, through the acquisition of Francesco Lucca's stock in 1887, he still continued his policy of opposition and actual sabotage against his operas.

Yet if Verdi occupied the most exalted place in Ricordi's hierarchy of living Italian composers, Puccini ranked immediately after. Ricordi early recognized that Puccini was of the royal line—he was the 'Crown Prince'—and, as we have seen, the failure of *Edgar*, far from shaking his belief, brought him more closely still to the young composer, whom he inspired with fresh hopes and courage. Giulio, who was Puccini's senior by eighteen years, soon developed for the fatherless youth an affection and a paternal concern which lasted till his death in 1912. The publisher—a frustrated artist with whom the commercial tradition of his family proved stronger than his creative urge—may have perceived in Puccini the embodiment of his own artistic aspirations and therefore nurtured and protected the young composer as his spiritual son. Inevitably, there were ups and downs in this relationship, vicissitudes caused by both artistic and private matters. Indeed, how could it have been otherwise seeing the differences in age, temperament and outlook between the two? A major crisis was to arise in 1903 in connexion with a sordid love affair of Puccini's, but the bond between publisher and composer was strong enough to survive even this test. It is indeed a matter for speculation whether the early path of Puccini's career, despite his outstanding gifts, would have run as smoothly as it did but for Giulio's clearing away of most obstacles. For Puccini no trouble and expense were spared; a constant look-out was kept by Ricordi and his assistants for suitable subjects, and libretti were commissioned and paid for on the chance that Puccini might utilize them. Most of them were rejected out of hand or after some reflection. Sometimes the crumbs that fell from Puccini's table were picked up by younger composers under Ricordi's wing: Riccardo Zandonai set the libretto of *La Conchita*, discarded by Puccini after he had done considerable work on it. 'Guide philosopher and friend'—this is how we may best describe the role that Ricordi played in Puccini's career. Whether Puccini's nature was such as to enable him to form close bonds of friendship with any person is another question, yet he certainly entertained feelings of filial devotion, of trust and of admiration for his great publisher—'the only person who inspires me with trust, and to whom I can confide all that is going through my mind' (*E*).

5

To return to *Edgar*. It was at Ricordi's instigation that in the summer of 1889 (not 1905, as generally stated) Puccini revised the opera, compressing its four acts into three, cutting out the last act, but grafting its closing scene—the scene of the murder of the one heroine by the other—on to the end of the present third and final act; also the music was altered in various places. In this new version the opera was due to be given at La Scala in the following spring; but owing to the illness of the tenor (De Negri) the project fell through—to the profound disappointment of the composer, who in a letter to Dide of 23 April 1890 lamented the loss of 'about 2,000 or 3,000 lire—all sacrosanct money on which I had counted and which I had partly spent in advance' (*E*). There were subsequently productions in several other Italian cities, including one at Lucca, where local patriotism rather than critical discernment appears to have been responsible for a wildly enthusiastic reception.* The opera also travelled abroad, the first foreign production being given in Madrid during the spring season of 1892. For this production Puccini, with the aid of Ricordi, at last succeeded in getting Tamagno for the name-part, expecting that the celebrated singer would redeem *Edgar* from its near-failure. Two months before the Madrid première (19 March) he wrote to the singer:

11 January 1892

Dearest Tamagno,

I know that you are about to leave for Madrid [for some other productions]. I take my courage in both hands and make bold to address to you a request—to ask you a very great favour which, if granted, will be of immense advantage to my career.

Edgar should have been given at the Teatro Reale [Madrid] last year, but time and circumstances to do with the repertoire prevented this. At the time I had been given the formal promise by the management, especially by Conte di Michelena, that this work of mine would be produced during the current season; rehearsals were already at an advanced stage—we were in fact near the date of the première—when I was notified that Durot had dissolved his contract and so my poor *Edgar* was left without a protagonist and without hope of a performance! Tetrazzini and Pasqua were to have been the other principal interpreters. This was for me a most ruinous disaster, as I had counted on the production of *Edgar* to give me an uplift which I need most direly, morally as well as materially. Hence my request, which I make bold to address to you, to sing the very important part of the protagonist. Courage and audacity is needed, what! But since I know you to be so kind-hearted, I took the liberty of putting this idea to you. Shall I be granted this request? I confess that I hope so.

The opera has now been reduced to three acts. Two years ago you saw the music and studied it so that it will not be new to you and give you little trouble to learn it. If you accept, you can be sure of my immutable and unlimited gratitude. Among the many misfortunes that have befallen me, this

* The new three-act version was first given at Ferrara on 28 February 1892; in 1901 and 1905 Puccini made some further alterations.

would at least be my good luck! I'm writing to you just as my heart dictates it, jotting down the words as they leap into my head. I am so excited when I think that perhaps . . . who knows? . . . you will sing my stuff!!

If you accept, please write me a line. It is in your power, dear friend, to render happy

your most affectionate
G. Puccini.

Tamagno's reply could not have been very encouraging, for within a week of that first letter Puccini wrote him two more letters, offering to send him a copy of the revised opera so that the singer should see for himself that the part of Edgar was not difficult, and flattering him by stressing his 'phenomenal faculty of learning quickly'; he also suggested coming to play the music to Tamagno. The rest of the persuading was done by Ricordi, who sent Tamagno letters and telegrams, one of which reads:

> I have just been notified that the Madrid affair has been clinched. Please forgive if I renew my urgent request of yesterday. The part is already known to you, all that is needed is to look at the latest variants. If you, with your talent and your kindness, will accept, then you will have given immense encouragement to a young man who really deserves it. . .[29]

Tamagno accepted; the rest of the Madrid cast too was outstanding, with Eva Tetrazzini, the sister of the famous Luisa, as Fidelia, and Pasqua as Tigrana. The conductor was the eminent Luigi Mancinelli, a musician of Toscanini's stature.* But despite the excellence of the artists, Edgar failed to make an impression. This Madrid production occasioned Puccini's first visit to a foreign country made in order to supervise the rehearsals in person. Ricordi wrote him encouraging words, admonishing him 'to take care of yourself because the climate of Madrid is treacherous, especially at night! . . . without mentioning other things!!!!' (M). For a production in Buenos Aires (1905) Puccini revised the work a third time. London heard the opera in an amateur production in April 1967.

In later years the composer came to disown this early brainchild. 'It was an organism defective from the dramatic point of view. Its success was ephemeral. Although I knew that I wrote some pages which do me credit, that is not enough—as an opera it does not exist. The basis of an opera is the subject and its treatment. In setting the libretto of Edgar I have, with all respect to the memory of my friend Fontana, made a blunder (una cantonata). It was more my fault than his.'[30]

Many years later he presented Sybil Seligman, an English friend of his whom we shall meet presently, with a vocal score of the opera, with marginal comments in which he directs his caustic wit against himself. The title, for example, is enlarged thus:

---

* For this production Puccini composed a special Prelude evoking the dawn of spring, with which the first scene opens. This piece was, however, never published, the present version of the opera beginning with a few bars of orchestral introduction.

E Dio ti Gu A Rdi da quest'opera!
(And may God preserve you from this opera!)

The finale of the second act is 'the most horrible thing that has ever been written'. Edgar's theatrical outcry in the third act: 'Sì, poichè Edgar vive!'—'Yes, for Edgar lives!', Puccini acknowledges with a laconic '*Menzogna!*' —'It's a lie!'; and when at the end of the opera the crowd breaks into repeated shouts 'Orror'—'Oh horror!', his comment is 'How right they are!' Only two numbers in the whole work are marked 'This is good!': Fidelia's aria 'Addio mio dolce amor!' and her lament 'Nel villaggio d'Edgar' —both, significantly, in Puccini's melancholy vein. *

From the period of *Edgar* date three of a small number of independent pieces which Puccini wrote after he had turned to opera. These are two minuets for string quartet, and *Crisantemi* for the same medium, written on the death of Prince Amedeo of Savoy (1890); this inspired little composition, which Puccini, in his own words, composed 'in a night', was to come in handy for the last act of *Manon Lescaut*.

* But a drinking-song, *La Coppa*, which belongs to the first version of the opera, was published separately and can occasionally be heard in the concert hall.

VI

The Turn of the Tide

I

DESPITE THE ENCOURAGEMENT and support lent him by Ricordi, the immediate prospects for Puccini after *Edgar* appeared bleak. So far as his creative development was concerned, this opera, he must have felt, had led him into a blind alley; yet it was not an altogether blind one, as the later discussion of the music will reveal. Puccini's material conditions remained precarious, while the burden of supporting a family with two growing children increased. In addition, the insistent Dr. Cerù was once more pressing for the repayment of his loan. In his despair the composer began to toy with the idea of joining his brother in Latin America where the fabulous fees which artists were said to earn among the large colonies of Italian immigrants seemed a potent enough inducement to forsake his native country.* Writing to Michele on 24 April 1890 he says:

> I don't know if I shall go into the country because I'm down on the rocks. If you're doing well where you are, I would come too, if there is some work for me. Write me about this. I'm weary of this eternal struggle with poverty! (*E*).

In search, it would seem, for cheaper quarters in Milan, Puccini had moved from his lodgings in Vicolo San Carlo to Via Solferino, whence he was compelled to move again to a house beyond the new Porta Monforte because 'I have been playing the piano at night. Now that I have been given notice, I go at it like mad' (*E*). A week after the above letter Puccini writes to his brother again:

Milan, 30 April 1890 [?]

Dear Michele,

Dr. Cerù has given me notice to pay him back the money which he spent in supporting me as a student in Milan, with the interest to date. He says that I have made 40,000 lire with *Le Villi*! As my only reply I am sending him now Ricordi's statement of account from which he will see that my share amounts

---

* The strong Italian element in the population of South America explains why Buenos Aires figures, almost invariably, as the first among the foreign cities where a Puccini opera was given soon after its first Italian production. Yet the general level of artistic appreciation there during the last quarter or so of the nineteenth century was not high.

In illustration of this I cite an amusing anecdote told by the great Italian actress Eleonora Duse. A patron who was about to buy his ticket for the performance of a new play engaged the cashier in the following dialogue: 'How many acts are we to have tonight?—Three.— Will the *prima donna* have many dresses to display?—I don't know.—Will she die at the end?—No, it's a comedy!—Oh! in that case I'll come tomorrow!' (*Schauspieler und Theater im heutigen Italien*, by Richard Nathanson. Berlin, 1893.)

to only 6,000 lire. What a difference! I should never have expected it. The chemist is worrying me and I shall have to pay your account of twenty-five lire. I am absolutely down on the rocks. I don't know how to go on. I'm still receiving from Ricordi the 300 lire a month, but that is an advance. It's not enough and I am accumulating debts month by month. Soon the worst will come and God help me then!

If I could find means of making money I would come where you are. Is there any chance for me there? I would leave everything behind and go. Write to me often and tell me about everything you are doing. Don't forget the house at Lucca. Nitteti [one of the sisters] has been left in great poverty, the poor girl! . . .

Last night I worked till three in the morning and then had a bundle of onions for supper. . . If you have saved anything, send it to me so that I can put it away for you!!!

I shall send you under separate cover *Edgar* and *Villi* which I shall get from Ricordi.

Be careful and live as thriftily as possible. See that you at least make money. I have no hope of that.

The theatres here are stingy and because of the critics the public becomes more and more difficult. God help me! I am ready, absolutely ready to come, if you write. I shall come and we'll manage *somehow*. But I shall need money for the voyage, I warn you!

Addio, addio! (E).

If Puccini was ever serious in his intention to emigrate (which may be doubted) the reply he received from Michele must have put him off it once and for all:

Dear Giacomo,

I warn you—do not come here! You cannot imagine what I have been through. What a life! I left Buenos Aires, where I worked like a slave, with nothing to show for it on account of the high cost of living. Then they told me that in the province of Yoyoy I would obtain a position teaching voice, piano and Italian for 300 *scudi* a month. I crossed the Andes, and after innumerable sufferings came at last to Yoyoy. Of course, as you might expect, the place is full of Lucchesi. . . But America does not suit me. If the gold market improves I shall return to Lucca. Meanwhile I am a little worried by the epidemic of influenza. My classroom is empty. . .[31]

This is the last we hear of the hapless Michele. When in 1893, after the tremendous success of *Manon Lescaut*, Puccini wanted to bring his brother back to Italy, Michele contracted the yellow fever and died a miserable death in a remote corner of a far-away continent.

2

For all that Puccini was 'weary of this eternal struggle with poverty', he was nevertheless working full steam at his next opera. In 1884, the same year which saw the first production of *Le Villi*, Massenet had brought out at the Paris Opéra-Comique his *Manon*, founded on the celebrated novel by the Abbé Prévost. The work had a phenomenal success and conquered the opera houses of the whole world. Though *Manon* did not reach Italy till 1893, it is certain that Puccini knew it from a vocal score several years beforehand, despite Fraccaroli's statement to the contrary.[32] Nor can there be any doubt that it was Massenet's success that induced him in the first place to try his hand at the same subject. A reading of the novel convinced him still further that in it he had indeed found 'the perfect subject'. 'Manon', he wrote to Ricordi in 1889, 'is a heroine I believe in and therefore she cannot fail to win the hearts of the public.'[33] Here at last was a subject with a plot, with an atmosphere and with characters ideally suited to his particular genius. It was the first time in his career that he was following his instinct in the choice of a subject and this rendered him impervious to Ricordi's repeated warnings of the risks in writing an opera bound to challenge comparison with the French masterpiece. Puccini, no musical historian, cannot be presumed to have known that Prévost's novel had also furnished the subject for at least four stage works earlier than Massenet's;* yet had such information been imparted to him it would have served—for a reason to be shown later—to confirm him still further in his decision to use it himself. When Marco Praga, one of the half-dozen collaborators on the libretto, also reminded him of Massenet's opera, Puccini's retort was 'Massenet feels it as a Frenchman, with the powder and the minuets—*con la cipria e i minuetti*. I shall feel it as an Italian, with desperate passion—*con passione disperata*'.[34] With this the matter was settled; but remembering his experiences with Fontana, this time, he writes to Ricordi, 'no idiotic librettist must be allowed to ruin the story. I shall certainly put my hand to the making of the libretto'.[35] It is with an entirely new tone of voice that Puccini now begins to speak.

It was characteristic of him throughout his later career that even when he thought he had lighted on the right subject, he would concurrently contemplate other material. Thus he kept two more subjects under consideration beside *Manon Lescaut*. Ricordi, always anxious to provide his favourite composer with a choice of libretti, had commissioned the playwright Giuseppe Giacosa to prepare a scenario the plot of which was laid in Russia. Puccini, however, turned it down declaring that it was unsuitable for him. 'How can one compose something', he wrote to the publisher on 19 July 1889, 'that one does not *feel entirely*? We should look for and should certainly find something that is more poetic, more pleasing, less sombre and with a little more nobility of conception' (*E*). For different reasons he also rejected a suggestion made by Praga for an opera based on one of Shakespeare's King Henry plays, than which anything less suited to Puccini it is hard to imagine. That Praga made such a suggestion at all may have had something to do with the fact that Verdi's *Otello* (1887) and rumours of his writing a *Falstaff* had revived interest in the operatic possibilities of the Shakespeare dramas.†

* See p. 317 *n*.

† The most notable instances of previous Italian operas after a Shakespeare play were Rossini's *Otello* (1816), Verdi's *Macbeth* (1847), and Franco Faccio's *Amleto* (1865), to a libetto by Boito.

The first person to be entrusted by Ricordi with the dramatic adaptation of Prévost's novel was Puccini's fellow-composer and exact coeval, Ruggiero Leoncavallo. The future composer of *I Pagliacci* was at that period still torn between following a career as a dramatist and writer and as a musician, for both of which he displayed equal gifts; this enabled him to be his own librettist for the majority of his operas and to place his literary services at the disposal of other musicians, as in the case of Puccini and later of a Portuguese composer.* At the age of nineteen Leoncavallo had published the text of his first opera *Chatterton* (not produced until 1896), which demonstrated his theatrical talent. Some ten years later he brought to Ricordi the complete libretto of his *I Medici*, the first part of a huge trilogy entitled *Crepusculum*, which was designed to present a picture of the Italian Renaissance in dramatic episodes drawn from the lives of the Medici, Savonarola and Cesare Borgia. (It is not certain whether he ever completed or published the remaining two parts of this trilogy.) Ricordi was so impressed by the libretto that he made a contract with Leoncavallo for *I Medici* and, in addition, commissioned him to write the libretto for *Manon Lescaut*. Puccini, however, was dissatisfied with the treatment and to all intents and purposes his collaboration with Leoncavallo soon ceased, though the latter was retained by Ricordi in the capacity of a general adviser.

The next writer to enter upon the scene was Marco Praga, a playwright of some repute. On his own admission Praga had never tried his hand at a libretto before. Yet Puccini insisted on his collaboration and Praga yielded because of 'the friendship and admiration I felt for Puccini' (*E*). Since a duplication of the scenes of Massenet's opera was so far as possible to be eschewed, the composer enjoined on Praga to ignore the French libretto and take the novel as his chief basis, at the same time keeping firmly in mind a work in the style of an *opéra comique*, i.e. a lyrico-sentimental opera with spoken dialogue. He gave this warning to Praga, presumably, to prevent the librettist from straying into grand opera, as Fontana had done in *Edgar*. Being exclusively a prose writer, Praga suggested for the versification a young poet and critic of his acquaintance, Domenico Oliva, who had just published a successful volume of verse. Puccini consented.

The complete libretto was ready in the early summer of 1890, when it was read by Praga and Oliva to Puccini and Ricordi at the latter's summer residence at Cernobbio, on Lake Como. Composer and publisher declared themselves delighted with it and on their return to Milan a formal agreement was concluded. With the libretto in his pocket Puccini betook himself and his family to Vacallo, a small village near Chiasso, on the Italo-Swiss frontier, where he had rented a little chalet. Already at that early period, love of the country combined with a profound detestation of living and working in Milan, especially during the summer—'this horrible soul-destroying Milan'—was beginning to emerge: 'to tear me away from the country', he wrote to Dide in April 1890, 'is to tear away part of my life' (*E*). At Vacallo an unusual welcome awaited him. Leoncavallo, who appears to have

* Augusto Machado, in *Mario Wetter* (Lisbon, 1898).

recommended the place to him, was staying there himself and had rented a house opposite Puccini's. When the latter arrived he was greeted by a huge canvas, attached to the door of Leoncavallo's chalet, which depicted a clown—a *pagliaccio*, thus indicating the opera on which Leoncavallo was working just then. The composer of *Manon Lescaut* retorted some days later by hanging out of his window the drawing of a large white hand—*manon* in Italian.

Puccini spent the summer and winter of that year at Vacallo, then went to live the greater part of 1891 alone at Lucca, while Elvira and the two children, in order to avoid further gossip and scandal—her husband was still living at Lucca—proceeded to Florence, where they stayed with her sister Ida Razzi. By September, Puccini at last found a permanent abode at Torre del Lago near Lucca, a village on the Lake of Massaciuccoli which he had once visited some seven years earlier and immediately liked. Thus, *Manon Lescaut* was composed in several places, with frequent journeys to Milan for discussions with his librettists and publisher.

3

What progress had the opera been making during this period? Puccini's satisfaction with the work of Praga and Oliva was shortlived. On getting down to their libretto he found things little to his liking, such as the treatment of the plot, the division of the acts and the spoken dialogue; above all, he felt that it no longer answered the criteria for an *opéra comique*. Giving vent to his exasperation he writes to Dide: 'The libretto which I have had redone again and again drives me to despair. Even now there isn't a poet to be found who would produce something good' (undated, *E*). Praga, however, did not approve of Puccini's suggested alteration on dramatic grounds, and finally declined any further collaboration, so that Oliva, whom the composer found 'more obliging', now carried on alone. Together they sketched a new third act, with its highly original scene of the Embarkation of the Prostitutes. In November 1890 we find Ricordi asking: 'and the Signora Manon, are you continuing your good relations with her?' (*M*). Puccini was, for since March he had been working on the music for the first act and for such other sections of Oliva's libretto as had found his approval. Yet it was not long before Oliva too fell into disgrace. As an example to illustrate to what extent Puccini had matured since *Edgar* as a man of the theatre and what attention he now paid to the minutest points in a libretto, the following letter to his publisher deserves to be quoted *in toto*:

Dear Signor Giulio,   Undated

    I have thought it advisable to send you Oliva's manuscript so that you should read it and get an exact idea of the defects and contortions it contains. True, there are some good things in it, but the quartet, for example, is hideous. I don't understand why here Oliva has discarded the original outline, which was so clear. The first scene between Geronte and Lescaut is good and so is the second scene with Manon, except for some shortening in the scene in which Lescaut goes to fetch the old man, who is hiding. Those asides seem to me too long. Then if you look at the manuscript you'll find some observations of mine where Lescaut talks to. Des Grieux. The outline is perfectly clear: 'Ah, my dear fellow! There are so many ways and means of making money when one is intelligent, etc. . .: cards, beautiful women, more or less young, etc., etc.' Instead, as you'll see from the libretto, all that is vague, contorted and long. . . Then look at my observations. I don't like that disappearance of Lescaut and Renato to prepare the refreshments; besides, the scene makes Renato play an odious part. However does Renato come to the point of leaving Manon at the disposal of the old man? You'll remember how we fought with Leoncavallo to avoid that!

And now, besides many other defects, we come to the quartet. How graceful, logical and interesting was that quartet in the original sketch! That *mythological* entry of Geronte, then Lescaut's *war in Poland* to distract Des Grieux. That explosion between Geronte and Manon! It was also better that they should sit down at the table, as we had decided! And where has it disappeared, that little drinking-song between the four, which fitted in so well? In short, that little quartet at the table which was rapid and rich, has now been replaced by another version that is endless and of a rhetorical loquacity, to the detriment of the clarity and rapidity with which the drama should unfold. The scene after Geronte's exit, that is, the ultimate scene, is all right. In brief, I am not at all satisfied and I believe that you'll share my view. At some points, the departure from the original idea has resulted in an improvement, but at many others it has been much for the worse.

I shall write to Oliva that the manuscript, with some remarks of mine, is in your hands. I beg and entreat you to talk to him and explain the contents of my letter and tell him anything that you think reasonable in your own mind.

Trusting myself to you, I am, believe me, with affectionate greetings,

Yours . . . (*E*).

(Most of Puccini's criticisms refer to details in the original sketch of Act II which differed from its present version.)

Oliva, 'more obliging' though Puccini had found him, lost his patience and finally refused to serve any longer as his 'galley slave'. The crisis was as usual solved by Ricordi. He first approached Giacosa, pretending that he was asking merely for advice in the matter of Puccini's libretto but really hoping for his active collaboration. Giacosa, however, who considered libretto-writing an uncongenial task, avoided the trap and suggested another playwright, the young Luigi Illica.★ Illica at first hesitated, insisting on a written consent from Praga and Oliva before he would take over from them. These in their turn made difficulties, which were, however, smoothed over, thanks to Giacosa's authority and tactful intervention. Illica's chief difficulty in reshaping the libretto lay in the fact that Puccini had already composed the music for certain scenes which could not be altered. All the same, there still was a great deal left in the Praga-Oliva version that needed modifications. Illica, for the purpose of enlivening the period atmosphere of Act II (Geronte's

★ Of both more will be said in connection with *La Bohème*. It appears that Illica was first introduced to Puccini by Fontana.

home) introduced the secondary characters of the Hairdresser, the Music Master and the Dancing Master; added in Act III (Embarkation at Le Havre) the charming song of the Lampionaio or Lamplighter with his little 'conzoncina'; extended the roll-call of the Prostitutes from a few names to twelve, with Manon's coming last, and suggested a brief orchestral peroration, a *tempo di marinaresca*, at the close of the act.

Nevertheless, by May 1891 Illica was no longer working alone! Puccini had found him wanting too, and he was now being seconded by Giacosa, who had, no doubt, been eventually persuaded by Ricordi to come to the rescue. On 18 May the latter was able to inform his composer that 'the two poets are working with great enthusiasm and it is indeed a pleasure to do business with two people so cultivated and charming' (*M*).

To afford the reader some idea of the active and often decisive role which Ricordi played in the fashioning of Puccini's libretti, also of his insight into matters dramatic and musical, I quote a few extracts from his letters to the composer from the time of *Manon*:[36]

4 March 1892 (to Madrid)

Herewith the excerpts of *Manon*. The scene appears to be quite animated but superfluous at point 3. Better to go directly from ☐ to ☐ ☐. It is necessary to divide the third act into two parts, lowering the curtain but continuing the music which, it seems to me, ought to describe the consequence of the turmoil of the arrest (Act III), then change itself little by little into a mood of sadness and become dark in colour at the beginning of the second scene, night, etc. etc. . . . The last words of Lescaut's (those which Illica has marked) seem necessary to me. All in all, it is a scene very *rapid* in its musical and dramatic effect. That is good. . .

22 July 1892

I'll see Illica, but alas! I observe that you want eight verses for the tenor . . . at the end of the second act!! [the present third act]. What you need is not eight verses but eight words: that might do. Consider that the whole dramatic action is in a state of suspense. The less the tenor declaims, the better, while the orchestra indicates the movement of the condemned toward the vessel. You must cut the thing short, short, short. And find just the *right* effect to ring down the curtain. I am afraid of that whole act. But I do not always want to be the one who grumbles. Instead, dreaming about Manon, regard the four masterpieces which I send you [four verses by Ricordi himself] worthy of a Salvatore Rosa. . .

2 August 1892

. . . The libretto, taken all in all, seems to me interesting, although in certain parts a little too puffed up and in other parts overloaded with episodes and with dramatic incidents; the music will solve many of these defects.

There is a quantity of characters who are episodic and useless. Merely annoying supernumeraries destined to frighten the impresarios and nothing else. Oh! how I cursed, seeing every so often one of these personages spring forth! Away, away! What need is there for a postilion? The host of the inn is quite capable of receiving the orders of Geronte. And that official who says three words in the second act? And then the officer who says two and a half?! *Mamma mia!* To the devil with all this uselessness! And how ugly is this whole business of the crinoline in which she [Manon] hides the jewels. It is a ridiculous action, unsympathetic and not true to life. Do you imagine Manon about to flee with her skirts lifted? . . .

For pity's sake, dear Puccini, don't make me suffer more agony on account of excessive length; your music is altogether beautiful, too beautiful. Don't let yourself be led astray by musical philosophy or by the libretto. Forward, forward, and quickly! . . .

5 August 1892

As far as I am concerned, in the finale of Havre I am little pleased with that embrace!! It doesn't ring true to life. How can one permit a young man to kiss a condemned woman, and in the front of the commander, the soldiers, and the entire populace? This offends common sense. How about this: Manon marches slowly with the others while Des Grieux begs her: 'I have obtained the permission'; then, half crying, half speaking: 'Manon, Manon, I follow you!' Manon turns, she falls to her knees, she lifts her arms to heaven in a gesture of joy and gratitude. Des Grieux runs toward Manon and the curtain falls. It's not so wonderful. No! But it is more believable. Consider it. . .

Small wonder that Puccini should have described his publisher as 'my best of poets, mender of other men's faults' (E).

4

Manon Lescaut was finished in October 1892, Puccini having left the most difficult Act III to be completed last. All in all, the work on it (including the libretto) had taken over three years, as against the one year which he had anticipated in his youthful optimism in 1889, when he wrote to Dide that he expected to 'finish an opera for this next season at La Scala' (E). Yet two more hurdles had to be taken before the publication of the score. One was the title, over which Puccini, always vacillating at the last moment, began to feel a sudden doubt, on account of its similarity to the title of Massenet's opera. 'Change the title?' exclaims Ricordi in a letter of 6 December 1892, 'that would be ridiculous, nothing more nor less, for a subject so well known.' Puccini acquiesced, but to distinguish it from Massenet's *Manon* his opera was called *Manon Lescaut*. The second obstacle lay in the manner in which acknowledgment should be made of the multiple paternity of the libretto, which in Puccini's words was 'by all and none'. To give the names of its five begetters—Leoncavallo, Praga, Oliva, Illica and Giacosa, not to mention Ricordi in the role of *accoucheur*—would have looked ludicrous on the printed page; moreover, none considered his contribution large enough to claim a major responsibility for the mongrel. Discreet anonymity was hence indicated, an anonymity that even extended to the father of the original story, the Abbé Prévost.* The opera was, therefore, published as simply '*Manon Lescaut*. Lyric Drama in Four Acts, Music by Giacomo Puccini'— assuredly a curiosity in theatrical history.

* It is only in an anonymous Preface to the published libretto that Prévost's name is mentioned.

The autograph score presents the usual appearance: many pages are crossed out; passages are pasted over with slips of music manuscript paper, with corrections written on them; Puccini's signs for sharps and naturals are frequently undistinguishable, and all kinds of hieroglyphics are addressed to the unfortunate copyist.* For the first time Puccini added metronome markings and adopted Verdi's practice of putting *ppppp* for the orchestra in order to ensure the softest possible dynamics. The autograph is not completely identical with the version we have now; some of the more important divagations will be mentioned later.

Manon Lescaut was given for the first time at the Teatro Regio, Turin, on 1 February 1893—precisely eight days before the première at La Scala of Verdi's swansong *Falstaff*. The choice of Turin, instead of La Scala where Puccini had originally hoped his opera would be staged, was due to the wily Ricordi, who feared that, after the failure of *Edgar* there, the Milan public might have cooled off toward the composer and would thus adopt an attitude of injurious reserve to the new work.† In January Puccini travelled to Turin to supervise the rehearsals. Writing to Elvira he expressed his conviction that, despite rumours to the contrary, 'I have done a successful piece of work. Here everybody is mad about it. Nevertheless, the execution will be wretched because the voices can hardly be heard' (undated, *M*). The chief cast were Cesira Ferrani in the name-part (she was to be the first Mimi in *La Bohème*), Giuseppe Cremonini as Des Grieux, and the conductor was the veteran Alessandro Pomé. The theatre was sold out and critics had come from all over Italy. In the event Puccini's apprehension as to the execution proved wholly unfounded. The opera was received with a tremendous enthusiasm, composer and artists taking as many as thirty calls. The papers were unanimous in their priase. Giovanni Pozza, giving in the *Corriere della Sera* the most detailed account of the performance, remarked on the progress the composer had made since *Edgar* and laid stress on the true Italian quality of his vocal style, a quality 'which is that of our race (*paganesimo*), of our sensuousness in art . . . Puccini instinctively draws back from Wagner's mystic profundity yet for all that he is not given to making concessions to trivial melodrama'—a shaft aimed at Mascagni and Leoncavallo. Pozza also drew attention to the important part played in this opera by the orchestra, which 'the modern style now demands and which is as it should be', but finds that at times Puccini goes too far in that direction and

---

* At various times Puccini made minor alterations in the opera (notably in Act IV), some of which were suggested by Toscanini. There are no fewer than six editions of the Italian vocal score, the last dating from 1960! The autograph folio score was never published, and there are two versions of the full quarto score published in 1915 and 1958, respectively. As Cecil Hopkinson, who had made a particular study of the Puccini vocal scores, writes: 'Of all Puccini's operas *Manon Lescaut* presented the greatest number of complexities with its many changes in the music. Among the twelve editions in five languages there are no fewer than six different versions of the piano and vocal score and two of the orchestra'. Cecil Hopkinson, *A Bibliography of the Works of Giacomo Puccini, 1858–1924* (New York, 1986), p. 8.

† It is possible too that he feared the close proximity of *Falstaff* at La Scala.

uses the brass on occasion to violent, strident effect. Though Pozza's notice reflects a slightly conservative and anti-Wagnerian attitude, yet what he said was as true as was the remark made by Giuseppe Depanis in the *Gazzetta Piemontese* that Puccini 'is one of the strongest talents among young Italian composers of opera'. The subsequent history of Italian opera proved Depanis right to the hilt. In short, *Manon Lescaut* achieved a success such as none of Puccini's subsequent and more mature operas were destined to enjoy at their first production; it placed him on the operatic map squarely and fairly and was the foundation of his international fame.†

A week after the première a banquet was given in honour of the composer in Turin, at which he was expected to make a speech. He had prepared some notes jotted down on the left-hand cuff of his shirt; yet as he was always shy, ill at ease and tongue-tied when confronted with a large public gathering, uses the brass on occasion to violent, strident effect. Though Pozza's notice reflects a slightly conservative and anti-Wagnerian attitude, yet what he said was as true as was the remark made by Giuseppe Depanis in the *Gazzetta Piemontese* that Puccini 'is one of the strongest talent among young Italian composers of opera'. The subsequent history of Italian opera proved when his turn came to reply to the numerous toasts, he forgot speech, cuff and all, and could bring out only a half-suffocated '*Grazie a tutti!*'

Manon Lescaut at once made its way through Italy and in its first year reached foreign cities as distant as Buenos Aires, Rio de Janeiro, St. Petersburg, Munich and Hamburg. The first English production was at Covent Garden on 14 May 1894, when Bernard Shaw, then a young music critic on *The World*, greeted it in most enthusiastic terms, concluding his long article with the prophetic words 'Puccini looks to me more like the heir of Verdi than any other of his rivals'.

Le Villi and *Edgar* had shown Puccini as a composer of great promise, *Manon Lescaut* brought the achievement. It raised his status and prestige overnight and outward signs of it were not slow in arriving. He was decorated with the Order of La Croce di Cavaliere, an honour received partly through the intermediacy of Depanis, who, on this showing, must have been a *rara avis* among critics. His one-time teacher Bazzini, now director of the Milan Conservatoire, offered him the post of professor of composition which had become vacant through the premature death of Catalani in August 1893; and Venice invited him to accept the directorship of the celebrated Liceo Benedetto Marcello. Yet if 'class-rooms' had already caused Puccini 'claustrophobia' when he was still a struggling artist, now that the tide had turned he was not likely to relinquish his freedom. Moreover, the royalties accruing from *Manon Lescaut* put an end to his straitened circumstances, ensuring henceforth a regular and handsome income. He repaid Ricordi the considerable debt for nine years of monthly advances, and out of piety he bought back his father's house at Lucca which had been sold after Albina Puccini's death. But the records preserve silence on whether old Dr. Cerù ever received his pound of flesh.

† Again we note the parallel with Verdi, in that he too achieved his first great success with his third opera, *Nabucco* (1842), which made his name known outside Italy.

TORRE DEL LAGO: THE ANCIENT TOWER
With Puccini's villa in the background

THE STUDY

TORRE BEL LAGO: PUCCINI ON A SHOOT- ING EXPEDITION ON THE LAKE OF MASSACIUCCOLI

WITH HIS WIFE IN THE GARDEN OF HIS VILLA

VII

Torre del Lago: 'Turris Eburnea'

I

A VISITOR, making the short trip from Lucca to Torre del Lago Puccini, as it is now officially called, might well wonder what it was that attracted the composer to this spot with such force that he made it his home for thirty years. All his operas from *La Bohème* onwards were worked out and, with the exception of *Turandot*, completed at Torre, but it was Puccini's habit to spend some of the winter months at his Milan flat (4 Via Giuseppe Verdi), where usually most of the orchestration was done. Torre itself is an unremarkable enough place lying in the flat plain that separates the foothills of the Apuan Alps from the Mediterranean. Even today it is no more than a large, dull village. Its sole attraction is the enchanting view it affords eastwards over the dark blue expanse of the Lake of Massaciuccoli to the green slopes on the opposite shore and, farther north, to the 'Puccini country' in the direction of Chiatri, where on a fine summer's day the white, red and blue houses of Quiesa, of Massarosa and of the climbing villages beyond shimmer and sparkle in the distance.

To reach the Puccini Villa, you are compelled to walk a mile or so along a straight dusty road, the Viale Giacomo Puccini, flanked on both sides by old, ugly-looking houses. At No. 222, the point where the road strikes the western shore of the lake, stands the composer's villa, erected in close vicinity to an ancient tower, since demolished, that gave the name to the village. Before the present quay was built, with its ineluctable *ristorante* at the edge, the water used to come within a few yards of the gates—convenient enough for Puccini to slip, armed with gun and game-bag, into his boat and row in the early hours of dawn, as was his wont, to the reeds and bulrushes that reach out into the lake on its southern side, where he would engage in the slaughter of wild duck, pheasant, teal, divers and moorhens. It was this richness in waterbirds that for Puccini rendered the Lake of Massaciuccoli the most beautiful lake in all Italy, though his visitors would find it somewhat less alluring—to Illica, for example, it was 'a bog', its greatest depth being no more than nine to twelve feet.

When Puccini first discovered Torre, in 1884, it was no more than a tiny fishing village counting, according to him, '120 souls and twelve houses'. Cut off from the busy world and dreaming away in rustic seclusion, the place then fulfilled three of Puccini's most urgent requirements: the living was cheap and a house could be rented at little expense, it provided perfect solitude and peace for his work, and the shores of the lake permitted unrestricted indulgence of his passion for wildfowling. Torre del Lago became his refuge from tiresome publishers, temperamental artists, lion-hunters and adoring society women. In a moment of lyrical effusion he once described it as his 'supreme joy, paradise, Eden, the Empyrean, *turris eburnea, vas spiritualis*, kingdom'.[37] When he settled at Torre in 1891, he first occupied part of a house which belonged to one Venanzio, keeper of the estate of the Marchese Carlo Ginori-Lisci, who was also the owner of the lake. The Marchese was soon to become an intimate friend of the Puccinis; *La Bohème* is dedicated to him. After some time Venanzio's house no longer met the composer's growing demands for comfort and space and he therefore rented a large villa in the vicinity, belonging to Conte Gratonelli of Siena. Here too his stay was brief, and when large royalties were beginning to flow in from *La Bohème* he decided to become a house-owner himself. There being no suitable property for sale at Torre itself, Puccini first thought of having a villa built on the opposite shore or on the hills above it. This plan, however, did not materialize and, at the suggestion of his Lucca friend, Alfredo Caselli, he bought in 1898 a sizeable estate at Monsagrati near Chiatri, a little township north-east of Torre, lying at an altitude of about 1,200 feet. Monsagrati afforded a splendid view of the lake and of the Tuscan Maremma down to the sea, but it was a wild and inaccessible spot. Unlike Verdi, who at Sant'Agata turned his hand from composition to agriculture—and with no less success—Puccini evinced little interest in a proper running of his estate and appears to have chosen Monsagrati for the sole purpose of composing *Tosca* there in complete solitude. In a letter to Ricordi he describes life at this place, thus:

Monsagrati, 31 July 1898

Dear Signor Giulio,

Hot! Hot! Hot! One sleeps by day and works by night! And the night here is really black—'I swear it, I swear it!' as Ferrani said.*

I am in a hideous, hateful place, amidst woods and pine trees which shut off all view, closed in by mountains and lighted by a broiling sun, with not a breath of wind. But the evenings are delicious and the nights enchanting.

I work from ten in the evening till four in the morning. The house is large and indoors one is very comfortable. All in all, I am very happy to have fled to this tedious place where the human being is the exception. We are really alone (*E*).

Elvira and Fosca—Tonio was then at a boarding school in Milan—disliked this place from the very beginning of their stay. In order to induce Puccini to leave, they are said to have enacted a ghost comedy with the help of some visitors who happened to be staying there, among them Carignani, to try to scare the composer during his night work. Since these spectral groans and moans did not seem to achieve the desired effect, Carignani finally appeared to Puccini in a white shroud. Whether this did the trick is

* Ferrani was Puccini's first Manon who sings these words in Act II.

somewhat doubtful, but Puccini seemed glad himself when he finally left Monsagrati in October; but he later blamed Elvira for it:

Brussels, about 1900

I gave my right eye for a crazy idea: Chiatri. If I could have at least heard you or Fosca say: 'True, it is uncomfortable and it cost a lot but we will be happy there, we will go there and you will be able to work in peace.' Never a word of encouragement, never one of kindness. Through the sovereign force of slow insistence I ended up hating Chiatri which, when I bought it and began its construction, I loved so much (M).

The move from Monsagrati was occasioned by the fact that the new villa which Puccini had started to build at Torre del Lago was now ready for occupation. He had bought the old house of his one-time landlord Venanzio, had it razed to the ground and a new building erected according to his own specifications, which, needless to say, he kept altering like his libretti. It was in this villa that he lived until his forced exodus in 1922 to Viareggio. Yet, in order to ensure a retreat into complete solitude, he retained the estate at Monsagrati and for the same purpose acquired later another villa high up in the Apennines, at Abetone, where part of *Butterfly* was composed. There is a friendly, warm and welcoming air about the villa at Torre del Lago which is in marked contrast to the cold and formal atmosphere that surrounds Puccini's palatial house at Viareggio. By the entrance to the garden stands Prince Troubetzkoy's famous statuette and the garden contains a magnificent palm. The interior of the villa, which is furnished in the opulent, heavy style of the late nineteenth century, has been preserved in more or less the same condition as its owner left it. Most of the ground floor is occupied by the study, a bright, spacious room with a large open fireplace. Opposite stands Puccini's Förster upright piano, which he had had provided with a special damper because of his habit of working at night. Next to the piano, on the left, there is the table with all his writing paraphernalia on it. Signed photographic portraits of artists are seen everywhere: Caruso, Maria Jeritza (Puccini's best Tosca), Gustav Mahler, with a dedication commemorating the Hamburg production of *Le Villi* in 1892, Franz Schalk, the witty director of the Vienna State Opera, and—Lehár.

What must assuredly be a unique curiosity in the house of an artist is the gunroom, immediately adjoining the study, with a chest replete with guns of all descriptions, with stuffed trophies of some magnificent water-birds staring fixedly at the visitor, with shooting boots of all makes and shapes neatly arranged in a row on the floor, and photographs hanging on the wall which show the composer and his cronies in hunting attire and evidently enjoying some huge joke.

After his father's death, Tonio Puccini had a small mausoleum built into the wall between the study and the gunroom; this contains the mortal remains of the composer, of Elvira, who died in 1934, and, since 1946, of Tonio himself, who like his father died of cancer. Their names and dates are inscribed on white Carrara marble. Affixed to one of the outside walls of the house there is a plaque which was unveiled on 28 December 1924, five weeks after the composer's death. It reads:

Il popolo di Torre del Lago pose questa pietra
a termine di devozione
nella casa
ove ebbero nascimento
le innumeravoli creature di sogno
che
GIACOMO PUCCINI
trasse dal suo spirito immortale
e rese vive
col magistro dell'arte
perché dicessero all'universa
ITALIA

(The people of Torre del Lago, in token of their devotion, have laid this stone in the house in which were born the innumerable creatures of fantasy which GIACOMO PUCCINI formed in his immortal spirit and brought to life with magisterial art that they should speak to all ITALY.)

2

At Torre del Lago Puccini soon became the centre of a small colony of writers and artists who like himself had settled there in search of peace and tranquillity.* Their usual meeting place was a kind of roadhouse, a shed rather than an inn, which bore the impressive name *Capanna di Giovanni delle Bande Nere*, so called after its owner, who was the local cobbler. There, greatly to Elvira's annoyance, her husband would spend a great deal of his time in convivial company—drinking the strong Tuscan wine, talking nineteen to the dozen and playing *scopa* and *briscola*, two popular Italian card games; later he added poker to them. In outward appearances his life at Torre del Lago seemed to pass in the blissful state of *far niente*.

When poverty compelled 'Giovanni of the Black Stripes' to emigrate to South America, Puccini proposed to his friends to purchase the place from him and turn it into a kind of club, a proposal that was put into effect with alacrity. No other name was more appropriate than *Club La Bohème*, indicating the character and purpose of the new venture as well as the opera on which its most distinguished member happened to be working just then. Signs were posted on the walls of the inn, with inscriptions partly in deliberately faulty Latin, partly in nonsensical Italian, but the spirit reigning in this 'club' is best illustrated in its so-called regulations. Thus:

No. 1. The members of the *Club La Bohème*, faithful interpreters of the spirit in which it was founded, pledge themselves under oath to be well and eat better.

* Among these were the painters Guido Marotti and Ferruccio Pagni, the co-authors of a lively book of memoirs, *Giacomo Puccini Intimo* (Florence, 1926), on which I have drawn for this sketch of life at Torre.

No. 2. Poker faces, pedants, weak stomachs, blockheads, puritans and other wretches of the species are not admitted and will be chased away.

No. 3. The President acts as conciliator but undertakes to hinder the Treasurer in the collection of the subscription money.

No. 4. The Treasurer is empowered to abscond with the money.

No. 5. The lighting of the *locale* is provided by a petrol lamp. Failing the fuel, the *'moccoli'* of the members are to be used. (This is a pun on *moccolo* which may mean 'candle stump' or 'blockhead'.)

No. 6. All games permitted by law are forbidden.

No. 7. Silence is prohibited.

No. 8. Wisdom is not permitted, except in special cases.

It is as though we heard the four Bohemians of the opera.

In the evenings, however, the club members would repair to Puccini's house for conversation and card games, but mostly without the composer's participation. Evening and night were his chief working hours, but, strangely enough, he liked the presence of people in his study,* provided that the company behaved as though he were non-existent. Woe to him who had the temerity to whistle some motive or tune the composer had been trying out on the piano; Puccini was good-natured and not easily roused, but this would send him into fuming rage. Another oddity of his was to wear a hat while composing. They were in all unusual circumstances in which *La Bohème* was committed to paper.

Puccini's chief relaxation from his work was his shooting expeditions. Specht has interpreted this passion as a Freudian expression of the composer's cruelty, a symbolic substitute for the gratification of his 'Neronic instinct'.[38] There is no doubt something in this interpretation. Yet, as I was assured on all hands during my stay in Lucca, shooting is a highly popular sport in Tuscany, owing to the many marshes and forests teeming with wild prey, so that to the Tuscans Puccini's passion has no pathological or morbid element in it. It may well be that it was not so much the actual shooting as the many hours of complete solitude watching for the prey wherein lay the fascination for Puccini—hours when his creative fantasy would work out problems that had baffled him within the four walls of his study. And from various accounts it is indeed doubtful whether he was a good shot. However, the fact remains that he pursued this sport with a relentless passion which frequently landed him in dangerous situations and brought him into conflict with the authorities. Thus, on one occasion when 'Sor Giacomo', as Puccini was familiarly called by the peasants, and his usual companion Giovanni Manfredi, nicknamed (in the Tuscan dialect) 'Lappore' for his white eyelashes, were out in their boat on a nocturnal expedition they were mistaken for poachers and were nearly shot by the gamekeepers of the Marchese Ginori's estate. On another occasion when the two tried their luck on the shore opposite Torre del Lago, they were arrested on the triple charge of shooting during the forbidden season, of trespassing and of being without possession of a permit to carry firearms.

* The same is recorded of Glinka and Scriabin.

The name of the chief culprit was sufficiently distinguished to create a minor sensation and news of the incident soon reached Ricordi in Milan. For some considerable time the publisher had been admonishing his 'sharpshooter' not to let 'your passion for birds seduce you away from music. . . Therefore one eye at the gun-sight but your thought at *Bohème*' (17 August 1893. *M*). Apprised of Puccini's 'crime', Ricordi now saw in its legal consequences what to him as the publisher appeared as a blessing in disguise:

21 September 1894

I have heard about your shooting prowess. Bravo, by Jove! But I believe that this time you are going to finish in prison. So much the better! Let them send you a piano and, instead of annoying wild beasts, you can blast forth gunshots of melody (*M*).

The case came in due course before a magistrates' court at Bagni San Giuliano, at which, thanks to the casuistry of his defending counsel, his friend Pelosini, the accused and his accomplice were found not guilty. Yet it was not until December 1894 that Puccini troubled to obtain a shooting permit from Ginori.

About the same time Puccini began to indulge in another sport, yet with less enthusiasm than he displayed for shooting. He was inclining to adiposity, on account of which his friend had nicknamed him '*uomo palla*'—literally 'human globe', and in order to reduce his weight he bought himself, in July 1893, a Humber bicycle for 220 lire—'a veritable patrimony'; Ricordi's comment was 'Ride your bicycle, but from one librettist to another!'. Thus began Puccini's passion for mechanical locomotion which in his later years led him to acquire several expensive motor-cars and a small fleet of motor-boats in which he would race on the lake from one shore to the other.

VIII

Maturity

I

WE RETURN TO OUR CHRONICLE of events following the success of *Manon Lescaut*. In that opera Puccini had reached the threshold of maturity; with his next work, *La Bohème*, he passed into it. Yet before this masterpiece saw the light of day, many hurdles had to be taken, and for some considerable time Puccini attempted to ride two horses simultaneously. This equestrian *tour de force* was preceded by a brief preliminary canter. As early as 5 January 1890, when in the throes of *Manon Lescaut*, Puccini informed his brother in South America that after that opera he intended to write one with Buddha as its central character—'but it will be years before it materializes. In the mean-time I am thinking about it' (E). For how long he thought, we do not know —probably for only a short time, as there is no more mention of this subject in his letters. In any case, it would have seemed a strange choice for Puccini and its chief attraction probably lay in the exotic ambience, even as it had been with Delibes and *Lakmé* (1883); indeed it is conceivable that Puccini was tempted by the Buddha subject in the hope of repeating Delibes' great success with a similar excursion into the Far East.

Far more serious than the plan for a *Buddha* was his intention to write a *La Lupa—The She-Wolf*, after a tale by Giovanni Verga, one of Italy's first realistic writers, from whose collection of short stories about Sicilian peasant life (which included *La Lupa*) Mascagni had derived the libretto for his *Cavalleria Rusticana*. There can be little doubt that Mascagni's sensational success with that work was largely responsible for Ricordi's decision to commission from Verga a libretto of a similar realistic character. At first Puccini was much impressed by it and for some time not only worked simultaneously at *La Lupa* and *La Bohème* but appears to have given pre-ference to the Verga subject, setting part of the libretto to music some of which he later incorporated in *La Bohème*. In the spring of 1894 he paid Verga a visit at Catania, where the Sicilian-born writer lived, for the purpose of discussing details of the libretto and also of acquainting himself with the local atmosphere and the folk-music of Sicily; he also took photographs of characteristic places and, at Ricordi's request, made notes about suitable national costumes to be used in the opera.

Puccini interrupted his visit to Verga by a short pleasure trip to Malta, where he made his first, somewhat disagreeable acquaintance with the English authorities, who arrested him as a spy, as he had aroused their suspicion by taking snapshots of the naval fortifications. None the worse for this experience he returned to Catania, where he continued his research into Sicilian lore. The care with which he set about these matters—a characteristic trait of Puccini's working methods which we shall encounter again and again—seemed a propitious portent for the 'Sicilian' opera. Yet, while still staying with Verga, already the first doubts began to cross his mind. On his return voyage to Leghorn, one of his fellow-passengers happened to be the Contessa Blandine Gravina, Cosima Wagner's daughter by her first marriage to Bülow. Anxious to make her acquaintance, Puccini effected his introduction in an unusual yet, in the circumstances, highly appropriate manner: he sat down at the piano in the ship's lounge and began to play from *Tannhäuser*. The introduction was made. The Contessa had heard of the celebrated composer of *Manon Lescaut* and in the course of her conversation inquired after his future operatic plans. When Puccini told her of *La Lupa*, outlining to her the plot in which the heroine, a woman consumed by a savage passion, is murdered during a Good Friday procession, the good Contessa, dismayed beyond description, besought him to abandon this drama of 'lechery and crime, and with a religious procession in it!' (she might almost have been referring to the future *Tosca*) 'it would bring nothing but misfortune'.[39] Whether or not it was the Contessa's pious horror that finally tipped the scales against *La Lupa*, the fact is that no sooner had Puccini returned to Torre del Lago than he sent Ricordi the following missive:

Torre del Lago, 13 July 1894

Dear Signor Giulio,

I delayed writing to you because I wanted time to reflect seriously on the things I am now about to say to you. Since my return from Sicily and my conversations with Verga, I confess that, instead of feeling inspired by *La Lupa*, I am assailed by a thousand doubts which have made me decide to postpone the composition until the play is staged.

My reasons are the many dialogues in the libretto, which are drawn out to excessive lengths and the unattractive characters, without a single *luminous* and appealing figure to stand out from them. I had hoped that Verga would give Mara [the heroine] more prominence and consideration, but it was impossible, given the existing plot. Also the observations he made in his last letters helped me to come to this decision. I do not think that you will be displeased by this! I only regret the time that I have lost, but I shall make up for it by plunging into *La Bohème* head over heels (*a corpo morto*). . .

Puccini then goes on to discuss certain points in the *Bohème* libretto; but the decision of abandoning *La Lupa* still troubles him and he returns to the subject in his concluding paragraph:

As to *La Lupa*, it is better to await the judgment which the public will pronounce on the play. In Sicily I found nothing of musical interest but I photographed types, peasant farms, etc., which I will show you when it will be convenient for you. Meanwhile, I have need of a letter from you which will set my mind at rest and not condemn my inconstancy which I would call 'belated insight'. But better late than never (*E*).

Ricordi accepted Puccini's reasons, but not without making reproaches to him:

18 July 1894

> No, I don't wonder that you made the decision that you did, though it saddens me. Again so many months lost, unfruitful! At least, I see your strong and resolute decision in favour of *Bohème*. . . Permit me, however, my dear Doge, to observe with my usual frankness that you have been a long time realizing that the dialogue in *La Lupa* is excessive—after you have begun to set it to music, after the newspapers have already announced the immediate appearance of the opera, after your voyage to Catania! Well, these are useless observations. . . I wish you a ticket for the most direct train to take you to station *Bohème* (M).

Puccini's letter to Ricordi is highly interesting for the revealing light it throws on him as a dramatist. He rejects Verga's libretto on the ground that it has 'unattractive characters, without a single luminous and appealing figure to stand out': this, surely, argues an aversion from pure *verismo*, with its predilection for sordid and unlovable characters. In the second place, he wishes to wait until *La Lupa* will be staged as a play before making up his mind whether or not to set it to music. In other words, its success as a *spoken drama* was to be for him the ultimate criterion as to the subject's effectiveness. Time and again he would make his decision dependent upon the impression made on him by the stage production of a play that seemed to him suitable for an operatic treatment. Thus, in connection with Gerhart Hauptmann's symbolist drama, *Hanneles Himmelfahrt*, which he considered for some time, he wrote to his friend, Riccardo Schnabl: '. . . whatever we do, I want to see the play in the theatre before making up my mind' (26 August 1911. *C.P.* Let.585). We now come to understand why four of his mature operas—*Tosca*, *Butterfly*, *La Fanciulla del West* and *Il Tabarro*—are all based on plays which had proved stageworthy in the theatre. From this two conclusions can be drawn. One is that in his mind's eye Puccini saw a subject, in the first place, in terms of pure stage action and only secondarily in operatic terms, that is to say, he conceived an opera above all as a spoken drama to which music was to lend a third dimension, thus aiming at *musical drama* and not *music-drama*—hence the extraordinary *stage* effect of his works. The second conclusion to be drawn from his remarks is that his preference for subjects taken from well-tried plays may have sprung from the supremacy in his considerations of the principle 'Safety first' or, else, from a measure of inner uncertainty as to what he really wanted. Though he finally always followed his own counsel, he needed outside encouragement and clarification of his ideas by others. What he once wrote to Clausetti, namely: 'I don't know what is needed, but I feel the need that someone comes and checks what is going on in mind. I can't tell you anything else' (10 November 1899. *C.P.* Let.214), Puccini uttered in many variations throughout his career.

2

As Puccini himself admitted much time had been lost over the abortive *La Lupa*. Yet even if this diversion had not occurred, it is permissible to doubt whether *La Bohème* would have been completed appreciably earlier than it was. We have seen that with *Manon Lescaut* the composer had begun to make increasingly severe demands on his librettists, demands which in *La Bohème* reached their maximum. The halting progress of the opera was largely caused by the innumerable difficulties which he kept raising with his poets over their treatment of the libretto, rather than by any slowness in the actual composition.

In view of the later *contretemps* with Leoncavallo, it is not unimportant to enquire who it was who first suggested drawing a libretto from Henry Mürger's celebrated and largely autobiographical novel, *Scènes de la Vie de Bohème* (1848), which also exists in a dramatized version, produced in Paris in the following year. Two persons are the most likely, Illica and Leoncavallo; though on the evidence available it is not possible to establish which of the two might claim priority. Illica was well versed in French literature, of which he was said to possess a large library, and he had been one of the collaborators on the libretto for *Manon Lescaut*, which had been an un- qualified success. Therefore, Illica may have reasoned, why not tempt luck again with a subject drawn from yet another famous French novel, a subject, moreover, which was bound to recall to Puccini his own experiences of gay poverty as a student at the Milan Conservatoire and which, more important, fitted so well into his peculiar emotional world? If indeed it was Illica who first stumbled on the Mürger subject, then the first vague ideas for a *Bohème* opera must have begun to float in Puccini's mind as early as the late autumn of 1892 when he was just putting the finishing touches to *Manon Lescaut*. There is at any rate an oracular sentence contained in a letter from Ricordi to Puccini, dated 19 September 1892, which might be inter- preted in that sense: 'I talked again with Illica. He first has to finish a comedy, then he will occupy himself with a subject that is *formidable* and *commercial*' (*M*). In addition, there is the solid fact that for some time Illica was in sole charge of the dramatization of Mürger's novel and that, swift worker as he was, he had the first act and part of the second ready by the early June of the following year. All this would seem to point to Illica as the 'first begetter' of the idea for a *Bohème* opera.

How great, on the other hand, is the probability that Leoncavallo might claim this honour? It is great indeed if we assume Leoncavallo to have been the *indirect* originator. About the time when Puccini was casting about for a new subject, Leoncavallo had already lighted on Mürger's novel from which he planned to fashion a libretto for his own use—as he indeed later did for his opera *La Bohème* (1897). At that early period he was still on a friendly footing with Puccini and Ricordi—a friendship, it must be added, that was by no means reciprocal—and it is not unlikely that in conversation with them Leoncavallo inadvertently dropped a word or two about his intention, thus drawing their attention to the French subject. It should be explained that, in view of the rivalries and intrigues that enlivened the operatic world of Milan at that period, the subject on which a composer happened to be working was considered a business secret, to be guarded as jealously as an inventor would guard an unpatented invention. There is perhaps no more striking illustration of this state of affairs than this letter from Ricordi, dated 6 June 1893, in which he sends Puccini the urgent warning:

> It is absolutely necessary that you keep *secret* the progress of the libretto from everybody, friends, admirers. If to trust is good, not to trust is better. An inadvertent word which slips out may serve as a guide to your rival in *Bohème* and give him ideas for his libretto. That would be a real misfortune. Prudence, therefore, and a great deal of it! . . . (M).

'Your rival' was of course none other than Leoncavallo, to whom Ricordi and Puccini would also refer by such flattering epithets as 'Leonasino', 'Leonbestia' and 'that grand Kaiser Leoncavallo'.* Ricordi's secretiveness in such matters went to such lengths that even when he had the complete score of the first three acts of *La Bohème* in his possession he would show it to no one. Writing to Puccini on 13 November 1895 he says:

> Of the third act I have as yet only one copy, which is being used by the copyist for checking the score. I cannot therefore let it go. But even if I could, I wouldn't let it out of my hands. The matter is too delicate and touchy; it would only cause all kinds of gossip. I need only tell you that after I called Signora Storchio [she later sang the first Butterfly] for an audition and told her I was looking for an artist of quick sensitivity who could speak words easily and behave graciously on the stage—that is all I told her: you know how close-mouthed I am in these affairs—very well, immediately afterwards I heard that Sonzogno [Leoncavallo's publisher] knew all about the interview. Not only that, but Leoncavallo was going around boasting that he knew the libretto, that it was a mess and contained nothing of Mürger's spirit; he had his opera and he was going to show the world what the true *Bohème* was like.
> Give out the parts? Never again! . . . At the opportune moment I will hand them over to the impresario with the injunction to guard them. . . That's how we did it with *Falstaff*. . . (M).†

It would appear that at the time when Puccini was already at work on *La Bohème*, Leoncavallo offered him his own libretto or a scenario which Puccini is said to have perused and rejected. Yet, while all this belongs to the

---

* Possibly on account of his Wilhelm II moustache.

† Ricordi's secretiveness, however, was surpassed by that of Richard Strauss. When Strauss was considering *Ariadne auf Naxos* (first version), he enjoined on his librettist, Hugo von Hofmannsthal, not to breathe a word about it to anybody, except Max Reinhardt (who was to be the producer). And when Hofmannsthal asked to name him examples of classical coloratura arias which might serve him as models for the form of Zerbinetta's great aria, Strauss, in mentioning some, again impressed on him to use utter caution, mention no name; no subject. It would be best to say nothing at all, just have them sung to you'. (See letters of 20 and 22 May 1911, in *Richard Strauss. Briefwechsel mit Hugo von Hofmannsthal*, ed. by Franz and Alice Strauss. Zürich, 1952.)

realm of conjecture and hearsay, we now come to documented facts. In March 1893, after his return from Turin where he had gone to supervise the production of *Manon Lescaut*, Puccini happened to meet Leoncavallo in a Milan café. In the course of the conversation he mentioned that he was busy on an opera after Mürger's novel whereupon followed a most un- pleasant scene in which Leoncavallo, fuming with rage, reminded his rival that he had shown him his own libretto the previous winter and now claimed priority rights on this subject.* The immediate sequel of this stormy meeting was to be read in Milan's two most influential papers. On 20 March *Il Secolo*, owned by Leoncavallo's publisher Sonzogno, brought an announcement to the effect that the composer had been working for some time on an opera *La Bohème*, and the next day *Il Corriere della Sera* carried a similar announce- ment about Puccini, yet without going into the question of a possible priority over his competitor. Puccini was more explicit in a letter he wrote to the editor of *Il Corriere*, in which his dislike of Leoncavallo can clearly be read between the lines:

> The declaration made by Maestro Leoncavallo in *Il Secolo* yesterday must convince the public that I have acted in perfectly good faith. For it is clear that if Maestro Leoncavallo, with whom I have been linked for a long time by vivid feelings of friendship, had first told me what he unexpectedly told me the other evening, I would not have thought of the *Bohème* by Mürger. But now—for reasons easy to see—I am no longer willing to oblige him as I would the friend and musician.
>
> For the rest, what does it matter to Maestro Leoncavallo? Let him compose and I shall compose, and the public will judge. Priority in art does not imply that one interprets the same subject with the same ideas. I will only stress that since two months, that is, after the first production of *Manon Lescaut* in Turin, I have been seriously working on this plan and have made no secret of it to anybody. (21 March, 1893. *C.P.Let.81.*)

Knowing Puccini's foible for coveting a subject already used or about to be used by another composer, one is permitted to doubt the absolute honesty of his remark that 'if Maestro Leoncavallo had first told me what he told me unexpectedly the other evening, I would not have thought of the *Bohème* by Mürger'. However, the announcement of Puccini's work on *Bohème* in *Il Corriere* brought forth from Leoncavallo a reply in the same paper the next day, while *Il Secolo* published another notice giving a number of details to prove that Leoncavallo's priority over this subject was indisputable.

In the event, it was Puccini who won the race, largely, it would appear, because Ricordi turned the fact of Leoncavallo's rival venture into a whip with which to lash on Puccini's Pegasus.† Leoncavallo's *La Bohème* was given in Venice on 5 May 1897, fifteen months after the première of

* On moral grounds, Leoncavallo was, perhaps, justified in this claim, but not on legal grounds, since Mürger's novel was by that time no longer subject to copyright and therefore free to be used by any dramatist or composer.

† Dramatic composers seem especially responsive to such treatment. Thus, Johann Strauss was prompted to write *Eine Nacht in Venedig* chiefly because he had heard that his rival Millöcker intended to use the same subject.

Puccini's opera, and, while more powerful in dramatic treatment and not without its impressive moments, it was destined to be eclipsed by his rival's more inspired and incomparably more poetic work. Yet it is interesting to note that at its first performance Leoncavallo's work* had a considerably greater success than Puccini's at Turin.

3

Before narrating the tortuous history of the genesis of La Bohème, let us seek closer acquaintance with the two literary members of the 'holy trinity' (Ricordi) which was to produce the trio of Puccini's most popular operas: Giacosa and Illica. Of the two, Giacosa was by far the more outstanding personality and the greater artist. To the world at large the name of Giuseppe Giacosa (1847–1906) is today known merely as that of one of Puccini's chief librettists; yet in his time Giacosa stood in the front rank of those Italian writers and playwrights whose works form the transition from the romanticism of a Carducci and Pascoli to the French-influenced realism in the last two decades of the nineteenth century. Giacosa was a gifted poet and essayist and the author of finely observed short stories; but, above all, he was a dramatist with a subtle psychological insight, with thirty-two tragedies and comedies to his name, of which Tristi Amori (1887) and La Dame de Challant (1891)—the first written for Eleonora Duse and the second for Sarah Bernhardt—won him international acclaim. Noteworthy too is his Il Trionfo d'Amore (1875) for its treatment of the 'Turandot' motive in a medieval Italian setting, which Giacosa invested with a profound symbolism; it is not improbable that this play, together with Bazzini's opera Turanda, drew Puccini's early attention to a subject which he was to use toward the end of his life.

For some years Giacosa was also lecturer on dramatic literature at Milan Conservatoire and, until his death, editor of La Lettura, a literary periodical of high distinction.

Among his intimates, who included Boito and Duse, Giacosa was affectionately known as 'Pin', while Puccini later nicknamed him 'the Giacosan Buddha', on account of his short, thick-set figure, his large paunch, his full beard and his meditative, avuncular countenance. Giacosa had first come into contact with the composer in 1889, when he had been preparing for him the abortive 'Russian' libretto, and then again in connection with Manon Lescaut; but with La Bohème this collaboration was to become a close and lasting one. That Ricordi should have been most anxious to enlist the co-operation of so eminent a writer as Giacosa for his favourite composer seems to argue the growing importance that was being attached in Italy to the literary quality of an opera 'book'—a new tendency that had, no doubt, been partly inspired by the example of Verdi's partnership with Boito, if not also by Wagner's operatic texts.

* It was, incidentally, in Leoncavallo's Bohème that the young Caruso achieved his first success.

In their work for Puccini there existed a kind of division of labour between Giacosa and Illica. While Illica would draw up the scenario and develop the plot in detail, Giacosa's assignment was to cast the prose text into verse, elaborate the lyrical situations, introduce a more balanced order into the succession of scenes and, generally, lend the libretto literary polish and refinement. Whereas Illica contended that in the last analysis a libretto was merely a canvas to be filled in, expanded or contracted by the composer, according to his requirements, Giacosa maintained that 'it was one thing to sketch out scenes more or less fully, but another to condense the subject into a few verses and, at the same time, try to throw the essential elements into relief and attend to the shaping of the scene and verse. Such detailed and intricate work needs time and patience and much toil' (Letter to Ricordi, 23 August 1896).[40] Giacosa would and could not be hurried. Unlike Illica, he was a slow and painstakingly conscientious worker attempting to reconcile the practical and less subtle exigencies of a libretto with the demands for literary quality. This was for him a hard task because he naturally inclined to approach it from the angle of the poet and playwright and was loth to consider a libretto as primarily a means to an end. In Giacosa there was a permanent conflict between his artistic integrity and his self-criticism on the one hand, and the wishes of publisher and composer on the other. 'I don't possess Illica's prodigious facility', he wrote to Ricordi on 28 July 1893; 'I cannot go on writing if what I have already done does not satisfy me.' And again, a little later: 'I can't dash down just anything that comes into my head.' Many, as we shall see, were the clashes between him and Puccini and Ricordi which on several occasions led to Giacosa's offering his resignation; needless to say, it was never accepted. By the time the Bohème libretto was completed, his irritation with Puccini's perpetual demands for alterations had reached such a pitch that he wrote to Ricordi (25 June 1895): 'I swear to you that I shall never be caught again writing another libretto.' Doubtless the fact that he was an acclaimed writer in his own right was apt to make Giacosa feel easily hurt in his professional pride when having to submit to someone else's wishes; hence his peevish reproach to Ricordi (after Bohème): 'It is certain that the authors of the libretto did not receive from you and your firm the hundredth part of the moral satisfaction which was accorded to the composer. And of the authors I was surely the one who was noticed less.' Giacosa's susceptibility to imagined slights was such that it sometimes prompted him to make unreasonable demands himself, as we shall have occasion to relate in connection with the Butterfly libretto. But at heart good-natured, accommodating and generous, he was unable after such outbursts of indignation to harbour resentment for long and in the end always yielded to the combined entreaties of composer and publisher to return to the fold. And oddly enough, though he kept complaining that the writing of libretti was for him a most uncongenial occupation interfering with his true vocation as poet and playwright—'for those few scenes [Bohème] I have wasted', he once wrote to Ricordi, 'more paper and racked my brain more than I have for any of my own plays'—on at least two occasions he volunteered to write one for Ricordi; yet what he had in mind was not an adaptation of another writer's novel or play but something entirely of his own invention: 'And you will see the result will be a pure work of art' (letter to Tito Ricordi, 3 February 1900).* There cannot be the least doubt that what tender lyrical poetry and verbal felicities there are in the text of La Bohème, Tosca and Butterfly, flowed in from Giacosa's pen. The element in which Puccini must have felt a particularly close affinity with Giacosa was the latter's insight into the female psyche, his *feminismo*, which characterized the treatment of his heroines in his plays and stories. (Is it not significant that out of Puccini's twelve operas, seven should be named after the heroine?) The measure of authority and respect which Giacosa commanded with Puccini (his junior by eleven years), with Illica and Ricordi, emerges from an obituary published by Illica in La Lettura, in October 1906, from which I quote the following excerpt:

> Those sessions of ours!†. . . Real battles in which there and then entire acts were torn to pieces, scene after scene sacrificed, ideas abjured which only a moment ago had seemed bright and beautiful; thus was destroyed in a minute the work of long and painful months. Giacosa, Puccini, Giulio Ricordi and I—we were a quartet because Giulio Ricordi, who was presumed to preside, would always leave his presidential chair and descend into our semicircle which was extremely narrow (two metres in circumference and rendered more narrow still and more close and uncomfortable by the mighty person of Giacosa), to become one of the most obstinate and most vigorous belligerents. . . Giacosa was for us the equilibrium, in dark moments he was the sun, on stormy days the rainbow. . . In that uproar of voices expressing different views and conceptions, Giacosa's voice was the delightful, persuasive song of the nightingale. . . And Puccini? After each session he had to run to the manicurist to have his finger-nails attended to: he had bitten them off, down to the bone!

Luigi Illica (1857–1919), playwright, librettist and journalist, was a writer of prolific industry but a far less important figure than Giacosa. He counts

---

* Nardi (op. cit.), incidentally, makes the interesting suggestion that Giacosa profited from his work as Puccini's librettist because it taught him greater precision of language for his own plays. In addition to the three Puccini libretti, Giacosa adapted his drama *Una Partita a Scacchi* for a one-act opera by an obscure composer, Pietro Abbà-Cornaglia, and sketched a scenario for an oratorio *Caino* for Don Lorenzo Perosi, a noteworthy composer of church music. He was also planning to write, in collaboration with Illica, a libretto for Mascagni, but nothing came of it.

It is worth pointing to a parallel between Giacosa and Hofmannsthal which lay in their concern lest their own work as playwrights should suffer on account of the time spent on the writing of libretti. Thus, Hofmannsthal reminds Strauss, politely but firmly, that in order to finish the libretto for *Ariadne* (first version) he was forced to postpone his work on a prose comedy for a whole year and also to interrupt his work on *Jedermann*, which cost him a great effort to resume again (18 December 1911). Strauss, on the other hand, paid Hofmannsthal a compliment such as Puccini could never bring himself to pay Giacosa: 'You are the born librettist—in my eyes the greatest compliment, as I consider it far more difficult to produce a good opera "book" than a beautiful play' (6 July 1908). (*Richard Strauss. Briefwechsel*, etc., op. cit.)

† These were mostly held at Ricordi's office.

for little in Italian literature and drama of his period but can claim a respectable niche as the author of thirty-odd* libretti. A swift worker, quick-witted and most resourceful, Illica's services were greatly in demand. But his was a difficult and unbalanced personality and, to judge from the description given by his friend, Carlo Gatti,[12] a rather unattractive one. Illica could be generous and noble—'*un galantuomo*', as Ricordi referred to him. Yet he was entirely unpredictable in his conduct, impulsive and possessed a biting tongue. He would fly into a fuming rage at the slightest provocation, actual or imaginary, especially when under the influence of alcohol which he apparently indulged to excess. He was self-opinionated, conceited and aggressive—traits that would land him in the most disagreeable situations: in a sabre duel with Cuzzo Crea, the editor of the conservative *Gazetta dell'Emilia*, Illica, who was himself an out-and out republican, lost half his left ear. Despite the high fees he commanded and despite the royalties accruing to him from his many plays, Illica would frequently find himself in financial straits, due to the extravagant style in which he chose to live. It was difficult to trace him in Milan since he was almost perpetually on the move from one apartment to another.

As a librettist, Illica lacked Giacosa's poetic vision and the latter's depth and richness of feeling. On the other hand, he excelled his collaborator, his senior by ten years, in the profuse invention of telling theatrical incidents and the elaboration of a given subject into a varied and flexible plot. Illica's eye for the stage was as keen as Puccini's (which is saying a great deal) and it was perhaps more practical than the composer's and Giacosa's. Never at a loss for an idea, he would often, on the spur of the moment, light on an effective way out of difficulties that had baffled the other two. On a preceding page we have briefly touched on the different views which Illica and Giacosa entertained on the essential nature of a libretto. As it happened, Illica himself expounded them clearly in a highly interesting letter to Puccini from which I quote a substantial excerpt below. What Illica has to say in it argues a curious mixture of a most penetrating insight into operatic dramaturgy with a shallow pragmatism concerning the role of poetic verse in a libretto. This latter attitude sprang largely from his firm adherence to the tenets of a naturalistic theatre, an attitude so much in contrast to Giacosa's poetic approach and then already on the point of being superseded by a different outlook on dramatic values. The immediate cause for Illica's letter was a violent tussle he had had with Puccini over the libretto for a *Maria Antonietta*, which was the chief apple of discord between him and the composer after the death of Giacosa. Illica writes:

> The form of a libretto is created by the music, only the music and nothing but the music. It alone, Puccini, is the form. A libretto is nothing but a sketch. Méry† puts it well when he says: 'The verses in an opera are only there for

---

* In addition to the three he wrote for Puccini, Illica's most important libretti were for Catalani's *La Wally*, Gnecchi's *Cassandra*, Franchetti's *Cristoforo Colombo*, Mascagni's *Iris* and *Isabeau*, and Giordano's *Andrea Chénier* and *Siberia*.

† Francois Méry (1797–1866) was a French playwright and author of a number of satirical writings.

the convenience of the deaf'. I shall therefore continue to give in every libretto importance only to the treatment of the characters, to the cut of the scenes and to the verisimilitude, in its naturalness, of the dialogue, of the passions and situations. . . . The verse in a libretto is nothing but a prevalent custom, just as it is to call those who write a libretto 'poets' * That which has real value in a libretto is the word. The words should correspond to the truth of the moment (the situation) and of the passion (the character). Everything lies in that, the rest is *blague*.

But today the decadence propagated by D'Annunzio, in corrupting the simplicity and naturalness of language, threatens (in the theatre) truth and logic (the two guardian angels which stand beside you when you compose), notably because they distort the word. (October 1907. *C.P.Let.*528).

If this demonstrates Illica's ideological limitations, what was his other chief failing as a librettist? Puccini seems to have put his finger on it when he wrote to Illica in February 1915: 'You have always had spirit! But at times you don't reflect and allow your fantasy to flow without let or hindrance' (*C.P.Let.*671). Illica, not unlike Puccini himself, was prone to be carried away by a momentary enthusiasm for a subject or for a solution proposed by him for some dramatic problem or other, and with his predilection for picturesque details in the plot would indulge in soaring flights of fancy. He needed control from outside, from a hand that would erect a dam to the 'flow' of his fantasy and divert it into more narrow and safer channels. This operation was successfully carried out by Puccini, Giacosa and Ricordi, but only after much heated controversy and discrimination. If the rebellious Illica eventually relented, this was in the first place due to the great authority which the 'Giacosian Buddha' exerted in their deliberations.

The bald fact is that Illica *by himself* was never able to satisfy Puccini. Is it not significant that, when after Giacosa's death in 1906 the composer was prepared to continue working with Illica, all projects devised by the two proved a dismal failure? Yet the proud Illica would not accept an associate, and all attempts on the part of Puccini and Ricordi to persuade him to this foundered on the rock of Illica's vanity and lack of self-criticism. For ever convinced that his own work was beyond cavil, he contemptuously scorned all association with another writer. On one occasion (again in connection with the abortive *Maria Antonietta*) he was so angered by Puccini's suggestion to share his work with a collaborator that he retorted: 'If I were impertinent, I would advise you, and perhaps with greater truth and more justification, that you should take a good musician as collaborator' (September 1907. *C.P.Let.*542). No doubt, Illica's refusal, after Giacosa's death, to accept an associate who would curb his wildly proliferating fantasy, was the principal reason why he and Puccini, try as they might, failed to come to terms with each other. But there is also the strong suspicion that Puccini, now fully mature, was beginning to outgrow Illica's naturalism and in addition was no longer willing to put up with the prima donna attitude of his temperamental librettist. Yet, with his characteristic aversion from making clear-cut

* In his own plays Illica would occasionally venture into verse which his friends chaffingly called *Illicasillabi*.

decisions, he avoided a complete break, continuing to deceive both Illica and himself that a collaboration would be fruitful. As we shall see in the case of *Maria Antonietta* and *Conchita*, Puccini was fully convinced that Illica would produce for him a satisfactory libretto. But the fact remains that *Butterfly* was Puccini's last opera which bears the name of Illica as one of the two librettists. With Giacosa's demise an important chapter closed in the relationship of the two surviving members of the former 'trinity', but looking back on this chapter we cannot but acknowledge that in Illica and Giacosa the composer had a most admirable pair of librettists who complemented each other to perfection. However fierce the quarrels he had with them, however strong the oaths and curses he heaped on them, the two represented the best team of collaborators it was his fortune to possess in his entire career. The nature of this collaboration seems to me most aptly summed up in what Mozart once wrote to his father in connection with *Die Entführung*:

> The best thing of all is when a good composer who understands the stage and is talented enough to make sound suggestions . . . meets an able poet.[42]

If *La Bohème*, *Tosca* and *Butterfly* have proved Puccini's most successful operas, his two 'able poets' must take an appreciable share in this.

4

The odds are that but for Giacosa's death in 1906 the 'trinity' would have continued to flourish, though the wonder is that it stuck together as long and as closely as it did. If his work on the libretto for *Manon Lescaut* had already given Illica a foretaste of what being Puccini's collaborator entailed, this was mild compared with Puccini's treatment of both Illica and Giacosa in *La Bohème* and the two following operas. Here, for example, is Giacosa, with the libretto for *La Bohème* all but completed, bursting out in a letter to Ricordi on 25 June 1895:

> I confess to you that I'm tired to death of this constant re-making, re-touching, adding, correcting, piecing together, extending on the one hand and reducing on the other. If it had not been for my friendship for you and because I wish Puccini well, I would at this hour free myself from my obligations with ill grace. I've written this blessed libretto from beginning to end *three* times and certain sections *four* times. How am I to finish at that rate? You have been generous enough to increase my fee by 200 lire, but please reflect that, since I delivered the last act complete, I have had to start work on it again, work which is trifling and uninteresting and on which I spent three to four and frequently five hours a day. In the time which I wasted on these patchings-up, I could have comfortably written four articles for the *Nuova Antologia* and for these I get paid 300 lire per printed page. This is not a fortune, true, but you must convince yourself of the absolute and urgent need in which I find myself of attending to other work, in order to earn what I require for my living.
>
> I swear to you, I shall never again permit myself to be caught with the writing of a libretto! . . . (N).

The *Bohème* libretto passed through many vicissitudes—even *after* the first production of the opera he demanded fresh alterations—before it met with the composer's full approval. As originally conceived by Illica, it consisted of four acts* and five scenes: 'La Soffitta' and 'Il Quartiere Latino' (Act I);—'La Barriera d'Enfer' (Act II)—'Il Cortile della casa di via Labruyère' (Act III)†—'La Soffitta' ovvero 'La Morte di Mimí' (Act IV). The major modification to the present version appears to have been made in December 1893 when the 'Cortile' act was thrown out in its entirety—no doubt because, though very lively and gay, it was essentially in the same vein as the 'Quartiere Latino' act with its crowd scenes.†

By the third week of March 1893 Giacosa received from Illica for versification what seems to have been a complete scenario which Giacosa acknowledges in these generous terms:

> I have read it and admire you You have been able to extract from a novel which seems to me exquisite but little suited to the theatre, a real dramatic action. The first acts are stupendous, but I cannot yet visualize the last act which seems to me very similar to many other acts. But one can find a solution. I very much look forward to a collaboration with you, you nimble and generous spirit. (22 March 1893. C.P.Let.82).

As already mentioned, Illica appears to have started work on the libretto in the autumn of 1892. Mürger's novel is crowded with characters and episodes which succeed each other in kaleidoscopic fashion, and it was no easy task to draw up a plot with at least a semblance of coherence, and select suitable scenes for the opera. Puccini's dissatisfaction with Illica's work, we recall, brought Giacosa on the scene in the early spring of 1893, and by the end of May he had already versified Illica's first act. On 31 May Giacosa gives news of this to Ricordi in this amusing poem:

Dolce Ricordi amato,	My sweet Ricordi,
vi sono molto grato,	I do adore thee,
dell'avermi aspettato	That for me with bated
con animo pacato.	Breath thou has waited.
Ho sempre lavorato,	How I've worked at it,
ho sempre dibrucato,	To prune and to pat it,
ho sempre tagliuzzato,	To cut and to mend;
ed è un lavoro ingrato,	Yet how thankless the end!
Or mi vedo arrivato	But now let's exult
ad un buon risultato.	At the splendid result.

* In *La Bohème* it is not quite correct to refer to 'acts' since in the full score they are called *quadri*—'scenes' or 'tableaux'; but in his letters Puccini himself often writes of 'acts'.

† The 'Cortile' act was largely based on Chapter IV of Mürger's novel, entitled 'Mademoiselle Musette', in which this attractive spitfire of a girl throws a party for the Bohemians in the court of her house while porters carry out her furniture since she has not paid her rent. Illica's final version of this act was published in the review, *La Scala*, of December 1958, with an excellent introduction by Mario Morini.

Puccini ha ormai sicura	Puccini has at last succeeded
trama alle note sue.	In getting all the sleep he needed.
Faremo la lettura	So let me read the thing to you
domani all' ore due,	Tomorrow on the stroke of two
in via degli Omenoni (N).★	At Via degli Omenoni.

Yet at the end of July, by which time he had completed the versification of the original second act (*Barrière d'Enfer*) and had all but done that of the last act, Giacosa's good humour vanished. Perfectionist that he was, he re-read what he had written, was dissatisfied and started again from the beginning, as he informed Ricordi in a letter of 28 July:

> The trouble is that the work I'm doing on this libretto is not artistic work, but minute pedantry and most wearisome. It will most certainly be finished and it needs an artist, but it is work that does not stimulate or possess inner warmth. An artist's work has its hours of toil and sweat, but in compensation it also has hours of inspiration when the pen follows the thought readily. But here there is nothing to lift the spirit. I assure you that I shall never again, at whatever price, undertake such a task, which I should want to carry out with conscientiousness. It has happened many times that I compared what I had already completed with what was still left to be done, and I rejoiced in the certainty that in a few hours I should be rid of it. But all of a sudden I got caught in a scene, in a verse, which tormented me for days, and with my critical mind now sharpened in the pain of so much labour, I found that all that I had already thought finished looked to me incomplete and feeble. I returned to Milan last evening. I have to go to Paris for my comedy [*Tristi Amori*]. But I won't go for many reasons, not the least of them being the thought of you and the libretto. . . Believe me, I am not wanting in good will (N).

A little over two months after the date of that letter the first impasse is reached: Giacosa decides to withdraw. It is interesting to read the reason which he gives to Ricordi in a letter that also attests the intellectual honesty of the man:

6 October 1893

> . . . I am giving up. I am sending you those few pages which, out of the many I have written, seem to me worth showing. In laying down my arms I confess my impotence. The second part of the first act ['Il Quartiere Latino' of the original version] presented me with an insuperable difficulty. I do not feel it! I am not inside it, I do not succeed in creating that illusion, that imaginary reality, without which nothing can be achieved. For those few scenes I have wasted more paper and racked my brain more than I have for any of my own plays. For a week now I have been stuck in the scene with the ear-boxing [Musetta and Marcello in Act III of the present version]. I must have rewritten it a hundred times, but I have not managed to write a single verse that pleases me. I worked last night from eleven to three in the morning and resumed again at half past seven; now it's five o'clock in the afternoon and that scene has not moved forward by an inch. I don't know if it is my fault or that of the scene. Perhaps both, or perhaps only mine. . .

★ The premises of the House of Ricordi, before it moved to its present address in Via Berchet.

If Puccini were not in such a hurry, if he could get busy with the third act which I am sending you all but finished, and if he gave me a little more time for this second act—then perhaps I could make myself find the strength again. But I have no right to claim such a sacrifice nor to request it and perhaps artistic reasons are against it. Since I despair of finishing the work in the short time allowed me and since it is myself and my insufficiency to which I attribute this shameful surrender—though (I assure you) I feel bitter grief because of you whom I wish well and whom I don't want to cause any difficulties—I take the heroic decision and withdraw from a task which, I am sure, Illica will be able to bring to its happy conclusion alone. To dash off things anyhow—that I don't want to do. To add verse after verse with the only purpose of getting to the end and then receive the agreed fee seems to me disgraceful and dishonest. I shall send you the work of two months of labour but I won't make you fret any more. . . There is one thing I beg of you and that is that, seeing how much damage I have inflicted on myself, you will not be angry with me into the bargain (N).

Needless to say, Giacosa's resignation was not accepted and, good-naturedly and patiently, he continued with his labours. At last, in December, Puccini appeared satisfied with the shape of the first two acts; but as at that period he was still pursuing the project of *La Lupa*, his attention was divided and this would explain why it took him another seven or eight months to come to the conclusion that the two acts of *La Bohème* needed a number of further alterations, especially the second act. In the same letter in which he gave Ricordi his reasons for temporarily discarding the 'Sicilian' opera (13 July 1894) he begs him

> to speak seriously now to Illica about the *Latin Quarter* act about most of which we are already in complete agreement. . . But the second act—the *Barrière d'Enfer**—does not please me much. I am annoyed by all that prattle (*cianfrusaglie*) and those episodes that have nothing to do with the action. We must find something different and more effective both as drama and as comedy. If Illica will read Mürger's novel, he will find valuable material there.
>
> To conclude, I am working hard and Illica or somebody else ought to finish this libretto to my satisfaction (*C.P.Let.*106).

It was now the turn of Illica to revolt, as will be seen from Ricordi's letter to Puccini, written six days later, in reply to the above letter:

> 19 July 1894
>
> . . . He [Illica] has almost decided to have nothing further to do with *Bohème*. He complains because he has expended much work and time fruitlessly, and sees himself used, cast aside, taken up again, and once more shoved away like a dog. I need not labour the point. The conclusion was this: I succeeded in making Illica go back to work on the *Latin Quarter*. But he wants me to tell you this: he is resuming work solely out of regard for me!! . . . As for the second act, he believes it wrong to treat cavalierly the work already done and to begin again from the ground up. He finds the scene at the barrier

---

* Puccini here is still referring to the original version of the libretto.

very good (and I am of his opinion) as it was conceived at first. As far as that is concerned, in the course of the work we can see what can be changed, cut, or modified. . . I am writing immediately to Giacosa to send me the second act. In all this hubbub and during all this storm, I see but one consoling ray of sunshine: that is the assurance that you are working at full speed and well. *Avanti* then! I remember the very beautiful beginning of the *Latin Quarter*. Ah! Doge, Doge!! How much, how much time lost!! (*M*).

Puccini's reaction to this was scarcely less violent than that of the offended Illica. To Ricordi on 21 July:

Dearest Signor Giulio,

I shall be at your office on Tuesday at ten in the morning.

I am surprised at Illica's irritation and find it strange. When he came here [Torre del Lago], we were in perfect accord—and he knew about *La Lupa*—and he deplored that I was not working on *La Bohème*, but assured me that he would always be ready to help me in anything. Now that I go back to him, he chooses to give himself airs. If he says now that I have sent him packing, whose fault is it? All I wanted was that the work should be what it ought to be: logical, terse and well balanced.

But at the moment it is none of these things. Must I blindly accept Illica's gospel? I have my conception of *Bohème* but with the *Latin Quarter* as we discussed it last time with Illica: with Musetta's scene, *which was my idea*. I want the death [of Mimi] as I had imagined it, and I shall be sure then of writing an original and vital work. As to the *Barrière*, I am still of the opinion that it doesn't please me much. To me it seems an act in which there is little that is musical; only the drama moves on, and that is not enough. I should have liked more occasions in it for music. We must not forget that there is plenty of action in the other acts. In this one I wanted a canvas that would allow me to spread myself a little more lyrically. . .

Illica should calm down and then we shall get on with the work. But I too want to have my say, as the necessity arises, and I am not prepared to do anybody's bidding. . . (*C.P.Let.*109).

But peace was soon restored again and on 22 August Ricordi was able to inform the composer that Illica had brought him the previous day the whole libretto of *La Bohème*:

. . . It seems to me now that we have really succeeded! The last act and the death of Mimi, especially, ought to call forth torrents of tears. I myself was much, much moved. Although it is only in three acts, the libretto seems to me long, but Illica and I have already come to an understanding, and it will be easy to shorten it here and there. Moreover, you can do it according to the dictates of musical necessity, as they will appear in the course of composition. . . (*M*).

Puccini, too, is gratified at last. Writing to Ricordi on 7 September, he says:

There is no doubt about its being an original work. And how original! The last act is most beautiful. So is also the *Latin Quarter*, but extremely difficult. . . The death of Mimi, with all that leads up to it, is very moving (*E*).

But, again, he presses for the elimination of superfluous details, such as a scene with a mountebank and certain extravagances (*bizzarrie*) in the text. Ricordi had meanwhile gone to Paris, in order to assist Verdi in the first French production of *Otello*,* whence he wrote to Puccini on 29 September:

> . . . The more I think of it, the more pleased I am with *Bohème*. In my modest opinion, the second, Latin act will be an arduous task, to give the whole scene a vivacious design, to make it run quickly, and not to leave any holes into which the cold wind may blow and create a void.
>
> It is difficult, but Puccini has broad shoulders and strong lungs! and then, are you the Doge or aren't you the Doge? (*C.P.Let.*119).

In that same letter Ricordi also refers to Verdi's astounding vitality:

> . . . Verdi, who in a few days will have completed eighty-one years, is rejuvenated this spring. Yesterday he was 'crazy' enough to arrange, preside at, and conduct the following rehearsals: twelve o'clock the chorus, from one to two orchestra, from two to half past two dance rehearsal, from half past two to half past five soloists at the piano, third and fourth acts!! I cry, Hosanna!!
>
> By the way, Tuesday, 9 October, Verdi has his eighty-first birthday.† If you want to telegraph to him here a word of congratulation, I am sure it will please him very much. In spite of his occupations, he has already mentioned you twice, what you are doing, etc., etc. . . (*C.P.Let.* 119).

Ricordi was evidently anxious to encourage Puccini in cultivating friendly relations with Verdi, which could only add to the prestige of the younger composer. When in June of the following year (1895) Verdi was at Montecatini to take the cure there, Ricordi advised Puccini to pay him a visit—'I am certain that it would give him the greatest pleasure'. What seems curious, however, is the fact that neither Fraccaroli, who wrote his biography[43] from information largely supplied by Puccini himself, nor Marotti and Pagni,[44] who belonged to the inner circle of the *Bohème* Club at Torre del Lago, make any mention of any personal meetings between him and Verdi.‡ Yet in the correspondence between Puccini and Ricordi the name of Verdi crops up very frequently. Each holds him up as precept and example to the other. Thus when Puccini complains of some unkind critic or other, Ricordi counsels him to adopt Verdi's attitude: 'he never concerned himself with criticism; he marched straight ahead on his way and now he is—what he is!! Even then we had no lack of fools. . .' (letter of 14 August 1895. *M*).

And when Ricordi, to his great puzzlement, found in the score of *La Bohème*

---

* 12 October 1894.

† Ricordi was out by one day: Verdi was born on 10 October.

‡ Yet Verdi's signed photograph, with its inscription to Puccini and dated 'Milano, 9 Febbraio 1893' (the date of the first production of *Falstaff*), suggests that such a meeting or meetings may have taken place.

... all kinds of possible and impossible indications. It is a forest of *p-pp-pppp*, of *f-ff-fff-ffff*, of slowing up and of going ahead, so that the conductors will lose their heads (*M*)

Puccini's reply was:

... As for the *pp*'s and the *ff*'s of the score, if I have overdone them it is because, *as Verdi says*, when one wants *piano* one puts *ppp* (*M*).*

We left Puccini expressing great satisfaction with the libretto of *La Bohème*, though he continues to find the *Barrière d'Enfer* act 'indigestible'. Hence Ricordi's gentle inquiry about its progress, couched in the form of a Latin poem of his own invention:

10 November 1894

Toc, toc!	Knock, knock!
Quid petis?	What is your request?
Jacopus Puccinius.	Giacomo Puccini.
Quare?	What for?
Ut videtur si laboret.	To see if he is working.
Laborat.	He is working.
Laborat? ad Bohemiam?	He is working? on *Bohème*?
Ad Bohemiam.	On *Bohème*.
Bene est! (*M*).	Good!

The *Barrière* act persisted for some time to cause difficulty and Ricordi offered valuable advice. He it was who suggested that Musetta should sing part of her waltz reminiscence offstage (from inside the inn) and he also advised the excision of many superfluous details, such as a little scene at the beginning of the act in which nuns from the nearby Hospice of St. Thérèse were to come down for their morning prayer to the accompaniment of four Matin bells.† He writes to Puccini on 30 June 1895:

Abolish many details. There are already too many details in the second act, and the opera would end by being a little comedy of episodes The atmosphere is at once created by the customs officers and by the others who appear. This is sufficient. More would not interest the public (*M*).

It was the last act, *The Garret*, which proved most troublesome of all. Requesting further alterations from Giacosa, Puccini, who was as adept a versifier as his publisher, humoured the touchy librettist in the following doggerel:

Ti rammento l'atto quarto,	I'll remind you, to Act Four
perch'io presto me ne parto.	I must quickly do some more.
Cerca, trova, taglia, inverti,	Seek and find, dissect and turn it,
ché tu re sei, tra gli esperti.	You, of experts the most learned.

* Thus, in the autograph score of Act IV of *Bohème*, the B minor chord which indicates the precise moment of Mimi's death is marked *ppppppp*.

† Puccini intended, as he put in an undated letter to Ricordi, to use in this scene a 'veritable arsenal: xylophone, bells, carillon, trumpets, drums, cart-bells, cracking of whips, carts, donkeys and tinkling of glasses'. The final version contains only glasses sounding a repeated C and four bells (E, C, D, G).

Ti ricordi di ridurre	Please remember what I mean,
le scenette in cima all'atto?	Give a climax to each scene,
Quando tutto sarà fatto,	Then, when all's done, with relief
qual sospiro emetterem!	What a sigh we both shall heave!
Ma la morte di Mimì	But the poor Mimì's demise
solo tu puoi preparar,	You alone can well devise,
poi con quattro Do Re Mi	And at last with DO RE MI
lancerem la barca in mar! (N).	We shall push our boat to sea!

The chief stumbling-block in the last act was a quartet for the four Bohemians in which they were to sing a toast to each other. This *quartetto brindisi* formed part of the scene of the general fooling preceding Musetta's entry when she arrives with the news of Mimì's illness. A lengthy and most detailed correspondence ensued on this quartet, largely because Giacosa had given each of the four characters lines in differing metres. Ricordi suggested omitting it altogether, but Puccini refused, though exclaiming:

> ... That toast will be *the death of me*! I don't know what to do about it—it's a serious matter unless I find some other idea for it. I shall leave it blank and they may speak it!!!! (undated, *E*).

The problem remained intractable, Puccini rightly feeling that the *brindisi* held up the action and that the main point of Act IV was, after all, the arrival of Mimì and her death. As late as 13 November 1895, some six weeks before the opera was finally completed, Ricordi sent him some verses for the quartet, signed jestingly 'Carducci'. They did not help and at last the composer decided to cut the Gordian knot by the simple device of making the three Bohemians interrupt Schaunard, just as he is about to begin his toast, by shouts of 'Basta!'

Also the scene of the dying Mimì needed, Puccini felt, more warmth and affection than it possessed:

> 'You will have a copy', he writes to Ricordi in the above-mentioned letter, 'of Act IV by you. Will you do me the kindness and open it at the point where they give Mimì the muff. Doesn't it seem to you rather poor at the moment of her death? Two more words, an affectionate phrase to Rodolfo, would be just enough. Perhaps I am being too subtle here, but at the moment when this girl, for whom I have worked so hard, dies I should like her to leave the world less for herself and a little more for him who loved her' (*E*).

Puccini's request for these and other alterations led to another temporary rift with Giacosa, who, overcome once again by a feeling of insufficiency, not only sent in his resignation but went so far as to disclaim all responsibility for the libretto, renouncing also the remuneration due to him. It was one of Giacosa's constant complaints that everybody but he was permitted to hear the music which Puccini had already written, so Ricordi, never at a loss for an astute move, played to him excerpts from the first and second acts. That this had the desired effect is seen from a letter of Ricordi to Puccini, dated 20 June 1895, in which he writes that Giacosa declared 'Puccini has surpassed all my expectations, and I now understand the reason for his tyranny over verses and accents' (*M*).

According to the dates on the autograph score, the orchestration of Act I was begun at Torre del Lago on 21 January 1895 and finished in Milan on 6 June, 'at two in the morning'; the orchestration of Act II was completed on 19 July and that of Act III on 18 September, both in Val di Nievole near Pescia, in the Apuan Alps. Puccini was staying there as the guest of his friend, Conte Bertolini, a sojourn that turned out to be little to his liking, as he wrote to Ricordi:

> I am sick and tired of this holiday, of this house, of this impossible place. I constantly think of my Torre del Lago. But I shall recover my strength next year, I swear it! (undated, *E*).

But it must not be thought that Puccini, though keeping his nose to the grindstone, as he now was, was prepared to forgo altogether his favourite sport. He accepted an invitation from Conte Ginori for two days' shooting at his beloved Torre del Lago where 'I will terrorize my adored palmipeds, which have long been panting for my murderous and infallible lead. Boom!' (undated, *E*). To this his publisher gave, for once, his unqualified blessing, seeing that the opera was now safely coming into port. Yet the expedition was eventually put off as Puccini felt that 'now that I have made a good start with my work I am going on with it' (9 October 1895, *E*). But he did interrupt his work on 5 October to travel with Elvira to Florence to see Sardou's *Tosca* which was being given there with the celebrated Sarah Bernhardt in the name-part.

Puccini put *Finis* to the score of *La Bohème* on 10 December 1895, at 'midnight, Torre del Lago' (not on 15 November, as generally stated), the opera having taken three years and nine months to complete. He later told Fraccaroli that when he had finished the scene of Mimì's death, he was seized by such emotion that 'I had to get up and, standing in the middle of the study, alone in the silence of the night, I began to weep like a child. It was as though I had seen my own child die'.[45] Of the four acts it was indeed the last which, revealingly, remained the composer's favourite and the only act which, on his own admission, he really cared to hear. Yet equally revealing of his temperament are the facts that, after finishing the death scene, he drew in the score the picture of a skull and crossbones, writing underneath 'Mimì', and that the happy birth of the opera was celebrated a few days later by a naïve masquerade, in which Puccini appeared accoutred in the robes of a Roman Emperor while his friends, paying homage to him, were dressed up, one as a Turk, another as an admiral and yet another as a priest.

5

It was Ricordi's wish that the first production of *La Bohème* should be given in Turin, where *Manon Lescaut* had been received with such tremendous enthusiasm and where, he doubtless felt, the public was especially well disposed toward the composer. At first Puccini made a dead stand against this plan, arguing that (a) the acoustics of the Teatro Regio were bad; (b) *non bis idem*; and (c) Turin was too near Milan. His wish was that the opera be first given at Naples and then in Rome; and he insisted on an all-star cast, conducted by the famous Leopoldo Mugnone, who had directed the première of *Cavalleria Rusticana*. To these demands Ricordi raised objections, both on artistic and financial grounds. In a long letter dated 12 October 1895 he advanced a number of counter-arguments, the first of which has quite a modern ring:

> . . . In regard to the cast and the observations which you submit, permit me to tell you with my usual frankness,* and do not take offence, dear Puccini, that they are uncalled for and unjust. Oh! yes, there was a time when everything depended on the virtuosity of the throat. For *Sonnambula* and *Norma* one had to have specialists. Today opera needs a homogeneous cast, the more intelligent the better! It is not the artist who is responsible for the success of the opera, but the opera itself.

Ricordi then goes on to cite two recent examples, Leoncavallo's *I Medici* and Mascagni's *Silvano*, in the first of which the famous Tamagno had sung and in the second De Lucia; and yet, he says, these two operas proved resounding failures. On the other hand, in *Falstaff*

> there was only one real artist in it, Maurel; all the others were almost mediocrities—including the *diva* Pasqua . . . including Pini-Corsi, who had a good voice but was a singer like a dozen others, and a trivial, second-rate actor. These and even that selfsame Maurel were *very bad* in their interpretations.
> It was the benison of our patient Verdi which gave them blood day by day, hour by hour, teaching them to pronounce the words, teaching them the sense of the words, all with that extraordinary patience which finally succeeded in obtaining a performance that was vivacious, lively and persuasive (*C.P.Let.* 142).

Coming to *La Bohème*, Ricordi suggests putting together 'a cast which is homogeneous, willing, animated by enthusiasm, and we will obtain what is needed'. The chief difficulty, he realizes, will be to find a good Musetta—'but I shall not cease looking for her and will try one, three, six, even among those whom at first we rejected'. He warns Puccini to beware of 'plunging opera into bankruptcy' by making extraordinary demands: 'Let us not force the impresarios toward expenditures which are impossible' and he concludes with a sting in the tail: 'Do not think that I am moved by tenderness toward impresarios, not at all! But I speak as a man of affairs, of long experience . . .' (*M*). Puccini must have recognized the force of these arguments, for he replied saying that he thought it best to leave the choice of the artists in his publisher's hands. As the latter had stated, the only real problem was to find a suitable artist for the part of Musetta, as it demanded the combination of a lively histrionic talent with a voice capable of light coloratura as well as lyrical

* In most of his letters to Puccini, Ricordi lays stress on his 'usual frankness'.

expression. Hence Puccini's mock-pathetic dialogue when the search proved for a long time unavailing: 'O Musetta, where are you? I am still in *mente Dei.*' All these controversies, incidentally, were taking place while the composer was still battling with the recalcitrant fourth act.

By December 1895 place and date of the first production were at last fixed: Turin—as Ricordi had intended it all along—on 1 February 1896, three years to the day after the première of *Manon Lescaut*. It should be added that the management of the Teatro Regio had met Puccini's criticisms by making structural alterations to improve both the acoustics and the stage lighting. Meanwhile Rome, Naples and Palermo were entering into negotiations for the opera. For Naples, incidentally, Puccini wanted as conductor Arthur Nikisch, a most curious choice which Ricordi nipped in the bud with 'what are you thinking of? To introduce a foreigner, no matter how worthy, into an Italian theatre? Don't dream of it! It would result in a *dies irae*' (29 November 1895, *M*).

The principal cast for the Turin production consisted of Ferrani as Mimi (she had been Puccini's first Manon), Pasini as Musetta, Gorga as Rodolfo,* and Wilmant as Marcello. The conductor, however, was not Puccini's original choice, Mugnone, but a young man not yet twenty-nine around whom a legend was already forming: Arturo Toscanini.† Toscanini was now the new musical director of the Turin Teatro Regio where on 22 December 1895 he had made musical history by giving the first separate performance of *Götterdämmerung*. Puccini and Ricordi afterwards agreed that they could not have been more fortunate in the conductor of the first *Bohème*.

In the second week of January, the composer and Illica, later joined by Ricordi, travelled to Turin to supervise the rehearsals. Elvira—much against her will, it would appear—remained at Torre del Lago—from the biographer's point of view a fortunate circumstance, since the separation occasioned a short correspondence in which Puccini made to his wife some interesting observations on the new work and the artists of this first production. Thus he believes and hopes that 'this time also I have succeeded and have hit the nail on the head' (11 January 1896, *M*). And some days later:

> . . . We are working like dogs. I assure you that the orchestration is really prodigious. It is as fine as a miniature. I foresee a great and sensational success if—the artists will do their part.

On that score he entertained some doubts. Mimi is 'good' and Musetta 'excellent', but he worries over the singers of Rodolfo and Marcello:

> . . . The first hasn't got such a bad voice, but I doubt whether he will last . . .
> The baritone is full of good will, but a terrible actor. All the real effects are being sacrificed, and, as you know, this opera needs vivacious acting. More-

---

* Puccini was forced to transpose down almost the entire tenor part.

† *Bohème* was not, as often stated, the first Puccini opera conducted by Toscanini; he had directed a number of performances of *Le Villi* before, and with his characteristic temerity introduced *Manon Lescaut* to Paris in 1894, thus challenging comparison with Massenet's opera.

over his voice is coarse, and Marcello is such a gentle man. In short, he is out of place. . . We shall see what Ricordi will decide. . . (undated, *M*).

We note the emphasis that Puccini lays on the acting in this opera.

For Toscanini he has nothing but boundless admiration: '. . . And the orchestra! Toscanini! Extraordinary!' They rehearsed in true Toscanini style—'today from eleven to 4.30 p.m. Tonight we rehearse from eight-thirty to midnight'. He found Toscanini 'highly intelligent' and, strange as it may sound in view of the great maestro's saturnine temper, he described him as 'a very sweet and nice man'. *La Bohème* was to mark the beginning of a lifelong though tempestuous friendship between the two men.

In these letters to Elvira, Puccini speaks with self-confidence and great optimism of the forthcoming première. Yet this is completely at variance with what he told Fraccaroli years later—that an atmosphere of diffidence, uncertainty and dark prognostication brooded over the rehearsals, so much so that he looked forward to this first night with the 'same joyous anticipation with which a prisoner condemned to death walks to the scaffold'.[46] Which of the two versions are we to believe? Both, I think. The truth seems that, in his state of nervous excitement during those weeks of preparation, his mood perpetually fluctuated between extremes, and that he was unwilling to give vent to his fears to Elvira. What may have contributed to his anxiety was the apprehension, well known in creative artists, lest the new work might not live up to the high expectations aroused by the previous one.

On the first night members of the royal family* and critics from all over Italy were present. Yet the reception accorded to *Bohème* only seemed to confirm the composer's misgivings. Admittedly from the public's point of view it was a success, if not an outstanding one. At no point did the audience evince the enthusiasm with which it had greeted *Manon Lescaut* in the same theatre three years before. The first act pleased and after Rodolfo's aria 'Che gelida manina!' there was a demand for a repeat and for Puccini to show himself on the stage—neither of which occurred: Toscanini was on the rostrum! The second act fell flat because the spectators felt bewildered by the kaleidoscopic changes of episodes in which they missed 'the cohesion and unity of the first act', as one critic put it (Pozza). The third act fared better and the final scene of the last act left the audience deeply moved. Puccini took five curtain calls. If the reaction of the public may be said to have been on the whole friendly, that of most critics was decidedly hostile. The sole voice that spoke with some measure of sympathy in this discordant critical chorus was that of the aforementioned Giovanni Pozza of the *Corriere della Sera*. He noted the remarkable advance Puccini had made since *Manon Lescaut*, pointed to the refinement of craftsmanship displayed by the new work, and called attention to one of the most salient features of the libretto: the successful blend of comedy and pathos, its happy mixture of smiles and tears. Yet to achieve this in the music had put, he felt, too great a strain on

* Princess Letizia of Piedmont, who enjoyed the reputation of an Italian Madame Sans-Gêne, had called Puccini to her box where he sat throughout the third act, tongue-tied and shy, his hands between his knees.

the composer. Nevertheless he predicted for *Bohème* 'a long future because it pleases no less those who seek in music merely delight than those who make higher demands'—a verdict which posterity has fully confirmed.

Other critics, recalling *Manon Lescaut*, declared that the new work could not bear comparison with it. *Bohème* showed 'a deplorable decline', it was an '*opera mancata*'—'a failure', written 'in haste (so it appears) and with little discernment and polish . . . often lapsing into the empty* and, sometimes, the puerile'; Puccini was given the advice to turn in future 'to the great and arduous struggles of art'. One of the most hostile critics was E. A. Berta of the *Gazzetta del Popolo*, who had a personal axe to grind, as he was said to have once submitted to Puccini a libretto which was rejected. Berta also made scathing remarks on Ricordi's new methods of advance publicity. For with *La Bohème* the publisher had introduced the kind of illustrated posters best remembered from the days of the silent film (and still to be seen today, on occasion) with the most melodramatic, harrowing scene displayed in lurid colours. Ricordi's posters were enlarged reproductions of the cover picture which adorned the vocal score;† in the case of *La Bohème* it showed the final scene of the *Barrière d'Enfer* act, with Rodolfo and Mimi walking off arm in arm and with the quarrelling pair, Marcello and Musetta, seen in the background. This was assuredly unobjectionable, but the same could scarcely be said of the later cover pictures for *Tosca* and *La Fanciulla del West*: for the first was chosen the scene in which the heroine places a cross on the body of the dead Scarpia while the second represented the scene of the poker game between the heroine and the sinister Sheriff, in which the stake is the life of her lover, who is seen leaning against the table bleeding from a shot wound and semi-conscious.‡

What the generality of the critics and of the public had been expecting of Puccini's new work was that it should continue in the path he had trodden in *Manon Lescaut*; instead, they were confronted with a light-weight opera, episodic in character, often conversational in tone and full of impressionist touches in the orchestration and in the harmony. In short, they were perplexed by the composer's novel and audacious style. As Carlo Bersezio put it in *La Stampa*:

> . . . In order to be original and new he has not disdained, here and there, the artificial and the whimsical (*barocco*), forgetting that originality may very well be achieved by traditional means, without a proud display of consecutive fifths (not really a pleasing effect) and without contempt for the good old rules of harmony.

The parallel fifths (at the beginning of Acts II and III) to which Bersezio refers with such irony were, to mix a metaphor, a thorn in the ears of the conservative critics of that period; but it is scarcely a complimentary

---

* In France the opera was later nicknamed *La Vide de Bohème*.

† Early editions still show it.

‡ The success of these posters induced Ricordi to attach to the firm a special advertising department which carried out orders for other commercial concerns.

reflection that none of these critics had spotted similar things in *Manon Lescaut*,* which opera they had praised to the skies only three years before. It is noteworthy that Verdi, then in his eighty-third year, took, in comparison, a more broadminded view of Puccini's 'crime' in *Bohème*:

> If he had eschewed those progressions of fifths, he could not have achieved the same significant suggestion of snow and ice (since that is the effect they are supposed to create), but it would have had the advantage of not grating on the ears. [47]

Another and less tangible factor partly responsible for rendering the critics unresponsive to *La Bohème* was the fact that its performance had been preceded, by six weeks and at the same theatre, by that of *Götterdämmerung*. Having imbibed so intoxicating a potion of Wagnerian transcendentalism they must have found it hard to descend to the world of everyday realities which surround the four Bohemians and their amours, a world that was bound to strike them as insubstantial and frivolous. This, at any rate, was the view of the intelligent critic who wrote in the Turin paper *Fanfulla*. To ridicule Puccini's detractors for judgments which appear to us unbelievably shortsighted and obtuse would be unjust; after all, their opinions were conditioned by the artistic tastes and fashions of their time. Yet it is impossible to suppress a smile when we read so cocksure a prophecy as that made by Bersezio that '*La Bohème*, just as it leaves no great impression on the mind of the spectator, will leave no great mark on the history of our opera'.

6

It is illuminating to compare Puccini's reaction after the première of *La Bohème* with that of Verdi after the fiasco which attended the first-night of *Traviata*. At that point in their respective careers both composers were of nearly the same age—Verdi forty, Puccini thirty-eight. Verdi laconically disposes of the whole matter in a letter to Tito Ricordi: 'I am sorry to give you bad news, but I cannot hide the truth. *La Traviata* has been a failure. Let us not inquire into the causes. That is the fact. Good-bye, good-bye!' [48] And here is Puccini, wounded to the quick, sadly shaken and full of self-pity:

> '. . . They even said', he told Fraccaroli, 'that *Bohème* would be taken off before the end of the season. I, who put into *Bohème* all my soul and loved it boundlessly and loved its creatures more than I can say, returned to my hotel completely heartbroken. There was in me sadness, melancholy, a wish to cry. . . I passed a most miserable night. And in the morning I was greeted with the spiteful salute of the critics.' [49]

We mentioned *La Traviata*. We may also mention *Carmen*, whose initial reception by the Press provides yet another chapter in the *chronique scandaleuse* of famous first-night failures. Admittedly the fiasco of *La Bohème* was by no means as devastating as that of Verdi's and Bizet's masterpieces, yet all three operas share this in common, that it was the realism of the subject which the critics found hard to stomach, and that with all three it was the public

* Des Grieux's song 'Tra voi, belle', Act I (see, Ex. 22b, p. 304).

—having, in the words of a French tag, more sense than Voltaire—which in the event vindicated the composer and proved the professional critics monstrously wrong.* By the end of February *La Bohème* had been given twenty-four times before sold-out houses. Then followed the Rome production, where, it is true, the reception was at first lukewarm. It was at Palermo, in the following April, that the opera achieved its triumph on the very first evening and whence its fame spread like wildfire through all Italy.

The conductor on this occasion was Mugnone, who, next to Toscanini, was Puccini's favourite interpreter.† Like so many stage artists, Mugnone was a superstitious man who regarded it as an ill omen that the first performance fell on Friday, 13 April. And what with the failure of an oboist to arrive on time, delaying the start by half an hour, and the Sicilian audience giving vent to their impatience by whistlings and shouts, the conductor's forebodings appeared indeed justified. Yet beyond these harmless incidents, nothing untoward occurred. The opera was received with enthusiasm, and numerous curtain calls for the artists both during and after the individual acts prolonged this performance to one o'clock in the morning. Even then the public would not leave, continuing to clamour for encores. Though half the orchestra had already gone and though the artists had already changed into their day clothes, Mugnone decided to repeat the whole of the last scene, beginning with the entry of Mimi—even in Italy a rare occurrence. Rodolfo is said to have sung without his wig and Mimi with her hair undone.‡

Two months after the Palermo production, the opera was given in Buenos Aires. It reached England the following year, when it was staged in English as *The Bohemians* at the Comedy Theatre, Manchester, on 22 April 1897. Ricordi chose Manchester instead of London because of the cool reception which the English capital had accorded *Manon Lescaut* three years previously. This Manchester production was the occasion for Puccini's first visit to England when he was accompanied by Giulio Ricordi's son, Tito, the composer's contemporary who about that time had begun to assist his father in the business. Neither of the visitors spoke English. A lively description of the pair is given by Herman Klein, music critic of the *Sunday Times*, who was present at the first night:

> I never saw two young men in a more despondent frame of mind or more certain of failure. Rehearsals had been going badly and it was impossible that the opera should succeed. However, their doleful anticipations were not to be realized. On the following morning we all travelled back to Euston in a saloon carriage that the railway company had courteously placed at the

---

* Cf. Hofmannsthal's remark to Strauss apropos of the first version of *Ariadne auf Naxos*: Erfolge macht das Publikum, nicht die Kritik'—'Successes are made by the public, not the critics' (23 July 1911). (*Richard Strauss. Briefwechsel*, etc., op. cit.)

† Yet fifteen years later when Mugnone conducted *La Fanciulla del West* at Naples, Puccini found that he was 'flabby and drags out the tempi to indecent lengths' (23 December 1911, *S*).

‡ The soprano on this occasion was Ada Giachetti, Caruso's first wife.

disposal of the musicians and journalists. We had with us a very different Puccini now—a merry, smiling fellow, with a plentiful supply of Italian jokes, and radiant with the recollection of genuine Lancashire feeling.[50]

Puccini's recorded impressions of the city were scarcely flattering: 'land of black smoke, darkness, cold, rain, cotton (but woe to anyone who does not wear wool!) and fog. A veritable inferno! A horrible place to stay at!'[51]

Five months later, on 2 October 1897, *La Bohème* was given at Covent Garden, also in English; the first production in Italian was staged there on 1 July 1899, when Nellie Melba sang Mimi.

Puccini also attended the first French production given in Paris on 13 June 1898. This was his first visit to the French capital, where he arrived, again accompanied by Tito Ricordi, at the end of April to supervise rehearsals. Though in later years he came to like the city, on this occasion he found little to please him there. This Paris visit produced three letters which shed a clear light on the psychology of the man. The first two letters were addressed to Ricordi. On 15 May, after discussing the artists and the rehearsals which 'are going very well', though he found their slowness 'phenomenal', he burst out into a tale of woe:

> I am not in a very happy state here. I should like to be out of here for the sake of my work. I cannot work here. My nerves suffer here from too much excitement and I have not the tranquillity which I need. An invitation to a dinner makes me ill for a week; I'm made like that and cannot change at the age of nearly forty. It is useless to insist; I am not born for a life in *salons* and parties! What is the good of exposing myself and cutting the figure of an idiot and imbecile? I see that this is what I am and it grieves me very much! But, I repeat, I am made that way—and you know me, only you; Tito does not and he constantly insists that I should make myself presentable, but with me to insist on this argument makes things all the worse!
>
> I do not want to make comparisons, because this would be ridiculous, but Verdi always did what suited him and, in spite of it, has made not a bad little career!
>
> So far, thank God, I have had my full share of success and that without having had to resort to methods for which I am not born! I am here for the sole purpose of making sure that my music is executed as it is written (*E*).

Ricordi replied to what he called these 'litanies' on the next day, pointing out that the composer's citation of Verdi was not exact. Verdi, he assures him, made a point of frequenting high society in Milan, in Paris, in St. Petersburg, London and Vienna. True he did it without pleasure, but he conformed to the 'uses and abuses of society. He found the remedy in a tranquil life which compensated him for the pills he had had to gulp'. Ricordi then reminds Puccini that times have since changed, that 'victory now is more difficult to attain and needs greater tact and strategy! Therefore arm yourself with philosophy and beware of comparisons of yourself with certain artist pigs!—who remain pigs no matter what they do' (*M*).

On 26 May Puccini writes a second letter to Ricordi which shows his nervous stamina on the point of utter exhaustion:

. . . The orchestra is having its first rehearsal today. What time has been lost with the *mise en scène*! They are of a slowness here which is unnerving and killing.

I have grown thin, and my disgust with *La Bohème* is such that I am in despair in trying to communicate a little enthusiasm and a little Italian vitality to those supine and passive employees. But I hope that the end of this *via crucis* is in sight. . .

I can hardly bear to have to wait for the moment when I can return to my quietness. How I long for it! (*E*).

The most self-revealing of these Paris letters, however, is the one that Puccini addressed to his friend Alfredo Caselli, a chemist at Lucca:

Paris, Tuesday, 10 May 1898
Dear Caselli,

I do not receive your letters every day and that is bad. Are you abandoning me in this *mare magnum*?

I am sick of Paris. I am panting for the woods with their sweet smells and fragrance, I am panting for the free movement of my belly in wide trousers and with no waistcoat; I pant for the wind that blows, free and fragrant, from the sea, I savour with dilated nostrils the iodic, salty air and inhale it with wide-open lungs!

I hate pavements!

I hate palaces!

I hate capitals!

I hate columns!

I love the beautiful columns of the poplar and the fir, and the vaults of shady glades where, like a modern Druid, I love to make my temple, my house, my study. I love the green expanse of cool shelters in forest ancient and young. I love the blackbird, the blackcap, the woodpecker! I hate the horse, the cat, the starlings and the lapdog! I hate the steamer, the silk hat, and the dress coat! (*E*).

This letter reveals a striking paradox between Puccini the man and the artist. He loathes the sophistication, the refinement, the nervous excitement of urban civilization, it induces in him an intolerable feeling of malaise and even nausea; yet his whole art is unthinkable away from the 'decadence' of modern life in the big cities, of which it is indeed a highly characteristic product. In Puccini's music we seek in vain for that feeling of sturdy rusticity which we encounter in many of Verdi's works; no breath of that invigorating, briny air, which he inhaled 'with wide-open lungs', blows through it— the spirit of the country, in whose simplicities Puccini's fretted soul would find its real happiness, is almost wholly absent from the world of his art.

IX

'Sardoodledom'

I

It WAS AS EARLY AS 1889 that Puccini had first thought of basing an opera on Sardou's drama *Tosca* (1887). On 7 May of that year—a little over two weeks after the première of *Edgar*—he expressed himself to Ricordi on the subject with a conviction which suggests that he must have been pondering this plan for some time:

> Dearest Signor Ricordi,
>
> After two or three days of bucolic idleness, so that I might rest from all exertions I have undergone, I realize that my desire for work, instead of diminishing, has returned more strongly than ever. I am thinking of *Tosca*. I implore you to take the necessary steps in order to obtain Sardou's permission. If we had to abandon this idea, it would grieve me exceedingly. In this *Tosca* I see the opera which exactly suits me, one without excessive proportions, one which is a decorative spectacle, and one which gives opportunity for an abundance of music... (*C.P.Let.31*).*

It is possible that Sardou refused his permission on the ground that Puccini was then an unknown composer in France. Or perhaps Puccini himself—at that period still sailing in the deep waters of romantic opera—began to entertain misgivings about the use of a subject of such realistic brutality as *Tosca*. Whatever the reasons, this topic is not mentioned again until six years later, in October 1895, when he specially went to Florence to see a production of the play, with Sarah Bernhardt in the title-role.

Meanwhile other subjects had sailed into his ken, soon to vanish again beyond the horizon, though one or two were to reappear later. Thus he evinced great interest in Maurice Maeterlinck's *Pelléas et Mélisande* and paid the Belgian poet a visit at Ghent. 'Alas', was Maeterlinck's reply, 'how willingly would I have given my poem to the composer of *La Bohème* had I not already given it to Debussy.'[52] Similarly, Puccini had read an Italian translation of Zola's novel *La Faute de l'Abbé Mouret* (1875), the story of a young priest's impassioned love affair with a 'romantic savage' *à la* Rousseau. This luridly erotic novel had aroused a wave of indignation in Catholic circles and it is, indeed, doubtful whether in the end Puccini would not

---

* The 'decorative spectacle' is a reference to the second of Sardou's five acts, which Puccini at this early stage appears to have wished to retain but which was omitted from the final libretto. It was Fontana who had first suggested Sardou's play to Puccini, and he was therefore much piqued when six years later the operatic adaption was entrusted to Giacosa and Illica.

99

have shrunk back from it, even as he did later from Pierre Louÿs's novel *La Femme et le Pantin*. Still he felt sufficiently attracted by it to sketch out a scenario and elaborate certain situations, among them, significantly, a love and a death scene in which the heroine ends her life by inhaling the intoxicating scent of flowers.* But Zola had already promised his novel to Massenet. Puccini, incidentally, appears to have made Zola's acquaintance first in December 1894 when, on the occasion of the latter's visit to Italy, the Society of Italian Authors gave a banquet in his honour, presided over by Giacosa and including among the guests Boito, Puccini and Leoncavallo.

There was yet another subject to which Puccini gave serious attention while already at work on *Tosca* and one that was to occupy him, intermittently, over a number of years. This was the last days in the life of Marie Antoinette, a heroine whose character and fate would have perfectly answered the type of Puccini's favourite female protagonist. The idea to dramatize this subject appears to have originated with the impresario Schürmann about 1897 which Illica took up intending to treat it in an entirely original manner. Having already made extensive researches into the history of the French Revolution for his libretto for Giordano's *Andrea Chénier*, he was thoroughly familiar with its atmosphere, and drew up a scenario containing no fewer than thirteen to fourteen scenes. The Queen was of course to be the dominant character but Puccini thought that for the sake of an effective dramatic contrast, the royal heroine ought to be opposed by a female revolutionary, a woman of the people, who was to be a contralto—an interesting point, in view of the composer's lack of sympathy for this voice category. However, owing to his waning interest in the subject—'were it not for the hoary and much exploited colour of the Revolution'—it was shelved for the time being.

What prompted Puccini, in 1896, to revert to the plan of an opera after Sardou's play? Generally, the growing vogue which realistic opera was enjoying in the 1890s, with Bruneau as the leader of this movement in France while in Italy its principal flagbearers were Mascagni and Leoncavallo; moreover, Giordano had in the same year produced his very successful *Andrea Chénier*, the plot of which showed points of strong resemblance with that of Sardou's *Tosca*. All in all Puccini must have felt that he could no longer lag behind his rivals. And *Tosca* contained all the essential ingredients for a veristic opera. Besides, Sardou's play continued to enjoy a sensational success since its first production in Paris in 1887—largely owing, it is true, to the acting of Sarah Bernhardt, who toured a number of European countries in it. Such success was, as we noted before, an important criterion for Puccini. Yet there were two more reasons which appear to have actuated him in his choice with particular force, the first of which brings Franchetti on to the scene.

* Puccini was to use this motive of floral suicide in a slightly altered form in *Suor Angelica*. Three other operatic heroines who die by a similar painless method are Selika in *L'Africaine*, Lakmé and Adriana Lecouvreur.

Alberto Franchetti (1860–1942) was a close contemporary of Puccini's who had been his fellow-student under Magi at Lucca, and who had later achieved a considerable reputation with his *Asrael* (1883) and *Cristoforo Colombo* (1892). In 1893 or thereabouts he signed an agreement with Ricordi for a *Tosca* after Sardou's play, and it is possible that it was Ricordi himself who had suggested this subject to Franchetti, seeing that Puccini's erstwhile enthusiasm for it had cooled off. Illica was entrusted with the adaptation and in the autumn of 1894 Franchetti and Illica travelled to Paris to discuss this matter with the French playwright. It so happened that Verdi, who was staying in Paris to prepare the first French production of *Otello*, and who was well acquainted with Sardou, attended one of the sessions at the playwright's home at which Illica read his libretto to the small assembly. Verdi was much impressed by it, especially by a long farewell to art and life which Illica had written for Cavaradossi to sing shortly before his execution, near the end of the last act. According to Fraccaroli,[53] the old master was so moved by these verses that he seized the manuscript from Illica's hand and read them out aloud in a trembling voice. No doubt for Verdi, then in his eighty-first year, this farewell expressed sentiments in tune with his own. That *Tosca* made a profound impression on Verdi is also attested by his biographer Gino Monaldi, who relates that once, when discussing with him the operatic suitability of Sardou's plays, Verdi told him that as early as 1870 the play-wright had sought to interest him in his *Patrie*, but Verdi had found the subject uncongenial. Yet there *was* a drama by Sardou, Verdi continued, which he would have liked to set to music were he not too old—*Tosca*, providing, however, that Sardou permitted him to change the last act. Verdi then proceeded to indicate to Monaldi the alterations he had in mind; but unfortunately Monaldi, beyond describing them as 'most beautiful', omitted to record them in his book.[54]

Verdi's reaction at this session at Sardou's was duly reported to Puccini by either Illica or Ricordi; this, combined with his knowledge that Franchetti planned to use the *Tosca* subject, served to place an extraordinarily high premium upon it in his eyes. He now decided that he must have *Tosca* by hook or by crook. But how was he to get it from Franchetti, who possessed the composing rights? Franchetti was a member of a wealthy Turin family, and it was said of him that his private means enabled him to pay for the productions of his operas, so as to have them staged in the most favourable conditions. He was, therefore, not likely to be tempted by the bait of a handsome financial offer into releasing the *Tosca* subject, least of all in favour of his rival Puccini. Another method of approach had to be found, and found it was by Ricordi, who had no doubt whatever which of the two composers would make a better job of this subject. Great as the success of Franchetti's two operas had been, it could not compare with that of *Manon Lescaut*. And so the wily publisher resorted to a stratagem that in modern parlance might be termed 'psychological warfare'. It was a most questionable ruse from the point of morality, but thanks to it the operatic world has been enriched by one of the most effective works ever written for the musical stage. With Puccini's full knowledge and consent Ricordi and his 'accomplice' Illica arranged a meeting with the guileless Franchetti in which they informed him that after prolonged reflection they had come to the conclusion that *Tosca* was a most unsuitable subject for opera. There was, they urged upon him, the brutality of the plot; there was the scene of Scarpia's attempted rape of Tosca, a scene too *risqué* for the theatre, followed, for good measure, by Scarpia's murder by Tosca which was bound to alienate the public's sympathy for the heroine; and there were many references to historical events in the play incomprehensible to a modern audience. Ricordi's plan worked to perfection. Franchetti's confidence in the success of a *Tosca* opera was thoroughly demolished, he relinquished his rights—whether for a consideration, is not known—and on the next day (it is even said the same day) Ricordi signed a new contract with Puccini!*

2

The turning of Sardou's play into a libretto caused, as was to be expected, far less trouble than had the dramatization of Mürger's novel for *Bohème*. For one thing, its dramatic structure could hardly be improved; all it needed to suit Puccini's purposes was, in the main, reductions and simplifications of certain scenes and of the dialogue. For another, there was at hand the libretto which Illica had fashioned for Franchetti and which could be used again with alterations. If there was a serious difficulty, it lay in Giacosa's profound dislike of the play, which struck him as being devoid of any lyrical and poetic situations and therefore hard to versify. He was convinced of its absolute unsuitability for an opera and declared that while *La Bohème* was all poetry and no plot, *Tosca* was all plot and no poetry, with puppets instead of real characters in it. It is interesting to follow Giacosa's criticisms in greater detail. After declaring himself profoundly convinced that the plot of *Tosca* was not suitable for an opera, Giacosa wrote to Ricordi on 23 August 1896:

> At a first glance it appears to be suitable because of the rapidity of the dramatic action and the self-evidence of its scenes. And this will the more readily appear to be the case at a first reading of the skilful synthesis which Illica has made of it. But the more one studies the action of each scene and tries to extract lyrical and poetic moments, the more convinced one grows of its absolute inadaptability to the musical stage. I am glad to have told you this now, because I am sure that I shall have occasion in the future to recall to you this letter of mine. The first act consists of nothing but duets. Nothing but duets in the second act (except for the short 'torture' scene in which only two characters are seen on the stage). The third act is one interminable duet.

In Sardou's play this duologue structure seemed to Giacosa justified, because, in his view, it was a play with only one protagonist and designed to display the virtuosity of a single actress (Sarah Bernhardt):

* Incidentally, Franchetti's next opera was *Il Signor di Pourceaugnac* (1897), after one of Molière's lesser-known comedies, the same comedy from which Hugo von Hofmannsthal partly derived the character of Ochs von Lerchenau for Strauss's *Der Rosenkavalier*.

But it is as well to note that even in the spoken theatre *Tosca* has never become part of the normal repertoire. It is a drama reserved for the virtuosity of an exceptional actress. On the operatic stage, however, this succession of duets is bound to result in monotony. Nor is this its worst defect. The greatest calamity lies in the fact that that part, which I should call the mechanical element, namely the joining together of incidents in the action, prevails over the poetry, to the latter's detriment. *Tosca* is a drama of coarse emotional situations, without poetry. With *Bohème* it was quite different, where the action is of no importance and where, instead, lyrical and poetic moments abound. In *Tosca* one has to throw the concatenation of events into relief and that takes much more space than it should, and permits little scope for the emotional development. . .

I have on purpose renounced all rest and all plans for a trip to the mountains. I have shut myself off in my solitude at Parella* and have attended to nothing else. I had started work on a play but I have interrupted it and don't reckon to resume it until I have finished the libretto. But I do not feel like dashing off just anything. . . If you, if Illica, if Puccini have had recourse to me, it was because you wanted me to see to it that the libretto was given poetry and the right shape. Well, to have, with difficulty, to join together all those minute points of the action and complete it within a short time is a very arduous task. Each scene costs me painful labour. I have to re-do it several times because I do not want to part with it until I am satisfied. . . Dear Ricordi, let us speak with frankness and clarity as is proper between good friends. If you prefer it, if you are annoyed at my artistic scruples, which hold matters up, then I am not only prepared to relinquish my work but to restitute part of the sum you had paid me in advance.† I have not failed in my duties. But artistic work is not the product of manual labour that is accomplished in a day. . . By the beginning of September you will have the whole of the second act, and a good bit of the third is already done. I have started on the lyrical portions, leaving to the last the job of joining it all together. But I repeat, if you wish to do without me, you are the boss and we shall always remain friends (*N*).

Ricordi, needless to say, ignored Giacosa's offer to withdraw and the latter continued to work with his wonted conscientiousness; but stung by the publisher's reproaches for his slowness, he retorted in the following (undated) letter:

You have fixed 6 December as the date at which *Tosca* must be delivered complete, with a fine of fifty lire for every day of delay. I swear to you I am not wasting one hour. But permit me to add that Puccini wastes an infinite number of hours—whether in hunting or fishing, I don't know. I understand very well that a composer cannot start with his work until he has the entire libretto in his hands. But he has in his possession the entire libretto, and two acts of it are in their definitive form. For the third act he has not only a clear outline of the individual scenes but also the substance and drift of the dialogue well outlined. . . *La Bohème* was begun and treated in quite a different manner. To be sure, if he wants the dialogue rendered definitive before he starts to

* Giacosa's native town, near Ivrea in the Val d'Aosta.

† The normal fee paid to a librettist by the House of Ricordi was 500 lire an act (then c. £25), but Giacosa and Illica received a special rate, plus a royalty of 6% for Author's Copyright.

compose, he has only to say so; but once the dialogue is really definitive, don't let him come afterwards and propose new alterations at every turn (N).

In a subsequent letter, dated 14 December, Giacosa criticizes the dramatic treatment of Scarpia:

> ... It seems to me that to finish the first act with a monologue and start the second again with a monologue sung by the selfsame character is rather monotonous. This is to say nothing of the fact that it is absurd that this Scarpia should waste time in giving a description of himself. A character such as Scarpia acts but does not express himself in words. You have told me that, from a musical point of view, the piece [Scarpia's monologue at the beginning of Act II] has its purpose, a point which I am not competent to argue about. But dramatically and psychologically that monologue seems to me absurd. However, I shall get down to it, but I decline any responsibility (N).

From a playwright's point of view, Giacosa was possibly right in his objections to this close succession of monologues; but he overlooked the fact that they were separated by an interval and that Puccini's musical treatment of them was entirely different—though this Giacosa could not have known at that stage.

When in 1898 Puccini, after having suddenly dropped the whole plan of *Tosca*, took it up again, Giacosa unburdened himself in a letter to Ricordi (8 September) compounded of bitter reproaches and sarcasm. He starts by asking whether all that was required of him was to jot down a dozen verses—'correct, sonorous and not ungrammatical'; for that, Illica and Puccini could have found a hundred other poets able to accomplish this task to their satisfaction and at a cheaper price. Giacosa then goes on to complain that while everyone else had heard Puccini's music, he had not had the honour of hearing a single note of it, a complaint also voiced by Illica but in far stronger terms. All the same, Giacosa was prepared to collaborate, in order to show his good will, and in token of it he was sending Ricordi the verses requested of him. But he adds:

> I have paid no attention to the dramatic element or the personalities of the characters or the psychology of the *signor tenore*, as you call him (for it seems that for you and Puccini, Mario Cavaradossi should be nothing but a *signor tenore*) nor have I paid attention to common sense. You wanted *lyrical verses* and we know that *lyrical verses* have nothing to do with psychology nor with dramaturgy. So let it be lyrical verses. Also, to please you, I have faithfully followed the metrical pattern which you sent me. The prosody won't be very satisfactory, but these verses of mine make light of the rules of prosody.

After demonstrating in detail the extent to which the pattern he was requested to follow in his verses offended against metrical rules, and after suggesting how it ought to be modified, Giacosa continues:

> That is what the rules of prosody demand but they do not square with the exigencies of the *signor tenore*, to whom I yield, before whom I bow my head and take my hat off so reverently. . . Even schoolboys will have a laugh at the libretto if they read it; but it is certain that people won't fall for it. . .

I wanted to rid my heart of that weight of bitterness which your letter has caused me. Having given you my reasons, I now shake hands with you in immutable friendship (N).

Let us now cross over to the opposite camp in this battle between librettist and composer. In the early part of July 1896 Puccini had been anxiously awaiting some material from Giacosa to start work; by the end of October he had the greater part of the libretto in his possession, and on 4 November he wrote to Ricordi in an elated mood:

> Long live Act II, carefully revised, repolished and speeded (?) along by Puccini's ink-blots. The third act will be really stupendous. At least, that is what it makes me hope for (E).

Only a few weeks before he had received yet another powerful confirmation that in choosing *Tosca* he had laid his hands on an excellent subject. For on 14 October Ricordi had written to him that he and Illica had paid Verdi a short visit of three hours. Verdi 'informed himself of what new works were in process and told me "Puccini has a good libretto! Fortunate composer who has that work in his hands!" Our Verdi is a good prophet!! Therefore *laboremus*!!' (M).

It is difficult to trace the growth of *Tosca* during 1897, there being a gap in the *Epistolario* for that year—possibly on account of Puccini's frequent personal meetings with his librettists and publisher. All the same, the complete absence, from this collection, of letters dating from that period appears somewhat strange.

From entries in the autograph score we learn that the composition of the first act was begun in January 1898; but in April work had to be interrupted because of the composer's visit to Paris for the first French production of *Bohème*. On this occasion Puccini paid his first visit to Sardou, on Ricordi's advice, to discuss the *Tosca* libretto, in the shaping of which the playwright himself wished to take an active part.* Of these sessions Puccini gave Fraccaroli the following amusing account:

> That man is prodigious. He was then more than seventy but there was in him the energy and agility of a youngster. Besides, he was an indefatigable and highly interesting conversationalist, talking for hours on end without getting tired. When he touched on an historical subject, he was a water-tap, nay, a fountain; anecdote after anecdote would pour from his lips in a clear and inexhaustible stream. Our sessions simply turned into monologues—most delightful, assuredly, but this did not make for much progress in our *Tosca*. However, he suddenly became compliant and readily agreed with the need for suppressing one act [Act II of the play] and to fuse the scene in the prison cell with that of the execution.[55]

---

* In addition to the libretto for *Tosca*, Sardou offered Puccini between 1903 and 1906 three more of his plays. Altogether, there is a round dozen of operas based on Sardou plays, the most important ones being Johann Strauss's *Der Karneval in Rom* (1873), after *Piccolino*, and Giordano's *Fedora* (1898) and his *Madame Sans-Gêne* (1915). Incidentally, Sardou's *Fedora* was another subject that Verdi appears to have considered at one time.

Sardou also wished to hear the music of *Tosca* which already existed, and Puccini played it to him on the piano, weaving into it melodies from *Manon Lescaut* and *Bohème*! Sardou was clearly impressed, but there was still the matter of the composing rights to be settled—for these he demanded the exorbitant sum of 50,000 francs, a sum, Puccini remarked, no one had ever dared to exact before, not even for a newly invented libretto or the music of a whole opera. Sardou finally agreed to accept 15 per cent of the gross takings.

In January 1899 Puccini paid Sardou another visit in Paris; for difficulties had arisen with the playwright over the final scene of the opera, of the nature of which the composer informed Ricordi in this graphic description:

Paris, Friday 13 January 1899

Dear and beloved Don Giulio,

This morning I spent an hour with Sardou and he told me various things he does not like in the finale. He wants that poor woman dead at all costs! Now that Deibler [the French executioner] is in his decline, the Magician wants to *take his place*! But I will certainly not follow him. He accepts her madness but would like her to swoon and die like a fluttering bird. Moreover, in the *reprise* which Sarah will give on the 20th, Sardou has introduced a large flag on the Castel Sant' Angelo, which flying and refulgent (he says) will make an enormous effect; he goes in for the flag (and that is nearer to his heart at the moment than the play itself).

But I am still for the lament of Tito and for the end—well, delicate and not *éclatant*.*

In sketching the panorama he wanted one to see the course of the Tiber pass between St. Peter and the Castello! I observed to him that the *flumen* flows past on the other side, under the Castello. But he, as calm as a fish, said: 'Oh, that's nothing!'†

A fine fellow, all life and fire and full of historico-topo-panoramic inexactitudes!... On Tuesday morning I must go and see Sardou again—the Magician has ordered it—perhaps he wants Spoletta to die too. We shall see! (E).

3

We return to the year 1898. In May Puccini was back in Italy from his first visit to Sardou and now threw himself into the composition of the opera in his mountain fastness at Monsagrati. From there he wrote on 18 August, at '2 a.m.', one of those characteristic nonsense letters to Caselli which always contain one or two self-revealing lines. He had caught butterflies and was sending them to his chemist friend at Lucca:

* This would suggest that Puccini, like Verdi before him, wanted to tone down the violent ending and that he possibly intended Tosca to sing a lament before her suicide, an idea apparently suggested by Tito Ricordi. The final version of the libretto, however, has the same closing scene as Sardou's play.

† Puccini treasured this sketch among his curiosities. He later told Fraccaroli that Sardou also got hold of a huge map of Rome and discoursed for another quarter of an hour on his impossible suggestion.

These butterflies may serve to give you the idea of the transient character of human miseries.

As corpses, let them remind you that when evening comes we must all die; while I am racking my brain in the silence of the night to give colour to the Roman heroine, I act as an executioner to these poor frail creatures.

The Neronic instinct manifests and fulfils itself (*E*).

On 18 August he began with the final scene of the first act, the *Te Deum* sung in celebration of the Austrians' supposed victory over Napoleon's army. Though well acquainted with the liturgy from his organist days at Lucca, he was anxious to achieve strict authenticity in every detail and therefore wished to make certain of the prayer which it is customary to recite in Roman churches during the Cardinal's procession from the Sanctuary to the High Altar on the occasion when a solemn *Te Deum* is celebrated. He first thought of the *Ecce Sacerdos*, but became doubtful, considering this prayer not quite suitable for the special effect he intended; it occurred to him that some old Latin sequences might serve his purpose. But where was he to find them? He first addressed himself to Maestro Vandini at Lucca, to whom he was soon sending missive after missive in a mock-furious tone:

> I said I wanted some words to be murmured, therefore I want them. Go to San Martino! ... Go to the Bishop! ... Go to Father Agrimonti, to Fathers Marianetti, Volpi and Pardini, go to the priests of Antraccoli! Whatever you do, find them, forward them to me. Ask Caselli, he will be able to find them in some corner of his junk-shop. ... Get the words for me or I'll become a Protestant. ... If you don't send me those prayers, I'll compose a 'Funeral March for Religion' ... Go to the Bishop! ... Tell him to invent something for me. If he does not, I'll write to the Pope and have him thrown out of his job on the grounds of his imbecility.[56]

But Maestro Vandini failed him. Then Puccini remembered Father Pietro Panichelli, whom he had first met in Rome in 1897; Panichelli later became an intimate friend of the Puccini family, who nicknamed him '*Pretino*'—'little priest'—and '*Cappellano di Casa Puccini*'—'Chaplain of the House of Puccini'.* In a letter to the priest of August 1898, Puccini was most explicit in his request for the words of a prayer, which for the sake of the phonic effect, should be murmured 'in subdued and muttered voices, without intonation, precisely as real prayers are said'.

> 'The *Ecce Sacerdos*', he continues, 'is too imposing to be murmured. I know that it is not usual to say or sing anything before the solemn *Te Deum*, which is sung as soon as they reach the High Altar, but I repeat (whether right or wrong) that I should like to find *something to be murmured* during the procession from the sacristy to the altar, either by the Chapter or the people; preferably by the people because they are more numerous and therefore more effective musically' (*E*).

* Father Panichelli later published his memoirs in *Il 'Pretino' di Giacomo Puccini Racconta* (3rd Ed. Pisa, 1949), a garrulous and naïve little book which gives a rather roseate picture of the composer but contains a number of hitherto unknown details about his private life.

But Father Panichelli was no more successful than Maestro Vandini, and it was ultimately Puccini himself who lighted on the suitable words in an old book of prayers:

Adjutorium nostrum in nomine Domini . . .
Qui fecit coelum et terram
Sit nomen Domini benedictum
Et hoc nunc et usque in saeculum.

As will be noted, the accumulation of the vowels 'o' and 'u' does indeed produce the dull, subdued sound which Puccini had in mind.

Father Panichelli was, however, able to provide the version of the plainsong to which the *Te Deum* is sung in Roman churches, there being a number of variants of this melody used in Italy. He also sent the composer a description of the correct order of the Cardinal's procession and of the costumes worn by the Swiss Guard. Panichelli was, moreover, instrumental in putting Puccini in touch with Maestro Meluzzi of St. Peter's; for Puccini was anxious to reproduce, in the third act of the opera, the authentic effect of the Matin bells, the *scampanio mattutino*, which are rung from the Cathedral; in particular, he wished to know the exact pitch of St. Peter's largest bell, the famous *campanone*, which Meluzzi established—not without difficulty, on account of the powerful overtones—to be E below the bass stave, which in fact is the note sounded by the lowest bell in Act III of the opera. Moreover, Puccini made a special journey to Rome and in the early hours of the morning climbed the ramparts of the Castel Sant' Angelo in order to obtain a first-hand impression of the bewildering sounds of the Matin bells, rung from different churches in the neighbourhood to announce the first *Ave Maria*.

It was through Alfredo Vandini, an old friend of the composer's from his Lucca days, who was now a civil servant in Rome, that Puccini approached Luigi Zanazzo, a Roman poet and librarian at the Ministry of Education, who provided him with the words for the charming little pastoral 'Io de' sospiri', which is sung by the shepherd offstage at the beginning of Act III. This quatrain is in the style of traditional shepherds' songs of the Campagna and Puccini's special request to Zanazzo was that the words should in no way refer to the actual drama of the opera. The fact that he sent the poet dummy verses to show what kind of metre he required, suggests that he had already sketched the music for this song.

If it has appeared to the reader that during his work on *Tosca* Puccini was not assailed by his usual doubts, this would be a false impression. Certainly they were less corrosive and less frequent with this opera, where, as we have seen, he had Verdi's encouraging words to fall back on at moments when his spirit faltered before his task. Nevertheless, there were periods when he indeed felt more than uncertain whether he had after all chosen a subject really suited to his particular genius. The clearest evidence of this is provided by a conversation he had on one occasion with Sardou.[57] Its gist was that Puccini thought it might be better if a French composer set the drama; to which Sardou replied that *Tosca* was a Roman subject and hence needed Italian music. Puccini then cited Verdi and Franchetti, both of whom had considered and finally rejected the subject. Sardou retorted that Verdi's rejection was due not to his being intimidated by the drama but to his old age—he was too tired to undertake a new opera. The fact, moreover, Sardou continued, that two composers had seriously considered his play was the best guarantee of its vitality, and this should serve Puccini as an encouragement. Whereupon the composer made the significant reply: 'But my music is tenuous, it is delicate, it is written in a different register. . . My previous heroines, Manon and Mimi, are different from Tosca.' This the choleric Sardou simply brushed aside by maintaining that there were 'no registers . . . there's only talent'. As to Puccini's three heroines—'it's all the same thing! . . . Women in love all belong to the same family. I have created Marcella and Fernanda, I have created Fedora, Theodora and Cleopatra. They are all the same woman'. It was a remark which plainly revealed Sardou's limitation as a dramatist and which applies *mutatis mutandis* also to the Puccini of the operas before *Il Trittico*.

Sardou subsequently claimed that it was largely owing to his powers of persuasion that Puccini wrote *Tosca*, and he even went so far as to declare that the libretto was superior to his play—which, needless to say, it is not. According to Puccini, who was present at the first Paris production of the opera on 13 October 1903, the septuagenarian playwright, exuberant and vital as ever, took full command at the rehearsals, throwing his weight about as though he were not only the author of the play but composer and producer of the opera as well. The French critics, incidentally, received the opera with scarcely less hostility than had their Italian confrères at its first production in Rome.

To return to 1899. The difficulties with Sardou over the last scene having finally been settled, Puccini returned to Torre del Lago and now began to work consistently at the second act, which he started, according to an entry in the autograph score, on 23 February, completing it on 16 July. Yet in a letter to Ricordi, undated but placed by internal evidence shortly after the completion of that act,* he still questioned a number of textual details, but he raised no objection to certain alterations in the 'torture' scene which Ricordi had made at Sardou's request. 'If that is how we can satisfy Sardou, let us do it. It makes no essential change in the scene' (E). It is interesting to note that over this scene there had previously occurred one of those now familiar clashes with his librettists who in an earlier version had made Cavaradossi sing, *during* his torture, a funereal aria which merged into a quartet with Tosca, the Judge and Spoletta. This formal piece Puccini found unacceptable from the point of view of dramatic truth, representing, as it did, a reversion to the obsolete convention of mid-nineteenth-century opera. In this matter the librettists soon yielded to Puccini's objection, but there was another bone of contention over which they fought until the opera was nearly completed. This was the famous Farewell to Life and Art which had moved

* In the *Epistolario* this letter (No. 58) is reproduced in a wrong chronological order, suggesting that it had been written some two or three years earlier.

Verdi so profoundly and which Cavaradossi was to sing before his execution. It was cast in a reflective and somewhat philosophical mood, with verses of an academic cut, whereas Puccini here wanted a stirring lament—the present 'E lucevan le stelle'—expressing a lover's anguish and despair at the thought of his final separation from his beloved—a truly Puccinian motive. Yet Illica, proud of these verses of his and recalling the impression they had made on Verdi, was adamant in his refusal to alter them, deliberately ignoring that Puccini's bent lay not in the direction of the rhetorical and heroic. What complicated matters was the fact that the composer had already sketched words and music for this scene, such as he felt would exactly limn the emotional situation as he saw it.[*] The arguments over the changes to be made were long-drawn and were not settled until Puccini, by singing and playing the music to them, brought his librettists round to his point of view. Giacosa wrote new verses adapting their metre to the rhythm of Puccini's melody but retaining from Puccini's dummy verses the two words 'Muoio disperato !' The composer later declared that admirers of that aria had treble cause to be grateful to him: for composing the music, for causing the words to be written, and for declining expert advice to throw the result into the waste-paper basket.[58]

The final act was completed on 29 September 1899 and the score dispatched to Ricordi without delay. But how great was Puccini's consternation when a few days later his publisher informed him of his reaction, which was as unforeseen as it was violent. In this letter—one of the longest he ever wrote to the composer—Ricordi said he had been so profoundly disturbed that he had not slept a wink the previous night. With 'a beating heart' and with 'full frankness' he had to tell him the truth as it appeared to him:

> . . . The third act of *Tosca*, as it stands, is a grave error of conception and craftsmanship . . . it would cancel out the splendid impression of Act I . . . and the overwhelming effect that Act II is bound to create, which is a true masterpiece of dramatic power and tragic expression !! . . . As to the duet between Tosca and Cavaradossi . . . it is fragmentary music, music of a small line that reduces the characters to pygmies . . . I find that one of the most beautiful passages of lyrical poetry—the 'O dolci mani'—is merely underlined by a scrappy and modest melody which, to make matters worse, comes from *Edgar*[†] . . . stupendous if sung by a peasant woman from the Tyrol, but out of place in the mouths of Tosca and Cavaradossi. In short, this duet, which ought to have been a hymn, if not a Latin hymn, though a hymn of love, is reduced to a few meagre bars. . . Where, in truth, is the Puccini of that noble, warm and vigorous inspiration? (10 October 1899. *C.P.Let.*208).

What was Puccini's reaction to these strictures? On all previous occasions Ricordi's words had carried so much weight with him. Now, in his pro-

---

[*] The autograph score suggests that in fact Puccini began the composition (or orchestration?) of the third act with Cavaradossi's lament, which was, significantly, one of the first musical ideas that had come into his head.

[†] See p. 376. According to Illica, Puccini also made use of some ideas in his sketches for the abortive *La Lupa*. (*C.P.Let.*221).

found conviction of having done the right thing, he replied in a singularly restrained and dignified letter which is worth reproducing in full.

> Torre del Lago
> 11 October 1899

Dearest Signor Giulio,

Your letter has been an extraordinary surprise for me. I am still under its impact. All the same, I am sure and convinced that if you re-read that third act, you would change your opinion! It is not pride on my part. No, it is the conviction of having given life as best I could to the drama that stood before me. You know how scrupulous I am in interpreting the situation or the words and how important it is to get down to this first. Your reproach about having taken a fragment from *Edgar*—this can be criticized by you and those few who are able to recognize it and it can be regarded as a *labour-saving device*. As it stands (if one rids oneself of the idea that it belongs to another work—Act IV of *Edgar*—which has been abolished anyhow) it seems to me full of that poetry which emanates from the words. Oh! I am sure of that and you will be convinced when you hear it in its proper place, that is, in the theatre. As to its fragmentary character, that was deliberate; this love duet cannot be a uniform and tranquil situation as is the case with other love duets. Tosca's thoughts constantly return to the necessity that Mario's fall should be well simulated and that his behaviour should appear natural before the shooting party. As to the end of the duet (the so-called Latin hymn which I have not yet had the benefit of seeing written by the poets) I too have my doubts about it—but I hope that in the theatre it will come off and perhaps very well.

The duet of the third act has always been the great stumbling-block. The poets have not been able to produce anything good (I am speaking of the end) and, above all, anything with true feeling in it.

They are academic, academic all the time—nothing but the usual amorous embroideries. I have had to contrive to get to the end, without boring the audience too much, and avoiding all academic stuff.

Mugnone, who heard this third act several times when I *sang* it to him, is so enthusiastic about it that he even prefers it to the fourth act of *Bohème*. Friends and members of my household have formed an excellent impression of it. So far as my own experience goes, I am not displeased with it either.

I really fail to understand your unfavourable impression. Before I set to work to do it again (and will there be time?) I shall take a run up to Milan and we shall discuss it, *we two alone*, at the piano and with the music in front of us, and if your unfavourable impression persists, we shall try like good friends to find, as Scarpia says, a way to save ourselves.*

I repeat, it is not pride on my part. It is only a defence of a work about which I have thought—and thought a lot.

I have always encountered in my dear 'Papa Giulio' great delicacy of feeling and an affection which, you may be sure, is reciprocated in full measure. And I am grateful for the interest you take in me and have always taken since that day when I had the good fortune to encounter you first.

I disagree with you about that third act; it is the first time that we do not

---

* In Act II, Scarpia says to Tosca about her lover: 'Volete che cerchiamo . . . il modo di salvarlo?'

see eye to eye with each other. But I hope and will even say, I am sure, that you will change your view. We shall see!

Toscanini is coming today—and perhaps I shall come back with him tomorrow or the next day. I shall wire to you.

I am still working at the prelude which is giving me much trouble, but it is coming along (E). . . .*

So far as we know Puccini altered not an iota in that act. Yet Ricordi's remarks on the duet, exaggerated though they are, contain more than a grain of truth, as we shall see in our later analysis of the opera.

Assuming the summer of 1896 as the period when work on the opera was begun in all seriousness, *Tosca* was written in a little over three years, the adaptation of the libretto taking less time than that of *Manon* and *La Bohème* —an indirect tribute to Sardou's stagecraft.

4

With the action of *Tosca* laid in Rome, Ricordi's choice (first suggested by Illica) of the Italian capital for the first production was as appropriate as it was diplomatic, and calculated to flatter the Romans' local patriotism and pride. But in the event his shrewd move proved not altogether successful. Ricordi had not reckoned with the traditional antagonism that existed, and still exists, between the Rome audiences and those of northern Italy, nor could he have foreseen that the disturbed political atmosphere of the times would contribute to the extraordinary tension which was to reign in the theatre at the première. This took place on 14 January 1900 at the Teatro Costanzi, where—a noteworthy coincidence—Mascagni's *Cavalleria* had launched veristic opera a decade before; *Tosca* was Puccini's first excursion into this genere.

The conductor was Mugnone and the three chief roles were sung by Hariclea Darclée (Tosca), De Marchi (Cavaradossi) and Eugenio Giraldoni (Scarpia). Darclée had been chosen less for her vocal accomplishments than for her striking beauty and great talent as an actress. Incidentally, it is generally stated that it was she who first introduced the costume and the diverse paraphernalia that has since become traditional for every Tosca to wear: the rustling silk dress, the large plumed hat, the long cane and the bouquet of flowers. This is not correct, for Sarah Bernhardt had already appeared thus apparelled at the first performance of the play in Paris, and the carrying of a cane and of flowers is demanded by Sardou in his stage directions; as a born man of the theatre he took, like Puccini, meticulous care with all details connected with the costumes, the scenery and the lighting of his plays.

Puccini was looking forward to the première with unusual confidence. Shortly before, he had written to Father Panichelli:

* From the autograph score, it would appear that Puccini composed this prelude (to Act III) last.

PUCCINI
(about 1900)

ELVIRA PUCCINI
(about 1900)

December 1899

... I believe that the opera will have an execution *hors ligne*. Mugnone will put all his great art into directing it and all the able artists (already inspired as they ought to be) will do wonders. This time I am in good hands: management, orchestra, artists and conductor. We have good hopes that the public will show favour and that the opera will be a success when it is seen on the stage. We shall see if my instinct is true... (*E*).

This letter was evidently written in reply to one by Panichelli, in which the priest must have made reference to the official receptions and banquets that were awaiting Puccini after the première. To this Puccini made the following retort:

... After the three sacramental performances (if I am not hissed at the first) I shall go into hiding in the woods which were a safe refuge for so long for Tiburzo and his companions.* There I shall give vent to my sportsman's rage and compensate myself for the sufferings experienced in thirty or thirty-five days of rehearsals.

Yes, in the green, rustic wilderness of the most splendid Maremma—the hospitable ground for nice people—I shall pass, I think, the best days of my life. But are you crazy? Ah, to be out shooting where there is really some prey, and after a success! It is the supreme moment when the spirit is at rest! I want to profit from it and shall plunge myself into it. Away with banquets, receptions and official visits! . . . (*E*).

In charge of the production was Tito Ricordi (1865–1932). Tito was the eldest of the publisher's four children; he had studied engineering, but faithful to the family tradition he now began to share his father's responsibilities in the firm. Unlike Giulio, Tito was impulsive, short-tempered, intransigent and dictatorial. The wealth and fame of his family had engendered in him in an arrogance which made him both feared and hated. There were frequent quarrels between father and son; in 1907 Tito threatened to resign from the firm, and eventually did in 1919; while with Puccini, who in playful irony used to refer to him as 'that queer capricious fellow *Savoia*' (the name of Italy's royal dynasty), he was to come to a head-on collision in connection with *La Rondine*. Yet Tito was a man of drive and initiative who knew his own mind: it was largely owing to his efforts that the firm consolidated its position in foreign countries by the establishment of new branches. He was one of the first persons in Italy to realize the importance of good acting and careful production for the success of a realistic opera. *Tosca* gave him a welcome opportunity to show his mettle as a producer: he paid attention to the minutest scenic details and worked indefatigably with the cast. But he committed a tactical error by bringing with him the stage-designer of La Scala, Hohenstein,† a fact much resented in Roman

* He was of German descent; in addition to those for *Tosca*, he had designed the costumes and scenery for *Manon Lescaut* and *La Bohème* and also the cover pictures for the vocal scores of these operas.

† The 'woods' were a reference to the wild forests of the Tuscan Maremma which extends along the coast and is an ideal hunting-ground for waterfowl.

artistic circles, and he created a storm of protest when he gave orders that no outsiders, including critics and relations of the cast, were to be permitted to attend rehearsals. Tito's conduct contributed not a little to the tense atmosphere in which the preparations of the opera proceeded. Rumours were put about that certain rivals of Puccini's and their followers intended to disturb the first night and hiss the opera, whatever its merits, and that Rome, jealous of its rank as the country's capital, was not going to permit itself to be influenced by what Milan and Turin thought of the composer and his 'facile' successes there.

The artists on that evening of 14 January at the packed Teatro Costanzi —some had received anonymous letters threatening them with violence— felt as though they were sitting on a powder-keg; they were indeed not wide of the mark. For fifteen minutes before the curtain was due to rise a police officer called on Mugnone in his dressing-room and informed him of the reported threat that a bomb might be thrown during the performance —in which case the conductor was at once to strike up the National Anthem! The fact that Queen Margherita, members of the government and senators were expected to attend lent colour to the rumours that a political assassination was planned. Mugnone wisely kept the news from Puccini; but he himself, a timid man by nature, who had had the grim experience of seeing several people killed by an anarchist's bomb at a performance conducted by him at the Liceo in Barcelona a few years before, descended to the orchestral pit like one condemned to death. The opera began with an ominous portent. The opening bars were greeted with whispers and noises which increased with Angelotti's stage entry and soon reached such a pitch that neither singer nor orchestra could be heard any longer. Shouts came from the audience: 'Stop! Down with the curtain!' Mugnone broke off and rushed up backstage trembling with fear and agitation. Yet the cause of the uproar proved a harmless one: a crowd of latecomers had tried to force an entry into the auditorium, and their attempts to reach their seats had led to violent protests on the part of those already seated. After a while calm was restored and the opera began again and remained undisturbed throughout the whole performance.

Puccini's biographers speak of a rival faction to which they ascribe the intention of wrecking the première of *Tosca* by the throwing of a bomb. It is not an implausible explanation. For similar methods of settling personal rivalries had been resorted to before in the history of the Italian theatre. As recently as March 1894, during a performance of *Otello* at the Teatro Nuovo at Pisa conducted by the young Toscanini, a bomb was thrown backstage but without causing any loss of life. The would-be assassin was never found, though suspicion fell on one of the artists who had been dismissed by Toscanini.[59]

It is equally possible to connect the rumours of an intended bomb-throwing at the *Tosca* première with the general political climate in Italy at the period. Since the termination of the unsuccessful war against Abyssinia in 1896, the country had been rent by much discontent and unrest, the chief cause of which lay in worsening economic conditions. There had been industrial riots both in the North and South which the government of King Humbert I had suppressed ruthlessly. Parliament was dissolved by royal decree at the end of June 1899. Even Puccini, despite his lack of interest in anything that lay outside the sphere of his art (and hunting), had been compelled to take note, however superficially, of these events; especially when, during his sojourn in Paris in the spring of 1898, disturbances had occurred in Milan which caused him concern for the safety of his family there. There had already occurred two attempts on the King's life by anarchists, the second as recently as 1897. The Queen's intended presence at the first night of *Tosca*—she did not arrive until the first interval—thus presented a tempting opportunity to a would-be assassin, and the King was in fact assassinated seven months later, at Monza on 19 July. Seen against this larger, political background, the rumours surrounding the première of the opera appear, therefore, in a more sinister light than has hitherto been realized.

There is no doubt that the extraordinary atmosphere in which *Tosca* received its baptism had an adverse influence on the quality of the performance and kept the audience on the edge of their nerves. Yet this would not altogether account for the unfavourable comments made by the generality of critics afterwards, though compared with those on *La Bohème* the strictures were less harsh, and in one or two instances even laudatory. The most sensible review came from Colombani in the *Corriere della Sera*, who pointed to the main problem which Puccini had had to face in this opera, namely to adapt the music to naked facts and swift-changing incidents and to a dialogue fragmentary, rapid and agitated: in all that, he declared, Puccini had been wholly successful. The composer, according to this critic, managed to ennoble an action which might have otherwise suggested 'the most reprehensible vulgarity'. Colombani considered the libretto to be an improvement on the play; from the purely operatic point of view he was right.* Nevertheless, he felt that it still suffered from the defects of the original drama—psychological poverty and an excess of melodramatic situations hampering the composer in the free play of his imagination. In fact most writers directed their shafts at the libretto rather than the music, finding it unsuited to Puccini's temperament, which at certain moments was 'suffocated' by it. All the same, the measure of importance that the Press perceived in the new opera may be gauged from the fact that the *Corriere d'Italia* devoted its entire front page to a discussion of it, offering congratulations to the composer but at the same time deploring that 'he should have attempted something the futility of which ought not to have escaped him'.

So much for the Press notices. As to Puccini, he thought that *Tosca* had been a near-failure, but, as with *La Bohème*, both he and his critics were proved wrong by the public. Twenty more performances were given before full houses at the Costanzi, and in that same year the opera was produced in a large number of other Italian cities. Again it was Buenos Aires

* See p. 360.

which staged the first foreign production, five months after the première, and this was immediately followed by London, where *Tosca* was first performed (in Italian) at Covent Garden on 12 July.* In this production Antonio Scotti made his first appearance as Scarpia—a role which he continued to play to perfection until his retirement from the stage thirty-three years later. Fernando De Lucia sang Cavaradossi.

The promptitude with which London accepted the work was a measure of Puccini's increased reputation since *La Bohème* (the latter, we recall, did not reach the English capital until twenty months after its Italian première). Like their Italian colleagues, the English critics directed their main attack at the libretto; they found the torture scene particularly objectionable and accused the composer of degrading the art of music by making it express physical agony. For this production Puccini came to London, arriving in June to attend rehearsals which 'go tolerably well but a little in the American style, that is, rather hurriedly and without much finish'.[60] But, writing to Elvira (in an undated letter) he hopes

> to have great success because the artists are very good . . . better than at La Scala . . . in the tragic moments Ternina is extraordinary. In moments of love and lightness, she has little *charme*. The second act, however, she does wonderfully, except the 'Vissi d'arte', which she sings a little like a German. . . . Scotti, marvellous; bad voice, but talent, and of grand stature in the part.
>
> In short, I hope that when you read this you will already have received a telegram. If instead it is a fiasco, call me a big idiot. A hundred thousand kisses. Topizio, who is going to bed (*M*).

This was Puccini's first London visit of any length, but he was hoping to leave soon. 'I have had enough of London. It is cold here—quite like autumn.' Among other things he went to see the slums, 'which interested me very much', and also attended a big party at Rothschild's; and he found London 'a better place to stay in and more interesting than Paris' (whence he had just come), 'but it is the question of language which depresses me. I don't understand a single word. I just know the numerals (the first ten) and a few addresses where to go by cab!'[61] In later years, however, he grew fond of London: 'immense movement, infernal, indescribable, Paris is nothing compared with it. The language impossible, the women most beautiful, splendid theatres and entertainments in profusion. The city is hardly beautiful but fascinating.'[62]

A few occasional compositions date from the period of *Tosca*. Of negligible worth, they provide the clearest evidence that Puccini's creative imagination depended entirely on the stimulus of the stage. In 1896 he wrote an orchestral march, *Scossa elettrica*, a humorous piece in which the 'electric shocks' of the title are administered by strokes on the percussion which punctuate the music*—a jest reminiscent of Wagner's youthful overture in B flat. In

---

* Cf. *Electric-Magnetic Polka*, by Johann Strauss the younger. Such titles reflected the sensation caused by the revolutionary discoveries which were being made at that period in the comparatively new field of electricity.

* The first English version was heard at the Shaftesbury Theatre in 1915.

1897 Puccini wrote for his hunting companions the march *Inno a Diana* (words by Fausto Salvatori), for chorus and piano accompaniment, the main theme of which foreshadows Rinuccio's Hymn in praise of Florence, in *Gianni Schicchi*. He later adapted the music for his *Inno a Roma*. From 1899 dates a marching-song, *Avanti, Urania!* for chorus and piano, to words by Renato Fucini, and composed for the launching of a ship of that name. To the same year belongs the well-known song *E l'uccellino*, also to words by Fucini, which Puccini wrote in memory of his Lucca friend, the physician Guglielmo Lippi, who had died of a typhus infection a few days after his marriage. The song, dedicated to Lippi's posthumously born son Memmo, displays a simple, childlike charm such as we find in the music of Mimi and Butterfly.

X

Intermezzo Strepitoso

I

NO SOONER was *Tosca* launched than Puccini felt already 'sick to death of being *inoperatic*',* as he wrote to Elvira in February, a mere month after its first performance; and in August he described himself to Ricordi as '*il vostro operaio disoccupato*'—'an unemployed workman of yours'. The search for a suitable new subject now began to be an obsession. Old plans were taken up and dropped again, and new ones considered.

Thanks to some recently published letters, addressed by Puccini and Ricordi to Illica,[63] we are now in a position to trace the course of Puccini's operatic projects immediately after *Tosca* with far greater accuracy than hitherto. He was still putting the finishing touches to his 'Roman' opera when he requested Illica (15 November 1899) to read *Pelléas et Mélisande*, a very strange suggestion, since he knew perfectly well and had, we recall, been told by Maeterlinck in person that this subject was in Debussy's hands.†
In the same letter he also reminded Illica of *La Faute de l'Abbé Mouret*—'although Zola had promised it to others; but who knows if after *Bohème* in Paris and *Tosca* (if it goes well) he might not change his mind?' The reason why Puccini reverted to this old subject was evidently a report he had read in a French or Italian paper that Zola had granted the composing rights to Leoncavallo, and this whetted his desire again. While in Paris during 1900, he asked Zola about this report, but Zola replied that the musical rights were still reserved for Massenet.‡ Puccini's gallery of 'might have beens' was further enriched by *La Glu*, Jean Richepin's verse play which deals with the theme of mother love, a theme holding great attraction for Puccini, as seen in *Butterfly* and *Suor Angelica*. There was, further, *Le Dernier Chouan* by Balzac, *Aphrodite* by Pierre Louÿs, who will figure more prominently later on, and *La Tour de Nesle* by the elder Dumas; and at the suggestion of his Lucca friend Baccelli, he even contemplated so unpromising a subject as episodes from the life of the Numidian King Jugurtha who came to a tragic end at the hands of the Romans. Similarly, in November 1899 Illica drew his attention to Dostojevsky's autobiographical *Memoirs of*

* The word *inoperaio*, which Puccini uses here, was coined by him as a pun, with the double meaning of 'being without work' and 'without opera'. The correct Italian expression would be '*inoperoso*'—'workless'.

† Also Maeterlinck's *Monna Vanna*, set in medieval Tuscany, was briefly considered in 1903.

‡ In the event, it was not Massenet but his pupil Alfred Bruneau who wrote, not an opera, but incidental music for a dramatized version of Zola's novel (Paris, 1907).

a House of the Dead recounting the Russian writer's experiences as an exile in Siberia, but Puccini who had already read it found that it would need a lot of work to adapt it for the operatic stage.* Another Russian subject proposed by Illica was *Siberia* of which he sent the composer an outline of the plot, but what the latter disliked in it were the 'Russian costumes *à la Feodora* (a reference to Giordano's opera of 1898) and the deportation scene which reminded him too much of his own *Manon Lescaut*.† Puccini also rejected, after showing a genuine interest in them, Victor Hugo's *Notre Dame de Paris* and *Les Misérables*, whose principal motive—the life-long feud between two men—was not one to appeal to him. Nor did anything materialize from Sardou's suggestion, made in May 1903, to set his play, *Gismonda*, to music. Equally still-born was the project for an opera after Gerhart Hauptmann's social drama, *Die Weber*, whose realism was not of the kind favoured by Puccini; ten years later his interest in another play by the eminent German playwright, *Hanneles Himmelfahrt*, was similarly short-lived. A one-act drama, *Don Pietro Caruso*, by the Neapolitan writer, Roberto Bracco, was rejected on account of its brutal action. Puccini further considered a *Lea*, after the drama by Felice Cavallotti, and made enquiries of the Spanish playwright, Angel Guimerá, about his Catalan drama, *Tierra Baixa*, but this had already been promised to Eugen d'Albert.‡ Then there was Rostand's *Cyrano de Bergerac*, later set by Franco Alfano who completed Puccini's sketches for the last two scenes of *Turandot*. And from Ricordi came the repeated suggestion to take up *Maria Antonietta*; but for Puccini this subject suffered 'from the faded and much worn colours of the French Revolution', though this did not prevent him from giving it most serious consideration several years later.

We must now devote some space to Puccini's repeated attempts at a collaboration with Gabriele D'Annunzio, attempts which began as early as 1894 and were continued for nearly twenty years, up to 1913. An association between Italy's most eminent living opera composer and her most important poet of the time would, had it born fruit, have paralleled that of Strauss and Hofmannsthal in Germany. But it proved abortive and the chief reason for this failure lay in the fact that the two artists, though close contemporaries, inhabited different spiritual worlds and therefore never succeeded in speaking the same language. On the face of it, their efforts to work together were genuine and serious enough, and even shortly before their relationship was to come to an end Puccini was able to write to D'Annunzio:

> I persist to have from you what I am looking for and need. You know little perhaps my hypersensitivity hidden under the mask of a big, strong man which makes me at first appear quite different from what I am. Only through familiarity and frequent meetings with me can one really come to understand

* This Dostojevsky subject was later used by Janáček for his opera, *From the House of the Dead* (1930).

† *Siberia* was set later by Giordano, to a libretto by Illica (1903).

‡ D'Albert's *Tiefland* (1903), based on Guimerá's play, represents the most successful example of veristic opera in Germany.

my timid nature. But you are a judge of men and I am sure you will intui-
tively understand what I am. I therefore persist that you should make vibrate
my musical spirit and with it bring my public to weeping, laughter and to
tender delight (27 August 1912. *C.P.*Let.601).

Yet the truth was that, despite this and similar utterances, in his heart of
hearts Puccini felt that a collaboration with D'Annunzio would never lead
to happy results. And there were other people, too—'those facile prophets
who whisper and trumpet it about' (D'Annunzio) that a combination
Puccini–D'Annunzio was doomed to failure.

The first attempt to bring the two together was made by Carlo Clausetti*
and dates back to the summer of 1894 when Puccini was in the midst of
his work on *Bohème*. Clausetti had apparently put out feelers to D'Annunzio
to interest him in writing a libretto for Puccini to which the poet reacted
favourably but he demanded an exorbitant fee. In requesting Clausetti to
obtain more reasonable terms, Puccini writes to him on 18 July 1894:

> For years and years it had been my idea to obtain something original and
> tender from Italy's first talent. Explain to him my kind of style—poetry and
> again poetry, tenderness mixed with pain, sensuality, a drama surprising and
> burning, and a rocketing finale (*C.P.*Let.107).

'Italy's first talent' was a fine and generous tribute. But this should be
compared with what the composer wrote to Clausetti twenty-six years
later about D'Annunzio:

> Everything you say I foresaw and felt long ago. The Poet has little feeling
> for the lyrical theatre.† Pass it in review and you will see that I am right. He
> always lacked the sense of true, pure and simple humanity. Everything is
> is always a paroxysm, a tightly drawn cord, an excess of expression (11
> November 1918. *C.P.*Let.736).

Yet in the mid-1890s, the period of Puccini's first enthusiasm for D'Annunzio, the poet, whose major works were still to come, had not yet developed
that intoxicating verbal opulence and that swashbuckling virtuosity in the
manipulation of far-stretched and extravagant similes which characterized
his later style, and this would account for the composer's eagerness to
collaborate with him. Yet for an unknown reason—it may well have been
D'Annunzio's impossibly high financial terms‡—nothing materialized on that
occasion. Six years later another attempt was made to harness them together

---

* Clausetti was a composer and author and later became manager of Ricordi's. He was
a devoted friend of Puccini's and there are a number of letters to him in which the composer
discussed highly interesting points of his dramaturgy.

† Puccini's judgment that D'Annunzio had 'little feeling for the lyrical theatre' is coloured
by a strong bias against him and is vitiated by the success of Pizzetti's *Fedra* and Zandonai's
Francesca da Rimini for both of which D'Annunzio wrote the libretto. And the list of other
works based on texts by the Italian poet is certainly not negligible: *Figlia di Jorio* (Franchetti),
Parisina (Mascagni), *La Nave* (Montemezzi), *Sogno d'un tramonte autunno* (Malipiero, unpubl.),
Canzone del Quarnaro (Dallapiccola) and *Le Martyre de Saint Sébastien* (Debussy).

‡ D'Annunzio's published correspondence shows that he well knew how to market
his great talent to the best pecuniary advantage.

when the intermediary was Paolo Tosti, the well-known song writer and a mutual friend of the two artists. If Tosti entertained the sanguine hope that a masterpiece would spring from such an association he could not have been more mistaken. By then D'Annunzio was already displaying the qualities in his writings which were poles apart from what Puccini looked for in a libretto. It is small wonder, then, that he should have greeted Tosti's suggestion with the following comment made to Illica:

> O wonder of wonders! D'Annunzio my librettist! Not for all the riches of the world. Too intoxicating and heady—I want to stand upright on my legs. . . . (15 May 1900. *C.P.Let.226*).

Nevertheless, he and D'Annunzio did get together, and the first of a series of subjects the poet was to suggest over a period of years was *Il Cecco d'Ascola*, later known as *L'Alchimista*, about which he told the composer at great length and promised to send him a scenario. But the matter did not develop further.

2

There was, however, one subject which at the time held him more forcibly than any other and which he might have used, had it not been for legal obstacles in connection with the composing rights. This was the celebrated novel *Tartarin de Tarascon* by Alphonse Daudet, a riotous burlesque on the grandiloquence and braggadocio of the author's fellow-Provençals, with a hero reminiscent of Don Quixote. On the face of it, it hardly seemed the right kind of material for Puccini; but it appears that, in reaction from the stark melodrama of *Tosca*, he now felt an urgent desire to turn to the other extreme and relax in a boisterous comedy. It was the first time in his career that his thoughts veered in the direction of comic opera, and another eighteen years were to pass before he was to compose one, *Gianni Schicchi*. How strong this urge was after *Tosca* may be seen from the fact that in addition to Daudet's novel he simultaneously considered Goldoni's *La Locandiera*,★ and *Daphnis* by the witty French writer Paul de Kock, which was set in ancient Greece, and therefore reminded Puccini of Saint-Saëns's comic opera *Phryné* (1893).

It was, however, *Tartarin* on which his mind was set. Its first mention occurs as a mere afterthought in the same letter to Illica of 15 November 1899 in which Puccini referred to Maeterlinck's *Pelléas*. Illica apparently paid no attention to his suggestion and it was not until six months later, during which period the composer himself had been considering other ideas but must have also given some thought to the French subject, that he returned to it:

Milan
16 May 1900

Dear Illica,

Have you *Tartarin* among your books? If so, read it and think of a scenario with six or seven scenes. That is all I can tell you at present. It's an idea that

★ Set by Salieri in 1773.

came into my head some time ago. I return to it, with little hope of finding something better. But it's not a bad subject, and I believe that this character, who was once popular, has such comicality in him that he would deserve to be covered with musical notes. The public has seen so much of tears that I believe it will not look with a surly face on the adventures of the Tarascon. . . (C.P.Let.227).

There were, however, two initial doubts in Puccini's mind—one that *Tartarin* might invoke comparison with Verdi's *Falstaff*, and the other that the action might be dominated by one character only (*unipersoneggiante*). But he soon brushed these doubts aside and by the end of May Illica submitted the outline of the plot whose merits and demerits Puccini discussed in a letter to the librettist in great detail (2 June). A week later (9 June), a day before the composer was leaving for the London production of *Tosca*, he wrote Illica another letter expressing unstinted enthusiasm for Daudet's subject, and adumbrating how he envisaged the final scene of the opera— Tartarin's triumphant return to his native Tarascon after his breathtaking adventures in the wilds of Algeria. Again we note Puccini's eye for an effective stage-picture and its details:

> . . . A large square with oleander trees of diverse colours, white houses in the style of those of Palermo and Malta, the sky a dark cobalt blue, sun, a large practicable bridge over the Rhône in the background. A big Farandole with chorus who come running ahead of Tartarin and his Tarascon march. Groups of singing and shouting villagers. . . All this with much gaiety and with the impetuosity of the southern French—orchestra, chorus, bands [on the stage] and bells—in short, a rapid and fulminant scene. It will consist of one musical number and the close must be gay, warm-hearted, radiant, rich and clamorous. We shall make this opera an original, diverting and youthful work! Strength and courage! I shall see you on my return (C.P.Let.232).

So far, so good. But the first hitch in this promising venture was caused by Illica. Bombarded by Puccini with letter after letter indicating how he ought to treat the subject, foreseeing great difficulties in tailoring it to the composer's exigencies and having embarked on this work single-handed, Illica lost heart. Giacosa, it should be added, had apparently withdrawn from the collaboration in a huff, either because he had been against the whole idea or, more probably, because of his resentment at not having been informed about it in time. Giacosa issued, moreover, a public denial of reports that had meanwhile appeared in the Press announcing his collaboration in Puccini's new opera. An additional damper on Illica's waning enthusiasm was put by the businesslike Ricordi, who advised him, before proceeding further with his work, to await the reply of an inquiry made of the Society of French Authors as to the position regarding the musical rights of Daudet's novel.*

Indeed, Illica himself had begun to entertain doubts about this subject in

---

* It appears that Puccini wanted to use not the first part of the novel (1872), but its conclusion, *Tartarin sur les Alpes* and *Tartarin Voyageur* (1885).

specific relation to Puccini, considering it too earthy and coarsely robust for his style. It so happened that he had for some time been engrossed in a subject of his own invention—a satire set in eighteenth-century Milan, which he regarded as far more suitable for the composer and which he now proposed to him, seeing that his mind was set on a comic subject. But Ricordi, for reasons which will become clear at once, did not look upon this new project with favour; and in trying to dissuade Illica from it wrote him an amusing letter encouraging him to adhere to the original idea of *Tartarin*:

16 July 1900

... I'm not ignoring your doubts about the merits of *Tartarin*: it will be difficult painstaking work, but it seems to me to lend itself to a spectacle *sui generis*, with eight or nine tableaux. Look only at *Cendrillon* by Massenet,* the libretto insipid and without life, the characters antiquated, and yet it filled the Teatro Lirico on nearly thirty evenings! Although there is no music in it, or only music which is whimsical (*barocco*). I believe that the public has its cycles like the farmer's soil. There were years when it suffered from indigestion from the big operas (*operoni*), with five acts and eight scenes! Then came the one-acts, the little acts, the simple operas, the Cavallerias and the Pagliaccis! Now we go back again to the spectacle and the *mise en scène*. To all this *Tartarin*, I believe, will lend itself. Certainly, I can see many difficulties ahead but it is not impossible. On the contrary. 'Impossible' is a word which did not exist in our dictionaries at one time—the time when we chatted amicably, argued and invented new ideas, but this did not make us draw the revolver! Nor did we believe in discontinuing our mutual friendships and esteem for each other! But those times belong to prehistory! The times of *Bohème*! Now we go this way and now that way! And like John the Baptist, the one draws strength from the waters of Giordano and does not want to taste the waters of other springs; the other chases after leaves to make himself a crown of laurels or a mattress to rest upon (*L*).†

Ricordi must have received an immediate reply from Illica expressing himself unconvinced by the publisher's arguments. Four days after the above letter (20 July), Ricordi again wrote to the librettist, once more impressing on him the dramatic advantages of the French subject over Illica's Milanese satire; the latter, he reasoned, was too subtle and elegant to appeal to a large public, to say nothing of the fact that it 'plays on a single emotional string'. Illica's indecision and hesitancies were finally resolved by the negative reply that arrived from the Society of French Authors, informing Puccini that Daudet had, some years before his death in 1897, sold the composing rights of *Tartarin* to an obscure French composer who had used it for an unsuccessful operetta, and who, pretending that he possessed exclusive

* A fairy-tale opera on the Cinderella subject (after Perrault) and the most successful French opera of the *Hänsel und Gretel* type (Paris, 1899).

† The piqued tone in the latter part of Ricordi's letter was due to the tantrums which Illica was now beginning to throw. In the last sentences the publisher gives vent to his annoyance that Illica was collaborating with Giordano, protégé of the rival firm of Sonzogno, while 'the other' who 'chases after leaves' was Giacosa, who had been devoting a great deal of time to the writing of his play *Come le foglie—Like the Leaves*—which was produced in January of 1900.

rights, refused to grant Puccini permission.* This involved story was not closed until five years later when Puccini, once again seized by the urge to write a comic opera, resurrected the idea of a *Tartarin*. In the spring of 1905 he had been informed by Daudet's widow that her husband's·novel was free again, and his immediate reaction was to ask Illica to prepare the libretto for which the French writer Maurice Vaucaire was to provide the French version. But that was as far as he went, for, strangely enough, the apprehension which five years before he had confidently brushed aside as a 'mere phantom' had risen up in him once more and could not be banished again; as he put it to his first English biographer, Wakeling Dry, on the occasion of the London production of *Butterfly* in July 1905: 'I have always thought when coming to the point that I should be accused, if I set *Tartarin*, of copying Verdi.'†

3

We revert again to the period immediately following *Tosca*. Our account of Puccini's exasperating search for a suitable subject would not be complete without a glance at his brief flirtation with the idea of turning Benjamin Constant's autobiographical novel *Adolphe* into a libretto. Being essentially of a highly self-analytical and reflective character, with little exterior action, the novel would have been extremely difficult to dramatize; besides, it did not present the kind of sentimental tragedy that would have fired the composer's imagination. Nevertheless, he considered it for some time— no doubt because Constant's hero has much in common with Prévost's Des Grieux and thus with Puccini's own hero in *Manon Lescaut*.‡ Like Des

* Émile Pessard whose *Tartarin sur les Alpes* was given in Paris in 1888.

† *Giacomo Puccini*, by Wakeling Dry. London, 1906.

Readers of Adami's *Epistolario* will recall an account he gives of a visit supposed to have been paid by Puccini to the dying Daudet, when the poet's noble face, now wasted by his malady, lit up at the thought that his Tartarin might become the hero of a Puccini opera. This sentimental story must be discounted on two grounds. One is that, if this visit did really take place, it must have been in 1897, the year in which Daudet died. Yet no mention is made of this visit either in Puccini's published letters of that period or in Fraccaroli's biography (op. cit.). It is most unlikely that the composer would have omitted to refer to this incident when he was in the habit of relating incidents of far less personal interest to him. The first time he mentions *Tartarin* at all was late in 1899, two years after this apocryphal visit. Secondly, even supposing that he had been to see Daudet, it is inconceivable that the poet would not have told him that he had already sold the musical rights of his novel to some other composer. And as we have seen, it was not until 1900 that Puccini received the inform- ation from the Society of French Authors that the novel was not free. Adami's story is but one of a number whose probability is vitiated by documentary or factual evidence.

‡ There are in fact many passages in Constant's book that might have almost strayed in from the novel by Prévost. Thus, Adolphe expresses himself in the same self-pitying words as Des Grieux: 'What have I not sacrificed for Elléanore! For her sake I left home and family; for her sake I have grieved my old father, who is still lamenting over me, far away; for her sake I am living in this place where my youth slips away in solitude, without glory, without honour and without delight.' Constant's novel later provided the subject for Montemezzi's *Hellera*, to a libretto by Illica (Turin, 1909).

Grieux, Adolphe is a weakling, he weeps at moments of emotional stress and he attempts suicide because of unrequited love—in short, a Wertherian character for whom Puccini, one presumes, might have felt the same sympathy as he displayed for Manon's hapless lover. On the other hand Adolphe's mistress, Elléanore—a composite portrait of the formidable Madame de Staël and of Anna Lindsay, with both of whom Constant had had a liaison—was not the type of heroine for whom Puccini could have found much use. It is interesting to see on what grounds he rejected *Adolphe* as an operatic subject. Writing to Ricordi on 20 November 1900, he says:

> . . . I have read *Adolphe* and found it very poor material indeed . . . no salient incidents except for the scene, visualized by Illica, of the Polish dance, with appropriate lament and love-scenes; all the rest is a true and sincere description of the internal struggle of a man who loves, but is tired of loving a woman older than himself and whom he does not respect. . . It is impossible to modify the ending, that is, find a different situation for the ending. Either in bed like Mimi, or on a settee like Violetta.
>
> I know that Illica can find means of making changes and adding incidents, but the subject is too similar to that of *Traviata*, without the aura of youth about the head of Violetta.
>
> The protagonist is already the mother of two boys of about eight or ten years old. In fact, I have not yet found *any* subject. I am in despair and am tormenting my mind . . . (*E*).

Puccini, however, was contradicting himself when he wrote that he had not yet found 'any subject'. He *had,* and moreover had decided in its favour— more or less—declaring in the selfsame letter that the more he thought about it the more it attracted him. Indeed, this subject had been haunting him since the previous summer and it was owing largely to unduly protracted negotiations with its author for the musical rights that the impatient composer had in despair continued his search for other subjects in so many different directions. The subject in question was the play *Madam Butterfly* by David Belasco.

4

In 1898, there had appeared in the American *Century Magazine* a realistic story entitled *Madam Butterfly* which dealt with the desertion of a little geisha by an American naval officer, to whom she bore a child after she had been abandoned by him. The author of this story, said to have been based on a true episode—this was later confirmed to Puccini by the wife of the Japanese Ambassador to Italy—was one John Luther Long. Long was a practising lawyer in Philadelphia and had never been to Japan; but his sister, a Mrs. Irwin Corell, the wife of an American missionary at Nagasaki, who knew the country from long first-hand experience, had provided him with. authentic details about its customs and manners; it is probable that she also told him about the sad episode of the geisha, who, as we learn from Long's story, had been converted to the Christian faith at the American Missionary House at Nagasaki.* Modelling his tale to some extent on Pierre Loti's once much-read novel *Madame Chrysanthème* (1887), Long had caught most convincingly the atmosphere of Japan at the turn of the century, when Western influence was asserting itself with increasing force. His story created a stir in America, so much so that immediately after its publication two well-known actresses, Maud Adams and Julia Marlowe, approached the author to obtain his permission for a stage adaptation. But it was David Belasco, then at the height of his fame as a playwright and theatrical producer, to whom Long eventually granted the dramatic rights and who, with Long's collaboration, dramatized the story. It is said that Belasco had been so impressed by its suitability for the stage that even before the agreement with Long was drawn up he had already written half his play. Being in one act, *Madam Butterfly* was given in a double bill with his farce *Naughty Anthony*, when first produced at the Herald Theatre, New York, on 5 March 1900; the name-part was taken by the famous actress Blanche Bates, a kind of American Sarah Bernhardt. Like Long's story, Belasco's play was an immediate 'hit',† and some seven weeks later Belasco brought it to London, where it was given, together with Jerome K. Jerome's *Miss Nobbs*, at the Duke of York's Theatre, on 29 April, with Evelyn Millard as Butterfly. The play repeated its New York success and ran before packed audiences until well into July. The London Press declared it 'a rare theatrical find, a gem of simplicity' and even the dramatic critic of *The Times* opined that 'in any other than an exotic setting this dramatic episode would be intolerably painful. Redeemed as it is by delicate grace and, above all, by strangeness of detail, the little play proves by no means as distressing as a bald recital may suggest, but tear-compelling merely. A tragedy to be sure, but a toy tragedy'. There were, however, critical voices objecting to the 'harrowing

* According to an article, published in the rivista *Jiji-Scingo* on 24 December 1935, Long had told Tamaki Miura, a celebrated Japanese interpreter of Butterfly, that the real Cio-cio-san's attempt at suicide was frustrated and that she remained with her child. This was confirmed by the director and secretary of the Nagasaki Museum who also declared that her name was Tsuru Yamamura; she was born at Osaka on 1 January 1851 and died at Tokio on 23 March 1899. Her son Tom Glover (or Tomisaburo Kuraba, the Dolore of the opera) was taken to Nagasaki by his father, a wealthy English merchant, and there became the pupil of Mrs. Corell's son. Tsuru could often be seen at Nagasaki wearing a cloak with the crest of the family Aghe-ha-no-cio-cio, which means 'farfalla'; and people therefore used to call her O-cio-san.

On the other hand, K. Watanabe, a Nagasaki historian, maintains that the butterfly crest is worn by all geishas, and that the real Cio-cio-san was the daughter of a *samurai* family, named Daté, whose head committed *hara-kiri* at Nagasaki.

As for the real Pinkerton, he may have been a Russian naval officer if credence is given to a story originating during the Russo-Japanese war of 1904. By then, however, Puccini's opera had *already* been produced! (see article, *La vera Cio-cio-san*, by Duiti Miyasawa. *Musica d'oggi*, January 1959).

† The sensational success of *Butterfly* prompted Belasco to further collaboration with Long which resulted in five plays, several of which again exploited the Japanese ambience, such as *The Darling of the Gods*; this was seen in London in a production by Beerbohm Tree, at His Majesty's Theatre, in 1903.

dénouement' which, they suggested, ought to take place offstage. Puccini, as we shall see, followed this advice in his opera half-way.

It was during that summer of 1900, when Belasco's play was still running in London, where Puccini was staying in connection with the production of *Tosca*, that either the then manager of Covent Garden, Frank Nielson, or Puccini's London Italian friends, the Angelis, suggested he might attend a performance of *Madam Butterfly*. As had been the case when he first saw Sardou's *Tosca*, he understood virtually nothing of the dialogue, but nevertheless came away profoundly moved by the play, in spite of or perhaps because of his inability to follow its dialogue; for this was excellent proof to him of the remarkable clarity and theatrical effectiveness of the plot. Butterfly and her fate struck deep chords in him and the exotic setting fascinated him. According to Belasco, Puccini came after the performance to the green-room, embraced the playwright and begged him to permit him to use *Madam Butterfly* for an opera. 'I agreed at once', Belasco relates, 'and told him he could do anything he liked with the play and make any sort of contract, because it is not possible to discuss business arrangements with an impulsive Italian who has tears in his eyes and both his arms round your neck.'[64]

5

Belasco was one of the most picturesque and amusing figures of the American stage in the period between 1890 and 1910; and, as we shall meet him again in connection with Puccini's *La Fanciulla del West*, it may be as well to spend a few moments in his company.

Belasco descended from a family of Portuguese Jews—originally named Valasco or Velasco—who, owing to the religious persecutions in the reign of Manuel I, had emigrated to England in the early sixteenth century. Theatrical talent was in the family: Belasco's father was a comedian whose meagre earnings suggested an artist of mediocre talent; his uncle, however, later made his name on the English stage under the pseudonym David James. When in 1848 the 'gold fever' broke out in California, the family emigrated to San Francisco, where David was born in 1853. Later, they moved again and settled at Victoria in British Columbia, where the boy was educated at a Roman Catholic monastery. Partly in sentimental recollection of his teachers but largely to flatter his histrionic sense, which was monstrous, Belasco wore in later years, evidently in imitation of Liszt, a clerical collar; he is seen adorned with this garment in every photograph. His sojourn under priestly tutelage was, however, short-lived. With the family's theatre blood in his veins, he escaped from the monastery and joined a travelling circus as a clown. It was the humble start of a sensational career. At the age of eighteen he turned actor, touring with various companies up and down the coast of California and playing any part that happened to come his way. He soon discovered that he also possessed gifts as a producer, with a particular bent for realistic stage effects. His conception of realism in the theatre went at that early period no farther than making the actresses pour real water on each other, as he did in one of his first productions of a stage version of Zola's *L'Assommoir* in 1879.

David Belasco was a kind of American Sardou, but coarser in psychological fibre than the Frenchman, on whom he modelled himself, and without the latter's wit and elegance. Like Sardou, several of whose plays he adapted for the American stage, he wrote boulevard pieces which covered every genre—farce, comedy, historical and romantic melodrama. Plays such as *Du Barry, Adrea* and *The Darling of the Gods* sailed in the wake of Sardou's shallow but highly spectacular historical tragedies. And like Sardou, he got involved in frequent lawsuits for supposed plagiarism.* Belasco's sphere was, in short, sensational plots and stirring emotional situations calculated to make a violent assault on the spectator's sensibilities. Today Belasco would have been among the most successful of screen writers. As a literary figure he was negligible: he had no points of contact with the intellectual trends of his time, and no intrinsic or pregnant ideas to advance. His sole aim was to entertain and stun a large public. His real merit lay in an imaginative eye for the *mise en scène* and in his sense of atmosphere. In these respects he appears to have played a similar role in the American theatre to that played by Stanislavsky in Russia and Reinhardt in Germany, setting a standard of perfection for the American stage such as it had not known before. To act in a Belasco production was considered a high distinction. The importance he attached to the minutest scenic details is seen from his own plays, where stage directions and descriptions of the settings often cover a page and more.† His special line as a producer was the creation of romantic illusion by cunning manipulation of the lighting and of painted curtains which resulted in an almost cinematographic effect—all done in order to saturate the audience in the atmosphere before the opening of the play. Thus the first scene of *Madam Butterfly* was preceded by a series of illuminated screens depicting in turn a ricefield, a garden of cherry blossom, and a snow-capped volcano in a sunset; the same device he employed in his *Girl of the Golden West*. It was no doubt an attempt to wed the novel technique of the cinema, then in its infancy, to the theatre. Belasco's greatest *coup*—one that earned him the epithet 'wizard of the stage'—occurred in *Madam Butterfly* in the scene of the geisha's night vigil. In order to mark the passage of time (twelve hours) Belasco counterfeited it by a series of changing effects on the open stage: dusk, the gradual appearance of the stars, the break of dawn accompanied by the chirping of birds, and sunrise; this silent scene played for fourteen minutes. Belasco himself declared, a few years before his death in 1931, that he had conceived this scene as a challenge to himself and considered it as 'my most successful effort in appealing to the imagination of those who have sat before my stage'.[65] Naïve and meretricious though these effects might appear to

* Thus, *The Darling of the Gods* contains a scene in which a military despot extorts information from a woman by compelling her to witness the tortures of her lover—a motive taken from *Tosca*.

† In a production of *The Darling of the Gods* he once shouted to the electrician at the switchboard: 'I don't want a mere moon. What I want is a *Japanese* moon'—words often quoted as a motto by other producers.

PUCCINI
CONVALESCING
AFTER HIS
MOTOR CAR ACCIDENT
IN FEBRUARY 1903

SYBIL
SELIGMAN

In hunting costume

Puccini in his motor-boat

In his first automobile

TORRE DEL LAGO

the theatregoer of today, in their time they were hailed as the dawn of modern stage technique. In conjunction with Belasco's insistence on a natural style of acting, they made an important contribution to the advancement of American stagecraft.[66]

As a man Belasco was the incarnation of vanity and naïve exhibitionism. A visitor calling on him at his office at the Belasco Theatre in New York (up to 1902, the Republic) was made to pass through a long corridor flanked by a row of flunkies, and would be announced by several gong-strokes before being admitted to the sanctum. There he would find the Great Man enthroned at an enormous table covered with all kinds of Oriental pottery and surrounded by Oriental screens, on which were pinned innumerable sheets from the manuscripts of his diverse plays. Clad in clerical black, a clerical collar round his neck—to which as a descendant of Portuguese Jews he could not lay even the semblance of a claim—and with a shock of white hair so arranged as to fall artistically over his forehead, Belasco would receive his visitor with genial condescension.

6

We have left Puccini at the point where 'among the thousand suggestions' for a subject that kept pouring in on him, he had found none suitable. This was in November 1900, some four months after he had seen *Madam Butterfly* in London. Yet during those months he had been agitating for *Madam Butterfly*, for which the negotiations with Belasco dragged on for some reason. This did not mean, however, that the composer had been altogether idle on the projected 'American' opera. He had, we recall, Belasco's verbal consent to adapting the play to a libretto, and in the confidence that sooner or later the negotiations—carried on through Ricordi's New York representative, Maxwell—would be clinched, he began in November to occupy himself with the subject. He first thought of writing a one-act opera with a prologue (the present first act), then considered that 'instead of one act [like the play] one could make two quite long acts—the first in North America [following Long] and the second in Japan. Illica would certainly find in the novel all that he wanted'.[67] The plan of an 'American' act was later discarded.

While Puccini thus kept ideas for *Madam Butterfly* simmering, an event occurred that made him desert his solitude at Torre del Lago and hasten to Milan. Verdi had died on 27 January 1901, and Puccini, together with Mascagni, Leoncavallo and many other Italian musicians, attended the funeral and the memorial concert given at La Scala on 1 February under Toscanini's direction. A month later the bodies of Verdi and his wife Giuseppina were taken from their temporary resting-place to be buried, in accordance with the composer's wishes, in the cemetery of the Home for Musicians in Milan (which Verdi had founded in 1895). It provided an occasion for the whole of Italy to pay the last tribute to its great son, and Puccini attended the solemn ceremony as the official representative of his native Lucca. (In 1905 he composed, in memory of Verdi, a short unpublished *Requiem* for chorus and organ (or harmonium), which bears the unmistakable fingerprints of the composer of *Tosca* and *Butterfly*.)*

The year 1901 arrived and still no word had come from America that an agreement had been reached with Belasco. It was not until early April—nine months after Belasco had agreed in London to give *Madam Butterfly* to the 'impulsive Italian'—that at last the contract was signed. Work on the libretto could now be begun in all earnest by Puccini's trusted Siamese twins—Giacosa and Illica. Compared with the arduous labour involved in the fashioning of the libretti for *Manon Lescaut* and *La Bohème*, the adaptation of *Madam Butterfly* proceeded with remarkable smoothness; like Sardou's *Tosca*, Belasco's play was a clever piece of stage-craft and needed, in the main, only extension into three acts. For meanwhile the composer had dropped his original idea of 'two quite long acts', insisting now and for a considerable time to come on a full-length opera in three acts. It was his sudden decision, subsequently, to revert again to the plan of a two-act structure that created the only really serious difficulty in the gestation of the libretto.

At Illica's suggestion Puccini met in spring 1902 the celebrated Japanese actress Sada Jacco, who happened to be visiting Milan in the course of a rapid tour through Italy and France where she appeared with great success in Japanese plays. He wished to hear her speak in her native language so as to obtain an authentic impression of the timbre of a female Japanese voice, with its peculiar high twitter. About the same time, he also had several meetings with the wife of the Japanese Ambassador to Italy, who 'told me many interesting things and sang me some native songs', promising also to send him a collection of Japanese folk music.[68] On being told the outline of the libretto she criticized, however, the choice of names for the different characters, considering them inappropriate, particularly that of Prince Yamadori, which she found to be 'feminine' and therefore unsuitable: according to the tradition of the Japanese theatre, the characters are given names suggestive of their sex. (As the opera shows, Puccini paid no heed to this custom.) In addition to all this information, he consulted collections and gramophone records of Japanese music and books on Japanese customs, religious ceremonies and architecture. He all but became a student of Oriental ethnography, as he did again some twenty years later for *Turandot*.

On 18 September 1902 he was able to report to Ricordi:

> *Butterfly* is going well. I have passed through an ugly and tempestuous period. . . But now it seems that things have quietened down a little. So *Butterfly* is progressing, not *à grande vitesse*, but progressing. I am at Act II, but I want now to begin to orchestrate some of Act I (E).

This letter, as reproduced in the *Epistolario*, makes no reference to the cause of that 'ugly and tempestuous period . . .', but we are probably not

---

* A facsimile page from the autograph score is reproduced in *Puccini nelle imagini*, ed. by Leopoldo Marchetti. Milan, 1949.

far from the truth in suspecting that it was one of Puccini's conjugal quarrels with Elvira over some amorous escapade of his.*

Puccini was now working steadily, pleased with the libretto which he found 'so well constructed and lyrical'. But suddenly a serious hitch occurred. We recall that he had finally settled on an opera consisting of three acts, the third of which was to play at the American Consulate at Nagasaki, when he suddenly changed his mind again, wishing to reduce it to the two acts. His reasons, given to Ricordi in a letter, were the following:

Torre del Lago
16 November 1902

Dearest Signor Giulio,

For two days I have been in my worst humour and do you know why? Because the libretto, as it stands, is no good after the end of the second act and the realization of this has very much distressed me. But now I am convinced that the opera must be in two acts! Don't get frightened!

The Consulate was a grave error.† The drama must move to its close without interruption—rapid, effective, terrible! In planning the opera in three acts we were making for certain disaster. You will see, dear Signor Giulio, that I am right. . .

Do not worry about the two acts. The first lasts a good hour, the second an hour and more—perhaps an hour and a half. But how much more effective!

In doing this I am sure of riveting the public's attention and not sending it away disappointed. And we shall have at the same time an opera with a novel shape to it and one long enough to fill a whole evening. I am writing to Illica.

Send me a word or two. I am firmly decided about this idea and am going ahead with the work (E).

Ricordi must have raised serious objections, for only three days after the above letter Puccini found it necessary to write him yet another reassuring missive. Whether he was wise in his decision remains an open question: the two-act structure of the opera was, no doubt, a contributory factor in the fiasco that attended the première; but seen in retrospect, I am persuaded that Puccini's instinct was right in thus dividing the work. We shall later have occasion to discuss this point more fully.

At first, however, Puccini did not have it all his way and the strongest opposition to his plan of telescoping the second and third acts into a single act was put up by Giacosa, who refused point-blank to have anything to do with it. We now witness the rare spectacle of Puccini genuflecting before his librettist and, like a lover who feels deserted by his lady-love, imploring him not to abandon him:

16 January 1903

Dearest Giacosa,

I left your house [the previous day] oppressed in spirit. . . I cannot bear the idea of seeing myself abandoned by you!

* The dots after that sentence suggest that either Puccini was unwilling to be more explicit to Ricordi or else, and more likely, that his explanation was suppressed by the editor of the *Epistolario*.

† Illica's principal purpose in devising this act was to vary the prevailing Japanese atmosphere of the drama by the introduction of a Western ambience.

Everything crumbles! What is now to become of poor *Butterfly* into which I am putting so much of myself?! Oh, in *La Bohème*, didn't you recast the last act twice and three times? Didn't you, on my advice, suppress the act which played in the courtyard? And that was not a bad thing after all. . . You do not see matters in the light in which I see them! How impossible that seems to me! You, a man of such clear vision!

My dear Giacosa, go back on your decision, return to the fold and collaborate, and seeing things more calmly you'll find that the work that has to be done is neither difficult nor long.

Don't desert me in the best of my operas. I await a line from you to set my mind at peace again (N).

Giacosa did not budge an inch but with sweet reasonableness expounded the reasons which decided him to withdraw. His reply, written immediately after the receipt of Puccini's letter, is worth quoting in full for its shrewd observations, which the initial fiasco of *Butterfly* proved only too true:

17 January 1903

Dear Puccini,

I too feel grieved, and profoundly so, at our dissent. I have worked on this libretto with more love than I put into the other two and was satisfied with my work. I assure you, I am not prompted to my decision by any feeling of resentment, despite the little consideration shown to me. You kept me waiting for two months. I begged Signor Giulio to settle quickly on the alterations which were to be made, since I had to start work on a play which, once started, I could not have interrupted. It is certain that if I had agreed with your ideas, I should now say to you: 'You have suited your convenience, now let me suit mine.'

But that is not the point. I am convinced—and the more I ponder it the more convinced I become—that the curtain ought to fall between the futile night vigil and Pinkerton's reappearance. The English play has no curtain there, but then the play is compressed into a single act. I can understand that it was not light-heartedly that Belasco made these sacrifices to the unity of the play because there, too, the entry of Pinkerton and Kate is bad. But if we, who had the sound idea of adding a first act, extraneous to the action, now fail to give the action sufficient development, we shall upset the equilibrium of the work and aggravate the defects of the play, to the point of rendering them intolerable. I am convinced that the result of fusing the second with the third act would be, musically, an act which would be interminable and too contrived. I am also convinced that your alterations would do away with many exquisite poetic details: I do not mean verses but poetry of an intimate, essential character. To sum up, the sketch which you brought me appears to me absurd, and I foresee (however splendid the music) a disaster with the public. And for that I will assume no responsibility whatsoever. The argument you advance about *La Bohème* is, in fact, in my favour. For you saw, once I had recognized that the suppression of an act was justified, I accepted it.

But here my artistic feeling does not agree. You will have your reason and it is best for you to adhere to it; I wish you good luck from the bottom of my heart. But seeing that there is such an absolute divergence of views between us, I must cease meddling further (though it goes without saying, my author's rights remain unaffected). Even to look at it, this work of unstitching would require painful and uninspiring labour. In order to preserve my artistic integrity and also not to arrogate to myself a merit which does not belong to me, I must let the public know what my collaboration consisted of, and I reserve the right to publish my scenes, all the scenes which had already found such enthusiastic approval on your part, on the part of Illica and Signor Giulio.

But, notwithstanding our divergence of views and notwithstanding the little consideration you have shown to me in your behaviour, I remain your friend and wish you all the best.

Postscript.—Would you like us to recast the whole libretto, following the English play from the beginning? It is risky, but a real work of art might result from it. I strongly believe in this (N).

In the end, however, the good-natured Giacosa yielded and did Puccini's bidding.

7

The orchestration of the first act was begun at Torre del Lago on 29 November 1902, but Puccini was still racking his brain over the second act. 'The work to be done', he wrote to Ricordi in an undated letter, 'is not great but it is essential to bind the whole together with a closer logic than there is in Belasco's play' (E). This problem, however, was solved without great delay, and Puccini was able to inform Ricordi that 'Illica left today (Sunday). The work is finished and we are more than thoroughly satisfied with it. We succeeded splendidly. The action now moves forward, straight and logical—it is a real pleasure. Ah! that act at the Consulate was ruining everything!' (C.P.Let.290).

With all the obstacles now cleared, Madam Butterfly seemed safely on the road to completion when Puccini met with an accident which brought his work to a sudden standstill. Soon after Tosca his passion for motor-boats had begun to extend also to motor-cars. He was the first inhabitant of Torre del Lago to yield to the lure of what was then a novel form of locomotion, and photographs of that period show the composer proudly sitting at the steering-wheel, with chauffeur's cap, goggles and all. A persistent throat complaint had made it necessary for him to consult a specialist at Lucca and on 25 February 1903 he drove there with his wife and son. The consultation over, the Puccinis dined at the house of Caselli. It was a foggy night and owing to frost the roads had become slippery. Caselli tried to persuade his guests to spend the night at his house, but Puccini, although he intended to see a dentist at Lucca on the following day, insisted on returning home, his reason being that he was anxious to press on with his work on Butterfly, and night was the time when he worked best. At a spot about four miles from Lucca, in the vicinity of the village of Vignola, the car, driven by Puccini's chauffeur, skidded on a sharp bend, rolled over the embankment, crashed into a field some fifteen yards below and overturned. Elvira and Tonio escaped with shock while the chauffeur, who was flung out of the car, sustained a fracture of the thigh. Puccini could not be found at first, until he was discovered lying under the overturned car, unconscious and nearly asphyxiated by the escaping petrol fumes. Fortunately a doctor, Dr. Sbragia, who happened to live not far from the spot where the accident occurred, had heard the crash, hastened to the scene and had Puccini carried to his house. There he diagnosed a fracture of the right shin and a number of contusions. The next morning Puccini was brought back in a motor-boat to Torre del Lago, where the fracture was immediately set, yet so badly that after a time it was necessary to break the bone again and reset it, which left Puccini with a permanent limp. Moreover, a wound sustained in the accident refused to heal and this led to the discovery that Puccini was suffering from a mild form of diabetes. His convalescence took a full eight months. At first he was unable to work at all—'I am all plaster-cast', he wrote to an (unidentifiable) friend on 18 March, 'my legs are emaciated, without flesh, and they have put me on a diet of five meals a day with strychnine and Karlsbad water. . .' (M).

Later in the spring he was able to resume work, though in a condition of 'semi-nursery'; he was permitted to leave his bed and repair to the piano by means of a wheel-chair, his 'automobile without fuel' (Puccini was, like Schumann, Wagner and Stravinsky, a 'piano' composer). Yet for a man of Puccini's temperament the slow recovery was more than he could bear. Writing to Illica on 13 May he says: 'I can't tell you how I feel! . . . Farewell to everything, farewell to *Butterfly*, farewell to my life! It's terrible! And I am now really completely discouraged. I try to pluck up courage, but I don't succeed in calming myself' (*C.P.Let.*313). Yet there was something besides his illness to aggravate his misery. This was a major crisis in his relationship with Ricordi which now reached its culmination. It came to a head through the fact of Puccini's curiously slow convalescence which the publisher suspected to be also due to a sordid cause (a venereal infection), a suspicion aroused in him by his knowledge that Puccini was carrying on an affair with a woman from Piedmont. After a long, studiously maintained silence which gave Puccini much to think, Ricordi penned on 31 May a letter which must have been one of the longest he ever wrote to the composer. The gist of this letter to his 'caro, amatissimo Puccini' was that, though the motor accident was the primary cause for the present state of his slow recovery, it was also due to things that had happened before the accident by which Ricordi implied Puccini's sexual excesses, and he reminded him of the many warnings he had given him and of the sacrosanct promises Puccini had made to mend his ways but had never fulfilled. After some more general remarks and vague allusions Ricordi comes down to brass-tacks, and not mincing his words, writes:

> But is it at all possible that a man like Puccini, that an artist who moves millions of people and makes them cry with the power and spell of his creation, can become a ridiculous and ugly toy in the meretricious hands of a vulgar and contemptible woman? . . . Does this man no longer possess the faculty of a fair judgment? . . . And does this man not realize the immense distance that separates love from repellent obscenity which destroys in a man

his moral personality and physical vigour? . . . This low creature, with the instincts of a whore, gains possession of the heart, mind and body of such an outstanding artist, and with sensual obscenity which would have led him to his moral and physical death, makes him a plaything in a way as to appear in his eyes as a good fairy, loving and inspiring! I say it and confirm it with loud voice—she is a base and vile creature. Isn't she a corrupt woman who gets him under her thumb and like a foul vampyre sucks his mind, blood and life?

Ricordi impresses on Puccini that only in an intense desire for work which had been so unfortunately interrupted, lies his salvation and he concludes with the peroration:

Who knows how great your impatience and feeling of rebellion will be when you read this letter! Poor boy!—But I don't regret it. I now feel calmer and alleviated and I say to this letter: go, penetrate his heart and persuade him in the name of God of the great, true and loyal affection which has dictated you, and with a similar affection I tenderly embrace you,

Suo Giulio Ricordi*

Ricordi may well have seen things in too lurid a light, and the terms in which he refers to the Piedmontese woman read almost like a description of the vamp Tigrana in Puccini's forgotten *Edgar*. Yet, if there are exaggerations in his letter, they spring from the profound and compassionate concern Ricordi felt for the spiritual and physical well-being of his 'caro, amatissimo Puccini'.

Not unexpectedly, to the composer this epistle appeared to be a 'real inquisition', and writing to Illica soon after its receipt he declared, perhaps by way of self-defence, that it is 'not convincing nor does it conform to the truth, and it is little generous to a certain person . . . without proofs one cannot level such accusations,† but suggestions and gossip had made him judge too harshly. He is also wrong with regard to my illness. I would like to answer him, but with my present tooth-ache I do not feel inclined. If I could only speak with him! What shines through his letter is his affection for me, and this is a great consolation for me. You know much I suffered from his silence towards me! This was a real cross. I would like to speak to him about it. I am not good at refuting things, especially by letter . . .,(*C.P.*Let.315).

In due course composer and publisher met, talked the affair over and finally cleared the air of the dark clouds of dust the incident had raised.

In late summer we find Puccini recuperating at the mountain resort of Boscolungo in the Apennines, whence he informed Ricordi on 29 August that he was 'fat and flourishing again like a chaffinch', yet still walking with great difficulty and always on two sticks'. The cure, according to his doctor, would be 'a lengthy affair' and 'it will be a year and a half at least before I

---

* This letter is quoted in full in Claudio Sartori's *Puccini* (Milan, 1858), p. 62–68, and with discreet omissions in the *Carteggi pucciniani*, Let.315, n.2.

† Puccini was to be cured of his illusion when the liaison with the woman ended and when, under some legal pretext, she raised in the following November claims of a financial nature which suggests that she was an unscrupulous adventuress.

can walk like any other Christian' (*E*). In the event it was almost three years before he discarded his stick. At Boscolungo a specialist from Bologna subjected 'my urine to infallible tests' when '*no trace* of glucose' was found; but this diagnosis proved wrong, for Puccini continued to suffer from diabetes till the end of his life. In the same letter he also informed Ricordi of the completion of the famous *intermezzo* which 'I think is good.★ From here to the close of the opera it will not take long and I think we could fix the première for Lent' (29 August 1903, *E*).

On 15 September Puccini finished the orchestration of the first act and the whole opera was completed on 27 December, 'at 11.10 p.m.'. Thus *Madam Butterfly* was composed in a little over three years, and would have taken less but for the accident.

Just as the score and libretto were about to be printed another storm blew up—this time between Giacosa and Ricordi. On 31 December the publisher had requested the librettist to give his consent to the omission from the published libretto of those verses in the part of Pinkerton (last act) which Puccini had not set to music. Giacosa, profoundly hurt in his pride as a poet, adamantly refused to comply and wrote to Ricordi:

1 January 1904

. . . I insist with all the power at my command that the whole text of the libretto must be printed. That mutilation might not matter to the composer but for the poet it is a most wounding offence. I cannot pass a scene which has no proper prosody, no syntax and no common sense. . . At the point where Pinkerton says

'Oh l'amara fragranza'

the poem is in tercines. . . Now the third verse of each tercine has been taken away. What harm is there in printing it even though the composer has not set it to music? . . .

Believe me, dear Signor Giulio, we ought to print a libretto that does not offend too plainly against literary and dramatic canons. The composer sets only that part to music which he finds to his taste. But to me it seems that the part of the tenor, reduced as it is already, disappears entirely in that interminable second act, to the greatest detriment of the balance of scenes and at grave peril for its success. Believe me, unless we give Pinkerton a little more to sing, the act is monotonous and boring. Puccini could have waited for another week to finish it and paid more respect to the equilibrium of the parts. I do not want to enter into discussion of what concerns the musical composition . . . I am only venting my doubts and fears and shall be the happiest man if the result proves me wrong. But the responsibility for the libretto is mine. . . Mark the verses which have not been set, if you like, but publish the text as it stands. . . I very much regret to put a spoke in your wheel★ on New Year's Day, but on further reflection I am sure you will agree with me (*N*).

★ This is the music accompanying Butterfly's night vigil, up to the following scene in the early morning—which in the original version was played before the open stage.

† Giacosa's idiomatic phrase was: '*piantarvi una grana*'—literally, 'to sow a grain in your way'.

From a practical point of view Giacosa's demand was unreasonable, and this Ricordi did not fail to point out with 'his usual frankness', but in an unusually bad temper:

3 January 1904

. . . Yes, you *are* putting a spoke in my wheel which grieves me very much! . . . One risks confusing the public and ruining the scenic and musical effect because people will not fail to notice that the composer did wrong in not setting the verses to music or that the poet wrote superfluous verses. . . If the verses are not included in the libretto, then no one will be puzzled— however good or bad they may be. I am speaking from practical musical experience and I tell you that what Puccini did was good—very good, and that we would ruin for him the effect of a scene which is unavoidably trouble-some. But how in heaven's name can you, a man of the theatre, believe that at that moment the *signor tenore* will stop before the prompter's box and expatiate on the qualities of poor Butterfly!!

You are Giacosa and therefore a splendid poet; yet not even Apollo, who as the God of the Sun is more splendid than you, would be able to produce suitable verses for that situation! . . .

For the rest, you said you have 'put a spoke in my wheel'; it is true and I shall prove it to you: When you write that Pinkerton sings in tercines . . . don't you remember any more that you added the third stanza subsequently yourself so as to satisfy Puccini, who had here some musical rhythm or other in mind, that he changed his mind afterwards and reverted to two stanzas only. I told you that very clearly one day when I had the pleasure of seeing you in my study while I was just comparing the words of the music with those of the libretto; and then you approved!!! . . . As for your suggestion that in order to write a romanza for the tenor he (Puccini) should jeopardize the production of his opera at La Scala. . . Go on! That is more than putting a spoke in my wheel—it's a proper Matterhorn which you pile on my shoulders!!! . . . (N).

Giacosa remained unconvinced. In an undated letter he replied to Ricordi:

I was in bed yesterday with a temperature. Your letter caught me in an exhausted state and I was not in a belligerent mood. On the other hand the dressing-down you gave me was so violent that I have no choice but to resign myself. All right: the poet may be wholly sacrificed. You had already induced me to accept the proposition that the two acts should be compressed—against all common sense—into a single act. I now resign myself also to this second imposition. But don't let us try to justify it by dramatic reasons. Pinkerton, you say, must not sing at that moment. But what about Cavaradossi? It seemed to you appropriate, did it not, that at the moment at which he learns of his freedom [Act III] he should sing those verses

'O dolci mani', etc.

which you and Puccini wanted? (N).

Giacosa then returns to the troublesome point about the tercines for Pinkerton and reaffirms petulantly his intention to inform the public later of what precisely his share was in the libretto; he closes with the parting shot:

'Now you are free to butcher my work as you please' (*N*). This letter stung Ricordi into the angry retort:

5 January 1904

... Seeing the line which our discussion has taken, I reply: Ah! no, by God, no! I don't intend to have your remonstrations afterwards! . . . Oh, no! oh, no! It seems to me ridiculous to anticipate that the omission of eight verse lines should be the cause of such a pandemonium. . .

I am among your oldest and most loyal admirers and therefore permit your admirer, when it comes to musical matters, to state that you are making an enormous mistake if you bring in the comparison with *Tosca*. Puccini was in fact uncertain whether to set those verses 'O dolci mani', but he was prompted to it by a mysterious feeling for a poetic rounding-off of the scene. A comparison is therefore not possible; this is an effusion of the most moving tenderness. Pinkerton, on the other hand, is . . . a mean American clyster [*sic*], he is a coward, he fears Butterfly and her meeting his wife, and so he beats a retreat. Puccini has composed agitated music for the orchestra which will explain Pinkerton's state of mind and which follows beautifully after a kind of trio in a slow tempo, Handel-like (*N*).

Ricordi then goes on to propose including Giacosa's hard-fought-for verses in the published libretto but without any special indication that they had not been set to music since the public would not be aware of that fact; if Giacosa will not agree to this, then he suggests appealing to Boito as the final arbiter. Giacosa agreed.

8

The first and in the end the only performance of the original version of *Madam Butterfly* was fixed to take place at La Scala on 17 February 1904. No effort was spared by the management, then under the direction of Giulio Gatti-Casazza,* to mount the opera in style. Tito Ricordi was the producer, the scenery was designed by the famous Parisian stage-painter Jusseaume and the cast was first-rate. Cio-Cio-San was sung by Rosina Storchio, a gifted and intelligent young artist whom Toscanini had recently introduced at La Scala; Pinkerton was Giovanni Zenatello and Sharpless Giuseppe De Luca. The musical direction was entrusted to Cleofonte Campanini, a contemporary of Puccini's who subsequently made frequent appearances in the Italian season at Covent Garden.

Never before had Puccini been so confident of the success of a work as he was with *Butterfly*—in his own words, he had poured into it all his heart and soul. At the rehearsals the enthusiasm of all participants—from the artists to the stage hands—was tremendous. At the end of the dress rehearsal the whole orchestra rose to a man to give Puccini a spontaneous ovation. On the day of the first night he sent Rosina Storchio a short note expressing the most sanguine expectation for the success of her performance—'Through you I am speeding to victory!' In previous years he had been at pains to discourage his family from attending any first night of his operas, not

---

* He later became the general manager of the New York Metropolitan Opera House.

wishing, as he told Fraccaroli, 'to expose them to the uncertainty of a first experiment'; but this time he felt so certain of himself that he made a special point of inviting his sisters, and he had his son, then a boy of eighteen, with him in the wings.

Puccini's hopes were dashed to the ground in a manner rare in the annals of operatic history and comparable with the scandal at the first Paris production of *Tannhäuser*. There is perhaps no better summing up of the events of that evening than that given by Ricordi in the March number (1904) of *Musica e Musicisti*:

First performance of *Madam Butterfly*, libretto by Illica and Giacosa, music by Puccini. Growls, shouts, groans, laughter, giggling, the usual single cries of *bis*, designed to excite the public still more; that sums up the reception which the public of La Scala accorded the new work by Maestro Giacomo Puccini. After this pandemonium, throughout which virtually nothing could be heard, the public left the theatre as pleased as Punch. And never before had one seen as many happy or joyous faces—satisfied as though all had shared in a general triumph. In the vestibule of the theatre the joy was at its height and there was no lack of those who rubbed their hands, underlining this gesture with the great words: *consummatum est, parce sepulto!* The spectacle given in the auditorium seemed as well organized as that on the stage since it began precisely with the beginning of the opera. This is an accurate account of the evening after which the authors, Puccini, Giacosa and Illica, in agreement with the publishers, withdrew *Madam Butterfly* and returned to the management the fee for the rights of production, notwithstanding the determination of the latter to produce the opera again.

It is worth describing the events of that evening in detail if only to perceive the depth of scandalous conduct to which an audience—or, at any rate, that part of it which had been influenced by intrigues and cabals—is capable of descending. After some initial noises, the first act, up to the entrance of Butterfly, was listened to in an ominous silence. The first disturbance occurred at the point where Butterfly sings 'Siam giunto' to the delicate Japanese theme on the orchestra: this passage was received with angry shouts 'That is from *Bohème*!'. Still, with the Italian opera public's known susceptibility to 'reminiscences' there was perhaps nothing exceptional in such shouts. The rest of the act passed quietly enough, yet made no impression at all except for the timid clapping of a few sympathetic spectators at the climax of the long love duet. The end of the act was greeted with hisses and catcalls. Still there were three curtain calls, two of which were taken by the composer limping on to the stage with a stick. The real fracas was reserved for the second act. There was a harmless incident on the stage when through a sudden swift movement Storchio's kimono billowed up in front. It was greeted with the ironic comment 'Butterfly is pregnant!'. Both her aria 'Un bel dì' and her scene with Yamadori were received with apathy. After the 'Letter' scene with Sharpless there was some applause, which turned, however, into an uproar of hisses, obscene sneers, laughter and ironic demands for '*bis!*' when Butterfly introduced her child to the Consul. Pandemonium reached its height at the end of Butterfly's vigil, during which scene (in the original version) the curtain remained raised, the orchestra playing the *Intermezzo* before the open stage. (In the opera as we have it now, Act II is divided in two parts, the curtain falling upon the night vigil, a procedure suggested to the composer by Illica as early as November 1902). In attempting to outdo Belasco in realistic details, Tito Ricordi had arranged for the imitation of a whole 'concert' of twittering birds in order to mark the break of dawn. The audience, by now in hilarious mood and treating the opera as a huge jest, capped this piece of silliness with its own brand of bird and animal cries. As one writer put it, La Scala resembled more a menagerie than an opera house. The fate of the opera was sealed. Though its tragic dénouement succeeded in damping the high spirits in the auditorium, the curtain fell to the accompaniment of derisive laughter, whistlings and howls.

It is my conviction—and other biographers have expressed themselves to the same effect—that the fiasco of the first *Madam Butterfly* was largely engineered. Admittedly Puccini had committed certain errors. In deciding to cast the opera in two acts, the first of which lasted nearly an hour and the second about an hour and a half, he had omitted to reckon with the limited stamina of the Milan public, which even as late as the 1900s had not yet grown inured to the length of a Wagnerian opera.★ After all, it was only a mere fifteen years since Catalani's violent fulmination against the cutting of *Die Meistersinger*; and we recall also Giovannina Lucca's monstrous suggestion to Wagner to compress the *Ring* into a single evening's entertainment. At any rate, the Milanese were not prepared to tolerate even a mild trial of their patience at the hands of a native composer. There were, in addition, a number of minor details—dramatic, scenic and musical—which collectively tended to render the first version of the opera less effective than the second, revised version—to what extent we shall see when we come to compare the two versions. Yet one thing is certain: the differences between them are not marked enough to provide the sole explanation for the flood of abuse and ridicule that was poured on the opera at its first production, while three months later, at Brescia, the revised version was received with tremendous acclaim. There was far more in that Milan fiasco than meets the eye. True, documentary evidence for the real causes behind it is lacking—even Puccini, as we shall see, confined himself to making only vague allusions to them; yet it is safe to suggest that the scandal at La Scala on that night of 17 February had all the appearance of having been the work of a well organized claque, hired by Puccini's enemies and rivals to wreck the performance with all means at its disposal—an object in which they had very nearly succeeded on the first night of *Tosca* in Rome.

A sidelight on the power which operatic claques exercised in those days at the big European opera houses is thrown by an account given by Feodor Chaliapin, who in 1901—three years before the première of *Butterfly*— sang the name-part of Boito's *Mefistofele* at La Scala for the first time in his life. In a reminiscence recently published in an English newspaper by an

★ Verdi, who knew his public, once expressed his apprehension to Monaldi that the first act of *Otello* lasted forty-two minutes—'two minutes more than necessary'. (Gino Monaldi, op. cit.)

anonymous correspondent,[69] Chaliapin gives the following description of the nefarious actions of the Milan claque:

> At this time in theatres all over Europe the claque was an institution. The claque leader would buy tickets in various parts of a theatre and install his agents in them. If the leader was paid enough his agents would applaud enthusiastically and give the performance the appearance of a popular success. But if he were dissatisfied or ignored there would be disturbances—whistling, barracking, and the shouting of insults. The custom was so firmly established that even the biggest stars paid the claques, not for their unnecessary applause but to avoid trouble and disturbance at a critical performance. Not only were ordinary theatres subject to the blackmail of these gangsters but even the State theatres. The public were helpless.

Chaliapin himself was paid a visit in his hotel room in Milan by the leader of the La Scala claque—'a very important person'—who had come to demand that the price for his goodwill be given to him in advance. A moment later, as the great singer narrated, this individual found himself rolling down the stairs!

To return to Puccini. What was his own reaction to the débâcle of *Butterfly*? In a letter to Camillo Bondi,* written the day after, he described it as 'lynching. Those cannibals didn't listen to one single note—what a terrible orgy of madmen drunk with hate!'; and four days later, on 22 February, when most Press notices had appeared, he writes to the same correspondent:

> I am still shocked by all that happened—not so much for what they did to my poor *Butterfly*, but for all the poison that they spat at me as an artist and as a man! And I can't explain why all this was done to me, who live far away from all human contacts. They have printed all kinds of things! Now they say that I am going to rewrite the opera and that it will take me six months! Nothing of the kind! I am not rewriting anything, or, at least very few details —I shall make a few cuts and divide the second act in two—something which I had already thought of doing during the rehearsals, but it was then too near the first performance. . . That first performance was a Dantean Inferno, prepared in advance. . . (*M*).

Though Puccini says he could not explain why all this was done to him† the explanation is not far to seek. By his serried successes since *Manon Lescau*, he had become a world figure and thus an object of intense jealousy on the part of his less fortunate confrères. He had, moreover, kept himself apart from his fellow-composers (though the uncomplimentary remarks he used to make about them in private remained no secret)—'away from all human contacts'—and he had refused to curry favour with influential persons, a trait we have already observed in his student days at the Conservatoire. Such conduct was little calculated to render him *persona grata* in Milan high society. 'There were people there [the first-night of *Butterfly*] who for years had waited for the joy of laying me low at whatever costs' (*M*). For these

* Camillo and Ippolito Bondi were Milan music-lovers who had been on friendly terms with the composer, apparently, since his student days there.

people Puccini had grown sufficiently fat on his ubiquitous successes to be now considered ripe for slaughter. Nor must we ignore the fact—and more will be said about it in another context—that there was a movement afoot among the younger generation of Italian musicians and critics to see the glory of their country's musical tradition not in the sphere of opera, but in that of instrumental music; and these were *ipso facto* hostile to Puccini.

The reception of *Butterfly* by the Press may be gauged from such sensational headlines as appeared the next morning: '*Puccini hissed*', '*Fiasco at La Scala*', and '*Butterfly, Diabetic Opera, Result of an Accident*'. On 20 February, a writer in *Il Secolo*, announcing the cancellation of the second performance of the opera and its substitution by *Faust*, gave it as his opinion that

> a second performance would have provoked a scandal which would have called for decided action on the part of the Milanese public, who do not relish being mocked. This opera is not one of those, like *The Barber of Seville*, which carry in them the seeds of resurrection. It reveals that Maestro Puccini was in a hurry. Importuned as he was to bring out the work this season, sick as he was, he did not find original inspiration and took recourse to melodies from his previous operas, and even helped himself to melodies of other composers. In his defence we must say that the libretto was artistically unfortunate. . . The opera is dead.*

Yet what was the verdict of the serious and fair-minded critics who tried to preserve an even keel in the hurricane caused by the first *Butterfly*? It was by no means as negative and damning as that of the majority of their colleagues. Some of their strictures are fully supported by a critical glance at the first version.† Thus, Giovanni Pozza of the *Corriere della Sera* criticized the length and disproportion of the two acts, suggesting 'many and courageous cuts', notably in the first act where the action loses itself in minute superfluous details, and where 'the music at times becomes unnecessarily repetitive and prolix'. He also faulted Puccini's insistent use of reminiscences—which 'was imprudent, risky and little pleasing'. What appears strange, however, is Pozza's statement that 'the synthetic form of Puccini's melodies is unable to express the rapid succession of changes in both the situations and the sentiments of the childlike Butterfly', when it is in this very opera that the composer evinces consummate skill in his accurate, supple musical reflection of the heroine's emotional vicissitudes. No doubt, as with *La Bohème*, the impressionist and fragmentary style of the work, combined with the novelty of its harmonic language, created obstacles for the ears of Puccini's older contemporaries who still regarded Debussy as an iconoclast. Pozza, however, fully acknowledged Puccini's genius in painting the exotic atmosphere, and singled out for special praise the 'Letter' and the 'Flower' scenes; though he came to the final conclusion

---

* An amusing footnote to Puccini's fiasco is provided by a Genoese bookseller and enthusiastic admirer of the composer, who expressed his indignation at the treatment of his idol by baptizing his newborn daughter—Butterfly!

† See pp. 397–99.

that 'the opera has not stood the test, I yet persist in believing that shortened and lightened it will rise again'. He was to prove right three months later.

9

The failure of *Madam Butterfly*—his favourite opera and the only one of his works which, on his own admission, he did not tire of hearing again and again in its entirety—was for Puccini a blow the bitter memory of which remained with him until the end of his life. Though the blow had stunned him with its unexpected violence, he recovered his spirits sufficiently to be able to write on 18 February, a day after the first night, to Camillo Bondi:

> . . . my *Butterfly* remains as it is: the most heartfelt and most expressive opera that I have conceived! I shall win in the end, you'll see—if it is given in a smaller theatre, less permeated by hatred and passion. Here I have withdrawn the opera and refunded the money, in agreement with my collaborators; and I shall not give it in Rome if I can free myself of that contract, because I am sure that even there I would have trouble, as the atmosphere is not serene— and besides, I don't want to give it there.* I shall give it in a smaller theatre, in another city, where there is tranquillity. Enough!—You'll see if I am right (*M*).

Puccini was right in feeling that a smaller theatre would be more suitable to *Butterfly*, which, with the exception of the first act, is an intimate domestic tragedy. At first Turin and Bologna were contemplated until Tito Ricordi suggested Brescia as the most suitable place for the second production. Unlike his father, who considered *Butterfly* a light-weight, not fully representative of the composer and almost beyond repair, Tito was convinced that it could be resurrected provided it were given in a theatre different in atmosphere from La Scala, and that certain alterations were to be made— '*piccoli lavorucci*', as Puccini called the work of revision. He himself would have preferred Turin, but later he was delighted at the choice of Brescia. Writing to his friend Vandini in Rome he says (undated):

> . . . Ah! if I could have my revenge I should rejoice, not so much on my account as because of all the rabble we know. We need a clamorous success, and shall I achieve it? Will the public, by that time, still remain influenced by the ill-will shown by everyone and everywhere? Let us place our hopes in the good, honest and valiant people of Brescia. . . Inform me about everything, even the scurrilous things—nothing surprises me any more now.[70]

The revised version was staged at the Teatro Grande, Brescia, on 28 May, when the part of Butterfly was taken by a new singer, Salomea Krusceniski, Rosina Storchio having in the meantime departed for Buenos Aires.† The audience, far from being a merely local one, contained a strong element of Milan's artistic world and thus lent the performance almost the appearance

---

* After the *Tosca* première Puccini nursed an intense dislike for the Italian capital for many years to come.

† 'You seem in your departure to be taking away the best, the most poetical part of my work', wrote the composer in his farewell letter to her on 22 February 1904 (*E*).

of a first night at La Scala. The evening was a triumphant vindication of Puccini's unshaken confidence in his work. No less than five numbers had to be encored* and the composer appeared ten times before the curtain. *Madam Butterfly*, 'rinnegata e felice'—'rejected and happy', as Puccini aptly quoted from the text, was launched on its swift conquest of the world. Again it was Buenos Aires which staged the first foreign production in July, with Storchio in the name-part and Toscanini conducting.† It reached Covent Garden in the following year, when it was given (in Italian) on 10 July 1905, and when the main cast consisted of a rare constellation of stars: Emmy Destinn (Cio-Cio-San), Enrico Caruso (Pinkerton), Antonio Scotti (Sharpless). The first English production in London took place at the Lyric Theatre on 16 August 1907.‡

Puccini was anxious that the opera be given in Paris at the first opportunity, considering the French capital as next in importance to Milan in the world of opera. For this production (28 December 1906) which was staged by the then director of the Opéra-Comique, Albert Carré, he agreed, at the latter's request, to make certain *ad hoc* alterations and cuts, which Ricordi, however, regarded as offending the composer's dignity. Some of these cuts were necessary because the singer of Butterfly, Marguerite Giraud, the wife of Carré, 'feels that the strain would otherwise be too much for her strength', and Puccini feared that without her the opera would be 'put on one side and that will be the end of it!'. His estimation of Madame Carré—or 'Madame *pomme de terre*', as he would refer to her in his private correspondence—was: 'she's weak and has little intelligence'.[71] This judgment is somewhat surprising, for Mme. Carré excelled in such delicate roles as Massenet's Manon and the Puccinian Mimi.

Thanks to Tito Ricordi's enterprise *Butterfly* was taken on a seven-months tour through North America between 1906 and 1907, a venture that had not been attempted before with an opera there. Puccini made a special journey to attend the New York production on 11 February 1907.

After the First World War it became a fashion to engage Japanese singers in the name-part to heighten the authenticity of the exotic ambience—

* Among them, Butterfly's aria, 'Un bel dì', the 'Letter' and 'Flower' scenes and the Humming Chorus which now concludes the first part of the last act.

† Toscanini's later view of the opera was nothing if not damning. He is quoted as saying that 'Puccini was very clever, but only clever. Look at Cio-Cio-San. She thinks he [Pinkerton] is returning at last. Listen to the music. Sugary. Look at Verdi in *Traviata*. Listen to the agitation of the music, the passion, the truthfulness'. (*Toscanini*, by Howard Taubman. London, 1951.)

Toscanini also thought Boito's *Nerone* in many ways superior to the best of Puccini's operas.

‡ A highly amusing though apocryphal anecdote is told in connection with a Manchester production of which Tito Ricordi was in charge. As according to the Lord Chamberlain's regulations young children were not permitted to appear in theatrical performances after a certain evening hour, Tito lighted on the idea of engaging a male midget for the part of Butterfly's young child. This worked splendidly for several performances until one night, at the point of the action at which Butterfly embraces her child, the midget was overcome by a feeling all too human in this situation and responded to his 'mother's' affectionate gesture with most unfilial passion. *Se non è vero è ben trovato!*

much to the dislike of the composer, who found 'these gramophone voices not very pleasant' (S). One wonders what his reaction would have been to the all-Japanese productions now being given in Butterfly's native land?

The completion of *Butterfly* all but coincided with the legalization of the composer's marital status. By the death of Elvira's first husband in 1903 the obstacle to a *de jure* recognition of their union had been removed and the church ceremony took place on 3 January 1904. The entry in the church register of Torre del Lago reads:

> Maestro Giacomo Puccini, son of Michele and Albina Magi, and Elvira Bonturi, widow of Narciso Gemignani, born at Lucca and resident in this village, having obtained the dispensation of the three canonical bans, being free of the impediment of crime and with no canonical impediment now existing against the valid and lawful celebration of their marriage, having been questioned *in facie Ecclesiae* and their consent *per verba de praesenti* having been received, were by me here [Father Michelucci], subscribed the third of January 1904, united in the holy bonds of Matrimony in the presence of the two witnesses, Dr. Rodolfo Giacchi and Giuseppe Razzi.[72]

Lean Years

I

EVEN FOR SO SLOW-WORKING A COMPOSER as Puccini, the interval of seven years separating *Butterfly* from his next opera, *La Fanciulla del West*, must be regarded as inordinately long.* What was the cause of it? A combination of three factors. First, with *Butterfly* the composer began to undertake more extensive travels than before—both in Italy and abroad—in order to supervise the productions of his favourite opera so that it 'should suffer the least possible ill-treatment'; this meant less time for his creative work. Secondly, he was growing tired of the line he had pursued in those 'old carcases—*Bohème, Butterfly and Co.*' and was now aiming at an opera 'modern in construction and moving'.[73] Yet in his searches for a subject that would lend itself to such treatment, he was striking out in directions which only after months of wasteful effort he recognized as blind alleys. And thirdly, in his private life he was to pass through a shattering experience, disruptive in its influence on his work. There is pathos in the fact that Puccini's prime of life should have been the least creative period of his whole career, a period at the beginning of which he had indeed been moved to write to Ricordi that 'never before have I felt time flow more swiftly and so intense a desire to go on. But *on*, not back!'[74]

In his searches for a new subject Puccini was not the man to allow grass to grow under his feet. While in the midst of the rehearsals for the La Scala production of *Butterfly* he already corresponded with Valentino Soldani about a *Margherita da Cortona* suggested to him by this Tuscan playwright in Florence shortly before. Its mysticism, its religious songs and the pristine atmosphere of the 12th century—all this seemed to have a strong appeal for Puccini who for two years toyed with this project on and off, finally to abandon it.† (He was to set a similar subject twelve years later in *Suor Angelica*). He also read Soldani's *Ciompi* and *Calendimaggio* finding the latter 'full of life and emotion' but criticized if for being 'troppo politico'—'Yes, I would have liked a political background but far more simple and with the drama more developed'. Nor did Illica's suggestion for one of Edgar Allan Poe's short stories fall on fertile ground, any more than did Ricordi's for a *Romeo e Giuletta*, while Puccini himself was thinking of Giacosa's *La Dame de Challant* which he soon declared to be little suited for him. The same, no doubt, was also true of Georges Rodenbach's

---

* In this calculation only the dates of completion are considered.
† Soldani later fashioned this subject into a play of that name.

symbolistic novel, *Bruges la Morte*, much acclaimed at the time.* And so the tale of Puccini's frantic searches continued. He even went to the Bible and thumbed through an old Lucchese chronicle by his medieval compatriot, Giovanni Sercambi; he wrote to Giacosa, after denying the truth of a newspaper report that he was contemplating to collaborate with the poet, Giovanni Pascoli—for suggestion for a new subject; and on 11 June he informs his sister Dide that he was already 'thinking and discussing the new libretto the title of which I must keep a secret for the moment' (*E*). The identity of this libretto is unknown. It may have been a *King Lear* or a *Benvenuto Cellini*, two subjects he referred to three years later in an interview given to American journalists in New York. He had been afraid of a Shakespeare opera, he then said, and doubted who among the singers could ever act in such a work, while in the story of the famous Roman goldsmith he found the love interest too diffused. But the truth was that Puccini was wearying of tragic subjects, of 'grand operas', and that, as after *Tosca*, he was again pining to try his hand at comedy. On 5 March 1905, he addressed himself to Giacosa, thus:

> What do you say to a comic opera? We could try and find a good subject, but one that will make people really laugh. Don't you think this would provide a respite for us as well as the public? By now the graves . . . and the altars have become filled with dramas of death and languor.
> Search in your files, in your memory, in old and brilliant comedies that you have seen, and find something that will have a special lyrical quality, worthy of musical notes and symphonic thoughts. Illica, to whom I wrote, favours Italian *opera buffa* (*N*).

And to Illica, on 21 March:

> . . . Have you thought of anything comic? But really comic? Signor Giulio wrote to me saying that it is more difficult to find a good comic subject than a tragic one. I knew this but one must overcome the difficulties. If one threw up the sponge at once! . . .† I have need to work *but I don't want to write grand operas*. The strings in me must vibrate. And, meanwhile, with that fatal idea of a grand opera in one's head, the years pass and one does nothing. I want three acts, comic or bold, but not more. Courage, therefore, and God may deliver you from *Marie Antoinette*. . . (*C.P.Let.*409).

* Rodenbach's novel, dramatized in 1901 as *Le Mirage* later provided the subject for the opera, *Die tote Stadt* (Hamburg and Cologne, 1920) by Erich Wolfgang Korngold who was much influenced by Puccini's and Strauss's style and in whose career the Italian composer showed genuine interest. Korngold began as an infant prodigy achieving his greatest successes in his two one-act opera, *Der Ring des Polykrates* and *Violanta* (Munich, 1916) and *Die tote Stadt*. He showed a sad decline in his subsequent works, notably those written in America where he emigrated in 1935. He died there in 1957.

† Ricordi was trying to dissuade Puccini from launching into a comic opera. Having considered *Butterfly* a mediocre work and not weighty enough, he now wanted the composer to redeem himself with the public by composing a grand opera of tragic import, such as *Marie Antoinette*, on which the publisher had set his heart. This explains Puccini's following sentences.

It seemed now comic opera or nothing. He thought again of *Tartarin*; he enquired of Illica whether he knew the satirical novel, *El Buscon ovvero Don Pablo de Segovia* (1626) by the ancient Spanish writer, Francisco Quevedo; and he was intrigued by the ironic suggestion to write an operetta before embarking on a more substantial work. This was the first time that the composer evinced interest in this light genre to which some nine years later he was to make a single and not very successful contribution. He considered a comedy by the Italian playwright Roberto Branco, but he also toyed with the idea of a *William Tell*, than which no more unsuitable subject could be imagined for Puccini; he appears, however, to have soon realized this himself, and thinking, no doubt, of Rossini's opera, he quashed the idea with 'I should for ever be the target for the thunderbolts of all Italian critics'.[75]

To divert his mind from his constant preoccupation with finding the right libretto, there arrived an invitation from the great Argentine paper *La Prensa* to attend in person a summer season of his operas at Buenos Aires, the bait being 50,000 francs, with paid passage for himself and Elvira. Five works were being given during June and July of 1905, including the almost forgotten *Edgar*, for the new production of which Puccini revised the opera a third time. Buenos Aires, with its large Italian colony, fêted the composer in grand style. This was Puccini's first transatlantic journey. In October, after returning for a few weeks to Italy, he came to London to attend some of the *Butterfly* performances given during a short autumn season at Covent Garden; owing to his trip to South America, he had missed the London première in July. It was on the occasion of this London visit that the foundation was laid for Puccini's intimate friendship with Sybil Seligman and her husband David, head of a well-known firm of London bankers. The composer had first met her shortly after the Brescia première of *Butterfly* at the London house of his old friend Paolo Tosti, the composer of pretty drawing-room songs, whom he had known since his struggling days in Milan. Tosti had settled in London about 1880 and became much sought after as a singing-teacher. He was music master to the Royal Family and one of his favourite pupils was Sybil Seligman, who is said to have had a contralto voice of exceptional beauty. She was passionately fond of opera, paid frequent visits to Italy, spoke fluent Italian and kept open house for visiting Italian artists.

According to information for which I am indebted to her sister, Mrs. Violet Schiff, Sybil's relationship with Puccini was at first by no means platonic, as has been affirmed by some recent biographers who have inevitably had to base their statements on the little that Sybil's son, Vincent Seligman, cared to divulge on this point in his book.[76] In publishing the collection of letters written by Puccini to his mother over nearly twenty years, Vincent very naturally drew a veil over the true nature of at least the early part of his mother's friendship with the composer, a friendship which the son in fact described as 'so alien to the traditional Latin temperament'. The truth is that it began as a passionate love affair and only with the years developed into one of the few genuine friendships which Puccini was able to form; it lasted to his death. But even in this relationship it is permissible to doubt whether the markedly egocentric composer was capable of reciprocating the large measure of devotion and concern shown to him on all and every occasion by his London friend. A woman of remarkable intelligence and artistic feeling, Sybil became his mentor and confidante in many private and professional matters; she was his 'Sybil of Cumae'— 'the person who had come nearest to understanding my nature', as Puccini once wrote to her. They exchanged a voluminous correspondence, of which Vincent published the composer's part, letters which constitute one of the best first-hand sources for information on the man Puccini, if not at present the best.

Knowing Puccini's anxiety to find the right subject, Sybil, in the autumn of 1905, promptly interested herself in the matter and made several suggestions which reflected credit on her literary taste but which were scarcely calculated to appeal to him: *The Light That Failed,** *Enoch Arden*, *Anna Karenina*, *The Last Days of Pompeii* and a story (unspecified) by Mérimée. Puccini, who knew some of these works, found them all unsuitable, though Tolstoy's great book contains elements out of which a typically Puccinian libretto might have been fashioned. Kipling's novel, which was unknown to him, he took the trouble to read in a French translation, later giving Sybil detailed reasons for his rejection. However, he encouraged her in further searches—'for you read so much and you are so clever and intelligent that I have hopes—then again English literature is not so well known as ours or French—so who knows that you may not make this lucky find for me'.[77]

In the autumn of 1906 Sybil made two more suggestions. Through Robert Ross, the literary executor of Oscar Wilde, she had been permitted access to two then unpublished plays, *The Duchess of Padua* and *A Florentine Tragedy*, of which she had copies made and sent to Puccini. No doubt Strauss's *Salome*, first performed in the previous year, had drawn her attention to Wilde plays as possible material for opera.† Puccini displayed special interest in *A Florentine Tragedy*, 'which I like very much', as he wrote to Ricordi from Paris on 14 November 1906. 'It's in one act, but beautiful, inspired, strong and tragic; three principal characters, three first-rate roles. Epoch, 1300'; and with a taunt at Strauss—whose music he disliked but not as much as Strauss disliked his—'it would be a counterpart to *Salome*, yet more human, more real and nearer the feelings of the *man in the street*' (E).

Ricordi's reaction to the entire project was summed up in the telegram he sent to Illica on 11 December: 'Absolutely necessary for the future good of the Doge to throw Florentine stupidity into fire' (L).

---

* Strauss, incidentally, was not the first to discover Wilde for the operatic stage. The French composer Antoine Mariotte wrote a *Salomé* earlier than his more successful rival yet it was not produced until 1908, at Lyons, where it survived precisely one performance.

† Kipling's novel had recently been adapted for the stage and was just then running in London with great success.

The play, which Wilde had left unfinished and which was completed by Thomas Sturge Moore, centres on a triangular situation between Simone, a wealthy Florentine merchant, his beautiful wife Bianca and the young nobleman Bardi. It contains little action, most of the scenes being taken up by Wilde's scintillating dialogue, and the plot is designed to illustrate the thesis that most people are blind to the value and the beauty of things in their possession to which they have to have their eyes opened by others endowed with more perception. The play ends with a duel between the two men in which the young nobleman is stabbed to death. It is only then that Bianca realizes for the first time the passion and boldness of her husband, whom she had always regarded as commonplace and cold. Taking no heed of the body of her dead lover lying on the floor, she advances toward Simone with outstretched arms: 'Why did you not tell me you were so strong?'—Simone: 'Why did you not tell me you were so beautiful?'

As it stood, *A Florentine Tragedy* was scarcely a suitable subject for Puccini, despite his enthusiasm for it,* though Ricordi's description of it as 'stupidity' was cruelly unjust. The composer discussed it at length with Illica, giving him detailed indications as to the modifications he wanted, yet for some unknown reason he subsequently deserted Illica for another writer, Arturo Colautti. But by April of 1907 the project was abandoned. This was, however, not the end of it. We have already noted Puccini's habit of returning, after years of oblivion, to his old discarded 'loves', and so it was with *A Florentine Tragedy*. Five years later—while staying at Carlsbad for the cure, in August 1912—he bethought himself of the play and Illica was to do the adaptation. At his request Sybil Seligman inquired from Robert Ross whether it was still free. It was. Ross, it is true, had promised it to Mariotte, the same French composer who had set Wilde's *Salome* before Strauss, yet he had not granted him the exclusive rights. In imparting this information to Puccini, Wilde's literary executor reminded him, with a scarcely veiled slight on Illica, that Sturge Moore had completed the play, and he strongly advised him to avail himself of this version. Puccini, however, remained loyal to his Italian librettist. In a letter to Illica, written in Munich on 5 August 1912, just before leaving to attend the Festival at 'Wagner's sanctuary', he developed his ideas of how Wilde's one-act play could be expanded into a two-act opera of sufficient length for a whole evening's entertainment. And in a subsequent letter (20 August) he suggested that Illica should make of it 'a Florentine night with some mystery in it (engraving *à la* Fortuny†), silken ladders, feminine intrigues, fornications' (*L*). Wilde's original was scarcely discernible in this 'Florentine Night'! But all these and other suggestions proved to small purpose, for by the early autumn of the same year we read that 'Alas! the *Tragedy* of Wilde has gone the way of others' (*S*).

---

* The play was published in 1908 and provided the basis for a one-act opera (1917) by Alexander von Zemlinski, a distinguished Viennese composer and conductor.

† A Catalan painter who had settled in Italy for a time.

2

To return to the period between *Butterfly* and Puccini's next opera, *La Fanciulla del West*. In his quest for new subjects Puccini now evinced a marked desire to search among the works of writers of high reputation and thus move with the advanced literary taste of the time. Although, owing to his inner limitations, this was to prove unsuccessful and ended in his choice of Belasco's crude and then already faded Wild West melodrama, the fact remains that in this musician, approaching the prime of his creative career, there was a strong urge to aspire to 'a higher form of poetry' and 'a profound renewal of my whole style', as Puccini wrote to D'Annunzio in August 1906. We have have seen that he was seriously interested in Wilde, and to Wilde we must now add the famous Russian writer, Maxim Gorky, for whom his enthusiasm waxed and waned during nearly four years. As this Gorky episode throws some light on the composer's growing preoccupation with the idea of a triple bill, such as he wrote in *Il Trittico* some ten or eleven years later, it deserves our closer attention.

It would appear that soon after *Tosca* Puccini conceived the plan for a trilogy of self-contained and strongly contrasted operas for which the plots were to be drawn from Dante's *Divina Commedia* or to be freely invented. Originally the operas were to bear the symbolic titles: *Inferno—Purgatorio—Paradiso*. It is very likely that Puccini's scheme was inspired by the passing vogue of the Parisian *Grand Guignol* which presented on one evening three contrasted subjects: something horrific, something sentimental and a farce. It may well be that also Offenbach's *Tales of Hoffmann*, with its three different plots, had something to do with Puccini's idea. Perusing Gorky's plays he seemed to have found the material for a trilogy in the Russian writer's *The Raft*, *Kan and his Son* and *The 26 against One*. What appears to have attracted him to these stories was the combination of a sombre and stark realism, a highly unusual atmosphere and the author's profound compassion for the social outcast, the 'under-dog'. Was there emerging in Puccini something like a social conscience which was to find an, admittedly, vague expression in the later *Tabarro*, or was it that in these Gorky characters he encountered that 'great suffering of little souls' which had always been a strong motive-force of his dramatic imagination ? It is hard to say. Of the three plays, *The Raft* and *The 26 against One* treat of the theme of man's inhumanity against his weaker fellow-man, while *Kan and his Son*, based on a Crimean legend, is in the vein of a cruel but poignant oriental story. In its general atmosphere and the character of a Tartar slave girl—affectionate and self-sacrificing as Liù—*Kan* at once recalls the later *Turandot* and is the first intimation of Puccini's attraction to a barbaric fairy-tale of the East. Similarly, *The Raft*, with its bleak depressing atmosphere of the river Volga which is enveloped in dense fog, with the entire action taking place on two floating rafts, and with a triangular situation between a young woman, a much older skipper and his young son, is singularly prophetic of what was to come in the later *Tabarro*. If in the end nothing was to materialize of this Gorky project, the reason for this was partly Puccini's own doubts and vacillations and partly Ricordi's persistent opposition to the scheme of three one-act opera.

In early 1906 D'Annunzio appeared again on the scene, this time with a suggestion for a legendary subject, *Parisina*, so treated by him that, as he wrote to Puccini on 23 January 1906, it would result in 'a poem in which life and dream are intertwined as in the soul of man', that 'the simplicity and robustness of the architecture' would be one of its essential virtues, and that it would have 'such clarity that the spectator could immediately grasp the development' (*C.P.Let.*469). This latter point was, as we know, one of Puccini's principal criteria for a good libretto, a point which no doubt he must have impressed on the poet. But by August he lost interest in this subject and now turned his attention to another legendary subject previously proposed by D'Annunzio—*La Rosa di Cipro*. But in the event this *Rose* failed to bloom and, though it showed a brief sign of life again in 1912, finally faded for good and all.

D'Annunzio's pride was deeply hurt and in a letter of 31 August he unburdened himself to Camillo Bondi, a mutual friend, in these sarcastic terms:

> . . . My contacts with the Maestro of Lucca have been sterile. He is overwhelmed by the power of Poetry. Two excellent outlines—*Parisina* and the *Rose of Cyprus**—seemed too grandiose for him. He went so far as to confess to me that he needs a 'small, light thing, to be put to music in a few months, between one trip and another'. And for this he came to the poet of *Francesca da Rimini*!
>
> The disillusionment has been very sad. Not art, but commerce. *Ahi mè!*
>
> I, with great cordiality, without regretting the time that had been lost (it was not entirely lost, because I learned many new things), gave him back that liberty which I love so dearly and respect in art and in life. Now he writes me a letter begging me not to abandon him and to give him a third outline, a more humble one, and more suited to his strength. I shall try one of these days. . . (*M*).

Given Puccini's working methods, it was highly unlikely that he could have wished for 'a small, light thing to be put to music in a few months between one trip and another'; or else he meant this in jest. Yet despite his pique D'Annunzio appeared eager to resume contact with Puccini to whom he offered himself again. Already in the spring of the following year he assured him that 'my old nightingale has woken up with the spring and would like to sing for you' (April 1907. Puccini to Ricordi. *E*.) Evidently the poet's 'nightingale' must have sung a tune little to the composer's liking as nothing materialized from this approach. And when five years later the two made another attempt to collaborate, the result was equally negative. D'Annunzio's resentment that his dealings with Puccini should have proved throughout so unsuccessful rankled with him for the rest of his life. While he mentions Mascagni and other composers frequently in his autobiographical writings, to Puccini he refers only once and in this oblique, damning fashion:

* *Parisina* was later set to music by Mascagni (Milan, 1913) and *Francesca da Rimini* by Zandonai (Turin, 1914), for which Tito Ricordi adapted d'Annunzio's play.

Ecco il lago Massaciuccoli   Behold, Lake Massaciuccoli!
tanto ricco di cacciagione   Of waterfowl enough to feed the nation,
quanto misero d'ispirazione![78]   But miserably poor in inspiration!

3

There *was* a project, however, that had progressed farther toward its full realization than any other contemplated by Puccini in those years between *Butterfly* and *La Fanciulla*. It was probably during Puccini's stay in Paris for the *Tosca* production, in the autumn of 1903, that his attention had been drawn to the novel *La Femme et le Pantin—The Woman and the Puppet—* by Pierre Louÿs, the French poet and writer and an intimate friend of Debussy's.* The novel, which had been published in 1898 and was thereafter dramatized for the French and German stage, achieved a *succès de scandale* at its publication. Even a present-day reader, inured as he may well be to the literary treatment of sexual pathology, is bound to register a shock at certain scenes presented by Louÿs with unsparing realism, but described in cool, dispassionate language that seems to render the novel the more fascinating to read. In it Louÿs portrays a *femme fatale*, Conchita Perez by name, who has much in common with Mérimée's Carmen. She too works in the famous *fábrica*, the cigar factory of Seville, and she too is a prostitute, but —this is important for her psychology—only in thought and behaviour. Brought up in a convent, she keeps her virginity as a sacrosanct possession. She becomes the mistress of the wealthy Matteo but refuses to yield to him, playing a cruel game in which she reduces this proud and aristocratic man to the state of a puppet tied to her by the strings of sexual serfdom. It is his doglike submission to her every whim that gradually engenders in her an almost murderously sadistic hate for him and that finally prompts her to a monstrous act of mental torture which she performs with the intention of driving him to commit suicide: with a young boy, Morenito, she simulates the sexual act in the presence of Matteo, who is made to witness it behind the grille of a doorway. Yet what Conchita achieves is to drive Matteo not into suicide but into a state of insanity in which he very nearly thrashes the life out of her. It is precisely this brutal treatment of her— '*Que tu m'as bien battue, mon cœur! Que c'était doux! Que c'était bon!*', Conchita shouts in perverse ecstasy—that awakens an erotic response in her and makes her at last give herself to Matteo. Henceforth it is Matteo who will treat Conchita *en canaille*, thus turning the tables on her and reducing her to a state of complete sexual servitude. Somewhere in *Thus Spake Zarathustra*, Nietzsche wrote '*Wenn du zum Weibe gehst, vergiss die Peitsche nicht!*'— 'When thou goest to the woman do not forget the whip!'—it might have furnished an apt motto for Louÿs. Yet his novel, it must be stressed, is devoid of all suggestion of obscenity and lewdness, despite its unbelievable realism. Its larger theme, treated with skill and psychological insight, is that of the ambivalence of love and hate, a theme which exercised on Puccini a magnetic

* Debussy set his exquisite *Chansons de Bilitis*.

attraction, as witness *Turandot*. The reasons why in the end he abandoned this subject will emerge presently, yet I venture the suggestion that something of Conchita flowed into the character of Puccini's cruel Chinese princess.

Few of Puccini's libretti, abortive or otherwise, passed through as many vicissitudes and caused him as much exasperation as that of *Conchita*, which was to be the title of the opera. There were countless conferences with Louÿs—called 'Inouï' or 'Épatant' by Puccini because these adjectives were foremost in the poet's vocabulary—and with Maurice Vaucaire, 'The Vicar', who had dramatized the novel. In June 1906 the agreement for *Conchita* was signed and Illica was entrusted with making an Italian version of Vaucaire's dramatization. Yet already in September Puccini's customary vacillation started; writing to Sybil on the 25th, he says:

> I am rather preoccupied about *Conchita*—or, rather, I am feeling weaker on the subject! What frightens me is *her* character, and the plot of the play—and then all the characters seem unlovable, and that is a very bad thing on the stage (*S*).

We recall that he had turned down Verga's *La Lupa* on precisely the same grounds. But on 5 October, only a fortnight later, 'Conchita is coming back to life' again, and so it was to continue, Puccini's interest waxing and waning, to the despair of his collaborators as well as of Ricordi, who had developed great enthusiasm for the subject, hoping perhaps (as he had hoped in *Edgar*) that with it the composer might write another *Carmen*. What infuriated the publisher in particular was Puccini's sudden decision to drop Illica from the work on *Conchita*. To make matters worse, Ricordi was fuming with rage because Puccini, instead of occupying himself with *Conchita*, had, off his own bat, commissioned an Italian translation of *A Florentine Tragedy*. This brought forth from the publisher one of those few sarcastic letters he ever had occasion to pen to his 'beloved Doge' during their long association:

19 November 1906

. . . Take care: if you renounce Illica you will not be able to use any of his ideas [for *La Conchita*] and that means—*da capo*.

As to your idea of having the tragedy by Wilde translated, bravo!—However, unless you have already made an agreement with somebody for the translation (an agreement in writing), you will need a translator as your first collaborator. Further—what rights do the heirs . . . of Wilde hold? That brings up collaborator No. 2!! Then you will need one or very likely several librettists—collaborators Nos. 3, 4 and 5. So it goes on and on! All right—kick out that bloodsucker of a publisher, who is swimming in his millions—what am I saying? in his milliards—while the poor, exploited composers

vanno raminghi e poveri	roam, homeless and poor,
cercando un pane agli uomini.	begging bread from people.
(*Dante*)	

Perhaps you will be astonished to read this. But between friends, as people who esteem each other and who love each other, one may be frank and call things by their right names. Regarding the millions that my firm is earning—just like that!—do you want to know, my dear Puccini, the truth? Up to now, *Butterfly* is a liability. . . What with the administrative expense, the personal representation, the journeys, more journeys, regal suites, banquets, and all the other incidental nuisances.

I am saying this because if all our affairs were to go like this, I would be constrained to roam 'homeless and poor', and perhaps the good Giacomo would come occasionally and take me out in his 275 h.p. automobile for a ride around the bastions. . .

None the less, long live *Madama Butterfly* and Giacomo, Doge and Imperator. You know very well that you are like a son to me, and my affection for you will always be the same, as well as my trust. I only wish to see clearly in this murky fog of the future. I cannot discern when the sun of *Conchita* will break through.

You can never say of me that I have not lent myself to all your desires. Even recently I resumed friendly relations with Illica just so that we might succeed in getting some results. Now we are at *sicut erat in principio*. That is the reason why today my liver is manufacturing enough bile to supply a whole stock company. . . As to all composers, French, English, German, Turkish, and Abyssinian—A Bunch of Idiots!! (*M*).

It is, in parenthesis, amusing to note that, half a century before, when Verdi took Giulio Ricordi's father, Tito, to task for his negligence concerning the Venice production of *Un Ballo in Maschera*, the publisher broke into a similar jeremiad about his losses. Verdi's uncompromising reply (which Puccini, with the same justification, might have made to Giulio) was 'You're wrong when you make a song and dance to me about your misfortunes and losses as if my operas were the cause of your ruin. Why in heaven's name, then, did you acquire them at all?'[79]

What amounted to a death sentence on *Conchita* was pronounced by Puccini in a letter to his publisher from which I quote extensively as it provides clear evidence of his aversion from the sexually *risqué* and characterizes his approach to psychological matters:

Torre del Lago
11 April 1907

Dearest Signor Giulio,

I have not replied to your letter immediately because it gave me, I confess, a shock and left me, I should almost say, with an unhappy feeling. For some days I have been intending to write to you but I had to wait for the right moment to come. I re-read your letter today and my impression has changed. I see in it how much affection you have for me and how great an interest you take in one who has always looked to you with feelings of trust and deference, joined with an unchanging affection.

I could write a great deal about the reasons which have influenced my project for *Conchita* to the point of wishing to abandon it.

It was not *fear* (confound that word) of the *pruderie* of the Anglo-Saxon audiences of Europe and America. It was not the example of *Salome* in New York.* My reasons are of a practical and dramatic nature.

If there had been anything (I will not call it fear) to preoccupy my thoughts, it would have been the parallel in musical colour and brilliance with *Carmen*. This is the one and only point which is justifiably bound to cause a headache to any composer.

During the long hours of reflection I have examined this subject with a critical eye, both from the point of view of the spectator and the composer of opera. I maintain that the character of Conchita remains for the spectator inexplicable, unless he has read the novel.

Then there are the diverse lines of a strange and continuous dialogue so often repeated (five and six times) and forming one single situation which turns round the only idea—*the woman and the puppet*, in other words, the advances Conchita makes toward Matteo and her withdrawals. Furthermore, there is the final scene which, as it stands (I am not referring to the brutal part), I consider impossible to perform, or rather, to be accepted on the stage unless one wants to show a spectacle so *nature* that even Aretino himself would not have dared it. And note that this final scene cannot be represented in any other way.

This is not to mention that there is no baritone part in it, that there is the problem of why Morentino is with Conchita in the 'grille' scene, and that the whole audience will think her to be what she is not. Nor do I mention the difficulty in providing the conclusive proof of her *virginity*, the essential point of the whole work. How are we to make the public understand that she has given herself, pure, for the first time and that all that she appeared to be was deceptive?

I do not deny that Louÿs's novel is more than fascinating. Perhaps we should have departed from it or at least treated the subject differently so as to make it more clear to the audience. In this way we might have found other contrasts, other variations, other episodes which would have taken away from that sense of monotony which it appears to have now... Vaucaire brought me a Conchita *tout à fait française*, devoid of any original character. It was I who turned the poet back to the right track and perhaps we followed the novel too closely, instead of using our imagination a little more (*E*).

By May the 'Spanish slut', as the composer had nicknamed the heroine, was buried for good and all, so far as he was concerned. But there arose some trouble with Louys—'*Inouï* has written me another idiotic letter claiming damages and indemnification for not having put his libretto to music'—a threat which Puccini shrugged off with 'ridiculous—*rigolo!* I haven't answered him yet because I'm too lazy'.[80] The libretto was later set by Zandonai, whose *Conchita* was successfully produced in Milan in 1911 and given in London the following year. Puccini's comment on this London

* Strauss's opera, given at the Metropolitan Opera House on 22 January 1907, had to be withdrawn after a single performance, on account of its 'appeal to the beast in man' and 'its disgrace to civilization'. Puccini, who happened to be in New York at that time for the production of *Butterfly*, was present at that performance and it is not improbable that, despite his statement to the contrary, the New York reception of *Salome* did have something to do with his final rejection of *Conchita*.

production was not without an undertone of jealousy; he wrote to Sybil in July 1912:

> The papers here speak of the success of *Conchita* and also give little snippets from foreign newspapers—this is what always happens to disguise a failure. To that one must add *Savoia's* [Tito Ricordi] great interest in this young author, who does not lack talent but who at present hasn't got that little something which is needed for the theatre. And then the libretto is one that I turned down—which seems to me to say something (*S*).

The truth is that Zandonai's opera was subsequently given in a great number of cities such as Rio de Janeiro, San Francisco, New York and Paris, and may, occasionally, still be heard in Italy. It should be added, however, that when Zandonai brought out his most successful opera, *Francesca da Rimini* (1914), Puccini found much to laud in it and declared its composer as one of the most gifted operatic writers of the younger generation.

With the rejection of his 'Spanish slut', however, the chapter of Puccini's abortive chases after suitable subjects was by no means closed. Thus in May 1907 he thought he had at last found what he wanted: it was the old, rejected *Maria Antonietta* who raised her guillotined head once more in his imagination. The libretto was to have a new plot designed by himself and confined to the last days of the hapless queen. He outlined the scenario to Sybil (in a latter of 9 May) as follows:

> I have sidetracked *Conchita* and I have even convinced Ricordi. *Today I can breathe again*—after so many days of struggle and the vilest temper. Tomorrow I shall see Illica about an idea I have—which seems to me a grand one! The last days of Marie Antoinette. A soul in torment—First act, prison; second act, the trial; third act, the execution—three short acts, stirring enough to take one's breath away. I'm absolutely taken up with this idea of mine. And I have found a title which seems to me fitting and appropriate because I couldn't call it *Maria Antionetta*, seeing that it deals only with the one episode of her tragic death. The title is *La Donna Austriaca*—what do you think of it? (*S*).

The opera was to have the queen as its sole protagonist—much in the manner of *Butterfly*—yet with many minor parts and a great deal of chorus in it. An agreement was signed with Illica, who was to be the librettist, and while in Paris in June 1907 Puccini obtained a large quantity of music dating from the time of the French Revolution. Yet in a letter to Ricordi of 14 September we read already the ominous sentence 'Illica must have a collaborator' and with that the *Austrian Woman* was allowed to die a natural and highly undramatic death. By that time poor Illica had been occupying himself with the libretto, intermittently, for nearly a decade!

Admittedly, in theory the character and fate of Marie Antoinette would, as I suggested, have suited Puccini's psychology most admirably. Yet even if the opera had turned out a masterpiece, as it might well have, it is very likely that audiences would have always confronted it with a certain prejudice. The great peril in using a familiar historical subject on the stage—

with a protagonist so well known from the history books—lies in the often observed fact that each spectator has formed in his mind's eye his own private picture of it and is therefore disappointed and even resentful if the author's picture fails to coincide with his own. Some such misgiving may well have been one of the reasons for Puccini's decision to abandon this subject for good; and this is to say nothing of the amount of historical authenticity which he would have been compelled to observe in plot and incidents, in order to obviate criticism for any possible distortion of amply documented facts—a necessity calculated to interfere with the free play of his dramatic imagination.

All these efforts in pursuit of the 'right' subject filled the long period from the summer of 1904 to the autumn of 1907. And even though Puccini had meanwhile lighted on the subject he was to use eventually, Belasco's play *The Girl of the Golden West*, for many months he was continuing to vacillate between it and *The Austrian Woman*, which two subjects 'have given me the courage of a lion' (S). He decided to tackle the French subject first, yet suddenly changed his mind in favour of Belasco's play, intending to resume the former thereafter. It is conceivable that but for his visit to New York early in 1907 Puccini would never have composed *La Fanciulla del West* and might perhaps have settled on *Maria Antonietta*, despite the risks involved. The odds are that the 'French' opera would have been a work far more inspired and more intrinsically Puccinian than the 'Wild West' opera.

XII

New York and After

IT WAS WHILE PUCCINI WAS STAYING IN PARIS in the autumn of 1906 for the
first French production of *Butterfly* that he received an invitation from
Heinrich Conried, then manager of the Metropolitan Opera House, New
York, to attend a six-weeks season of his operas there in January and February
of the following year. In addition to *Bohème* and *Tosca*, it was to include
Manon Lescaut, never staged before at that theatre,* and the most recent
Butterfly. For the mere supervision of the new productions the composer
was offered the tempting sum of 8,000 dollars. No sooner had he accepted
the invitation than he regretted it profoundly: the thought of going to
America was 'now getting on my nerves. Whyever did I accept?' he
exclaimed in a letter to Ricordi of 15 November (*E*). The invitation, however, had arrived at a moment when, for several reasons, Puccini found
himself in the doldrums, a mood that about this period began to seize him
with increasing frequency. He therefore hoped that this radical change of
atmosphere might help to improve his state of mind. He had arrived in Paris
in the last week of October for the rehearsals of *Butterfly* expecting to make
only a brief sojourn there; but owing to a series of delays the opera could
not be given until 28 December, so that he was forced to kick his heels in the
French capital for more than two months. There was, it will be recalled, the
irritating and inadequate Butterfly of Madame Carré; there was her husband
Albert Carré whose 'fussiness about the *mise en scène* . . . is enough to turn
one's hair grey'.[81] There was Pierre Louÿs plaguing him about *Conchita*—
'he won't let me alone, not a bit of it; he's a sticker, that fellow'.[82] And there
were those hateful luncheon parties, dinners and receptions; and to blacken
the composer's mood still further, he was still without 'his' libretto. His
Paris letters to Sybil are punctuated with expressions such as: 'I see everything through dark-coloured spectacles—I'm tired to death of everything,
including opera—I would like to be in London or at Torre del Lago or in a
wood where the foliage is thick—all I want is to be allowed to retire into
my shell', and so on. They are the expressions of a born introspective compelled by circumstances to turn extrovert. Puccini even asked Sybil whether
she knew of 'some medicine that raises the morale'—and the prescription
for the medicine was promptly sent from London, but we do not know
what its nature was. Puccini, in short, seemed at the end of his nervous tether
in those autumn months of 1906. This may have been partly responsible

*The first American production, though, took place at Philadelphia as early as 1894.

for his description of the music he then heard in Paris as 'frightful'. The only work he found 'truly interesting, despite its sombre colour, unrelieved like a Franciscan's habit', was Debussy's *Pelléas et Mélisande* which 'has extraordinary harmonic qualities and a most transparent instrumental texture'.[83] Elsewhere he criticized Debussy's opera as being too much tinged in 'a greyish monochrome. The theatre must have variety; it is the only thing that is successful. Uniformity is disastrous'.[84] Variety of colour is indeed an outstanding feature of Puccini's operatic style, though he temporarily lost sight of it in his *Suor Angelica*, to the disadvantage of that work.

At last the day arrived when Puccini was able to leave Paris, with its 'épatant, inouï, Opéra-Comique, Ritz, Rue de la Paix, Faubourg Saint-Honoré, Champs-Elysées'[85] and embark for New York on the *Kaiserin Auguste Viktoria*, where he had booked 'a cabin amidships and a vomitorium for Elvira'. The boat was delayed two days by fog so that Puccini did not arrive until the day of the first performance of *Manon Lescaut*—23 January: 'I landed at six and at eight o'clock I was already at the opera' (S).

While he expressed great satisfaction with this production,* he was far less pleased with that of *Butterfly*, about which he wrote to Sybil some weeks later (18 February):

> I have had all I wanted of America—at the opera all is well, and *Madam Butterfly* was excellent, but lacked the poetry I put into it. The rehearsals were too hurried, and the woman [Geraldine Farrar] was not what she ought to have been. Also as regards your *god* (*entre nous*) I make you a present of him—he won't learn anything, he's lazy and he's too pleased with himself— all the same his voice is magnificent (S).†

Puccini's marked lack of reverence applied to a number of 'gods', including Toscanini and Melba. When he heard, for example, that Melba was too ill to be able to appear in *La Bohème* he expressed his regrets to Sybil but thought 'that Mimi will be pleased to be *unsung* by her'![86] Again, a famous German conductor‡ who prided himself on his fine interpretation of *Tosca* was told by Puccini, after attending a performance, that if he (the conductor) had been in Italy they would have shot *him*, instead of Cavaradossi.[87] Similarly, when Puccini heard rumours that, in a Vienna production of *La Bohème* in 1919, Leo Slezak, a celebrated tenor blessed with a mountainous

---

* The three chief parts were sung by Lina Cavalieri (Manon), Caruso (Des Grieux) and Scotti (Lescaut).

† 'Your *god*' was Caruso, who sang the part of Pinkerton. Puccini, incidentally, may be said to have been indirectly responsible for Caruso's early fame. As a young and unknown singer in Italy, he was introduced to Puccini at his home at Torre del Lago, by a mutual friend, so as to have the composer's views on his voice. Caruso sang to him Rodolfo's aria 'Che gelida manina'; after a few phrases Puccini, who accompanied him, suddenly stopped, turned round on his piano stool and asked him: 'Who sent you to me? God?!'

Caruso was not slow to make use of Puccini's verdict, which in fact helped him a few days later to obtain the role of Rodolfo in a production of *Bohème* at Leghorn, where the director of the theatre had at first been unwilling to let him sing that part. (*Caruso*, by T. R. Ybarra. London, 1954.)

‡ I was unable to establish his identity.

circumference, was to sing the part of Rodolfo, he wrote to a Viennese friend that Slezak would create the effect 'of an elephant wooing a weasel'.[88]

New York both fascinated and bewildered Puccini with its tremendous vitality and nervous haste. He went sightseeing with Elvira and indulged his childlike love for mechanical gadgets by gazing at shop windows which displayed the latest models of refrigerators and motor-cars. He bought a magnificent motor-boat and had it shipped to Leghorn to add to his growing fleet at Torre del Lago. This purchase, incidentally, was made with the 500 dollars paid him by a wealthy autograph-hunter for writing out the opening bars of the Musetta Waltz. He was much interested in the gramophone, foreseeing a great future for the industry then hardly out of its infancy, and in an open letter to the *New York Herald* gave his views on the question of royalties for mechanical reproduction of music. It was either on this or on a later occasion that he made the acquaintance of Thomas Edison, an enthusiastic admirer, who in 1920 sent him a signed photograph with the fulsome inscription 'Men die and governments change, but the songs of *La Bohème* will live for ever'. Puccini also knew Marconi, whom he first met in London in 1911.

Fêted, lionized and interviewed, he had had after three weeks 'all I want of America', and yearned to return to his retreat at Torre del Lago. It was, possibly, during this New York visit, lasting five weeks altogether, that he composed two piano pieces, *Foglio d'Album* and *Piccolo Tango*, scented drawing-room music, which was published in America as late as 1942.*

While in New York, in the hope of finding a new subject Puccini went to see a number of plays, including three by Belasco: *The Music Master, The Rose of Rancho* and *The Girl of the Golden West*. To the last-named his attention had already been drawn in Italy the previous autumn by his friend Piero Antinori. It was no longer a novelty, having been first produced at Pittsburgh in 1905, but it was just then running at the Belasco Theatre in New York before full houses. Like *Madam Butterfly* Belasco had written it for his favourite actress Blanche Bates and it was with her as the heroine that Puccini saw *The Girl of the Golden West*.† Belasco achieved his most sensational effects by a realistic cinematographic representation of the local atmosphere. Thus, before the opening of the first scene, the audience was shown on moving curtains a panorama of the Cloudy Mountains of California, with the heroine's log cabin nestling against the rocks; then followed a view of the exterior of the 'Polka Saloon' (in which the first scene was laid) while from within issued the strains of a 'coon' song. Instead

---

* I am not altogether convinced of their authenticity, and my inquiry of the publishers for information remained unanswered.

† I cannot withhold from the reader a few quotations from the letter Belasco wrote to Blanche Bates on the completion of the play. After assuring her that the part of Minnie would fit 'you from your dear little feet up to your pretty head', he continues, 'it's a *bully* part . . . the characters call you "The Girl". The models of the play are fine—the last scene of all, *In the Wilderness*, is a gem. There are some beautiful speeches in the play—very Batesesque! The lines just crackle and the situations are human'. (The letter is reproduced in *The Life of David Belasco*, op. cit.)

of the usual theatre orchestra, Belasco employed a band of authentic Californian minstrels consisting of a singer, a concertina, banjo and 'bones' (xylophone), which played such old songs as *Coal Oil Tommy*, *Rosalie*, *Prairie Flower*, *Pop goes the Weasel*, and so on. At one point in the first act there appeared an old minstrel singing *The Old Dog Tray* and it was then, according to Belasco, that Puccini, who had so far shown no perceptible enthusiasm, exclaimed 'Ah, there is my theme at last'.* Belasco omitted nothing to drench his audience in an authentic Californian atmosphere. But his *pièce de résistance* was the imitation of a blizzard in the second act for which he employed an 'orchestra' of thirty-two 'players' operating wind and snow machines.

All the same, to judge from what Puccini wrote to Tito Ricordi on 18 February, the general impression which he took away with him of this and the other Belasco plays was not overwhelming:

> . . . Here too I have been trying to find new subjects but there is nothing useful or, rather, complete enough. I've found some good hints in Belasco, but nothing definitive, or solid or complete.
>
> The atmosphere of the *Wild West* attracts me but in all the plays I have seen I found only good scenes here and there. Never a clear, simple line of development; it's all a hotchpotch and sometimes in very bad taste and *vieux jeux* (E).

It is possible that his preoccupation at that time with *Conchita* and *Maria Antonietta* made Puccini on this occasion less receptive to *The Girl of the Golden West*; though, despite his little knowledge of English, he had had no difficulty in following the simple and self-explanatory situations, and a seed was sown in his mind. A few weeks later Belasco received from him a letter from Paris, to the effect that he had been thinking a good deal about *The Girl* and felt that, with certain modifications, it might easily be adapted for the operatic stage. 'Would you be good enough to send me a copy of the play?' he asked. 'I could then have it translated, study it more carefully, and write to you my further impression.' In June Puccini was in London and, according to Vincent Seligman, it was Sybil who tipped the scales in favour of the play and who commissioned an Italian translation of it. By the middle of July Puccini had made up his mind to set it to music, and already at that early date he envisaged a different ending from Belasco's, namely a scene showing a manhunt (as we now have it in the opera) in which Puccini originally intended to have eight or ten horses on the stage! With the help of Sybil he at once set about procuring popular American music of the 1850s as well as authentic Red Indian songs. Illica being occupied with the libretto of *Maria Antonietta*, which, we recall, was to be the next opera after *La Fanciulla*, Puccini entrusted the adaptation of Belasco's play to the writer Carlo Zangarini†—no doubt because his mother hailed from New York and Zangarini himself knew English. Zangarini had been suggested to him by

---

* *The Life of David Belasco*, op. cit. The minstrel with his song is retained in the opera .

† Zangarini was responsible for numerous libretti, among them for Wolf-Ferrari's successful *I gioielli della Madonna* and Zandonai's *Conchita*.

Tito Ricordi—'a present from *Savoia*'—as Puccini was to call him later for reasons not difficult to guess. In early September Giulio Ricordi must have expressed some concern about the slow progress of the work, for in a letter of 14 September the composer is at pains to assure him that

> . . . I have not gone to sleep nor am I cooling off toward the subject of the *Wild West*. On the contrary! I am thinking of it constantly and I am sure that it will turn out a second *Bohème*, that is, unless my brain and energy fail me (*E*).

In another letter sent to his publisher shortly afterwards, Puccini again stresses the curious point of *The Girl* promising to become a second *Bohème*, 'but more vigorous, more daring, and on an altogether larger scale' (*E*). In fact no two operas could be more dissimilar, unless Puccini was thinking of a similar treatment of the crowd scenes.

While waiting for Zangarini to complete the libretto, Puccini paid a brief visit to Vienna in the second half of October, to supervise the first Austrian production of *Madam Butterfly*, given there on 31 October; this was, incidentally, the last novelty to be staged at the Hofoper before Gustav Mahler resigned as director. Mahler who, we recall, had conducted the first German production of *Le Villi* at Hamburg in 1892, developed a strong dislike of Puccini's later operas and for years refused to accept them for the Vienna Hofoper. Given his spirituality and ethical idealism, Mahler's antagonism to Puccini is not difficult to understand. *Tosca* he once declared to be a '*Kunstmachwerk*', a clever conflation of the separate expressions: *Kunstwerk*—art work, and *Machwerk*—concoction or bungling work. Nor did, to Puccini's intense resentment, *Manon Lescaut* and *Bohème* find favour with Mahler. Puccini could never forget that on the occasion of the first Vienna production of *Bohème* at the Theater an der Wien, on 5 October 1897, Mahler, who was present, burst into ironic laughter. Yet, though deeply hurt, he pocketed his pride and requested a Viennese friend of his, Baron Angelino Eisner, to try his best with the 'impregnable Mahler' to persuade him to give the first German production of *Tosca* at the Hofoper. It was in vain—this opera was never given there while Mahler remained director. *Bohème* was performed at the Hofoper but not until 1903, and *Butterfly* followed in 1907 which was the occasion for Puccini's present visit to Vienna.* He was little pleased with this production, finding the artists 'hard and unsympathetic' and lacking 'the diction or the naturalness which is necessary in *Butterfly*'. The name-part was sung by the celebrated coloratura soprano Selma Kurz—'fairly good, not very intelligent, but I don't dislike her'.[89]

* Strangely enough, it was Mahler who introduced Leoncavallo's *Bohème* to Vienna only a year after its first production at Venice (1897). He also showed great interest in Mascagni whose *L'Amico Fritz* he declared to be 'a decisive advance on *Cavalleria rusticana*', and, very curiously, felt that there existed 'many points of contact' between him and the father of *verismo* (from an unpublished letter to Mahler's sister Justine, 27 January 1893). In reality no two composers could have been more dissimilar, and the affinity which Mahler considered to exist between him and Mascagni was a deception accounted for by the fact that the Austrian symphonist was then a comparatively young man and hence not sure of the true nature of his own genius.

Vienna was one of Puccini's favourite cities, and Puccini one of Vienna's favourite composers. In 1914, a few months before the outbreak of the First World War, he was decorated by the Emperor with the Order of Franz Josef. But in the early 1900s Puccini had looked on the metropolis of the Austro-Hungarian Monarchy with little love: memories of the Austrian occupation of Lombardy were still alive in the Italian mind, to say nothing of the thorn of the Austrian South Tyrol lacerating Italy's side. When, however, Vienna's imperial splendour vanished with the collapse of the Habsburg Empire in November 1918 and the city became the impoverished capital of a small country, though still able to preserve its cultural life, especially in music, Puccini developed genuine affection for it, feeling as much at home there as he did in any other foreign city. Thus, writing to Sybil from Vienna on 17 May 1923, he says:

> . . . You who are so fond of me would be pleased to see how your Giacomo is fêted by these people here who are so hospitable and so agreeable. Vienna is a really musical city—I believe that even today, when it is forsaken and so different from what it used to be, it is still the leading city in the world— magnificent orchestras, concerts, amazing choirs, and a splendid Opera House of absolutely first rank (S).

To return to the libretto of *La Fanciulla*. On 30 January 1908 Puccini was able to inform Sybil that it was 'a really beautiful libretto—it is not fully built, but the foundations have been laid' (S).* Yet with Puccini such outbursts of optimism were deceptive. Some two months later, Zangarini had already become 'that wretch of a poet who refuses to have a collaborator . . . but tomorrow the matter will be decided with the assistance of a lawyer', as Puccini wrote angrily to Sybil on 8 April (S). Zangarini, however, acquiesced and was now paired with the writer Guelfo Civinini, whose chief task it was to curb his colleague's wild flights of imagination and reduce the libretto to more manageable proportions. At last Puccini was able to retire to his mountain eyrie at Chiatri, whence he wrote to Sybil in a rather disgruntled mood:

22 June 1908

> I've taken refuge here in order to work, but I'm doing very little; un- doubtedly *The Girl* is more difficult than I thought—it's on account of the distinctive and characteristic features with which I want to endow the opera that for the time being I've lost my way and don't go straight ahead as I should like to. I may also be influenced by my physical condition and the appalling boredom of this cursed spot.† Lucky you who live in a country of great resources—in Italy I can't find a single town that is possible to live in. Wherever you go, you see envious faces and you are treated as Cain treated Abel! It's like this in our country, especially for anyone who rises above the common level, and to a peculiar degree in the realm of Art (S).

* After Puccini's death, Zangarini told Vincent Seligman that the real librettist of *La Fanciulla* was not he but the composer (S).

† By 'my physical condition' Puccini was referring to a throat trouble that had started the previous May and had grown worse so that he had to consult the distinguished laryngologist Gracco at Florence.

At the beginning of August, the torrid heat at Chiatri and his own rest-lessness combined to drive him to Abetone, but at the end of the month we find him already back at his beloved Torre del Lago where 'life is much as usual . . . and now I am seriously getting down to work'.[90] Yet this peace was of short duration, for early in October, a mere fortnight after the date of the above letter, there began the first act of a domestic tragedy which ended in the suicide of an innocent young girl and nearly wrecked the composer's marriage. Before relating these events, however, let us first direct the limelight on the two personalities who were the chief actors in this sad drama—Giacomo and Elvira.

XIII

Giacomo and Elvira

I

WHAT MANNER OF MAN was Giacomo Puccini? He will have emerged from
the preceding pages with a number of characteristics to which new traits
must now be added, to gain a rounded picture of a personality by no means
as simple and homogeneous as has been represented by the majority of his
biographers.

On the surface, it is true, Puccini appeared uncomplicated enough. All
who knew him in his private life emphasize his infinite charm, his gentleness,
his direct and affectionate manner, his kindness and his modesty, which
remained unchanged even at the very height of his fame. Also his friends
speak with delight—and his letters confirm it—of his sense of humour,
coupled with a caustic wit whose shafts he would often direct against himself.
It was largely in his dealings with his librettists and artists that his good nature
forsook him and his tongue became capable of mordant, wounding remarks.
Yet the essential Puccini was *un simpatico*, as the Italians call the possessor of
such engaging qualities. In the company of his intimates Puccini would
throw off the habitual reserve he displayed on public occasions and behave
like the big schoolboy which he remained in one corner of his personality
all his life. Puccini was then like one of the four Bohemians depicted in his
opera. In his younger days he could be gay to the point of recklessness,
freely indulging his bent for practical jokes and obscene language. It was in
such moods that he would deliver himself of Rabelaisian doggerels—all of
them unprintable, though some *were* printed.* I reproduce here an example
which I prefer to leave in the mitigating euphony of the Italian original.
This 'poem' was a New Year's Greeting for 1899, sent by Puccini to his
Lucca friends:

Cacca di Lucca

Cacca di Lucca è sempre senza pecca
Anche se è fatta in fretta da Baldracca
Sia nera, gialla or rossa come lacca
Cacca di Lucca è sempre senza pecca.

Sia secca, o a oliva cucca, o a fil di rócca
O fatta a neccio come fa la mucca
Il suo profumo acuto mai ci stucca
Cacca di Lucca è proprio senza pecca.

Giacomo Puccini[91]

* Even as were Mozart's scatological letters to his cousin, Maria Anna Thekla.

166

There was a strong streak of coarseness and vulgarity in Puccini—one part of him was of the earth earthy, springing from that sturdy Tuscan soil from which his first ancestor had come.

But such pronounced extrovert traits were far outweighed by a peculiar shyness, a feminine sensibility and a morbid vulnerability. Adverse criticism he found most difficult to accept and, as is so often the case with such natures, he would react, by way of self-defence, by making rash, ill-considered and wounding remarks even about his best friends (including Ricordi), when they happened to express disapproval of his conduct in certain private and professional matters. Puccini dreaded publicity and displayed an exaggerated respect for newspapers and their critics. Unflattering comment would render him miserable for weeks on end. (We recall his suicidal despair after the fiasco of the first *Butterfly*). Diffident of his own powers, he would suspect enemies where there were none and could never accept those ineluctable detractors who are the lot of every outstanding artist. This man to whom entire continents paid tribute, was happiest in the rural solitude of an obscure Tuscan village because there he found the physical and spiritual protection against his vulnerable nature and was shielded against the detested but unavoidable contacts with the big cities (especially Milan), their large crowds, public receptions and banquets. The banquet given for him after the première of *Manon Lescaut* was one of the innumerable occasions to show how diffident, tongue-tied and boorish he could be in public. He aptly said of himself: 'Sono tanto orso'—'I'm such a bear'.

While healthy and strong in body—at any rate until the last year or two of his life—he displayed from his earliest youth an almost morbid over-sensitivity. His instinctive reaction to the slightest obstacles in his private— though not in his professional—life was that of the snail which withdraws into its shell at the merest touch from outside. Of all this Puccini was fully aware; as he wrote to Sybil on 6 April 1906:

> . . . you know, I make the great mistake of being too sensitive, and I suffer too when people don't understand me and misjudge me. Even my friends don't know what sort of man I am—it's a punishment that has been visited on me since the day of my birth. It seems to me that you are the only person who have come nearest to understanding my nature—and you are so far away from me!! (*S*).

And again, to the same correspondent, on 3 February 1907:

> . . . I'm so tired of this life; . . . and all my nerves are worn to shreds! How I long for a little calm! Believe me, our life is not to be envied—the texture of our nerves, or at any rate of mine, can no longer stand up to this drudgery, these anxieties and fatigues (*S*).

He was highly sensitive to changes in the weather and the seasons, which influenced his working mood. In his private letters allusions to the weather occur frequently and his autograph scores bear such recurring laconic entries as '*piove!*'—'it rains!'—and '*bel tempo!*'—'fine weather!'*

Puccini's was the decadence that is not an uncommon phenomenon in the last member of a dynasty of creative artists. From about 1907, when he entered the high summer of his life, his hypersensitiveness increased to the point of hypochondria. He began to complain about all kinds of ailments, most of which proved imaginary. In December 1920 he was concerned about some slight pain in his chest which he believed to be *angina pectoris*. To Sybil he writes some nine months later that 'I've got something—I don't know what it is—which makes me feel ill and especially depresses my spirits' (*S*). The periods of mental fatigue grew longer and more exhausting; but for such periods he might well have composed more operas and completed *Turandot*. How apposite was Illica's description that 'Puccini is a clock-work which is rapidly wound up and as rapidly runs down'. This was said in 1893 when the composer was a comparatively young man. With advancing years he grew increasingly prone to such labile moods and he more than ever gave way to self-pity—a common feature of the Latin temperament—finding more and more causes to lament his lot, which to the outsider was bound to appear a highly enviable one. He was famous, wealthy and in a position to gratify every whim—which he did. Yet he found life an intolerable burden.

Before he reached fifty years of age, he began to be tormented by the prospect of growing old and of death.† This would show even in such trifling matters as reading a programme that gave the date of his birth—'I detest that "Puccini *born* . . ." it always reminds me that in a few years will be added "*died* . . ." '92 We can readily imagine his feelings when in February 1921 a report was published in a Roman paper and at once spread to all the four corners of the globe that Puccini was dying. Letters and telegrams began to pour in to his family at Torre del Lago and to his publisher in Milan. It was not Puccini who was gravely ill but Fucini whose name had been mis-spelt when the news was telegraphed to Rome from the poet's home town, Empoli. Puccini, then still enjoying robust health, might have replied with Mark Twain that the news of his death was greatly exaggerated.

More and more he became obsessed by the fear of senescence and seriously toyed with the idea of undergoing an operation for rejuvenation. The first time he appears to have been thinking of this remedy was in the summer of 1920 when he had just embarked on *Turandot*, and wished to consult a Berlin surgeon. Three years later, his wish having become more insistent, he wanted to see a Viennese surgeon who had started experiments in this direction.‡ As he wrote to Sybil on 26 January 1923:

* To the reader living in the British Isles, where the weather forms a favourite topic of conversation, Puccini's constant references to it may seem nothing extraordinary, but for an Italian they assuredly are.

† Tchaikovsky, too, is said to have suffered from this fear. The hero of Oscar Wilde's *The Picture of Dorian Gray* exclaims: 'When I find that I am growing old I shall kill myself!'

‡ Presumably Professor Eugen Steinach. It was, incidentally, Steinach who, in November 1923, performed such an operation on Sigmund Freud, in the hope that the rejuvenation it

I think in March I shall go to Vienna to see that doctor! I've met a South American gentleman here [Viareggio] sixty-seven years old, who tells me that the operation is nothing at all and that the benefits are extraordinary—he says he feels as though he were twenty-five again, and that it no longer tires him to walk and his mind is fresh and agile, etc., etc.—why shouldn't I do it too? My dear, my life is my own and means the whole world to me—so why not? I have such a fear and such horror of old age! (S).

And seven months before his death, he intended to consult another specialist, Serge Voronov of Paris, famed for his experiments in restoring the aged to youthful vigour by grafting on to their reproductive glands those of apes. According to Panichelli,[93] Puccini would have submitted to this operation but for his diabetes.

The ground-bass of Puccini's life and his art was an ever-present melancholy—'I have always carried a large load of melancholy [*un gran sacco di melanconia*] with me. I have no reason for it, but so I am made and so are made all men who feel and who are not altogether stupid'.[94] This melancholy showed in his *povera faccia*—so well known to his intimates—in the veiled, distant glance of the eyes and the drooping corners of the mouth. It has been suggested that his was the characteristic Tuscan sadness, *la mestizia Toscana*. His fellow-Lucchese, Catalani, evinced it too—in his countenance and in his music, which is marked by an expression of delicate despair. Yet in Puccini there was also the sadness of the man and artist who, for all the immense popularity he enjoyed, was compelled by his inner nature to withdraw into himself—'to spin round him', as Strindberg once put it, 'the silk of his own soul'. The essential Puccini was an introvert and thus a lonely man. There is a most self-revealing letter to Illica written in the prime of his life and at the height of his fame which deserves to be quoted in full:

Torre del Lago, 24 November 1903

Dear Illica,

Write to me often, I am here alone and sad. If you only knew how I suffer. I have such need of a friend, but I have none, and if there is someone who loves me, he does not understand me. I have a nature so different from that of others. It's only I who understand myself and that gives me great pain. But mine is a constant pain which never leaves me alone. Nor does my work give me pleasure, and I work because I must. My life is a sea of sadness in which I am becalmed! I seem to be loved by no one; understand, by no one; and so many people say how enviable my lot is! I was born under an unhappy star! Even you don't understand me as I would like to, and perhaps you don't even sympathize with me! I would like to talk to you and pour my heart out! But you are so far away, and then to hear lamentation is certainly not pleasant. (*C.P.Let.*332).

'I seem to be loved by no one' is patently not true. Puccini here is projecting his own failing—his inability to form a deep and close attachment to

promised might delay the progress of the cancer from which Freud was to suffer for the remainder of his life. (See *Sigmund Freud. Life and Work*, Vol. III, by Ernest Jones. London, 1957.)

any person—on to other people; he attributes to *them* and to the world at large a defect in *his own* psychological make-up. The same sentiment yet couched in more poetic terms he expressed about a year and a half before his death when on 3 March 1923 he penned some verses found afterwards among his papers:

Non ho un amico	I am friendless
mi sento solo,	And alone
anche la musica	Even music
triste mi fa.	Saddens me.
Quando la morte	When death comes
verrà a trovarmi	To call me
sarò felice a capo di riposarmi.	I shall find happy repose
Oh com'è dura	Oh, how hard is my life!
la vita mia!	Yet to many I seem happy.
eppur a molti	But my successes?
sembro felice.	They pass . . . and little remains.
Ma i miei successi?	They are ephemeral things:
Passano . . . e resta	Life runs on
ben poca cosa.	Toward the abyss.
Son cose effimere:	The young take pleasure in life,
la vita corre	Yet who heeds it all?
va verso il baratro.	Youth is soon past
Chi vive giovane	And the eye scans eternity.
si gode il mondo,	
ma chi s'accorge	
di tutto questo?	
Passa veloce	
la giovinezza	
e l'occhio scruta	
l'eternità.[95]	

This last farewell possesses no literary quality yet there is irresistible poignancy in its simplicity and sincerity—it is the same with his music. Linked to a sense of spiritual loneliness and isolation, and perhaps springing from it, was a sense of weariness, a *taedium vitae*, that even his creative work was often incapable of silencing.*

* Flaubert provides, in several respects, a striking parallel. He too was obsessed by the fear of senescence, he too suffered from periods of neurotic fatigue which slowed down his work, he too was tormented by despair and frustration. In many of his letters it is indeed as though we heard Puccini's voice: 'But if you knew how weary I am sometimes! . . . I suffer from perpetual melancholy which I try to silence with the loud voice of Art; and when the siren voice fails I cannot tell you how exhausted, exasperated and bored I am'. (To Madame de Chantepie, November 1857.) And again: 'How bored and weary I am! The leaves are falling, I can hear a bell tolling, the wind is soft and enervating . . . Have you ever considered the sadness of my existence, and how much determination I need in order to live? I spend my days absolutely alone, with no more company than if I were in the depths of Central Africa. Finally, in the evenings, when I have worn myself out to little purpose, I manage to write a few lines, which I find loathsome the next day. There are gayer folk, certainly. The difficulties of my book [*L'Éducation sentimentale*] overwhelm me.

Was Puccini's tedium—his *noia*—evidence of an inner void? The life of his mind was wholly in his operas, and up to *Turandot* they reveal no spiritual aspirations, no sublimity of thought. Outside his creative work he displayed no inclination for any artistic or intellectual relaxation. True, he was an avid reader, yet his interest in literature was largely utilitarian—an endless search for the 'right' subject. He wrote verses, but they are slight and inferior. He wrote copious letters, indifferent in their literary quality, though he could be witty and picturesque in his descriptions. He was a shrewd judge of human nature, a perspicacious and frequently scathing critic of his artists, and he knew more about the theatre—at any rate his kind of theatre—than most of his contemporaries. Oddly enough, though, while he took an active part in the productions of his operas, he was never tempted to conduct them—as did Verdi, Wagner, Strauss and several of his Italian rivals like Mascagni and Leoncavallo.

2

In his views on the music of other composers Puccini was, unlike so many creative artists, remarkably broad-minded. Among the great masters of the past Beethoven represented to him the essence of music—'*Beethoven è la musica!*'; and he was especially fond of such movements as the Allegretto of the Seventh Symphony and the Scherzo and Adagio of the Ninth. In opera Verdi was his idol. Yet he placed Wagner on almost the same pedestal: *Die Meistersinger*, *Tristan* and *Parsifal* were his favourites. During his work on *Turandot* he glanced again at the score of *Tristan*, only to put it down again with the words: 'Enough of this music! We're mandolinists, amateurs: woe to him who gets caught by it! This tremendous music destroys one and renders one incapable of composing any more!'[96] His greatest admiration was reserved for *Parsifal*, which he could not hear often enough. During a visit to Vienna in 1923 he had decided, on account of the length of the opera, to attend an act each performance, in order to enjoy it the better— yet once he found himself in the theatre he stayed to the very end. It was not the huge superstructure of Wagner's religious and philosophical thought that fascinated him, but the sensuous orchestral colouring, with its evocation of an intoxicating mystical atmosphere.*

The music of his contemporaries Puccini followed with a critical yet absorbed interest, adopting and adapting certain modern devices in harmony and orchestration to his own purposes. In this he seemed to be motivated by genuine intellectual curiosity as by an apprehension that, unless he moved with the times, he might be considered old-fashioned and conserva-

---

Have I aged? Am I worn out? Yes, I think so. That is at the root of it. Then what I am doing is not pleasant. I have grown timid. I have taken seven weeks to write fifteen pages and they are still not up to much' (to Madame des Genettes, October 1864).

* Debussy too admired *Parsifal*, and for the same reasons—declaring it to be 'one of the most beautiful monuments raised to the imperturbable glory of music'. (Quoted in *Debussy*, by Edward Lockspeiser. 2nd ed. London, 1951.)

tive. The charge made against him at the time of *Butterfly* that he kept repeating himself, troubled him considerably. Writing to Clausetti in connection with *La Fanciulla del West*, he says:

> To renew oneself or die! . . . I promise myself that, if I find the right subject, I shall always do better in the direction I have taken, and sure not to remain behind' (9 July 1911. *C.P.Let.*583).

In his desire to keep abreast of contemporary development he sat almost like a young student at the feet of important composers of the day. Embittered at the poor reception accorded to part of his *Trittico* and suspecting that the music had not been considered modern enough, he is reported as saying to the critic Gaianus: 'When you come to Viareggio, I will show you my scores of Debussy, Strauss, Dukas and other. You will see how worn they are, because I have read, re-read, analysed, and made notes all over them. . .'[97]

Yet Puccini's attitude to contemporary music displayed a curious ambivalence, as will be seen from the following letter to Simoni, written some time before he made the above remark to Gaianus:

Viareggio
1 May 1922

Dear Renato,

> Tell me the truth—you have no longer any confidence in me! Why haven't you yet sent me the third act [*Turandot*], as promised? Have you done it? Perhaps not—and I, here, torment myself because it seems to me that you have lost your confidence in me. You think perhaps that my work is useless— that may well be true. There is something wrong with the taste of the public that goes to hear the new music. It loves and endures music that is illogical and without good sense. Nowadays there's no more melody or, if there is, it is vulgar. There is the belief that symphonic music is the thing, whereas I believe that it is the end of opera. One does not sing in Italy any more— instead, you have crashes, discordant chords, and insincerity—pale, opalescent and lymphatic stuff.
>
> All Celtic* diseases—true syphilis from across the Alps.[98]

And on 25 March 1924 to Clausetti:

> Nowadays atonality is the thing and one alters one's style as one likes; and he who deviates most thinks himself on the right road. We shall see. But in opera not the smallest conquest has been made. Three or more hours of this stuff are killing. It's all right in the concert hall where one adds Beethoven and other composers declared 'old hat' who refresh the spirit and serve to blot out the wearisome scribbles of those who seek the new at all costs (*C.P.Let.*886).

In view of the achievements of Malipiero and Pizzetti, Puccini's remark that 'in opera not the smallest conquest has been made' was both unfair and objectively untrue.

Among modern composers Puccini reserved his highest esteem for Debussy—an esteem, incidentally, that was not reciprocated. On the other

---

* Puccini plays here on the double meaning of *celtico*: 'Celtic', 'nordic', or 'venereal'.

hand, his attitude to Richard Strauss was guarded and circumspect. Strauss saw in Puccini his most serious rival in opera and envied him his greater popularity, but insinuated on more than one occasion that he considered his music as 'Schund'—'trash'; Puccini, on his part, evinced a genuine interest in the German composer's symphonic poems—especially and significantly in Tod und Verklärung—yet for his operas he displayed no liking. We do not know what his views were on Der Rosenkavalier, which, it may be suggested, would have appealed to him on account of its more lyrical and vocal style more than Strauss's two previous operas. As he once wrote to Sybil: 'Elektra! A horror! Salome passes—but Elektra is too much!'[99] Yet despite this verdict Salome left its mark on certain pages of La Fanciulla. When Franz Schalk, the director of the Vienna Staatsoper, once showed him the score of Die Frau ohne Schatten, Puccini, after glancing through it, pushed it aside with the laconic comment: 'It's logarithms!'[100]

Of Stravinsky's music Puccini was at first unable to make anything. Seeing a production of Le Sacre du Printemps in Paris in 1913, he found the music 'sheer cacophony but strange and not without a certain talent. But all in all, it is the stuff of a madman'.[101] Yet in the end Stravinsky's rhythmic and orchestral audacities made their impact on him, as shown in Il Tabarro and Turandot. He was also interested in Schoenberg and made a special journey to Florence in May 1924 to hear a performance of Pierrot lunaire under the composer's direction.* The work was a closed book to him, and yet, despite his aversion from atonality, in his comment Puccini was anything but negative. His prophetic words were: 'Who can say that Schoenberg will not be a point of departure to a goal in the distant future? But at present—unless I understand nothing—we are as far from a concrete artistic realization of it as Mars is from Earth.'[102] At the other extreme of the scale lay Puccini's interest in the music of Franz Lehár, with whom he stood on terms of friendship—a fact that served Puccini's detractors as an argument against his music.† No doubt he sensed in Lehár's sentimental vein an affinity with

* In June 1921 he attended in Vienna the first performance of Schoenberg's Gurrelieder but failed to be impressed by it. On this occasion he renewed his acquaintance with Mahler's widow, Alma Maria, to whom he said that he had come to the concert to hear something radical, but was hearing Wagner. That did not interest him . . . all this he knew already. He was quite angry. Alma replied that the second part of the Gurrelieder was much daring, but he left in the interval. Later he told her he had come to admire Schoenberg's work! (See Alma Mahler Werfel, And the Bridge is Love. Memories of a Lifetime. London, 1959).

† Schoenberg is reported as having ridiculed Puccini as an 'avant-courier' of Lehár, while at other times he considered him greater than Verdi and superior to him in skill. (Mahler-Werfel, op. cit.)
After the composer's death Schoenberg wrote on 28 January 1925 a letter to Alfredo Casella in which he thanked him for his article in Anbruch in which Casella described the meeting of the two composers after the Pierrot lunaire performance in Florence. Schoenberg continues: 'His death has very greatly shaken me. I would have never thought that I shall never see this great man again! And I am proud that he was interested in me, and grateful to you that you told my enemies about this honouring event'. This letter appeared in Italian in Casella's autobiography, I Segreti della della giara (Florence, 1941). Its German original was kindly placed at my disposal, through the intermediacy of the Roman critic, Fedele D'Amico, by Yvonne Casella, the composer's widow.

his own manner. Yet when the two musicians met in Vienna in 1922, and when Lehár told him of his intention to write a full-scale tragic opera, Puccini's advice—prompted, possibly, by his own experiences with *La Rondine**—was to stick to his last—operetta.†

3

In his outlook Puccini was a materialist with a strong element of the *bourgeois* in him. His philosophy of life—if so largely instinctive an attitude can thus be called—was an all but untrammelled hedonism. It may be that his nerves needed the titillation of sensual pleasures: the excitement of the hunt, the thrill of speed in cars and boats, the delights of the table—though here his diabetes would permit him only restricted indulgence—and, last but far from least the pursuit of amorous adventure. There appears to have been present in Puccini an extraordinary abundance of animal sexuality. Did he not once say: 'On the day on which I am no longer in love, you can hold my funeral!'[103] Yet, unlike the true Don Juan who is in love with the *idea* of love and for whom the conquest of the female essentially represents an unconscious attempt to clutch at this elusive image, Puccini seems to have been driven to his countless adventures by a mere sexual urge and also, one ventures to suggest, by an irresistible need to suppress irrational doubts about his virility and to assert himself. In this light the sexual act seems to have represented to him a means to an end—temporary release from those unconscious pressures and the restoration, so far as this was possible, of an inner equilibrium; it was not the physical expression of any profound emotional and spiritual attachment to a woman. Revealing of his psychology is the fact that the many women with whom he committed infidelities were, with one or two exceptions, insignificant, obscure and socially inferior creatures. For reasons to be hazarded in a later chapter, he seemed indeed to be driven to this female type. We recall Ricordi's fulmination against the affair with a Piedmonese woman—'una bassa creatura, dagli instinti putanieri'. That a high degree of sexual vitality such as Puccini possessed, does not exclude the possibility of forming emotionally valuable attachments to a woman is illustrated by the lives of Byron and Wagner. Their relationships with diverse women were, while they lasted, deeply felt and acted as a potent leaven in their creative imagination. Nothing of this kind happened to Puccini: there was no woman in his life who played the role of a Teresa Guiccioli or a Mathilde Wesendonck. Indeed, it appears that Puccini was altogether incapable of ever experiencing true love—not even with Elvira, who after the initial stage of their union may be said to have been the Minna to Puccini's Wagner. And yet the axis round which the imaginary

* See Chapter XVII.

† The failure of Lehár's opera *Giuditta* (Vienna, 1934) proved the soundness of Puccini's advice. It was, in fact, Lehár's later attempt to emulate, after the First World War, a pretentious quasi-operatic style that contributed to the decline of his own music and that of twentieth-century Viennese operetta in general.

world of his operas revolved was woman in true love, a heroine whose whole existence is consummated in her boundless devotion to the man. It was with these creatures of his fantasy that Puccini formed the close attachments which were absent from his life in the real world. Manon, Mimi, Tosca, Cio-Cio-San, Angelica and Liù—these were his true loves, and on his own confession he wept with 'nostalgia, tenderness and pain' while composing their music. Yet—and this is important—the Puccinian heroine is almost invariably a woman who by virtue of her very devotion unwittingly accumulates a heavy load of guilt which she must be made to expiate by slow suffering and the ultimate destruction of herself. This is the perennial theme of the Puccini operas. Was there concealed behind it a wish-fulfilment, a compensation in the world of his imagination for what could not be achieved in his physical life? Or, to put it differently, was Puccini's highly characteristic treatment of his heroines the symbolic re-enactment of a 'play' that was being permanently staged in his unconscious fantasies? In short, was a neurotic fixation—to be more precise, mother-fixation—the real and all but exclusive subject of his operas? The second part of this book will afford us the opportunity to try to answer this question.

4

Elvira was by all accounts a difficult woman—self-willed and self-assertive, obstinate, haughty, dogmatic and very much conscious of her position as the spouse of an illustrious man. Her temper was uncertain; she could be provoked easily and would make the most wounding remarks in a harsh, rasping voice. The superstitious fisherfolk of Torre del Lago attributed to her the possesion of 'la iettatura'—'the evil eye'. Her background had been that of a small provincial town, the same milieu from which Puccini too had sprung, yet from which he gradually succeeded in emancipating himself while Elvira was never able to achieve this. She was rigidly conventional, narrow-minded, ungenerous in her sympathies and, so far as is known, interested in nothing beyond what concerned her family. She was a faithful and devoted wife, and a dedicated mother to whom her children, notably Tonio, were deeply attached.

A true Tuscan woman, she was full-blooded in her love of Puccini, and it was this that inspired in her the courage to commit the one and only act in her life by which she flouted the moral code of her class. Had she not deserted the respectable home of her first husband and eloped with a young struggling artist, thus tarnishing her character and exposing herself to material insecurity? With the upbringing she had had, Elvira must have suffered—at any rate during her early association with Puccini—a sense of profound humiliation and shame; we recall that a period of nearly twenty years elapsed before this union could be sanctioned by the laws of man and God. The vexations, the indignities, the slights to her self-respect—it must be borne in mind that she lived in Catholic Italy of the 1890s and came, like her husband, from a petit bourgeois milieu, with its narrow and rigid moral code—could not fail to exercise their influence on Elvira's spirit. All this may also explain why her love for her husband became excessively possessive and jealous; being a woman of a remarkably strong will she dominated him. When a woman of such character traits as Elvira's lives with a man inferior to her in will-power but superior in most other respects, she can ruin his happiness and peace of mind—but not his genius.

Admittedly, despite his many engaging qualities, Puccini was by no means easy to live with. He was not without his share of guilt in the strains to which this relationship was subjected almost from its very inception. No wife—short of being an angel or a moron—could be presumed to steer the matrimonial ship on an even keel all the time; Elvira was neither angel nor moron, yet she might have proved a more successful pilot had she possessed a generous heart and insight into her husband's mentality—had she possessed 'more judgment and sense', as Puccini once wrote to her.

There were two factors that more than any other bedevilled their marriage. One was Puccini's unwillingness to make Elvira a true companion of his *creative* life; the other, her pathological jealousy.

It is questionable—and we have no evidence to prove the contrary—whether Elvira, despite the music lessons she had had in her youth, possessed any true understanding for her husband's work or for music at all; she was definitely his intellectual inferior. Whether justified or not, Puccini's deliberate exclusion of her from the most vital sphere of his life amounted to a denial of all intelligence in her and engendered in Elvira a mounting sense of resentment and inferiority which she attempted to conceal under the cloak of contempt for everything connected with art. Her attitude only served to alienate Puccini still further from her. 'You sneer when the word "art" is pronounced. This has always offended me and offends me still', he wrote to her as late as 1915—after nearly thirty years of life together! Puccini, it is true, frequently wrote her letters, with long accounts of such things as rehearsals, new productions, artists and current events in the theatre—but this was essentially in the nature of gossip. He scarcely ever touched on intrinsic artistic issues, on problems that profoundly troubled him as a creative artist; and one supposes he rarely discussed them with her in the intimacy of their home. She, in turn, felt lonely and deserted; she would often accuse him of treating her with icy coldness—'like a piece of furniture'—and of taking everyone into his confidence but her.

Elvira, it must be stressed, was extremely proud of her husband's successes and fame; but at the same time she could not help perceiving in them a major cause for her own isolation and her feeling of inferiority. A letter she wrote to Puccini, then on a visit to New York on the occasion of the first production of *La Fanciulla*, makes pathetic reading:

30 November 1910

The fact that you did not allow me to go with you, and the way in which you expressed that prohibition, hurt me deeply. I shall not get over it.

Remember this. You deprived me of a great satisfaction, that of participating in your triumph. . . The only thing that consoles me is the thought that at least you are happy without me—I wish that everything goes well, just as you desire, that you enjoy a great triumph, and that no shadow, even the faintest, comes to disturb your peace. Now you are a great man, and compared to you I am nothing but a pygmy. Therefore be happy and forgive me if I have annoyed you with my lamentations (M).

Elvira did not fail to become gradually aware that, while for her husband the *grand monde* was all smiles and compliments, it had little more than a cool, formal nod of acknowledgment for her as la Donna Puccini. Again, there was a marked contrast in the public behaviour and appearances of the two. From a rather uncouth youth, Puccini had grown into a man of the world, polished and urbane; while Elvira—despite the wealth that surrounded her and her many travels abroad—remained a provincial. And whereas Puccini looked in his middle age more personable, more distinguished and in a sense younger than he had in his thirties, Elvira's beauty had paid its toll to the passage of time in the prematurely aged look of her face, with deep lines round her eyes, her lips habitually tight, the corners of her mouth drawn; this lent her an expression of severity and bitterness. As the years passed, she became withdrawn, unsociable, and hostile to her husband's intimate friends, whom she suspected of aiding and abetting him in his amorous escapades. And while he passionately loved life in the country —on his own admission the *sine qua non* for his creative work—she was for ever fretting to escape (as Puccini put it with irony) 'from the heavy burden of green nature' to the bustle of life in Milan.

Elvira was, in short, her own worst enemy. The major source for her own misery and the misery she caused her husband lay in her nature. Puccini put his finger on it in a revealing letter written from Berlin on 14 March 1913, in reply to one of her usual reproaches for not having been permitted to accompany him on his journey:

. . . Here it is not like Paris, where even if you remain alone, you can enjoy yourself. Here you would have been furious. I assure you, and you know it as well as I, that you would have been on tenterhooks here, and then the journey would have become feverish and painful. In short, it is time that you understand certain matters. We are always together, either at Torre or in Milan, and once in a while a man wants a mite of liberty—that is not a crime. You fabricate God knows what phantoms, and you suffer. But be tranquil. I always think of you and with you, and when you are good and less grim I remain with you very willingly. But you have a tragic soul. That is it. Your enormous pessimism, that is your enemy. It does not permit you to enjoy life. You also communicate it to me. That is why from time to time you make me wish to be alone, to rid myself of that continuous black which surrounds you and which makes you suffer morally, and in consequence physically. . . Well, if you want to come and if it makes you sad not being here, do as you please. I cannot say more. . . (M).

The gnawing worm in Elvira's 'tragic soul' was a congenital, tormenting jealousy which made her 'fabricate God knows what phantoms' and which, in its extreme manifestations, suggested, as we shall see, persecution mania; it was the single major cause of their interminable quarrels. Admittedly, Puccini's conduct provided abundant justification for her jealousy; everyone in his intimate circle knew of his frequent infidelities, but he was candid enough to confess to them. 'Mine is the guilt. But it is my destiny that I must be guilty', he wrote to Elvira on one occasion.[104] Egocentric artist that he was, he claimed a certain measure of conjugal freedom, arguing that he needed his little amours as a stimulant to his work—a typically male argument, to be sure. He tried to reason with Elvira and convince her of the insignificance of his love affairs:

30 August 1915

. . . Your suspicions mislead you into the most undignified investigations. You invent women in order to give free play to your policeman's instinct. Everything appears serious, large, weighty to you while it is nothing, a mere negligible nothing. . . You have never looked at these matters as do other women who are more reasonable—Good God! The world is full of such things. And all the artists cultivate these little gardens in order to delude themselves into thinking that they are not finished and old and torn by strife.* You imagine immense affairs. In reality, it is nothing but a sport to which all men more or less dedicate a fleeting thought without, however, giving up that which is serious and sacred; that is, the family. . . Let time and circumstances do their work. Do not oppose me with that vehemence and assiduity that you have adopted. Everyone has within himself a measure of rebellion. It is natural. See to it that my house be not odious to me and burdensome, that I find here a cupful of jollity and calm instead of this continuous and discouraging aggravation. Such a state embitters a disposition however good, irritates and renders the soul desirous of other and different sensations. The wife of an artist has a mission different from that of wives of ordinary men. This is something you have never wanted to understand. Indeed you sneer when the word 'art' is pronounced. This has always offended me and offends me still. I, more than you, seek peace. I seek to lead with you and to finish with you a life which would have been less parlous if you had had more judgment and sense. Good-bye! I kiss you. Be calm. Wait for me. I shall always be your Topizio (M).

Yet Elvira was never able to accept her husband's marital heterodoxy and look with a tolerant eye on his cultivating 'these little gardens'. In her obsessional jealousy she would on occasion be prompted to actions both absurd and pathetic. A beautiful young singer who called on Puccini in connection with some professional matter found herself threatened by Elvira with an umbrella and ignominiously chased out of the house; and as she ruefully admitted in later years, she was in the habit of putting camphor in Puccini's trouser pockets, and mixing the wine or the coffee with an anaphrodisiac, whenever an attractive woman guest happened to be invited to dinner at their home. In short, Elvira provides a classical illustration of the

* Puccini was then in his fifty-seventh year.

old German pun: '*Eifersucht ist eine Leidenschaft, die mit Eifer 'sucht was Leiden schafft*'—'Jealousy is a passion which seeks with passion that which causes suffering'.

5

The first violent rift in their union appears to have occurred in 1891, by which time Puccini and Elvira had been living together for about six years. He was then still closely attached to her, addressing her in his letters by a variety of pet-names: *Elviretta—Cecetta* ('Little Pea')—*Cicina* ('Birdie')—*Porchizia* ('Piglet')—*Topizia* ('Little Mouse'), and signing himself '*Topizio*'. There is no reason to suppose that he had yet been unfaithful to her, but Elvira's suspicions were already awake. In the spring of that year, Puccini was living at Lucca while Elvira stayed somewhere in the neighbourhood—an arrangement designed to prevent giving fresh food to the malicious local gossips in his native town. Besides, mere tact demanded this temporary separation since Elvira's husband was living at Lucca. Some kind friend had insinuated to Elvira that Puccini was tired of her and wished to leave her. Her immediate reaction was to want to rush to Lucca in order to find out the truth. In a long letter dated 23 May 1891 Puccini tries to prove to her the falsity of her friend's story, and continues:

> . . . And now as to us two—please convince yourself that you cannot come to Lucca; if you only knew what they say and do, my relatives, his, the whole city! Therefore it is impossible for you to come to Lucca; you would force me to leave and not find me there. A serious situation which would harm us both; if you were going to be with your mother, it could still be done, but even then it would be a bad situation. In these few days I have understood what kind of village it is that we live in. Please don't create trouble for me—be patient; Viareggio is not the place for you or for me either. I don't know what to advise you because the matter is quite involved. . . You know how hard I must work, as everything depends on my work [*Manon Lescaut*], and I don't have the peace of mind that I need; I beg of you, think of me and make the sacrifice of being patient and staying where you belong—don't worry about me—I am and will always be your Topizio, and the time will come when we shall be calm and happy. . . (*M*).

Her mind poisoned by the venom of suspicion, Elvira must have interpreted his explanations as subterfuges. She repeated her wild accusations, as the following reply suggests, sent her by Puccini from Milan, where he had gone for consultations with Ricordi:

4 June 1891

> . . . Why don't you remain as calm as possible? What reasons can there be for you to be so upset on my account? You say that you have to tell me *certain things* in person. For my part, I have nothing to blame myself for; I have always acted and always will act loyally toward you—no subterfuges, no idea of leaving you, of betraying you. My only desire is to be able to finish *Manon* in peace. I have committed myself (if I weren't to keep my word I should be ruined) and it must be ready for Turin next Carnival. In November,

if we can wait so long, I'll come and fetch you to resume our life—to live together eternally with our baby until it is time for him to enter boarding school. . .

Have faith in me; good God, what more can I tell you? Every day the same complaints, the same oaths, and you know me well enough not to have any doubts. If you continue I shall be hurt. You know I am your love and you are my only and true, holy love. . . (M).

This was the tone and temper of their correspondence when Puccini still professed to be in love with Elvira. With the passing of years his friendly expostulations grew fewer and fewer and were replaced by despair at her unceasing complaints. In 1900, when both had reached full maturity, Puccini wrote her the following (undated) letter from Brussels:

You write me a letter full of discomfort and sadness. And I? We are strange two beings. But a little of the guilt is yours, dear Elvira. You are no longer the same, your nerves dominate you, no longer a smile, no longer an open mien. In my own house I feel myself more of a stranger than you do. Oh, the beautiful intimacy of our first years! Now we pass months (at least I do) in a house which belongs to others. I do not say this in order to complain about Ida, Beppe, etc* No. They are all good people, very sweet people. But their continuous presence in our midst has expelled our intimacy. You are always bored in the country and I love it so. You have need of your relatives in order to make the heavy burden of green nature seem lighter. This is what has given me a shock I hope not an irreparable one, to our dear past intimacy . . .

I think always of the beautiful times which are past. In those days we were materially not well off, but for all that we were not less content. You are unhappy? I am doubly so. . . I see no way out. Your letter gave me such pain! . . . (M).

The estrangement between husband and wife continued to widen in an atmosphere of growing mutual exasperation. This was the background for the tragedy now to be related, and it provides the explanation for the violence with which it was enacted.

* Relatives of Elvira.

XIV

Tragic Interlude

ELVIRA WAS A SEVERE TASKMASTER with her servants. With the exception of Guicche—an old factotum who, as often as not, would turn a deaf ear to the scoldings of his autocratic mistress—domestics did not remain long in her service. It was different, however, with Doria Manfredi, the daughter of a local family at Torre del Lago. She was sixteen at the time when she entered the employ of the Puccinis—soon after the composer's car accident in February 1903; and she appears to have been engaged in the first place to act as nurse during his convalescence. Doria had accepted the post against the wishes of her family, having been warned by everyone at Torre of Elvira's uncertain temper and jealous disposition as well as of Puccini's susceptibility to female charms. Yet the girl seems to have regarded it a privilege to serve in the house of the illustrious composer. Doria was by all accounts a gentle, modest girl, childlike in her devotion to her master and mistress; but in her adoration of Puccini there was, as later events suggest, an element of girlish hysteria. Vincent Seligman, who well remembered her, affirms that there was literally nothing that she was not prepared to do and that, in fact, the whole household revolved round her.[105] Doria was a rare domestic pearl.

She had already seen five years of service when, in late September or early October 1908, Elvira began to suspect her of what she later described as 'immoral conduct' with her husband. It appears that the first insinuations came from one of Elvira's interfering relatives, whose continued presence in the house Puccini had always found so exasperating. Whether there was any truth in their innuendoes we shall never know. Puccini declared later that he had merely been fond of the girl on account of her devotion as a servant. It may be that he felt, in fact, attracted to her and had indulged in a harmless flirtation; yet, as was to be subsequently established beyond doubt, she had never been his mistress.

Elvira began a veritable war against Doria, levelling wild accusations at her, pretending to possess proof of her misconduct, and bruiting it about that she had caught her and Puccini in the act—'the most infamous lies! I defy anyone to say that he ever saw me give Doria even the most innocent caress!' Puccini wrote to Sybil after the tragedy.[106] Doria was given notice. Not content with this, Elvira went around Torre branding the girl as a social outcast, and in her fury and desire to persecute her still further demanded of the local priest, Father Michelucci, that he intervene with Doria's family and persuade them to compel Doria to leave the village. When meeting her in the street, which was unavoidable in so small a place, in the presence of witnesses Elvira would hurl into her face that she was

> a slut, a tart, that she was a whore because she was the mistress of her husband, that she [Elvira] was then going to the lake to look for her husband, that sooner or later, as sure as there was Christ and a Madonna, she would drown her. . .[107]

Appalled by his wife's conduct and the scandal this wretched affair was beginning to arouse, Puccini adopted at first the line of least resistance and fled to Paris, whence he wrote to Sybil in early October:

> I'm all by myself and I've taken refuge here! I couldn't stand it any more; I've suffered so much. Elvira has given Doria notice, saying that she is a ―― without a *shadow* of proof.
> Life at Torre had become absolutely unbearable for me; I'm only telling you the truth when I say that I have often lovingly fingered my revolver! And everyone (including you) says that I am the happiest man in the world!
> I'm going to stay here a short while, and then out of force of habit I shall have to return to that Hell. . . (*S*).

He began to suffer from insomnia and was forced to take veronal so that 'my face is mottled like a Winchester gun'. After a short sojourn in Milan, he was back at Torre, whence he informed Sybil:

> 20 December 1908
>
> I can write a little more freely today because Elvira has gone to Lucca, where her mother is ill—it's a ghastly, horrible life—enough to drive one to suicide!
> My work goes on [*La Fanciulla*], but so slowly as to make me wonder if it will ever be finished—perhaps I shall finish first! As for the 'Affaire Doria', Elvira's persecution continues unabated. . . I've seen the poor girl secretly once or twice—and the sight is enough to make one cry; in addition to everything else, she's in a very poor state of health. My spirit rebels against all this brutality—and I have to stay on in the midst of it! If it hadn't been for my work which keeps me here, I should have gone away, and perhaps for ever. . . I can only go on, hoping for the best and that things will settle down again. . . (*S*).

Things did not 'settle down again'; on the contrary, they grew so much worse that Puccini was now seriously considering leaving his wife. Writing to Sybil he says:

> 4 January 1909
>
> I'm still in a state of the greatest unhappiness—if you only knew the things my wife has been doing and the way she has been spying on me! It's an appalling torment, and I'm passing through the saddest time of my life! I should like to tell you everything, but I don't want to torture myself further; it's enough if I tell you that I don't want to live any longer—certainly not with her. To go far away and create a new life; to breathe the air freely and rid myself of this prison atmosphere which is killing me. . . (*S*).

The climax of this sordid drama was reached on 23 January, when Doria, completely unnerved and distraught by Elvira's persecution, attempted suicide in her mother's home. She died five days later. For months after Puccini was haunted by the vision of that poor victim: 'I can't get her out of my mind—it's a continual torment. The fate of that poor child was too cruel.'[108]

Of the events leading up to this tragedy, Puccini himself gave an abbreviated account to Sybil in the following letter:

Rome
6 February 1909

It's a long story and too sad for me to relate now—I'll merely give you a summary of the facts.

Elvira continued to persecute that wretched child, preventing her even from taking a walk, and telling tales about her all over the village—to her mother, her relations, the priest and everyone. All my friends and relations and I myself told her to stop it and calm herself; but she wouldn't listen to anyone. I made my peace with her and told her to forget about the past and be satisfied that the girl was no longer in the house. She promised to do so; but the same evening I found her out of doors hidden in the dark, *dressed in my clothes*, to spy on me. I said nothing and left the following day for Rome.

Elvira was supposed to go to Milan; instead, she remained for three more days at Torre, and during that time did everything and said everything she could to the mother, repeating again that her daughter was a —— and that we used to meet each other in the evenings in the dark. She told one of Doria's uncles that his daughter used to carry letters between us; and, meeting Doria in the street, she publicly insulted her in the presence of others. Her brother wrote to me in a rage that he would like to kill me because I was his sister's lover—and that my wife had said so herself. In a word, poor Doria, faced with Hell in her own home and dishonour outside, and with Elvira's insults still ringing in her ears, in a moment of desperation swallowed three tablets of sublimate, and died after five days of atrocious agony.

You can imagine what happened at Torre; Elvira left for Milan the day of the poisoning; everyone was against me, but even more against Elvira. By order of the authorities a medical examination was made in the presence of witnesses, and she was found to be *pure;* then public opinion turned round entirely against Elvira. There are some other painful details which I shall omit.

The position now is that I can go back to Torre, and I *shall* go back. But Doria's family have brought an action against Elvira for public defamation. We're trying to see if we can stop the action, though I'm not directly taking part in the negotiations. In any case, Elvira will never be able to go back to Torre—or she would be lynched (S).

Puccini had hoped to persuade the Manfredi family to withdraw their action by offering them a handsome sum of money, but his offer met with a complete refusal, for Doria's relatives were set on retribution. The necessary papers were filed on 1 February and the case put down to be heard at the Pisa court on 6 July.

Meanwhile Elvira had gone to live in Milan, taking Antonio with her, while Puccini remained at Torre. For all the revulsion he felt for the 'horrible things and barbarities' that had been committed, he was now anxious to offer her, through Tonio, advice as to the line of defence she ought to adopt at the forthcoming trial, placing little trust in the lawyers whom Elvira had engaged; in that he was justified, as the outcome of the case was to prove. He counselled his wife to plead that, deceived by appearances, she was led to treat Doria badly, and that she deplored the tragic results, 'not having the slightest idea that such could be possible'.[109] Still pretending in her obstinacy to have evidence of Doria's guilt, Elvira took no heed of his advice.

On 16 June—three weeks before the trial was due to open—Puccini wrote to Sybil as follows:

> . . . Elvira's lawyers are doing their best to ruin her and me by giving conflicting advice, but I can understand that they want to pile up the costs so as to make a better meal, and in order that the case should be more sensational, thus giving them additional advertisement. The lawsuit, which looks rather black for Elvira, will be heard on 6 July; I've done everything I possibly can here by speaking to Doria's brother, but he is implacable. He's determined to bring the action, failing which he has sworn to kill Elvira—and I believe he is quite capable of carrying out his threat. I am not personally involved; in fact he told me that he wishes me well, but that, before she died, Doria bade him avenge her on her mistress, though no harm must befall her master because he had always been so good to her, etc. That, in a word, is the wretched story I have to tell. . . I can't work—it's a real crime that is being committed, to torture in this way a poor fellow who has never done anyone any harm—or at least never intended any (S).

Among the documentary evidence cited against Elvira at the trial were four of Puccini's letters, written to Doria and her mother respectively. In a letter addressed to the girl, dated 26 October, he tried to comfort her by stating that

> I know that I have a clean conscience in regard to you and I am desolate to see you thus sacrificed and slandered. I declare openly that I am fond of you because you were always a good girl in my house. Nobody can say anything bad about you. Whoever does, lies and commits the greatest injustice. . . (M).

And to her mother he declared, in a letter of 21 November:

> . . . there is not a shadow of truth in all that has been whispered. It is the result of vicious people who have turned my wife's head. I have always considered your daughter as a member of my family (M).

Another piece of damning evidence against Elvira was a note left by Doria, to the effect that she was wholly innocent of what her mistress had accused her.

Elvira was ill advised by her lawyers to stay away from the trial on the plea of sickness. The defence put forward on her behalf was feeble and unconvincing and Elvira was found guilty on three counts: defamation of character, libel, and menace to life and limb. She was condemned to five months and five days of imprisonment, a fine of 700 lire for damages, and the payment of all costs.

On 8 July, two days after the verdict, Elvira, who was in Milan nursing Tonio, who had fallen ill, wrote to her husband:

> ... This last blow has demolished me and surely I shall not get over it easily. Everybody has condemned me... And now what shall we do? Appeal? What will be my defence? Tell the truth? But you know that this, now more than ever, is impossible without hurting chiefly you. What will the world say? That you let your wife be condemned? And shall I have to go to prison? That you do not desire, I hope... (M).

These are incredible words. In the face of all the evidence—including the result of the post-mortem examination proving that Doria had died a *virgo intacta*—Elvira still remained convinced of the truth of her accusations. It was obvious that she had by now lost her senses. Two days later she told Puccini in another letter that she found his protestations ridiculous as she did not doubt him any longer, and a week later wrote that had she the courage she would throw herself out of the window if it were a little higher.

On 21 July, Elvira's lawyers lodged an appeal. In her defence they put forward that she was a person inexperienced in legal matters, that her mind had been poisoned by the evil talk of her friends, that her threat to the girl to drown her in the shallow waters of the lake could not be taken seriously, that in her regrettable conduct she had been actuated by jealousy due to her love for her husband, and that the girl, as had been attested by her doctor, was inclined to hysteria.* According to Elvira, Doria had some years previously taken arsenic because Puccini had found fault with her.

Elvira pleaded guilty on the count of libel but denied the charges of defamation of character and menace to life and limb. While her appeal was being considered, Puccini once more approached Doria's family offering them the considerable sum of 12,000 lire to withdraw their action. Possibly because they found this offer too tempting to resist, or because they felt that Doria's honour had now been fully redeemed, the Manfredis withdrew the action and on 2 October the Court of Appeal removed it from the files.

The 'Affaire Doria' caused an unprecedented sensation in Italy. Newspapers carried detailed reports of the court proceedings, some giving lurid descriptions of the circumstances in which the girl had died. It provided Puccini's enemies and rivals with a heaven-sent occasion to wag their tongues and gratify their *Schadenfreude*—which according to some psychologists is the keenest of joys. Puccini did not exaggerate when he described this period as 'the saddest time of my life'. He, who had always dreaded strangers prying into his private life, now saw it dragged in the mud; and he considered the honourable name of the Puccinis besmirched. In his despair he even felt that his own position was 'irretrievably ruined'. The tragedy had grievously affected his spirits and his work; all who met him remarked how much older he looked.

What had grievously added to his misery was the fact that at one stage his own son had turned against him. Like his mother, Tonio was convinced of

* Ironically enough, Dr. Rodolfo Giacchi, who testified at the trial and who had carried out the autopsy, had been one of the witnesses at Puccini's belated wedding in 1904.

his father's guilt and had at first taken her side in the conflict, though, as
Puccini pointed out to Elvira, Tonio ought to have 'enough judgment and
sentiment to distinguish good from bad'.[110] Tonio, then in his twenty-third
year, had left for Munich without informing his father, in order to escape
the distressing atmosphere of his home. Here is Puccini's comment, in a
letter addressed to his son in Munich on 7 April:

> What have I done to deserve this treatment?·To others you confide that
> you will go to Munich, from me you hide your plan. . . You are hurting me
> and yourself. I do not deserve this new affront added to all those which I
> have received from my family.
>
> As to what is going on in our house, you judge wrongly. Very wrongly.
> You have let yourself be led astray by assertions which are contrary to the
> truth. . . (M).

To get away from it all, Tonio decided at one moment to emigrate to
Africa; but his father managed to dissuade him:

19 April 1909

> . . . For God's sake abandon this idea of Africa, where ninety-nine out of a hun-
> dred perish. You have not the physical fibre necessary for such a climate. . . (M).

What course did Puccini's relations with Elvira take after the tragedy?
At first he contemplated permanent separation from her. Yet he was not a
vindictive man and, after a few weeks, considered that temporary separation
would be punishment enough for her. And though he stressed, when he
heard of Elvira having 'grown very thin and that she is wretched and
unhappy', that 'nothing will induce me to alter my decision, and for the
first time in my life I pray that I shall not be moved by feelings of pity or
compassion',[111] he had already been moved by such feelings. Only two
months after Doria's suicide he had written to Sybil that 'Elvira too deserves
pity because the chief fault was not hers', implying that the real culprits were
his wife's relatives, who had poisoned her mind with false insinuations; they
were the same 'unscrupulous persons' whom he later suspected of having
influenced Elvira against Sybil herself.

The initial step toward a reconciliation was taken in May, when husband
and wife met in Milan for the first time since the previous January. The outcome was disheartening. As Puccini informed his son from London on 24 May:

> After having met your mother, I became very sad because I see that her
> behaviour towards me remains the same, nothing conciliatory, always the
> same violence, and above all an unwillingness to recognize that the cause, the
> principal cause, of her and our misfortune is she herself. . . Believe me, my
> dear Tonio, the future looks black for us. I have every intention of returning
> to her, but I do not wish to humiliate myself. . . (M).

A second meeting with Elvira, in Milan on 9 June, found her in the
same mood as before. To a letter she wrote him a day or two afterwards
Puccini made, on 12 June, the following reply:

> I have no wish to quarrel. You write me a letter which does not even deserve
> an answer, so unjust and false is it. . . I repair the harm that I have done?

That's really too much! You who, with your morbid jealousy and with your entourage, have poisoned my existence, now demand that I prostrate myself and beg your pardon? You are mad! Very well, do as you like. I am leaving. . . If you wish to return to me, I shall always be ready to take you back. If you want to conduct your defence in the way you say you do, go ahead. I have nothing to fear—nothing. There are a million people who will attest my honesty and probity and the sincerity of my life as man and artist . . .(*M*).

Like her husband Elvira was passing through the most miserable period of her life, and she too suffered grievously under the blow dealt to her family life. At last her defences broke down and on 26 July—twenty days after the trial—Puccini was able to inform Sybil from Bagni di Lucca:

> I was in Milan because Tonio had been ill. Now all three of us are reunited again here, and it seems as if life is going to be less unpleasant. Elvira seems to me to have changed a great deal as the result of the hardships of the separation which she has endured—and so I hope to have a little peace and to be able to get on with my work (*S*).

Elvira was now a chastened woman and life at Torre resumed, outwardly at any rate, its old routine. But the upheaval had been too great, the experience too shattering and the recriminations between husband and wife too wounding; the discordant echo of this tragic interlude continued to reverberate through their marriage, though in diminishing force, for a long time. It was, in fact, not until the period of *Turandot*, during the last three or four years of Puccini's life, that their relationship grew affectionate again, and that both felt a sense of belonging together. Puccini and Elvira were then in their early sixties: serenity and resignation—the solace of approaching old age—descended upon them, and this is the picture which the composer conjures up for Adami, eighteen months before his death:

> Elvira and I are here [Viareggio], the two ancients, like two old family portraits, raising our eyebrows from time to time at the cobwebs which tickle us. We sleep, we eat, we read the *Corriere*, and with four notes in the evening the old composer keeps life going.[112]

The last words Puccini spoke on his deathbed concerned Elvira. Whispering to his stepdaughter Fosca, he is reported to have said: 'Remember that your mother is a remarkable woman!'

There is small doubt that the 'Affaire Doria' was a major if not indeed the sole factor responsible for the temporary decline of Puccini's creative curve during the period which produced *La Fanciulla* and *La Rondine*—both works which, despite fine craftsmanship, reveal signs of an exhaustion in his inventive faculty and of a reduction in his powers of concentration. Nevertheless, this tragic episode proved artistically not altogether negative. 'Always I have before my eyes the vision of that poor victim', Puccini had said. It is more than probable that Doria's character, her suffering and ultimate fate, were at the back of his mind when he portrayed the Nun in *Suor Angelica* and the little slave girl Liù in *Turandot* in such poignant colours. In those two heroines, so truly Puccinian, he appears to have paid homage to the memory of a gentle, childlike creature. Doria's tragedy is perhaps the only instance in Puccini's life when a profound experience in the world of reality was transmuted in the crucible of his artistic imagination. But Doria's mortal enemy, too, found her portrayal. It is my conviction—and more will be said on this point later—that Elvira contributed traits to two of her husband's heroines, heroines who re-enact precisely the role which she had played in those 'horrible things and atrocities committed' against Doria, the role of a persecutor: the Aunt of Sister Angelica and the Princess Turandot.

XV

Recovery

THE AMOUNT OF WORK that Puccini was able to do on *Fanciulla* during those disturbing months from October 1908 to July 1909 was negligible. In August, however, he was in harness again and informed Sybil on the 22nd of that month that he felt 'a little quieter now' and that the opera was 'beginning to take life and strength'. Though his diabetes was giving him trouble again, compelling him to live 'on a régime—no bread, but douches and injections'— he yet felt 'strong, and my brain is clear', hoping to finish his work soon, as he wrote to Sybil on 30 September. By then the second act was nearly completed. In November he began the third act, which, however, made such slow progress that on 9 April of the following year he informed her: 'I've still got the whole of the third act to do, and I'm beginning to be a little fed up with Minnie and her friends. Let's hope that the third act will satisfy me as much as the other two.' In point of fact it was to turn out the best of the three and was completed on 6 August, while the first two were finished on 21 January and 9 April 1910 respectively. The news of the completion of the opera was announced to Sybil on 15 August, with a sigh of relief and the curious statement '*The Girl* has come out, in my opinion, the best opera I have written'. Puccini sadly deceived himself; but then he always thought his most recent opera his best.

A minor difficulty arose over the choice of the Italian title. *La Fanciulla dell'Occidente d'Oro*—the literal translation of Belasco's title—was a mouthful; the shorter *La Fanciulla dell'Occidente* signified next to nothing; *L'Occidente della Fanciulla* lent itself to a *double entendre*. Then there was the composer's objection, whether in jest or otherwise is uncertain, to using '*Fanciulla*' at all in the title 'because of the last two syllables, which, I fear, might be applied to me'.* Hence the proposal to call the opera *La Figlia del West* or, alternatively, *L'Occidente d'Oro*. It was Mrs. Seligman, faithful to the time-honoured tradition of her country, who suggested a compromise in the hybrid *La Fanciulla del West*, which found the composer's approval. It was possibly at her instigation, or at that of Paolo Tosti, that Puccini dedicated the opera to Queen Alexandra, who, like her husband King Edward VII, was fond of opera and counted *La Bohème* as her favourite among the composer's works. The Queen later acknowledged the dedication with the gift of a diamond-and-ruby pin and a letter of thanks—'most flattering indeed

---

* Puccini refers to the word '*ciullo*' signifying 'stupid' or 'daft'. (Letter to Ricordi of 13 July 1908, *E*.)

to me—I was greatly touched by it', wrote Puccini on 26 June 1911 to Sybil, who had advised him on the formalities required for obtaining the Queen's consent to the dedication.

The first performance of La Fanciulla del West was fixed to take place at the Metropolitan Opera on 10 December 1910. Being an 'American' opera by an Italian composer of world-wide fame, it was but natural that Gatti-Casazza, who was biased in favour of an Italian repertoire, should have secured the first production for his opera house. To add to the glamour, he invited Puccini to New York to come as guest of the management and to supervise the preparations. The cast for the chief roles was a resplendent one: Emmy Destinn in the name-part, Caruso as Johnson and Pasquale Amato as Sheriff. The conductor was Toscanini. Puccini sailed from Genoa in early November, accompanied by his son and Tito Ricordi, who was in charge of the production. Elvira remained at home. According to Vincent Seligman, whose statement is based on her letters to his mother, 'one visit to New York [in 1907] had been more than enough' for her. Yet this seems to have been merely a face-saving excuse before the Seligmans, for in the aforementioned letter to Puccini, Elvira expressed her resentment at not having been permitted to join him.* The tension between husband and wife caused by the 'Affaire Doria' had evidently not yet subsided.

The production of La Fanciulla was one of the most spectacular events in the annals of the Metropolitan Opera. The publicity had been set in motion as early as in the previous May when the agreement for the New York performance was signed, and it reached gigantic dimensions near the date of the first night. The demand for tickets was so big that the management resorted to stringent measures to prevent trafficking in tickets. Even so, tickets are said to have been sold at thirty times their box-office price, which, anyhow, had been doubled for the première. For the second performance the prices were quadrupled!

Puccini was in high spirits. Writing to Elvira on 7 December he said:

> The rehearsals are going very well. I believe it will be a success and let's hope it will be a big one. Tomorrow is the dress rehearsal. After the perform-ance there will be a supper and reception at the Vanderbilts' and perhaps others to follow—what a pleasure! . . . The opera emerges splendidly, the first act a little long, but the second act magnificent and the third act grandiose. . . Caruso is magnificent in his part, Destinn not bad but she needs more energy. Toscanini, the zenith!—kind, good, adorable—in short, I am content with my work and I hope for the best. But how tremendously difficult it is, this music and the staging! . . . (M).

Though Tito Ricordi was the chief producer, Belasco was invited to assist and he did it with a will, determined 'to make the artists act as well as sing'; as he said after the first-night, 'they were all wild with enthusiasm. I was never so much bekissed in my life!'[113] In the third act, the so-called 'Puccini Act', which was largely of his own invention, the composer had the

* See p. 176.

satisfaction of seeing eight horses on the stage, just as he had envisaged it. Yet he had to consent to the alteration of one episode in 'his' act. In his ignorance of the American public's susceptibilities in racial matters, he had made the character of Billy Jack Rabbit, a Red Indian, carry out lynch law by hanging the condemned Johnson on a tree, an idea inconceivable on the American stage of that period. The Red Indian was replaced by one of the gold-miners, who are all whites. Similarly Puccini's libretto had originally demanded that the gold-miners should wear cowboy costumes. These and other changes were made at the rehearsals.

Outwardly the first production of *La Fanciulla* represented a triumph for Puccini such as he had never enjoyed before or was ever to enjoy again in his career. Fourteen curtain-calls greeted the artists at the end of the first act and nineteen after the second when Gatti-Casazza appeared on the stage and on behalf of the management placed on Puccini's head a massive silver crown adorned with ribbons in the national colours of Italy and the United States. By the end of the performance no less than fifty-two curtain calls had been taken, and the audience, beside itself, flung bouquets of flowers at the composer and his artists. Typical headlines in next morning's papers ran: 'Puccini Tells How He Set a Game of Poker to Music—Strange and Curious Scene in *The Girl*! One of the Strong Features of the Opera—All Written at Night.' Or: 'An International Première—America Proud of *The Girl of the Golden West*—Under Two Flags—A $20,000 House—Riots over Puccini', and so on.

New York critics overreached themselves in superlatives, except for Richard Aldrich of the *New York Times* who noticed it with reserve and confined himself in the main to its novel features, such as its advanced harmonic and orchestral idiom in which he detected the influence of Debussy. The opera was given at the Metropolitan Opera House altogether nine times in that season, repeating its success in Chicago and Boston immediately after. The first European opera house to produce it was Covent Garden, where it was staged in Italian, in the presence of the composer, on 29 May 1911.* The first Italian production took place in Rome at the Teatro Costanzi two weeks later, again with Toscanini conducting. Like the rest of Puccini's operas. *La Fanciulla del West* made the round of the world during the next few years; but for a number of reasons to be considered later it failed to establish itself. Even in the composer's own country it is now rarely heard and then usually in open-air performances, to which its spectacular last act laid in the Californian forest lends itself particularly well.

* The first production in English was given at Liverpool in October of that year.

XVI

Out of Work Again

I

THE ILL-LUCK which since *Madam Butterfly* had dogged Puccini's search for a suitable subject persisted after *La Fanciulla*. Almost three years were to elapse, 1910 to 1913, before he found the subject for what was to be the first of his three one-act operas: *Il Tabarro*. Not that there had been any lack of choice—there never was in Puccini's case. But now that he and various friends began to explore the highways and byways of world literature more assiduously than ever before—to say nothing of the libretti and ideas which descended on him uninvited almost daily—the choice of subject had indeed become embarrassing. What was the reason for his increasing indecision? The answer is that Puccini's artistic aims and aspirations were undergoing a certain change—he appeared no longer satisfied with a simple sentimental story such as had been his bent for so long; he felt a growing desire to strike out in the direction of something which, to judge from the following subjects, contained elements of the mystical, fantastic and symbolic. Thus as early as September 1910, when the ink on the score of *La Fanciulla* had scarcely dried, he was anxious to read Maeterlinck's symbolic fairy-tale *L'Oiseau bleu*, published in the previous year, and in 1913 he showed a similar interest in the same author's *Marie Madeleine*. He was still searching when in January 1911 Sybil Seligman suggested to him Sudermann's realistic play *Johannisfeuer*, for which she had gone to the trouble of making an Italian translation. He turned her suggestion down with a comment that indicated the goal toward which his thoughts were now travelling:

8 February 1911

. . . I consider that the plot is not an interesting one to put to music— there is no fluttering of the spirit behind the words, that something which evokes music, the divine art which begins, or ought to begin, where the words cease . . . in fact, at the point at which I have now arrived in art, I need to find something loftier, more musical, and more original. . . (S).

'Loftier and more original' subjects he was destined to find, yet none 'more musical' in his sense than those of *Manon Lescaut*, *La Bohème* and *Madam Butterfly*.

Other equally abortive suggestions made by Sybil at that time were Richard Blackmore's romantic novel *Lorna Doone* and *Sumerun*, a 'wordless play' or mime after a tale from the *Arabian Nights*, which Max Reinhardt had staged at the London Coliseum in the spring of 1911. Puccini rejected the latter with the remark that 'the East does not tempt me very much' though nine years later he yielded to this temptation with remarkable results. On the other hand he was seriously interested in *Liliom*, one of the most successful plays by Ferencz Molnár. But his enquiry met with a refusal since the Hungarian playwright preferred his work, as he put it, 'to be remembered as a play by Molnár, not as an opera by Puccini' (*M*). And for a time he also thought of Gerhart Hauptmann's visionary play, *Hanneles Himmelfahrt*.

We note that the subjects so far mentioned were all tragic, yet it was the field of comedy into which the composer now ardently wished to launch out. Possibly this was a delayed reaction to the sad events of 1908–9. Yet ever since *Tosca* he had entertained, on and off, the idea of writing a comic opera, and after *La Fanciulla* this was once again uppermost in his mind. In an interview given to a *New York Herald* reporter in December 1910, he confessed to being tired of tragic subjects, adding that he wanted his next opera to be a 'good lusty comedy'. Eleven months later, in a letter to Sybil of 19 November 1911, he enquired whether she knew of 'any grotesque novel or story or play, full of humour and buffoonery? I have a desire to laugh and to make people laugh'. He thought he had at last found his kind of subject in the charming Spanish comedy *Anima Allegra—The Cheerful Soul—*by the brothers Joaquin and Serafin Quintero. Though in the event nothing was to come of it, as Puccini felt that it was a subject more suitable for a Spanish composer,* this play was instrumental in introducing to him a new librettist, who, later, became one of his most devoted friends— Giuseppe Adami (1878–1946). Adami was a prolific playwright in a light, graceful vein and a music critic; after the composer's death he published the invaluable *Epistolario* and an intimate biography of him. At the time at which Puccini first met him, he was a young man of thirty-three and a protégé of Giulio Ricordi's, on the libretto of whose unfinished opera *Tappeto Rosa* he had done some work. Giulio, happy to see his vacillating 'Doge' at last settle on a subject, recommended Adami for the operatic adaptation of the Spanish comedy. Puccini at first appeared not satisfied with his new colla- borator, and wished to associate him with Zangarini, the first librettist of *La Fanciulla*, stressing, however, in an (undated) letter to Ricordi that he would not like to leave Adami out of the work for *Anima Allegra*.

> . . . he defers to me and is affectionate, and since the director of all the operation will be myself, I shall make the two librettists the vassals to the Doge. . . (*E*).

In the event Adami remained his chief collaborator, expending a year's hard work in order to render *The Cheerful Soul* more cheerful still for the composer. Yet Puccini grew increasingly apprehensive—as he had in the case of Louÿs's *La Femme et le Pantin*—because of the similarity of atmosphere between the comedy—it dealt with characters and incidents drawn from the life of the Spanish gipsies—and *Carmen*, although the plots had not a whit in

---

* He had also read another play of the Quintero brothers, *Los Flores—The Flowers—*but did not care for it either. *Anima Allegra* was subsequently offered by Tito Ricordi to Manuel de Falla, who also turned it down.

common. In order to allay his misgivings, the obliging Adami offered to transplant the action to Holland, a suggestion which Puccini accepted after some hesitation. Yet by the end of 1913 the whole project was dead and buried.* It is amusing to observe that Puccini, while plagued by no scruples when choosing subjects which had already been used or considered by others —*viz.* Massenet's *Manon*, Leoncavallo's *La Bohème*, Franchetti's *Tosca*— evinced a wholesome fear of any subject that in his eyes displayed the slightest resemblance to Bizet's masterpiece. He felt perhaps less compunction in abandoning *Anima Allegra*, when with the death of Giulio Ricordi on 6 June 1912, the main driving spirit behind this project had disappeared, and so the plan of a comic opera was again shelved.

Puccini would not have been Puccini without simultaneously pursuing other subjects. He thought of Washington Irving's *Rip Van Winkle*, of *Trilby*†, the elder Dumas's *Les Trois Mousquetaires* and of plays by Heine. At Carlsbad in the summer of 1912 he briefly revived the idea of *A Florentine Tragedy* after Wilde. Furthermore, Illica and the critic Giovanni Pozza submitted to him a Russian subject of their own invention, and a meeting took place in Milan in mid-September, but nothing useful resulted from it. With justifiable but rarely expressed pride in his achievements, Puccini afterward wrote to Illica (3 October 1912): '. . . to put into the world another opera which has no power to strike with tremendous force, is no job for me who for good or ill have to this day called myself Giacomo Puccini'.‡ (*C.P.Let.*605). The failure to light on a suitable subject threw him into his customary mood of despair, eliciting from him two letters, addressed to Illica, which are worth quoting, as the first attests his growing interest in novel techniques of stage production, and the second gives us the kernel of his operatic credo.

Boscolungo Pistoiese
5 October 1912

. . . Production in the theatre possesses a special importance, particularly if one tries fresh methods. I've seen a spectacle by Reinhardt and remained struck by its simplicity and effectiveness. Even if a subject is not brand new (and what is really new in this world?) one can succeed in making it appear original through new scenic means. . . (*C.P.Let.*606).

The second letter, written three days later and obviously in reply to one by Illica, runs:

Torre del Lago
8 October 1912

. . . I'm in a perfidiously bad humour because I don't think we shall ever find the *quid* which I need for *my theatre*. I have written to you about production,

* Adami's efforts, however, were not in vain, for his libretto was later set by Franco Vittadini in *Anima Allegra*, Rome, 1921.

† In February 1912 the stage version of George du Maurier's novel had had one of its innumerable revivals in London under Beerbohm Tree to which the Angelis had drawn the composer's attention.

‡ At this period the composer appeared especially conscious of his eminence. In a letter to Sybil, written a few months before the above letter to Illica, he said: 'Puccini must compose something *extra*. . .' (Carlsbad, August 1912, S.)

not because it is a gospel with me but a secondary element and simply a means whereby to achieve diversity. I too know well that we need a 'sound kernel', but I assure you that our musty old *mises en scène* have become tiresome, and for me there is something to praise and to derive profit from if one tries to abandon the old ways (so long as this is done with critical taste and not out of a thirst for the new at all costs). Don't you know about the things they have done and are doing in Russia and in London and in Germany? I admire any kind of attempt toward unhackneyed *productions*.

To turn to ourselves. I told you that I still want to *make people weep*: therein lies everything. But do you think that this is easy? It's terribly difficult, dear Illica. In the first place, where is one to look for a subject? And will our imagination find that sacrosanct, that enduring thing? We are not out to make original departures nor do we rack our brains searching for something new. Love and grief were born with the world and we, our kind who have passed the half-century, know well the impact of both the one and the other. We must therefore find a story which holds us with its poetry and its love and grief and inspires us to the point that we might make an opera of it. But I repeat to you (not that I have any doubt in you, never!), I feel a little shaken in my faith and it begins to desert me! Do you think that during all this time (since the last note of *Fanciulla*) I have sat with my hands crossed in my lap? I have tried all and everything, and what has so far remained on my fingers is nothing but the ashes of the dead. *Addio*, I feel weary and in despair (*C.P.Let.607*).

This was one of the last letters Puccini wrote to his quondam librettist. When in early 1913 he was searching for suitable subjects for the *Trittico* and was also in difficulties over the libretto of *Due Zoccoletti*, he sought, rather half-heartedly, to enlist Illica's assistance, but his appeal was in vain. And so we arrive at the end of the chapter Puccini-Illica, an association which since Giacosa's death in 1906 had brought nothing but mutual disagreeableness and frustration. Used and abused by the composer, the librettist was now cast off like a piece of old rag; and what added a certain pathos to this development was the fact that, while Puccini was to march on to further successes, Illica, who had catered for a whole generation of Italian opera composers, now receded into the background. Younger librettists were entering the field, and indeed one of the reasons why he had been dropped by Puccini for good was the fact that shortly before the composer had found in the young Adami a devoted collaborator who was for ever willing to do his bidding.

Yet before Adami was to be put into harness, Puccini bethought himself again of D'Annunzio with whom he had made his peace in 1907, after their contretemps over the abortive projects for *Parisina* and *La Rosa di Cipro*. The subject suggested by D'Annunzio in June 1912 was *La Crociata degli innocenti*, based on the Children's Crusade of 1212, which was one of the strangest episodes in all medieval history. Its first outline greatly appealed to the composer but when the finished libretto reached him in January 1913, the plot had undergone so radical a metamorphosis from the original that Puccini curtly dismissed it with the withering comment: 'D'Annunzio had given birth to a small, shapeless monstrosity, unable to work or live.'[115] Nevertheless, he was to try his luck once more with the erratic poet and this, fairly soon, in connection with the *Trittico* which now began to loom large on the horizon.

2

We recall that the first idea for three one-act operas to be given together as an evening's entertainment occurred to Puccini soon after *Tosca*. We also remember that he returned to his plan in the years immediately after *Butterfly* when he thought of a trilogy based on tales by Gorky, but then shelved the whole project. The fact that in 1913 he reverted to it and this time carried it into effect was probably due to the combination of three factors. First, the death of Giulio Ricordi in 1912 had removed the chief opponent to this scheme, secondly, Puccini had not yet found a subject substantial or suitable enough to yield the material for a full-length opera; and thirdly, one-act operas required of him a less sustained concentration and effort since he seems to have not yet regained full command of his creative energy after the tragic events of four years before.

In June 1913 he thought he had found the three contrasting subjects for what was later to be called *Il Trittico—The Triptych*.* The first of these subjects was to be drawn from the one-act play *La Houppelande—The Cloak* —by the French writer Didier Gold, which Puccini had seen in Paris at the Théâtre Marigny in the spring of 1912. Though *Grand Guignol*, with two brutal murders on the open stage, the play differed from the general run of such dramas in its unusual atmosphere, which was that of the sordid life of Paris bargees on the River Seine at the beginning of this century. The play was first produced in 1910. On account of its striking local ambience it ran for several years, and it was precisely this ambience which fascinated Puccini. The libretto for the second opera was to be written by D'Annunzio,† and that for the third, a comic opera, by the French novelist and playwright Tristan Bernard. Yet no more was heard of d'Annunzio's libretto, the subject of which remains unknown; and Puccini's repeated attempts at a collaboration with the Italian poet came to a disappointing close. Nor did anything materialize from Bernard's two suggestions: his own fairy-tale *La Peau de l'Ours—The Bearskin*—(1907), and a satirical grotesque, the action

* Charpentier also conceived the idea, some years after Puccini, of writing a *Triptyque* (*L'Amour au Faubourg—Comédiante—Tragédiante*) which never materialized, however.

† It is worth mentioning that Puccini first wanted D'Annunzio to provide all the three episodes or at least two of them. Writing to the poet from Karlsbad on 27 August 1912 he says:

> Not a big thing: find me two or (better) three acts which are varied, dramatic and inspired by every sensitive chord. Little acts dealing with gentle and little things and people like your Sirenetta (a character in D'Annunzio's *Gioconda*) . . . You can introduce as many characters as you like and put also three or four women on the stage. A woman's voice is so beautiful in a small group; have children, flowers, grief and love. (*C.P.Let.601*).

Puccini's last sentence conjures up *Butterfly* and is prophetic of his *Suor Angelica*.

of which was laid in the African jungle.* Puccini's quest for the two missing episodes of the trilogy continued, leading him to consider the comedy *At the Barn* by Anthony Wharton, which he saw in Milan in September 1913 under the title *Mollie*; he also sounded out G. B. Shaw, an author possibly least suited for Puccini's theatre, Sacha Guitry, and the 'popular firm' of Robert de Flers and Armand de Caillavet for a comic subject, and he thought of Anatole France's *Comédie de celui qui epouse une femme muette*. As late as spring 1916 when he was already treating with Forzano (see p. 184), he considered briefly a two-act play (its title is unknown) by the author of *La Houppelande* to fill the remainder of his triple-bill, while Adami searched in Dickens who was one of the composer's favourite writers.

Meanwhile the adaptation of *La Houppelande* had been entrusted to the writer and politician Ferdinando Martini, suggested to Puccini by Giovacchino Forzano whom we shall meet presently and whom the composer had approached in the first place to collaborate with him. A septuagenarian and a slow and fastidious worker, Martini had produced no more after several months than the Italian equivalents of the *apache* names which Gold had given to his characters, and a few verses—the play was in prose— of a high literary quality which was entirely unsuited for bargees. Confronted with an ultimatum, couched by Puccini in friendly yet unequivocal terms, Martini relinquished his task with the somewhat disdainful remark that 'the writing of libretti was not my line of country'.[116] Adami, who had for some time been anxious to get his teeth into it himself, was now handed over the play and completed the libretto, according to him, within the space of a fortnight. This was in late 1913, yet the opera did not see the light of day until three years later.

What was the cause of this delay? In the last resort it was the tug of war which now began between Puccini and the House of Ricordi, culminating in his temporary break with the firm. On Giulio's death in June 1912, Tito Ricordi had succeeded him as the head of the firm and, being no longer controlled by his father, began to apply without let or hindrance those autocratic and even brutal methods for which he was feared and which in 1919 led to his final resignation from the firm. Tito was the type of tycoon who, if it suited his purposes, would not shrink, metaphorically speaking, from walking over dead bodies. His and Puccini's were incompatible temperaments. Their relations, already strained during the last three years of Giulio's life, now went from bad to worse and a clash between them was bound to occur. A first warning was given by Puccini to Sybil in a letter written only a few days after Giulio's demise:

---

* It centred on a negro who once served as an object of amusement to visitors of the *Jardin d'Acclimatisation* in Paris. On his return to his native village, he takes his revenge for this humiliation by capturing a group of white explorers, whom he exhibits for an entrance fee to members of his tribe until the time when they are ripe to be roasted at the stake. The negro and his tribe were cannibals!

Poor Signor Giulio Ricordi! You simply can't imagine how grieved I am at his death! From now on everything is in the hands of *Savoia*—we're in a nice fix! But on the very first occasion that he tries any of his tricks, I shall leave the firm—you can be quite sure of that, I promise you! (*S*).

In his subsequent letters to Sybil, Puccini makes repeated complaints about Tito's hostility to him but says little about the possible reasons for his publisher's behaviour. It appears that Tito, intolerant and short-tempered, was, unlike his father, not prepared to put up with the composer's every whim—least of all with his constant vacillations regarding the choice of subjects, vacillations that grew increasingly frequent with advancing years. It may also be that he felt somewhat contemptuous of Puccini's feminine vulnerability. What is certain, however, is that Tito was anxious to encourage a new talent in the person of Riccardo Zandonai—even as Giulio had encouraged the young Puccini a generation before—and he patronized Zandonai, with a deliberate cold-shouldering of the older composer, who could not but feel jealous and slighted. (We recall what Puccini's comment had been on the London production of Zandonai's *Conchita* in July 1912.)* The gradual deterioration in Puccini's relations with Tito is graphically reflected in his letters to Sybil.

By January 1913 the publisher had become 'more impossible than ever—I have found out that he is actually my enemy—or at least the enemy of my music!' By early May of the following year Tito's treatment of him was 'most inconsiderate—he behaves to me as though I were nothing but a bit of scrap iron'; and a fortnight later:

> ... a storm is brewing which I fear, or rather hope, will soon burst. You can believe me when I say that this fellow is a real *pig*, and that his behaviour to me is most Jesuitical; I know that he has said of me that I shall never write any more—is that the way to behave after twenty years during which I brought honour to his firm as well as many millions of profit? And I am treated without the least respect or consideration. It's a disgrace! I wish I were ten years younger—but although I am already getting old, I can still give him a nasty pill or two to swallow.[117]

3

This was the background against which took place the odd affair of the *Two Little Wooden Shoes* and the still odder one of *La Rondine*—*The Swallow* —Puccini's excursion into the land of operetta. The first involved him in a complicated legal tangle and the second resulted in his break with 'Savoia'— to say nothing of the time and labour expended on what in the first case proved an abortive project and, in the second, a 'bird' with half-broken wings.

Two Little Wooden Shoes was one of the later romances by the English-born writer Louise de la Ramée, better known under her pseudonym

---

* See p. 156.

Ouida, who made her name with a number of widely read novels in which she depicted fashionable society in Victorian England in highly romantic yet, for her time, daring colours. An eccentric woman, Ouida became dissatisfied with what she regarded as an artificial mode of existence in her native England and settled in Florence, where she embarked on an extravagant style of living and gradually squandered the considerable fortune she had made with her successful novels. At one period she lived also at Lucca and at Massarosa, some two miles away from the northern shore of Puccini's Lago di Massaciuccoli. Ouida died poor and lonely at Viareggio in 1908.

Most of her novels were translated into Italian, including the *Two Little Wooden Shoes* (1874)—*Due Zoccoletti*—to which Puccini's attention had been drawn as early as 1898 by the critic Giovanni Pozza. But this was the period when *Tosca* was in the making and the composer took little notice of Pozza's suggestion. According to Adami,[118] it was one evening at Torre del Lago, probably in February 1914, when he and Puccini were having one of their frequent meetings in connection with some libretto or other, that the composer accidentally glanced across the lake to the twinkling lights of Massarosa, and suddenly remembered Ouida and her long-forgotten novel. It now seemed to him to possess all the right qualities and Adami was commissioned on the spot to prepare a scenario. We can understand Puccini's enthusiasm for *Two Little Wooden Shoes*, though it was hardly one of those 'loftier and more original' subjects to which, on his own admission, he had aspired after *La Fanciulla*. The novel belongs to the genre of *tragédie larmoyante* such as Puccini had set to music in *La Bohème* and *Butterfly*; and using Ouida's material would have meant a reversion to the style of those 'old carcases' of which he had grown 'sick and tired'.

In her later years Ouida had become the champion of lost causes, the protector of the 'underdog', making 'the unequal fight of the strong against the weak, the fierce against the feeble, the subtle against the simple, the master against the slaves' the theme of several of her novels, including *Two Little Wooden Shoes*, from which this quotation is taken. The book illustrates her favourite theme in a story of a simple, trusting woman who perishes on account of her love for a cruel and cynical male. Bébée, a flower-girl from Brabant, falls in love with a Parisian painter, Flamen, who has come to Brussels and uses her as model for a projected Gretchen portrait. Touched by her childlike innocence and trust, the painter resists the temptation to seduce her, and, his portrait completed, he returns to Paris promising the girl to return in the following year. Bébée waits in vain, and at last, on learning by chance that he is ill and lonely, she walks all the way from Brussels to Paris on her wooden clogs, arriving in a state of utter exhaustion, only to find that the painter is living in a luxurious studio and surrounded by a company of disreputable women—a 'kind of *Venusberg*', as Ouida put it. Heartbroken, Bébée returns to the little hut in her Brabant village, her clogs worn down, and drowns herself in a brook 'among the water-lilies'. This story of Innocence Betrayed is told by Ouida in a style that strikes the present-day reader as cloying to the point of nausea; yet Bébée herself, who has much in common with Puccini's little geisha, Cio-Cio-San, is drawn with a sympathy and compassion that renders her and her fate truly moving. Ouida was at her best in the evocation of a pastoral idyll and the description of the world of little things—children, animals, flowers—in the midst of which she places the wraith-like Bébée. I venture to suggest that Bébée was resurrected, to some extent, in the character of the nun Angelica, a conjecture strongly supported by the fact that a number of lines in the 'Flower' scene of *Suor Angelica* recall passages from the novel and that Puccini used some musical sketches he had made for *Due Zoccoletti* for the opening scenes of his later opera.

Puccini was anxious to acquire the *exclusive* rights of Ouida's novel, the chief reason being to prevent Tito Ricordi from getting hold of it and throwing 'a noose round my neck'.* Thinking that 'a Mr. MacMillan who lives in St. Martin Street' was the owner of the copyright, he made, through Sybil, enquiries in London, only to be told that Chatto & Windus were the publishers of Ouida's novels but that the copyright was held by the executor of the authoress's estate, an Italian lawyer at Viareggio.† While these enquiries were proceeding, Puccini published in March, in the *Corriere della Sera*, an announcement that he was planning an opera called *Due Zoccoletti*, based on Ouida's novel, stressing his exclusive rights to the subject. No sooner had this announcement appeared than he was approached by the Viennese firm of Herzmansky-Doblinger with an offer for a contract for which Puccini's terms were 400,000 Austrian crowns (£16,000) and 40 per cent royalties! 'It will be a nice little sum of money to put by for a rainy day. And good-bye to *Savoia*—but he has really brought it on his head...'‡ Yet things were not to develop as smoothly as Puccini hoped. In fact, by wishing to acquire the exclusive rights of the novel he stirred up a hornets' nest. First Mascagni declared that he had found the subject independently of Puccini and that he was determined to use it too. 'Let him if he wants to,' wrote Puccini to Sybil on 1 June 1914, 'I've nothing to be afraid of—by now I have become accustomed to doubles; the two *Manons*—the two

* Letter to Sybil, 16 April 1914 (*S*). It is not without interest that he also wished to obtain the cinematographic rights. It appears that a few months previously an American film company had in vain offered him the fabulous sum of a million lire (£40,000) to write the music for a film; such an offer in the days of the silent film when ready-made music was invariably used to accompany the screen narrative must surely be accounted unique. It was possibly this offer which subsequently suggested to Puccini the idea of also making a film version of the opera and which, therefore, induced him to acquire the exclusive rights of the novel.

† Puccini's error arose from the fact that Macmillan were the publishers of Ouida's last book while most of her previous novels, including the *Two Little Wooden Shoes*, had been published by Chatto & Windus.

‡ Letter to Sybil, 24 April 1914 (*S*). The London firm of Chappell appears also to have been interested in the new opera.

Bohèmes—the . . . four *little wooden shoes*.'* There was also Tito Ricordi working behind the scenes to pocket *Two Little Wooden Shoes* for his firm. There was Tauchnitz of Leipzig, who maintained that his firm held a monopoly as the publisher of English fiction on the Continent and claimed compensation. And there was finally Ouida's shrewd Italian executor, to whom Puccini had previously paid the sum of 1,000 lire to establish his priority over the other interested parties, but who now declared that since Ouida had died intestate and had left no next-of-kin, her legitimate heirs and the owners of her copyright were her Italian creditors.† The matter grew so involved that it had to be put in the hands of the court at Viareggio, which after some deliberation decided that if there existed a copyright in the novel at all—a point that appeared impossible to establish with any certainty—it should be sold at auction in the interest of Ouida's creditors. Adami gives a vivid account[119] of this auction, held on 18 March 1915 at the Viareggio court. There were present: Puccini, Mascagni's lawyer, Ouida's creditors and Ricordi's legal representative, Dr. Cantù, while the literary expert called by the judge was Giovacchino Forzano, who later became the librettist of the last two episodes of Puccini's *Trittico*. It was Ricordi's representative who acquired the 'imaginary' copyright for the sum of 4,000 lire and handed the purchase document with a generous gesture to Puccini! The futility of Puccini's efforts to acquire a right that did not really exist was increased by the fact that before the end of the year *Two Little Wooden Shoes* joined the long string of Puccini's other discarded subjects, never to be thought of again.

* Mascagni's opera, whose title was changed to *Lodoletta—The Little Lark*—with a libretto by Puccini's later librettist Forzano, was produced in Rome in 1917. This is the least obscure of the four works based on a Ouida novel, one of which is *Sigma*, by Frederick Cowen (Milan, 1893, and London, 1894).

† Owing to·her extravagant life Ouida left on her death a whole string of debts and it was said at the time that her few belongings had been seized by the Italian Government to repay her many creditors. (*Ouida, A Study in Ostentation*, by Yvonne F. French. London, 1938).

XVII

War Years

I

WHILE THIS TUG OF WAR for the rights in Ouida's novel was proceeding, Puccini had not been idle about his own work. He had started on the composition of *Il Tabarro* and he had entered into negotiations concerning *La Rondine*.

The egg in which this ill-fated bird was hatched had been laid in Vienna in October 1913, when Puccini visited the Austrian capital on the occasion of the first production of *La Fanciulla* at the Hofoper. The plan had originated in the heads of Otto Eibenschütz and Heinrich Berté,* the enterprising directors of the Carl Theater, which, together with the Theater an der Wien, was the foremost home of Viennese operetta. The two Viennese were certainly justified in their assumption that an operetta, half gay and half sentimental, might be a tempting proposition to make to the composer of *La Bohème*. All Puccini was requested to write were eight or ten musical numbers, the rest being spoken dialogue, which was the traditional form of the Viennese operetta—itself an offspring of the marriage of Viennese *singspiel* and French vaudeville. For this small labour he was offered a fee variously reported as between 200,000 and 400,000 Austrian crowns (*c.* £8,000 to £16,000), plus 50 per cent royalties! This was a sum that might indeed have tempted our composer, had he really been the 'commercialized music-merchant' that his enemies chose to see in him. Admittedly Puccini used to pride himself on being a 'good money-getter', and pecuniary advantage was not an aspect he lost sight of—any more than Verdi or Richard Strauss—yet artistic considerations always came first with him. He showed a mild interest in the Viennese offer but eventually declined with thanks. Operetta, he felt was not his line of country—'I will never compose an operetta', he wrote to his Viennese friend Baron Eisner, 'comic opera, yes—like *Rosenkavalier*, but more amusing and more organic'†. Moreover, strained though his

* Berte, a prolific composer of ballets, operettas and operas, is best known for the world success of his *Das Dreimäderl Haus—Lilac Time—*(1916), a sentimental *singspiel* on the life of Schubert, with music suitably and unsuitably chosen from his works.

† 14 December 1913. (*C.P.Let.*638). The view, incidentally, which Puccini expressed about the Strauss opera was evidently coloured by his prejudice against the German composer.

relations then were with Tito Ricordi, loyalty would not permit him to desert to another publisher. But things were to turn out differently.

In the early spring of 1914, Puccini found himself again in Vienna, the occasion being a new production of *Tosca* in which a rising young star, Maria Jeritza, made her début in the name-part.* In previous years it had been customary for Puccini to be accompanied by Tito on his travels to foreign cities, but on this occasion Tito announced that he was too busy to come. The grounds for his refusal seemed reasonable enough. He had just produced *Francesca da Rimini* by his protégé Zandonai at Turin (19 February), for which he had himself adapted the libretto from d'Annunzio's famous tragedy; and as the opera was shortly to be given at Naples it was more important to him to attend this new production than to look after *Tosca* in Vienna, an old work, after all, the supervision of which could be safely left in the hands of Puccini and Carlo Clausetti, a representative of the firm delegated by Tito to accompany the composer. Though deeply hurt in his pride, Puccini acquiesced in this arrangement. Then two days before the Vienna performance was due, Clausetti was bidden by Tito to proceed to Naples immediately where he was urgently needed. Again pocketing his pride, Puccini begged Tito in a telegram to permit Clausetti to postpone his departure at least until after the first performance of *Tosca*, to which the publisher wired back: 'Impossible to accede to request. I order Clausetti to leave immediately.'[120] Puccini thereupon dispatched a letter to Tito, expressing himself in no uncertain terms about the treatment meted out to him and making veiled threats as to his future connection with the House of Ricordi. Tito ignored this letter. The composer, now feeling humiliated and incensed by this new affront, decided to pay Tito back in his own coin: he signed with the Viennese directors the contract for *La Rondine*. It was an act of revenge, but little good was to come of it.

2

In order to understand the difficulties and embarrassments in which *La Rondine* was to land Puccini, it is useful to glance at some of the clauses of his contract:

1. The composer reserves to his person all the rights of the operetta for Italy and South America.
2. The first production is to be given in Vienna in the German language.
3. The subject is to be chosen by the Viennese directors and is to be

* Not in 1907, as generally stated. Jeritza was to become a celebrated interpreter of this role as well as of that of Minnie in *La Fanciulla*; Puccini himself later declared her his best Tosca and 'one of the most original artists I have ever known' (S). It was, incidentally, Jeritza who by an accident introduced the half-lying position in which most Toscas now address their 'Vissi d'arte' to Scarpia. In her tussle with the Roman Chief of Police she had, during a rehearsal, slipped to the ground, a position which Puccini considered in perfect keeping with the emotional situation at that moment and which he asked her to retain.

dramatized by a librettist of their own choice, A. M. Willner,* after the composer's approval of it.

4. The Italian version of the libretto is to be made by a dramatist of the composer's choice, who must be permitted a reasonably free hand in his adaptation.

So far, so good. Yet when in the early summer Puccini received Willner's scenario he found it 'a poor, pitiful thing'. The Viennese, however, undismayed and admitting the inferiority of Willner's work, presently submitted another subject which Willner was to fashion into a libretto, in collaboration with another Vienna writer, Heinz Reichert.† The new libretto was ready in July and in order to make certain of their bargain the Viennese travelled to Milan, four of them descending on Puccini together—Eibenschütz, Berté, Willner and a Baron Eisner, a Vienna friend of the composer's who had taken an active part in all these negotiations. The libretto was read to Puccini in French! The plot, borrowing heavily from *La Traviata* and *Die Fledermaus*, centred on a woman of aristocratic birth but doubtful reputation —The Swallow of the title—who after a shortlived flight into the world of true love and romance with a poor young man returns to her golden nest, feathered by a wealthy Parisian banker. Puccini's reaction, if not enthusiastic, was not unfavourable—'the plot is not bad and it doesn't displease me', he afterwards reported to Adami, who had been kept in the wings.[121] All details were settled to mutual satisfaction and the Vienna party returned home, convinced of having at last bagged their rare and precious bird—Puccini. Yet they reckoned without the capricious nature of their prey, nor did they foresee the legal complications which were to arise owing to the war, the clouds of which were gathering fast in the European sky.

Eight or ten musical numbers—it seemed indeed a trifling affair. A less conscientious artist than Puccini might well have considered the whole assignment as little more than a potboiler, to be tossed off in a trice for the sake of the handsome fee. Moreover Puccini's name would have been sufficient guarantee for the Viennese to accept anything from his pen, irrespective of quality. Yet not even this trifle could induce him to lower his standards. He settled to work with all his wonted care and circumspection, Adami having meanwhile made the Italian version of the libretto. And though the outbreak of the war at first 'absolutely stupefied' him, rendering him 'unable to work any more', by the middle of September he had sufficiently recovered from the shock to write to Sybil:

Milan
14 September 1914

. . . now I've started again, and I'm pleased about it. *La Rondine* is the title of the small opera, which will be finished in spring; it's a light sentimental

---

* Willner was a well-known Viennese writer and the librettist of, among a number of stage works, Lehár's *Der Graf von Luxemburg*, *Die Dollarprinzessin* by Leo Fall, and Goldmark's *Ein Wintermärchen*, after Shakespeare's *A Winter's Tale*. It was, incidentally, Willner who, acting on behalf of another Vienna publisher, had, in 1913, offered Puccini the sum of 400,000 Austrian crowns for *Two Little Wooden Shoes*.

† Willner and Reichert later concocted the 'book' for *Lilac Time*.

opera with touches of comedy—but it's agreeable, limpid, easy to sing, with little waltz music and lively and fetching tunes. We'll see how it goes—it's a sort of reaction against the repulsive music of today—which, as you put it so well, is very much like the war! (S).

He composed several of the required set-pieces, though with a growing dislike for the whole venture. The spoken dialogue, he considered, was a serious limitation to spreading himself in the music, and the plot no longer convinced him. Already by the third week of November he felt 'utterly discouraged', and intended to 'send the contract back to Vienna and start thinking of something else. . . La Rondine is a solemn piece of obscene trash (porcheria). I curse the moment when I signed the contract in Vienna'.[122] But the resourceful Adami came to the rescue. He abolished the spoken dialogue, replacing it by lyrical verses, and made various alterations in the plot and the characters, with the result that Puccini now had a well-tailored libretto of quasi-operatic cut before him. The Viennese directors, informed of this, not only raised no objection but were overjoyed at the prospect of getting a full-length opera, instead of the original ten numbers. The contract was changed accordingly, Adami becoming the sole librettist while Willner and Reichert were to be responsible for the German adaptation. Yet, for all that The Swallow had now grown new and more attractive feathers, Puccini found little pleasure in it. He bombarded Adami with missive after missive asking for alteration after alteration to help his bird take wing. In view of the labour spent on Turandot, Adami possibly exaggerated when he later wrote that never had his work been 'more exhausting, more worrying, more arduous, more infuriating, more difficult and more desolating' than that for the libretto of La Rondine.[123] He sketched no fewer than sixteen acts before the three acts were born which satisfied the composer. Oddly enough, to his friends Puccini hardly made any mention of his difficulties; on the contrary, he appears anxious to pretend that the work was proceeding smoothly and that he was enjoying it all. In April of the following year (1915) the opera was nearly finished, as he informed Sybil; but Puccini's 'nearly' meant another year before the music was completed 'for those gentlemen, our enemies, and now I've got to wait'.[124] Owing to Italy's declaration of war on the Central Powers on 14 May 1915, Austria had become enemy country, and communications with the Viennese ceased; and since the contract stipulated for the first production of La Rondine in Vienna, there seemed nothing for Puccini to do but to put the score in his bottom drawer and await the end of the conflagration, which it was then impossible to foresee. It is true that in August 1915 he met the Viennese publishers on neutral territory (Zürich) and tried to persuade them to cancel the contract, but they would not hear of it; all he achieved was the alteration of a minor clause—Vienna still remained the venue for the première.

La Rondine was completed by Easter 1916. If Puccini was contractually bound to Vienna for its first production, he was, however, not bound to have it published in Austria, seeing that he possessed all the rights for Italy. Since the summer of 1915 he had been offering the work to Tito Ricordi, with whom he had made an uneasy peace after the contretemps over the Vienna production of *Tosca*. Yet Tito kept stalling, and finally declared, as Puccini wrote to Sybil from Monte Carlo on 1 April 1917:

> I had written an opera that hadn't come off, and that was bad Lehár! I insisted so much that he should take the opera that I positively degraded myself before 'him! But he would not have anything to do with it—and now he will be sorry, because *La Rondine* is an opera full of life and melody—it will appeal to you very much (*S*).

It is worth noting that Puccini did not volunteer this information to Sybil until *after* the seemingly successful production of *La Rondine*. Whether Tito's refusal was an act of revenge for Puccini's desertion or whether he was really convinced that the opera was 'bad Lehár' remains uncertain. In the light of the future fortunes of *La Rondine* he certainly displayed foresight in not wishing 'to have anything to do with it'.

The news of Puccini's difficulties with Ricordi must have leaked out, for in the spring of 1916 there appeared a *deus ex machina* in the person of Lorenzo Sonzogno, the head of Ricordi's rival firm, who declared himself prepared to publish *La Rondine*. He had, he said, been in touch in neutral Switzerland with the Viennese publishers, who were willing to sell him all their rights in the work, including that of the first production. Owing to war conditions, Sonzogno thought it best to give the opera at Monte Carlo. Greatly relieved, Puccini came to terms with Sonzogno, who in his turn clinched the deal with the Viennese, and the composer later received as his fee the sum of 250,000 lire. *La Rondine* is Puccini's only stage work not published by Ricordi.*

Meanwhile *Il Tabarro* had safely come into port, and for some time Puccini was in two minds whether to give this opera alone in Rome or Turin or together with *La Rondine* at Monte Carlo. In the end he decided in favour of the operetta, postponing the first production of *Il Tabarro* until the completion of the other two one-act operas of the original scheme, neither of which was as yet in sight.

The première of *La Rondine* took place at Monte Carlo on 27 March 1917, the main cast consisting of Gilda Dalla Rizza (Magda), Ines Farraris (Lisette) and Tito Schipa (Ruggero); the conductor was Gino Marinuzzi. The work was received with all the signs of a triumphant success: there were flowers and orations and the Press next morning spoke of 'rich inspiration, freshness and youthful charm'. Not that the public of Monte Carlo can be credited with much critical discernment, least of all the type of public that gathered there during the war years. And *pace* the Monegasque critics, while *La Rondine* cannot be denied charm and technical mastery, it is precisely 'rich inspiration' and 'freshness' in which the work is lacking, and its hybrid character, in my view, sealed its ultimate fate. Shortly after the première it was given in the principal Italian cities—Bologna, Milan, Rome, Naples— and in South America (Buenos Aires and Rio de Janeiro). In 1919 the composer revised the opera—'it's going to be made much simpler and much

---

* His later *Inno di Roma* was also published by Sonzogno.

more easy to sing'[125]—yet this did not help to render the flights of *The Swallow* more frequent. In October 1920 it eventually reached Vienna, its original destination, where it was given at the Volksoper.* The reception was lukewarm. Puccini, however, put this down to a mediocre cast and made yet a fourth version which, but for changes in the libretto, is almost identical with the first (Monte Carlo) version.†

It is amusing to learn that the composer considered *La Rondine* 'just the thing for a London theatre', his reason being that it was 'a melodious opera and the subject is a *moral one*', as he wrote to Sybil on 11 June 1917 (S). Vincent Higgins, then manager of Covent Garden, was approached by Mrs. Seligman, but at first refused to consider a production, saying that Puccini would do much better to 'concentrate on a new work rather than waste time trying to revivify dead horses like *La Rondine* and *Suor Angelica*'.[126] (The latter work had been completed in September 1917.) After repeated interventions by Mrs. Seligman, Higgins finally agreed to put on *La Rondine*, on condition that it was altered, as he said, to suit British taste. This entailed introducing spoken comic dialogue—the very thing to which Puccini had objected in the original libretto—adding a part for a low comedian and a new 'happy ending'. Puccini reacted to these suggestions with indignation, protesting to Sybil that the work was not an operetta but a lyrical opera. Therefore 'Good-bye to *Rondine* in London, unless they have lyrical opera in the Covent Garden repertory—that is if Higgins wants the theatre to be used as it used to be'.[127] This is the last we hear of Puccini's persistent attempts to foist *La Rondine* on London, which was seen on the English stage not until 1965, though a potted version of it was heard in a B.B.C. studio broadcast in 1938.‡

3

It is not without irony that the least successful of Puccini's mature works should have involved him in a political scandal on an international scale and cast serious aspersions on his patriotism. The trouble started soon after the outbreak of hostilities in 1914. Italy was then still neutral, but public opinion in the country was deeply divided between the Germanophiles, in the majority at that stage of the war, and the pro-Allied sympathizers. The Church, owing to its historic links with the Habsburg dynasty, was Austrophile; the Court, again, sympathized with Germany, in which attitude it was supported by the big banking and industrial interests; and the political parties on the left looked on Kaiser Wilhelm's country as the birthplace of Marx and Engels. With France, on the other hand, relations were traditionally strained, especially since her occupation of Tunisia.

* The German adaptation of the libretto was made by R. S. Hoffmann, not by Willner and Reichert, as originally stipulated in the contract.

† For an account of the vicissitudes *La Rondine* experienced from its birth and its different versions, see Cecil Hopkinson (*op. cit.*), pp. 35–42.

‡ It was produced in New York in 1928 and again in 1936.

Puccini appeared to favour the cause of the Central Powers, at any rate during the initial phases of the war. For France he evinced little sympathy, largely for personal reasons, as his operas had been violently attacked in certain quarters there, while in Germany and Austria he enjoyed almost unchallenged successes. He was reported as having even said that, so far as he was concerned, the Germans could not capture Paris too soon—a statement which caused the first serious rift between him and the Francophile Toscanini, who, it is suggested, now avoided meeting the composer, as he would have slapped his face![128]

Now if Puccini's Germanophile attitude had been the result of a honest political conviction—after all, the whole of Italy was divided on this issue at the outbreak of the war—one could not have blamed him for this, at any rate as long as his country remained neutral. But his partisanship for the Central Powers, ill-concealed behind a pretence of neutrality, was largely pragmatic and sprang from fear for the fate of his operas in Germany and Austria. The prelude to a series of most disagreeable happenings was the publication in a German newspaper of an article calling for the boycott of Puccini's operas, as the composer had been reported to have signed, in common with other eminent artists and writers (Leoncavallo, Saint-Saëns, D'Annunzio, Maeterlinck, Shaw), a manifesto protesting against the bombardment of Rheims. The truth, however, was that Puccini did not figure among the signatories to this manifesto and for the simple reason that he had not been invited to sign. He therefore issued a public denial of that report and went on to declare that, though he had never been anti-German, he entertained feelings of friendship and gratitude for any country in which his music was being performed—France, England, Germany, Austria, America and so on; besides, as an Italian (Italy was then still neutral) it was his duty to show himself publicly as impartial.[129]

Meanwhile the English novelist, Hall Caine was preparing the so-called *King Albert's Book** in which representative men and women throughout the world paid tribute to the heroism of the Belgian King and his people and expressed their condemnation and horror of Germany's unprovoked aggression against a small neutral country. A number of distinguished musicians contributed to it with short compositions or prose tributes, such as Debussy (*Berceuse héroique*), Mascagni, Elgar, Saint-Saëns, Messager and Paderewski, but again Puccini's name was not be found among theirs.†
Why? Simply, because he was still hoping that by adopting a strictly neutral attitude he might be able to spare his operas in Germany the fate suffered there by Leoncavallo's and Mascagni's which had been banned from all theatres. This explains the content of the letter he wrote to the editor of the *King Albert's Book:*

* It was published in early 1915 and sold for the benefit of the *Daily Telegraph* Belgian Fund.

† Adami, however, states that Puccini intended to write a kind of funeral march for Hall Caine's *Book* which he later turned into the great monologue of Michele in *Il Tabarro*. (*Giacomo Puccini, op. cit.*)

Dear Mr. Hall Caine,

On my return from a journey I found your letter awaiting me. You are asking me for something which I would have done willingly because I, too, have been moved by the sad fate of Belgium and have admired the heroic defence of her people under the courageous leadership of King Albert.

But I received already from other quarters the request to sign tributes and protests. To all I replied that I wished to remain in the background and therefore did not want that my name appeared in public. I am telling this only to you and beg you to forgive my reserve.*

As was to be expected, his explicit denial of an anti-German attitude and the emphasis he laid on his strict neutrality were at once interpreted in France as an implicit admission of his sympathies for the Central Powers. His statement caused a violent uproar in the French Press, which had never been inspired by any excess of friendly feelings for the composer. The attack was led by Léon Daudet, son of Alphonse and editor of the nationalist paper *L'Action Française*; also some Italian papers joined in the fray, Italy being just on the verge of entering the war on the side of the Allies. Even the composer's most intimate friends now began to suspect that there was some substance in those French diatribes, including Sybil; hence his explanatory letter to her:

Milan

23 February 1915

No, dear Sybil!—my little denial (which perhaps would have been better if I hadn't made) has been travestied by my enemies in France into an assertion which is untrue. I repeat to you that it isn't the French—that is, the people of France—but those incapable colleagues, people like X, Y, Z and Co., who for a long time past have been working and writing against me— it is they who have let loose the storm. . . (S).†

Whatever their truth, these accusations were as nothing compared with the abuse heaped on Puccini two years later when news of the imminent Monte Carlo production of 'my Austrian opera', *La Rondine*, spread to France. Now it was not only the composer but also all the artists, as well as Raoul Gunsbourg, director of the Monegasque opera house, who were torn limb from limb. Daudet went so far as to accuse them of 'culpable commerce with the enemy' and of being no less than traitors to their country. This compelled Puccini to publish, early in April 1917, yet another long statement, in which he refuted Daudet's charges point by point. He opened by saying: 'My life and my art are the most valid testimony before the whole world to my feelings as a patriot'; he then proceeded to a detailed account of the origin and history of *La Rondine*, and concluded by averring:

---

* Reproduced in Sartori, *op. cit.*

† 'Those incapable colleagues, people like X, Y, Z and Co.' was a reference to such Parisian composers as Leroux, D'Indy and Dukas who in 1913 had combined in vehement attacks against Puccini and the invasion of the French repertory by Italian opera. When Puccini visited Paris after the war he wrote to Adami that the Opéra-Comique would like to give his *Rondine*—'but they are afraid of being *shot* because I dominate the theatre too much and have the great defect (*sic*) of making too much *argent*!' (Paris, 9 July 1920, *E.*).

'The accusation of M. Daudet boils down to this: I have taken away from our enemies that which was their property and given my opera to an Italian publisher. If that is my crime I have reason to be proud of it'.* With this the whole disagreeable affair was closed; yet in order to give more tangible proof of his Allied sympathies, he instructed the Paris Opéra-Comique to donate an entire year's royalties from the performances of *Tosca* to a fund for soldiers wounded in the war.† Whatever the pros and cons of this *cause célèbre*, its violence is chiefly accounted for by the fact that in the 1914–18 war hostilities did not stop at the trenches but extended also to the sphere of art, so that plays, operas and other compositions by 'enemy' artists, including even some of the great masters of the past were banned. (This chauvinist attitude was not adopted during the Second World War, despite the greater fierceness with which it was fought and despite the fundamental ideological issues at stake.)

Admittedly Puccini's erstwhile declaration of his neutrality contained an equivocal element, but there could at no time have been the slightest doubt of his patriotism. His was a patriotism free from the militant, histrionic manifestations of a d'Annunzio; on the other hand, it had no such deep roots as Verdi's love of his fatherland—Verdi, who had regarded Italy's defeat at the hands of the Austrians in the Battle of Custozza as a personal humiliation. Perhaps in his heart of hearts Puccini realized the futility of modern war. Through his letters of that period there runs a thread of horror and despair at the sufferings brought on humanity by the conflagration. His correspondence in previous years had been almost exclusively confined to his artistic and private affairs; but it now began to widen both in scope and sentiment, and a hitherto unknown note of compassion is sounded. At the beginning of the war he wrote to Sybil:

Milan
22 December 1914

... at least we're not at war; this is a selfish remark to make, I know, but I cannot do otherwise than make it—war is too horrible a thing whatever the results; for whether it be victory or defeat, human lives are sacrificed. We live in a terrible world, and I see no sign of this cruel state of things coming to an end! (*S*).

Although he had, as we have seen, expressed strict neutrality at an early stage of the war, yet he confidently hoped for an Allied victory—even before his country had joined them. England, whose 'poise' had always filled him with admiration, 'is certain to come out of the war well, because she is so wise and strong'—words written to Sybil as early as 14 September 1914.

* For the full statement, see Fraccaroli (*op. cit.*), p. 160.

† In Italy he displayed the same patriotic gesture when in February 1918 he allowed the proceeds from the 25th anniversary performance of *Manon Lescaut* at Turin to go the families of fallen soldiers. Similarly, he composed a little song, *Morire?*, for tenor and piano (text by Adami) which was issued, together with unpublished compositions by Boito, Franchetti, Giordano, Leoncavallo, Mascagni and Zandonai, by Ricordi in 1917 and sold for the benefit of the Italian Red Cross.

With Italy's entry into the war there was now added to his abhorrence of the general slaughter a father's anguish for his son. For Tonio, 'a fine, big fellow and a splendid son', had at once enlisted as a volunteer in the Army Motor Ambulance, serving at the front for most of the time. Tonio was a civil engineer by profession.

One of Puccini's favourite diversions was foreign travel. This now ceased and the enforced immobility engendered in him a feeling not far short of claustrophobia. To Sybil, on 27 April 1916:

> ... How I long to travel! When will this cursed war be over? It seems to me like a suspension of life! ... Here one languishes; between the green earth and the sea the seeds of hatred against this enforced calm are beginning to develop within me... (*S*).

His life at Torre, though, ran smoothly enough, despite his lamentations to Sybil that

> ... I'm here alone and mournful like an Elegy; the wind is blowing and the cold has returned. Elvira is always in such black spirits that I feel a longing to get away—but living alone like a dog makes me so unhappy! [130]

He was now approaching his sixtieth year. 'How unjust it is', he wrote to Sybil on 5 November 1918, 'that one should grow old—it makes me simply furious, confound it! And to think that I won't surrender and that there are times when I believe I'm the man I used to be! Illusions, and also a sign of—strength!'

Puccini was not mistaken in his last words. He had by then completed his Triptych, two panels of which turned out masterpieces.

XVIII

'A Sign of Strength'

I

WE RECALL that in the late autumn of 1913 Puccini had started on the actual composition of *Il Tabarro*, vainly hoping for d'Annunzio and Tristan Bernard to provide him with the subjects for the last two episodes of his triple bill. Then followed his entanglement in the affair of Ouida's novel and his excursion into operetta, in consequence of which work on *Il Tabarro* had to be put aside and was not resumed until summer 1915. There were still a number of points in the libretto that had to be ironed out. As it stood it seemed to Puccini weak, full of useless details, and, so far as the close of the love scene between tenor and soprano was concerned—the '*sobborgo*' or 'suburb' duet, as he called it—lacking in inspiration. Writing to Adami in an (undated) letter he besought his poet, in playful exaggeration, 'with feet and hands clasped, to put some warmth into them [the closing lines of the duet] and give me an end with wings; or, if without wings, then something to make an effective ending' (*E*). By May 1916 he had finished a good half of the opera and was more than satisfied with it, though both the verses and the music of Michele's great monologue were to be radically altered after the first production. The opera was completed on 25 November, the weather at Torre being 'fine' on that particular day, as we learn from an entry at the close of the autograph score.

Yet while work on this opera was proceeding, the anxious composer had missed few opportunities of reminding Adami that the subjects for the two remaining parts of the Triptych were still out of sight. Writing to him on 29 May, he lamented:

> . . . This is a gadfly that stings me continually. But, for all that I think and scrutinize my thoughts of today and yesterday, nothing emerges that is of any use to me. It is sad, very sad, because time is flying. . . (*E*).

In the event, it was not Adami but another playwright, Giovacchino Forzano, who squashed Puccini's 'gadfly' with two well-aimed strokes—the libretti for *Suor Angelica* and *Gianni Schicchi*. We first met Forzano for a moment at the auction of the copyright of *Two Little Wooden Shoes*, where he acted as the court's literary expert.

Forzano (b. 1883) was a man of many parts. He had studied medicine and law, had been for a time a baritone singer and then a journalist, was editor of the Florence paper *Nazione* and later turned playwright and producer, in which latter capacity he worked at La Scala and the Teatro Reale of Rome.

He was a picturesque personality, eloquent but somewhat pompous in his utterances and difficult to deal with. Nevertheless, Puccini put him into harness and was to be fully rewarded. Informed of the idea of presenting three short but strongly contrasted operas on one evening, Forzano, after some search, recalled a sketch that he had made for a one-act play intended for a touring company. Both its subject and its setting were out of the common: a young nun, who after learning of the death of her child, the fruit of a sinful passion, commits suicide in a convent, the action taking place at the end of the seventeenth century. *Suor Angelica*, as the play was called, appealed to the composer at once. There was the character of the heroine, possessed of a sweetness and pathos such as had been missing from Puccini's heroines since *Butterfly*. Hardly less important was the mystico-religious ambience which Puccini knew so well from his Lucca days as a young organist. Moreover, after his sister Iginia had risen to become Mother Superior at the Convent of Vicopelago, Puccini would often go to see her there. He was lax in his religious beliefs, if not actually an unbeliever, as his priest friend Panichelli suggests;[131] yet as a man of the theatre he had always been fascinated by the colourful spectacle that surrounds the Roman Catholic service in a Latin country; and he knew, as he proved in the first-act finale of *Tosca*, the never-failing effect on the stage of the potent mixture of religion with eroticism. We also call to mind his abortive attempt, as far back as 1895, to obtain Zola's permission to use a subject with the same ingredients, *La Faute de l'Abbé Mouret*, as well as his intention to write a *Santa Margherita da Cortona*. He therefore accepted Forzano's subject with alacrity and set to work without delay. As with *Tosca*, he again called on the services of Father Panichelli, who found for him the appropriate Latin prayer for what Puccini later described as the *Marcia Reale della Madonna*, the marching-hymn sung by a celestial chorus during the 'Miracle' scene at the close of *Suor Angelica*. He also paid Iginia's convent a number of visits, to steep himself in the authentic atmosphere—just as he had when he had climbed up to the platform of the Castel Sant'Angelo in Rome, while *Tosca* was in the making. The realistic vein in him would not permit him to leave anything to chance in the details of the setting. After the completion of the opera he even went so far as to test its impact on his sister's nuns—his '*cuffie*' or 'bonnets'— playing and singing the music to them; and seeing them deeply moved and some even in tears, he felt assured of the effect of the work on its future audiences; but his assurance was to prove false.

2

While Puccini was still at work on this '*opera claustrale-monacale*, begun in February or March 1917, Forzano, a quick worker, submitted to him the scenario for the last episode of the *Trittico*. The germ of it was found in the 30th Canto of the *Inferno*, where Dante in a single tercine recalls the shade of the Florentine rogue Gianni Schicchi and his trick of impersonation whereby he bequeathed to himself a handsome legacy and the best mare in Buoso Donati's stable. In one of his comic doggerels, Puccini put the whole plot of the opera into a nutshell:

S'apre la scena	Up goes the curtain
col morto in casa.	The rich man is dead
Tutt'i parenti borbottan preci	Kith and kin mumble prayers all round his bed.
viene quel Gianni—tabula rasa	Gianni the wily, aware of their greed
fiorini d'oro diventan ceci.[132]	Turns their gilt lilies into a weed.

It is uncertain which of the two, Puccini or Forzano, must take the credit for the brilliant idea of developing a plot from Dante's few lines. Fraccaroli ascribes it to Forzano; Adami, on the other hand, asserts that it was Puccini, who for some time previously had been in the habit of carrying about a pocket edition of the *Divina Commedia* to read on his many train journeys. A letter to Adami of 2 September 1915 contains a sentence that appears to refer to the genesis of *Gianni Schicchi*: 'I have a tiny little idea (*ideuccia*) but I fear that it might not stand on its feet. I shall tell you later' (*E*). In view of his long-standing intention to draw upon Dante for a trilogy, it is probable that Puccini was, indeed, the first begetter' of the whole idea.

Whatever the true circumstances, the fact is that when Puccini received Forzano's libretto in the early summer of 1917, he was so delighted with it that he decided to put his 'nun opera' aside for a while; in his own words it was 'not an easy one'. He forthwith embarked on *Schicchi*, announcing this intention to the librettist thus:

Dopo il *Tabarro* di tinta nera	After *Tabarro* of the black hue
sento la voglia di buffeggiare.	Surely some fun is my well-deserved due.
Lei non si picchi	My dear Giovacchino, forgive me, I burst
se faccio prima quel *Gianni Schicchi*.	With impatience to start on the comedy first.

It is likely too that Puccini's desire to turn to comic opera and 'to laugh and make people laugh', as he had put it to Sybil, was by way of an escape from the oppressive realities of the war. Yet his enthusiasm was shortlived, as we gather from a remark to Adami in an (undated) letter:

> . . . I fear that ancient Florence does not suit me, nor is it a subject that would appeal much to the public at large; because I write for all the races of men! And these include the negroes when they have fully developed (what pretensions!) (*E*).

He stopped work on *Schicchi* and turned back to *Suor Angelica*, which he completed on 14 September 1917, while the comic opera was finished on 20 April 1918. These dates, entered by the composer in the autograph scores,* disprove the statement, made by all his biographers, that the middle episode of the *Trittico* was completed last.

Marotti and Pagni, in their memoirs,[133] give an amusing account of how the collective title was found. At a session in Puccini's home Forzano and a number of the composer's intimates tried, as if for a crossword puzzle, to

---

* Owing to his weakening eyesight, Puccini now used music manuscript paper with specially widely-spaced staves and wrote in pencil instead of ink.

hit on a word denoting a trinity of things. Half in jest, the most impossible suggestions were made: *triangolo, treppiede, trinomio, tritono* and so on until it was Marotti who lighted on *trittico*. All were aware, though, of the questionable aptness of this title for a succession of three operas which are entirely unconnected.*

A feature of the genesis of the last two operas of the *Trittico* was the remarkable speed with which Puccini composed the music, which all in all took him no more than a year or so. He appeared to be working with newly found energy, and for once in his career he did not seem unduly assailed by his perennial doubts. Partly responsible for this swift progress was the excellence of Forzano's libretti. Forzano was a more than averagely gifted playwright and, unlike Puccini's previous librettists, was not hampered by having to adapt his 'books' from an already existing novel or play; for that very reason he was not fettered by any of Puccini's own ideas, as might have been the case if *Suor Angelica* and *Gianni Schicchi* had already been treated for the stage or in a work of fiction.† Thus Forzano was able to work with greater freedom than his predecessors. So far as we know, his collaboration with Puccini proceeded with unwonted smoothness and resulted in two libretti more coherent in conception and of a higher literary quality than the majority of the composer's previous texts.‡ It was a pity that this association, despite later efforts to continue it, terminated with the *Trittico*.

3

With the whole of the Triple Bill complete by the end of April 1918, the original intention was to stage it in Rome, but this proved not feasible since owing to the war many artists were serving in the forces. It was therefore decided to accept the offer of the Metropolitan Opera to give the first production in New York, where it took place on 14 December 1918. This was only just over a month after the signing of the Armistice, when private travel was still hedged round with so many difficulties that Puccini, to his profound disappointment, was unable to attend. It was the first time in his career that he had not been present at the baptism of one of his brain-children.

The principal singers of the New York cast were, for *Il Tabarro*: Claudia Muzio (Giorgetta), Giulio Crimi (Luigi) and Luigi Montesanto (Michele); for *Suor Angelica*: Geraldine Farrar (Angelica) and Flora Perini (Zia Principessa); for *Gianni Schicchi*: Giuseppe De Luca (Schicchi), Florence Easton (Lauretta) and Giulio Crimi (Rinuccio). The conductor was Roberto Moranzoni. The comedy had an immediate success, but the other two

* But see p. 421.

† It is worth quoting what Forzano replied to the composer when the latter approached him in 1912 with the request to adapt Gold's *La Houppelande* for him: 'Caro Maestro, I wish to write a libretto for Giacomo Puccini based on a subject of my own invention and not to adapt as usual the subject of somebody else'. Giovacchino Forzano, *Come li ho conosciuti* (Radio italiana, Turin, 1957), p. 13, and also quoted in the *Carteggi pucciniani (op. cit)*.

‡ On his own admission, the literary aspect of the libretto of *Schicchi* cost Forzano a great deal of trouble.

operas were received with marked coolness, especially *Suor Angelica*, which the composer, with a father's love for his weakest child, considered the best of the three. Later he came to detest the whole of the *Trittico*. The first European production was staged at the Teatro Costanzi, Rome, on 11 January 1919, conducted by Gino Marinuzzi, not Toscanini, as has been stated.* Yet again, it was the 'Florentine' opera which stole the limelight from its two sister works; and this was to happen at all theatres where the *Trittico* was given in its entirety. Thus in London—where it was staged for the first time at Covent Garden on 18 June 1920 in the presence of·King George V and Queen Mary, with the composer and his two librettists also present—*Schicchi* was declared 'a gem, a masterpiece of comic opera', while *Il Tabarro* was dismissed as 'Puccini *réchauffé*' and *Suor Angelica* as 'anaemic'.†

For some time Puccini considered his Triptych an indivisible whole and was much grieved to see it 'brutally torn to pieces' when theatres began to drop *Tabarro* and *Angelica* in succession. After the first Vienna production he wrote to Sybil:

Milan
20 January 1921

> . . . I have protested to Ricordi's for giving permission for *Tabarro* and *Schicchi* without *Angelica*—it makes me really unhappy to see the *best* of the three operas laid on one side. In Vienna it was the most effective of the three with the good Lehmann (she's German, it's true) but a fine, delicate artist—simple and without any of the airs of a prima donna, with a voice as sweet as honey. . . (*S*).‡

Yet after a production of the entire *Trittico* at Lucca in 1921 the composer himself came to the conclusion that it was too long for an evening's entertainment and he ceased to object to the Cinderella treatment meted out to the first two operas. For a number of years *Schicchi* continued on its own, usually paired with *Cavalleria* or *I Pagliacci* or, as in London, with *Salome*; but latterly *Il Tabarro* has begun to be appreciated as the masterly study it is in concentrated drama and atmosphere.

---

* The principal cast on this occasion was, for the first opera: Labia (Giorgetta), Di Giovanni (Luigi), later known as Edward Johnson, and Galeffi (Michele); for the second opera: Dalla Rizza (Angelica), a singer highly appreciated by Puccini, and for the last: Galeffi (Schicchi), Dalla Rizza (Lauretta) and Di Giovanni (Rinuccio).

Soon after the première, Puccini's friends founded—as a pendant to the *Bohème* Club of a quarter of a century before—a *Gianni Schicchi* Club at Viareggio, where he had taken up temporary residence.

† First productions in this country of the individual operas in English were given: *Schicchi*, Covent Garden, 15 January 1924; *Suor Angelica*, Royal Academy of Music, 21 July 1931, and *Il Tabarro*, Sadler's Wells, 23 October 1935. The complete *Trittico* was not seen again in London until 1957 (Sadler's Wells).

‡ This writer, then a student, recalls Lotte Lehmann's moving interpretation of the Nun, which indeed lent the opera a poignancy he has not experienced since in any other production. It was as though Puccini had written this part especially for her.

The *Trittico* was responsible for bringing to a head the tension which had existed between Puccini and Toscanini since the early years of the war. In late 1913 or early 1914 Puccini had asked the conductor for his views on the libretto of *Il Tabarro* and the latter with brutal frankness declared that it was the worst kind of *Grand Guignol*, in extremely bad taste and unworthy of Puccini.[134] The composer, however, remained unimpressed. Soon after the Rome première it was reported to Puccini that Toscanini had said 'all sorts of nasty things about my *Trittico*', so that when he heard that Toscanini was to be engaged to conduct the London production, he besought Sybil to intervene with the management of Covent Garden to prevent this. He wrote to his English ambassadress:

Torre del Lago
16 March 1919

. . . I've heard about Covent Garden—I protested to Ricordi's because I don't want that *pig* (*porco*) of a Toscanini; he has said all sorts of nasty things about my operas and has tried to inspire certain journalists to run them down. He didn't succeed in every case, but one of his friends (of the *Secolo*) wrote a beastly article under his inspiration—and I won't have this *God*. He's no use to me—and I say, as I have already said, that when an orchestral conductor thinks poorly of the operas he has to conduct, he can't interpret them properly. This is the reason from the point of view of Art which I have expounded; there remains the personal question, and I shall do all I can not to have him; I have no need of *Gods* because my operas go all over the world—they have sufficiently strong legs to walk by themselves. If you see Higgins* or any of the others tell them too that I don't want this *pig*; if he comes to London, *I shan't come*, which would be a great disappointment to me—I can't object to this *God* because my contract with Ricordi's doesn't give me the right, but I'll do and say everything I can so that it should be known and so that he should know it himself. . . (*S*).

In the event it was neither Toscanini, who apparently withdrew, nor Sir Thomas Beecham, who had at one time been considered, nor Mugnone, who was vetoed by both Puccini and Ricordi, but Gaetano Bavagnoli who conducted the London production. Yet after no more than two years we find Puccini and 'that pig Toscanini' on friendly terms again, at any rate outwardly; it was Toscanini who directed the gala performance of *Manon Lescaut* at La Scala, given in celebration of the thirtieth anniversary of its first production, and it was he who conducted the memorable première of the posthumous *Turandot*; the *Trittico*, however, he never touched.

Into the period after the *Trittico* falls the *Inno di Roma* (1919), to words by Fausto Salvatori, written at the suggestion of Prince Prospero Colonna, who felt that Rome needed a kind of national hymn. This short choral march, dedicated to Princess Iolanda of Savoy, was first performed in the presence of the King at the Rome Stadium in June 1920. Under Mussolini's régime it was adopted as one of the official Fascist hymns.†

* Then manager of Covent Garden. † In a letter to his wife of 26 March 1919 the composer described his *Hymn* as 'una bella porcheria' (*C.P.Let.751*). It was published by Sonzogno as Ricordi, to whom he had offered it first, declined to accept it,

XIX

Aftermath of War

I

WE HAVE SEEN how the war, with the restrictions it imposed on foreign travel, had caused Puccini a feeling of claustrophobia. With the cessation of hostilities his thoughts immediately turned to journeys abroad. There was, however, an additional reason which made him wish to leave Italy for a time and even to settle elsewhere. The aftermath of the war had brought disturbed political and economic conditions—inflation had set in owing to the devaluation of the currency, the cost of living was rising steeply, and there were strikes and unrest in the industrial centres where factories had been seized by the workers. Lenin's gospel was being preached in the North and South rendering the country an easy prey to Communism and creating the conditions which gave birth to Fascism. Puccini had never been one to face unpleasant realities with equanimity, least of all, realities of a political order. He refused to perceive in the political changes of the time the symptoms of a general social *malaise* which was most strongly felt in Italy and Central Europe. For ever a *laudator temporis acti*, he imagined himself threatened in his bourgeois existence, and was now troubled by a sense of insecurity, artistic as well as material; in his pessimism he predicted inevitable disaster for Italy. It was by way of an escape that he now began to plan long distant journeys—to India, to the Far East, to Brazil—and for some time seriously considered emigrating altogether. After his visit to London in the late spring of 1920 he returned home in a despondent mood and wrote to Sybil:

Torre del Lago
1 July 1920

I am so sad here, so very sad—how different the life is from London! Italy is really in a bad way . . . and I can't stand Torre much longer. I wouldn't mind leaving Italy either—certainly if things don't improve I shall have to come to a decision of one sort or another—but it's going to be difficult for me, who am already an old man, to see good order restored in my country. What a contrast I find here with the orderliness and prosperity of London! There one really feels the heartbeats of a great country, whereas with us it's disaster—oh, the war! and oh, the Allies! In this way one advances like a crab! . . . (*S*).

In these last exclamations Puccini merely voiced the general sentiment of his countrymen that Italy, although belonging to the victorious nations, had come out of the war cheated of her spoils and sadly impoverished. For all his admiration for England, he now could not suppress a feeling of envy and resentment when he remarked to Sybil that 'now, as always, Albion has known how to look after her own interest'.[135]

In October 1922 Mussolini made his famous March on Rome, establishing himself as head of the new Government.* Puccini, whose first reaction to these events was tepid, made merely a passing reference to them in a letter to Adami of 30 October: '. . . And what do you think of Mussolini? God give, he is the man we need! He is welcome if he will reform our country and give it a little peace!' (E). If Puccini confessed to any political creed at all, it was, like that of the majority of the Italian *bourgeoisie* of his generation, based on the principles of a constitutional monarchy. Besides he was personally acquainted with members of the royal family, who took a genuine interest in his person and in his work. Yet once Fascism became established, this did not prevent him from sympathizing with the ideas and ideals of Mussolini. If we are to believe what his two intimates, Marotti and Pagni, record in their memoirs,† the composer became, like so many others, honestly convinced of the need for his country to be ruled by a firm hand. He was made an honorary member of the Fascist Party and was highly gratified when in 1924 he was nominated a *Senatore del Regno*—'Senator of the Realm'—which in letters to his friends he jestingly turned into *Sonatore del Regno*—'Player of the Realm'. Yet it is more than doubtful whether Mussolini spoke the truth when, in his official obituary tribute in 1924, he declared that Puccini himself had requested admission to the party.

2

Into this unsettled period fell Puccini's move from Torre del Lago to Viareggio, where he lived for the few remaining years of his life. It was a sad moment for him when at the end of December 1921 he was compelled to leave his beloved lake—'the greatest sorrow of my life', he wrote to Sybil in half-serious exaggeration. His exodus had been necessitated by the erection of a peat factory near his villa, the noise and stench rendering his further stay there intolerable. 'Curse those modern industrial developments', was his comment. Another—and in view of Puccini's nature—quite plausible reason responsible for driving him out of his '*Turris Eburnea*' may have been the fact that after the war communist agitation and unrest in the big cities were beginning to spread also to small rural communities. Symptomatic of this was an incident related by Del Fiorentino as well as Sartori.‡ Puccini, while one day traversing the Lake of Massaciuccoli with Del Fiorentino in his

* The future dictator, though, took care to leave the March to be organized and carried out by others, he himself travelling to Rome in a sleeper!

† *Giacomo Puccini Intimo.* They reproduce what is purported to be Puccini's *ipsissima verba*, yet the whole tone and language in which his words are couched are so unlike his customary utterances that one suspects that the two writers presented a highly coloured version of what he actually said. The book was published in 1926, two years after his death, and Fascism was still a young, strong movement.

‡ *Immortal Bohemian* (op. cit.) and *Puccini* (op. cit.).

motor boat, passed a fisherman who shook his fist at him and shouted: 'Now it's your turn, but soon *we* shall be in power!' According to Del Fiorentino, the composer did not seem unduly disturbed, but the lines on his face suddenly deepened and returning home he said to his companion:

> A new spirit is rife in Italy. It is a mortal disease which spreads over the whole world and has also affected our Tuscany. I have never done intentionally anything wrong to anybody. I have also tried to do good to some people. Why then does this man hate me? There was hate both in his voice and gesture.

Shortly after this incident Puccini decided to build his new villa at Viareggio where in fact he had bought ground as early as spring 1915. This suggests that he contemplated the move to Viareggio before Torre de Lago became such an unpleasant place to live at. But it may well have been that the changing political atmosphere at Torre was a contributory factor in prompting him to leave it for good. Puccini disliked Viareggio, yet on account of the sea air it was an agreeable place to live, and convenient for him, since, being a mere five miles' distance from Torre, he could drive to the lake in almost no time whenever his shooting passion seized hold of him. (He also owned a shooting-lodge in an inaccessible part of the Tuscan Maremma, the Torre della Tagliata, where part of *Turandot* was written.) At the time of his move from Torre, Viareggio was not yet the fashionable resort which it has since become, but was just beginning to develop from the small fishing-village where a century before Shelley's body had been washed ashore and cremated in the presence of Byron. In 1922, incidentally, the community of Viareggio wished to commemorate the centenary of Shelley's tragic death by the burial of the urn containing his ashes near the spot where his body had been found. For this purpose a committee was formed under the chairmanship of the writer Enrico Pea, a friend of Puccini's; and the composer approached Sybil in January of the following year for a donation 'for this noble cause.'

Puccini's villa at Viareggio (part of which is now occupied by a commercial firm) was built by the architect Pilotti, the same who was later responsible for the construction of the small mausoleum in the composer's house at Torre. The villa stands in Via Buonarroti at the far end of the town, near the long Promenade which runs along the sea front for a mile or so, and is flanked on one side by the spacious Piazza Giacomo Puccini. Its front faces the main road connecting Viareggio with La Spezia, along which now roars an interminable stream of noisy traffic. But in the early 1920s it must have been a quiet spot if Puccini chose to have his new home built there. The large forest of pine trees which borders the road—the whole region is famous for its *pinete*—has fortunately been left untouched. The villa itself is an impressive, almost palatial building, but rather sombre and uninviting and thus in contrast to the friendlier house at Torre. It is built of red brick, with a gabled roof under which runs a relief showing ancient Greek masks and lyres; wide steps lead up to the portal and a long veranda. The building

ILLICA   ELVIRA PUCCINI
TOSCANINI?

PUCCINI, TITO RICORDI

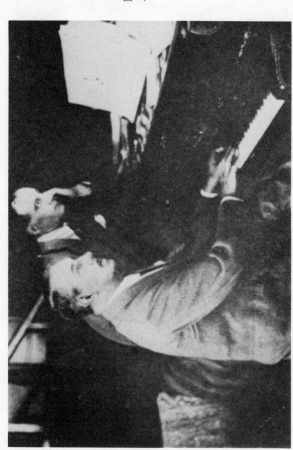

PUCCINI AND HIS SON, TONIO, IN THE VILLA
AT VIAREGGIO (At the time of *Turandot*)

Left: RENATO SIMONI
Centre: PUCCINI
Right: GIUSEPPE ADAMI

is surrounded by a large garden with pine trees of which early in 1924 Puccini had twelve trees cut down because of Elvira's constant complaints of humidity and lack of air—'it breaks my heart to have to do it', he wrote to Adami. At the time when he occupied the villa its many rooms were luxuriously furnished and there were three pianos, one of which—a Steinway grand—stood in the composer's spacious, airy study, from the windows of which he had an unimpeded view of the sea. This study was connected by a small private staircase with his bedroom, so that he did not disturb anyone when going to bed after working late. With his childlike love of mechanical gadgets,* Puccini had all kinds of contraptions installed in the new house. At a touch on a secret spot on the brass plaque fixed to the entrance gate the latter would silently open. Again, concealed pipes led up the branches of the trees so that at the turn of a tap they would spout water in profusion and the delighted composer could walk round in the artificial rain with an umbrella! Despite his regret at having had to leave his villa at Torre, he became greatly attached to the new house and showed an increasing reluctance to leave it for any length of time.† He now preferred to discuss his various problems with his librettists by correspondence, and this possibly accounts for the fact that in the *Epistolario* his letters to Adami concerning *Turandot*, most of which was composed at Viareggio, far outnumber those written in connection with his previous operas.

3

We have run ahead in our chronicle of events and must now return to the year 1918 to follow the course Puccini had been pursuing in his operatic plans after the *Trittico*. Scarcely two months after he had put *finis* to it, he wrote to Sybil:

Viareggio
29 June 1918

> . . . I have in mind a subject, full of emotion, in which the leading parts are those of two boys (they would be women in the opera)—a subject which I regard as being suited to the taste of every country but particularly to that of the British public. . . (S).

The source and title of this curious subject, which was to contain two *travestiti* roles, are unknown, and so is the reason why Puccini regarded the subject as particularly suited to the taste of the British public. However, he appeared very anxious for his London confidante to find him an English publisher for the projected opera, someone, as he wrote, who by making a good bid for it would steal a march on Tito Ricordi. Once again he and 'Savoia' were at loggerheads; he now wanted 'to get out of the clutches of these publishers of ours' and, as with *La Rondine*, to revenge himself on the arrogant Tito. Yet strangely enough, despite Sybil's efforts, no English

* Alban Berg is said to have shown the same trait

† The villa was almost completely plundered in the war; and an American soldier took away a large amount of letters and other documents which on his return home he deposited with the New York Public Library. Part of this material was published in Marek's book. op. cit.

publisher could be found willing to consider an undertaking of such indubitable financial advantage as the acquisition of a Puccini opera.

By August, however, the composer was no longer interested in the project, having meanwhile made his peace with Tito, nor did he ever again mention that 'subject, full of emotion'. Tito, incidentally, left his father's firm in 1919, Puccini hinting to Sybil that his publisher had been made to resign because, owing to his extravagant ventures in trying to discover new operatic talent, the firm had sustained serious financial losses. Now that Tito was out of luck—'the Prince of Savoy without a crown'—Puccini forgot their numerous squabbles and pitied him. Tito, who settled in Paris, later fell on hard days.

In June 1919 Puccini and Elvira came to London—it appears to have been their first journey abroad since the end of the war. Starved as he was of the theatre and more than ever on the look-out for a new subject, he went to see a large number of London productions, among them two that may possibly have directed his thoughts to a 'Chinese' opera or, at any rate, resuscitated his slumbering interest in an Oriental subject. One of these was the musical comedy *Chu Chin Chow*, the great 'hit' of the war years which had been running since 1916; the other was the play *Mr. Wu*.* About this time Forzano proposed to Puccini a *Cristoforo Sly*, the idea for which he had found in the prologue to *The Taming of the Shrew*. Puccini displayed sufficient interest to encourage Forzano to prepare a libretto—meanwhile Forzano was also writing a play on this subject—but by the summer of 1920 the composer suddenly dropped the whole project with 'Sly is no good. Forzano is unhappy about it, and so am I—for his sake. But what can I do?'[136] How typical of his perennial inner uncertainty was the fact that only a month later (August 1920) he wanted to await the first production of the spoken drama, *Sly*, before coming to a final decision. It remains doubtful whether Puccini's rejection was due to dissatisfaction with the subject or with the librettist's treatment of it. Forzano subsequently turned *Sly* into a play which enjoyed great success in Italy and was also seen in London in the summer of 1921, when the name-part was taken by Matheson Lang, whose attention to the play is said to have been drawn by Sybil Seligman. In its skilful blend of pathos and comedy, with scenes originally and vividly conceived, and with an ending reminiscent of that of *Butterfly*—Sly cuts his vein just before the arrival of Dolly—this play† might well have answered Puccini's operatic criteria but for the fact that the heroine plays no conspicuous part in it. For Dolly—not unlike Pinkerton in *Butterfly*'s tragedy—represents little more than the catalyst in the drama of Sly. An even more potent reason for Puccini's dismissal of *Sly* was, most probably, the fact that meanwhile he had lighted on a subject which began to exercise an irresistible fascination on him. This was *Turandot*.

* This melodrama by H. M. Vernon and H. Owen was later used by Eugen d'Albert as the basis for his opera of the same name, produced posthumously at Dresden in 1932.

† It later provided the libretto for Wolf-Ferrari's opera *Sly—La Leggenda del Dormiente Risvegliato* (Milan, 1927).

XX

Swansong

I

THE CHOICE OF THE SUBJECT for Puccini's last and greatest masterpiece appears to have come about in a highly adventitious manner. Since *Il Tabarro* Adami had been unable to find any suitable material for his exacting taskmaster, and the libretti for the remaining two episodes of the *Trittico* had been provided by Forzano. It so happened that during the summer of 1920 Puccini was staying at Bagni di Lucca and there he renewed his acquaintance with Renato Simoni. Simoni (1875-1952) was an erudite and scholarly writer; he had been editor and subsequently dramatic critic of the *Corriere della Sera* and, at time of his meeting with Puccini, edited *La Lettura*, which he had taken over on Giacosa's death in 1906. He was the author of comedies in the Venetian dialect and—most important from Puccini's point of view—the librettist of Giordano's successful opera *Madame Sans-Gêne*.* Simoni seemed to the composer the right man to associate with Adami, hoping that the former's wide knowledge of dramatic literature would be useful in finding a fruitful subject. His expectation was to be fulfilled, though not immediately.

During one of his post-war visits to London—presumably in the spring of 1919—Puccini had seen at His Majesty's Theatre the dramatic adaptation which Beerbohm Tree had made of *Oliver Twist*, which seemed to him to possess operatic possibilities, in particular that part of the play which centred on the hapless Nancy. The heroine and her subsequent end at the hands of the brutal Bill Sikes, the lurid atmosphere of low life in Victorian London—all this struck a responsive chord in the composer's imagination. At his suggestion Adami and Simoni now set out to fashion from the Dickens novel a libretto to be called *Fanny*, changing for an unknown reason the heroine's original name. By the spring of 1920 they presented him with a fully versified first act and a detailed scenario of the two remaining acts. But it all proved a wasted labour, for Puccini politely but firmly declared himself dissatisfied with their work. He may have felt that *Fanny* was too similar in general character to *Il Tabarro*; but there was another, stronger motive for his rejection. As he informed his two librettists, a conventional sentimental melodrama no longer attracted him and he wished henceforth to 'strike out on unbeaten tracks'. His mind, he said, was turning in the direction of some

---

* New York, 1915. Simoni had also revised the text of Paisiello's *Nina* for a revival in 1910 and later provided the libretto for *Il Dibuc* (1934) by Lodovico Rocca, which found much acclaim in Italy. He was a Gozzi scholar and the author of a play, *Carlo Gozzi* (1903).

fantastic, fairy-tale subject which was at the same time human and moving. According to Fraccaroli and Adami, this important conversation took place in summer 1920, during one of his flying visits to Milan, a few hours before he was due to take the train back to Torre. The three had repaired to a restaurant for luncheon when Simoni threw out a last suggestion: 'And what about Gozzi? What if we reconsidered Gozzi? A fairy-tale which would perhaps be the synthesis of his other typical fables? I don't know . . . something fantastic and remote, interpreted with human sentiment and presented in modern colours?' (E). It appears that it was Puccini who now proposed Gozzi's *Turandotte* (1762), a play based on the ancient legend of the cruel Chinese princess whose heart is softened by her experience of true love. He remembered seeing the play in Berlin, in Max Reinhardt's production of a German adaptation by Karl Vollmoeller,* with incidental music by Busoni. Busoni, it should be recalled, later wrote a two-act opera *Turandot* after Gozzi's play—which was given at Zürich in 1917 in a double bill with his *Arlecchino*. This Zürich production may well have suggested to Puccini to try his hand at Italian subjects of the same provenance, *commedia dell'arte* in *Schicchi* and a Gozzi fable in *Turandot*. Moreover, his thoughts may have reverted to *Turanda* by his one-time teacher Bazzini; and there was in addition the verse-drama *Il Trionfo d'Amore* by the late Giacosa which made use of the psychological motive underlying the Gozzi play and which, in fact, Simoni considered worthy of close study.

The crucial meeting in Milan is supposed to have ended with Simoni's having a copy of *Turandotte* sent over from his home to the restaurant, and Puccini took it with him to read on the train journey to Torre. It is worth mentioning that Simoni's copy was not of the original Gozzi play but of the version Schiller had made of it in 1803, translated back into Italian by Andrea Maffei—the same Maffei who had adapted Schiller's *Die Räuber* for Verdi's *I Masnadieri*. It was the Schiller version which served Puccini's initial purpose.

So much for the account of the genesis of the *Turandot* libretto as given by Adami and Fraccaroli. But from Puccini's letters to Simoni published in the *Carteggi pucciniani* this account is inaccurate in at least two important details. The first time that the subject of *Turandot*, most probably suggested by Simoni, was mentioned, was not in summer 1920 but either in late 1919 or early 1920, and that by the time Puccini's meeting with his librettists in Milan was supposed to have taken place, the composer had already decided on this subject and given Simoni general direction as to how he thought it ought to be treated:

> . . . Reduce its number of acts (from five in Gozzi to three in the opera) slim it down and make it effective and, above all, heighten the passion of Turandot who for so long has been buried in the ashes of her great pride. . . . To sum up, I am of the opinion that *Turandot* is the most normal and most human of all Gozzi's plays (18 March 1920. *C.P.*Let.766).

* Not Schiller, as generally stated.

Amazingly, Puccini's view tallies completely with the motives which Gozzi is presumed to have pursued when writing his *Turandotte*.

To correct another inaccuracy in Adami and Fraccaroli. It appears that Puccini did not see in person the Reinhardt production in Berlin but, as he wrote to Simoni in the above letter, was told about it by a 'foreign lady in Rome' who described this production as being 'most remarkable and original'. Puccini later obtained some scenic material from Berlin.

2

Puccini was fully aware that with *Turandot* he was moving on to a higher plane than that of all his previous operas. He wanted, as he put it, '*tentar vie non battute*'; he felt that in this opera 'an original and perhaps unique work was in the making', and he wrote to Adami only six months before his death: 'Hour by hour, minute by minute I think of *Turandot*, and all my music that I have written up to now seems to me a farce ('*burletta*') and pleases me no more.'[137] The last four years of his life were wholly devoted to this opera, years marked in turn by high hopes and abject despair. His dissatisfaction with his poets increased at the same rate as his striving for utter perfection. Never before had his mind been invaded by such tormenting doubts about any subject. A new and disquieting note of mistrust in his own powers creeps into his correspondence, also a feverish urgency to complete this opera. Reading his letters of that period, with their persistent exhortations to his poets to hurry, their unceasing reproaches for the supposed neglect of his person—can we avoid the feeling that in some mysterious way Puccini sensed that the sands in the hour-glass of his life were running down and that *Turandot* would never be finished? It was in a moment of such presentiment that he penned to Adami a letter (undated), moving in its gentle sadness and humility and rare in the clarity with which he perceived the limitation of his creative orbit:

17th, 11.20 p.m.

Caro Adamino,

I touch the keyboard of my piano and my hands get dirty with dust! My writing-desk is a sea of letters—and not a trace of music! Music? It is useless. I have the great weakness of being able to compose only when my puppet executioners (*miei carnefici burattini*) move on the stage. If I could be a pure symphonic composer (?) I should then cheat time and my public. But I am not! I was born many years ago—so many, far too many, almost a century . . . and the Almighty touched me with His little finger and said: 'Write for the theatre—mind well, only for the theatre!' And I have obeyed the supreme command. Had He intended me for some other profession . . . well, I should perhaps not now find myself without the essential material. Oh you, who say you are working, while instead you are really doing quite other things—films, plays, poetry, articles—and never think, as you ought to think, of a man who has the earth under his feet and who yet feels the ground receding under him with every hour and every day, as if a precipice would swallow him up! I receive such nice and encouraging letters. But if,

225

instead, one act arrived of that glittering Princess, would that not be better? You would give me back my calm, my confidence, and the dust would not settle on my piano any more, so much pounding would I do, and my writing-desk would have its sheets of music paper with a thousand staves! Oh, you of the city, have more serious thought for one who is waiting in the country. . . (E).

Although as implacable in his demands as before, Puccini now no longer commanded 'these terrible poets of mine' in the tone which he used to address his past collaborators. He now cajoles them, begs them on his knees, pleads with them and entreats them to have pity on 'an ageing man'. He has names of endearment for Adami whom he often addresses as 'Caro Adamino', concluding virtually every letter to him with 'saluti affetuosi' or 'embraces', and rarely omitting to enclose special greetings for Simoni. More than ever he indulges his predilection for play on words, puns and neologisms.* Thus in the letter quoted on p. 210 the reader may have been puzzled by the apostrophe 'Karadà', a contraction of 'Caro Adami', and so spelt as to suggest an Eastern name, in keeping with the Oriental subject that now occupied the composer's mind. In another letter he refers to his two librettists by the epithets attaccaticci—vento—bestie bovine ('sticky ones'—'wind'—'bovine animals'), adding in explanation the synonyms colla—bora—tori ('glue'—'north wind'—'bulls'), which, ranged together, form the word 'collaboratori'.[138]

3

Thanks to numerous letters to Adami, Simoni and Sybil Seligman, the genesis of Turandot with its many vicissitudes can be followed in detail and almost week by week. Initial misgivings that its exotic atmosphere might recall that of Butterfly were soon dispelled and Puccini set out to familiarize himself with it with his customary thoroughness. He obtained some scenic material from Reinhardt's Berlin production and studied books about old Chinese music, with descriptions and drawings of different instruments which he intended to use on the stage, but not in the main orchestra.†

In autumn of 1920 Puccini was again at Bagni di Lucca, where his friend Baron Fassini lived. The Baron had spent many years in the Italian consular service in China and possessed a large collection of Chinese objets d'art, among them an ancient musical-box which played the Imperial Hymn and another tune. Both these tunes Puccini used in the opera.

About this time the librettists submitted to him the first draft of the

* Puccini shared this quirk with Mussorgsky, who often introduced a fantastic element into his puns which is absent from Puccini's.

† Both Fraccaroli and Adami (op. cit.), refer to a collection of Chinese music which the British Museum is said to have lent Puccini. This is not true, as the statutory regulations permit no such loan. It is, however, possible that someone on behalf of Puccini—Sybil Seligman perhaps—consulted relevant literature there. I have myself found some of the authentic tunes which the composer incorporated in Turandot (and Butterfly) in collections at the British Museum. (See pp. 385–86 and 469–71.)

complete scenario, which found his approval. While they now proceeded with its elaboration, Puccini bombarded them with advice and suggestions. Thus, in referring to the stock characters from the old *commedia dell'arte* which Gozzi had introduced into his play, he admonishes them in an undated letter:

> . . . Don't make too much of those Venetian masks—they are to be *clowns* and philosophers who here and there risk a joke or an opinion (well chosen, as also the moment for it), but they must not thrust themselves on the attention and be petulant (*E*).

At one moment the poets, not quite certain themselves about the effect the masks would create, decided on their complete elimination. While Puccini's first impulse was to agree, he suggested (also in an undated letter):

> it might just be possible that by retaining the masks *with discretion* we should have an Italian element which, in the midst of so much Chinese mannerism (for that is what it is), would introduce a touch of our life and, above all, of sincerity. The pointed observations of *Pantalone and Co.* would bring us back to the reality of our life. In short, do a little as Shakespeare often does when he introduces three or four extraneous characters, who drink, use blasphemous language and speak ill of the King. I have seen this done in *The Tempest*, among the Elves, Ariel and Caliban* (*E*).

In July Puccini began with the first sketches for the music but was forced in October to interrupt his work to attend the first production of *La Rondine* and *Il Trittico* in Vienna, though his thoughts were no the new opera. 'And *Turandot* sleeps?' he asks Adami in a letter from Vienna of 20 October:

> The more I think of it the more it seems to me the kind of subject that one wants nowadays and that suits me down to the ground (*E*).

Yet back at Torre del Lago we find him again in the grip of black despair. In this state of mind he writes Adami a letter, dated 10 November, which throws a highly illuminating light on the working of his creative imagination. After referring to his inborn melancholy (this part of the letter has already been quoted on p. 169), he continues:

> . . . I fear that *Turandot* will never be finished. It is impossible to work in this way. When the fever abates, it ends by disappearing altogether, and without fever there is no creation; because emotional art is a kind of malady, an exceptional state of mind, an over-excitation of every fibre, of every atom of one's being—and so one could go on *ad aeternum* (*E*).

By about Christmas 1920 the versification of the first act was completed and Adami joined the composer at Torre della Tagliata in the Maremma for a reading. It was a resounding fiasco. To saturate the act in Chinese atmosphere, Adami and Simoni—who was by way of being a Chinese scholar—had crammed it with so many ethnographical details, most of them irrelevant to

---

* It may be that at one moment Puccini, searching for a 'fantastic, fairy-tale' subject, had toyed with the idea of this Shakespeare play; just as had Hugo Wolf in 1890, to whom, incidentally, the suggestion had also been made by a friend to write an opera after a Gozzi play.

the action, that the manuscript had swollen to no less than ninety pages. 'But this is not an act, this is a lecture!' exclaimed the disconsolate Puccini. It was too verbose, too literary and ineffective. The two librettists must then have performed a surgical operation at high pressure, for already by the middle of the following January Puccini was able to inform Sybil: '. . . at last I've got a fine first act—we are really on the right road'. Yet his optimism was to be trusted about as much as sunshine in April. Three months later he was again in the doldrums. On 21 April 1921, he wrote to Sybil Seligman:

> . . . I'm very, very down. I don't seem to have any more faith in myself; my work terrifies me, and I find nothing good anywhere. I feel as though from now on I were finished—and it may well be that this is so; I am old—this is literally the truth—and it's a very sad thing, especially for an artist. And then Milan stifles me with its affairs, its commerce, etc.; there's no breath of art here—the most profound indifference to everything that isn't *money*, and greed to accumulate a fortune—*Cambronne!*★ (*S*).

Yet in pouring out his heart to Sybil he omitted to mention that in the actual composition of the first act he was advancing at a good pace. In fact he was already clamouring for the final text of the second and third acts, appealing to his librettists with these amusing lines (12 June 1921):

> . . . I need the second act in a few days. I also need to feel myself caressed a little and to wag my tail like a faithful dog. But, instead, so far as you two are concerned, I pull a long face and keep my tail low! (*E*).

By and large, the composition of the first act had proceeded without delays and was completed in August. The serious difficulties arose over the second of the three acts and this explains why Puccini suddenly conceived the idea—as he had done during his work on *Butterfly*—of telescoping the last two acts into a single one. He writes to Simoni on 13 September 1921:

> . . . That second act! I find no way out, perhaps I torture myself because I have a fixed idea: *Turandot* must be in two acts only, what do you think?... Cut down incidents, eliminate others and arrive at a final scene in which love explodes . . . I can't advise you on the right structure but I feel that two more acts is too much. *Turandot* in two great acts! And why not? It's all a question of hitting on the right finale. Do it as in *Parsifal* with its change of scene in the third act—a kind of Chinese Holy Grail? Everywhere roses and everywhere love? Think about it and tell Adami. I am sure you will find it and all will be well. I am almost convinced that three acts for *Turandot* are too much. I am anxiously awaiting your letter. (*C.P.Let.816*).

It is not entirely improbable that Busoni's *Turandot* which is in two acts, suggested this scheme to Puccini and he stuck to it for some time, ignoring however that in his libretto such foreshortening of the action would have rendered the psychological transformation of the heroine still less convincing than it is in the final three-act version.

Puccini felt dissatisfied with what his librettists had sent him, and in making

★ The *mot de Cambronne* is the famous bisyllable uttered by the distinguished French general on a certain occasion and used by Frenchmen on all suitable and unsuitable occasions.

no bones about it he must have received from Adami an ill-humoured letter.
Replying, he took occasion to vent his views on the aesthetics of the theatre:

Rome
11 November 1921

Dear Adami,

It grieves me to read your letter. Do you think I am doing this because the subject has lost its attraction for me? By God, no!...

I feel that as that act [2nd] stands, it does not convince me nor can it convince the listener. The theatre has its fixed laws: to hold the interest, to surprise and to move or to make people laugh. Our act must have interest and surprise... (E).

Then there was the great love duet, near the end of the opera, which was to prove an almost insurmountable obstacle to the completion of the work. For Puccini this scene represented the core of the opera—it was to be, as he put it to Adami:

... the *clou*—but it must contain something great, audacious and unexpected and not leave things simply as they are at the beginning and interrupt it by off-stage cries from people arriving. I could write a whole book on this subject. But it is late. I'm going to bed—cursing a little because I am far from satisfied! (E).

A week later he returns to the question of the duet, exclaiming to Adami: 'The duet! the duet! It is the nodal point, all that is beautiful and vivid in the drama converges on it!' (E). And very much later—to be precise, two months before his death when scenic and textual details still remained to be settled—he described to Adami what he considered to be the spiritual essence of this love duet:

... It must be a great duet. These two beings, who stand, so to speak, outside the world, are transformed into humans through love and this love must take possession of everybody on the stage in an orchestral peroration...*
(E).

It was the most bitter irony of fate that this duet was never finished—this duet for which the composer summoned all his creative energies, in which he aspired to something exalted and lofty, and which was to convey his message to the world: the triumph of all-conquering love over the inhumanity of man. An unconscionable time was expended on recasting the text, and when at last it had been moulded into the form which found the composer's approval, after four previous versions rejected by him, he had to abandon his work, never to resume it again. Yet Puccini's failure to complete this particular love duet cannot be merely ascribed to the onset of his tragic illness; it seems to have sprung from something deep down in himself, from obstacles in his unconscious mind whose relevance to the fundamental

---

* In the *Epistolario* this letter appears under the date '16 November 1924' when Puccini was already under treatment at the Brussels clinic, which renders it most unlikely that he wrote this particular letter as late as that. Adami must have either misread the actual date or made an error when editing this collection. In the English edition the letter has been redated with the more probable month of September 1924.

psychology of the man and artist will occupy us in the second part of this book.

4

The many difficulties experienced during his work on *Turandot* impressed themselves on the composer to such a degree that at one stage he was near to throwing the opera overboard, and in fact began to turn his thoughts to another subject. Again it was Sybil in whom he confides in despair:

> Torre del Lago
> 20 October 1921

> . . . *Turandot languishes*. I haven't got the second act as I want it yet, and I don't feel myself capable any more of composing music; if I had a charming, light, sentimental subject, a little sad and with a touch of burlesque in it, I think I could still do some good; but with a serious subject—a *really* serious subject—no. . . (*S*).

It was as though he now recoiled from his own daring in striking out 'on unbeaten tracks'. On 5 November he gave Sybil the disquieting news that

> *Turandot* will end by going to the wall. . . I'm looking for something else with Forzano with an eye to London (*S*).

This 'something else' was *Chinese Play* by Forzano. Puccini sent a copy of the play to Sybil, whose views were favourable, and she advised him to set it to music. But in the meantime the composer had changed his mind. He too liked the play, as he assured her in a letter written at the end of December,

> but I've got *Turandot* and I can't change now. You say I should use the music I've already written, but it's not possible—you know how I fit the words exactly to the music. . . (*S*).

But this would not have been the first occasion in his career that he used music composed for one opera in another.

This letter was written in Rome. Puccini had gone there in December to attend a meeting at the Ministry of Education to adjudicate in a prize competition for operas by young composers. The sense of duty that inspired the individual members of this jury may be gauged from what Puccini said in a letter to Adami of 21 December:

> . . . I am thinking of the twenty-five operas which I ought to be judging but which I am not judging because I'm left alone. Mascagni is at Pisa conducting his *Marat*.
> Toscanini has given up for a thousand reasons of his own. Bossi has his son competing and has therefore made off.* Cilèa is at Naples. There remain d'Atri, who has given proof of musical judgment but . . . and Rosadi who

---

* Enrico Bossi, a notable composer of organ and chamber music and a celebrated organ player. His son, Renzo (b. 1883), made a name as a conductor and opera composer. He set Oscar Wilde's fairy-tale *The Nightingale and the Rose*.

hums the Masses of my eighteenth-century ancestor. . . *Ergo* I am not plucking this bird! . . . (E).

Meanwhile reports had appeared in the newspapers about Puccini's dissensions with his poets over *Turandot*. The latter 'are simply furious' wrote the composer to Sybil on 23 December, and in the vein of a school-master who has brought recalcitrant pupils to see reason again he adds:

> And now they've recognized how wrong they were and are going to work enthusiastically along the lines of my suggestions. . . (S).

Again he voices doubts about *Turandot*, which 'terrifies me', and again he hints at another subject—this time the adventures of the eighteenth-century rogue Cagliostro:

> This idea occurred to me in the train today when I was reading a review about him. He seems to me a great character, this Count Cagliostro—do you know Dumas's novel? But it would need a lot of historical research in order to construct a play for the stage, half heroic and half comic with a touch of the fantastic too. .'. (S).*

It is significant that Puccini here uses the adjectives 'heroic', 'comic' and 'fantastic'—qualities which precisely fit the general character of *Turandot*.

At the time of this letter the composition of the second act of *Turandot* was well advanced. Though Puccini found it hard work he nevertheless enjoyed it. Good progress was also reported by his librettists on the third act, though 'these lazy fellows' kept him waiting for it till July. For once Puccini was in the best of spirits, 'most comfortable in the new house at Viareggio', as he wrote to Sybil on 29 May, and both gratified and proud that 'all the world over my operas still hold their own—I've had quite a good six months—about 400,000 lire [*c.* £16,000]'. This sum, moreover, did not include the heavy damages he had been paid for the plagiarism of his music perpetrated by an American dance composer in a ragtime. This piece, ironically enough, had been published by the New York branch of Ricordi! It may well have been this windfall that prompted him to buy in January 1923 'a marvellous new car, an eight-cylinder limousine Lancia—90,000 lire!' He also acquired a new motor-boat, proudly announcing to Adami that it 'does over twenty-five miles an hour'. For all his anxious frettings and fits of despair over *Turandot*, of which he was thinking 'day by day', Puccini was not the man to renounce his pleasures.

Moreover, he suddenly got it into his head that he wanted to be decorated with a British order and wrote to Sybil:

Viareggio
16 June 1922

> . . . I see that for many years I have reigned over Covent Garden and I am glad of it; but now that I am an old man I think I might have received some form of recognition from your great country. The father no less than the son, the present King [George V], loved and love my music; I know

---

* This subject was used by Johann Strauss in his delightful operetta *Cagliostro in Wien* (Vienna, 1875), and Richard Strauss contemplated it for an opera to follow *Elektra*.

that, whether at the Opera or at Court, they wanted and they want songs from *Bohème*—and never once have they thought of that author who, too, has reigned for so many years in their home on the throne of the music of the theatre. That's the end of my outburst, which is moreover a passing thought that has just come to me, and has died as quickly as it was born; for if there is one man in the world who does not care for knick-knacks to be put on his evening dress, I am that man—and the real meaning of my outburst is that I love your country and want to go on reigning there. And since 1894! —*Manon*! (*S*).

It was a whim of childish vanity of which Sybil, apparently, took no notice.*
Soon afterwards Puccini went with a party of friends on a motor tour that took them to Switzerland, Germany and Holland. It was on this trip that an incident occurred which in retrospect seems like an ominous portent. On the night of 28 August the party stayed at an hotel at Ingolstadt in Bavaria. During dinner Puccini swallowed a goose bone which became stuck in his throat, causing him such pain that a doctor had to be called to remove it. (With his love of puns, the composer afterwards referred to this incident as '*in gola sta*'—'it sticks in the throat'.) After his death the suggestion was made that an injury caused to his throat, either by the bone or in the process of removing it, might have set off the cancer of which he was to die two years later.

On his return from this trip, in the autumn, work on the opera was taken up at once, but it progressed only haltingly and in November Puccini was again on the verge of giving it all up. Some time earlier his librettists must have persuaded him to abandon his idea of a two-act opera, but now he returned to it, declaring in a letter to Adami of 3 November 1922 that the three-act form was 'a great mistake'; after describing how he visualized that telescoped second act in which 'the basis must be the love duet', he makes the crucial suggestion which was to give the opera its tragic twist and its most moving scene:

> . . . I believe that Liù must sacrifice herself because of some sorrow but I don't see how this can be developed unless we make her die under torture. And why not? Her death could be an element in softening the heart of the Princess. . . (*E*).

If Puccini had indeed used this motive of Liù's suicide *affecting* the heart of Turandot, he would have eschewed what must be accounted a serious psychological flaw in the dramaturgy of the last act.†

Five weeks after that letter, when he had completed the whole of the first act and nearly finished the second, Puccini was more than ever before determined to throw the opera away and try some other subject. To Adami on 11 December:

> . . . If I had found that little subject I had been looking for and which I

---

* At any rate, my inquiry at the Lord Chamberlain's Office as to whether any approach had been made to procure a decoration for Puccini elicited a negative answer.
† See p. 446.

still hope to find, it would be on the stage by now. But that Chinese world!
I shall come to some decision or other in Milan—perhaps I shall return to
Ricordi their shekels (*soldi*) and cancel the contract (*E*).

In point of fact Adami had already proposed to him another subject—
to be set in eighteenth-century Venice—and the composer was anxiously
awaiting further news about it, asking the librettist the significant question:
'But will there be some sorrow in it? At least a scene to make one weep?'
This 'Venetian' opera he subsequently decided to tackle after *Turandot*. (In
the previous September Luigi Motta, the Italian translator of *Anima Allegra*,
submitted to him the scenario for a *Casanova* but Puccini found the third
act not good enough although the subject interested him).

The early part of 1923 brought two events which gave the composer
immense pleasure. On 1 February La Scala celebrated the thirtieth anniversary
of the first performance of *Manon Lescaut* by repeating the magnificent
production given there under Toscanini at Christmas 1922. It was 'a miracle
of execution and enthusiasm', Puccini wrote to Sybil on 5 February; and a
large banquet was afterwards given in the composer's honour, with nearly
500 guests present—'at last Milan has honoured me!'. Puccini was profoundly moved by Toscanini's performance. All his old quarrels with the
conductor were forgotten. He wrote to him on the following day:

Milan
2 February 1923

Dear Arturo,

    You have given me the greatest satisfaction of my life.

    In your wonderful interpretation *Manon* became a far better work than I
had thought in those far-off days—you performed this music of mine with
such poetic feeling, such *souplesse* and irresistible passion.

    Last night I truly felt the greatness of your soul and all your affection for
your old friend and companion of those early struggles.

    I am happy because you showed, above all, such an understanding for the
spirit of my passionate youth of thirty years ago! My beloved creature in the
hands of Arturo Toscanini! I thank you from the depth of my heart![139]

As part of a Puccini festival the Vienna State Opera also commemorated
the *Manon Lescaut* anniversary with a special production to be given in May,
with Lotte Lehmann and Alfred Piccaver in the leading parts. Yet, owing to
the tenor's illness and other obstacles, the production had to be postponed
several times and was in fact not staged until 5 October. Puccini, in the
company of his son and a friend, motored to Vienna at the beginning of
May in his new Lancia car and was fêted in the Austrian capital 'as if I were
the Emperor or the Crownprince'.* As we recall, he was deeply impressed

* On this occasion he saw *Butterfly* with Selma Kurz—'nearly a disaster'; *Tosca* with
Jeritza (who originally was to have sung Manon)—'sublime! A mad success! over 50 curtain
calls!'; and *Bohème* with Kurz and Piccaver—'she is a bit too old but not yet as old as
Melba', he wrote to Sybil(*S*).

He also attended at the Vienna Opera a performance of Strauss's ballet, *Josefslegende*,—
'there were enough nude Eves in it to turn the head of St. Francis', he commented to Adami
(*E*).

by the musical life of a city courageously trying to rise from the ashes of a lost war, and writing to Sybil on 17 May about 'the splendid Opera House of absolutely first rank', he added, 'it really is a shame that an immense city like London shouldn't have a good and permanent Opera House'. This thought lingered in his mind for some time, for when in October he paid yet another visit to Vienna to attend the *Manon Lescaut* production he harped again on the theme of a permanent opera house for London, emphasizing to Sybil that he had spoken about it to several English newspaper correspondents in Vienna.*

During this stay he learned that the Austrian Government were planning to give a special season of Viennese productions in London to include works by Wagner, Strauss and Puccini. This plan did not materialize, but Puccini was so impressed by this method of national propaganda that he decided to propose a similar plan to the Fascist Government. On his return home he sought an audience of Mussolini to submit his views and also discuss the project of erecting a National Opera House in Rome. The Duce brushed this latter subject aside with the argument that there was no money available; in his dictator's megalomania it had to be 'a project grandiose enough to be worthy of Rome, or nothing!'.[140] Intimidated by his curt rebuke, Puccini dared not put forward his idea of sending Italian opera productions abroad.

As to his work on *Turandot*, he had meanwhile once again changed his mind as to the number of acts the opera should have, now definitely settling on three. Though he had been in possession of the provisional libretto for the third act since June of the previous year (1922), it was not until June of 1923 that he at last got down to its composition in earnest but working 'not exactly feverishly'. In November the music of Liù's death-scene was finished, as yet without the proper verses—once more he had outpaced his librettists, as he had done several times before when a situation, merely outlined in the scenario, had fired his imagination; on such occasions the music welled up in him so that the words had to be fitted to it afterwards. In order to give Adami an indication of the kind of verse metre he needed for Liù's final scene, he jotted down two quatrains which in the event were set to music as they stood, except for one or two minor modifications. He also sent Adami the verse-pattern for a section of the Trio of the Masks in Act II, with characteristic assonances in it, designed to evoke a Chinese flavour.[141] In December he began with the orchestration of Act II, completing it at the end of the following February (1924); then without a break went straight on to the scoring of the last act, although his poets were still labouring on the verses for the love duet, of which they had already produced four different versions.

* If Puccini evinced at this period such interest in opera houses, the reason for it lay, it would seem, in the fact that in the previous February he had been appointed president of a committee at Lucca to supervise the rebuilding of the Teatro del Giglio, near the main square of the town. For that purpose Puccini asked Sybil Seligman for the plans of London's Gaiety and His Majesty's theatres, which he considered the most commodious theatres of the British capital.

5

It was towards the end of 1923 that Puccini began to complain of a sore throat and an obstinate cough; but, having suffered from this ailment virtually all his life, he attached little importance to it—the less so as work on the opera was progressing at a good pace, with his whole mind now bent on completing it. Yet his throat would not give him peace, and in March 1924—by then *Turandot* was complete, except for the last two scenes—the composer consulted his own doctor as well as a Milan specialist, neither of whom discovered anything to cause alarm. They put his complaint down to rheumatic inflammation and, on their advice, Puccini underwent a brief treatment in the last week of May at Salsomaggiore, a health resort near Parma. But, as he informed Sybil from there on 1 June, 'my throat is just the same—the cure hasn't made any difference. They say I shall be better later—we'll see' (*S*). On his return to Viareggio in early July he toyed with plans to visit Switzerland, France and Bad Gastein in the Austrian Alps, hoping that a change of air would ameliorate his complaint. But in the event he did not move from Viareggio, nor did his work on the opera prosper. As he wrote to Adami on 1 September:

Dear Adamino,
I am starting today writing letters again. I have been passing through tremendous crises—also with regard to my health. That trouble in my throat which has tormented me since March seemed a grave matter. I feel better now and also have the assurance that it is rheumatic in origin and that with treatment it will improve. But I have had some very sad days. That is why I have not written to anybody, not even to you, which is saying a lot!!

Clausetti came here yesterday and I said *Yes* for La Scala. I wonder if it was wise? I shall resume my work, interrupted six months ago! And I hope soon to see the end of this blessed Princess.

Now I can see the horizon clear in all directions (*E*).

All that remained to be done of the opera was to complete the love duet and the finale of the last act—which Puccini considered to be a matter of but a few weeks. On 7 September Toscanini, who had become artistic director of La Scala in December 1921, visited Puccini at Viareggio to hear some of the music and discuss details of the forthcoming production fixed for the spring of 1925. The tension that had existed between them had completely subsided, and the meeting ended in mutual satisfaction.* In his joy Puccini wrote on the very same day a letter to Adami which bears

---

* There had been a sharp set-to between the two men in the previous April, in connexion with Boito's posthumous *Nerone* to be staged under Toscanini at La Scala, about which Puccini had expressed himself unfavourably. This deeply hurt the conductor who had been a personal friend and admirer of Boito and had, in collaboration with Vincenzo Tommasini, completed *Nerone*, left unfinished at the composer's death in 1918.

witness to the importance he attached to the conductor's judgment and approval of his new work:

7 September 1924

Dear Adami,

Toscanini has just left here. We are in perfect agreement and I breathe at last. A load (*incubo*) has been taken off my chest which had oppressed me since April.* We discussed the duet which he did not like much. What is to be done? I don't know. Toscanini will perhaps ask you and Simoni to come to Salso. I'll come too and we shall see if a way could be found to improve the situation. I see only black before me. I have already grown silly over this duet.† Speak also to Renato about it. And we must get out of this difficulty because I'm at my last gasp. . . PS. The little I played to Toscanini made an excellent impression (*E*).

The meeting Toscanini was to call at Salsomaggiore took place late in September, and at the beginning of October composer and conductor met once more at La Scala, where in a rehearsal room, in the presence of Simoni, Puccini played those parts of the opera which Toscanini had not yet heard. Toscanini was deeply disturbed at the sight of the composer, who looked depressed and evidently felt very ill; but none suspected at this stage that the shadow of death had already fallen upon him.

On 8 October Puccini was at last able to inform Adami that he had received from Simoni the verses for the love duet—'they are really beautiful, they round off and justify the duet'. In the same letter he also made suggestions for the manner in which he wished the scene of the Three Masks to be staged at the opening of the second act, illustrating his idea with a diagram and referring to a Vienna production of Strauss's *Ariadne auf Naxos* in which the masks arrive on the stage by stairs leading up to it from the orchestra pit; this, however, he considered a solution not to be recommended for La Scala. The letter is signed 'Giacomo Puccini—*Sonatore del Regno*'.

It was Sybil Seligman who, apparently, was the first to suspect the hideous truth. Visiting Puccini at Viareggio at the end of August, she grew alarmed at his persistent complaint about a pain in his throat and confided her fear to Tonio. Greatly perturbed, Tonio urged his father to consult yet another doctor, but Puccini procrastinated, fearing to be told that he was indeed suffering from some serious malady. Yet in the course of October the pain increased to such an extent that he finally did consult a specialist at Viareggio, who, like his colleagues before him, discovered nothing suspicious, beyond a slight inflammation deep down the throat; he advised Puccini to take a complete rest, abstain from smoking, and to consult him again in a fortnight's time. If this allayed his family's fear, it did not allay Puccini's. Unknown to them, he consulted yet another specialist in Florence, who, after a careful examination, diagnosed a '*papilloma*' (a small nipple-like protuberance) under the epiglottis, and expressed the hope that it was not a malignant

---

* A reference to the *Nerone* incident.

† Puccini here uses a more graphic expression which it is impossible to render in English: '*ho fatto un testone da elefante*'—'I have grown an elephant's head'.

growth. Puccini returned home in a state of utter perturbation and in asking Tonio for the meaning of that medical term revealed to him his secret visit to the Florence specialist. Tonio immediately communicated with the latter and after a second consultation was told the shattering truth that his father was suffering from cancer of the throat in so advanced a stage that an operation would be futile. Yet Tonio refused to accept the death verdict, without trying to explore all possibilities of at least prolonging his father's life. While dissembling the true nature of the complaint from both his parents, he arranged for another examination of his father on 20 October by three eminent specialists, one of whom was called from Naples.* They confirmed the previous diagnoses but suggested treatment by X-ray as the only method likely to arrest the rapid progress of the disease. This kind of treatment was then in its infancy and there were only two clinics known in the whole of Europe where the method had been tried out with success: Berlin and Brussels. The decision fell on the Brussels Institut de la Couronne under Dr. Ledoux. As has often been observed with cancer patients, Puccini himself did not suspect, consciously at all events, the real cause of his complaint, though he sensed that he was very gravely ill. In this state of mind he wrote to Adami:

Viareggio
22 October 1924

Dear Adamino,

What shall I tell you? I am going through a most terrible time. That trouble in my throat torments me more morally than physically. I am going to Brussels to consult a famous specialist. I am leaving soon. . . Will they operate on me? Shall I be cured? Or condemned to death? I cannot go on like this any longer. And then there is *Turandot.* . . (E).

Before his journey to Brussels, Puccini had one more meeting with Toscanini in Milan for further discussion of the forthcoming production. Tonio had informed the conductor of the nature of his father's malady, wishing to warn him against making definite arrangements for the Scala production until they knew whether the composer would ever complete the final act. It was on this occasion or soon after that Puccini is said to have uttered the tragically prophetic words: 'My opera will be given incomplete, and then someone will come on the stage and say to the public: "At this point the composer died!" '[142]

On 4 November Puccini set out on his journey to Brussels accompanied by his son and Carlo Clausetti, representing the House of Ricordi. Elvira, apparently still ignorant of the true nature of her husband's illness, remained with Fosca at Viareggio on account of a severe bronchitis. They intended to join the composer in a week or two, but in the event only Fosca travelled to Brussels, arriving on Sunday, 23 November—a day before the crucial part of the treatment was due to begin at the clinic.

* Professor Gradenigo; the other were Drs. Torrigiani and Toti of Florence.

The composer had taken with him the sketches for the love duet and the finale of the last act—thirty-six pages in all—hoping to complete them in Brussels. On the journey he spat blood profusely but pretended to make light of this alarming symptom. His entry into the clinic he announced to Adami laconically:

Brussels

Here I am! Poor me! They say I shall have six weeks of it! Who would have imagined this! And *Turandot*? (undated, *E*).

Dr. Ledoux's treatment was to proceed in two stages, of which Puccini gave a detailed description in a letter (undated) to his friend Angiolino Magrini at Viareggio: ·

Dear Angiolini,

Many thanks for your kind and affectionate letter. I am crucified like Christ! I have a collar round my throat which is a very torture. External X-ray treatment at present—then crystal needles into my neck and a hole in order to breathe, this too in my neck. But say nothing about it to Elvira or anyone else.

The thought of that hole, with a rubber or silver tube in it—I don't yet know which—terrifies me. They say that I won't suffer at all and I must just put up with it for eight days so as to leave undisturbed that part of the throat which is to be treated. For to breathe in the normal way would upset it. And so I must breathe through a tube! My God, what horror! I remember that an uncle of Tabarracci's went about with a tube all his life. After eight days I shall breathe through my mouth again.

What a calamity! God help me. It will be a long treatment—six weeks—and terrible. But they assure me that I shall be cured. I am a little sceptical about it and am prepared for anything. I'm thinking of my family, of poor Elvira. From the day of my departure my malady has grown worse. In the mornings I spit mouthfuls of dark blood. But the doctor says that this is nothing serious and that I ought to calm myself now that the treatment has started. We'll see.*

During the first stage of his treatment Puccini was not confined to bed and was permitted to leave the clinic. He went to see among other things a performance of *Butterfly* at the Théâtre de la Monnaie—the last music of his he heard.

The external radium application at first seemed to result in some improvement of his condition and hopes began to rise. Writing again to Magrini, his thoughts even reverted to shooting in his beloved Maremma:

17 November 1924

Dear Angiolini,

Things are as before. External treatment but I seem to feel better. Here too we have a dry Siberian cold. Today I went out for luncheon and passing the market I saw such a lot of fowls on the stalls. What a shame! It makes no impression on me!

* At Tonio's request, Magrini came to Brussels, where also Toscanini's wife, Carla, had arrived. This and the following letter are reproduced in Panichelli's memoir without date. (*op. cit.*)

Even when I am cured I cannot go to the Maremma because of that blessed opera. I don't know what I shall do afterwards. Meanwhile I hope to get well or, rather, I shall try to. Greetings to all of you—happy and healthy young men. How sad is my life! And in a few days' time what cruel surprise may be in store for me! I am speaking of the internal application of the radium needles. . .

On the morning of 24 November, Dr. Ledoux proceeded to the second part of the treatment. Puccini's throat was punctured and seven needles inserted into the tumor. The operation lasted three hours and forty minutes, yet on account of his heart the patient had been given only a local anaesthetic. During the following three days Puccini's condition gave rise to a guarded optimism. Admittedly his morale was low, he suffered agonizing pains in his wound, he was plagued by thirst, he was fed by liquids administered through the nose, and he was unable to speak, communicating by means of gestures and scribbled notes; but Dr. Ledoux was satisfied with his progress, trusting his patient's robust constitution to pull him through. In reply to an inquiry from the Théâtre de la Monnaie on 25 November, he even committed himself to the statement: 'Puccini en sortira', and he planned to remove the radium needles in a few days. On the afternoon of 28 November, Fosca sat down to pen the following lines to Sybil:

Everything is going well and the doctors are more than satisfied: our adored Papa is saved! Saved—do you understand? Certainly he has suffered a good deal, but from now on this terrible part of the cure is over, and he will only have to submit to the boredom of convalescence. There is no more physical suffering, and far less moral suffering; it is only his nerves which have been upset, so the doctors assure us, by the radium which is at work. His throat is no longer swollen; the radium has destroyed the tumours. I believe that on Sunday or Monday [this letter was written on the previous Friday] they will remove the needles and then this ghastly week will be over. It's true that he is reduced to a shadow, but the doctors assure us that he will very quickly recover; he has a strong constitution, his heart is absolutely sound, and his diabetes has given no cause for anxiety. But how painful it is, Sybil dear, to see him with that hole in his throat, and being fed by the nose through a syringe. . . (S).

This letter, begun at 4 p.m., was not sent off. (Fosca enclosed it in another letter to Sybil as a pathetic comment on the irony of fate, a fortnight after Puccini's death). Towards six o'clock of the same afternoon Puccini suddenly collapsed in his chair: against all expectation his heart had given way under the strain of the treatment. The needles were removed at once and he was given an injection, in the hope that his heart failure might prove only a passing crisis. The death agony lasted for ten hours, during which time the Italian Ambassador called and the Papal Nuncio, who gave Puccini, still conscious, the last sacrament. He died at four o'clock on the morning of 29 November.*

* Dr. Ledoux was so shattered by this sudden turn of events that, driving home in his car afterwards, he is said to have fatally injured a woman pedestrian.

The funeral ceremony took place on 1 December, conducted by the Papal Nuncio at the Church at Sainte-Marie which lies in a quarter of Brussels with a predominantly Italian population. The body was then taken by train to Milan where on 3 December the official obsequies were performed by Cardinal Tosi in the Duomo. Toscanini and the Scala orchestra played the Requiem music from *Edgar*. Amid torrential rain Puccini's mortal remains were then conveyed in a solemn procession to the Cimitero Monumentale for provisional burial in Toscanini's family tomb. All Italy was in public mourning, flags fluttered from official and private buildings and La Scala was closed. Two years later, on the second anniversary of his death, the coffin was brought to Torre and placed in the mausoleum which Tonio had had erected in the villa by the lake. At this last ceremony, Puccini's friend, the conductor Bavagnoli, performed with an orchestra music from his operas, and Mascagni spoke the funeral oration.

The Puccini estate, which included the villas at Torre, Viareggio, Chiatri and his paternal home at Lucca, was assessed at £800,000 (present value). He had left no formal will but only a letter written, it appears, before his car journey to Vienna in 1923. In it he appointed his son as sole heir and Elvira as the beneficiary from his estate, bequeathing only a small monthly endowment to his sole surviving sister Nitteti. He had been close-fisted all his life and made no such generous gesture as had Verdi, who left one half of his great fortune to the Home for Musicians in Milan and the other half to charitable institutions at his native Busseto and other places. Not even his beloved Torre was considered in the will. Subsequently, several of his sisters' descendants contested his bequests to Tonio, on the ground that Tonio was an illegitimate son and that his paternity was indeed doubtful. The action did not succeed; by virtue of a decree promulgated by the Fascist Government, children born out of wedlock acquired the status of legitimacy through the subsequent marriage of their parents.

At the suggestion of Toscanini, the task of completing the final scenes of *Turandot* was entrusted to Franco Alfano, a meritorious opera composer of the younger generation, who himself had once planned an opera on the same subject. The first production was given at La Scala on 25 April 1926—seventeen months after Puccini's death; Toscanini conducted and the three principal roles were sung by Rosa Raisa (Turandot), Maria Zamboni (Liù) and Michele Fleta (Calaf).* On that evening the performance terminated with the scene of Liù's death, when Toscanini laid down the baton and turning to face the audience, made the first and last public utterance in his life. He said: 'Here, at this point, Giacomo Puccini broke off his work. Death on this occasion was stronger than art', or words to that effect,[143] thus fulfilling the composer's prophecy. The next evening the opera was performed with Alfano's ending.

The première of *Turandot* might almost have been wrecked by a political scandal of the first order. It so happened that Empire Day, which fell on

* Puccini had originally wanted the young Beniamino Gigli to sing this part, and also thought of Giacomo Lauri-Volpi who later became an outstanding interpreter of Calaf.

MANON LESCAUT, ACT I

TOSCA, ACT II

21 April, was being commemorated by the Fascist Party with a celebration in Milan to which Mussolini had especially come from Rome. The management of La Scala considered it therefore their duty to invite the Duce to honour the first-night of *Turandot* with his presence. Toscanini's anti-Fascist views were well known and he had been a red rag to Mussolini ever since that notorious occasion in the autumn of 1923 when a gang of young Blackshirts had forced their entry into La Scala, where Toscanini was just conducting Pizzetti's *Debora e Jaele*, and commanded him to play the Fascist hymn *Giovinezza*, which he refused to do. Mussolini, on being now invited to attend the première, and recalling that Scala incident, would only accept on condition that the Fascist song be played at the beginning of the opera. But he did not reckon with the rock-like stubbornness of a musical dictator. Informed of the Duce's wish, Toscanini confronted the directorate of La Scala with the curt ultimatum: either *Turandot* is performed without that hymn or else they would have to find another conductor. Toscanini won the day—there was no *Giovinezza* and no Duce to mar the baptism of Puccini's swansong.

SECOND PART

The Artist

La principale règle est de plaire et de toucher; toutes les autres règles ne sont faites que pour parvenir à cette première.—*Racine*.

The theatre has its fixed laws: it must interest, surprise, touch, or move to laughter.—*Puccini*.

XXI

General Features—Verdi and Puccini—Fundamental Aesthetics of
Italian Opera—Melodrama (Libretto) and Opera—Realism—Zola's
Formula and Verismo—Anti-Operatic Tendencies in Italy—Puccini's
'French' Sensibility—Three Aspects of Atmosphere: Documentary;
Poetic; Psychological—Atmosphere versus Character.

I

IT IS A SIGN OF GENIUS if an artist has been able to create a world which by the
force of his imagination and gifts he compels us to recognize as peculiarly
his own. This is not necessarily synonymous with greatness but it argues a
high degree of individuality—one of the most precious of creative gifts.
Puccini was such an artist. The world he created in his operas is distinctly
his own, with an emotional and dramatic climate as personal as is his musical
style. Puccini is not only an important fact in operatic history but he represents a definitive and consistent point of view in musico-dramatic thinking.
There is something like a specifically Puccinian concept of opera. Admittedly,
his concept is narrow—though he did attempt to enlarge it in his last period
—and tarnished by neurotic features. Compared with the microcosm created
by the greatest of musical dramatists, his orbit is limited—limited in subject-
matter, range of characters and musical depth. Puccini does not engage us
on many levels, as do Mozart, Wagner, Verdi and Strauss. Yet he remains
an unsurpassed master on his own and most characteristic level, which is
where erotic passion, sensuality, tenderness, pathos and despair meet and fuse.

Where, then, is Puccini's place in the hierarchy of creative artists? He is
unquestionably a major artist, but is he a great one by the highest standards?
Perhaps the fairest answer is that he was a potentially great dramatic composer
who was prevented from attaining his full stature by the limitations and
contradictions in his make-up. He possessed burning intensity of feeling
but no profundity and no spirituality. On his own admission he had 'more
heart than mind' and though he considered his untrammelled emotionalism
a weakness, he persisted in it to the end of his life. He commanded the power
of complete self-identification with his dramatic characters, notably his
heroines, but little detachment. His instinct for the theatre was extraordinary
yet he stumbled as a dramatist on more than one occasion. His technical
accomplishments were stupendous, yet he dodged some essential problems of
dramatic composition. He could never be tedious, prolix or long-winded,
but he could never be sublime. In brief, Puccini is a borderline case between
genius and talent, between the great and the not so great. And like similar
composers—Berlioz, Tchaikovsky and Mahler spring to mind—he is

difficult to portray in the round, but for this very reason he makes a fascinating subject for study.

For a variety of causes we may feel out of sympathy with the world of the Puccini operas. There is his all-pervasive eroticism and sentimentality; he deliberately aims at our tearducts: two of his three most celebrated operas are 'tear-jerkers' *in excelsis*. There is his streak of vulgarity—inevitable in fullblooded artists instinct with animal vitality, as witness the younger Verdi, Tchaikovsky, Strauss, Elgar, Balzac, Zola and Dickens. There is Puccini's calculated assault on our nervous sensibilities. And there is—perhaps most fundamental in causing a resistance to him—the ethos, or rather, lack of it, of his art. Puccini does not set his sights high. Yet in saying this we imply a moral judgment that is bound to interfere with our aesthetic judgment. Works that are genuinely admired by the world at large must possess some value even if they offend the taste and principles of the *élite*. We may in cold blood accuse an artist of holding a view of life which as a statement of moral and spiritual values strikes us as shallow or even false, yet we cannot withhold our admiration from him if he succeeds in transmuting this view into artistic terms of such intensity, conviction and imaginative qualities as will make it perennially interesting and persuasive. This, clearly, is Puccini's case, who thus remains 'modern' in the same sense as do Mozart, Wagner, Verdi and Strauss.

The supreme test of an opera composer—and, for that matter, of any dramatist—lies in his power to compel us even against our will to identify ourselves with his characters, to make us feel as they feel while we are spectators in the theatre. The born musical dramatist is the one who has it in him to arouse our sympathy with his *dramatis personae*, not merely in the colloquial sense of 'feeling *for*' but in the original meaning of 'feeling *with*' or com-passion. He will establish a close *rapport* between the men and women in the audience and those on the stage, and this *rapport* will also extend to the 'evil' character, the villain of the piece. Puccini achieves this. For all their repulsiveness, in which hate and sadism are the dominating emotions, Scarpia, the Aunt in *Suor Angelica* and Turandot force us, through Puccini's *music*, to 'sympathize' with them as much as we do with the Manons, the Mimis, the Butterflies and the Liùs. But with these, needless to say, we feel in addition real compassion—they touch and move our hearts. In virtually every opera Puccini affects the spectator in this truly dramatic manner. Even in the early *Le Villi* and *Edgar* and those less successful works of his maturity, such as *La Fanciulla del West* and *Suor Angelica*, there is at least one scene of such compelling effect. We may afterwards question the means by which he obtains his ends and even the ends themselves, but while we are spectators we are held by the spell of his theatre. What more can be asked of a musical dramatist? And when all is said, an artist has the right to be judged in the first place by his strokes of genius and not by his lapses. Henry James once wrote that 'an artist is fortunate when his theory and his limitations so exactly correspond'. Puccini is a perfect illustration of this. He belongs to that small group of artists who know exactly what they are about and are able to gauge accurately the measure of their creative powers. Puccini was aware where the boundaries of his genius lay and seldom made the mistake of venturing beyond them, for the very good reason that within their scope he was able to achieve all he set out to achieve. For all the regeneration of his style to which he began to aspire since *Butterfly* and which, technically, he realized in full measure, he remained faithful to himself. Puccini was an artist of rare integrity whose recognition of his limitations—expressed with such touching sincerity in his famous letter to Adami (see page 225)—does not make him a *petit maître* any more than it made Chopin, Hugo Wolf or Ravel or, to turn to literature, Maupassant or Chekhov—all artists of genius with an acute awareness of the extent of their creative range. Nor was Puccini a mere miniaturist, a composer of *musiquette*, as he has been represented by some biographers. True, he confessed to a predilection for '*le cose piccole*'—'the little things'—but this is only one aspect of his art. He was equally drawn to the big and fullblooded things. *Tosca* and *Turandot* are as much part of the essential Puccini as are *La Bohème* and *Butterfly*. Moreover, artists who are as conscious of the scope of their creative fancy as Puccini rarely fail to achieve a perfect adjustment of means to ends. They are stylists knowing instinctively how best to adapt their imagination to the technical exigencies of any given medium and vice versa. Not for nothing was Puccini the scion of four generations of very respectable musical craftsmen. Allied to his high-grade professionalism there were his gifts for melting lyrical melody, for the impassioned dramatic phrase, for refined and pliant harmony and a multi-coloured orchestra. It is this combination of qualities which raises Puccini above the level of the majority of opera composers of his time and largely defines his eminence.

From *Le Villi* to *Turandot* we note a continuous advance toward more complete technical realization of his dramatic intentions. And with this went a constant assimilation of various technical devices developed by his contemporaries. Like Verdi, but to a larger extent, Puccini kept abreast of his time, yet the individuality of his style remained unaffected. The Puccinian stamp is as unmistakable in the Wagnerisms of *Manon Lescaut* as it is in the Debussyean touches of *Butterfly* and *La Fanciulla* and the Stravinsky passages of *Il Tabarro* and *Turandot*. Puccini the man was by no means a fully integrated personality, but the artist in him succeeded in creating a style which represents a perfect amalgam formed in the crucible of an individual, imaginative mind.

2

Puccini has often been called the successor of Verdi. He himself would in all probability have disclaimed any right to a *proxime accessit*, for he was modest and conscious of his lesser stature. None the less, the epithet of successor and even heir is apt, so long as we do not stretch its implications too far. A comparison between the two is inevitable and will serve to throw additional light on Puccini's own position in the central tradition of Italian opera. Yet such a comparison must start from the premise that Verdi was as unique an artist as was his great contemporary across the Alps. Verdi found in Puccini as much or as little a successor as Wagner found in Richard Strauss. We note, incidentally, the curious repetition of an antithesis between north and south in the history of opera, an antithesis expressed in the pairs Gluck-Piccini, Mozart-Cimarosa, Weber-Rossini, Wagner-Verdi and Strauss-Puccini.

This is not the place to expatiate on what made Verdi such a towering figure in nineteenth-century Italian opera. But a few points may be noted in order to illuminate the chief difference between him and Puccini. Verdi's uniqueness lies in the elemental masculinity of his whole art. A spouting volcano, the eruptions of his genius—his *terribilità*—link him with artists of such magnitude as Michelangelo, Shakespeare and Beethoven. Moreover, Verdi was a product of the *risorgimento*, that awakening in the national spirit which inspired Italy to fight for political freedom and unity, realizing at long last the dream dreamt three centuries before by Machiavelli. Verdi himself was a spiritual fighter for those national ideals, and the man and his aspirations are clearly reflected in his art, in its tragic heroism, its ideals of justice, truth, family bonds, patriotism and loyalty of man to man. Such artists as Verdi are rare phenomena and can have no real successors.

Puccini's, on the other hand, was a splintered, neurotic personality, feminine in many ways and rooted in man's strongest biological urge—sexuality. To put the difference between the two artists into an extreme form we may say that while the ground-bass of Verdi's operas is a battle cry, of Puccini's it is a mating call. The psychological chasm that thus separates the two is revealed in a flash by that incident in connection with the original libretto of *Tosca*. While Verdi was deeply moved by the Farewell Hymn to Life and Art, Puccini could do nothing with it and had it altered to a lament in which the hero, about to face the execution squad, recalls the hours of sensual passion with the heroine.

Also the Italy in which Puccini grew up was different from the country which Verdi knew in his early life. After her successful struggle for unity Italy settled down to consolidate her political gains and a period of prosperity and relaxation followed. While Verdi's art proclaims the peasant origin of its creator's every fibre, Puccini's springs from the climate of a settled *bourgeoisie*. If Verdi wrote in the first place for national audiences, Puccini addressed himself to *l'homme moyen sensuel*, in fact to the international *bourgeoisie*. In saying this I do not imply a Marxian dialectic or use the term *bourgeoisie* in a pejorative sense but merely wish to indicate the changed social and spiritual atmosphere in which Puccini worked. (It is one thing to relate Puccini to bourgeois ideology and another to attempt to explain the artist *entirely* in terms of middle-class society, particularly of the Italian *bourgeoisie* at its most developed as represented by Milanese society. This is the view adopted by some recent Italian critics who thus continue—though, admittedly in a more responsible and more sympathetic way—the essential arguments advanced in the first decade or so of our century by

Torrefranca and others (see pp. 263–264). Rightly or wrongly, non-Italian musicians who see in Puccini a more complex and transcending figure, consider such a view as too narrow and over-simplified. The historico-social environment is undeniably a very important factor in the formation of an artist's personality but cannot define the *whole* of his creative orbit, which contains elements quite independent of the time and place in which he lived.)★

The picture of Puccini's time is complicated by the fact that there occurred changes in Continental art at the turn of the century which were symptoms of a radical shift of values. I am referring to the period of the *fin de siècle* from which Puccini is inseparable, although Italy, so far as opera was concerned, was too secure in its old traditions, too robust and resilient to be radically affected by the 'decadent' spirit emanating from Central Europe and France.

But in certain essentials there were close links between Verdi and Puccini. What united them was their common view that opera represented the central tradition of Italian music, a tradition which began with Monteverdi and terminated with Puccini. *Turandot* is the end-product of a continuous development of more than three hundred years. If we inquire into the constant elements of this tradition, the general answer will be found in the quotation from Racine which heads this part of the book: 'the principal rule is to please and move; all the other rules are only made to lead up to that first'. Racine's is possibly the most concise statement ever made of the first principles governing the dramatic and operatic stage in Latin countries. They may be summed up in three words: 'Direct human appeal.' To gratify our senses and move our hearts—Racine's *'plaire'* and *'toucher'*—represent the dramatist's supreme aim, to which he must harness all his imagination, technical resources and material. Since their early beginnings, Italian and French opera have rarely lost sight of those fundamental principles. From Monteverdi to Verdi and Puccini, and from Lully and Rameau to Massenet, Bizet and Debussy, the Latin composer has always endeavoured to subordinate 'all the other rules' to that 'first rule'. In parenthesis, the most perfect equilibrium between these two aims is to be found in Mozart, whose basic conception of opera was Latin, yet with an added depth flowing from the German element in his supra-national genius.

If there is a difference between the French and the Italian approach to the sensual and the emotional, it is a difference of emphasis. Rational, sophisticated and largely concerned with matters of refined taste—*le goût*—the French aim at a neat balance between those two aesthetic goals, at times being inclined also to lay greater stress on the appeal to our sensibilities than our emotions. The Italians, on the other hand, fullblooded, closer to nature and hence more direct and instinctive in their art, have mostly gone the other way about it. They are more intent on stirring our emotions than delighting

★ An interesting parallel to this is found in German critical writing on Richard Strauss whose art—so the the argument runs—must be seen springing exclusively from the middle-class mentality characteristic of the Germany of the Wilhelminian era.

our senses. For the Italian opera composer the abiding theme is that of the simple passions of the heart shown in conflict with one another. It is the elemental polarity of pleasure versus pain that provides the dramatic main-spring for Monteverdi no less than Puccini. Traditional Italian opera is tethered to the primary emotions and their polarity is brought into play to create a simple human drama in terms of love—hate, joy—sadness, rapture—despair. If Monteverdi wrote that 'contraries greatly move our mind . . . this is the purpose which all good music should have',[1] Puccini asked for a libretto 'full of passion and pain', for 'grande dolore in piccole anime' yet also for 'episodes, delicate, luminous, exquisite . . . and with a touch of gay, fresh laughter'.

The consequences springing from such a conception are several and are of intrinsic importance for our appreciation of the aesthetics of Italian opera. They explain the high emotional tension, the strong contrast of moods, the unfailing dramatic impact, and musically, the concentration on *melody* as the most direct and vital element to appeal to our senses and feelings. Melody in its most immediate form is song—hence the supremacy of the singing voice in Italian opera. Of all the instruments the human voice is the most natural and the most potent in creating sensuous and emotional effects. For the Italian opera composer the voice all but stands for the entire character, and therefore delineation of character is to be achieved primarily through the singing voice. Furthermore voice is an extension of sex into sound and thus functions as a characterizing force *par excellence*. The mere contrast of male and female voice is instinct with drama. Add to this the power and sensuality of the true Italian voice and the dramatic thrust and vibrating quality of the Italian language and it becomes clear why Italian opera through the ages has always achieved its principal effects by vocal means. This bondage to the voice also explains why Italian opera of the eighteenth century became the soil from which sprouted such vocal excesses as the *coloratura* aria and the cult of the vocal virtuoso (*prima donna* and *primo uomo*) and of the *castrato*.* In the Italian *cantilena* speech, thought, emotion are brought together in complete unity, so that we often gain the impression as though the musical phrase sprang into being at the very moment in which it is being sung. It is this that gives the Italian opera aria its irresistible dramatic effect. There is no difference in fundamental aesthetic approach between such famous arias as Arianna's 'Lasciatemi morire', Desdemona's 'Piangea cantando' and Cavaradossi's 'Muoio disperato'. Monteverdi, Verdi and Puccini, separated though they are by temperament, period and style, seek to achieve an identical aim: to express a simple yet intense emotion concentrated into a pregnant vocal melody, and thus stir the heart. I have advisedly chosen as examples three laments because the lament is the occasion in Italian opera (as indeed in most operas) for music of the most poignant appeal. Arianna's Lament, which in Monteverdi's own

* In the nineteenth century this narcissistic stage of Italian vocalism was gradually dying out but we still find traces of it in the style of the middle-period Verdi and in the early Puccini. The part of Musetta shows the last flicker of the tradition.

words was 'the most essential part of the opera', is said to have moved his contemporaries to tears. Puccini too said that he wanted in his music 'to make the world weep—therein lies everything'. Monteverdi complained to Alessandro Striggio, the librettist of *Orfeo*, that he could not write suitable music for the winds in *Le Nozze di Tetide*: they were not human beings and did not speak—how could he then write music for them? Puccini's demand to his librettists was for something 'passionate and moving', for 'not too much psychology but sympathetic understanding of human grief'. Monteverdi stood at the dawn of Italian opera and Puccini at its sunset, yet both they and the long series of intervening composers display the four great features of Italian operatic art: *umanità—sincerità—passione—effetto*. *Effetto* does not merely stand for the obvious theatrical effect but is also to be understood as describing the supreme dramatic moment. No true Italian opera is without those four features, though their manifestations necessarily vary according to period, taste and style. Yet an aesthetic which lays such stress on the untrammelled expression of human feelings runs the risk of an excessive emotionalism and a kicking over the traces, dramatically and musically. This is precisely what happened in *verismo*, with which we shall deal later.

In the eyes of Italian, and for that matter of most French, composers the opera house represents not a temple, not a moral institution—as Schiller and Wagner conceived the theatre—but rather an arena in which large and heterogeneous audiences are brought together to be entertained pleasingly or movingly or both. Verdi composed, as he once said, with 'one eye on art, the other on the public'. Puccini insisted on 'a subject that would appeal to the public at large; because I write for all races of men'! Italian opera of the nineteenth century addresses itself to majorities and aims at a broad appeal. Bellini, Donizetti, Verdi, Puccini and his contemporaries would have readily endorsed Defoe's proposition: 'If any man were to ask me what I suppose to be a perfect style of language I would answer, that in which a man speaking to 500 people, all of common and various composites, idiots and lunatics excepted, should be understood by them all and in the same sense in which the speaker intended to be understood.' They would have subscribed, no less readily, to what Baudelaire said with deliberate hyperbole: 'Any book which is not addressed to the majority—in number and intelligence—is a stupid book.' The reverse side of such a liking for broad appeal and popularity are features which sometimes strike non-Italian audiences as vulgar and naïve. There is certainly an aspect of Italian opera which offends the sensibilities of the rigid purist, the highbrow, the aesthete, the man of perilously refined tastes; but only a bold man would claim that to relish lusty fullbloodedness in art is incompatible with aesthetic enjoyment—it may indeed be a sign of a healthy, unwarped artistic instinct. I quote Baudelaire again: 'The autocrats in thought, the distributors of praise and blame, the monopolists of the things of the mind, have told you that you have no right to feel and enjoy— they are the Pharisees.'

In such a conception as we have just described opera remains primarily a drama of emotions, and it will rarely aspire to be a drama of ideas, as has German opera since Wagner (Strauss, Pfitzner, Schreker, Berg). It will eschew intellectuality, 'deep' thought, metaphysics, *Weltanschauung*, complex psychology and elaborate literary conceits. Hence the choice in Italian opera of a simple human drama as subject and of a libretto so fashioned that it will provide the composer with a plot, characters and situations from which a maximum of emotional and dramatic expression can be extracted. Such a libretto will furnish him with sharp contrasts of mood and swift-moving action, to heighten the tension and counteract the slow tempo inherent in a sung text. If Verdi asked for 'powerful situations, virility, spirit and pathos', this is matched by Puccini's demand for something 'passionate, moving . . . and of varied scope' and for action that 'must move forward to the close without interruption, rapid, effective, terrible'.*

Now in what type of libretto can such desiderata best be fulfilled? Evidently in one of a melodramatic cut. This brings us to a problem, not important only for our later consideration of Puccini's dramatic style but fundamental to operatic dramaturgy of, roughly, the last century and a half. It is the *raison d'être* of melodrama on the lyrical stage. Tempting though it would be to study this problem in detail here—one hitherto much neglected in operatic aesthetics—this would take us too far for our present purpose, and I shall therefore confine myself to a few essential points. Melodrama appears, broadly speaking, to have met the most immediate needs of the majority of romantic and modern operas because it provided those elements on which dramatic music seems to thrive best: passions shown in their nakedness and brought to white heat in 'strong' situations, characters drawn in black and white, and rapidity of action. Owing to the retarding nature of vocal music—and in Italian and French works it is, with rare exceptions, the singing character and not the orchestra which is the chief vehicle of the action—there is far less time in opera than there is in a play for elaboration of plot and character development, so that the time factor assumes in opera an importance greatly transcending that in the spoken drama. Thus in a libretto the drama must be presented in a compressed form. It was largely Wagner, and to some extent Strauss from *Rosenkavalier* onwards, who ignored the time factor successfully, allowing the action to unfold gradually and putting characters on the stage not only consistently developed but rich and complex in their psychology.

On the spoken stage melodrama has been known since the Elizabethan plays; but it does not seem to have entered opera until the French Revolution in the so-called 'terror' and 'rescue' operas, with their scenes of violence,

* Cf. the Preface to *Alceste*, signed by Gluck but written by his librettist Calzabigi: 'By good fortune my designs were wonderfully furthered by the libretto, in which the celebrated author, devising a new dramatic scheme, had substituted for florid descriptions, unnatural paragons and sententious, cold morality, *heartfelt language, strong passions, interesting situations . . . and an endlessly varied spectacle*'. (My italics.)

cruelty and excessive passions—of which the greatest and only surviving example is Beethoven's *Fidelio*. What could be more melodramatic in that noblest of noble operas than the scene in the dungeon where the 'villain' Pizarro is about to kill the 'virtuous' Florestan, but is prevented by the unexpected intervention of the 'faithful' Fidelio in her spine-chilling cry: 'Töt' erst sein Weib!'—'Kill first his wife!' Melodrama dominates the subsequent grand operas of Rossini, Meyerbeer, Halévy and the Verdi of the early and middle periods, seeking to achieve its most striking effects by means of violent emotional contrasts in combination with huge spectacular scenes. Drawing on the contemporary novels of romantics like Scott, and Hugo, the libretto becomes a hotchpotch of all sorts of crudely interwoven intrigues—amorous, religious, political and historical; a late descendant of these is Puccini's *Tosca* where sex, religion and art enter into a strange but effective fellowship, against a background of important historical events. Grand opera also throve on medieval legends, with their grotesque superstitions and general air of lunacy, all of which were readily accepted by a public that delighted in the Gothic novels of Mrs. Radcliffe and the fantastic tales of E. T. A. Hoffmann. We only need to recall Weber's *Der Freischütz* and its French counterpart, *Robert le Diable* by Meyerbeer, to say nothing of the operas by Spohr, Marschner and the young Wagner. This supernatural atmosphere lingered on in Italian opera during the 1880s and 1890s, as exemplified in Catalani's *Loreley* and *La Wally* and Puccini's *Le Villi*. With the advent of realism in literature, it was inevitable that the operatic libretto should follow suit, spicing the old romantic ingredients more pungently from ordinary everyday life. We witness this already in *Traviata*; but it was really *Carmen* that opened the gates for a flood of the kind of half-romantic and half-realistic melodramas which provided the chief pabulum for Puccini and his contemporaries in Italy, France and Germany. Melodrama certainly answered the essential requirement of an operatic aesthetic rooted in the primary forces of the theatre. Indeed, if we were to draw up a list of the viable operas of the nineteenth and twentieth centuries, we should find that the majority are based on libretti of such a nature. Even *Otello*, the greatest tragic opera Italy has produced since Monteverdi's *Orfeo*, contains a melodramatic touch in the strangulation scene of Act IV. It also offends against the most elementary canons of dramatic truth in Desdemona's brief arioso which she sings *after* Otello has suffocated her.* (Puccini, a more modern composer, would never have committed such post-mortem offences.) And for that matter, what are the most dramatic situations in *Salome*, *Elektra*, *Wozzeck* and *Lulu* but melodrama which is lent an added *frisson* through the introduction of pathological traits—in fact *Grand Guignol* of a psychological order. Germans, since Wagner's Kundry and Klingsor, have always shown a liking for characters of a complex and perverted psychology. And melodramatic elements are of course present in many great classical

---

* A parallel case is Gilda's duet with Rigoletto, after she has been stabbed to death and her body been disposed of in a sack.

and modern tragedies—from the ancient Greek dramatists* to Shakespeare, Schiller and Ibsen; but we do not recognize them as such because of the different ideological premises on which these tragedies are based, and because no such emphasis is laid upon them as in pure melodrama. In the latter, those powerful dramatic agents—'strong' situations and conflict of passions—are used almost constantly and as a result tend to displace character. The character is often reduced to a mere function of the plot, is unable to develop on account of the rapid action and displays the simplest and most fundamental emotions often expressed in the crudest fashion. Character in melodrama is, as it were, only one storey high.

Why is it, then, that while modern taste dismisses melodrama on the dramatic stage, it accepts it so readily in traditional opera? The answer lies in the nature of music which can and mostly does raise melodrama to a higher plane. It can even turn melodrama into drama or tragedy, as in *Aida*, *Carmen* and *Butterfly*. Music has an ennobling and idealizing power. It can tone down (but also intensify) excess on the stage. It can add emotional and psychological depth to the characters, and because it needs room to assert its lyrical quality it has a retarding effect on rapid action. An opera in which music is no more than the servant of the action would be intolerable. Furthermore, genuine dramatic music has its own logic, it can bridge gaps and camouflage flaws in the dramatic structure and psychological motivation. There are, indeed, precious few operas with a libretto watertight in every respect, least of all where the plot is a melodramatic one; yet fused with the music it *appears* watertight or its faults seem to matter little, as we shall see in the detailed discussion of Puccini's operas. Melodrama and music in the hands of a born dramatic composer coalesce into an entity which is not only more than the sum of its two constituent parts but indeed different from them. It is in that new entity that musical drama has its being. The majority of audiences have found this entirely acceptable, the proof of which is the undiminished popularity enjoyed by operas based on libretti which with our modern contempt of melodrama and our demands for psychological verisimilitude and literary quality we should reject out of hand on the spoken stage.

We mentioned realism. Here again we are confronted with a problem that impinges on Puccini's style and one that we may best approach by a few generalities. Realism in the sense of psychological truth has been known in opera since Monteverdi. Did he not write, though in a different context, that 'the modern composer builds on the foundation of truth'? But in opera to build on the foundation of truth and to represent truth as it is found in life are two entirely different things. The first leads to the highest form of realism: imaginative truth; the second to its crudest form unvarnished truth or naturalism, which is not the stuff of the stage, least of all of opera.† The

* What is it but melodrama when Oedipus commits patricide and incest and then blinds himself while Jocasta hangs herself?

† Cf. Verdi's trenchant remark: 'Ah, progress, science, realism!... *Ahi, ahi!* I am a realist as long you wish, but ... Shakespeare was a realist too, but he did not know it. He was a realist by inspiration, we are realists by design, by calculation'. (In a letter to Ricordi, 20 November 1880. See Appendix to *Copialettere*, op. cit.)

stage is there to create an illusion of life but not to photograph it. The truth of life sprawls, flickers, flares up in the most unlikely places and at the most unexpected moments, it is utterly unselective and contradictory. It is not a formula for opera. It is in the replacement of illusion by crude reality that realistic opera, so far as its libretto is concerned, overshoots its aim.

Opera is a patterned, contrived thing and the most artificial form of drama; but over and above this there is the fact that music, from which opera receives its very lifeblood, abhors naturalism. Music is, paradoxically, both an abstract and an emotional art or, rather, its effect on the listener is both abstract and emotional. When it merely imitates physical reality it ceases to be music in the true sense. Its real task in opera is to convey an imaginative realism through tone symbols which have the qualities of expression, suggestion and evocation. Genuine dramatic music is in the first place interpretation and not imitation, expression and not description. And when faced with ideological or intellectual concepts which are characteristic of literary realism, the true dramatic composer will reduce them to their emotional substratum. His actual realism resides not in the music but in the kind of subject chosen and the kind of characters brought on to the stage. True, this will have its influence and also condition to some extent the style of the music, but the music, in order to gratify our senses and stir our emotions, will have to retain its qualities of expression, suggestion and poetic evocation. Mozart went to the root of the matter when he laid it down that dramatic music must certainly be dramatic but it must be music too. Or more explicitly, 'passions, whether violent or not, must never be expressed in such a way as to excite disgust, and as music, even in the most terrible situations, must never offend the ear, but must please the hearer, or in other words must never cease to be *music*. . .'[2] Puccini on the whole always fulfilled those conditions. Whatever the realism of his subjects and the brutality of certain situations—we recall here *Tosca*, *La Fanciulla* and *Il Tabarro*—he has always known how to extract from them the emotional essence and translate it into terms of real music. To each of Puccini's operas there is what Zola, in referring to novel writing, called *le côté poème*.

It is the libretto, then, which represents the chief realistic element in realistic opera. Our next question is: what are the salient features of such a libretto? I can do no better than quote what Zola once wrote about the realistic novel. The passage reads like a set of rules for a realistic libretto and, incidentally, demonstrates to what extent literary realism not only encouraged but demanded a melodramatic treatment:

> Gone is the time when the reader was kept in suspense by a complicated dramatic but improbable story; the sole object is to register human facts, to lay bare the mechanism of body and soul. The plot is simplified; the first man one comes across will do as a hero; examine him and you are sure to find a straightforward drama which allows full play to all the machinery of emotion and passion.*

* From a speech to the Congrès Scientifique held at Aix-en-Provence in 1866, in which Zola surveyed the development of the novel from the earliest Greek specimens down to the nineteenth century. See *Emile Zola*, by F. W. J. Hemmings. London, 1953.

We note here three important points. There is, first, an implicit demand to abandon mythological, historical and dynastic subjects and turn to subjects drawn from everyday life, with characters often standing on the lowest rung of the social ladder—'the first man one comes across will do as a hero'. Hence the gallery of 'low life' characters in opera from about 1870 onwards: prostitutes, poor students and artists, workers, peasants, soldiers and so on. There is, secondly, Zola's demand for 'full play to all the machinery of emotion and passion'. In other words, *le droit divin de la passion* is established as the prime motive in the drama, and more often than not the dénouement is brought about by a passionate crime and/or suicide—as first seen on the operatic stage in *Carmen* and exemplified in the fate which Puccini reserves for several of his heroes and heroines. It is in this special emphasis on passion, on the instinctive in the human being, that realism shows its close link with romanticism, the decadence of which it, in fact, represents in a sense. Lastly, Zola demands a simple, straightforward story, of which Puccini's self-explanatory plots provide excellent examples.

All this seemed new on the surface. It is customary to date the birth of realistic opera from *Carmen* (1875) though its labours began as early as *La Traviata* (1853). Both indeed represent landmarks in the development of realistic opera, reflecting the growing trend in contemporary French literature—*La Traviata* the early and romantically tinged realism of Dumas *fils* and Mürger, *Carmen* the later realism of Mérimée, Flaubert and Zola, which was more factual and documentary and less poetic, yet more searching in its analysis of the social and psychological aspects of life.

But a certain realism has always been present in Italian art and is indeed a trait of the Italian national character. Episodes and figures drawn from low life are the source material for Boccaccio's *Decameron* and the *novellieri* of the Renaissance as they are for the *commedia dell'arte* and *opera buffa*.

So far as tragic opera was concerned, before both the advent of French realism and the historical fusion of French grand opera with the older type of *opéra comique*, with its 'simple folk' characters, there was Verdi, who had entered upon the realistic path as early as in *Luisa Miller* (1849). Similarly, the gloomy and violently dramatic situations characteristic of realistic opera were also anticipated by him in such works as *Ernani* (1844), *Rigoletto* (1851) and *Trovatore* (1853), where some of the protagonists are shown in the white heat of a consuming passion.* It is also significant that Verdi was much tempted to set Sardou's *Tosca*.

It now becomes clear why the seeds of French literary and operatic realism should have found so fertile a soil in Italian opera of the last decade of the nineteenth century, though admittedly Italian literature of that period first reflected Zola's preachings and prepared the soil in such writers as

---

* Characters set in an atmosphere of utter gloom and writhing in a paroxysm of savage passion and suffering have never been achieved on a more impressive scale than by another great Italian realist—Dante in the *Inferno* of his *Divine Comedy*. Nor does it seem to me a mere coincidence that Zola, the father of modern literary realism, should have been an Italian by descent.

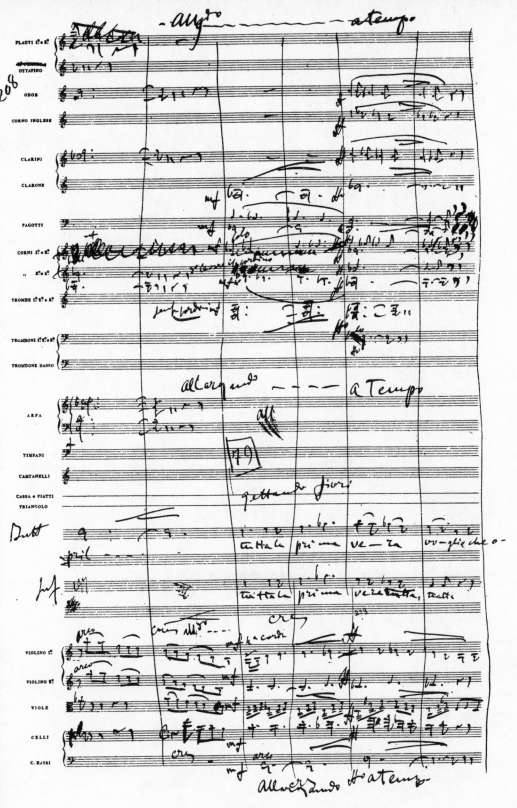

MADAM BUTTERFLY, ACT II, PART I

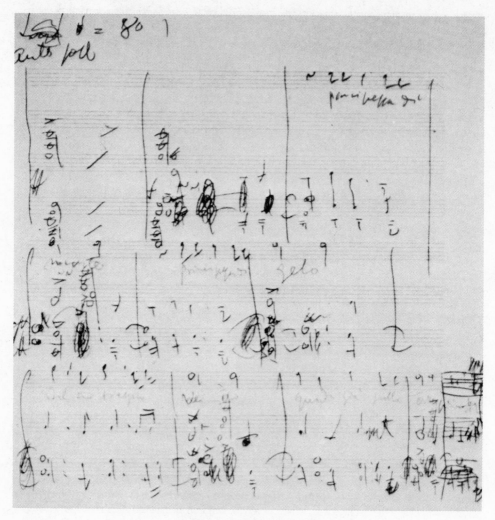

TURANDOT, ACT III
Beginning of the Love Duet (left uncompleted)

Luigi Capuana, Giacosa and, above all, Giovanni Verga (1840–1923), whom we encountered in connection with Puccini's abortive project *La Lupa*.

We also recall that *Cavalleria Rusticana* was based on a dramatized story from Verga's *Vita dei Campi*, a collection of short stories depicting the life of Sicilian peasant and fisher folk, a life of endless toil, endurance, strong passions and swift vengeance. It was published in 1880, ten years before Mascagni's opera. Yet Italian operatic realism known as *verismo* (*vero* = true) was not a mere translation of a foreign concept into the vernacular but something closely corresponding to a fundamental trait in the Italian national character. Now, given the dynamic Italian temperament and its natural bent for truth, and given Verdi and the general constellation of opera of that period, it was hardly surprising that the high-powered spark of French realism should have caused the Italian powder keg to explode with an elemental force. It is in the nature of an explosion to be short and sharp, but its reverberations may continue for some time after.

4

Pure *verismo* did not last longer than a decade or so, after which it gradually petered out, but its echo was still to be heard in the 1920s and 1930s: in Puccini's *Il Tabarro*, in *Káta Kabanová* (1921) by Janacek, who in fact had created a Czech brand of *verismo* as early as 1904 in *Jenufa*, and in Shostakovich's *Lady Macbeth of Mtsensk* (1934). Yet while *verismo* was at its height in Italy, it exercised its influence in all operatic countries, especially France, *vide* Massenet's *La Navarraise* (1894), Bruneau's *L'Attaque du Moulin* (1893) and *Messidor* (1897), and *Louise* (1900) by Charpentier. Germany, reacting more slowly, made its chief contribution in D'Albert's *Tiefland* (1903) and Schillings' *Mona Lisa* (1915); nor would it appear a mere coincidence that *Salome* and *Elektra* followed after *Tosca*. Yet with the French, notably Bruneau, there runs a thread of symbolism and a 'message' through their operatic realism which is absent from their Italian contemporaries. Thus Bruneau, the bulk of whose stage works are based on subjects drawn from Zola novels, was, as Martin Cooper puts it, 'a passionate believer in Zola's humanism and "vitalism" '.[3] The larger theme underlying his operas is the conflict between spiritual and physical forces in which, as Zola saw it, human beings must suffer and perish. Charpentier again, in his 'musical novel' *Louise*, touched on contemporary problems such as free love, the relation of parents and children, the misery of poverty and the temptation to which *les pauvres* are inevitably exposed. At the same time, the story contains a strong romantic element in the love of Louise for Julien, but the real heroine of the opera is Paris, the great city at once mysterious, seductive and fatal. This interpenetration of romanticism, social realism and symbolism was typical of *fin de siècle* art and we sense it too in so late a work as *Il Tabarro*.

In the Italian realists we do not generally perceive such overtones. Far more earthbound than their French counterparts, they were almost exclusively concerned with presenting a cross-section of ordinary life in a melodramatic plot, the action of which has no universal significance and no larger theme; but on the credit side of their ledger we must enter such items as concentration of the action by the omission of distracting dramatic details, extreme vividness of plot and characters, an elemental drive and melodic vitality. The verists thus followed Zola in what he postulated for contemporary opera: 'un drame plus directement humain, non pas dans le vague des mythologies du Nord, mais éclatant entre nous pauvres hommes, dans la realité des nos misères et des nos joies. La vie, la vie partout, même dans l'infini du chant.'⁴ Does it not sound like a direct echo of Zola when Leoncavallo puts in the mouth of the Prologue of *Pagliacci*:

> Our author tonight a chapter will borrow from life with its laughter and sorrow! Is not the actor a man with a heart like you? So 'tis for men that our author has written. And the story he tells you is true!*

It is significant, too, that the story of this opera as well as of *Butterfly* is based on a real incident. Yet in the later stage of *verismo*, a contemporary subject was no longer *de rigueur*, any subject would do as long as its plot provided the kind of characters and situations required by the veristic creed. The French Revolution and its aftermath became a favourite setting (*Andrea Chénier* and *Tosca*) and also remoter historical periods (*Francesca da Rimini, La Cena delle Beffe, Suor Angelica, Mona Lisa*).

The paramount feature of *verismo* is excess, the uninhibited inflation of every dramatic and emotional moment. Climax follows climax in swift succession and moods are no sooner established than they are destroyed. And since excessive tension cannot be sustained for long, the one-act becomes the favourite form of veristic opera. Characters are presented over-lifesize and are swept along in a whirlwind of passions in which sex becomes the driving force. Erotic desire is always thwarted and thus leads to acts of insensate jealousy and savage revenge, acts—and this is characteristic—almost invariably committed on the *open* stage so as to score a direct hit at the spectator's sensibility. Thus in Puccini's *Tosca* we are shown the actual execution of Cavaradossi, whereas in Sardou's play it takes place behind the scenes. And while in Belasco's *The Girl of the Golden West* there is merely talk of lynching Johnson, in Puccini's opera we are made to witness how the noose is placed round the hero's neck.† Don José's *crime passionel* in Act IV of *Carmen* was the point of departure for all those scenes of stabbing, strangling, execution, suicide and attempted rape that are found in realistic opera of the following period.

With such *données* in the libretto, it was inevitable that the music should be in an almost unbroken state of excitement and agitation. Short, broken-up declamatory phrases alternate with sharp rocketing fragments of melody

---

* This is the official translation, which has, however, not the force of the original: 'L'autore ha cercato pingervi uno squarcio di vita. Egli ha per massima sol che l'artista é un uomo e che per gli uomini scrivere ei deve. Ed al vero ispiravasi.'

† Strauss once wrote to Josef Gregor, apropos of a certain scene in *Daphne*: 'Nothing must take place behind the scenes, not even the killing of Leukippos. Theatre and not literature!'

and the naturalistic shout finds its way into the aria, now dubbed *aria d'urlo* (*urlo* = howl or yell). Thus Mascagni wrote about his *Il Piccolo Marat*: 'It has muscles of steel. Its force lies in the voice which does not speak nor sing: it yells! yells! yells!'[5] No doubt the last duet between Don José and Carmen, with its frenzied ejaculation, provided the most immediate model for such cries, but they are already anticipated in the tremendous vocal explosions in the Verdi of the early and middle periods, and found even in *Otello*. Already in Puccini's pre-veristic operas, the wholly romantic *Manon Lescaut* and the largely romantic *La Bohème*, we find such naturalistic *cris du coeur* in the parts of Des Grieux and Rodolfo. The character of the Italian operatic voice encouraged such an intensification of vocal expression, of which French voices would have been incapable. As to the orchestra, it displays an almost obsessive use of tremolo and a predilection (as in the early Verdi) for blatant and inflated effects, with the brass in marked prominence. *Con (tutta) forza* becomes a frequent dynamic marking, to say nothing of violent contrasts between *ff* and *pp*. To a large extent the musical aspect of *verismo* represents a hypertrophic growth of features of the Verdian style. Considered as a movement, *verismo* was partly the reaction of the Mediterranean spirit against the mythological, symbol-laden, remote world of the Wagnerian music-drama, which in the 1880s had found such ardent admirers amongst the younger Italian composers—much to Verdi's concern and alarm. In retrospect, though, his fulminations against the perils of *germanismo* appear exaggerated. Native opera was too securely anchored in the national tradition to be cut off its moorings by the northern wave. But Verdi, an Italian of Italians, could not have reacted otherwise and his decision to break his long creative silence with *Otello* was largely prompted by the desire to prove in the teeth of all the Wagnerian enthusiasm around him that the fundamental principles of native opera, its *italianità*, could still hold their own. *Otello* was a single-handed act of defence of those principles, though Verdi could not altogether escape the *Zeitgeist*, any more than other composers. In spirit, it is true, *Otello* was a negation of all that Wagner stood for, but in its technique it demonstrated the degree to which Verdi had recognized the general gains which the Bayreuth master had brought to dramatic composition as such. In a sense *Otello* represents a solution by a great Italian of the problems thrown up by the German music-drama.

It is from the technical style of *Otello* that the Italian realists took their chief bearings, though they made more deliberate use than Verdi of the various Wagnerian devices (already seen in the pre-realist *Manon Lescaut*), e.g. application of the leitmotive but in a rather crude and inconsistent form; the abandonment of separate, self-contained numbers (still retained in *Cavalleria*), with the orchestra now providing continuity and itself achieving greater significance, though still a subordinate means of dramatic characterization; and lastly, the avoidance of extended formal ensembles since they offended, it was held, against the principle of dramatic truth. Thus Puccini during his veristic period proper—*Tosca* to *Fanciulla*—avoids such concerted ensembles, nor are his love duets real duets but essentially duologues in which only toward the climax the two voices unite.

For all their insistence on being 'true to life', the verists could, of course, not do without certain conventions of traditional opera. Like Verdi, they believed in the magnetism of the solo aria as the focus of lirico-dramatic expression; and, like Verdi, they too composed 'with one eye on art, and the other on the public'.* Nor did they disdain the insertion—characteristic of the older *opéra comique*—of purely musical numbers which may or may not arise out of the action and which serve the double purpose of delighting the ear and lending colour to the atmosphere: *brindisi* or drinking-songs (still present in *Otello*), dances, vaudevilles, little choruses and so on. Puccini has such pieces in every one of his operas; perhaps the most enchanting echoes of this past tradition are heard in Colline's little song about his old coat, in Musetta's waltz and, on a large scale, in the Trio of the Masks, in Act II of *Turandot*.†

5

We have outlined the essential features of *verismo* and the question now arises whether Puccini's position is wholly defined by an exclusive reference to this movement. If the answer is yes then it must be conceded that Puccini is the verist *in excelsis* and his *Tosca* the high-water mark of *verismo*. All the characteristic features of this style can be studied in this opera, dramatic no less than musical, though its setting was not 'modern' or 'contemporary' in the sense which Zola and the early verists postulated for realistic opera. Yet in all other respects it faithfully conformed to their canons. In acknowledging Puccini's pre-eminence we cannot ignore the other members of this movement whose initial leaders were Mascagni and Leoncavallo. Both Mascagni (1863–1945) and Leoncavallo (1858–1919) are, to all intents, one-opera composers, their fame resting on *Cavalleria Rusticana* and *I Pagliacci* respectively. But Mascagni's opera forms an historical landmark in Italian opera of the nineteenth century and was a striking novelty for its time.‡ Verdi, than whom there was no shrewder judge, found in it, after an initial hasty dismissal, 'such sincerity' and prophesied for the young composer a great career. '*Cavalleria*', he declared, 'has all the elements of success.'[6]

Mascagni has a long series of operas to his name and by no means all in the style with which he is commonly associated. He himself declared at the time of the romantic *Isabeau* (1911) that '*verismo*, of which I had been so fervent an adherent, has run its course', which did not prevent him, however,

---

* In their support they might have quoted a witty saying by La Harpe about Gluck's *Alceste*: 'Tous les arts sont fondés sur des conventions, sur des données. Quand je viens à l'opéra, c'est pour entendre la musique. Je n' ignore pas qu'Alceste ne faisait ses adieux à Admète en chantant un air; mais comme Alceste est sur le théâtre pour chanter, si je retrouve sa douleur et son amour dans un air bien mélodieux, je jouirai de son chant en m'intéressant à son infortune.' (*Journal de Politique et de la Littérature*. 5 October 1777. Quoted in *Source Readings in Music History*, ed. Oliver Strunk. London, 1952.)

† See also, *Cavalleria*: Turiddu's Siciliana; *I Pagliacci*: Nedda's Bird Song.

‡ The publisher Sonzogno, in whose prize competition it was discovered, even doubted whether it would be effective on the stage.

from reverting to it in *Il Piccolo Marat* (1921). The chief trouble with Mascagni lay in the fact that he did not follow his true instinct, which was for more or less pure *verismo*, and that he ventured into spheres for which his gifts were less well suited: idyllic comedy in *L'Amico Fritz*, romantic tragedy in *I Rantzau* and *Ratcliff*, Goldonian *commedia dell' arte* in *Le Maschere*, and exotic symbolism in *Iris*. *Iris* (1898) represents the first excursion by a modern Italian opera composer into the alluring atmosphere of legendary Japan and may well have kindled in Puccini the desire to try his hand at a similar subject. *Butterfly* is of course far superior, but *Iris* displays harmonic and orchestral subtleties with which we would not have credited the composer of the coarse-grained *Cavalleria*. Mascagni (like Puccini after him) knew how to turn to advantage devices from Debussy, whose music began to cross the Alps in the late 1890s. Indeed, it would be unfair to judge Mascagni solely on the technical crudities of his most celebrated opera, which he wrote when barely twenty-six years of age. His subsequent works show a considerable advance in craftsmanship and contain many incidental touches of beauty; but in contrast with Puccini, Mascagni was an artist of little self-discipline who had been spoiled for the rest of his career by the sensational success of his early years. He appears to have recognized as much himself, and once remarked: 'It was a pity I wrote *Cavalleria* first. I was crowned before I was king.'[7] No doubt there was a more elemental outpouring of melody in Mascagni than with Puccini, he was more of a *Musikant*; and to many of his Italian contemporaries he represented 'l'italianissimo genio', never belying 'the characteristics of our race'.[8] Yet Mascagni never fulfilled the hopes he had aroused in *Cavalleria*, which appears to have been written in an outburst of youthful creative energy, after which the composer quickly burnt himself out.*

Much the same can be said of Leoncavallo. Though less gifted than Mascagni in direct and forceful melody he was an appreciably finer craftsman, as is shown by even the most superficial comparison of *Cavalleria* with *I Pagliacci*, written at the age of thirty-three. Like Puccini and Mascagni, he had an inborn sense of what was theatrically effective, and he had the advantage over both in being his own librettist for the majority of his operas and operettas, of which he wrote some twenty. But in art quantity has never been a passport to greatness and the inventive quality of Leoncavallo's operas deteriorated in direct ratio to his output. Still it is a fair guess that his *La Bohème* (1897) would still be heard outside Italy but for Puccini's enchanting masterpiece on the same subject. Leoncavallo treated Mürger quite differently from Puccini and introduced scenes of sombre dramatic power. His is an opera that cannot be dismissed lightly. For this

---

* In this connexion it is not without interest to read what Puccini thought of *Iris* and its composer. 'For me this opera which has such beautiful things in it and is scored in a most brilliant and colourful way, has this fundamental defect: the action is not interesting and languishes and flags for three acts... You, who are his true friend, should tell him that he ought to return to the passion and the lively and human feelings with which he began his career in such a brilliant manner'. (To Alberto Crecchi, 21 January 1899. *C.P.Let.*201).

reason, and also because the comparison throws indirect light on Puccini as a dramatist, a brief discussion of the Leoncavallo work will be found in the third part of this book. Nor is *Zazà* (1900), which in its time enjoyed considerable success, an altogether negligible work. The heroine, a *café concert* singer, and her milieu are portrayed in authentic colours, which Leoncavallo knew from his own experience, having had to eke out a precarious living as a pianist in such surroundings before the finger of Fortune touched him with *I Pagliacci*.

Giordano (1867–1948), four years younger than Mascagni, was, with Leoncavallo, one of the first composers to apply the formula of *Cavalleria* in *Mala Vita* (1892), a work of almost repulsive brutality. He too is, so far as non-Italian audiences are concerned, a one-opera composer. Despite his subsequent works such as *Fedora* (1898), after Sardou's play, *Siberia* (1903), and several others in the veristic vein, only *Andrea Chénier* (1896), whose action recalls that of *Tosca*, survives on the international stage.* Montemezzi (1875–1952) and Zandonai (1883–1944), representing the second generation of verists, set their main course in the direction of a realism tempered by neo-romantic and impressionist features, as in the former's *L'Amore dei tre re* (1913) and the latter's *Francesca da Rimini* (1914), after d'Annunzio's tragedy. Zandonai's first great success in *Conchita* (1911), a subject which Puccini contemplated for some time but which, it will be recalled, he finally rejected, led to the hope that in him realist opera had found a new leader—a hope that proved illusory. It is undeniable that all these and other composers of that period knew how to build effective dramatic scenes, possessed the gift of melodic warmth and exuberance, and that especially the younger ones, who came under the growing influence of Debussy and to some extent Strauss, display high technical competence. Yet Puccini towers head and shoulders above them by dint of his superior inventive powers as a musician, his sense of the inner laws governing action and music, his instinct for balanced dramatic structure, and his constant awareness that opera, however dramatic in conception, is not all action, movement and conflict but must have moments of repose, moments of lyrical contemplation and poetry. In his letters to both his actual and potential librettists we find him time and again stressing the fact that opera is different from spoken drama and that the libretto has to be adapted to the poetic exigences of the music. Hence his repeated exhortations to them to allow him scope for 'spreading his colours more lyrically', for 'an affectionate little phrase' and for 'episodes, delicate, tender, luminous, and exquisite'. And no one before and after him was ever endowed with such sensitive antennae for the poetry of *le cose piccole*, the little unimportant things in the lives of little unimportant people, as he shows in *La Bohème* and *Butterfly* and the first half of *Suor Angelica*. Such qualities cannot be reconciled with those of a whole-hogging verist, as he has been represented. He neither began nor ended his career as such; and it is signifi-cant that he allowed nearly ten years to elapse after Mascagni's *Cavalleria*

* Its sensational success may indeed have acted as an additional incentive for Puccini to set Sardou's drama.

before he unfurled his own veristic flag in *Tosca*. Thus the long answer to the question posed at the beginning of this section must be that there is a dimension in Puccini which reaches far beyond the narrow confines of pure *verismo*.

6

But, paradoxically, it was Puccini who became the chief target of those virulent attacks which during the first decade of the twentieth century the Italian *avant-garde* launched against *verismo* and indeed all opera. Puccini found his Hanslick in the musicologist Fausto Torrefranca, the intellectual leader of this anti-operatic movement and the author of a book with the significant title *Giacomo Puccini e l'opera internazionale* (1912) in which the composer was torn limb from limb. The hypersensitive Puccini must have suffered profoundly under this assault on all that his art stood for, but he suffered in silence. He made no public retort, and his private correspondence contains merely vague allusions to this painful interlude. Torrefranca's attacks started from the narrow and one-sided premise that the great tradition of Italian music was not to be found in opera but the instrumental music of the seventeenth and eighteenth centuries. In his quixotic tiltings Torrefranca went so far as to declare that opera was a mongrel and did not at all reflect the native genius for music. The rot, according to him, had set in with Monteverdi, while Puccini illustrated 'all the decadence of present Italian music, all its cynical commercialism, all its pious impotence and the triumph of internationalism'. Torrefranca concluded with the prophecy that 'in a few decades hardly anything will be remembered of Puccini's works'. This was written in 1912! Behind all these polemics was a strong conviction, shared by all the young composers of the time and chief among them Pizzetti, Malipiero and Casella—all three born in the early 1880s, a generation after Puccini—that native opera had run its course and had become effete, and that a new *risorgimento*, a rejuvenation of Italian music, could be brought about only by the assimilation of the spirit and style of the great instrumental masters of the past: Frescobaldi, Corelli, Veracini, Vivaldi and others.* The monopoly that opera enjoyed in the musical life of the nation was deeply resented and vocalism condemned, and the stage was finally reached when the young iconoclasts clamoured for a ban on all those composers who had exclusively devoted themselves to opera. Mascagni retorted by saying that he would write a symphony only when he felt his imagination exhausted. And we recall Puccini's ironical remark to Adami: 'If I could be a pure symphonic composer (?) I should then cheat time and my public.' By diverting creative energies from opera to instrumental music the *avant-gardistes* hoped to achieve that '*ristabilimento dell'equilibrio*' which they so much desired and which was in fact brought about in the large amount of instrumental music that has been composed in

---

* It is worth noting that the renascence of English music started, partly, from similar premises and about the same period.

Italy in the first half of this century. (This process had already begun in the 1880s with such older composers as Martucci, Bossi, Sgambati and Sinigaglia.)

The new anti-operatic movement was both idealistic and nationalistic. Idealistic because it wished to turn away from the *bourgeois* mentality of realist opera with its lack of spirituality and high moral values; nationalistic because it demanded an art exclusively nurtured in old Italian soil and freed from the influences of both late German romanticism and French impressionism. In a thoughtful book,[9] which includes a fairly balanced study of Puccini, Pizzetti reproached the entire impressionist school for its over-refinement, its growing exclusion of the life of the emotions, 'its prodigious faculty of stifling the will to live'; on the other hand, he accused Puccini and other Italian realists of having sinned in the opposite direction by their emotional excesses and their superabundance of vitality, which, so ran his argument, defied full translation into satisfactory aesthetic expression.

Yet, not unexpectedly, the extreme position occupied by these young firebrands of the 1900s was gradually relinquished with growing maturity. Casella (1883–1947), Malipiero (1882–1973) and, especially, Pizzetti (1880–1968) began to turn their attention to the operatic stage, albeit guided by aesthetic and stylistic ideas different from those of Puccini.* Admittedly, Pizzetti with his ten operas to date, and Malipiero with a dozen or so, may be said to have opened fresh paths for the post-Puccinian opera, but they are paths, not avenues. Neither Pizzetti's adherence to a pervasive declamation of the voice part and his reduction, for dramatic reasons, of the static lyrical element to a minimum, nor Malipiero's elimination of all dramatic dialectics and of character development—thought-provoking though these innovations be in themselves—have so far succeeded in producing specimens of that universal appeal which Verdi, Puccini and the 'old melodrama' of the last century still continues to command. Aesthetic theories that tend to by-pass the natural laws of the theatre have little chance of leading to results of an enduring nature. It is a sobering comment, too, on these high-minded reformers and on the present-day state of Italian opera that the only modern Italian composer whose operas have asserted themselves on an international scale happens to be applying the much-decried Puccinian canons. This is Gian-Carlo Menotti (1911), who has been living in America since 1928. Endowed with an extraordinary sense of the stage he has the advantage over Puccini in being his own librettist, but on the plane of musical originality and memorability of invention the comparison with Puccini ceases to be profitable.

7

'Internationalism' was one of the charges levelled against Puccini by the phalanx of young nationalists. Translated into musical terms it largely signified the French influence on his style. Influence is perhaps not an apt description, for it was not so much the adoption of certain technical features,

---

*Pizzetti's first opera *Fedra*, to a libretto by d'Annunzio, dates from 1905.

such as impressionist harmony and orchestration, but a deep-seated affinity with French sensibility that links Puccini with France. There was something in his psychological make-up—just as there was in Tchaikovsky's—that readily responded to French 'feeling', which is the reason why Puccini's relationship to the Italian 'nationalists' strikes us as somewhat similar to that of Tchaikovsky and the Russian nationalists. Tchaikovsky, too, was accused of internationalism. Puccini's 'Frenchness', so marked in the operas of his middle period, is the more noteworthy as pure Tuscan blood ran in his veins. In his pronounced leanings toward France Puccini stands apart from the rest of his Italian contemporaries; indeed, his historic significance may be said to lie partly in the fact that he created a type of opera which fuses the fullblooded *passione* of the Italian with the sophisticated, refined *sentiment* of the French.

Of Puccini's twelve operas, five have subjects taken from French authors and in four the setting is France, to say nothing of the many French subjects he considered during his career but did not set for one reason or another. Similarly, the true Puccinian heroine is bi-national in her parentage. One root of her family tree is formed by the more fragile and gentle women in Verdi—Luisa Miller, Gilda, Leonora (of *La Forza del Destino*), Violetta, Desdemona and Nannetta, while the other root leads to the soubrette type of French opera—Mignon, Marguerite, Micaëla, Manon and Lakmé, who themselves are descended from the young girl and her confidante in *opera buffa*. Thus Puccini's Anna, Fidelia, Mimi, Butterfly, Magda, Giorgetta, Angelica and Liù are as capable of the intensity, the emotional incandescence and dramatic accents of those Verdian heroines as they are capable of the refined emotional shades, the elegance, the delicate charm and sweetness of the French *petites amoureuses*.* Hence the characteristic blend, in the vocal style of these roles, of a broad sensuous *cantilena* with diminutive melodic fragments, and of resonant bright colour with a discreet, intimate timbre. On the other hand, Tosca and especially Turandot are direct descendants of the great dramatic heroines of Verdi. As to Puccini's men, the tenors are mostly of mixed Italo-French origin, but Calaf is very nearly· of the calibre of Radamès. Puccini's baritones and basses are all of pure Italian blood, none more so than Gianni Schicchi, in whom Puccini revived the rogue of the old *opera buffa*.

* It is worth drawing attention to the type of heroine which the Viennese novelist and playwright Arthur Schnitzler created in the '*Süsses Wiener Mädel*'. Schnitzler's 'Sweet Viennese girl' might have almost stepped out of Mürger's *La Vie de Bohème*. She is a little sempstress or a typist or a shopgirl, lives in a small room, dreaming the dream of romantic love until she meets the man to whom she gives herself with complete abandon and single-hearted tenderness. This is how the poet Anatol describes her in Schnitzler's play of that name (1893): 'She isn't fascinatingly beautiful, she isn't particularly elegant, she isn't at all clever . . . but she has the graceful charm of an evening in spring, and the wit of a girl who knows how to love. And she says nothing very special, all she says sounds so childishly simple, unless you hear the tone of her voice with it.' This type of girl which Schnitzler drew from the Vienna of his days is a cousin of the Parisian midinettes and grisettes, and since she displays affinities with Puccini's typical heroines, we appreciate the better Vienna's great partiality for his operas.

Puccini has often been called the Italian Massenet. This is only a half-truth, for he possessed an incomparably richer fund of sheer music and far more vitality than his French counterpart, though the latter's formative influence on the Italian composer's early melodic style is undeniable.* What links the two musicians is a refined, languid eroticism, a feeling of delicate despair, and the truly Gallic elegance of their craftsmanship. And both possessed a highly developed sense of atmosphere which rendered them indefatigable travellers on the map of operatic geography.

With Puccini atmosphere was as integral a part of his dramatic world as the plot—the very air in which his characters have their being. He said to Adami when first contemplating the subject of *Il Tabarro*: 'It's a violent thing, brutal, wounding almost, but effective—that life on the river, that colour of the Seine, that background of Notre-Dame!'[10] He saw atmosphere here not only as a mitigating element in the plot, but also as a source of inspiration. As a realist Puccini possessed a highly developed sense of environment which, as with Zola and Flaubert in their novels, led him to cultivate an almost documentary realism in certain operas in order to reproduce the illusion of authenticity. If Zola, for example, spent months in the slums of Paris or in the coal-mines of Northern France so as to be able to create a scientifically accurate ambience in *L'Assommoir* and *Germinal*, or if Flaubert noted down medical details about arsenical poisoning for *Madame Bovary*, this is on a par with Puccini asking, at the time of his work on *Tosca*, for the text of certain Latin prayers, for precise details about the costumes of the Swiss Guard, and making a special journey to Rome to hear with his own ears the morning bells of the various churches in the neighbourhood of the Castello Sant' Angelo. Similarly, when Flaubert made intensive archaeological studies preparatory to his writing of *Salammbô*, this is matched by Puccini consulting books on the ethnography and music of Japan and China for *Butterfly* and *Turandot*.

Puccini's exoticism, however, is only partly an expression of his predilection for authentic atmosphere, nor is it merely a means whereby to colour it from without: it springs from a deeper source which is his instinctive imaginative response to the *emotional* overtones of the exotic ambience. Its ultimate purpose is to create *poetic* atmosphere. This explains why the various authentic tunes of Japanese, North American and Chinese origin which he uses in his three 'exotic' operas are not merely included as apt quotations but are intimately worked into the texture of the music. They represent, moreover, a fertilizing material whose characteristic inflections are assimilated into his own idiom, so much so in fact that there is no intrinsic dichotomy between his 'exotic' and 'Western' manner—hence the homogeneity of style in *Butterfly*, *Fanciulla* and *Turandot*. The fructifying influence of this material on Puccini is almost comparable to that exercised by native folk-song on composers such as Vaughan Williams, Bartók and Falla.

* See Exx. 5 (p. 292) and 32 & 33 (p. 339).

The evocation of a poetic atmosphere serves also those exquisite impression-ist mood-pictures which are found in all his mature operas. Nature is made to reflect the mood of his characters, and it is almost invariably desolate nature at dawn in which is mirrored the despair of his heroes and heroines: the grey morning at Le Havre in *Manon Lescaut*, Act III; the bleak winter morn-ing at the 'Barrière d'Enfer' act of *La Bohème*; the leaden dawn breaking over the snow-capped Californian forest in *Fanciulla*, Act III. In *Tosca*, on the other hand, Puccini achieves a calculated contrast by opening Act III with an evocation of the pristine freshness and peace of a Roman morning, which, but for the stealthy appearance of the 'Scarpia' motive, gives no hint of the terrible things that are to follow shortly. To the same order of atmosphere painting belong those scenic vignettes and tableaux which the impressionist in Puccini so cleverly dovetails into the action. Every act of *La Bohème* contains such scenes; in *Butterfly* there is the geisha's night vigil and the preceding 'Flower' scene, with music of the utmost fragrance and tender-ness; and in *Turandot* there is the nostalgic Trio of the Masks. Admittedly such scenes are static, holding up the essential action, and Verdi would not have tolerated them; but with Puccini they form part of his dramatic con-cept, and who will deny that they add to the life, variety and colour of his theatre?

To Puccini's documentary realism and poetic evocation we must now add a third aspect. This is atmosphere as the nerve-centre of his drama, affecting the musical portrayal of his protagonists and determining the individual character of each opera. Admittedly, his dramatic world was restricted and revolved around an immutable axis: love as tragic guilt pre-sented in a compulsive recurrent pattern. Yet over and above it, each of his operas possesses a peculiar musical tone or climate or ambience, or whatever we care to call that something which, despite stylistic similarities, sets one work apart from another and gives it a distinctive personality. To take a few examples. *Bohème* conjures up the spirit of eternal youth, its joys and sorrows, its smiles and tears, the bliss and pathos of young love. *Butterfly* recaptures the quaintness, daintiness, the childlike innocence and humility which the West at one time associated with Japan and its diminutive people. Again, the fascination of *Tosca* and *Turandot* resides, primarily, in an air of evil and sadistic cruelty—suffocating, seeping into everything and rotting the very fibre of the characters—though the musical means employed in the two operas display a marked difference of style. And only a composer endowed with a deep-rooted sense of atmosphere like Puccini could have conceived a work such as the *Trittico*, the *raison d'être* of which lies in the concentrated dramatic effect achieved by the sharpest possible contrast of three different atmospheres. It is in this ability to bend his invention so completely to the particular psychological ambience of a given opera that lies a measure of his power as a musical dramatist. And it is a highly characteristic feature of his musico-dramatic technique that he establishes this ambience at the very opening, catapulting us into it by a motto theme which captures with a single stroke the atmospheric essence of the drama. He once said to Adami, revealingly: 'The difficulty is, how to begin an opera, that is, how to find its musical atmosphere. Once the opening is fixed and composed, there is no more to fear.'[11]

Yet a composer with whom atmosphere forms so integral a strand in the fabric of his dramatic thoughts runs the peril of seeing his characters as emanations of it. It is indeed often difficult to distinguish in Puccini between what is delineation of character and what of atmosphere. The two tend to blur. This hybrid nature of his musical portraiture forms one of the fundamental differences between him and Verdi, for whom character came first and atmosphere second. Puccini's musical characters are not so much individualities with a life of their own as projections of atmosphere, incarnations of emotional states and, in the last analysis, symbols of his own unconscious drives and tensions. They speak less for themselves than for their creator. In so far as they do strike us as individualities, they achieve this largely by virtue of the peculiar dramatic atmosphere in which they move.

XXII

Puccini and the Fin de Siècle—Psychological Mainspring of his Art—Love as Tragic Guilt and its Compulsive Pattern—Latent Symbolism of Plot and Characters—The Puccinian Heroine and her Antagonist—Puccini's Limitations.

I

WE HAVE ALREADY TOUCHED on the way in which Puccini's mind worked. Before attempting to probe farther and shed more light on his secret creative processes, it will be relevant to try to see him against the background of that fascinating period of which he was a characteristic product: the romantic decadence or *fin de siècle*.

As always in periods when old beliefs disintegrate and new beliefs can only just be discerned on the horizon, the *fin de siècle* was an age spiritually unsettled, self-questioning, self-divided and marked by inner contradictions about the significance of life and art. Nietzsche, its most percipient commentator, described it as the period of 'transvaluation of all values'. What largely brought this about was the emergence of an acutely scientific spirit embodied in such men as Marx, Darwin and Freud, a spirit that gradually undermined the foundations of the old order of things, which up to about the last third of the nineteenth century had been thought of as solid and unshakable. As for the artists and writers between 1880 and 1910, the majority reacted with feelings of disillusionment, frustration and despair. The moral, social and aesthetic standards which they had been taught by their elders to set store by, were now shown to be tottering. In music, the pervasive pessimism in the works of such composers as Puccini, Mahler and Debussy was in part a reflection of the spiritual *malaise* of their period. With Puccini and Mahler there is, in addition, a suggestion of the existential *Angst*, of helplessness in a world of hard brutal facts and resignation to the sadness which they saw at the roots of life. Puccini's verses,* artless as they are, echo essentially the same sentiment to which Mahler gave such poignant expression in the *Farewell*, the last movement of his *Song of the Earth*.

The chief gain for the artist in this process of 'transvaluation' was a sharpening of his antennae for things of the outer and inner world and, in consequence, a considerable enlargement of his field of vision. We notice in the arts two parallel and complementary developments. On the one hand there is an increasing and almost microscopic exploration of man's outer world, his physical and social surroundings, his milieu and the influence it exercises on his character and conduct. On the other there is an urge to

---

* See p. 170.

look more deeply into the inner man, to probe the hidden recesses of his mind and convey their secrets in artistic terms, often esoteric and symbolic in character. The corollary of this introspective probing was to be seen, in literature, drama and opera, in the cultivation of almost imperceptibly fine shades of feeling and of nervous sensibility, notably the erotic sensibility which was subtilized to the point of extreme refinement and also shown in the form of sexual perversion. The *fin de siècle* is the period of the discovery of the ugly, of disease, physical and mental, and of abnormality as a fertile theme for artistic treatment. The early prophets of French realism, Dumas *fils* and Mürger, referred to themselves as members of *l'école poitrinaire*, that literary school which provided the subjects for two operatic master-pieces, *La Traviata* and *La Bohème*. But it was later writers—Ibsen, Strindberg, Wilde, D'Annunzio, Wedekind, Hofmannsthal, Thomas Mann and others—who in drama and novel dealt, in terms at once more realistic and psychologically more penetrating, with the themes of mental and physical dis-integration and pathological sex. In *Salome* the heroine is a sexual pervert indulging in necrophilism, in *Elektra* she is obsessed with a desire for matricide. *Tosca* has in Scarpia an erotic sadist whose pathological trait is even more marked in Sardou's play than in Puccini's opera. The tendency to present neurotic heroes and heroines persisted into the 1920s and 1930s: there is Turandot, a symbol of love-hate, a woman torn between sadistic cruelty and meek submission to the male; there is Alban Berg's demented soldier Wozzeck, the butt of his sadistic superiors, and there is the nympho-maniac Lulu, whose kisses are kisses of death; and there is the hero of Hindemith's opera with the telltale title *Murderer, the Hope of Women* (1921), to say nothing of the lurid eroticism of some of Schreker's operas. The procession is carried on in our time by the hero of Britten's *Peter Grimes*, by Claggart of the same composer's *Billy Budd* and the chief characters of his *The Turn of the Screw*.

A salient feature of *fin de siècle* art is that emphasis is constantly shifting, that the demarcation lines between realism, impressionism and symbolism overlap and blur: truth will ally itself with romantic idealism, the 'slice of life' with veiled, dreamlike images, cruelty with over-refinement, the *frisson* with the idyllic, the trite with the exquisitely poetic, overstatements with mere hints, the bang with the whimper. It is a far cry from the serene, balanced world of classical art, an art that knew only rational man whose life was controlled and ordered by reason. His passions were assumed to reside in watertight compartments, and to spring from rational causes, and the erotic emotion was largely brought into play as a lofty heroic sentiment, as we still perceive in Verdi. In romanticism, however, the artist gains a gradual aware-ness of the irrational in man, of the chaos under the surface, of the 'demon' in the self. Hence the dominant role played by eroticism—both in its instinctive and spiritual expression—in romantic drama and opera, *vide* Wagner. Romanticism may indeed be defined as the irruption of the irrational into classical art, but the true nature of those dark, disturbing forces was no more than vaguely sensed. It is the *fin de siècle* artist who may be said to have arrived at a clearer recognition of the role played by the unconscious, and to have accepted irrational man both as a reality and as material for artistic treatment.* The *fin de siècle* invited the uninhibited projection of the artist's self into his work, with all his deep-seated urges and conflicts. He was now given full liberty to relive his unconscious fantasies in symbolic form; or, as Freud said, the creative artist is the only man able to put his neurosis to positive use through its sublimation into a work of art.

2

SCHUMANN: Wir würden schreckliche Dinge erfahren, wenn wir bei allen Kunstwerken auf den Grund ihre Entstehung blicken könnten.

(We should learn of terrible things if in every work of art we were able to peer into the root of its origin.)

NIETZSCHE: Art und Grad der Geschlechtlichkeit eines Menschen reichen bis in die letzten Zipfel seines Geistes hinauf.

(The nature and the degree of a man's sexuality reaches up to the last recesses of his mind.)

This, then, is the period background against which Puccini must be placed if his artistic personality, with its inner contradictions and morbid traits, is to be fully comprehended. It is indeed conceivable that an artist of his kind would not have flourished in an age serene in outlook and settled in its moral and artistic values. That Puccini displayed certain neurotic features will have already emerged—we recall his tormenting *folie de doute*, his destructive self-criticism, his recurring spells of lethargy and frustration. His music mirrors him with almost photographic faithfulness in its suggestion of anguish and dread ('*come un tremito*'—'like a shudder'—is a direction mark often encountered in his scores) and in the expression of mortal despair rising to almost unendurable intensity in his arias of lament. 'Muoio disperato' is the heart-cry not only of Cavaradossi but of virtually all his tragic heroes and heroines. Mood and pace are in a restless flux, *tempo rubato* and tugging syncopations all but destroy a firm rhythmic structure, and generate a feverish excitement in fast-moving passages and an enervating languor in the slow music. The profusion of dynamic details and expression marks strewn over virtually every page of his scores, reveal (as they do in Mahler) an almost obsessional concern to indicate the finest emotional shades. With *Manon Lescaut*, if not already in parts of *Le Villi* and *Edgar*, the music begins to create the impression of having been written by a man driven by ceaseless nervous pressure, a state of mind which he himself appears to have felt as something abnormal. Did he not write to Adami: 'Without fever there is no creation, because emotional art is a kind of malady, an exceptional state of mind, an over-excitation of every fibre and every atom of one's being'? Music born of such pressure cannot be expected to display serenity, emotional equilibrium and spiritual poise. But such pressure was merely a symptom, a manifestation of a conflict played out in

* It was between 1895 and 1899 that Freud laid the foundation of psychoanalysis, publishing his *magnum opus*, *The Interpretation of Dreams*, in 1899.

the composer's unconscious of whose true significance he seemed wholly unaware. What was this significance?

I have already ventured the suggestion that it is to be sought in a neurotic fixation which may be defined as an unresolved bondage to the mother-image. To this hypothesis I have been led by certain data in the composer's private life but, above all, by the kind of operatic subjects he used and his highly characteristic treatment of them. To throw more light on what I assume to have constituted the psychological mainspring of his dramatic world, let us now turn to analyse his libretti and consider them as a psychiatrist examines his patient's dreams, in the expectation of obtaining an insight into the nature of his deep-rooted conflict. I beg the reader's indulgence if in the following pages I adopt the language of a clinical case-history, but I hasten to assure him that in all this I am guided by the over-riding principle that where psychology leaves off, aesthetics must begin.

Our inquiry must start with the question whether Puccini's tragic operas possess a central and recurring theme and, if so, what is its nature. There is such a central theme and, as it happens, it is defined in a line given to one of his own characters: the Street Song Vendor of *Tabarro* sings: 'Chi ha vissuto per amore, per amore si morì!'—'Who lived for love, died for love!' This line, which was developed from one in the original play, might stand as the motto for ten out of Puccini's twelve operas. Its significance is paramount —an equation of love with death, of life-enhancing with life-destroying forces, of Eros with Thanatos. To put it differently, it is the concept of love as tragic guilt to be atoned for by death—a perennial theme in drama and opera which has nowhere been shown in such grandeur and elaborated to such psychological and metaphysical depths as in Wagner's *Tristan*. With Puccini, this theme carried no such implications; with him it was, essentially, the expression of an erotic nihilism which stands in *apparent* contrast to the hedonism displayed in his private life. What is striking, however, is the peculiar dramatic pattern in which he presented this theme and the con-sistency with which he adhered to it from his first to his last opera. The Puccinian libretto is so fashioned as to render the heroine the pivot around which the whole drama revolves, a heroine one of whose specific character traits is her true and unbounded love. This, in the composer's view, seems to constitute a guilt for which she must be punished by physical or mental suffering, gradually grinding her down until she perishes. In this pattern the male characters perform, with one or two exceptions, the role of catalyst (the tenor lovers) or of persecutor (baritones).* In *Suor Angelica* and *Turandot* the part of the persecutor is assigned to a female character—the Aunt in the former, the Chinese Princess in the latter; but this is for a reason which it will be more opportune to discuss in a later context.

Now the ubiquity of this theme in Puccini's operas, combined with its presentation in an essentially unvarying pattern—does this not argue a

* Strindberg, another *fin de siècle* artist, evolved in his plays the obverse pattern, showing the male mentally persecuted and driven into a corner, like a hunted animal, by a woman of pathological cruelty.

compulsive automatic choice, just as do certain themes in Wagner's operas? Does it not suggest that behind this choice was concealed an *idée fixe* which compelled him to return to such themes again and again? To draw a wider circle and include some symphonic composers: there is Beethoven with the compulsive idea *per ardua ad astra*; there is Tchaikovsky with his 'destiny hanging over me like the sword of Damocles'—a theme which, most probably, sprang from a guilt feeling engendered by his homosexuality and one which seems to have inspired not only the Fourth Symphony but also the Fifth and Sixth—for all three works tell the same emotional tale; and there is Mahler with whom certain inner conflicts form the recurrent topic of his symphonic discourses. All these are 'committed' artists in a specific sense, compelled to create works whose immutable motto remains *mea res agitur*, though they are but dimly aware of the compulsive nature of their solipsism. At the other end of the scale stand such wholly 'uncommitted' artists as Richard Strauss, who appears to have been almost entirely free of neurotic fixations—hence his protean facility in dealing with a multitude of different themes. With equal ease and success, Strauss was able to portray Don Juan, Till Eulenspiegel and Don Quixote, conjure up the atmosphere of a *bourgeois* home in the *Sinfonia Domestica*, express the pathological frenzies of a Salome, evoke the pathos of an ageing woman in *Rosenkavalier*, entertain us with the quips and quirks of *commedia dell'arte* in *Ariadne*, and discourse on the perennial problem of music versus words in *Capriccio*.

To return to Puccini. His is a striking illustration of what Flaubert once wrote about the compulsive character in an artist's choice of subject: 'One is certainly not free to write on any subject. One does not choose one's subject, but is chosen by it. The secret of a masterpiece lies in the conformity between the subject and the author's nature.' Puccini nearly always chose the kind of subject most closely conforming to his nature, or more precisely, to his unconscious fantasies. Inevitably in his choice he was partly guided by the dramatic and musical suitability of a subject, partly by the prevailing conventions and fashions of his time; but he would, in the last resort, settle on a subject only if he sensed an affinity in it with his own inner world. He would then proceed to have this subject so treated as to yield the kind of action, characters and atmosphere which he felt to be the dramatic symbols of the images, drives and conflicts present in his unconscious. Hence the essential identity of all his tragic subjects, hence the identity of their dramatic pattern, hence the similarity in the characterization of his favourite type of heroine, and hence also the close family likeness of certain musical images, notably those associated with such prime situations as love and death, scenes of lament and of mental and physical torture.

We now come to the crucial question: what was the nature of these unconscious fantasies? The answer to this ought to reveal the latent and, indeed, ultimate significance of what Puccini was under compulsion to present on the stage. It is here that the assumption of his failing to sever his early bondage to the Mother promises to throw an illuminating light. Puccini was a boy of five when he lost his father; he was brought up in a wholly feminine environment presided over by a relatively young mother, endowed with a powerful will and great initiative; as a boy he was surrounded by five sisters, who, psychologically speaking, represented so many duplications of the mother-image; he was his mother's favourite child and the bond between them was close and affectionate, and his sorrow at her death was altogether exceptional. Such an atmosphere was likely to establish a particularly strong fixation on the mother and cause an intolerable pressure in a fatherless boy. There are several ways of escape from such pressure, depending on the interaction of complex factors. For example, had Puccini been passive of temperament and weak in his natural instincts, the odds are that in later life he might have turned his back on the female sex. But he was, on the contrary, a boy full of vigour and resilience, given to asserting his personality, and charged with a high degree of maleness. Yet it would appear that a strong bondage to the Mother remained. Symptoms of this are seen in the persistent stresses and strains to which his conjugal life was subjected, though, admittedly, his wife contributed a considerable share to this unhappiness. Still more revealing are his innumerable infidelities committed with obscure and socially inferior women. In other words, Puccini's attempt to escape from his fixation was an avoidance of superior women—and Elvira was superior to him in her strong will-power—leading him to fleeting associations in which the partners represented the obverse of the powerful Mother; partners who attracted him for their submission, thus permitting him a feeling of dominance and mastery, which he apparently needed in order to counteract his unconscious dependence on the Mother. Now it has been observed that a man thus shackled is prone to guilt feelings in his love relationships since in his unconscious such a relationship would seem to bear the stigma of incest. In order to diminish his irrational guilt and thus enable him to establish some kind of erotic *rapport* with the 'other' woman, he has no choice but to denigrate her in his fantasies, and may in actual life choose her from a sphere inferior to his own. His fixation to the past—his reliving of an early stage of the child-mother relation—demands the choice of an 'unworthy' woman standing far below the exalted Mother; for this will give her the passport, not to his love, of which he is incapable on account of his unconscious bondage, but to his acceptance of her as a sexual partner. It now becomes clear why Puccini was never able to form a close and absorbing attachment to women, why no woman could ever inspire him in his creative life, and why he never allowed his wife to share in it. This reading of his essential psychology will also help us to explain the type of heroine we encounter in his operas and the peculiar treatment she suffers at his hands.

3

'I am nothing but a poor little girl, obscure and good for nothing,' sings Minnie, the heroine of *Fanciulla*. This is an apt description not only of herself but, essentially, of Puccini's favourite type of heroine—all women tarnished in one way or another and all social outcasts. There are first the girls of doubtful virtue who form the majority—Manon, Mimi, Musetta, Butterfly and Magda (in *La Rondine*). (The peasants of Torre del Lago showed the right instinct when they jokingly referred to Puccini as '*il maestro cuccumeggiante*'—'the composer of harlot music'.) There is Liù, a slave girl, and hence an inferior creature. As for Tosca, she is, it is true, a celebrated singer but her immorality lies in her free association with Cavaradossi; she is, moreover, an artist and therefore suspect in the eyes of conventional *bourgeois* morality. And there is that oddest of all Puccini heroines, Minnie, a pure angel who yet consorts with the riff-raff of a gold-mining camp in the Wild West and who is not above some first-rate cheating. Giorgetta again, who hails from a low Parisian suburb, is an adulteress, and the nun Angelica, though of exalted birth, has disgraced the name of her family by an illegitimate child. In brief, each of these heroines shows a serious flaw in her character and stands at the bottom of that height on which Puccini had enthroned the Mother. It is, precisely, because of their degraded position that he was able to fall in love with his heroines, display such extraordinary empathy with them and achieve so complete an identification with their personalities. For them he wrote his most inspired, poetic and poignant music, music in which his creative potency—I employ this noun advisedly— is felt to be at its full strength.

And, as though wishing to compensate them for their moral and social unworthiness, he invests them with the most endearing traits. They are gentle, tender, affectionate and childlike, and they love to the point of self-sacrifice. They are those 'luminous pleasing figures', that 'something beautiful, attractive and gracious' of which he wrote to his librettists. In comparing them—as will be done in the latter part of this book—with their original models in the relevant novels and plays, we are struck by the extent to which the composer sought to transmogrify his fair sinners into shining little angels; he attempts to whitewash them almost beyond recognition and surrounds them all with the halo of romantic love. And for all that they are morally tainted, there is, even with such lights-o'-love as Manon, Mimi and Musetta, not the faintest suggestion of lubricity or lasciviousness in them; nor are any of his heroines, with the exception of Turandot, afflicted with such pathological traits as are the female protagonists in certain operas of Strauss, Schreker and Berg. It is even possible to speak of an aura of chastity surrounding his little heroines and it is significant that in *Tosca* Puccini greatly toned down the text which Sardou had given to Scarpia in the scene of his sexual paroxysm.* There is the equally significant fact of his revulsion from Strauss's *Salome*, and of his final rejection of Pierre Louÿs's sex novel *La Femme et le Pantin* as a subject.

There remains his predilection for inflicting suffering and torture on his heroines. How do we account for the fact that Puccini's passionate love for them must always be accompanied by a sadistic impulse? Why must he always kill that which he loves and act the role of a Bluebeard? He him-

---

* See comparison of dialogue, pp. 354-58.

self recognized this tendency when he jokingly referred to his 'Neronic instinct', and confessed in his famous letter to Adami that he could only compose 'when my puppet executioners are moving on the scene'. Two explanations suggest themselves. One is provided by the marked ambivalence in his personality, which compels him to love and hate simultaneously, or, as Freud once pointed out, the thought 'I should like to enjoy your love' may also mean 'I should like to murder you'.[12] Puccini's Turandot is the very embodiment of the love-hate impulse.

The second answer lies in the probability that for all their 'unworthiness' Puccini felt unconsciously that his heroines were in some way rivals of the exalted mother-image. He may even have identified them with it to some extent, so that loving them carried with it an incestuous implication. But as his conscious mind could never allow the admission of such a forbidden desire, it had to be repressed, though the 'guilt' remained but was now transferred from himself to his heroines. Having soiled the Mother they had to be punished for a crime committed by himself. This retribution is visited upon them with a manifestly sado-masochistic enjoyment which proves the 'primitive' nature of Puccini's sex fantasies. We now appreciate the reason why scenes of suffering, torture and death exercised such a fascination on his creative imagination—they were, so to speak, the grit in Puccini's oyster. Even in his most ecstatic love scenes, almost invariably placed in the first act, when the sun of romantic love seems to shine in all its radiance on hero and heroine, there is somewhere on the distant horizon an ominous cloud, some suggestion in the music (sometimes in the text, too, as in *Butterfly*) of the impending catastrophe. But it is despairing passion and pain which release the full springs of his imagination; and nowhere is Puccini more himself, nowhere does he reveal more strikingly his whole being as an artist and man, than in the lament. In these arias he expresses not only the feelings of his dramatic characters caught in extremity, but also his own pathetic despair at being condemned for ever to remain a prisoner in the cage of his neurosis: to be compelled to murder his loves.

It may have been a vague awareness of the nature of these unconscious urges that was the real cause of those long spells of abysmal and often suicidal melancholy which occasionally seized Puccini from the early years of his creative career, and which found its facial expression in that '*povera faccia*' so often observed by his intimates and strangers alike. This 'poor face' is also in his music and it is graphically mirrored in those ineffably sad melodies of his—those dragging, sagging, broken-backed themes in the minor key—which form one of the most individual aspects of his musical style.*

With the regularity of a pendulum Puccini swings between extreme expressions of his guilt complex. Now he chooses a subject marked by delicate poetic eroticism and presenting a gentle and diminutive heroine to whom he applies a subtle, slow-working form of sadism—an illustration of Nietzsche's observation that 'the refinement of cruelty belongs to the springs

* See examples on pp. 291–92.

of art'. Next he turns to a subject saturated in an atmosphere of stark brutality, with a heroine of a stronger emotional fibre with whom his cruelty takes the form of direct violence. If we mark the two types of operas plus and minus respectively, the following pattern emerges:

Le Villi (+)	La Fanciulla (—)
Edgar (—)	La Rondine (+)
La Bohème (+)	Il Tabarro (—)
Tosca (—)	Suor Angelica (+)
Butterfly (+)	Turandot (+ —)

Considered as genres, the works marked with (+) are, in some senses of the term, opéra comique and those marked with (—) approach grand opera, with Turandot achieving a synthesis of both.

The reader who has followed me thus far may well have wondered how those two seemingly un-Puccinian characters, the Aunt and Turandot, fit into the pattern of his heroines. They stand at the opposite pole to that of his 'little women', they are haughty, cruel, imperious, unlovable characters; and both, significantly, are of an exalted rank. I venture to suggest that they are essentially nothing other than a projection of Puccini's own mother image—not, of course, of the real mother who was anything but a monster, but of the idea formed of her in his unconscious, under the pressure of his conflict between a guilty longing for her and moral censorship. This idea demanded translation into an exalted and unapproachable dramatic character because only thus could the Mother figure be temporarily removed from the dark sphere of his unconscious. Puccini invests both the Aunt and Turandot with cruel traits partly by way of a defence mechanism, but largely, I suggest, because he saw in the Mother the ultimate source of his unconscious guilt and of the mortal agonies he suffered in having to persecute and kill the heroines he loved. In order to pacify the godlike Mother, whenever he succeeded in loosening the fetters binding him to her, by loving the 'degraded' heroine, the latter had to be offered up as a sacrificial animal. The symbolism of this ritual act is most sharply brought out in the suicides of Angelica and Liù. In the case of the slave girl this compulsive act provides the true motivation for her self-sacrifice. In the actual drama it appears as useless and futile and merely superimposed in order to introduce a moment of tragic poignancy. This results in the most flagrant psychological error Puccini ever committed as a dramatist, namely engaging our sympathies for the wrong heroine; Liù is after all no more than an episodic figure in the opera. But more of that later.

The real antagonist of Puccini's frail heroines is the cruel Mother. In the majority of his operas she exercises her baneful influence from behind the scenes, as it were, but in Suor Angelica and Turandot she is presented to us in flesh and blood and confronted with her 'rival' in what are the most dramatic solo scenes in these two operas. It is most revealing of the symbolic role played by Turandot in the composer's unconscious fantasies that when in the great love duet in the penultimate scene of the opera he attempts to show her gradual transformation from the cruel Mother into the loving and sub-missive woman, he fails to convince us. In the light of all that has been said the two pairs—the Aunt and Angelica, Turandot and Liù—take on a significance which lies outside the context of the actual drama and which springs solely from the composer's unconscious conflict. Nor does it seem fanciful to suggest that the portrayals of the Aunt and the Chinese Princess are partly coloured by Puccini's experiences with Elvira in the notorious Doria tragedy, and that Wife and Mother are fused in these two characters just as Angelica and Liù echo the pathetic Doria.

What of Puccini's male characters? They too are symbolic projections: in the tenors he is the romantic lover, in the baritones he is the killer of his heroines. He plays both roles because he loves and hates simultaneously. In the 'Torture' and 'Execution' scenes of Cavaradossi and the manhunt of Johnson, Puccini seems to take sado-masochistic pleasure in punishing him-self for his 'guilt'. That he should have conceived the majority of his tenor lovers as somewhat weak, effeminate characters is perhaps a reflection of himself who in private life was gentle, affectionate and yielding. But it also argues the presence in his unconscious of only a dim father figure. Roberto in *Le Villi*, Edgar, Des Grieux, Rodolfo, Pinkerton, and Ruggero in *La Rondine* are such feminine heroes; yet with growing emotional maturity his lovers take on a more virile, almost heroic quality, e.g. Johnson, Luigi, and especially Calaf—a development which may be said to have begun in the half-sentimental, half-heroic character of Cavaradossi.

In the big baritone roles, on the other hand, the composer gives free rein to his erotic sadism, enacting his twin role as the primitive He-Man and the grim avenger of the soiled mother-image. Geronte is a spiteful old roué who causes the ultimate downfall of Manon; the force that drives both Scarpia and Rance is frenzied lust combined with murderous impulse, Michele again commits a brutal *crime passionel*. Sadism of a kind is also present in the rogue Gianni Schicchi, who takes a malicious pleasure in duping the predatory heirs of Buoso Donati and who relishes their fear when he reminds them of the dire punishment—the severance of one hand—that Florentine law reserves for the forger of wills. Not for nothing was Schicchi hauled up for Puccini from Dante's *Inferno*!

It is only in the secondary bass and baritone roles that the composer succeeds in getting away from sadism, and not in all of them, as witness the Sacristan in *Tosca* and the three Masks in *Turandot* (one of whom is a low voice). On the other hand Marcello, Schaunard and Colline are delightful harmless group figures and exponents of the Bohemian atmosphere, while the Consul in *Butterfly* is a sympathetic, warm-hearted onlooker playing a similar part to that of the Chorus in ancient Greek tragedy. Admittedly, there is variety in Puccini's low-voiced male roles. Yet we realize his limitations as a creator of great masculine figures when we call to mind the wide range of such characters which Verdi, Wagner and Strauss put on the stage in their basses and baritones, characters not only richer and larger as dramatic personalities but also actuated by motives other than erotic desire. This is specially true of Verdi's great father-figures—father-figures also in a deeper, psychological sense—such as Rigoletto, Germont, Philip II and Amonasro, who represent the very embodiment of authoritative masculinity. There is no such character to be found in Puccini, which provides perhaps the best evidence that in his unconscious he avoided a strong Father through fear. Guglielmo in *Le Villi* is modelled on Verdi and uncharacteristic of Puccini, while the Emperor in *Turandot* is, revealingly, far more senile than he is in Gozzi's drama, where he plays a very active role. It is not from Verdi's fathers but from his villains and comic rogues—Francesco Moor, Count Luna, Iago and Falstaff—that a direct line runs to Scarpia and Gianni Schicchi.

4

We have seen how Puccini was under a compulsion to equate love with guilt from which it follows that the representation of love as an exalting and cathartic power lay outside his range. This is clearly suggested in the finali of those three operas where he attempted to interpret love in such terms but failed: *Suor Angelica*, *Fanciulla* and *Turandot*. The miracle which is to indicate to the nun that divine grace has pardoned her sin remains a *stage* miracle, impressive though it is. In the other two operas love is shown as a liberating force—in *Fanciulla* even as an instrument of moral redemption, though Puccini the musician fails to rise to the occasion in those very scenes where this idea is to be conveyed in all its force. The final scene in the snow-clad Californian forest, with the lovers now united and bidding farewell to the dejected crowd of miners, is certainly moving as a scenic picture, but musically the composer can do no more than introduce a choral repeat of the Minstrel's song (not his!) with which he opened the opera. In the great love scene between Calaf and Turandot in which the heroine is to be shown transformed from a man-hating Amazon to a loving woman there is, it is true, an abundance of lyrical ideas; yet this duet, intended to be the crowning climax of the whole opera, the apotheosis of all-conquering love, fails to move the spectator. It is laboured and uncertain in its sense of direction. The immense toil the composer expended on this scene, the untold alterations he demanded in the text, and above all the nagging doubts he felt about its ultimate effect—all this, I suggest, can be interpreted as a sign of his psychological inability to feel himself entirely into such a situation.

Yet the fact that Puccini should ever have been prompted to attempt such an interpretation of love cannot be regarded as merely accidental. It would appear to suggest greater emotional maturity than we observe in his middle-period operas. Technical maturity he had achieved as early as *La Bohème*, but emotional maturity did not begin until *Fanciulla*, the first opera in which love is no longer represented as disruptive force. In order to shed more light on this important change in Puccini, we must for a moment revert to the Aunt and Turandot, characters in whom we are at last brought face to face with the Mother. Yet we are bound to ask why it is that, if Puccini was in fact tethered to her from his earliest days, he did not project her image on to the stage before *Suor Angelica*, which belongs to his last period. In the preceding operas the Mother played, as I suggested, an invisible role, acting from behind the scenes as a kind of Grey Eminence. Why then her emergence, in flesh and blood, in a late work? It would appear that this fact has a close connection with the age at which Puccini wrote *Suor Angelica* and *Turandot*—the former when he was fifty-nine and the latter when he was sixty-two. These are the climacteric years in a man's life, the years when, owing to biological changes, a more detached and less self-interested view of Eros begins to assert itself. It is the age when true maturity—emotional, intellectual and spiritual—is reached. In Puccini this is to be perceived, apart from other signs, in his ability to loosen at long last the iron grip in which he had been held by the powerful Mother. He now becomes sufficiently free to present her in a concrete symbol, in a dramatic character invested with all those 'terrible' traits associated with her in his unconscious. The repressed image was finally allowed to emerge from the dark sphere in which he had imprisoned it for so many years. The release, thus brought about, from an intolerable inner pressure resulted in a 'happiness' which now permitted him also to change from a concept of love as a disruptive element to one of a benign force. This process, started in *Fanciulla* and continuing with growing strength in *Suor Angelica*, reached its apogee in *Turandot*, where it is shown in concentrated form in the transformation of the heroine from the cruel Princess into the loving woman. (Nevertheless, he wrote his most inspired music for Liù, a character who still represents love as tragic guilt.) If this change in Puccini's interpretation of Eros is perhaps the most striking symptom of his emotional maturity, there are, in addition, several other pointers to it.

To begin with, we note that in three of his late-period operas the composer turns to *Italian*-derived subjects—*Suor Angelica*, *Schicchi* and *Turandot*; in other words, after excursions in all his previous works to foreign lands, he now returns to his *Mother*-land, the symbolic significance of which is manifest—a partial reconciliation with the mother-image, which has no longer any terrors for him. To put it differently, he returns to the Mother as an adult man, as master in his own home. Equally significant, in *Schicchi* he revives the genre of native comic opera (*opera buffa*) paying tribute in it to his own Tuscany and her capital Florence—even as the fully mature Wagner paid tribute to his native Germany in the *Meistersinger*. But also the very fact that Puccini wrote a comic opera is in itself a sign of his having broken the spell which the theme of love as tragic guilt had exercised on him; and we at last have an explanation for the fact that, despite his repeated intention since 1895 to compose a comedy, as many as twenty-two years had to elapse before he was able to put this plan into effect. It is noteworthy, too, that his last three operas represent a departure from the realism of the previous works toward subjects remote in time and tinged with a fantastic element. The plots of both *Suor Angelica* and *Schicchi* read like tales from ancient Italian chronicles, while the ferocious sex war fought in *Turandot* takes on an air of unreality characteristic of legend and fairy-tale. Even in the lurid *Tabarro* we sense something veiled and unreal.

Similarly, in Puccini's general musical style we perceive a change, already heralded in *Fanciulla*. His *cantilena* grows firmer and more incisive in outline, and the invertebrate lyrical phrase yields to themes of greater expressive vigour with more sweep and amplitude than before. Admittedly such gains must be set against a certain loss in spontaneity and incandescence. The Puccini of the *Trittico* and *Turandot* appears, not unlike the late Verdi, more intent on succinct characterization, on the achievement of strict dramatic truth, than on entrancing us with sensuous, heart-easing melody. We miss his characteristic *morbidezza*, the melting softness and insinuating feminine grace possessed by his operas up to and including *Butterfly*. It is illuminating, too, that his all but ubiquitous *tempo rubato* is now offset by long stretches of *tempo giusto*, and harmonic and orchestral details are touched in with remarkable economy and point. In the *Trittico* and *Turandot*, notably in the music of the Three Masks, we feel that every note is in its right place and that there is not one too many. Puccini's full maturity is also seen in a more objective approach to character: his emotional identification is now matched by greater detachment—he stands almost as much outside as inside his *dramatis personae*. Climaxes overcharged with emotion to the point of hysteria occur far less frequently, and veristic explosions and cries are confined to a mere handful of bars in *Tabarro* and *Angelica*. Puccini's last period may indeed be described as his 'classical' period when he achieved a sublimation of his unconscious urges beyond his reach during his preceding development. It is, in fact, arguable whether *Trittico* and *Turandot* could ever have been written during his years of mother-fixation and obsession with a biological urge. This was the period comprising those three operas on which his world-wide fame is based, and which are precisely those that aroused the strongest hostility in certain quarters, a hostility not merely confined to the Italian *avant-gardistes* of the 1900s. Busoni, for example, found *Butterfly* so 'indecent' (*unanständig*) that at a Vienna production in 1908 he walked out of the theatre half-way through the performance; but some twelve years later he expressed his unreserved admiration for *Il Tabarro* and *Gianni Schicchi*, which he declared to be masterpieces. Busoni's change of attitude reflected the view of a great number of 'serious' musicians who had in former years regarded Puccini as a mere business man, and as a purveyor of sentimental *Kitsch*.* Puccini himself was aware of this change in his whole approach, when he said at the time of *Turandot*: 'All the music I have written so far seems to me just a farce in comparison with the music I now write.'

In casting a comprehensive glance over Puccini's three periods one is reminded of what E. J. Dent wrote in connection with Mozart:

> The musician's three ages may be described in various ways. We may say that in the first he is asserting himself and trying to obtain an audience: in the second he has obtained his audience and is trying to develop himself

* An academic luminary referred to it as musical *marijuana*.

to the fullest extent compatible with remaining in touch with it: in the third he has become indifferent to his audience, and writes only for himself.[13]

There is perhaps no surer sign of an artist having attained complete maturity than when he begins to write exclusively for himself, as Puccini did in his *Trittico* and *Turandot*.

Puccini was an instinctive artist and thus reflects in his art compulsive fantasies with far greater immediacy and force than other artists of a similar disposition, who because they are endowed with stronger intellectual fibre and a more reflective mind are capable of achieving a high degree of sublimation. With Puccini we feel too near our own primitive impulses; he cuts too near the bone, or rather the nerve, and thus sets up a resistance in many spectators. Yet his late works prove that there was a greater artist in him than is suggested by the operas of his middle period. With advancing years he succeeded in adding a cubit to his stature, writing in *Gianni Schicchi* and *Turandot* two works that can almost be mentioned in the same breath as Verdi's *Otello* and *Falstaff*. There is no knowing what he might later have achieved had he lived to the ripe old age of a Verdi or a Wagner. Puccini, like Tchaikovsky, was a musician of whom it may be said that the inner man acted as a retarding and even inhibiting force on the artist. His essential limitations were far more psychological than artistic, wherein lay the tragedy of a potentially great artist. But I feel I cannot close this chapter without posing a final question: would Puccini have been Puccini, the creator of an operatic world with a dramatic and musical climate so peculiarly its own, without those 'terrible things' from which his art sprang?

XXIII

Dramaturgy and Musical Style

PUCCINI: 'The basis of an opera is the subject and its dramatic treatment.'

I

PUCCINI'S ESSENTIAL APPROACH to musical drama is embodied in that remark. It was the fashioning of the libretto, i.e. the drama *on the stage*, that claimed his first attention and to which he devoted more time and labour than to the writing of the music. With Puccini, as indeed with every born dramatic composer, work on the libretto was as much a creative act as setting it to music. Whatever criticism might be raised against the limitations of his subject-matter, or however questionable certain details might be found from the psychological or dramatic angle, the overriding fact remains that his libretti are eminently stageworthy, offering him precisely the kind of opportunities which he needed for the full exercise of his gifts. Puccini did not aim at music-drama but at musical drama, which is not quite the same thing, but in his own way he aimed at a *Gesamtkunstwerk* in which the whole apparatus of the stage—singing, acting, words, facial expression, gesture, movement, costume, scenery and lighting—is harnessed to the singers and the orchestra to create a maximum of dramatic effect. He insisted for example on the utmost clarity of verbal enunciation and on lighting effects following closely the musical changes and being regulated 'with a most attentive *ear*'.* He was obsessed with the importance of the precise moment at which the curtain rose or came down—'a curtain dropped too soon or too late often means the failure of an opera'. Puccini's stage directions are far more elaborate than Verdi's, especially after *Tosca*, and his operas require singer-actors of more flexibility in their histrionics than is called for in most of Verdi's.

The paramount question which will occupy us in the following pages is Puccini's dramaturgy, the form and structure of his libretti. Broadly, his technique has much in common with that of the great writers of the short story. To begin with there is the plot, which in Puccini always displays a

* This and some of the following quotations, which are presumed to have been the composer's *ipsissima verba*, have been taken from *Puccini. Interprete di se stesso*, by Luigi Ricci. Milan, 1954. Ricci was for many years attached to La Scala and assisted Puccini in the supervision and the production of his operas. The book is a first-hand record of observations made by the composer during rehearsals and the author also discusses in it many points raised by Puccini in connection with phrasing, tempo, dynamics and so on. For producers, conductors and singers alike this book is an invaluable guide.

clear and logical design, with a definite point of departure, a middle and an end. The plot was for him the chief means to direct and hold the spectator's interest and he always demanded that it should be straightforward and simple in development, so that the action and its motivations should remain, so far as feasible, self-explanatory. He insisted on what he called '*l'evidenza della situazione*', which should enable the spectator to follow the drama even without understanding the actual words. This in fact was one of the supreme criteria for himself when in his perennial searches for a suitable subject he attended productions of plays in foreign languages.

Puccini's gifts included one which any playwright might envy him and which is found only in a mere handful of opera composers. This was what the French call *l'optique du théâtre*, an eye for the purely visual effect of a scene. Puccini wrote to Adami while at work on *Turandot*: 'Be sparing of words and try to make the incidents clear and brilliant to the *eye* rather than the *ear*.'* There is not a single opera of his without at least one scene that is uncommonly striking as a spectacle and that seems to have fired his musical imagination in an equally striking manner. To name some noteworthy instances: the 'Requiem' scene in *Edgar*, the Embarkation in *Manon Lescaut*, scenes laid against a background of wintry, desolate nature such as we find in *La Bohème* (Act III) and *La Fanciulla* (Act III), Butterfly's Vigil, the Miracle at the end of *Suor Angelica*, Liù's funeral cortège, and the '*Te Deum*' scene and Execution in *Tosca*. From this same sense of the purely visual springs Puccini's predilection for dumb-shows where he relies largely on stage action to create the dramatic effect, confining himself to writing what is little more than incidental or situation music, but in closest *rapport* with the happenings on the stage. This is superbly illustrated in the silent scene which follows Tosca's murder of Scarpia, and the scene of the Aunt's arrival and departure in *Suor Angelica*. Nor must we omit to mention Puccini's masterly use of dramatic pauses—especially at points of the highest tension where they achieve a degree of eloquence far beyond the power of any words or music. He himself referred to such pauses as '*musica sottintesa*'—'implied music'. There is, in addition, his sense of what Verdi called '*la parola scenica*', a verbal phrase so turned as to make its point in the simplest yet most concentrated manner and thus clinch a situation tellingly. He knew, too, how to apply Verdi's operatic maxim once expressed to Ghislanzoni: 'There are moments in the theatre when poets and composers must have the talent to write neither poetry nor music.'†

Puccini's dramatic technique recalls that of the short-story writer in the extraordinary economy with which he treats his material. With the sole exception of *La Bohème*, sub-plots contained in the original plays and novels were eliminated, and historical and local details were excised unless they helped to evoke the essential atmosphere. The characters, too, are reduced to such traits as were strictly relevant to his dramatic purposes, though information about their background and history is imparted by a

* My italics. Letter of 21 September 1921 (*E*).
† Letter of 16 August 1870, written in connection with the libretto of *Aida*.

deft accumulation of small details. Owing to his peculiar psychology, the emotional range of Puccini's characters is narrow; so far as his lovers are concerned, its extremes are defined on the one hand by hysterical ecstasy, and on the other by mortal despair. And like most operatic realists, Puccini tends to upset the dramatic equilibrium by laying too much emphasis on 'strong' situations, which in works such as *Tosca* and *La Fanciulla* almost suggest that they were the be-all and end-all of the entire drama.

Concentration was one of Puccini's dramatic axioms, yet there is a positive as well as negative aspect to his application of it. On the one hand it results in swift action and steadily mounting tension; once the action gets under way, there is little lingering and dispersion of interest, and the composer sees to it that it is given suspense and surprise by well-timed incidents and drawn rapidly to its conclusion. Five of his operas observe the classical unities of time, action and place—an imponderable but important factor contributing to the concentrated effect of his drama. In his full-length operas *Tosca* and *Turandot* the action takes place within less than twenty-four hours; while in the works of the *Trittico*, the one-act form inevitably compels the composer to observe the unities strictly. In stage-time the action here takes no more than a few hours, yet for all the condensation each of the three episodes is so aptly constructed that it represents a foreshortened version of a full-length drama, with proper exposition, development and dénouement.

Yet in his concern to achieve maximum concentration, Puccini sometimes overshoots the mark. It leads him to over-compression and the suppression of dramatic and psychological details necessary for fully convincing motivation of the characters and the action. Not that he stands alone in this: over-compression was, as Dyneley Hussey well puts it, 'the blind spot in Verdi's dramaturgy',[14] as it has been in that of most composers who set a melo-dramatic libretto. It is, for example, responsible for the jerky development shown by some of Puccini's characters. Thus the psychological transition is missing between the timid and almost monosyllabic Manon in Act I and the haughty, voluble courtesan in Act II, though extenuating circumstances here are the composer's relative inexperience at that period and his understandable wish not to sail too closely to Massenet's opera. But Mimi's separation from Rodolfo in Act III of *La Bohème* is insufficiently motivated, and the same is true of Cavaradossi's sudden afflatus of heroic enthusiasm for Napoleon in Act II of *Tosca*. There is in fact only one character in Puccini's full-length operas presented in steady psychological development: Butterfly, who grows before our eyes from the child-wife of Act I to the tragic heroine of the end of the opera. In more concentrated fashion such continuous development is to be observed in Michele and Angelica.

2

Let us now turn to an examination of the musico-dramatic structure of the individual acts. The first act is inevitably the best constructed and the longest, though mostly lasting less than an hour and, in the two four-act operas, only a little over half an hour.* Nearly always Puccini begins with what he called *'il motivo di prima intenzione'*, the motto theme embodying the work's essential spirit. The dramatic knot is smoothly and tightly tied, and almost invariably the chief *dramatis personae* make their entries successively. This is a characteristic device of Puccini's permitting the spectator to become acquainted with one character before the next appears. The most important character is always introduced last. Stage proceedings are usually opened by the lyrical tenor, who presents his visiting card in an aria of warm-hearted, youthful sentiment. While the action unfolds, informative details and atmosphere are almost imperceptibly touched in. The full measure of Puccini's dramatic mastery is seen in those difficult openings where he has to deal with a group of characters and where the action shows constant variations in momentum and mood.† Having introduced his tenor and some subsidiary figures, set the atmosphere and thus put the spectator in a receptive frame of mind, Puccini now proceeds to introduce his central character—usually the heroine, but in some operas it is a male character.‡ In introducing the heroine the composer resorts to a highly characteristic device, one which, to my knowledge, had been employed only once before him—by Delibes in *Lakmé* (1884). This is to herald the heroine's entry by her voice: Mimi, Musetta, Tosca, Butterfly are first heard offstage before they appear on the scene and deliver their first aria. Puccini here plays on the universal urge to *see* a person whom we hear speak or sing in the distance. By withholding the immediate gratification of this desire Puccini creates tension so that we demand to see the owner of the voice with heightened expectancy and this in turn renders her entry more dramatic.§ To the heroine of *Turandot*, however, he applies precisely the opposite device—the Princess is first seen but, like a Victorian child, not heard; the reason for this will be discussed in a later chapter. Most of Puccini's first acts are pivoted on the 'boy meets girl' situation or a similar one in which two characters exchange their respective *curricula vitae*, each informing the other about their background and their history. (It is a foible of Puccini's to make one of the pair refer

---

* The playing time of the individual acts, as checked by Ricci (op. cit.) at Scala productions under the composer's supervision, is as follows:

Manon: 37 min.	*Bohème:* 35 min.	*Tosca:* 44 min.
42 min.	18 min.	40 min.
23 min.	25 min.	28 min.
18 min.	29 min.	1 hour, 52 min.
2 hours	1 hour, 47 min.	
Butterfly: 48 min.	*Fanciulla:* 55 min.	*Tabarro:* 52 min.
47 min.	45 min.	*Angelica:* 55 min.
30 min.	24 min.	*Schicchi:* 50 min.
2 hours, 5 min.	2 hours, 4 min.	2 hours, 37 min.

† *Manon Lescaut, Bohème, Fanciulla, Angelica, Schicchi* and *Turandot.*
‡ Scarpia, Johnson, Schicchi.
§ In *Butterfly* this device is also applied to male characters and becomes there almost an obsession.

longingly to a *piccola casa*, some simple abode—preferably in the country—where he or she has lived or would like to live or return to with the other, now that their hearts have found each other.)* This scene corresponds to the *racconto* or narration of earlier opera and provides the first occasion for an ecstatic love duet. Here again we note a very characteristic feature that reveals Puccini's sense of the theatre: he counteracts the static effect of the love duet by momentary interruptions of the mood, interruptions coming from other characters: the '*Momus*' calls of the Bohemians, for example, or Suzuki's stage 'business' during the rather long duet between Butterfly and Pinkerton. In *La Fanciulla* the interruption is a dramatic and ominous one. Masterly, too, is Puccini's treatment of the first love scene between Cavaradossi and Tosca, in which the heroine's suspicious nature prompts her to break up the lyrical mood three times in dramatic recitatives. Also a number of solo arias are tethered to the action, however tenuously, through interjections by other characters.† All these are, perhaps, small points, but it is in such seemingly negligible details that the composer's dramatic instinct manifests itself at its most subtle.

Puccini's arias and duets always arise out of the situation, or, to put it the other way round, the course of the action is always so directed as to demand culmination in a lyrical effusion just at the point where it occurs. While the duets are extended pieces comprising several sections, most arias are brief, simple binary structures—an A-A´ of which the second section is merely a slightly varied and orchestrally richer repeat of the first. The straightforward artless structure of such arias may be said to be in itself a reflection of the characters' psychology, in other words, form is here employed as a means of dramatic characterization.‡ But there are exceptions, such as the arias sung by Rodolfo and Mimi at their first encounter, which display a more elaborate pattern. It is chiefly in his two early operas, in the parts of Roberto (*Le Villi*) and of Tigrana (*Edgar*, first version) that Puccini wrote extended arias of the Verdian type, while in his mature operas only 'In questa Reggia' (*Turandot*) represents an aria of similar dimensions and dramatic force. It is surprising, however, that Scarpia, who plays so dominant a role, should content himself with arias as simply built as those of his victims Cavaradossi and Tosca. This fact, combined with a marked lyrical expression, leads to the impression that Scarpia received somewhat inadequate treatment at Puccini's hands, so far as his characterization in a solo piece is concerned.

Most of Puccini's first acts show a clear division into two halves, the first

---

* *Manon, Tosca, Fanciulla, Rondine*; in *Butterfly* the lovers are already in their little house on the hill!

† E.g. the opening arias of Rodolfo, Cavaradossi, Calaf and Turandot.

‡ The charge raised by an eminent English musicologist that it was the business man in Puccini that prompted him to write arias of precisely the length of a 78 gramophone record can be dismissed as nonsense. Brief arias, especially cavatinas, happened to be written long before the invention of the gramophone; and commercial recording did not start seriously until the early years of the twentieth century, by which time Puccini had already written his three popular favourites.

half being lively, the second more static, preponderantly lyrical and closing with a love duet. This is specially true of his operas of the *tragédie larmoyante* type. In his 'grand operas'—*Tosca* and *Turandot*—the close is formed by a big choral scene of sinister grandeur and majesty.

The second act introduces the first important turning-point of the drama in a well-prepared *scène à faire* between the lovers or between them and their antagonists, a scene usually clinched by a *coup de théâtre*: the arrest of Manon, the murder of Scarpia, the shooting of Johnson and so on. It is usually in the second act that the heroine is given another big aria, Butterfly being even presented with two.

The final act is almost invariably the shortest,* which is consonant with Puccini's demand for a rapid dénouement; it represents the most sombre and moving part of the opera, always including a heart-rending lament for heroine or hero. Puccini's final acts contain far less fresh musical matter than the preceding acts, as he prefers to follow Verdi's precedent in *Rigoletto* and *La Traviata* and operate his system of 'logical reminiscences'. This is a most powerful device in the hands of a dramatic composer, and Puccini achieves with it some telling psychological effects as well as irresistible poignancy, witness the last scenes in *La Bohème* and *Butterfly*. Characteristic, too, is his use of reminiscence at the very close of an opera, where he quotes a theme associated with a previous situation. This is most exquisitely done in *Manon Lescaut*, with the Minuet from Act II, but in *Tosca* the quotation from Cavaradossi's lament has no conceivable relevance to the heroine's suicide. And Puccini is tempted to thunder out the theme on the full orchestra —a device of realistic opera which Bizet appears to have been the first to employ in the last finale of *Carmen*.

3

Dramatic structure in opera being one thing and musical structure another, our next question will concern itself with the manner in which Puccini makes the two reinforce each other. There is in the first place the problem of musical coherence and continuity between the various scenes. Like all post-Wagnerians, Puccini uses continuous orchestral texture and the leitmotive. True, in *Le Villi* and the first version of *Edgar* he still clings to the old pattern of separate numbers or set pieces, but this disappears with *Manon Lescaut*, though the seams remain noticeable. Even as late as *Turandot*, the skeleton of the old 'number' opera still shows through.

Nor is Puccini's leitmotive deployed with any strictness or consistency, admirably dramatic though it is in character. He will use the same theme to denote now a character, now a situation, now an atmosphere, and now to add a purely musical interest to the orchestral texture, without perceptible reference to the drama on the stage. Mostly he applies it in the manner of the old 'reminiscence', merely altering the original tempo and transposing it to another key. This method may be likened to Homer's when he attaches stereotyped

* See the timings on p. 286.

epithets to his heroes, irrespective of the situations in which they find them-selves. Thus Achilles is always 'Achilles of the swift feet' and Odysseus 'Odysseus of the nimble wit'. The instances are rare—and we shall draw special attention to them later—where Puccini transforms the rhythmic and harmonic structure of a theme, and still rarer where the intervals are altered according to the psychological situation at a given moment. It is not without its significance that such metamorphoses occur, invariably, in the leitmotives of his female characters, notably of the Aunt in *Suor Angelica* and the heroine of *Turandot*. Another peculiarity of his is to reveal the full significance of a leitmotive *a posteriori*, that is, in a later context than the one in which it is first heard.

Puccini's treatment of the orchestra as a means of achieving musical coherence shows only a semblance of symphonic technique, but it would be unfair to chalk this up against a composer for whom the centre of the drama always lay on the stage. Puccini creates continuity not by interweaving his themes but largely by juxtaposition. And this brings us to his characteristic mosaics in which diminutive melodic 'squares', not longer than a bar and often even less, are repeated, varied or treated sequentially, after which the same process is continued with the next 'square'. This technique may have been making a virtue of necessity, for Puccini's melodic invention tends to be shortwinded. On the other hand, the mosaic is characteristic of *opera buffa*, e.g. Pergolesi, Mozart and Rossini, and it may be that Puccini deliberately adopted this method of melodic structure from that genre. Yet he handles this technique with such masterly skill, adjusting, dovetailing and ranging together his little squares with such ease that his mosaics do indeed create the impression of musical organisms. To subject them to formal criticism and take them to pieces would be like smashing a kaleidoscope in order to see what is inside. It is only when Puccini applies the mosaic on a larger scale, as for example in the extended love duets of *Manon Lescaut* and *Butterfly* and the 'Torture' scene of *Tosca*, that organic continuity suffers and that we miss the absence of a truly symphonic technique.

Puccini employs two more means for achieving musical cohesion and unity. One is casting entire scenes and even whole acts in a quasi-instrumental form, his favourite pattern being a rondo-like scherzo, of the type he wrote in his early *Capriccio Sinfonico*. This is the musical structure of the opening scenes of *Manon Lescaut*, *La Bohème* and *Butterfly*, while the love duet and the 'Flower' scene in the last-named opera approximate to a *Bogen* or arch form. Act I of *Turandot*, again, suggests something like the four con-trasted movements of a symphony.

Puccini's other device for obtaining coherence is the harmonic one of key relationships and progressive tonalities, though this is an aspect more pronounced in his pre-impressionist style. Thus an act may be anchored in a basic key or it may begin in the tonic and close in the key of the dominant, sub-dominant or relative major. As to his use of progressive tonalities, it undoubtedly served the purpose of dramatic characterization, especially when we consider the choice of keys at the opening and closing of an opera.

The progression is mostly from major to minor, but there are exceptions. Moreover, Puccini manifestly attached emotional and symbolic significance to certain tonalities. Thus, we note a predominance of minor keys in the final acts, with F♯ minor, C♯ minor and E♭ minor reserved for scenes of anguish and despair. In *Tosca* and *Butterfly*, B minor (Beethoven's 'dark' key) is also associated with such moods, *vide* the laments of Cavaradossi and Cio-Cio-San. For his ecstatic love scenes he mostly selects the bright keys of A, E♭ and F, while A♭, D♭ and G♭ are associated with tender and nostalgic sentiments.

4

When Puccini wrote that 'without melody, fresh and poignant, there can be no music', he unwittingly put his finger on what is his own greatest single gift. It is indeed arguable whether, for all his extraordinary sense of the theatre and his consummate technique, his operas would have achieved the immense popularity they enjoy without his inventive powers as a melodist. It is in this that he proclaims his deep roots in the true tradition of Italian opera, and his successorship to Verdi, though admittedly his fund of melody is less rich and varied than the older master's. Puccini's melodic power is concentrated in the lyrical aria; but he was too good a dramatist to subscribe to the absurd axiom which Giordano once enunciated, half in jest and half seriously: 'Find a good song, and then build an opera around it!'[15] He even thought in later years that Tosca's 'Vissi d'arte' tended to hold up the action.

The Italian quality of Puccini's lyrical arias lies, above all else, in the sensuous warmth and melting radiance of the vocal line. Like Verdi's, this line is predominantly diatonic, which largely accounts for its euphony;* yet in contrast to Verdi's which is marked by skips and leaps in arpeggio, Puccini's unfolds in step-wise progressions. Except at climaxes, his vocal line lacks the dramatic stab and thrust of Verdi's dramatic *cantilena* and it is never shot out, torpedo-like, at the beginning of an aria, as it so often is with the older composer. The Puccinian aria starts, more often than not, in a slow hesitating manner, with the vocal theme, in some cases, first given to the orchestra while the voice glides in, chant-like, on soft reiterated notes,† as we frequently observe in Massenet and Debussy. Altogether, Puccini's melodic style—though this applies, chiefly, to the works of his middle period—has a feminine character. Tender, graceful, coaxing and infinitely supple, his *cantilena* conjures up the movements of gently caressing hands, movements both languorous and nervously excited.‡ It is *la phrase décadente* of Thomas, Gounod and Massenet transplanted to an Italian clime—richer in emotional expression, more sensuous and more pregnant. More pregnant, because

* Even in *Manon Lescaut*, with its Tristanesque harmonies, the melody remains essentially diatonic.

† Cf. Rodolfo's 'Che gelida manina' and Cavaradossi's 'E lucevan le stelle'.

‡ Similar features characterize the intense lyricism of Alban Berg, which earned him the nickname 'The Puccini of Dodecaphony'.

Puccini—like Verdi, Wagner and Strauss—possessed the ability to concentrate into a single phrase the driving emotion of a character in a situation and the predominant atmosphere of a scene. The characteristic Puccini melody gathers up all there is to be expressed at that particular moment in the drama. It fuses words, action, emotion and the pure vocal sound into a complete unity—hence its intensity and irresistible effect on the spectator. (But sketches show that the initial version of a Puccinian melody is not always as well tailored and dramatically apt as it appears in the final version). Yet while Verdi reserves this sort of concentrated melody for the high points of the drama, the verist in Puccini was tempted to aim at its perpetuity, as though the spectators had to be held in a state of feverish excitement. In the early and late operas, however, this is less marked; there the melody shows sweep and balanced periods, while in the operas of his middle period it tends to become aphoristic, more flexible and irregular in structure.

Perhaps the most individual type of Puccinian *cantilena* is represented by those ineffably sad strains which we described before as *povera faccia* melody. They are significantly reserved for those moments in the drama when a character is caught in an extreme situation, usually facing death. Certain stylistic features are constant here, e.g. the slow, dragging pace, and the minor key; the downward trend of the melodic line with its drooping intervals— mostly fifths which by their effect of finality seem more responsible than any other interval for the impression of perpetual stopping and starting;* and the vain effort to counteract this downward tendency by a forced screwing up of the line. There is about these limping, spineless tunes an air of utter weariness and helplessness—some are like naked despair crying out aloud. Each one of Puccini's tragic operas contains such a melody, from the early *Le Villi* to the late *Turandot*.

Ex.4

(a) "Le Villi"

(b) "Manon Lescaut"

Ah! Ma - non, mi tra-disce il tuo fol-le pen-sie - ro:

Sem - pre la stes - sa! Sem-pre la stes - sa!

* The reason why we associate the falling fifth with finality resides in the fact that it represents the fundamental cadential step, from dominant to tonic.

(c) "Madam Butterfly"

O me, sce - so dal tro - no dell'al - to Pa - ra -
- di - so guar - da ben fi - so, fi - so

(d) "Turandot"

The historic roots of this kind of melody are to be traced back through Bellini and Donizetti* to the *lamento* of seventh-century Italian opera. But with Puccini there is also a French element present, derived from Massenet, e.g. Manon's elegiac 'Voyons, Manon!' and notably her Farewell 'Adieu, petite table!':

Ex.5

(a) Andante

A - dieu, notre pe - ti - te ta - ble, Qui nous réu - nit si sou - vent!

Orch

(b) "La Fanciulla del West" Act. III
Johnson

Ris - par - mia - te lo scher - no Del - la mor - te

Orch

Puccini has similar passages in which a sad *arioso* in a minor key is punctuated by orchestral chords in a monotonous rhythm. But the concentrated poignancy and tension of his 'poor face' melodies, such as we find in his arias of lament and farewell as well as in certain duets and choruses, bears so individual a stamp that their stylistic affinity with Massenet's is only just perceptible.

* See, for example, the aria 'Una furtiva lagrima' in *L'Elisir d'Amore*.

Another fingerprint of Puccini's melodic style and one which effectively contrasts with his slow *cantabile* is the *ballabile*—those dance-like, pirouetting themes which are found in every opera of his, mostly in the opening scenes before the noose begins to tighten round the characters' necks. As with Tchaikovsky, of whom this feature is equally characteristic, Puccini's *ballabile* with its lilting six/eight and two/four rhythms and its light *staccato* is of French origin. This style of writing is associated with the whole gamut of light-hearted emotions, from youthful gaiety (*La Bohème* and *Butterfly*), through the playfulness and insouciance of lovers (*Tosca*), to grotesque comedy (the Sacristan in *Tosca* and the three Masks in *Turandot*).

Another important aspect of Puccini's melodic style are his recitatives, which are always treated in a *stilo misto* or mixed style, fluctuating between an expressive *arioso* and a light conversational *parlando*, but are never without some melodic interest. Puccini's recitative is essentially a modern application of the old accompanied recitative; and while the Verdi of *Falstaff* pointed the way to a more flexible and subtle handling, the younger composer added a nervous pliability of line and a more tender lyrical note, without thereby affecting the natural inflections of the verbal phrases. Puccini's recitatives may be said to represent modern Italian speech-song at its most varied and supple, as witness the conversational scenes in *La Bohème* and *Butterfly*.*

His harmonic style displays a similar flexibility and variety. Indeed, next to his melodic invention, it is in the range and richness of his harmonic palette that he evinces his superiority over his Italian contemporaries. By turns delicate, fragrant, bitter-sweet, brilliant, piquant and pungent, his harmonies are in a constant flux, reflecting his own nervous tension no less than the emotional ebb and flow of the drama. His ear for harmonic colour is nowhere more in evidence than in his three 'exotic' operas. Puccini always kept his harmonic style up to date, assimilating contemporary developments into his own manner. Thus he began with the simple chromatic 'alterations' and the secondary sevenths and ninths of pre-Wagnerian romantic harmony (*Le Villi* and *Edgar*); turned to *Tristan* harmonies in *Manon Lescaut*, in which he also ventured passages in parallel fifths, before Debussy; and under the subsequent influence of the French Impressionists he cultivated, often to surfeit, parallel *organum*-like progressions (of common chords, secondary sevenths, and chords of the added sixth), unresolved discords, and augmented triads. From the early 1900s he began to make increased use of the whole-tone scale (*Tosca* to *La Fanciulla*); and later he experimented with bitonality, chords of the fourth, and naked, harsh dissonances (*Turandot*). Had he lived longer it is certain that he would have availed himself of dodecaphony and quarter-tones.

Some of Puccini's harmonic devices are employed merely for colour effects, others again are pressed into service for dramatic characterization and atmosphere-painting. Thus a succession of (mainly) minor triads invariably denotes sadness or sinister forebodings:

* See, Ex. 29, on p. 337.

Ex.6

(a) "Manon Lescaut" Act. II

Best pedal on A

(b) "La Boheme" Act. III "Death-knell" motive

(c) "Turandot" Act. I Procession to the scaffold

Again, for a desolate atmosphere he uses long-sustained pedals, of which the opening of Act III of *Manon Lescaut* is an excellent example. To this order belong also such harmonic monotones as repeated tonic-dominant basses and drones. The brutal wrenching of tonalities in *Tosca*, *La Fanciulla* and *Turandot* is self-explanatory, as is, in these same operas, the frequent presence of the whole-tone scale and the *diabolus in musica*, i.e. the augmented fourth.*
It is not without its psychological significance that the majority of Puccini's melodic and harmonic fingerprints emerge in situations charged with 'negative' emotions—pain, despair and sadness. But the list would not be complete without referring to his *ostinati*, those melodic-rhythmic mono-tones in an ominous and funereal vein. Invariably cast in a minor key, they are the heralds of catastrophe in every one of his tragic operas, from *Manon Lescaut* onwards. The poignancy that the composer extracts from such *ostinati* is best illustrated in such scenes as that of Butterfly's first reaction to the Consul's hint that Pinkerton may never return, and the scene of Angelica's mortal agony after she has learned from the Aunt of her child's death. Terrifying, on the other hand, is the processional march accompanying the preparations for Cavaradossi's execution, which generates so unbearable a tension that we almost sigh with relief when at last we hear the salvo of the firing-party. Puccini's *ostinato* is a form of concentrated musical sadism, its impact on our nervous sensibilities being a kind of mental torture.

* Ever since Glinka's *Russlan and Ludmilla* (1842), the whole-tone has been associated with the suggestion of something evil, sinister, strange or supernatural.

Verdi had employed melodic-rhythmic *ostinati* to establish a dramatic mood firmly and to impress it insistently on the spectators, e.g. Violetta's 'Morò! la mia memoria', in her duet with Germont *père* in Act II of *Traviata*; but neither Verdi nor any other musical dramatist handled this device to such effect as Puccini. Which brings us to the role played, in his operas, by the orchestra.

5

This role is manifold and essential. His orchestra becomes at once a more active and more articulate partner in the drama than it is in Verdi; for no composer who, like Puccini, had witnessed in his youth the triumph of music-drama could afford to ignore the advances made by Wagner in orchestral technique for the enhancement of dramatic and psychological moments. Nevertheless, Puccini proclaims his Italianism in the fact that, however important his orchestra in relation to the drama itself, notably in his later operas, the hard core of his musical texture remains the singing voice. Yet there is great variety in the functions allotted to Puccini's orchestra. In addition to providing continuity, it often acts the part of a Greek chorus, commenting upon, warning, anticipating and often revealing a character's most secret emotions and thoughts. This latter role it fulfils with the greatest subtlety and penetration in *Butterfly*—in which Puccini came nearest to psychological music-drama. But as a result of the kind of plot and characters we encounter in Puccini his instrumental commentary strikes us, in comparison with that of Wagner and Strauss, as constricted and lacking in depth, though there are occasional sudden intuitions and revealing flashes. Even more important is the part played by his orchestra in engendering atmosphere—not only in terms of documentary realism and poetic evocation but as the nerve-centre of the drama.

Already in *Manon Lescaut* but especially from *Bohème* onwards we note how Puccini's 'French' sensibility manifests itself in an instrumental texture that is at once light, diaphanous, supple, piquant and frequently self-effacing. There are the muted, delicate tones of orchestral chamber music,★ there is the scattering of a handful of tiny motives and chords to add point to the recitative, and there are the complete silences. Like Massenet and Debussy Puccini calibrates an instrumental passage as though it were a filigree, set with the expertise and loving care of a master jeweller. It is in such passages that the *fin de siècle* artist in Puccini displays an ear for the most refined and complex sensory stimuli, an aristocratic sensualism which relishes sound for its purely intoxicating effect on the nerves.

At the other end of the scale we encounter the strong, saturated colours of Italian Renaissance paintings. There are Puccini's massive *tutti* and there is his 'lazy' device of doubling, trebling and even quadrupling a vocal melody in octaves, most frequently on the strings—a device known as *violinata*. Puccini has been clapperclawed for this, and deservedly so, for he uses it to excess, notably at the climax of an aria or a love duet. Yet we might point to

★ It is noteworthy how often Puccini substitutes the softer bass-clarinet for the bassoon.

the fact that such unisons occur also in Rossini, Spontini, Bellini, Donizetti, Verdi and others;* indeed, this device belongs to a tradition dating as far back as the Neapolitan opera of the eighteenth century. Rousseau drew attention to it in his celebrated *Lettre sur la Musique Française* (1753) where he refers to the 'frequent accompaniments in unison which are observed in Italian music and which, reinforcing the melody, render its notes more soft and mellow and less tiring for the ear'; far from condemning it, he considers 'this unity of melody . . . to be an indispensable rule no less important in music than the unity of action in tragedy'. What lies behind these frequent unisons is, no doubt, the urge to impart to the vocal line a maximum of sensuousness and emotional warmth, to lend it vibrancy as pure melody, in brief, to crown what is the soul of Italian opera. But, as always in art, when maximal effects are aimed at without restraint, they tend to offend our sensibilities; they certainly do this with Puccini.

Puccini always employs a large orchestra, which is considerably reinforced in his 'grand operas'. Yet as with Verdi, the basis remains the mellow expressive strings, and it is, significantly, in the first half of his lyrical arias and love duets that they are introduced alone or with slight support from other instruments. The woodwind, on the other hand, come into their own in comic and grotesque scenes, or scenes of youthful gaiety. The brass mostly serves to mark a mounting tension and to underline the climaxes; in the three 'exotic' operas it is used, together with woodwind, to paint local colour, and here Puccini enlarges his arsenal by all kinds of percussion instruments and bells. Each of his mature operas has its peculiar orchestral tone, in accord with the dramatic atmosphere. There could hardly be a stronger contrast than that between the liquescent, diaphanous hues of *Butterfly*, on the one hand, and the red-tinted *fauvisme* of *Turandot*. Also within the same opera there is a noticeable change in the colour scheme as the drama unfolds. Similarly, Puccini extends the use of the orchestra as a characterizing agent to single instruments, associating them with the protagonists: the clarinet with Cavaradossi; the double bass, cellos and violas with Scarpia and the Aunt; upper woodwind with Butterfly and Liù; strings and cor anglais with Angelica. Nor can the student of Puccini's scores ignore his feeling for pictorial detail and his graphic touches of realism, e.g. the 'snowflakes' of *Bohème*, the 'storm' of *Fanciulla*, the 'out-of-tune barrel organ' of *Tabarro* and so on. And there is another amusing idiosyncrasy not surprising, perhaps, in this passionate wildfowler—almost every opera contains 'bird music': the 'robins' of *Butterfly*, the 'turtle-dove' of Scarpia's first aria, the 'cuckoo' of *Tabarro* and other unspecified varieties in *Suor Angelica* and *Gianni Schicchi*. Further inmates of Puccini's operatic menagerie are the 'three mice' to which Butterfly likens herself, her child and the nurse, while peering through the holes of the *shosi*, the 'braying ass' in Minnie's 'class' in *Fanciulla* and the 'miaowing cat' in *Tabarro*.

* See *Traviata*, Act II, duet between Violetta and Germont and the latter's aria 'Un padre ed una suora'. And as Martin Cooper points out (op. cit.), Bruneau, too, displayed a predilection for string passages in unison.

6

Like Verdi, Puccini was a master of big choral scenes; they occur in ten out of his dozen operas. His choruses are not merely scenic props and musical fillings, but are often treated as a collective character taking an active part in the drama, as they do in *Manon Lescaut*, *La Fanciulla* and *Turandot*. Even when the chorus is not directly involved in the action, it is called on to impart life and movement to a scene; Puccini achieves a most vivid impression of the bustle of crowds by an effortless to-and-fro between the chorus and the soloist—witness the opening acts of *Manon Lescaut* and *Butterfly*, and Act II of *Bohème*. Furthermore there are Puccini's 'atmospheric' choruses of humming voices, on and off stage, nowhere employed to more magical effect than in the scene of Butterfly's night vigil.

Puccini's choruses are mostly set in the syllabic, note-against-note fashion which was traditional in Italian opera; but he achieves a semblance of polyphony through skilful division of the four voice categories and the introduction of rhythmic contrast and variety. His customary procedure—in this, too, he continues a native tradition—is to entrust the leading melody to the orchestra which thus forms the solid backbone of the homophonic texture, to add fragments of that melody or little countermotives in the voice parts and gradually to fill up the canvas until he arrives at a *tutti* where chorus and orchestra combine to present the main theme.

This mastery of the choral medium may, perhaps, be taken for granted in a musician descended from four generations of church composers, who himself took the first creative step of his career in religious music. In point of fact, in his church compositions he proves himself a fluent contrapuntist and adept manipulator of the ancient scholastic devices. It is, hence, the more surprising that a composer with such a background should all but eschew real polyphony in his operatic choruses. Even *Suor Angelica*, which, one would have thought, offered golden opportunities for the display of contrapuntal ingenuity, notably in the 'Miracle' scene, failed to tempt him. Or did he, like Strauss, hold that counterpoint was out of place in opera?

THIRD PART

The Work

'And Almighty God touched me with His little finger and said: "Write for the theatre—mind well, only for the theatre!" And I have obeyed the supreme command.'—*Puccini*.

XXIV

Youthful Compositions: Mass, Capriccio Sinfonico, Chamber Music, etc.

PUCCINI'S NON-OPERATIC WORKS afford conclusive evidence that he needed the stimulus of the stage to fire his imagination: unless it was tethered to a libretto, it failed to soar. But the fact is noteworthy that of his compositions written before he embarked on his operatic career, the youthful Mass and the *Capriccio Sinfonico* display his gifts of melody, harmony and instrumental colour to far more telling effect than the occasional pieces he tossed off in his maturity.

I. MASS

This work, published in 1951 under the ambitious title *Messa di Gloria,*★ was called by Puccini simply *Messa a 4 voci con orchestra.* Yet it is in all but name a Solemn Mass, for tenor, baritone and bass solo,† mixed chorus and large orchestra, and represents the most ambitious of his youthful compositions. Despite its immaturity, the Mass proclaims a composer with a fund of fresh, spontaneous melody and of remarkable technical assurance. Like most Italian church music of the nineteenth century, it tends to a secular and operatic style, revealing influences from Bellini, Verdi and even Gounod; the *Credo*, for instance, might have stepped out of a Verdi opera:

Ex.7

and the *Gloria* contains a quick-march tune in comic-opera style. It is in keeping with the secular character of this Mass that we find few traces in it of liturgical material, such as Puccini later introduced into the *Te Deum* of *Tosca* and some scenes of *Suor Angelica*. Another striking feature, one that lends the work its Puccinian stamp, is its expressive lyricism. Thus the *Gratias* for tenor solo might almost have been written for Des Grieux or Rodolfo (Ex. 8).

A number of choruses, too, are in this lyrical style, such as the opening of the *Kyrie* which indeed sets the mood for the whole work; the composer later borrowed from this opening for the 'Church' scene in Act I of *Edgar*.

★ See p. 20. † The absence of a soprano solo is curious.

Ex.8 Andante sostenuto

Gra - - ti - as, gra - tias   a - gi - - mus ti - bi,

a - gi - - mus ti - bi

Generally, his choral treatment displays an admirable breadth and flow as well as fluent part-writing and a varied texture, with canon and *stretto* or close imitation effectively brought into play. Puccini's contrapuntal skill may be seen from this excerpt from the fugue *Cum Sancto Spiritu*:

Ex.9

FUGUE SUBJECT

Cum — san - - cto spi-ri-tu — in glori-a

men   in   glo - ria

A — • — men   a — men

—men cum san- — cto cum

De - - i pa - tris. A - - - -

De — i pa-

a — men a-

san — cto

This mettlesome four-part fugue, with its leaping subject, contains three expositions, and the coda deftly combines the fugal subject with the opening theme of the *Gloria*. The only passages in which the young composer loses his grip occur in the extended (thematic) interludes, two of which suffer from *rosalias*.

The Mass shows a remarkable advance in its harmonic idiom on Verdi's *Requiem*, written only a few years earlier. In addition to a pervasive chromaticism (but of the pre-*Tristan* kind), we already find fingerprints of the later Puccini in such things as the tritone and series of parallel chord-progressions, all of which lend the Mass a somewhat restless character. No less characteristic is the conspicuous part played by the orchestra, as in preludes, interludes and postludes; we also note a predilection for delicate hues (with woodwind in prominence) alternating with more massive, 'brassy' colours. Following both tradition and the Verdi of the *Requiem*, the young Puccini cannot have enough of trumpet fanfares, introduced in suitable and also some unsuitable places.

In setting the Ordinary he evinces a noticeable partiality for the more dramatic portions of the liturgy. Thus the *Gloria* and the *Credo* represent the most extensive movements of the work, the first consisting of no less than nine different sections. The *Crucifixus* for baritone solo is remarkable for a plangent melody in E minor, with suggestive *appoggiature* of the kind we shall encounter in the operas, where they are often marked *'come un sospiro'*—'like a sigh'. The *Agnus Dei* is a charming chorus in Puccini's *ballabile* style, but entirely unsuitable as a conclusion for a Solemn Mass. I suspect that this piece had originally no connection with the work and that in 1880, when the composer was anxious to complete the Mass in time for the Feast of San Paolino, he simply added that little chorus, most likely on account of its wistful pastoral feeling which at a pinch could be associated with the sentiment of an *Agnus Dei*. This piece eventually found its way into Act II of *Manon Lescaut*, where, as a Madrigal (!), it is sung to relieve the heroine's boredom during her morning toilet.

2. CAPRICCIO SINFONICO

Just as the Mass represents the most important work among Puccini's church music so does the *Capriccio Sinfonico* among his few orchestral compositions. The 'symphonic' of the title must, however, be taken with a grain of salt. The *Capriccio* was written by way of a school-leaving exercise for the Milan Conservatoire, and in it the young composer is seen trying, rather self-consciously, to display what he had acquired of symphonic technique. He makes several attempts at thematic development and contrapuntal combination of themes but these are the least convincing passages of the work, for Puccini's ideas are song-like or operatic and thus unsuitable for symphonic elaboration (E. 10). As in the operatic potpourri overtures of the period, the themes are loosely strung together like beads on a string. The standard by which symphonic skill was judged in Italy in the 1880s could not have been very exacting, since the *Capriccio* moved so eminent a critic and Wagnerian connoisseur as Filippi to describe its composer as 'a specifically symphonic talent'. A later writer, Alfredo Coppotelli, maintains that lack of symphonic skill was characteristic of all composers of Puccini's generation and he attributes this defect to insufficient training at the conserva-

Ex. 10

toires. Melodic invention was esteemed the chief accomplishment, facility in counterpoint and harmony being of secondary importance.[1] The alluring feature of the *Capriccio* lies in its rich flow of melodies, of which we count no less than seven in this comparatively short work. Its form is ternary: a grave introduction, a lively main section, *Allegro*, and a repeat of the introduction enlarged, modified and containing reminiscences of the middle section. The *Capriccio* of the title refers to the *Allegro*, a scherzo in three/eight time, now bubbling over with gaiety, now adopting a more subdued lyrical expression. In its opening idea we recognize the boisterous motto-theme of *La Bohème*:

Ex. 11

The fact that Puccini was able to lift a theme bodily from an early work and transfer it to one written more than ten years later, and yet avoid any impression of stylistic discrepancy, argues a certain precociousness in that youthful composition, which also provided a quarry for *Edgar*, the Requiem Mass (Act III) of which is based on the slow introduction of the orchestral piece. I quote from it a theme which represents the prototype of those sombre processional strains in minor and marked by narrow melodic steps, which we find in such great choral scenes as the Embarkation of *Manon Lescaut* and the Persian Prince's march to the scaffold in *Turandot*:

Ex.12

The full score of the *Capriccio* was never published; it was written for large orchestra, including a cornet and the obsolete ophicleide, instead of the modern bass tuba. A piano-duet version was brought out in 1884.

3. CHAMBER MUSIC AND OTHER PIECES

Most of Puccini's chamber music is student exercises dating from his years at the Milan Conservatoire and written for string quartet—fugues, a Scherzo and a Quartet in D. They are of no interest beyond displaying a natural feeling for the medium and foreshadowing the many intimate string passages of the operas. Two Minuets for string quartet were composed at a somewhat later date and are published. These are charming pastiches in the eighteenth-century manner, with elegant frills, such as Puccini wrote for the scene of the dancing lesson in Act II of *Manon Lescaut*, where he actually quotes a few phrases from the first minuet. A last echo of these pastiches is heard in the *Tempo di Gavotta* of *Tosca*.

On the other hand, *Crisantemi*, also for string quartet, is characteristic of Puccini's melancholy vein. Written in 1890, on the death of Duke Amedeo of Savoy, it is an inspired threnody in one continuous movement, rhapsodic in structure and clinging to the minor mode. Its two principal themes reappear in the last act of *Manon Lescaut*:

Ex.13

The rest of Puccini's *pièces de circonstance*, already discussed in the biographical part, are without exception inconsiderable trifles.

XXV

Le Villi

Principal Characters

Guglielmo Wulf	..	..	..	.. Baritone
Anna, his daughter ..	..	..	.. Soprano
Roberto	..	..	..	.. Tenor

Villagers—the Villi—Spirits

The action takes place in a village in the Black Forest.

THE SUBJECT of Puccini's first opera is best known to modern audiences from the version in Adam's celebrated ballet *Giselle ou Les Willis* (Paris, 1841), Theophile Gautier's plot being based on a legend related by Heine in his essay on German spirits and daemons which may have been known to Fontana.* According to Heine, this legend was familiar in parts of Austria but seems Slavonic in origin. Its affinity with the German legends of Loreley and Undine is manifest. Fontana's choice of it as an operatic subject was probably suggested by the undiminished success enjoyed by Adam's ballet, a conjecture supported by the fact that Puccini's opera too contains a ballet. Moreover, under the influence of the German romantics (Weber, Spohr, Marschner and the early Wagner) Italian opera of the 1880s passed through a shortlived vogue for subjects combining the supernatural with the theme of expiation and redemption so dear to the hearts of German romantics. The most representative Italian example of this genre is Catalani's *Elda* (1880), better known in its revised version as *Loreley* (1890). Yet ghost stories of the sombre, eerie kind, such as northern Germany has relished since the Middle Ages, are unknown in the Mediterranean countries, nor do southern audiences care for the representation of moral themes on the operatic stage, which explains why interest in native products of this type soon waned. If Catalani's opera is still given an occasional performance it is on account of the fine music it contains. There can be little doubt that his success with *Elda* provided an incentive for Puccini and his librettist to try their luck with a similar subject.

In accordance with the conditions stipulated in Sonzogno's prize competition, *Le Villi* was originally conceived in one act and this compelled Fontana to compress the plot so much that its most dramatic episodes— Roberto's seduction by the courtesan, his treachery and Anna's death—

---

* *Über Deutschland II. Elementargeister und Dämonen* (1834). Fontana appears to have been something of a German scholar, for he was responsible for the Italian translation of the libretti of *Tiefland* and *The Merry Widow*.

were not shown at all but merely referred to in the text. This bad piece of stagecraft could have been mended when the composer later extended the opera to two acts for its second production, but there was probably not enough time left for this. Inexperienced though he was in matters dramatic at that period, Puccini showed the right instinct when he felt the need to fill the gap in the plot by *musical* means. This was the insertion of a symphonic intermezzo between the two acts which is to tell the spectator about the intervening events. It consists of two parts: *L'Abbandono—The Desertion*—and *La Tregenda—The Spectre*—both pieces being prefaced by explanatory verses which the composer intended to have read to the audience, though no mention is made of this dramatic *pis aller* in any notices about the production. *The Desertion* movingly expresses Anna's longings, her grief and final death in a lyrical vein, which, with its nervous triplet passages, foreshadows the mature Puccini.* So as to leave no doubt in the spectator's mind as to the precise meaning of the music, the main curtain was raised halfway through it, to show behind a veil-curtain a funeral procession wending its way across the stage and chanting 'O pura virgo, requiescat in pace!' (Could Puccini have known of Weber's original intention to have the curtain raised in the overture to *Euryanthe* in order to show Emma's ghost hovering above the tomb?) Naïve as this procedure may seem to us, it provides the first instance of Puccini's eye for a suggestive stage-picture, a scene which, incidentally, is prophetic of Liù's funeral cortège in *Turandot*. *The Desertion* is followed by the ballet of the Villi, a conventionally gay tarantella which utterly belies its title *The Spectre* and which, despite its piquant harmony, is too reminiscent of the *Carmen* Overture. But, if it was the Intermezzo, notably its first half, that largely prompted Verdi to his remark about Puccini 'introducing symphonic passages for the mere pleasure of letting the orchestra fly',† there are, in addition, extended orchestral preludes and postludes to the arias and duets which witness to Wagner's influence.

Yet *Le Villi* is still a 'number' opera consisting of ten set-pieces and containing the traditional *coro d'introduzione* and *preghiera* or prayer. Puccini's chorus of rustics disports itself in graceful music that might almost have stepped out of Thomas or Gounod, and the general dance in which the celebration of Anna's betrothal to Roberto culminates is not a robust *Ländler*—as would have been appropriate—but a drawing-room waltz in the minor, à la Delibes. The Prayer, again, echoes passages from *Lohengrin* and *Parsifal* but shows skill in handling a large concerted ensemble, with a canon to lend it solidity of texture as well as an authentic religious stamp.

As to the principal characters, Fontana conceived them merely to provide Puccini with a soprano, a tenor and a bass, which makes it all the more remarkable that the composer succeeded in breathing musical life into such puppets, especially the lovers. And this, one imagines, was possible largely because the underlying theme of the opera was the true Puccinian one of

---

*This piece left its mark on the famous 'Preghiera' of *Cavalleria*; indeed a number of 'Mascagniisms' turn out, on closer inspection, to have grown on Puccini's tree.

† See his letter, p. 41.

love as tragic guilt. Each of the three characters has a set-piece of considerable length, of the *scena ed aria* kind we encounter in earlier Italian opera.

Anna is the first in the gallery of Puccini's frail heroines, and though in her opening Romanza she recalls Thomas's Mignon, she already shows the typical Puccinian blend of *morbidezza* and ardour:

Ex.14

Almost throughout the opera, Anna is characterized in that vein until her final duet with Roberto where as one of the Villi she almost reaches the stature of a dramatic heroine in Verdi (Ex. b).

It is Roberto, however, who kindles Puccini's imagination to incandescence, notably in the 'scena drammatica-romanza' of Act II, a monologue extending to no less than eighteen pages in the vocal score—possibly the longest solo scene in all Italian opera. None of Puccini's later lovers is characterized in as many shades of anguish, passion and despair and with the same active participation of the orchestra as is the hero of his first opera.[*]

This monologue is of particular interest as it clearly reveals the formative influences at work on Puccini's early operatic style. Its spiritual father is the Verdi of *Trovatore* and *Rigoletto*; but we also observe how Puccini, under the Wagnerian spell, draws on the orchestra to lend full force to one of Roberto's climaxes, at the same time modelling the instrumental texture on that in which Bizet often presents the Carmen motive:

Ex.15

[*] This was the aria that prompted Teresa Stolz to comment to Verdi that, except for occasional high notes, the tenor's voice was drowned by the orchestra. (See her letter on p. 42.)

(b)   "Le Villi" Act II

The textural identity is obvious: an agitated tremolo sustaining the harmony, beneath which a short incisive *ff* motive is repeated, varied and treated sequentially. The impression is one of emotional paroxysm, even of a certain brutality; this is the kind of texture we encounter in the '*agitato*' melodies of the later verists.

Lastly, there is Catalani whose influence is strongly felt in Roberto's melancholy *romanza* in B♭ minor, 'Torna ai felicidi'; Puccini manifestly fashioned it after an aria in the same key from Catalani's *Dejanice* (1883):

Ex.16

(a)   (Catalani)

(b) **(Puccini)**

Andante mesto

Tor - na ai fe-li-ci di do-len-te il mio pen-sier,—

ridean del maggio i fior

Both arias are characteristic of *la mestizia toscana* which the two Lucchese musicians shared in common. But even in this first operatic essay Puccini finds for the expression of his 'Tuscan sadness' musical equivalents at once more inspired and more poignant than we encounter in any of Catalani's operas. Similarly, Roberto's subsequent prayer in C minor, 'O sommo Iddio!', could have been penned by no one but Puccini.* It is the first instance of those 'weeping willow' melodies in which the young composer speaks with his own, authentic voice and which belongs to the type of themes that will occur, in a form terser and more subtle of articulation, in his mature operas, invariably shortly before the final catastrophe. Roberto's prayer stands at this point of the drama—the truly Puccinian 'muoio disperato' situation.

Guglielmo too benefits from Puccini's close proximity in this opera to Verdi's dramatic style, especially in his second-act monologue 'No! possibil non è' in C minor, which is prefaced by a long orchestral introduction expressing his grief at the death of his daughter. Guglielmo is clearly a descendant of Verdi's great father-roles but Puccini is unable to sustain this characterization for long, though he succeeds in rescuing the aria from floundering in sentimental piety by a dramatic epilogue that foreshadows the close of Michele's great monologue in *Il Tabarro*.

In retrospect it is not difficult to see why *Le Villi* was greeted with such acclaim on its first production, prompting the aged Verdi to one of the few favourable comments he ever made on the young opera composers of his time. People instinctively sensed the dramatic blood coursing through a work which even in its eclectic and conventional portions breathes theatre air and communicates the emotions of the characters with unfailing

* Ex. 4a. The composer himself seems to have regarded this idea as the finest of the entire opera, as he used it in the orchestral Prelude to Act I as well as in the choral Prayer.

directness; to say nothing of the youthful fire and engaging spontaneity that informs it from beginning to end. Neither Catalani nor Franchetti nor Smareglia nor any other Italian composer of Puccini's generation, sailing under the twin flags of Verdi and the German romantics, achieved in their early operas the imaginative level that characterizes the best pages of *Le Villi*.

XXVI

Edgar

Principal Characters

Edgar	..	..	.. Tenor
Gualtiero	..	..	.. Bass
Frank, his son	..	..	Baritone
Fidelia, his daughter	..	..	Soprano
Tigrana	..	..	.. Mezzo-soprano

Villagers, Soldiers, Monks and *Courtiers.*

The action takes place in Flanders in 1302.

ALFRED DE MUSSET's *La Coupe et les Lèvres* (1832), a verse drama in five acts, is a baffling piece in its mixture of introspection and melodrama, of exalted lyrical poetry and rhetorical bombast. What with its interminable monologues and its haphazard succession of scenes flouting all laws of dramatic structure, it is clear why this play has remained unknown. *La Coupe*, however, was not designed for the stage but as a 'book' drama in which Musset, untrammelled by the exigencies of the theatre, could give full rein to his lyrical effusions and indulge those dark broodings on life and love which were the perennial theme of this *poète maudit*.* His hero Frank (Edgar in the opera) is the mouthpiece for the expression of his own romantic agonies, a character created somewhat in the image of Faust—self-questioning, self-divided, and in revolt against God and man. In his search for the meaning of life and for spiritual happiness, Frank embarks on a career of wild military adventures, associating himself with a mysterious courtesan, Monna Belcolore. Tired of her charms and disgusted at himself, he returns to his native village in the Tyrol—the wild mountains have an obvious symbolism—and seeks purification of his soul in the love of the innocent Déidamia, the sweetheart of his early youth; but just before the wedding the bride is stabbed to death by the revengeful courtesan—hence the title of the play, *Betwixt Cup and Lips*. If we disregard Musset's melodramatic trappings, *La Coupe* is essentially a drama of spiritual quest, and in its language often anticipates the esoteric beauties of the later French symbolists.

Of all this nothing survives in Puccini's opera. On transferring the action from the Tyrol to Flanders in the Middle Ages, Fontana concentrated on the

---

* Musset wrote *La Coupe* after the failure of his *La Nuit Vénitienne* (Paris, 1830), when he renounced the theatre but not the dramatic form. He published it, together with a comedy, under the collective title *Un Spectacle dans un Fauteuil*, thus indicating the non-theatrical conception of the play.

melodramatic elements in Musset's play and let fly in such spectacular scenes as Edgar setting fire to his home, the mock funeral with its subsequent *coup de théâtre*, and the stabbing of Fidelia on the open stage. If in *Le Villi* he had provided the composer with the minimum of action, in *Edgar* he went to the other extreme. The result is an opera in the tradition of Meyerbeer which faithfully answers to Wagner's famous description of grand opera: 'a dramatic gallimaufry, monstrously motley, historico-romantic, diabolico-religious, bigoted-voluptuous, frivolous-lighthearted, mysterious-impudent and sentimental-rascally.' Fontana's characters are deprived of the aura of mysticism which surrounds them in Musset, becoming earth-bound figures drawn in a primitive black-and-white. The two heroines are re-baptized Fidelia and Tigrana, names indicating their temperaments with elephantine subtlety. The reason why Fontana resorted at all to Musset's obscure play for an operatic subject was, no doubt, the resemblance of its plot to that of *Carmen*, and in the process of turning it into a libretto he made this resemblance still stronger: the Moorish vamp Tigrana corresponds to Bizet's gipsy girl, Fidelia to Micaëla and Edgar to Don José, while Frank, to whom he transferred the name of Musset's hero, seems to have been modelled on the Torreador. But Fontana, seeking to surpass Bizet's librettists, worked into his story the theme of moral redemption reminiscent of *Tannhäuser*, but setting it in an atmosphere reminiscent of *Il Trovatore*. Still, his concoction served one useful purpose: it compelled Puccini, though with misgivings and reluctance, to tackle a subject not only far more dramatic but also larger in scope than that of *Le Villi*; he had to extend his creative range if he was to do justice to a plot which in its violent contrasts of character and situation heralded the advent of *verismo*. (*Cavalleria Rusticana* came out a year after *Edgar*!) However preposterous the libretto, in *Edgar* Puccini grew in stature, not 'by leaps and bounds' as Specht asserts, but by a cubit or two. In retrospect, this opera might be taken as a study for *Tosca*, especially for the character of Scarpia, who has psychological as well as musical traits in common with Tigrana. Similarly, the potent mixture of diabolism, lust and, religion, in which lies the fascination of the *Te Deum* scene of the later opera, is already present in a scene of Act I of *Edgar*, in which Tigrana vaunts her seductive charms to the hero, to the accompaniment of religious music heard from a nearby church. It was for this scene that the composer drew on the *Kyrie* music of his early Mass.

Edgar is the only opera of Puccini's which contains a full-length part for a mezzo-soprano, a voice little favoured by him in his later works, and providing further evidence that Bizet's heroine was then much in his mind. Nor does it seem a mere coincidence that, like Carmen's part, that of Tigrana has two alternative versions, one low and simple, the other high and florid. In fact, the 'tra-la-la and roulade school' which Bizet had thought 'already dead and buried' still survives in *Edgar*, not only in Tigrana but also in Fidelia, though Puccini's *coloratura* is often highly dramatic, in the style of Verdi's middle-period operas.

On the face of it, Tigrana was a heroine as un-Puccinian as can be imagined;

yet her musical portrayal turns out to be the richest and most varied one among those of the protagonists—Puccini seems to have been capable of a wider range of characterization of heroines than his later operas suggest. Tigrana is given the most dramatic music, and not until *Turandot* shall we find again such powerful and wide-ranging phrases as:

Ex.17

This excerpt comes from the first (four-act) version of the opera (1889), to which we have to turn in order to perceive Tigrana's full dramatic stature as a she-devil or *'demonio'*, as Edgar calls her. There she has no less than four great arias, one in each act, of which 'Ah, se scuoter della morte' in E♭ minor, sung at Edgar's bier, is an impressive piece of poignant dramatic expression. In the second (three-act) version (1892) Puccini mutilated her role by ruthless excisions, leaving her not much more than her leitmotive to indicate her savage nature:

Ex.18

A striking instance of the unscrupulous manner in which the composer curtailed her music is provided by the present second-act duet between her and Edgar. The gentle, coaxing strain in which Tigrana sues for Edgar's love—a scene reminiscent of Manon and Des Grieux in the 'Saint-Sulpice' scene of Massenet's *Manon*—cannot possibly, we feel, be the music of a woman of savage instincts; but the puzzle is solved if we cast a glance at the first version in which this music was given to Fidelia! In revising the opera the composer manifestly felt that Tigrana must sing a duet with Edgar before their final separation, and thus he simply transferred Fidelia's music to her, not caring that through this labour-saving device he threw Tigrana's character wholly out of focus at that particular moment in the drama. Admittedly Tigrana's music in the first version impresses by its dramatic power and melodic sweep, but her portrayal there must be said to be more Verdian than Puccinian in colours. This was possibly the prime reason for the composer butchering her part in 1892, while leaving that of the gentle Fidelia all but intact.

Fidelia is limned in tender and passionate music bearing the true stamp of Puccini's lyricism. She introduces herself in a charming pastoral, 'Oh fior del giorno', which foreshadows the 'Flower' music of Butterfly, and her third-act aria 'Nel villaggio', with its soaring lines, might not be amiss on the lips of Tosca in her love duet of Act I.* Another inspired aria is 'Addio, mio dolce amor', also in Act III, culminating in a *cantilena* of remarkable amplitude, one of the finest ideas of *Edgar*:

Ex.19

Andante assai calmo

O Ed-gar, la tua me-mo-nia sa - rà il mio sol pen-sie-ro!

Edgar is a cross-breed between Verdi's Manrico and Puccini's later Des Grieux. As a military hero he is delineated with firm, vigorous strokes, as for example in the solemn curses he heaps on Tigrana, 'O lebbra, sozurra del mondo'† in B minor, near the end of the opera, which in its emphatic dactyls is clearly modelled on the 'Miserere' of *Il Trovatore*. Yet more inspired as well as more characteristic of Puccini is the portrayal of the weakling Edgar torn between his two loves. His long monologue of Act II, 'Orgia, chimera dell' occhio', is a splendid piece in an ardent lyrical vein, reaching its high point in the aria:

Ex.20

Andante espressivo

p

O so - a - - ve vi - sion —— di quell'al - - ba d'a-pril!

The feminine endings here spring from the conception of the melody and not, as in most other cases, from the characteristic accentuation of the Italian language.‡

Edgar gave the composer his first opportunity to prove his mettle in big choral scenes and it was probably due to his promptings that Fontana allowed the crowd—in contrast to the villagers in *Le Villi*—to take an active part in the drama at crucial moments, most impressively so in the scene of the monk's revelation of Edgar's crimes. True, the choruses here owe much to Verdi and also Ponchielli (*La Gioconda*), as witness the sharp-chiselled lines, the leaping intervals and the tremendous rhythmic thrust:

* The opening theme derives from an Adagietto for Orchestra of 1883. *Edgar*, incidentally, is a veritable magpie's nest of ideas 'stolen' by the composer from his early works. In its turn it provided (in the original version) some music for *Tosca* (see p. 358).

† 'You leper, filth of the earth.' This is a choice specimen of Fontana's linguistic prowess in this opera.

‡ A typical example of the latter is Edgar's ironic apostrophe to Tigrana in Act III, 'Bella Signora'.

Ex. 21

The Requiem Mass of Act III, however, is a wholly original piece, despite its main theme having been taken from the *Capriccio* of six years before, and is nothing less than masterly in its treatment of concerted voices.

In fact, Puccini's advance in musical craftsmanship since *Le Villi* is seen on virtually every page of *Edgar*: in the greater flexibility of the vocal lines, the plasticity of the recitatives, the support lent by the orchestra in dramatic situations and in the considerable enlargement of the harmonic vocabulary.* The opera begins in D major and closes in B minor.

It was not in the music but the libretto that lay the primary cause for the failure of *Edgar*. The subject was already dated when it was set, and Puccini was justified in later calling the whole venture a '*cantonata*'. As a stage work it is indeed a 'blunder', but it is still interesting as a study of the growth of his dramatic style and as a testimony to his inventive powers. Ricordi was right when he said that he sensed the worth of *Edgar* and read in it 'all hopes for the future'.

* E.g. unresolved suspensions, parallel shifts of dissonant chords, chords of the 11th and 13th, and long pedals. Thus the whole of Tigrana's song 'Sia per voi', Act I, rests on a drone E♭–B♭.

XXVII

Manon Lescaut

Principal Characters

Manon Lescaut	Soprano
Lescaut, her brother and Sergeant of the King's Guard	Baritone
Chevalier Des Grieux	Tenor
Geronte de Ravoir, Treasurer-General	Bass

Time: Second Half of the Eighteenth Century

I

THE ABBÉ ANTOINE-FRANÇOIS PRÉVOST D'EXILE (1697–1763) was little more than a prolific hack, but he succeeded in producing a single masterpiece which gained him a niche in French literature. *Manon Lescaut* (1731), written in all probability during his exile in London, is an autobiographical novel. In it this twice-renegade priest recounted experiences of his turbulent youth, and for once setting aside the routine of a writer of popular adventure stories transmuted these experiences into terms of art. The novel, which was intended as the sort of cautionary tale fashionable at that period, has often been likened to a Racine tragedy, for its theme is the classic one of the conflict between reason and passion, virtue and vice, illustrated in the fatal fascination of a young nobleman for a seductive but perfidious woman, and treated with the dignity and moral purpose of French classical drama. The downfall of the two lovers is the logical outcome of their characters, and if Prévost arouses in us a deep sympathy for the hero it is because Des Grieux's weakness is that of universal human nature. The novel reads almost like a play: its action is swift and stripped of all superfluities and its language is direct and simple. Add to this a series of striking episodes and the allurement of its setting, which is the corrupt Paris of the Regency, and it is clear why Prévost's novel has continued in its popular appeal for upwards of two centuries and provided such ready material for dramatic treatment, with Massenet's *Manon* and Puccini's opera as the most successful examples.*

Before dealing with Puccini's libretto some additional remarks on the novel are called for. *Manon Lescaut* is essentially a study of the psychological involutions of a man caught in a struggle between his better self and his

---

* As early as 1765 it was turned into a play by one J. Ch. Brandes. Scribe made it the basis for a ballet by Halévy (1830) and also Auber's *Manon Lescaut* (1866), which is *opéra comique* in both the generic and literal sense of the term. Balfe in England drew on it for his *Maid of Artois* (1836).

instincts, of 'un caractère ambigu, un mélange des vertus et des vices, un contraste perpétuel de bons sentiments et d'actions mauvaises' (Prévost). This portrayal is carried out with insight and sensibility, especially in those passages of self-analysis which Prévost puts into the mouth of the Chevalier. Consider for example Des Grieux's reaction after the receipt of a letter from Manon in which she tries to explain away her desertion of him for the rich M. de G. M. and in the same breath assures him of her true love:

> I could never describe the state I was in when I had read this letter, and to this day I cannot decide what sort of emotions swirled round in my soul. It was one of those unique situations, the like of which has never been experienced before: you cannot explain to others because they have no conception of what is meant, and you cannot unravel them for yourself because, being unique, they have no connection with anything in your memory, nor even with any known feeling at all. And yet, whatever my emotions were, certain it is that grief, rage, jealousy and humiliation all had a share in them.[2]

It is passages like this that lend Des Grieux a psychological depth which we inevitably miss in both Massenet's and Puccini's operas, in which he is a sentimental lover pure and simple; in the French work he is refined and always an aristocrat, in the Italian work an impulsive youth, unrestrained and even hysterical in the expression of his feelings. But there are moments in Prévost, too, when the Chevalier cannot master his passions and gives vent to morbid self-pity like Goethe's Werther, whose delicately adjusted sensibility he shares.

Another problem in adapting the novel for opera lay in Prévost's presentation of his material. *Manon Lescaut* is a story within a story: a 'Man of Quality' (the author) meets on one of his journeys a poor young man whom he befriends and who out of gratitude feels moved to tell him the tragedy of his life. The novel is thus a statement of the male point of view, and we see Manon largely through the eyes of her lover;* and it is significant that Prévost makes no mention of her in the Preface in which he sets out the purpose of his tale, giving it the title *L'Histoire du Chevalier des Grieux et de Manon Lescaut*, though it was called *Manon Lescaut* within a few years of its publication. Manon is a far less complex character than her lover but a fascinating illustration of feminine frailty. Like Carmen, her coarser-grained Spanish cousin, she stands beyond good and evil. She is not immoral but amoral, and must act as she does because she is a creature of mere instinct. Des Grieux can, hence, truthfully say of her: 'elle pèche sans malice, elle est légère et imprudente, mais elle est droite et sincère.' The pathos in the character of the Chevalier springs from the fact that while he recognizes the girl for what she is, he remains enslaved to her to the last moment of her pitiful end. Prévost made him the central figure of the novel, yet in a dramatization Manon must, for obvious reasons, be elevated to the same level of importance as her lover. In Massenet's opera she dominates the drama; in Puccini's we are nearer to Prévost's conception.

* Mérimée adopted the same method in his novel *Carmen*.

2

Had Puccini adhered to the scenario which Praga submitted to him,*
he would certainly have incurred the charge of copying Massenet, but
the probability is that his libretto would not have turned out the broken-
backed affair it surely is in its final version. In Praga's original draft the first
three acts were more or less identical with the corresponding acts in the
French opera, and Act IV was similar, too, to Massenet's final act, except
for the setting. This draft had the advantage that, as in Massenet, it showed the
gradual decline in the lovers' fortunes, and brought out the fatal flaw in
Manon's character with convincing clarity. But, as we recall, misgivings
about this close similarity to Massenet prompted Puccini to ask for the
complete elimination of the original Act II (the wretched ménage of the
lovers in Paris), which was substituted by Act III (the present Act II); and
this latter act was to be replaced by 'a situation dramatic, gripping and
picturesque', which became the present Embarkation act. If we examine the
libretto as we have it now, the following picture presents itself: After a perfect
exposition of the drama in Act I, the action takes an unbelievable jump in
Act II, where the little ingénue we met at Amiens confronts us in Paris
as the flash mistress of the wealthy Treasurer-General, Geronte, and already
tired of her association with this old roué. How and why she became a
courtesan we only learn indirectly afterwards.* Equally important, we are
shown neither Manon and Des Grieux in their shortlived idyll after their flight
from Amiens† nor her subsequent desertion of the Chevalier, which forms so
poignant a scene in Massenet. And that it should be Lescaut who is instrumental in bringing the two lovers together, thus acting against his own interest, must strike us as irreconcilable with his true character. To sum up, Puccini
presents us with psychological inconsistencies and established facts in Act II
which are bound to baffle even the least critical of spectators. Yet, from the
point of view of dramatic structure, this act is extremely well built, bringing
out the contrast between a Manon bored with the splendours of her present
life and a Manon whipped into passion by Des Grieux's sudden arrival;
from this moment the emotional temperature rises in a steep curve, reaching
fever point with the arrest of Manon.

Act II forms the centre of the whole drama. Between it and Act III
there is another big gap in the action, though, as in *Le Villi*, Puccini bridges

* Illica noticed this unexplained change but not until he saw a performance of Massenet's
Manon in Milan in October 1893, that is, seven months after the first production of Puccini's
opera. In order to rectify to some extent this dramatic defect he inserted, towards the end of
Act I, a new dialogue between Lescaut and Geronte in which the former speaks in unequi-
vocable terms of his sister's fatal love of pleasure. This dialogue begins with the words:
'Parigi . . . È là Manon . . .Manon già non si perde'.

† Puccini's instinct was right when he asked Illica in the spring of 1891, for such a scene
where everything should be 'love, spring, youth . . . Manon e Des Grieux—happy lovers—
lavishing caresses on each other and playful like two young lovers' (*C.P.*Let.52). It will
remain a mystery why he did not insist on the inclusion of this scene and the only explanation
is that he feared it might turn out to be too similar to Act II of Massenet's opera.

it with a symphonic intermezzo in two parts, entitled *The Imprisonment* and *The Journey to Le Havre*, prefaced with explanatory lines from Prévost. Act III, *The Embarkation*, showing Manon at the nadir of her 'career' and centring on the roll-call of the twelve prostitutes, is most striking but, so· far as the essential action is concerned, adventitious, unless Puccini had made his heroine die in it. It was developed from a brief and wholly unimportant episode in Prévost,† possibly at the composer's suggestion, and it is more than probable that one motive for introducing it was to gratify his desire for the utmost humiliation of the heroine. Another, purely dramatic, motive must have been to present a situation uncommon on the stage and gripping in its visual effect, to say nothing of the excellent musical opportunities it offered. These Puccini seized with both hands. But having decided on an Embarkation act, he was now compelled to put his lovers to the inconvenience of undertaking a voyage as far as the New World, simply for Manon to die there and for Des Grieux to throw himself on her body, all of which they could have done with equal ease on board ship. Had Puccini clinched the opera in some such fashion, it would not have had the lame ending it has. For with his final act, *In America*, he committed the biggest dramatic blunder of all. Completely devoid of action, this act gives the impression of having been tacked on, largely to afford him an opportunity of indulging a long unrelieved lament. Nor did Puccini's librettists make it sufficiently clear why Manon and the Chevalier should have found themselves in such dire circumstances in the wild American desert. All we hear in explanation is Manon's 'Alas! my beauty has caused new misfortunes, they wanted to tear me away from him', which must remain obscure unless the reader turns to Prévost, in which he learns that Des Grieux fought a duel with one Synelet, the nephew of the Governor of the French Colony, who coveted Manon and who was supposed to have been killed in that combat. In order to avoid certain punishment, the pair make their escape across a vast plain to seek asylum in an English colony, and it is on this flight that the girl perishes of exhaustion. In Massenet, Manon dies on the road to Le Havre and so as to shorten her death scene his librettists, following Prévost, tellingly lead up to it with the episode of Lescaut's abortive raid on the guards escorting the transport. By introducing this dramatic episode they saved Massenet's closing act from the inevitable risk of monotony which indeed kills Puccini's nearly stone dead. In his fascination for scenes of mental and physical suffering the voice of the dramatist in him—then not yet strong enough anyhow—was completely silenced. It is in fact one of the serious flaws of this opera that Puccini, in contrast to the French composer, presents his lovers, for the best part of the drama, as caught up in such situations. Misfortune comes to them too soon—their decline starts as early as the second half of Act II and the opera has *four* acts—and thus renders the opera top-heavy with grief and despair.

* The *dis*embarkation of the prostitutes at New Orleans.

3

We now come to the question: to what extent, if any, did Puccini succeed in recapturing the peculiar French atmosphere of Prévost's novel?

Baudelaire, once speaking of Laclos's famous *Les Liaisons Dangereuses*, described it as 'un livre essentiellement français'. The same may be said of Prévost's *Manon Lescaut*. It is indeed one of the few subjects—Pushkin's *Eugene Onegin* and *Boris Godunov* are others—that demand a composer born and bred in the author's own country and instinctively at one with his mentality, if the resulting opera is to radiate the peculiar spirit of such a subject. Puccini, for all his inspired response to it—and *Manon Lescaut* must be reckoned as his richest opera so far as sheer musical invention is concerned—could not hope to rival Massenet in the re-creation of a French atmosphere. But the Italian was fully aware of his limitations on that score. Did he not say to Praga: 'If Massenet felt his subject with the powder and the minuets, I shall feel it with desperate passion'—'*con passione disperata*'? Which was the only sensible approach at that stage of his creative development. It is conceivable that a few years later, when his 'French' sensibility had grown more pronounced, witness *Bohème*, he might have given us a *Manon Lescaut* at once more refined, more elegant and more piquant.

Massenet's *Manon* is a masterpiece, which Puccini's is not. But, then, we must allow for the fact that Massenet was Puccini's senior by sixteen years and had reached, when he wrote his opera (1883–4), the zenith of his career, while the Italian was just beginning to get into his stride. Nevertheless, the younger composer scores over the older one on three counts—by his inexhaustible fund of melodic ideas, by the sensuous warmth and exuberance that characterizes his music in general, and by the comparative modernity of his harmonic and orchestral idiom.

Manon Lescaut might be defined as the work in which Puccini first found himself as a musician. It displays most of the characteristics of his mature style, some already brought to full bloom, others still inchoate. Moreover, it is the purest of his representative works, free from those deliberate assaults on our sensibilities to which we are exposed from *Tosca* onwards. In it the composer displays a romantic and wholly poetic vein, betraying no signs—admittedly, to the dramatic disadvantage of the opera—of the calculating man of the theatre we know from his later works. The music has the high seriousness of youth, and a dark fire of despairing passion smoulders in it which in the second half of the drama blazes out into the fiercest flame. It is significant, for example, that no other opera of his contains such an abundance of minor tonalities. Unconcerned with dramatic and psychological niceties, Puccini pours out, with youthful recklessness, a wealth of melodic ideas such as is found in none of the later operas. In Act I he writes two extended love duets where one would have been sufficient, and in Act II where he presents Manon in an elegant eighteenth-century Parisian *salon* he resorts to a Madrigal, an extended Minuet and a Pastoral. Again, in the subsequent scene between Manon and Des Grieux, he squanders his melodic fund to the extent of ten

321

different themes; and in the final act the dramatist is seen to abdicate altogether in favour of the musician.

One of the chief weaknesses of the opera lies in Puccini's failure to achieve sufficient contrast in the characterization of his lovers. Des Grieux, the most feminine of his tenor heroes, is portrayed in music that could readily be interchanged with that of Manon, without falsification of his essential character. True, in Act I the composer makes a half-hearted attempt to delineate a more reflective and more masculine aspect of Prévost's young Chevalier in a long-breathed cello theme* which owes something to Massenet's own 'Des Grieux' motive. But he soon discards this for good, and henceforth it is a tender languishing phrase which stands throughout for Des Grieux and his love:

Ex.22 **Andante lento espressivo**

In contrast to Massenet's and indeed to his own later method, Puccini allows his hero a greater share of arias and cavatinas than he does his heroine. Des Grieux introduces himself with 'Tra voi, belle brune', a fetching little air in a lightly ironic vein, the middle section of which includes the first parallel fifths in Puccini's operas, though no critic appears to have noticed them at the time (Ex. 22b). There follows Des Grieux's first big aria, 'Donna non vidi mai', which is, however, merely a repeat of the first duet. (Ex. 22a) transposed a third up to B♭ so as to achieve more vocal brilliance. In Act II the hero turns from the young *Schwärmer* enthralled by Manon's fatal charms to the despairing lover filled with dark forebodings. As such he is well caught in the plangent 'Ah, Manon, mi tradisce' (Ex. 4b, p. 274). In Act III his dirge-like processional 'Ansia eterna' in D minor is as much a reflection of his own mood as of the bleak dawn that breaks over Le Havre; and a tenebrous, oppressive effect is obtained by the sustained pedals in the bass.†

* A few bars before [12].

† Catalani's *La Wally* contains in the orchestral prelude to Act IV a piece in similar vein and of similar texture which was not lost on Puccini. Also the part of Manon reveals on occasion Catalani's influence, notably from his *Loreley*, e.g. the heroine's *arioso*, 'E quando non', in the love duet of Act I of that opera.

The heartrending orchestral strain to which Des Grieux presently addresses Manon, standing behind the grille of her prison window ('Ah! Manon, disperato') derives from the first of the *Crisantemi* themes (Ex. 13a, b) while the second provides the poignant opening for the final act. Des Grieux's second big aria in the opera occurs toward the end of Act III where he works himself up into a paroxysm of grief. It plainly echoes Gioconda's famous 'Suicidio!' from Ponchielli's opera:

while the Chevalier's violent outcries, in the later part of his aria, 'Guardate, pazzo son!', bear testimony to the growing influence of *verismo*.

Like Des Grieux, Manon has her leitmotive, manifestly inspired by the inflection of the verbal phrase yet at the same time recapturing something of that '*air charmant de tristesse*' of Prévost's heroine:

Ex. 24

This is one of the few themes in the opera which undergo transformation according to changes in the dramatic situation, illustrated in the chromatic version (Ex. b) which characterizes Manon in her state of complete exhaustion in Act IV. From the 'Manon' theme is also derived the 'Death' motive (Ex. c) we first hear at the unexpected arrival of Des Grieux in Act II, where it provides a characteristic instance of Puccini's ominous hints at the later tragedy. What little music Manon has to sing in Act I contains no suggestion of the little coquette whom we first encounter both in the novel and the Massenet opera; she is presented there as a sad young girl with no hope for the future. Puccini reserves his fuller portrayal of her for Act II, in which he shows her first as the haughty courtesan and then the passionate lover. In the first half of the act he resorts to those eighteenth-century pastiches mentioned before, of which the so-called Madrigal (the former *Agnus Dei* of the Mass) is an enchanting example of vocal chamber-music, with the mezzo-soprano first echoed and then supported by four women's voices. The Minuet for the scene of the dancing lesson has a wistful Trio in A minor which Puccini, taking a leaf out of Massenet's book, recalls poignantly at the moment of her death.

The first indication of the passionate side of Manon's nature comes in her aria 'In quelle trine morbide', truly Puccinian in the undulating vocal line and the tugging syncopations. But it lacks real glow and its second part represents merely a transposed repeat of Lescaut's previous aria, tacked on somewhat perfunctorily, because of its reference to 'that humble little dwelling' which Manon now recalls longingly amidst the cold and lifeless splendour of Geronte's mansion. Puccini's afflatus is not kindled until the love scene, which contains some of the most passionate pages he ever penned. It is the second act of *Tristan* seen with Puccini's eyes, with the lovers' rapt 'Ah, vien' corresponding, on a purely emotional plane, to Tristan's mystic 'O sink hernieder, Nacht der Liebe!'. Puccini here pays full tribute to Wagner in his frequent quotations of the 'Tristan' chord, in yearning sevenths, chromatic modulations, and a surfeit of sequences:

Ex.25

(The plaintive orchestral Intermezzo between Acts II and III is unblushingly Tristanesque, containing on its last page an almost literal quotation of Tristan's 'Isolde, Liebe!' (Act II).)

Yet Puccini is unable to bind his long love scene together by musical means: his profuse invention of themes is not equalled by the power to work them into a coherent whole, and the result is a kaleidoscope rather than an organism. Yet the last part of this duet is not altogether as haphazardly constructed as it seems. There are two distinct sections, the first—in two/four time, based on the key of Bb minor and agitated—describes Manon's frantic attempt to win Des Grieux back; the second, in which the Chevalier yields to her entreaties, flows along in broader, more tranquil phrases in three/four, culminating in one of those hymn-like strains rare in Puccini and symbolizing freedom and hope:

Ex.26

This theme provides, appropriately, the close for Act III, where it is thundered out by three trumpets in unison like a fanfare to mark the reunion of the two lovers and their departure for the freedom of the New World.

The emotional counterpart to the great love scene of Act II is the death scene of the final act which indeed may be said to occupy its entire length. It is essentially a lament in duet form, lasting as long as eighteen minutes

and thus failing on the dramatic plane. The music is saturated in the most despairing sombre colours ever resorted to by the composer. It scarcely leaves the minor mode, the melodic lines droop and sag in Puccini's character-istic manner, in the harmony 'sighing' *appoggiature* and doleful chromatic turns abound, and the pace drags and lurches. The centrepiece of the act is Manon's dramatic *scena* 'Sola, perduta, abbandonata' in F minor, a study in Puccini's use of a melodic *ostinato* for the purpose of achieving monotony.*
Thirst causes Manon to fall into a delirium, suggested with great dramatic force in the later part, but the contrast is not sufficiently marked to redeem the aria as a whole from its fatal uniformity of mood. A glance at the death of Mimì, where he puts not a foot wrong and where the brevity and economy of the scene are its great features, shows the measure of Puccini's growth as a musical dramatist in the few years that separate *Manon Lescaut* from *Bohème*.

With Lescaut and Geronte, who are episodic figures, we may deal briefly.†
While in Massenet, Manon's brother is allotted no fewer than three arias, an indication of his importance there, in Puccini he has the solitary 'Sei splendida' of Act II, music of a lyrical languor and a certain nobility of expression out of key with this noisy, raffish fellow, even as is the brief *arioso* 'Vedo, Manon' in Act I, in which he encourages Geronte to take a 'paternal' interest in his sister—a coaxing pentatonic phrase that we might not be surprised to encounter in *Butterfly*.

Puccini was more successful in his characterization of Geronte, who is given a sinister touch in those low-lying discords which accompany his brief soliloquy in Act I, expressing his intention to abduct Manon:

Ex. 27

This is one of those purely harmonic motives such as Puccini invariably reserves for his villains. When it returns in Act II, in the scene of the mirror in which Manon mocks Geronte's age, it is suggestively altered in pitch, rhythm and orchestration.

Manon Lescaut has important choral scenes in Acts I and III. In the opening

---

* See the descending phrase on alternating solo oboe and flute, which all but dominates the piece.

† The student Edmondo of Act I is no more than a group character, a singing super, though his opening, 'Ave, sera gentile', in F♯ minor (Ex. 28), is an entrancing song, full of youthful exuberance. He does not occur in Massenet and was very likely introduced in faint reminis-cence of Tiberge, Des Grieux's friend and mentor in Prévost's novel.

act Puccini still adheres to the traditional *coro di introduzione*, but builds it up like a scherzo, based on this rocketing pentatonic theme:

Ex. 28

The contrasting 'trio' is formed by Des Grieux's aforementioned 'Tra voi belle'. The whole section is prefaced by a scintillating orchestral introduction, part of which serves to round off this choral scene. Of similar structure is the following scene of the card game, the energetic main theme of which was taken from the composer's early Quartet in D major. The trio is a waltz *à la* Delibes sung in close harmony by the women only and forming a gay background for the nefarious dialogue between Lescaut and Geronte. An exquisite piece of vocal chamber-music is the finale of this act, in which the chorus—light, airy, and *pp*—repeats in E major Des Grieux's mocking song of the opening scene.* All these choruses belong in style to comic opera but the chorus of the Embarkation act is pure grand opera and possesses a dramatic impact comparable to some of Verdi's great ensembles. The gradual build-up of the tension from disjointed fragments to full chorus is nothing if not masterly. There is the populace of Le Havre, some laughing, others sneering, and others outraged at the sight of the prostitutes being shipped off to America. There is Lescaut inciting the crowd against the soldiers in agitated triplets; there is the Sergeant calling out the girls' names in a matter-of-fact voice which cuts through the choral texture like a sharp knife. And there are Manon and Des Grieux to crown the climax with their poignant *cantilena*. Not until the first-act finale of *Turandot*, which like the Embarkation chorus is in the sombre key of E♭, shall we encounter again a scene in Puccini's operas as memorable in invention and as gripping as a stage picture.

* The autograph score shows that Puccini here originally intended a grand-opera finale in a style far too pretentious for this light-hearted act.

XXVIII

La Bohème

Principal Characters

Mimi	..	..	..	..	Soprano
Musetta		..	..	..	Soprano
Rodolfo, a poet ..		..	..	..	Tenor
Marcello, a painter		..	..	..	Baritone
Schaunard, a musician ..		..	..	..	Baritone
Colline, a philosopher ..		..	..	..	Bass

Time: About 1830—Paris

I

THE CHARGE HAS BEEN LEVELLED at Puccini by some literary critics that with his opera he had erected a tombstone for Mürger's *Scènes de la Vie de Bohème*. Quite the contrary appears to be the case. If Mürger's novel is still read nowadays, this is largely, I believe, on account of its being 'the book of the opera'. Henry Mürger★ (1822–61) was a minor figure on the Paris literary scene of his time and regarded his *Scènes*, which was to bring him fame and fortune, as a mere pot-boiler, which indeed it was in origin. He himself believed that his true bent was for poetry, but he produced only mediocre verses in which he shows himself prone to morbid gloom—in contrast to the mood which inspires his novel. *Scènes* first appeared in serial form in the literary magazine *Le Corsaire* between 1845 and 1848. Encouraged by the success of these sketches, Mürger adapted them for the stage, in collaboration with Théodore Barrière, as a five-act play, *La Vie de Bohème*. This was first produced on 22 November 1849 at the Théâtre des Variétés before a packed audience which included Louis Napoleon and members of artistic and literary Paris who had come chiefly out of curiosity, for it was known that Mürger had drawn his characters after well-known figures in Parisian Bohemia. The play was a *succès fou* for the twenty-seven-year-old author, who wrote after-wards: 'I dreamed I was the Emperor of Morocco and had married the Bank

★ This is the correct spelling of his name. As Henri Murger he had written his first story for Arsène Houssaye, the editor of *L'Artiste*, but wished it to appear under a pseudonym. At Houssaye's suggestion he changed the French 'i' in the cognomen to the English 'y', as this would look more elegant and distinguished. This vogue for the English and things English is also reflected in a character of Mürger's novel, the eccentric Englishman Mr. Birn'n who was evidently modelled after Lord Byron. He is the 'lord o milord' to whom Schaunard refers in Act I of Puccini's opera.

To lend his surname also a foreign (German) flavour, Mürger placed the diaeresis over the 'ü', arguing that this would facilitate its correct pronunciation abroad.

of France'.[3] He received a congratulatory letter from his idol, Victor Hugo, was presented with the coveted red ribbon of the Légion d'Honneur, and was offered a contract by a great publishing firm (Michel Levi) for the issue of the *Scènes* in book form (1851). For this he revised and rearranged the original sketches and added a preface in which he stated his views on Bohemian life and the moral lesson to be drawn from it. The book was widely read and translated into several languages. It brought Whistler from Washington to Paris and found several imitators, among them George du Maurier with *Trilby*, which Puccini considered as a possible subject in 1912 but rejected on account of its resemblance to *La Bohème*. The libretto of the opera is based on both the book and the play.* After more than a century Mürger's novel is still responsible for the picture which popular imagination has formed of Bohemian life. Not that Mürger was the first to write of the joys and sorrows of struggling young artists and their *amours*, living a hand-to-mouth existence; but he was the first to see this life with an imaginative eye and recapture the atmosphere of Montmartre and the Latin Quarter of the 1840s in a series of vivid and colourful tableaux. *Scènes* is not a literary masterpiece but essentially high-class journalism. Mürger himself had lived the sort of life he describes and his early death at the age of thirty-nine is said to have been hastened by the dissipations and privations suffered in his youth. If several characters in his novel die of consumption it was because this disease, brought on by fast living and poverty, had taken a heavy toll among his friends.† In *Scènes* we thus perceive the first stirrings of realism in French literature, a fact which indeed aroused controversy between the upholders of the romantic tradition and the younger generation of writers. The brothers Goncourt called the book 'a triumph of Socialism' though nothing was farther from Mürger's mind than to write a political tract. All he aimed at was to portray '*la jeunesse qui n'a qu'un temps*' and portray it without a hint of prudery or censoriousness. If *Scènes* contains a message at all it is that Bohemia is perhaps a necessary stage in an artist's development and that the sooner he grows out of it the better for his art; in his last chapter Mürger shows us Rodolphe and Marcel settled down to steady, solid work and a *bourgeois* existence. In one of his many epigrams he describes Bohemia as 'the preface to the hospital, the morgue or the Academy', and his famous last words before he died were '*pas de musique, pas de bruit—pas de Bohème!*'. What makes his novel still worth reading is its perfect blend of comedy and tragedy, of humour and pathos. With the lightest of touch Mürger pictures 'this gay terrible life' and shows himself a writer of charm, observation and a ready wit, directing well-aimed shafts at certain fashions in the social, artistic and political life of Paris under Louis Philippe. Puccini's libretto retains some of these allusions as well as the hyperbole and meiosis in which Mürger delighted.

* Mürger originally called the book *Scènes de la Bohème* and the play *La Vie de Bohème*, while the title of the opera is *La Bohème*.

† The heroine of *La Dame aux Camélias* (1848), who dies of the same disease, was also drawn after an authentic person—Marie Duplessis, Dumas's mistress.

When we sit and watch *La Bohème*, few of us realize—nor is this necessary for our enjoyment—that the *dramatis personae* are images, at two removes, of authentic persons. Puccini's librettists rightly eliminated most of Mürger's direct clues and concentrated on the emotional essence of the story, which in conjunction with the evergreen music invests the Bohemians with a universal appeal and makes the spectator feel that this is youth as he might find it in any great city at any period. Nevertheless, it is of interest to trace Puccini's characters, through Mürger's novel, back to their historical models.

Mürger moved in a circle of artists and writers several of whom later achieved eminence, such as Courbet, Baudelaire, Banville, Gautier, Champfleury and Gérard de Nerval; these contributed to the portrayal of his Bohemians in a general way. Yet there were others, intimates of Mürger, who served him as more individual 'sitters'. In Rodolphe, we know, the author depicted himself, and the present-day interpreter of Puccini's romantic lover would no doubt be horrified if he were expected to appear exactly as Mürger describes his hero:

> . . . a young man whose face could hardly be seen for a huge, bushy, many-coloured beard. To set off this *prognathic hirsutism*, a premature baldness had stripped his temples as bare as a knee. A cluster of hairs, so few as to be almost countable, vainly endeavoured to conceal this nakedness. He wore a black jacket with tonsured elbows, which allowed a glimpse, when he raised the arm unduly, of air-holes at the places where it debouched into the sleeves. His trousers were perhaps black; but his boots, which had never been new, seemed to have already made several world tours on the feet of the Wandering Jew.[4]

Rodolphe is editor-in-chief of two fashion magazines, *L'Écharpe d'Iris* and *Le Castor*; for the latter he is attempting to write the article with which we see him occupied in the opera just before Mimi's entry. The manuscript which provides the fuel for the stove in the gay opening scene of the opera is that of a drama entitled *Le Vengeur*, of which Rodolphe has made so many versions that he can afford to burn them all except the latest, for which he eventually succeeds in securing a performance. He inhabits a room at the top of the highest house in Paris, 'a sort of turret', delightful in summer but in winter 'Kamchatka–Col St. Bernard–Spitzbergen–Siberia'. The room is adorned by a stove, with an aperture like a 'gate of honour specially reserved for Boreas and his following'. Mürger's Rodolphe, like Puccini's Rodolfo, is the idealist who alone among his fellow-Bohemians believes in true love, which he thinks to have found at last in Mimi.

Mürger's Marcel is a composite figure drawn after Champfleury and two well-known painters of the period, Marcel Lazare and Tabar. Tabar worked for some time on a great historical painting *The Crossing of the Red Sea* which he was unable to complete because of the expense of procuring the necessary models and costumes; he therefore altered it into the less expensive

Niobe and her Children slain by the arrows of Apollo and Diana which he exhibited in the Salon in 1842. This gave Mürger the idea for those amusing vicissitudes which Marcel's picture, *The Crossing of the Red Sea*, suffers. The painter had been working for five or six years and for as many years the jury had been rejecting it, so that after so many journeys from the artist's studio to the Museum and back 'the picture knew the way so well that, if it had been put on wheels, it could have gone to the Louvre by itself'. Every time, before submitting it to the jury, Marcel changed some details as well as the title: *The Crossing of the Rubicon—The Crossing of the Beresina—The Crossing of the Panoramas* (a street in Paris). It finally ended as a grocer's shop sign, with a steamboat added and the title altered to *In Marseilles Harbour*. This is the famous picture on which we find Marcello working in Act I of the opera and which turns up as the inn sign in Act III.

The model for Schaunard was one Alexandre Schanne who dabbled in the arts but later settled down to a more prosaic but more lucrative occupation manufacturing children's toys. In 1887 he published his memoirs *Souvenirs de Schaunard* in which he provided the clues for some of Mürger's Bohemians. In the novel he was originally called Schannard but by a printer's error this became Schaunard and Mürger never troubled to correct it. Schaunard's nose has the singular distinction of being 'aquiline in profile and snub in full face' and he speaks with 'a voice like a hunting horn'. In the novel he is a painter and musician, in the opera only the latter. He has written several symphonies, among them a 'mimetic' symphony, *On the Influence of Blue in the Arts*. He composes on a piano on which the note D is badly out of tune, a detail which Puccini reproduces in the Latin Quarter act where Schaunard is made to buy in a junk shop a hunting-horn whose note D is of uncertain intonation. This is realistically indicated in the orchestra by the clash, on the horn and trumpet, of D♭ against E♭.

Colline, the fourth male member of the Bohemian circle, is a composite character in whom Mürger immortalized two other friends. One was Jean Wallon, a student of theology, who wrote religious tracts and kept his pockets crammed with books. The other was the mysterious Trapadoux, called 'The Green Giant' because of his enormous height and his greatcoat which was so ancient that its original black had faded to green. In the novel Colline is a 'hyperphysical' philosopher who makes his living by giving lessons in 'mathematics, scholastics, botanics and various other sciences ending in *ics*'. He is always seen wearing a nut-coloured greatcoat whose 'durability made one think that it was built by the Romans', and in its pockets he carried about a whole library. In the opera Colline buys his famous garment in Act II only to sell it again in Act IV to buy cordials for the dying Mimi.

Puccini's old *beau* Alcindoro, whom Musetta treats with such ignominy in Act II, has no direct model in Mürger. The librettists manifestly derived this grotesque character from Carolus Barbemuche, a young poet and dandy in the novel, who is eager to be accepted by the Bohemians into their circle and for that purpose treats them collectively and severally to the most sumptuous repasts.* The first of these Lucullan feasts takes place at the Café Momus, which was situated at 15 Rue des Prêtres Saint-Germain l'Auxerrois, and whose proprietor himself had literary aspirations; it was the rendezvous of the four Bohemians, where they were known as the 'Four Musketeers'. From this episode Puccini's librettists developed the brilliant Latin Quarter act; but in the novel the Bohemians do not sit *outside* the Café Momus on a cold Christmas night as they do in the opera. The composer and his librettists must have been thinking of the covered Galleria Vittorio Emanuele in Milan when they planned this scene. Again it was the keen dramatic eye of Illica which first noticed this offence against verisimilitude. But it was only a week before the opera was fully completed, that he became aware of it and inserted in the libretto stage directions to the effect that the interior of the Café Momus is so crowded on Christmas Eve that some guests are forced to sit outside. It is curious that neither he nor Giacosa nor Puccini discovered this lapsus earlier and, as Mario Morini remarks, for spectators who have not carefully read the libretto, Illica's explanations remains non-existent. (*C.P.* Let.147, n.2).

Puccini's Benoit, boasting of his extra-marital escapades, is an exact replica of Rodolphe's landlord in the novel, while the doctor, whom Marcello goes to fetch in Act IV and who plays an important part in the novel, was drawn by Mürger after his friend, a certain Dr. Piogey, who died young. So much for Puccini's male characters.

As to Mimi and Musetta, both are composite characters in the novel. At least four of Mürger's mistresses had lent traits to his portrayal of Rodolphe's *petite amie*. There was, to begin with, his very first love, Marie-Virginie Vimal, blue-eyed, fair, frail, gentle and with the small white hands of which Mürger made a fetish. She is the heroine of every one of his subsequent books about Parisian Bohemia.† But her soul was not as white as her hands. She ran off with one of the author's friends, became involved in a criminal fraud, was arrested as an accomplice but later acquitted and went on the streets. Her desertion drove the young Mürger almost to suicide and this is the mood in which he pictures the hero of his novel in the chapter '*Epilogue des Amours de Rodolphe de Mademoiselle Mimi*'. Marie Vimal's place was soon taken by Lucille Louvet, a charming midinette who through starvation contracted tuberculosis and died in her early twenties. In the novel she is pictured partly in Francine and partly in the dying Mimi of the penultimate chapter. In real life Lucille was nicknamed 'Mimi'—hence the famous phrase with which the Mimi of the opera introduces herself to Rodolfo. Lucille's premature death preyed on Mürger's mind for a long time and he has told us about her at greater length in one of his later books. Another girl

---

* Barbemuche, whom Mürger draws with tongue in cheek, is said to represent a caricature of two of the author's personal enemies: Charles Barbara and Baudelaire. Some of the artists parodied in the novel hit back in kind, though in the years of his fame Baudelaire boasted of the early notoriety he had achieved through his intimacy with members of the original *Bohème*.

† *Le Pays Latin, Scènes de la Vie de Jeunesse, Les Buveurs d'Eau, Madame Olympe*, but none of these repeated the success of his first novel.

whose features coloured the portrait of Mimi of the novel was Juliette, a Shakespeare-loving grisette whom Mürger introduces in the amusing episode entitled *Roméo et Juliette*. Like her predecessors, she died young. According to Schanne's *Memoirs*, Mimi's portrait contained also traits of Mürger's young cousin Angèle, who later married a respectable husband. Mürger himself eventually settled down with Anaïs Latrasse, a young married woman and something of a blue-stocking, with whom he lived a happy *bourgeois* life till his death in 1861.

Mürger's Musette was partly drawn after one Marie Roux, the mistress of the poet Champfleury. At one time she had stood model for Ingres, and she was the owner of 'a pretty out-of-tune voice' on account of which Mürger nicknamed her 'Mademoiselle Bagpipe'. The other model for Musette is said to have been the wife of Pierre Dupont, the patriotic work-man-poet of Lyons and an intimate friend of Baudelaire. Madame Dupont made no bones about her promiscuous love affairs and thrived on them. In 1863 she set out on a voyage to Algiers, 'fortified' with 40,000 francs in her pocket, and was drowned.★ In the novel Musette is an intelligent and spirited girl, 'with some drops in her veins of the blood of Manon', an allusion which may well have suggested to Puccini's librettists the idea of associating Musetta in Act III with an elderly dandy; in Mürger she specializes only in young lovers. Coquettish and attractive to all men, she loved luxury and pleasure; but she was an adventuress with a heart of gold who really loved only one man, Marcel, yet was always unwilling 'to lock up her liberty in a marriage contract'. After a feverishly amorous career she finally became the wife of a respectable postmaster who, ironically enough, happened to be the guardian of a former lover of hers.

3

In a preface to the libretto, Illica and Giacosa indicated the principles by which they were guided in their dramatization of Mürger's novel and which they paraphrased thus: (1) to reproduce the essential spirit of the novel; (2) to remain faithful to Mürger's characters; (3) to reproduce, meticulously, certain details of the atmosphere; (4) to retain the general outline of Mürger's narrative and follow his method in presenting the story in distinct tableaux; (5) to treat the comic and tragic episodes with the freedom required by the dramatization of a novel. To have achieved all these aims, as they did, was indeed a *tour de force*. For Mürger's novel is crowded with incidents and characters some of whom pop up in a variety of different contexts and under different names. Furthermore, *Scènes* is not a closely knit novel but an almost casually arranged series of impressions, with no real plot to hold it together. The composer's and his poets' skill is seen in the fact that while they retained those undramatic features of Mürger's they succeeded in creating one of the most effective of all works for the musical stage. Admittedly the sequence of

★ In 1850 Schanne exhibited a painting of his called *Portrait of Mme. Pierre*, who was, presumably, Madame Dupont.

acts is loose, there is no strong dramatic motive to propel the action forward nor do the characters develop, but remain passive figures to whom things just happen; and Mimi's tragedy does not spring from the drama but is an adventitious element. The thin thread on which the plot hangs is her love affair with Rodolfo, and in order to add some missing links to the chain of incidents, the librettists resorted to the dubious dramatic device of prefacing each act with descriptive quotations from Mürger. Yet in retrospect the libretto of *La Bohème* must be judged a bold experiment in an impressionist stage technique by means of which a captivating atmosphere and striking yet essentially static episodes are made to take the place of a developing dramatic action. It was this novelty of approach which first told against the opera with Italian critics. Puccini himself never repeated this experiment but he found an imitator in Charpentier with his *Louise*.*

We recall that the opera was originally planned to have five scenes the third of which was being laid in the 'Courtyard of the House in Labruyère Street'. There was great wisdom in abolishing this scene which to a large extent duplicated the gay atmosphere of the 'Latin Quarter' act, and thus tended to tip the dramatic balance too much towards the comic. Now we have a perfect equilibrium: two gay and two sad acts, to say nothing of the correspondence as well as contrast that obtain between the happenings in Act I and Act IV. In addition, to have opened the opera with the 'Garret' scene was, dramatically and pyschologically, a masterstroke, for this scene enables the spectator to perceive the Bohemians first in their private world and thus fix them and their relationships to one another more firmly in his minds than would have been possible in the bustle of the 'Latin Quarter' act where our attention is, inevitably, divided between the soloists and the crowd. And by reserving the entry of Musetta with her Alcindoro for the second act, which was Puccini's idea, a dramatic element is introduced into this essentially static tableau of Parisian life.

Each of the four acts is concise, elegantly tailored, vivid and swift in its changes of scenes; and each ends with a theatrically effective situation. Puccini's great advance as a musical dramatist since *Manon Lescaut* is seen, *inter alia*, in the admirable economy with which he handles his many characters and scenes, notably that of Mimi's death. In addition, a great many details which in Mürger are distributed over the whole novel and associated with different personages and situations are neatly brought together and, often, concentrated in a single scene. With the exception of Mimi's death, there is not a scene in the opera which occurs in quite the same context or manner as in the novel where, incidentally, the story goes backwards and forwards in time. Nor must we overlook the skill with which the librettists adapted Mürger's easy conversational flow of language to Puccini's purposes.

In the process of reducing the numerous characters which people Mürger's

* I have it on reliable authority that Richard Strauss envied Puccini the success of *La Bohème* and for a time contemplated an opera of a similar character.

novel to a more manageable number, Schaunard and Colline lost the *amantes* with whom both were encumbered in the novel, and both are, inevitably, rather sketchy figures in comparison with their originals. And while Mürger aimed at the presentation of a group picture, with the two contrasting pairs of lovers nicely balanced against one another, in Puccini Marcello and Musetta are reduced to comic foils to the sentimental Rodolfo and Mimi. At the Paris production of *Bohème* (1898) the singer of Schaunard (Fuyère) was so splendid that Puccini regretted having allotted this character so little music of his own to sing. In the original (Turin) production Schaunard did have a solo in Act II, which was, however, subsequently eliminated, as were also a number of passages in other roles, all in order to tighten up the dialogue. In some instances these excisions were carried out with such carelessness that they resulted in obscurities in the remaining dialogue and even in the loss of important details of information.★

The operatic characters are painted in much the same colours as their prototypes in the novel—with one exception. This is Mimi, who in the opera is romanticized almost beyond recognition; in Mürger in fact she proclaims herself a direct descendant of Prévost's light o' love. After living with Rodolphe in a garret for eight months she begins to cast about for richer prey and to treat her lover abominably, and it is not until the long-suffering young idealist has obtained irrefutable proof of her infidelities that he sends her packing after a scene in which he all but strangles her. In Puccini's gentle hands Mürger's little gold-digger becomes all sweetness and innocence. When we first meet her she is living 'sola, soletta' and if she cannot go to church *always*, as she assures Rodolfo, yet she never omits to say her prayers; and when in Act III the lovers decide to separate, one of the few things she asks him to return to her is a prayer book. Of the less likeable side of her nature little is said in the opera. Most revealing of the concern with which the composer sought to whitewash his Mimi is his suppression, in the quotation from Mürger prefacing Act I, of certain lines which would have completely destroyed our illusions: 'at certain moments of boredom or bad temper her features assumed an appearance of almost savage brutality, so that a physiognomist might perhaps have recognized the signs either of a profound egotism or a complete lack of sensibility.' On the psychological reasons that moved the composer to cast a mantle of innocence on his fair sinners we have already commented earlier. Yet as it happens, Mürger himself provided the model for Puccini's all but pure Mimi.

Readers of the novel will recall the charming episode entitled *Francine's Muff* (unconnected with the main narrative), in which Francine is painted

★ Thus, in the present Act III, we are asked to believe that Rodolfo had told Marcello not a word about the reason—his quarrel with Mimi—which brings him to the inn at the crack of dawn. All we learn from Marcello's line to Mimi is that Rodolfo 'came just before dawn and overcome by fatigue he threw himself on a bench where he slumbers fast'. Yet in the original (uncut) version Marcello says: 'He came just before dawn, *without telling me why . . .*' which explains Marcello's surprise at Mimi's arrival at the inn.

Similarly, Rodolfo's reference in the same act, to 'un Moscardino (dandy) di Viscontino' remains obscure, owing to the abolition of the 'Courtyard' scene (see p. 82).

in the same roseate colours as Puccini's heroine. The alluring scene of Mimi's first encounter with Rodolfo is derived from that episode yet with the alteration of one significant scenic detail, manifestly for the purpose of representing Mimi in an innocent light. In the incident of the lost key, as told in the novel, it is the *girl* who finds it but quickly hides it so as to have an excuse for remaining in the room with her new friend (a sculptor named Jacques D.), while in the opera it is the young man who resorts to this ruse.

But the claim of Puccini's librettists that the idea of fusing the character of Mürger's Mimi with that of Francine was theirs cannot be accepted. This fusion was anticipated by Mürger himself in his play *La Vie de Bohème*, the heroine of which, Mlle Mimi Pinson (Chaffinch), is the image of Francine. That Illica and Giacosa drew substantially on the play is proved by a number of other parallels, some of which deserve mention.*

In the play, in contrast to the novel, the pair of sentimental lovers are made the leading characters and Mimi dies surrounded by all the Bohemians —precisely as happens in the opera. Similarly Musette, who in the novel is absent from the scene of Mimi's death, is present in the corresponding scene of the play; to show her as the compassionate girl she is, Mürger makes her go out to sell her bracelet for money to buy a muff for Mimi's freezing hands —a detail taken over from the Francine episode in the novel and made poignant use of in both the play and the opera; strangely enough, though, Puccini at first objected to the introduction of this 'muff' detail, declaring it a poor idea. Again the scene of Musetta's waltz in Act II of the opera was obviously suggested by the fact that in Act IV of the play a wealthy young widow gives a sumptuous party to which the four Bohemians and their womenfolk are invited and at which an offstage orchestra plays waltzes.†

4

Mürger's *Scènes* is, like Prévost's *Manon Lescaut*, a highly characteristic product of the Gallic mind; yet in Puccini's *Bohème* we no longer feel any discrepancy, as we do in his preceding opera, between the spirit of the subject and its operatic treatment. By the time he began the composition, his 'French' sensibility had developed to a such degree that he was able to identify himself completely with the particular atmosphere of his subject. Even so French a Frenchman as Debussy was moved to declare that 'if one did not keep a grip on oneself one would be swept away by the sheer verve of the music. I know of no one who has described the Paris of that time as well as Puccini in *La Bohème*'.[5] Countless performances year in year out‡

.* In a letter to Ricordi (13 July 1894) the composer explicitly asked the publisher to get Illica to search for valuable material in Mürger's other works.

† Mürger's play was with incidental music. Originally it was to have had a happy end, with Mimi being sent to Italy to recuperate; but Mürger's collaborator, Barrière, insisted that Mimi, like Puccini's Liù, 'must die'.

‡ It is said that the number of performances so far given of *Bohème* is the highest ever attained by any serious stage work, including plays.

have blunted our ears to the fact that Puccini's is one of the most original creations for the lyrical stage and the first opera in history to achieve an almost perfect fusion of romantic and realistic elements with impressionist features. In it Puccini speaks for the first time wholly in his own voice, and though he is tempted here and there to allow his lyrical bent too much elbow-room, by and large the dramatist has now completely caught up with the musician. Moreover the lessons learned from Massenet have now reached full deployment in the elegance and delicate shape of his lyrical phrases, especially those associated with the two sentimental lovers, while the Verdi of *Falstaff* is seen to have exercised a fruitful influence in the many vivid conversational passages. But Puccini excels Verdi in giving his little snatches of dialogue, despite their natural (realistic) inflexions, a slight lyrical and, thus, expressive touch. In his own words he wished 'there to be as much singing, as much *melody*, as possible'—even in so tiny a phrase as:

Ex. 29   Rodolfo

Seg-ga vi-ci-no al fuo-co... A-spet-ti... un po' di vi-no...

In *Bohème* we also become for the first time aware of Puccini's *Kleinkunst*, his penchant for the musical depiction of minute scenic details by which inanimate things suddenly spring to poetic life: the gay flicker of flames in the stove, Rodolfo sprinkling water on Mimi as she swoons, the ray of sun that suddenly falls on the face of the dying girl and so forth. It is perhaps in this sphere that his chamber-music style is seen at its most exquisite. Equally noteworthy is his calculated choice of instruments for the characterization of persons and scenes: chiefly strings for Rodolfo and Mimi; woodwind for Musetta and the rest of the Bohemians; the full orchestra, with especially brilliant effects on the brass, for the *Latin Quarter* act, and chamber music for the intimate scenes between the lovers. Mimi's death is a particularly memorable instance of this, with its half-lights (low-lying strings, wood-wind and harp) and solo passages as tenuous as the lines of a Japanese print.

The melodic style shows an increasingly free, almost improvisatory character: the phrases tend to overlapping and irregular patterns,* in the comic scenes the aphorism prevails, just as does Puccini's flexible mosaic—all of which combines to give an impression of the utmost spontaneity and naturalness. In the harmony we observe pointillistic touches, discords are often resolved in elliptical fashion, especially at the end of a scene where a pause serves to allow the first harmony to evaporate before the next is sounded. And as noted already in *Manon Lescaut*, though there it is only

---

* See the Christmas Carol, Act I, 16: 3+3+2+2+3 etc., Mimi's 'Oh! Sventata!', Act I, one bar after 27: 3+2+3+2 etc., Act II, seven bars after 1: Puccini harnesses a 5/8 figure to a 2/4 metre which has an almost Stravinskyian look. Indeed the opening of the 'Latin Quarter' act with its outdoor orchestration foreshadows the 'Shrove-Tide Fair' in *Petrushka*. Was this a case of unconscious influence on the Russian composer?

tentative, harmonic progressions are raised to the status of characterizing motives often consisting of no more than a sequence of parallel fifths, as in the 'Death Knell' and the 'Snow Flakes' figures (Exs. 6b and 36). Yet, with all this freedom in the harmonic idiom, the composer still believes in the cohesive power of central keys and the dramatic symbolism of progressive tonality. Thus, Act I is, broadly, centred on C, Act II begins in F and ends in B♭, while Act IV, which leads to the tragic dénouement, moves from C major to C♯ minor.

5

Let us now turn to a consideration of the characters. The chief *dramatis personae* being Rodolfo and Mimi, they are, of course, allotted the largest share of the music. The young poet introduces himself in the famous 'Nei cieli bigi', taken from the abortive *La Lupa* where it was to have been sung in praise of the radiant Sicilian sky and the fuming Mount Etna, whereas now it is associated with 'grey skies and fuming chimneys'. This is one of the many instances in which Puccini ignores the verbal sense originally attached to the musical phrase and uses the latter simply because it happens to fit equally the mood of another character or situation—here the exuberance of Rodolfo:

Ex. 30

This is his leitmotive. For the full portrayal of the romantic lover we have to wait until his encounter with Mimi where he has his great aria—really two arias linked by an *arioso* in which love's awakening, from the utmost tenderness to passionate ecstasy, is conveyed irresistibly. 'Che gelida manina' is one of the purest and most fragrant melodies that ever came into Puccini's head. We note the chant-like opening in *pp* and the disembodied beauty of the orchestral texture, with muted strings drawing a filigree against the vocal lines which is gently continued by the solo harp. Rodolfo gains heart in the *arioso* 'Chi son?' and then proceeds to describe his poor poet's life in 'In povertà', which is a rhythmic variation of his leitmotive, after which he breaks out into the passionate ardour of

Ex. 31

which henceforth stands for the idea of romantic love. Throughout the opera Rodolfo's music is marked by such leaping anacruses, diatonic steps, restless changes of the rhythmic shape and 'emotional' triplets.

Mimi is caught in a masterly musical vignette. 'Mi chiamano Mimi' is cast in the form of a free Rondo (A–B–A–C–D–B) in which the composer, with much psychological finesse, points different aspects of her nature. The childlike simplicity, her main trait, is at once limned in her leitmotive; it inevitably recalls the phrase with which Massenet introduces Manon in the first act of his opera, yet the Puccinian stamp is clearly seen in the tritone and the drooping cadential figure:

Ex. 32

(a) (Manon)

(b) (Mimi)

The composer clearly distinguishes between the little seamstress going demurely about her trivial daily tasks and the romantic girl dreaming of love's spring, as she does in the expansive 'Ma quando' which forms the climax of this mosaic of ariettes. And how true to her psychology is the simple *parlando* 'Altro di me', with which she casually concludes her artless little tale.

In his portrayal of the second pair of lovers, Puccini renders Musetta a more articulate musical character than her Marcello. Like Mimi, she introduces herself in a manner reminiscent of Massenet's Manon—the elegant courtesan of the *Le Cours-la-Reine* act—in a sprightly, capricious three-bar theme:

Ex. 33

(a) (Manon)

(b) (Musetta)

The coaxing Musetta, the coquette enamoured of her own feminine charms and naïvely proud of her attraction for all men, is admirably captured in her famous waltz. With its swaying, languid melody in the style of a French slow *Valse*, it fits the character of Musetta like a glove, though originally it was, oddly enough, a 'nautical' piece—another instance of Puccini's making apt use of previous material in a new context.* In this piece, inserted for its own, musical sake rather than to advance the action, the composer pays tribute to the tradition of the older type of *opéra-comique*.

Marcello, it must be admitted, is treated rather cavalierly. He has no solo aria, asserting himself only in a quartet and duet. Like his friends Schaunard and Colline, he is less an individual character (which he is in Mürger) than a group figure, and all three are often associated with the 'Bohème' theme, which Puccini lifted from his early *Capriccio* (Ex. 11). Strangely enough, although Schaunard and Colline are less important characters than the choleric lover of Musetta, they have, in contrast to him, their own leading-motives—the musician a kind of French quick-march and the philosopher a gruff, lapidary phrase:

Ex. 34

But Puccini, never too meticulous in his use of characterizing ideas, employs Ex. a for general 'Bohemian' purposes too. He has also sketched in the episodic figure of the landlord Benoit, meek, timid, and somewhat bizarre but naïvely self-important when it comes to boasting of his amorous adventures in 'Non dico una balena'.† The music of Benoit, with its faint echo of Beckmesser's, provides the first evidence of Puccini's possession of a grotesque vein.

* This waltz had come into being as a piano piece. The idea for it occurred to Puccini one day out shooting on his beloved lake at Torre del Lago, as he sat in his boat gently rocked by the waves. Its next appearance was at the ceremony of launching a battleship at Genoa, for which occasion he had been invited, together with Mancinelli and Franchetti, to compose something. It was probably performed there in an orchestral version.

But before it could be used a third time, i.e. put into the mouth of Musetta, Giacosa had to find a suitable text. In order to give him a sample of the required verse-metre, Puccini sent him this 'poetic' line: 'Coccoricó, coccoricó, bistécca'—'Cock-adoodle-do, cock-adoodle-do, beefsteak', which Giacosa transmuted to 'Quando m'en vo', quando m'en vo' soletta'.

† An amusing detail here is the squeaking seconds on the woodwind as Benoit expresses his dislike of 'thin' women.

The hallmark of *Bohème* is the astounding sleight-of-hand with which Puccini manages an incessant interplay of action, characters and atmosphere. It all seems in the nature of an inspired improvisation, yet analysis reveals a well-organized ground-plan which takes care of musical coherence and musical contrasts: Thus Act I shows a sharp division into two halves. Like the opening act of *Manon Lescaut*, the first half is in the character of a bubbling Scherzo-cum-Rondo, with snappy two/four and six/eight rhythms and with the 'Bohemian' and 'Rodolfo' themes playing the part of *ritornelli* in this profuse flow of ideas. Certain self-contained episodes stand out. There is the charming description of the flickering flames, devouring Rodolfo's manuscript with chords of the added sixth so laid out as to suggest bitonality Gb major against Eb minor:

Ex. 35

There is the delightful 'Christmas Eve' song, 'Quando un olezzo', archaic in flavour with its parallel (organum-like) fifths and reminiscent of a French carol.* And there is, by way of an extended lyrical trio, the insinuating music which accompanies Benoit's unwelcome visit.

With Mimi's timid knocking at the door the mood changes at a stroke, the orchestra stealing in softly, *lento*, with her theme (Ex. 32b) which tells us who is without. The brilliant, gay lights of the first half of the act are now turned down to a soft glow, and as the love scene unfolds the strings take over from the woodwind, the tonalities become more settled and the quicksilvery *parlando* of the four Bohemians yields place to slow and sustained melodies. This second half of Act I provides a *locus classicus* of Puccini's art in gradually building up an extended love scene to a poetic climax. At first, all is light conversation, though a sinister hint is thrown out in the 'illness' theme which punctuates Mimi's fit of coughing. Rodolfo's solicitous questions and her brief answers are small talk, but small talk that has never been made to sound more enchanting in a musical setting. A few broken-up phrases of *arioso*, pauses, and an insignificant little *ostinato* on the strings *pizzicato*, that is all; but we seem to hear the heart-beats of two young people irresistibly drawn to each other. In the following scene—the search for the lost key, again a trivial incident—the music gains in warmth and substance and leads with an exquisite transition to the central portion of the duet—the two arias already discussed. With his subtle sense of balance Puccini now feels that a change of mood is indicated. To have immediately followed the arias with a proper duet—the two lovers not having sung together so far—might have spelt monotony, and so the situation is disturbed by the impatient calls of the

* Act I, at [16]

other Bohemians who have meanwhile been awaiting Rodolfo in the courtyard. After this interruption the ensuing duet, entirely made up of reminiscences from Rodolfo's aria, at last unites the lovers in an impassioned embrace to the strains of the 'love' motive (Ex. 31). But they leave the scene in muted ecstasy, the music only whispering the melody of 'Che gelida manina'.* Puccini was never to surpass the delicate poetry of this love scene.

Admittedly the *Latin Quarter* act is, with the exception of Musetta's waltz, not as memorable in invention as the *Garret* act. Its outstanding feature lies in the vivid evocation of Christmas Eve in a Paris boulevard, with the interest shifting constantly between the crowd and the soloists until both are united in the final climax of the Military Tattoo. In contrast to the tender intimacy of Act I Puccini writes 'outdoor' music conjuring up the buoyant and vibrant air of a Christmas Fair. Yet for all the apparent casualness in which the scenes succeed each other, the act is more or less firm in its musical structure consisting of four distinct sections, each with its own thematic material, though this freely overlaps, and with the last three scenes anchored in definite keys. The general atmosphere is at once established with the 'Christmas Eve' theme now scored for three trumpets, *marcatissimo*, in close harmony, and punctuated by the excited shouts of the chorus. In the ensuing scenes the music fluctuates between, on the one hand, the racy 'Latin Quarter' music, the various street cries and the children's excited greetings of Parpignol and his toys, and, on the other, the lyrical episodes in which the Bohemians come to the fore. Here we note the leisurely 'Promenade' theme† and Rodolfo's ecstatic 'Dal mio cervel' which deftly varies the poet's leitmotive (Ex. 30). A point often missed in the theatre is that, on Rodolfo's introduction of his sweetheart to his friends, 'This is Mimi, a gay flower-girl', the orchestra anticipates the 'Death Knell' motive of Act III (Ex. 6b, p. 277).

The second section, opening with Musetta's entry, unfolds in the key of A♭ and is all but dominated by the 'Musetta' theme (Ex. 33b). With the third section in E major we arrive at the lyrical core of the act. This is Musetta's alluring waltz, first sung as a solo (though with Puccini's usual interjections from other characters) and later repeated in a sextet to round off the whole scene. Purely as vocal ensemble, the sextet is an admirable piece, but Puccini dodges individual characterizations. It is only Musetta who is suggestively limned in her wide skips and staccato patter, though the fact that Marcello doubles the waltz melody is, no doubt, to be taken as an indication that the painter has at last yielded to the charm of his fickle mistress. The link with the finale is cunningly effected by the offstage drum-rolls of the approaching Tattoo, into which the last strains of the waltz merge. This last section, in the key of B♭, is based on an authentic French march of the time

---

* Unfortunately, Puccini's demand that the last phrase be sung *pp perdendosi* is ignored by most singers, some tenors even taking it into their heads to correct the composer by doubling Mimi's C *in alt*, though their final note is E.

† Twelve bars after [4].

of King Louis Philippe and fragments of previous themes are added as in a mosaic.* Yet in this finale the composer is seen to make things easy for himself, introducing one reminiscence after another, with only one new tune, Musetta's 'E dove s'è'; but with the exception of the latter, we fail to perceive their strict relevance to the happenings on the stage. His whole concern appears to have been to provide a spectacular diversion with the Tattoo and join together his vocal and orchestral forces anyhow, to create a rousing climax, which he indeed achieves.†

In Act III, the *Barrière d'Enfer*, the first deep shadows begin to fall on the love affair of Rodolfo and Mimi. An initial indication of this is given in the orchestral introduction, an evocation of a bleak morning in February, by means which could not be simpler or more telling: a shuddering tremolo of bare fifths on the cellos sustained as a bass pedal for over a hundred bars, and above it a succession of bare parallel fifths on flutes and harp, suggestive of falling snowflakes, all cold and brittle as glass:

Ex.36

BASS : D - A

As in the third act of *Manon Lescaut*, where the song of the Lamplighter served to introduce a momentary touch of gaiety, so here a pervasive air of desolation is lightened for brief spells by gay snatches of song coming from inside the inn, among them fragments of Musetta's waltz, thus telling us of her presence—an idea of Ricordi's which Puccini accepted, as it fell in with his predilection for introducing offstage voices. Add the interjections of the customs officials and the gavotte-like music of the milk vendors, and the result is a perfect genre-picture.

In the following scenes further traits are added to the portraits of Mimi and Rodolfo. In her duet with Marcello, 'C'è Rodolfo?', with its drooping phrases, halting syncopations and nervous triplets, the girl shows her anguish at her lover's changed feelings for her. Rodolfo, on the other hand, is seen to go through several emotions—impatience, bitterness and the torments of jealousy; but it must be confessed that the music here is neither distinctly expressive of those emotions nor particularly inspired, except for

* The march is scored for a stage orchestra comprising four piccolos, six trumpets in B♭ and an equal number of side-drums.

† Among the various improvements made by Puccini in both text and music in the light of subsequent performances, there is an important one at the close of Act II. Originally it ended with a few words sung by Alcindoro while the crowd of the Bohemians and students were already leaving the stage—assuredly, an anticlimax or 'ghiacciaio' (lit. 'glacier') as Puccini called it, and as it was also felt by Ricordi and the poets. The addition of the final chorus as we now have it—'Eccola! Il bel tambur maggior!'—repeating the previous march, and of a few concluding bars on the orchestra, was made in spring or summer of 1896.

the A minor section 'Mimì è una civetta', an impassioned lament in the vein of Des Grieux's 'Manon, sempre la stessa'. It is not until the moment when Rodolfo is overcome by despair and tells Marcello of Mimì's mortal illness that Puccini fully rises to the occasion, in 'Mimì è tanto malata', with a sombre figure in the orchestra sounding like funeral bells (Ex. 6b). Tension is added to this scene by the fact that Mimì overhears him, unseen by her lover, and so is given the first intimation of the sad end that is awaiting her.

The music for the concluding Farewell, 'Addio, dolce svegliare', is bodily transferred from a song *Sole e amore* which Puccini wrote in 1888 for the magazine *Paganini*:

Ex.37

Il sole al - le - gra - men - te batte ai tuoi ve - tri——

This song, now provided with different words, is repeated twice, but with an effective contrast at the first repeat when the duet turns into a quartet with the addition of the furious patter of Musetta and Marcello, who are engaged in one of their perennial quarrels. The act ends in a mood of tranquil rapture similar to that of Act I, Mimì and Rodolfo singing their last line as they slowly walk off the stage hand in hand.★

The setting and dramatic structure of Act IV is the same as that of the opening act, yet with the difference that its first half now reveals a tense, febrile quality, a high-pitched brilliance, as though the four Bohemians vaguely sensed the imminent tragedy and were trying to conceal their malaise in artificial hilarity. The rhythms now are tauter, the phrases more fragmentary and the orchestration is harsher, even ferocious at times, with the brass frequently in action,† especially after Schaunard and Colline have joined their two friends. But before plunging into this mood of forced gaiety, Puccini inserts one of those poetic vignettes so characteristic of his dramatic style. This is the charming episode in which Rodolfo and Marcello contemplate with nostalgic affection the knick-knacks left them by their inconstant mistresses. Their exquisitely tender and dreamy duet 'O Mimì' suggests a momentary escape from reality and Puccini seems to indicate its parenthetical character in the context of the action by enclosing the text in brackets. After gathering up this wistful mood in a brief orchestral postlude —a last glance backwards to past memories—in a unison for solo violin (Rodolfo) and solo cello (Marcello), the composer turns again to action

---

★ At Mimì's words: 'Vorrei che eterno durasse il verno!'—'Would that the winter lasted for ever!'—Puccini quotes on the oboe, twice, the opening of the 'Bohème' theme (Ex. 11), the exact relevance of which to the present situation remains obscure. Perhaps the passage is intended to suggest that visions of her past happiness with the Bohemians, when she first met Rodolfo, are flashing through Mimì's mind.

† Note, for example, the striking contrast in the scoring of the 'Bohème' theme at the respective openings of Act I and Act IV.

and brings us down to earth with Rodolfo's 'Che ora sia?' 'What may be the time?'

With few notable exceptions, one of these being the above duet, the music for Act IV is made up of reminiscences, a fact to which strong objection was taken by both critics and the public at first; yet Puccini's use of themes and motives from the gay Acts I and II in this new context is psychologically astute and logical. Moreover, he makes the orchestra the chief narrator of the unfolding tragedy, e.g. at the violent jerk from the chord of B♭ to that of E minor when Musetta unexpectedly bursts on the scene with the news of Mimi's imminent arrival; or Mimi, now a shadow of her former self, being caught in this version of her leitmotive, scored for cor anglais and violas above a shuddering bass:

Ex. 38

or again, Musetta's subsequent account of her chance meeting with the dying girl, 'Intesi dire', which is accompanied by syncopations like the spasmodic beatings of an anguished heart. On several occasions the orchestra tells the spectator of a turn in the action which has not yet been realized by the characters themselves. Thus the sudden shift from D♭ major to B minor at [29] informs us that Mimi has fallen into a sleep from which she will never wake; similarly, when toward the end of the opera Rodolfo asks in tones of fear, 'What is the meaning of this coming and going, why do you look at me like this?', it is the orchestra alone which gives the answer in a heart-rending threnody.

From a dramatic point of view, we might, in the scene of Mimi's death, question the insertion of Colline's little song 'Vecchia zimarra', which tends to delay the action and distract our attention from the heroine. Colline's intention to sell his coat could have been indicated in a phrase or two, and that in fact was originally the case; but having cut an earlier aria for him, the composer no doubt felt that this lovable character had received too meagre a musical treatment, and so added this song at the last moment. Yet who would miss Colline's apostrophe to his old garment, so moving in its gentle sadness and so poetic an example of the composer's skill in breathing life into inanimate things.

Puccini would not have been Puccini had he not immortalized Mimi's last moments with one of the most inspired melodies that ever sprang into his head. Her 'Sono andati' is sadness incarnate, with its vocal line descending scale-wise an octave down to middle C, darkened by the doubling on

Ex.39 Andante calmo

So - no anda - ti? Fin-ge - vo di dor - mi - re, per - chè

vol - li con te so-la re-sta - re   Ho tan-te co - se che ti vo-glio

di - re   o u-na   so - la   ma gran-de come il ma - re

the cellos and punctuated by the throb of funereal chords (Ex. 39). Yet he could not resist the temptation to follow the practice of *verismo* and repeat this poignant theme in the orchestral epilogue at the very close of the opera, where it blazes out on the full orchestra *tutta forza*, the opening brass chords striking down on the spectator like the knife of a guillotine.*

After her sustained C minor melody the dying Mimi summons her last strength in the soaring phrase 'Sei il mio amor'; as she grows weaker the music becomes increasingly transparent and attenuated until it is reduced to the merest whisper when, already in a delirium, the girl recalls her first meeting with Rodolfo on that far-off Christmas Eve, the orchestra now stealing in with the strain of 'Che gelida manina' in colours of disembodied beauty. There are few closing scenes, including the finale of *Traviata*, to equal that of Mimi's death in pathos and the power to move the spectator to compassion.

* The last four bars repeat the final cadence from Colline's song—manifestly for no other reason than that it happened to suit the mood at the close of this orchestral peroration.

Before leaving *Bohème* it will be opportune to cast a brief glance at Leoncavallo's sister-work (1897), if, largely, for the purpose of making us realize, in an indirect fashion, the excellence and, indeed, uniqueness of Puccini's opera.

Leoncavallo drew for his libretto on other novels of Mürger's besides the *Scènes*, also on some of his poems, and to that extent his opera is richer both in incidents and literary images than Puccini's. The work is in four acts and, faithful to the tenets of documentary realism then in vogue, Leoncavallo gives the specific date on which the action of each act takes place (at quarterly intervals), the drama beginning on Christmas Eve 1837 and terminating on Christmas Eve 1838. In contrast to both Mürger and Puccini, he made Marcello (tenor) and Musetta (mezzo-soprano) his leading characters, while Rodolfo (baritone) and Mimi (lyric soprano) remain episodic figures until the final act in which the composer-librettist suddenly changes the dramatic course by switching over to the death scene of Mimi, in order to obtain a tragic ending. In consequence, the unity of the action and its equilibrium is gravely upset.

Like Puccini, Leoncavallo retains Schaunard and Colline but burdens the latter with a female encumbrance, the simpleton Euphemia of the novel, and also introduces Mürger's young fop and would-be poet Barbemuche. As with Puccini, his first two acts are designed to depict the gay and frivolous aspects of Bohemian life* but in turning to its more serious side in the following two acts Leoncavallo overshoots the mark. As the out-and-out verist he was, he laid undue emphasis on sordidness, misery and violence, presenting scenes charged with savage passions as when in Act III Marcello, in a fit of insensate jealousy, attempts to strangle his faithless Musetta. This is a far cry from the amusing set-to between the pair in Puccini's Act III or from the gentleness and poetry with which he treats the lovers' quarrel of the other pair in the same act. In other words, Puccini's perfect blend of laughter with tears, of comedy with pathos, is absent from Leoncavallo's treatment, to say nothing of the inferiority of his craftsmanship. Nor does Leoncavallo evince his rival's homogeneity of style; he darts from Tristanesque chromaticism to plain diatonic writing and from Viennese waltzes to pastiches of eighteenth-century minuets and gavottes. None the less, it cannot be contested that in his later acts Leoncavallo succeeds in achieving a considerable dramatic impact, notably in dark, gloomy scenes reminiscent of Verdi at his most sombre. Thus, Rodolfo's *scena* 'Scuoti, o vento!' is a very stirring piece in that vein and deserves resuscitation. Indeed, in a crudely dramatic sense, Leoncavallo's *Bohème* may be said to be superior to Puccini's. Yet the main reason for its all but total eclipse—it can occasionally still be seen in Italy—lies in its lack of poetry and of memorable lyrical invention.

* Incidentally, Leoncavallo's opera contains an act very similar to the 'Courtyard' scene in the original scheme of Puccini's *Bohème* libretto.

XXIX

Tosca

Principal Characters

Floria Tosca, a celebrated singer	..	..	Soprano
Mario Cavaradossi, a painter	..	..	Tenor
Baron Scarpia, chief of police	..	..	Baritone
Cesare Angelotti ..	..	..	.. Bass

Rome—June 1800.

I

SHORTLY AFTER THE FIRST PRODUCTION of the play (24 November 1887), as happened frequently in his long career, Sardou was accused of brazen plagiarism. First came Ernest Daudet, the brother of Alphonse, who contended that some details of the plot came from his play *La Saint-Aubin* in which the heroine was a singer and the action of which took place on the eve of Napoleon's battle at Marengo. Like Sardou, Daudet had written his play for Sarah Bernhardt and the scandal was not without its piquancy, as Daudet declared that he had read the manuscript to her, thus insinuating that she had given away the plot to his rival. The second accusation came from the American playwright Maurice Barrymore, who asserted that the motives of Scarpia's infamous bargain with Tosca and his double-crossing resulting in the death of the two lovers had been stolen from his play *Nadjeska* (1884).* Whatever the truth, Sardou refuted all these charges. He pointed out that being a voracious reader of history he had hit on the subject of *Tosca* in an episode of the religious wars in sixteenth-century France. This episode is said to have occurred at Toulouse where the Catholic Connétable de Montmorency had promised a Protestant peasant woman that he would save her husband from execution if she gave herself to him. She consented and her reward was to see next morning her husband's corpse suspended from the gallows.⁶ Incidents of this kind are likely to have taken place in times of war and revolution in many countries, and a similar incident forms the subject of a folk ballad still sung in the Italian province of Emilia.

Sardou, never too scrupulous in borrowing ideas from other writers—like Molière, he took his material wherever he found it—may well have elaborated that supposedly authentic incident into a double murder and suicide, either from Barrymore's play or possibly Victor Hugo's prose drama *Angelo, Tyrant of Padua* (1835), or Ponchielli's *La Gioconda* (1876), Boito's libretto being based on this play. Indeed the parallels in the story as

* Barrymore was the founder of the famous theatrical family.

told by Sardou and by Boito are too close to suggest a mere coincidence: like Tosca, Gioconda is a singer though merely of street ballads; like Tosca, she is of a madly jealous disposition, and this is played upon, for his nefarious purposes, by the Scapia-like Barnaba, a spy in the service of the Venetian Inquisition; and like Tosca, Gioconda is confronted with the choice of either yielding to Barnaba or forgeiting the life of her lover Enzio; but rather than suffer the fate alleged to be worse than death she stabs herself when Barnaba demands his price.

Yet another possible source for Sardou's drama may be in the life-story of the French revolutionary poet André Chénier,* who may indeed have provided the model for the painter-hero, the Chevalier Mario Cavaradossi, while Sardou's motive of the unknown blonde woman who is seen to frequent the church supposedly to pray—the Marchesa Attavanti of both the play and Puccini's opera—appears to have been derived from Scribe's *Adrienne Lecouvreur*, on which the Italian composer Cilèa later drew for his opera of that name.

2

Sardou's ingredients for *Tosca* were sex, sadism, religion and art, mixed by the hands of a master-chef with the whole dish served on the platter of an important historical event. Yet if his play is sheer melodrama it is melodrama at its most consummate—Shaw's *Sardoodledom* raised to the *n*th degree. On closer examination it is seen to represent an ingenious blend of elements from character-drama, the psychological thriller, *Grand Guignol* and the historical play. It is character-drama because the whole tragedy springs from Tosca's abnormal jealousy—for without this fundamental trait in her Scarpia could not have worked his devilish stratagems even as Iago could not have worked his without Othello's fatal disposition. Sardou by implication acknowledges his indebtedness to the Shakespeare tragedy in Act II of his play, when Scarpia is suddenly struck by the idea of using the Marchesa Attavanti's fan, the linchpin in the drama, to the same purpose, as he avers, as Iago used Desdemona's handkerchief. (This important detail is in Puccini's opera transferred to Act I.) *Tosca* is also a psychological thriller in that Sardou, after enmeshing his characters in a net carefully and adroitly laid, shows us their different and swiftly changing reactions in minute detail, as he pulls the net together with gradually increasing speed. Whatever may be said against Sardou's treatment in other respects, he proves himself a master in analysing his characters with economy and verisimilitude. *Grand Guignol* with a vengeance are the torture scene, the Execution, an attempted rape, a murder and two suicides. At the end we count no less than four corpses—Angelotti, Scarpia, Cavaradossi and Tosca—and as Puccini jokingly remarked to Ricordi: 'Perhaps Sardou will insist on killing Spoletta too.' Small wonder that after the first production of the play Sardou was nicknamed 'the Caligula of the theatre'.

The historical element, so dear to Sardou's heart but not to Puccini's,

* Illica's libretto for Giordano's best-known opera was in turn coloured by Sardou's *Tosca*!

lies in the authentic background of Napoleon's invasion of Italy in 1800 and his victory over the Austrians at Marengo on 17 June, against which the action unfolds. But this background is more than just trappings, for Sardou makes dramatic use of an important historical motive—the conflict in Italy between the Republicans and the Royalists—in the persecution of Angelotti and Cavaradossi by Scarpia, who is the tool of Royalist autocracy and the forerunner of those real chiefs of secret police which modern totalitarian countries have produced. Sardou also introduces military and political events in the action: in Act II a fête is given at the Palazzo Farnese to celebrate General Mélas's supposed victory over Napoleon's army, at which Tosca is to sing in a cantata by Paisiello. This celebration comes to an abrupt end with one of Sardou's typical *coups de théâtre* when the news is brought in that the Royalist army had after all been defeated at Alessandria, and this gives Tosca the welcome opportunity to leave and seek out Cavaradossi in his country villa, where she suspects him to be with the Marchesa Attavanti.

In this second act, built up as a magnificent stage spectacle, Sardou introduces such authentic personages as Maria-Caroline, Queen of Naples, 'august daughter of the Empress Maria Theresa, sister of Marie Antoinette of sad memory, and worthy and glorious wife of His Majesty King Ferdinand the Fourth', as the Sacristan reverently informs Cavaradossi's valet in Act I. In addition there is the Austrian General Froehlich, the Duke of Ascoli, Paisiello and others. Sardou also attempts to present a picture of Roman society ridden by intrigues and idle gossip, and indulges his satirical vein by allowing his characters to make caustic comparisons between the Italians and the French. The latter are represented by Vicomte de Trévilhac, an *émigré*, who detests Napoleon, but at the news of his victory cannot help exclaiming '*I* am beaten . . . but *we* have won! Vive la France!' Similarly, when the conversation turns to the subject of the Marchesa Attavanti, some of the characters discourse on the subtle differences between a married woman's lover and her *cicisbeo*. As in Puccini's opera, the Marchesa never appears in person in the play and the frivolous conversation is carried on at the expense of her fatuous husband, who is present. Sardou, incidentally, began his career with satirical comedies in which he castigated the morals of French society.

This then was the general character of the play. It certainly furnished Puccini a subject for a most powerful contribution to the growing body of veristic opera. The task of fashioning it into a libretto was a far easier proposition than in the case of *La Bohème*, where Mürger's novel had to be recast in the dramatic form. Sardou's play presented an almost ready-made libretto; yet 'almost' covers a number of important modifications. Puccini soon realized that the play could not be used in precisely the shape which its author had given it. He was not interested in the historical sub-plot with its many authentic details—to his way of thinking, superfluous trimmings— any more than he was interested in the political and ideological implications of the drama. Puccini's all but complete elimination of the sub-plot which in Sardou's Act II does, indeed, distract the spectator's attention from the essential drama, adds greatly to the tautness of the operatic plot, to say nothing of the fact that the classical unities of time, place and action were strengthened. Of Sardou's by-play Puccini retained just enough for the spectator to see the drama in a general historical perspective, concentrating on the central dramatic and emotional situations. But in thus reducing the characters and action, he inevitably presents us with some *faits accomplis* not always quite obvious to the spectator, and Sardou's well-knit, logical structure as well as his characterization suffers in the process. The play was in five acts and brought no less than twenty-three characters on to the stage, while the opera has three acts with only nine characters, five of whom are subsidiary plus one voice, the Shepherd of Act III. And while Sardou, in unfolding his drama, proceeded, like a chess-player, by slow, well-timed moves, Puccini preferred swift dramatic strokes and a close sequence of strong situations, so that Giacosa was not far from the truth when he complained that, whereas *Bohème* was all poetry and no plot, *Tosca* was all plot and no poetry.* Certainly the plot tends to override the characters, notably in Act II; and where Sardou draws his characters in the round, slowly adding touch after touch to his portrayals and thus allowing them to grow before our eyes, Puccini is compelled to foreshorten psychological development, especially in the case of Scarpia, and in the event to deprive his characters of that biographical perspective which they possess in Sardou. Admittedly, the characters and the essential action in the opera are self-explanatory, yet it is perhaps as well to listen to the opera with Sardou's fuller and more articulate presentation at the back of our minds.

3

Thus we learn that Mario Cavaradossi is the descendant of an ancient family of Roman patricians. (In the play he is addressed as 'Excellency'.) He inherited his great fortune as well as his liberal, anti-Royalist outlook from his father who frequented in Paris the society of Diderot and d'Alembert and stood on terms of friendship with Voltaire. Cavaradossi's mother was French and a great-niece of the philosopher Helvetius. He himself was brought up in Paris during the time of the Revolution when he worked in the studio of the great painter David. Family affairs brought him to Rome, but the chief reason for his prolonged stay there is Tosca, the great singer and idol of the Roman populace whom he met at the Teatro Argentina about a year before the drama takes place. Cavaradossi is an intellectual who tries to bring some enlightenment to the mind of his piously devout Tosca; he gives her *La nouvelle Héloïse* to read, but it bores her since the characters 'do nothing but talk and never make love'. Soon he will be leaving with Tosca for Venice where she is to fulfil a season's engagement, and thus turn his back on Rome for good. The Eternal City is not a safe place for him. Although he does not engage in any revolutionary activities, he is suspect in Royalist circles on account of his upbringing and his sympathy for Napoleonic

* See his letter on p. 102.

France. He dresses in the French style and wears a goatee which, as the Sacristan avers with horror in Act I, is an outward sign of atheism.*

In order to mislead the authorities as to his true political convictions, Cavaradossi has offered his services to the Jesuit Chapter of Sant' Andrea della Valle to paint a mural in the church. From these few details it is not difficult to perceive that Sardou's Cavaradossi represents a more individual and more mature character than Puccini's impulsive tenor.

Tosca too emerges from the play as a somewhat grander, more imperious figure than she is in the opera—a prima donna *pur sang*, throwing her tantrums at the slightest provocation, no respecter of persons and by turns impatient, capricious, amorous and religious. To show her in the role of a spoiled Diva, Sardou has in Act II an amusing little scene between her and Paisiello. They are about to begin his cantata when the following dialogue develops:

> P.: Are you ready, Diva?
> T.: Yes, yes, I am ready. Let's get on quick!
> P.: B natural, isn't it?
> T.: No, B flat!
> P.: Oh!
> T. (*violently*): B flat!
> P. (*turning to the orchestra*): B flat, B flat, gentlemen!
> (*At that moment the Queen arrives, taking her time to get to her seat.*)
> T. (*sotto voce*): Good God! When is she going to sit down, *that* Queen?
> Scarpia: Gracious me! Not so loud!
> (*The Queen takes her seat.*)
> T.: At last!
> P. (*to Tosca*): Maestoso?
> T.: Yes!
> P.: Largo . . . Largo. . .
> T.: You bore me.
> P.: Yes, charming lady! (*To Scarpia:* She has her nerves, you know!)

Paisiello is throughout represented as an obsequious figure anxious to ingratiate himself with the Queen so as to wipe out the incriminating memory of his sympathy with the Republicans. He later enjoyed the patronage of Napoleon, who was a great admirer of his music.

Tosca's two great faults, Cavaradossi informs Angelotti in Act I, are her jealousy and her excessive religiosity. She hides nothing from her Father Confessor and being an ardent Royalist she might, her lover fears, betray Angelotti whom she considers 'a criminal and an enemy of God, King, and the people'. It is wiser not to let her into their secret, says Cavaradossi to his friend; besides, 'the only really discreet woman is one who knows nothing'. In Puccini, however, we never perceive Tosca at the height of her

---

* This explains why the Sacristan of the opera mutters to himself something about the painter's impiety and 'those dogs of Voltairians who are enemies of the Holy Office', remarks whose relevance is not made at all clear by Puccini.

insensate jealousy. Sardou, on the other hand, anxious to bring out this trait of hers, designs in Act II a special scene—shortly before the performance of a cantata—in which Tosca, roused by Scarpia's insinuations, is prepared to let the cantata go to perdition, Queen or no Queen, and rush off, as she supposes, to surprise Cavaradossi and the Marchesa Attavanti in their love idyll. Nor has Sardou omitted to give us some sensational details of Tosca's phenomenal rise to fame. She was a wild, untamed creature tending goats in the fields near Verona when Benedictine nuns took pity on her and brought her up in their convent. Hence her piety which is in such strong contrast to Cavaradossi's libertarian views and plays a fairly important part in both play and opera. In the convent she began to show unusual musical gifts. At the age of sixteen she had already become a youthful celebrity and it was then that the great Cimarosa heard her and tried to remove her from the convent, to make an opera singer of her. A fierce tug of war ensued over the soul of Floria Tosca between the nuns of Verona and Cimarosa, and the Pope himself was appealed to as arbiter. At an 'audition' at the Vatican the Pope was so moved by her singing that he declared her free to devote herself to an artistic career. 'You will soften all hearts as you have done mine. You will make people shed gentle tears, and that is also a way of praying to God.' Tosca's début was in Paisiello's *Nina* at La Scala, then came the San Carlo Theatre at Naples and the Fenice at Venice, and at the time of the action she is thrilling audiences at the Argentina in Rome.

As to the biographical background of Scarpia, we learn from Sardou that his cognomen is Vitellio, a detail suppressed by Puccini, because there is at once more force and a symbolic ring in the single name 'Scarpia'. Scarpia hails from Sicily, the classical land of brigands.* At the time of the action he has been not more than a week in Rome, where he had been sent by the King of Naples to keep an iron hand on Napoleon's sympathizers. In Sardou he is portrayed as though he had stepped out of the Spanish Inquisition, a fanatic and an utterly ruthless zealot hiding his true nature behind a mask of nauseating sanctimoniousness. In Puccini, on the other hand, Scarpia has more of the traditional romantic stage villain in him, his brutality is toned down and he is altogether more mellifluous and insinuating in his manner than is the character of the play. It is also noteworthy that the motive which, in Sardou, drives Scarpia in pursuit of Angelotti and makes him subject Cavaradossi to third-degree torture is at once a more personal and stronger one than in the opera. As the Queen warns Scarpia in Act II, only a week had gone by since his arrival in Rome and already Angelotti, who had been a prisoner at the Castel Sant' Angelo, had made a successful escape. Rumours, the Queen says, are going round in the city that this escape might not be unconnected with the fact that Angelotti's sister is the Marchesa Attavanti—'a wealthy and beautiful woman!' adds the Queen meaningly; if Scarpia cannot hunt down Angelotti

* In 1919 the French composer Georges de Seynes attempted an unsuccessful imitation of Puccini's *Tosca* in his two-act opera *La Mafia* in which a leader of this secret Sicilian society plays a similar role to that of Scarpia.

soon his own head might be at stake. There is no hint of this in Puccini at all. Moreover, it is not until Act IV of the play that Sardou reveals Scarpia as the satyr he is; up to then he conducts himself with the cold, formal and detached air of a high police official who, in suppressing dangerous subversive elements, is merely doing his duty by his King. Puccini, forced as he was by condensation of the action to forgo showing his gradual development, introduces Scarpia as a compound of bigotry and profligacy as early as Act I. On the other hand, when Sardou arrives at the *scène à faire* of Act IV (in the opera this corresponds to the scene of the bargain between Scarpia and Tosca of Act II), he pulls out all his stops to depict Scarpia in his frenzy of love-hate. Scarpia is here presented as a sexual sadist to portray whom in all his lurid colours it would have needed the Strauss of *Salome* and *Elektra* or the Berg of *Wozzeck* and *Lulu*. Now despite the fact that this scene must have struck to the very depth of Puccini's unconscious fantasies, it is significant that he shrank (as he did in the case of Louÿs's *La Femme et le Pantin*) from presenting it with the same degree of violence and lust which it possesses in Sardou. He shortened it considerably, softened the language and introduced in Scarpia's aria a further emollient. Yet for all that, the successive stages of Scarpia's waxing rage, as shown in Sardou, are retained. To illustrate the skill displayed by the composer and his librettists in their work of condensation as well as lyrical expansion of Sardou's original scene, I reproduce the two texts side by side. The comparison, moreover, provides an object-lesson in the adaptation of a spoken scene to operatic purposes:*

SARDOU	PUCCINI
Scarpia: Now then! Pray be seated! A glass of Spanish wine! (*He pours it out*) In this way we shall feel more at ease to talk about the Chevalier and find a means how to extricate him from this bad business.	*Scarpia*: My poor little supper was interrupted. Why thus dishearten'd? Come, sweet sorrow-stricken lady, be seated here! Devise with me some plan whereby we may contrive to save him. And then—be seated!— we'll talk it over. Meanwhile this cordial. 'Tis Spanish wine. Pray taste it, 'twill raise your spirits.
Tosca: I'm not thirsty nor hungry— except for his freedom!... Well now, to the point! (*She resolutely takes a seat before Scarpia's table and pushes the glass away*) How much?	*T.* (*contemptuously*): How much?
S. (*pouring out*): How much?	*S.*: How much?
T.: It's a question of money, isn't it?	*T.*: Your price, man?

* Puccini's text is given in the official English translation.

S.: Shame on you, Tosca! You don't know me at all. . . . Yes, you've seen me fierce and implacable when I discharged my duty; that was because my honour and life are involved in it: Angelotti's escape has brought disgrace on me—inevitably. But once my duty is done I'm like a soldier who is no longer an enemy when he has discarded his weapon. Before you stands Baron Scarpia who has always applauded you and admired you to the point of fanaticism. But tonight my admiration has taken on a new character. Yes, up to now, I saw in you only the great interpreter of Cimarosa and Paisiello. But our contretemps has revealed the woman in you, a woman more tragic, more passionate than the artist ever led me to believe, and a hundred times more admirable in the love and pains of real life than you are on the stage! Ah, Tosca, you found accents, cries, gestures, attitudes! . . . No, it was prodigious. I was impressed to the point of forgetting my proper role in this tragedy. I would have applauded you simply as a spectator and declared myself conquered by you!

T. (*always uneasy, under her breath*): Would to God it were so!

S.: But do you know what held me back? In all my enthusiasm for you who fascinate and intoxicate me, who are so different from all those women who have been mine, there is jealousy, a sudden jealousy. It bites into my heart. Fancy, all these rages and tears for that Chevalier who, between ourselves, is not worth so much passion! Ah! The more you plead for him the more you strengthen in me an obstinate urge to keep him in my power and make him expiate for so much love. Yes, upon my word, I want to punish him for it! I hate

S. (*laughing*): Venal my enemies call me. Yes, venal they call me. But to ladies fair I do not sell myself for paltry sums of money . . . no, no! To beauteous ladies I do not sell myself for paltry sums of money.

Scarpia's aria: No, if my plighted fealty I must betray I'll choose some other payment. This hour I've long awaited! Goddess of song, you have scorned me and braved me. 'Twas your beauty that made me love you, 'tis your hatred that has enslaved me! When I saw your cheeks bedewed with tears of consternation, shed by lustrous eyes that fiercely sparkled with scorn and detestation! When you clung to your lover like an amorous tigress! Ah! 'Twas that moment I vowed thou should'st be mine!

SARDOU	PUCCINI
him because his luck is undeserved. I envy him the possession of a woman like you to such a degree that I shall not let him free, except on one condition—to get my share!	
T. (*leaping up from her seat*): You!	T. (*horrified*): Ah! Ah!
S. (*still seated, holds her back by the arm*): And I shall get it!	S.: Wholly mine! Wholly mine!
T. (*bursting into laughter while she violently tries to free herself*): You imbecile! I would rather throw myself out of that window!	T.: No! Far rather will I kill myself!
S. (*without stirring, coldly*): All right! Your lover will follow you! Say 'yes' and I'll save him—'no' and I'll kill him.	S.: Your Mario's life I'll hold in pawn for yours!
T. (*looking at him horrified*): You abominable scoundrel! What horrible bargain by means of brute force and terror!	T.: Think you I will contract so hideous a bargain?
S.: *Bon, ma chère*, but why this violent language? If the bargain doesn't suit you, well, go then!—the door is open. But I dare you—you will scream, insult me, invoke the Holy Virgin and all the saints! Waste time with useless words! After that, you'll say 'yes!'.	S. (*divining her thoughts*): I will not force you to stay. You are free to go, fair lady.
T.: Never! I shall wake the whole town and shout out your infamy.	
S. (*sipping his wine, coldly*): That won't wake the dead! (*Tosca stops short with a gesture of despair. Scarpia continues*) You detest me very much, don't you?	S.: But your hope is fallacious. It were in vain to ask our gracious Queen to pardon a dead man! (*Tosca makes a gesture of horror and disgust*) How you detest me!
T.: Oh, God!	T.: I do!
S. (*as before*): Well and good! I'll tell you how I love you. (*He puts the wineglass down on the table*) A woman	S.: 'Tis thus I love you!

who gives herself willingly is not
worth speaking of. I have had my fill
of those! (*He advances toward Tosca*)
But to humiliate you with all your
scorn and rage, to break your resistance and twist you in my arms—By
God, that's where the savour of it
lies. It would only spoil the feast for
me if you gave in!

*T. (leaning with her back against the
writing-desk)*: You demon!

S. (one knee on the divan): Demon!
Be it so! What fascinates me, you
haughty creature, is that you should
be mine in all your rage and pain—
that I should feel the struggle and shock
in your soul—feel how your unwilling
body shudders at the caresses forced on
it—how your flesh is the slave of my
flesh! What revenge for your contempt of me, what vengeance for your
insults, and what refinement of
voluptuousness that my pleasure
should be your punishment. Ah, you
hate me! But I, I want you and I
promise myself a diabolic enjoyment
from the union of my lust with your
hatred!

T. (goes to the table): Of what union
were you born, you savage beast?
It couldn't have been the breast of
woman that suckled you!

S. (advancing toward her): Go on!
Continue! Insult me! Spit your contempt into my face, bite and tear me!
All this whips up my desire and makes
me covet you still more!

T. (trying to escape, terrified): Help,
help!

S.: No one will come! You only
waste your time with these useless
shrieks. Look, it's getting brighter on

T.: Do not touch me, you demon!
I hate you, I hate you, I hate you, you
coward, you villain!

S.: What matter? Hatred like yours
and love are kindred passions!

T.: Villain!

S. (trying to seize her): Mine!

*Tosca shrieks for help. Distant drum-rolls
are heard.*

S.: Listen to the drums approaching,
leading the escort of men about to
die on the scaffold. And time is passing.

the horizon and your Mario has not more than a quarter of an hour to live!

T.: Oh Almighty God! God the Saviour! That such a man should live and that You should allow him to do these things! Do You not see him? Do You not hear him?

S. (*jeering*): Ha! If you count on Him!... Angelotti hangs already on the gallows. (*She draws back in horror*) It's now the turn of the other! (*calling*) Spoletta!

T. (*rushing to the window*): No, no! Save him!

S. (*walks up to her, takes her by the left hand and is about to embrace her*): Do you consent?

T. (*slips out of his arms and throws herself at his feet*): Pity! Mercy! Oh God! You've had your revenge! I've been punished and humiliated enough. I lie at your feet. I beseech you! I implore you to forgive me for all I said. I'm humble now. Have pity on me! Pity!

S.: Well, then, we're agreed, aren't we? (*He lifts her up and tries to embrace her*)

T. (*frees herself with a cry of disgust*): No! No! I don't want to! I couldn't! I don't want!

Enter Spoletta.

(*Pointing to the window*) There they have raised up a gallows-tree. 'Tis your will then that your lover should die in another brief hour.

Tosca's aria: 'Vissi d'arte'.

S.: Too lovely art thou, Tosca, and too enchanting to be resisted. I have the worst of the bargain. A life I barter against a minute of thy favour!

T. (*scornfully*): Go! Go! You make me shudder! Go! Go!

S. (*hearing a knock on the door*): Who is there?

Enter Spoletta.

Puccini, however, did not altogether discard the text of Sardou's scene, but put some of it into Scarpia's monologue in Act I. The play is in prose, mostly matter-of-fact dialogue, while the libretto is almost throughout in rhymed verse which also has the effect of mollifying some of Scarpia's worst utterances. Moreover, the Tosca and Cavaradossi of the play are a rather prosaic pair of lovers unlike the characters portrayed in the opera.

Of Puccini's subsidiary characters only Angelotti deserves a closer glance because he too has a past history in Sardou's play, where he is more prominent and invites greater sympathy than in the opera. Cesare Angelotti is the descendant of a noble Roman family, one of whose members was the founder of the chapel at the Church of Sant' Andrea della Valle in which Angelotti seeks refuge after his escape. Angelotti is an ardent Republican who was driven out from the Parthenopian Republic established at Naples by Napoleon in 1799. After its suppression by King Ferdinand IV he fled to Rome, where he was appointed Consul of the equally shortlived Roman Republic and was later thrown into prison. As he informs Cavaradossi in Act I of the play, it was thanks to his sister's influence with the Royal Governor of Rome that he had become a 'forgotten prisoner' who, the Governor hoped, might receive an amnesty on the election of a new Pope. But the Court of Naples had now dispatched the fearful Baron Scarpia, who, as Cavaradossi remarks, has forced every woman that ever came to intercede with him on behalf of a prisoner to submit to his desires. This thorough-paced scoundrel had also pursued the Marchesa Attavanti but without success, and anticipating a move on her part to get her brother free, Scarpia decided to send Angelotti back to Naples for swift execution so as to give, as we read with some puzzlement, 'Lady Hamilton the joy of seeing him hang from the gallows'. Why had Nelson's mistress been dragged in? Sardou has the explanation at hand, an explanation which illustrates his foible for enlivening his drama with spurious historical touches. Some twenty years before the time of the action, Angelotti was living a life of pleasure in London, and spending one evening in 'Waux-hall' was accosted by one of those lights-o'-love who nightly swarmed in these gardens in search of clients. She was 'a prodigiously beautiful' creature, and he enjoyed her venal favours for a week. On the death of his father, Angelotti settled in Naples, where he had inherited a considerable property in the neighbouring country. Dining one evening at the house of Prince Pepoli, he was introduced by his host to the English Ambassador 'Sir Hamilton' and his enchanting wife, in whom he recognized to his stupefaction his 'facile conquest' of Vauxhall Gardens. The recognition was mutual. Although Lady Hamilton did not then exercise the influence on Queen Marie Caroline that she did later, she was already a power at the Neapolitan Court. Incensed by the hostility which she evinced toward Napoleon and the Republicans, Angelotti imprudently told the company where and how he had first made her acquaintance. Two days later his house was searched and his papers seized; nothing incriminating could be found, but some perfidious hand had smuggled into his library some volumes of Voltaire, which was sufficient to send him to the galleys for three years. After his release he engaged in those political activities which finally landed him in the Castel Sant' Angelo, from which he had just escaped when the drama opens.

4

Sardou's play was close-knit, logical in construction and with every detail strictly relevant to the action. If the play was to yield the kind of libretto Puccini required, it needed a certain amount of loosening so as to make room for lyrical episodes, and a considerable amount of condensation, music being by its nature a retarding element. In this process of adaptation Puccini and his collaborators were guilty of illogicalities, unmotivated details and sketchy characterization. Yet music has a way of covering up what might be defects in a spoken drama. Seen in this light Puccini's *Tosca* emerges as his most concentrated full-length opera, holding the *spectator*—if not always the *listener*—in the closest grip from beginning to end. Not least responsible for this effect is the ingenuity with which the task of modification and transposition of telling dramatic points from one scene to another was carried out. Some of the cleverest alterations may well have originated in Sardou's own brain, and perhaps the voluble, impulsive playwright did not altogether exaggerate when he declared that the libretto was superior to this play.

In broad outlines Puccini's Act I is identical with Sardou's opening act, but with modifications. Sardou begins with a long scene in which the garrulous Sacristan and Cavaradossi's valet gossip about the painter, thus allowing the playwright to pass on to us important information about this character. Angelotti, who has been hiding in the Chapel since the previous evening, overhears this conversation. Puccini on the other hand opens with direct action. Angelotti, having just made his escape, is seen arriving at the church in prison garb, distraught and seeking for the key to the Attavanti chapel. Again, in Sardou, Angelotti and Cavaradossi meet for the first time in their lives and so a long scene is devoted to their mutual introduction in which we learn all those biographical details about the various characters related on a previous page. Sardou needs this scene to bring out the community of spirit which unites the two men—their love of freedom and hatred of tyranny and clericalism—and so provides a strong motivation for Cavaradossi's resolve to help Angelotti in his escape from Rome. In Puccini, the two men had known each other from the past, and had apparently been friends, so that long explanations become superfluous and the painter's swift decision to assist Angelotti appears sufficiently plausible. What is, however, not made plausible in the opera is Scarpia's sudden arrival at the church later on in the act. What made him come straight from the Palazzo Farnese just to the very place where Angelotti sought refuge? Do we have to allow the Chief of Police an intuition which would have done credit to Sherlock Holmes? No. For the explanation we have to turn to Sardou, where we learn that Angelotti's jailer, a certain Trebelli, had been bribed by the Marchesa Attavanti to succour her brother in his escape. After the discovery of the empty prison-cell, the jailer was arrested and under torture disclosed the full details of Angelotti's plan, of which he had been informed. Similarly, it is most unlikely that Angelotti in the opera could have made his way to the church in prisoner's garb in full daylight. In Sardou, he had already changed in his cell into ordinary clothes which his sister had provided for him. There are several other such loose ends in Puccini's first act, yet all in all the exposition of the drama is most adroit and when the curtain rings down on the magnificent *Te Deum* scene, which is merely hinted at in Sardou, the spectator is left in no doubt why the characters behave as they do.

Puccini's Act II, laid in Scarpia's room at the Palazzo Farnese, is a skilful compression of scenes taken from several acts of the play. Yet because of this very compression the composer was compelled to throw at our heads a whole packet of 'strong meat', introducing in quick succession those horrific scenes which Sardou distributes over his Acts III and IV: the interrogation and torture of Cavaradossi, Scarpia's infamous bargain with Tosca, his attempt at rape and finally his murder. Sardou's Act II takes place in a spectacular setting in a *salon* at the Palazzo Farnese which stresses the political and military aspects of the drama. Of this act Puccini retained only two important episodes. One is the intended performance of the festive cantata, which in the opera is sung offstage and provides the background for the sombre scene of Scarpia's interrogation—a master-stroke in the simultaneous suggestion of two strongly contrasted emotional spheres. The other episode is that of the arrival of the shattering news of Napoleon's victory during the festive assembly which brings Sardou's act to an abrupt close. In the opera this piece of news is given to Scarpia at the end of the torture scene when it inspires Cavaradossi to the triumphant revolutionary song which whips up Scarpia's rage to such a pitch that he gives orders to take the prisoner straight to execution. Like Sardou's Act III Puccini's Act II ends with a dumb-show in which Tosca's religious piety is demonstrated in an unblushingly theatrical manner. (Sardou conceived this scene in order to provide Sarah Bernhardt with an opportunity for mime and facial expression, in which she excelled.) There is, however, one subtle alteration in Puccini's treatment of that scene. With Scarpia's body lying on the ground, Sardou gives Tosca as her last words the lines: 'And the safe conduct? What have I done with that?', after which she proceeds to extract the document from the dead man's hand and finally places candles on either side of the body and a crucifix on his breast. Puccini evidently felt these prosaic words as an anti-climax and he cut them, clinching the scene with a line spoken in a low voice: 'E avanti a lui tremava tutta Roma!'—'and before him trembled all Rome'. Incidentally Puccini's 'tutta *Roma*' is far more suggestive of the baneful power Scarpia wielded than Sardou's 'whole *city*'. This change was Puccini's own idea, yet strangely enough his librettists first wished to strike out the whole of this last line. Another of these alterations which recall Verdi's demand for the 'theatrical phrase' occurs in the previous scene where Scarpia was originally made to ask the distraught Tosca 'Tu m'odii?'—'Do you hate me?', which was changed into the more telling 'Come tu m'odii!' —'How you hate me!'★

Sardou's fifth and final act consists of two scenes, both laid in the Castel

★See dialogue on p. 356.

Sant' Angelo, the first in the chapel reserved for prisoners condemned to death, the second on the platform outside. The first scene was designed to show the courage and the anti-clericalism of Cavaradossi: being under the impression that a priest is waiting outside the cell, ready to pray with him in his last hour, the painter curtly refuses such assistance with the words: 'Death in itself is a tiresome enough business not to be made still more so by such ceremonies.' But instead of the priest it is Tosca who now enters the cell. She tells her lover of her murder of Scarpia and of the macabre circumstances in which she obtained the safe conduct for them, and then instructs him how to feign death at what will be a sham execution. Cavaradossi is then led away while Tosca remains behind, having been advised by Spoletta to stay in the cell until the execution is over. There she hears the volley from the firing squad. In the following scene she is seen rushing up to the platform only to find Cavaradossi dead, after which the action rapidly proceeds to its close, as in the opera.

These two scenes of Sardou's last act are telescoped into Puccini's Act III which plays on the platform and thus we actually see the execution; equally significant, Tosca is made to be present at it, the composer wishing no doubt to extract for the spectator's benefit the last ounce from a spine-chilling situation. Whatever objection may be raised to this brutal assault on our nerves *and* eardrums, as sheer theatre Puccini's modification represents a master-stroke, to say nothing of the effect which Tosca's presence has on us who now see our own suspense reflected in her behaviour during the sombre ceremonial preceding the execution. This is, to my mind, the only scene in the whole opera that arouses in the initiated spectator real compassion for Tosca; he knows that her lover will be done to death, whereas she does not.

In addition to this major alteration there are several minor ones which throw light on the workings of Puccini's mind. Two of these may be mentioned. Cavaradossi's cynical refusal of any comfort before his execution, which in Sardou occupies a brief scene, is completely eliminated in the opera, the painter declining the offer with a simple 'No!' This excision was manifestly made in deference to the religious susceptibilities of the Italian public, though Cavaradossi's atheism was, as Panichelli intimated in his book, largely shared by the composer. The second modification occurs at the very end of the last act. In the play Spoletta, Sciarrone and the execution squad are still on the scene when Tosca arrives and discovers the deception which Scarpia has played on her. In an access of mad fury she shouts at the soldiers: 'Yes, I've killed your Scarpia! Killed him, killed him, do you understand? With a knife, and I would plunge it into his heart again and twist it round! . . . Oh, you shoot! . . . I kill with the knife! Yes, go and see what I've done to that monster whose corpse still murders. . .' Spoletta, thinking that the death of Cavaradossi had upset the balance of the poor woman's mind, pays no heed to what she says, yet when confirmation is brought by two soldiers of the truth of her words, he rushes after her, exclaiming, 'Ah, demon, I shall send you where your lover is!' Tosca's last retort is to fling herself over the balustrade, with '*J'y vais, canailles!*' Puccini shortened this brutal scene considerably, bringing Spoletta and Sciarrone on to the platform only toward the very end—which has also the advantage of focusing our attention wholly on the heroine. At the same time he replaced the abusive line she has in Sardou by words expressing a religious sentiment: 'Oh, Scarpia, avanti a Dio!'—'Scarpia, God will be our judge.'

5

If *Edgar* was Puccini's first but unsuccessful attempt, *Tosca* represents a brilliant achievement in breaking away, so far as subject-matter was concerned, from *tragédie larmoyante*, and, in respect of musical style, from *opéra comique*, to which genre both *Le Villi* and *Bohème* belong. He now presses forward in the direction of something heroic and larger than life and the result is nearly grand opera, a work marked by sombreness sustained from the first page to the last. The intimate miniatures of *Bohème* are now replaced, though not altogether, by a much broader manner. A powerful trenchancy informs the majority of themes and motives, some of which become the graphic equivalents of an actor's dramatic gestures. The melodic lines gain in amplitude and we note the emergence of diatonic scale-motives invested with a forceful thrust. The orchestra speaks in harder and less flexible tones than in *Bohème*, and though we encounter passages of true orchestral chamber-music*—indeed even torture-chamber music (Act II)— Puccini now tends to oppose rather than blend the various instrumental groups, and assigns the percussion an important role. The harmonic idiom is markedly dissonant, with frequent and abrupt tonal shifts, wrenching the music out of one key into another. An entire new feature is the pervasive use made of the whole-tone scale for the characterization of Scarpia, while an intense chromaticism is associated with the music of Angelotti. Characteristic too are the frequent dynamic marks *con tutta forza, con violenza, ruvido* (rough), the innumerable *sfz*, and the prevalence of *ff* and *fff*.

The price Puccini had to pay for setting so high-powered a drama with so 'plotty' a plot is seen in its loose and sometimes shoddy musical texture. The cinematic sequence of strong situations scarcely allows him to develop his musical material. In his somewhat naïve efforts to apply the Wagnerian technique pervasively, he invents 'labels' for situations and objects† of more incidental interest and thus assembles some sixty leitmotives which are reiterated in his usual fashion and/or plastered together with the addition of the *tremolo*—the verist's maid-of-all-work. This is the aspect of *Tosca* (prominent too in *Fanciulla*) that can least bear critical examination.

But such defects are scarcely noted in performance, partly because of the

* See, for instance, the delicate 'reminiscences' for four solo celli and two solo violas expressing the thoughts that pass through Cavaradossi's mind before he sings 'E lucevan le stelle'.

† Angelotti's 'flight' and his 'search for the key', 'the food basket', 'the knife' with which Tosca stabs Scarpia, and so forth.

drama on the stage, but mainly because the music coils and recoils itself round the action with snake-like suppleness. *Tosca* is musical drama (not music-drama) *par excellence*. One is almost tempted to lay the stress on the noun were it not that the work in the last analysis lives through its music. Sardou's play has disappeared into limbo, while Puccini's opera proclaims its vitality year in and year out in countless productions. Indeed the wonder is the amount of sheer musical invention that went to its making, invention kindled by a subject which, on the face of it, seems to defy operatic treatment and would assuredly have defeated a lesser composer.

6

Among the musical characters Scarpia claims our first attention, not only because he is the activating force of the drama but also because he is Puccini's first major role for a low male voice. After what has been said about the composer's psychological limitations in the portrayal of such roles, it will be especially interesting to see how far he brought Scarpia to life in the music. Broadly, he is more successful in limning Scarpia in short, incisive motives than in arias and other sustained music, where he is apt to fall into a lyrico-sentimental vein; and sentimentality is the last quality to be associated with this Chief of Police. The essence of Scarpia—his ferocity—is caught at the opening of the opera in a musical image as astounding in its simplicity as it is graphic in its suggestiveness:

Ex. a has no melodic 'face', it is, so to speak, musically inhuman; its evocation of a sinister and brute force derives from a harmonic progression of unconnected (parallel) chords based on the whole-tone scale. Except for such more external alterations as rhythmic diminution and changes in dynamic and instrumental colouring, this motive undergoes no intrinsic transformation, which is of course no new thing in Puccini; but the very rigidity with which he treats Ex. 40a *throughout* the work seems deliberate

and intended to suggest the immutable cruelty of Scarpia.* Of the many
subsidiary motives associated with Scarpia, Ex. 40b, another whole-tone
phrase and as inflexible as 40a, gains importance in Act II where it seems
to stand for his determination to achieve his object at all costs.

Scarpia is also reflected in characteristic instrumental timbres: low-lying
strings and woodwind in the more tranquil sections, massive brass and percussion in the dramatic passages, and, perhaps most noteworthy, the almost
ubiquitous double-basses whose dramatic use Puccini is likely to have studied
in Act IV of Verdi's *Otello*; and attention must be drawn to the Iago-like
trills and whirls on the cellos which accompany Scarpia's phrase in Act I
'Or tutto è chiaro'.

The first scene in which Puccini attempts to draw a fuller portrait of
Scarpia is the *Te Deum* scene beginning with 'Va, Tosca!'. According to the
stage directions, he is to be shown in turn as 'sardonic', 'ironic', 'ferocious',
in the grip of 'erotic passion' and 'awakening as though from a dream'.
Rarely has an operatic scene provided such an opportunity for the musical
suggestion of a character's swiftly changing emotions, but has Puccini really
seized all his chances? The answer is no; the *simultaneous* musical characterization of a religious atmosphere and of Scarpia passing through his various
states of mind would have required the genius of a Wagner or Verdi,
and this was beyond Puccini's power. Admittedly, Scarpia's voice part
is marked by leaps and chromatic turns but in essential outline and rhythm
it follows the religious music in the orchestra. Puccini eschews a crucial
problem of dramatic composition such as is presented by this scene; but
the man of the theatre, in contradistinction to the musical dramatist, would
not be beaten. He achieves his effects by a clever combination of non-
musical means, scenic, histrionic and verbal: scenic, through the contrast
between this vile character and the religious background; histrionic, through
the singer's gestures and facial expression; verbal, through the clarity with
which Scarpia's utterances are allowed to reach the spectator, orchestra and
organ being toned down and the chorus reduced to a murmur. It is not
until Scarpia, seized by a religious fervour, joins the chorus in the second
verse of the *Te Deum* that the music resumes its characterizing role. Thus,
looked at from a purely musical point of view the *Te Deum* scene is not a

---

* It is a matter of speculation whether Puccini knew Berlioz's *Damnation of Faust* in
which Mephistopheles is represented in this phrase:

Ex. 41

In *idea* this is strikingly similar to the 'Scarpia' motive. Like it, it also contains a *diabolus in
musica*—the augmented fourth. If this resemblance is merely coincidental it would confirm
an often observed fact that in dramatic music similar images tend to kindle similar musical
symbols in the minds of composers widely separated by temperament, style and period.

great piece.* Puccini's real concern here was to close the act with a grand
scenic spectacle—the Cardinal's solemn procession and the subsequent
Thanksgiving as background for the scheming Scarpia—and in this he
succeeds so admirably that the scene must be reckoned one of the most
impressive finali in all opera. It is Puccini at his Meyerbeerian best, which is
unquestionably better than the best of Meyerbeer.

What of the first of Scarpia's two second-act arias, 'Ella verrà', which
represents his erotic credo? For one thing, it lacks real afflatus, for another it
is largely cast in a sentimental vein more suited to Cavaradossi, and, in fact,
the baritone's opening phrase bears a family likeness to the tenor's 'Qual
occhio' of Act I. It is only in the middle section, 'Bramo. . . La cosa', that
something of Scarpia's true nature is conveyed in the violent zigzagging of
the vocal line. Puccini cannot, however, resist the temptation to introduce
various descriptive touches, piquant in themselves, but somehow out of
place in this aria.†

Puccini is more successful in Scarpia's second aria, 'Già mi dicon venal',
an extended monologue comparable to the *scena ed aria* of the older operas,
which convincingly conveys gradual progress from mocking irony to the
savage passion of 'Ah, in quell' istante'. However, before Scarpia reveals
his true intention to Tosca, the orchestra has already given his thought away
in the eruptive 'Lust' theme:

Ex. 42

while his waxing desire is expressed in the impassioned *cantilena* 'Già mí
struggea', marked by feminine phrase endings and throbbing syncopations
on the orchestra. To sum up, it is rather by the role he plays than by the
music he sings that Scarpia makes his impact, a criticism which also applies,
though in a lesser degree, to Puccini's treatment of the title-role of *Gianni
Schicchi*.

For the most inspired vocal writing we have to turn to the music of the
two lovers, which displays a sweep and breadth and sinew recalling Verdi
and foreshadowing the heroic style of Calaf and Turandot. To take Tosca

---

* Its main material derives from an unpublished church work (1880), while the actual
Te Deum melody is one in traditional use in Roman churches.

The orchestra here includes high and low bells, the latter tolling an *ostinato* F–B for no
less than seventy-three bars, a bass drum, an offstage cannon; and on the stage, four horns
and three trombones *ab lib.*, which enter, significantly, on Scarpia's joining the chorus in the
actual *Te Deum*.

† The harp arpeggios at 'guitar chords', the clarinet flourish at 'horoscope of flowers'
and the bird-calls at 'cooing like a turtle-dove'.

first. Puccini's portrayal of her contradictory nature is particularly felicitous and varied. There is the piously religious Tosca offering flowers to the Madonna (Ex. 43a), there is the romantic girl visualizing her love retreat in the country (Ex. 43b) and there is Tosca in her ardent passion for Cavaradossi (43c):

Ex. 43

These are her principal motives. Her capricious vanity and jealousy come to life in the nervous broken-up recitatives of her opening scene with Cavaradossi and her first encounter with Scarpia where her *arioso*, 'Ed io venivo' in F♯ minor, sounds the first tragic note in her music. Tosca at the height of her agony at seeing Cavaradossi suffer under torture is caught in the following phrase, similar in build to Mimi's C minor theme (Ex. 39)

as will be seen in the step-wise descent of the pivotal notes from C down to D:

Ex. 44

Ah! più non pos-so! Ah!— che orror!— Ah!- ces-sa-te il mar-
-tir! è trop-po sof-frir! Ah, non posso più, ah! non posso più!

The phrase conjures up the gesture of wringing the hands. And, lastly, there is the woman at the end of her strength, appealing in pathetic tones to Scarpia for mercy for her lover and seeking to soften his heart by a recital of her pious actions. This is the Tosca of 'Vissi d'arte', her only set-piece in the opera, which, as we recall, Puccini later did not much care for as he considered that it held up the action. This aria is essentially a lament and hence the title 'Prayer', by which it is generally known, seems inappropriate. Strangely enough, the composer has little fresh to say in a situation which we should have expected to touch off the spring of his melodic imagination. Except for an introduction in E♭ minor, the ecclesiastic, faburden-like harmonies—they are manifestly intended to characterize the religious Tosca—the main body of the aria is a patchwork of reminiscences which can be defended on grounds of dramatic relevance but which smacks too much of a labour-saving device. Nevertheless, it is a piece of splendid vocal effect and, despite Puccini's later view that it retarded the action, fulfils the need for a lyrical effusion after the grimness of the preceding scenes.

Cavaradossi is first introduced in the suave, flowing aria 'Recondita armonia', which, but for its slow pace, might have equally well suited Rodolfo at the opening of Act I of *Bohème*, so similar is it to 'Cieli bigi' in sentiment and musical texture. After all, both are young artists! Strictly speaking, Cavaradossi's is not a solo aria, as his lyrical musings are punctuated by the Sacristan's grumbles, which serve, however loosely, to knit this static piece into the context of the action. The scoring, in which harp and woodwind are prominent, has a delicious fragrance, and especially beautiful is the orchestral introduction in which the gentle flow of parallel fourths and fifths mirrors the painter's movements, as he passes with light strokes of the brush over his canvas.

Like Tosca, Cavaradossi has his own characterizing theme, which also stands for his love of her:

Ex.45

Andante sostenuto

Qual oc-chio al mon - do può star di pa - ro all'arden - te oc - chio tuo ne - ro——?

The scalar ascent of the opening as well as the later curve of the phrase links this theme with the Tosca motives, Ex. 43a, b. The heroic aspect of the painter —his love of liberty and his defiance of tyranny—is brought out in the agitated march-like trio, 'L'alba vindice', the most rousing tune Puccini, the least revolutionary of men, ever penned.*

Lastly there is the portrayal of the hero in extremity, his celebrated farewell to life and love, 'E lucevan le stelle'. The text of this aria calls for special comment. Except for Puccini's own contribution of the two significant words 'Muoio disperato!', the image evoked by his librettists for this particular situation seems to me utterly false. Is it likely from a psychological point that a man about to face a firing squad will allow his last thoughts to linger on a sexual image scarcely veiled in its suggestion?† That the memory of the painter's past intimacies with Tosca should invade his mind in his very last hour and, moreover, that Puccini should have accepted this motive—he may even have suggested it himself—provides, I suggest, a striking illustration, not only of the irrepressible force of sheer erotic concepts in him, but also of the compulsive link in his unconscious between the love-death instincts. It made him ignore the psychological improbability of this motive in just the situation in which his hero finds himself. Yet it is precisely because this was a situation that struck to the heart of his unconscious fantasies and thus became invested with a most powerful emotion that he was able to write what must, assuredly, be reckoned as the most poignant music of the whole opera. In Cavaradossi's lament he seems to express the quintessence of his despair at being always compelled to equate love with death. This aria is not merely suggestive of tears and sighs, it *is* tears and sighs (Ex. 46).

Admittedly the music is emotionally overcharged to breaking-point, tempting many tenors to an hysterical rendering of it; yet it remains within the bounds of pure lyricism and constitutes, perhaps, the finest example of melodic *verismo*. Puccini conceived it in the manner of an improvisation, as though it came into Cavaradossi's head on the spur of the moment. An

* But see p. 375.

† The English translator of the libretto has completely neutralized the original Italian of Cavaradossi's lines: 'Oh! dolci baci, o languide carezze, mentr' io fremente le belle forme discogliea dai veli!'

Ex. 46

Svani per sempre il sogno mio d'a-mo-re l'o - ra è fug - gi - ta—

—e muo-io di - spe - ra-to!

arioso rather than a formal aria, it shows a pervasive *rubato* and an asymmetrical phrasing (5+7+3 bars); the extension of the second phrase (5+2 bars) momentarily brings D minor into the orbit of B minor, thus adding a fresh harmonic colour. And how telling is the contrast between the two stanzas. In the first stanza Cavaradossi recites his words pensively against the orchestral melody which steals in on the solo clarinet, *dolcissimo, vagamente, rubando*; in the second stanza the tenor takes over this melody *con grande sentimento*, the strings doubling it in three (!) octaves.

It is to be noted that throughout the opera Cavaradossi is generally associated with warm, mellow instruments: first the clarinet and then the horn and cellos. Tosca on the other hand is characterized by the upper strings and the brighter woodwind (flute, oboe), and Angelotti, too, has his special instrument in the cor anglais.

Angelotti is no more than an episodic figure, but Puccini has associated him with at least half a dozen leitmotives—all brief and incisive, partly chromatic, partly whole-tone, and all suggestive of extreme agitation. Of these I quote the two most important:

Ex. 47

Vivacissimo con violenza

(a)

(b)

The first suggests the fugitive as he staggers into the church, ragged, emaciated and trembling with fear, while the second is associated with his anxious search for the key of the chapel.

7

Owing to the kind of plot with which Puccini was confronted in *Tosca*, his first act shows a division into three sections instead of the usual two, each with its distinct atmosphere but each containing a great variety of musical scenes. In passing it may be noted in this act that at no time are more than two of the four principal characters on the stage, and they are introduced one by one so as to impress themselves on the spectator's attention. Puccini dispenses with an orchestral introduction and boldly opens with the 'Scarpia' motive (Ex. 40a)—the motto of the opera—catapulting us *in medias res.**
The first part of Act I, which terminates with Tosca's unexpected arrival, is generally marked by agitated music and introduces the first of the many dumb shows characteristic of this opera. The whole of Angelotti's first scene is mime, the music suggesting his movements and unspoken thoughts during his frantic search for the key to the chapel. When he finally lights on it, suppressing a cry of joy, the music gives out the 'Scarpia' motive *ff robusto-pp*! Dumb show is also part of the scene in which the Sacristan inspects the church. He is afflicted with a nervous tic (not in Sardou), a recurrent convulsion of the neck and the shoulders and provides the only comic relief in this otherwise sombre opera.

With Cavaradossi's entry the music at once takes on a rich sensuous colour. As he mounts the platform to contemplate his painting of Mary Magdalene, whose original is, as the Sacristan later says, 'the unknown lady who has been coming here lately to pray devoutly to the Madonna', the orchestra reveals the painter's secret thoughts by quoting the noble 'Attavanti' theme

Ex.48

followed at once by the 'Tosca' motive. Cavaradossi's ensuing aria represents the first point of lyrical repose, after which the action is resumed again in the crucial scene with Angelotti. Tension is added by Tosca's impatient offstage call '*Mario!*'.

With the lovers' meeting we arrive at the central musical scene of Act I. Puccini appears so anxious to seize on this great opportunity for lyrical music that dramatically he starts with it too soon, overlooking the discrepancy between the state of irritation and suspicion in which Tosca enters and the

---

* In *Salome* and *Elektra* Strauss adopts the same procedure.

languid 'Tosca' melody on the orchestra. But in itself this extended love scene must be accounted one of the finest in all Puccini's operas, witness its masterly disposition from a dramatic point of view, its unflagging musical invention and the delicate fragrance of its instrumental colours. It consists of four separate sections, the second of which—Tosca's lilting 'Non lo sospiri'— is almost a solo aria. But the lyrical mood dominating the whole scene is not allowed to interfere with the action, which is adroitly carried on in the intervening recitatives. A sense of coherence is lent to this long duet by a recurring cadential figure, Tosca's insinuating *ballabile* (Ex. 43d) and by the key pattern of the first three sections: Ab–Db–Eb.

The duet over, the action moves with increased speed and reaches its greatest momentum in the chorus of the clerics, acolytes and choristers called together by the Sacristan to hear the joyous news of Napoleon's reported defeat. This ensemble echoes the Dance of the Apprentices in *Die Meistersinger*. One of the most powerful dramatic strokes in this opera occurs when at the height of these jubilations Scarpia makes his unexpected entry, his motive (Ex. 40a) cutting off the chorus in the middle of their phrase: a sudden hush falls upon the crowd as though seized by an evil spell. This marks the beginning of the third and last portion of the act. Scarpia's interrogation of the trembling Sacristan is caught in this suggestive passage, one of the rare instances in which Puccini resorts to a contrapuntal combination of themes:

Ex. 49

Scarpia's inspection of the Attavanti chapel, his finding of the telltale fan, and his gradual piecing together of details of incriminating evidence is dealt with in Puccini's famous mosaic of relevant and irrelevant 'reminiscences'. Tosca's return launches an alluring duet with Scarpia and is an excellent example of the composer's skill in the suggestive use of an *ostinato*—here a bell-like figure on the orchestra doubled by real bells:

Ex. 50

This duet admirably serves to paint Scarpia as a sanctimonious creature playing on Tosca's jealous disposition; but in the following recitative he becomes too much of the stage villain punctuating Tosca's outpouring with some melodramatic asides.

The ensuing *Te Deum* scene has already been discussed and all that remains to add is that Puccini rounds it off to grandiose effect by blazing out the opera's motto in triumphant fashion.

Act II represents, from a dramatic and musical point of view, a unique *tour de force* in which Puccini ventured to the very limits of operatic realism, without failing in his task as musician. Admittedly, 'naked truth' rears its ugly head in Cavaradossi's torture scene, in Scarpia's frenzied shouts of lust and the hoarse ejaculations of his death agony. Yet these and other things must be accepted as part of the veristic creed and on balance they do not seem to weigh too heavily if seen against the total of real music which this act contains. Moreover, Puccini always remains within the emotional key of the action and cannot be accused of such crass stylistic aberrations as Strauss was guilty of in the Viennese waltzes introduced into the closing scenes of *Salome* and *Elektra*.

Few operas contain an act as remorseless in its mounting tension as Act II of *Tosca*, which has five great scenes, each representing a further vicious turn of the screw. The first scene begins quietly enough showing Scarpia at the Palazzo Farnese sitting at his table and taking his meal. His thoughts are revealed in the orchestra, which in turn quotes the themes of 'Firm Purpose', 'Tosca', 'Angelotti' and 'Cavaradossi'. The first indication that festivities are in progress in another part of the palace, festivities in celebration of the Austrian victory over the French, comes in the *Tempo di Gavotta* offstage and momentarily breaking up the oppressive atmosphere.* This is followed by Scarpia's aria in which, after the first hints given in Act I, he now fully discloses himself as the satyr he is.

Cavaradossi's arrival opens the second scene, the peculiar effect of which lies in the fact that two entirely different worlds are simultaneously suggested in the music. There is the painful interrogation on the stage, proceeding to one of Puccini's ominous march themes (scored for low flutes and basses, *pizz.*):

Ex.51

* In Sardou's Act II we are invited to hear *on* the stage what amounts to an orchestral concert: a Minuet, a Gavotte, a Saltarello with chorus and the 'Andante of Haydn's Symphony in D' (the 'London'?).

and there is the singing, offstage, of the festive cantata heard through the open window. Dramatic contrast could not be stronger. Like the *Tempo di Gavotta*, the Cantata is an apt pastiche—originally Puccini here intended to use some of Paisiello's own music—and Tosca, who takes part in it, shows her mettle as a famous singer in the dramatic flourishes reaching up to C *in alt*, which the composer has given her.

The third great scene begins with Tosca's entry, the orchestra giving eloquent expression to her troubled state of mind. After Cavaradossi has been led into the torture chamber Scarpia tries to worm a confession out of Tosca, which he does to rocking, barcarole-like music; but being unsuccessful he presently utters a veiled threat, at which point Puccini introduces the first of his torture themes, one which almost conjures up the image of 'a fillet of steel encircling his temples' and gradually tightening:*

Ex. 52

Andante sostenuto

The first climax is reached in Tosca's agonized cry 'Non è vero!' with its violent wrench from D minor to C minor. And so the tension is gradually built up until it reaches explosion-point in Tosca's great phrase: 'Ah! Più non posso!', with its tremendous octave-leaps, downwards from C and B♭ *in alt* (Ex. 44). Her defences now having broken down she betrays Angelotti's hiding-place, a scene in which Puccini makes masterly use of pauses. Suspense grows again when Sciarrone enters with the startling news of Napoleon's victory, inspiring Puccini to a trio† in the heroic vein in which

* It was at this point of the action that Puccini's librettists originally intended an aria for Cavaradossi *while* under torture, which was to grow into a formal quartet with Tosca, the Judge and Spoletta.

† It opens with an orchestral introduction based on the 'Attavanti' theme whose relevance here is anyone's guess.

Cavaradossi reveals himself as an ardent revolutionary. This comes rather unexpectedly since Puccini, unlike Sardou, had scarcely vouchsafed us a hint in previous scenes that the painter entertained such strong political views. And sticklers for dramatic verisimilitude are bound to stumble over the fact that Cavaradossi, who a moment or two before was brought in from the torture chamber in a state of utter exhaustion, should suddenly find the strength to break, 'with great enthusiasm', into a paean of liberty, and in the process deliver himself of a high B♮ and some high A♭s. This about the only instance in Act II where operatic convention gets the better of Puccini the dramatic realist.

The fourth scene, centring on the infamous bargain, is musically the richest of the act, and contains the aforementioned arias of Scarpia and Tosca and the latter's *arioso* 'Mi vedi supplice' in E♭ minor: Puccini was aware that operatic laws demanded more lyrical music after the grim alarums of the preceding scenes. Passing mention may be made of one of those minor dramatic strokes so characteristic of this opera. At the moment when Scarpia can no longer contain his desire for Tosca and is about to proceed from persuasion to physical action, the ominous sound of distant drum-rolls is heard, the indication that the gallows is being erected for Cavaradossi. This not only serves to bring Scarpia's vile attempt to a sudden halt but, equally important, his explanation to Tosca of the significance of these drum-rolls strikes terror into her heart and so prepares the mood for her ensuing 'Vissi d'arte'. This detail of the drums is absent from the corresponding scene in Sardou.★

The fifth and last scene must be accounted as among the most macabre in all opera. The nerve-tautening atmosphere is caught by one of Puccini's finest inventions in a tragic vein, the whole ten-bar phrase being played by the first violins on the G string and muted:

Ex. 53

Its continuation (Ex. b) marks the precise moment at which, noticing the knife on Scarpia's table, Tosca conceives the idea of his murder. It is a pity

★See dialogue on p. 357.

375

that afterwards Puccini lapses into mere *bruitisme*, instead of developing these motives for the actual stabbing of Scarpia. What follows is all mime, the return of the F♯ minor melody (Ex. 53a) accompanying Tosca's washing of her hands, adjusting her hair before the mirror, taking the safe-conduct from the dead man's hand and so forth. (But significantly Puccini omits Sardou's detail of Tosca cleaning the stain of blood on her dress.) As she proceeds to perform the religious ceremony, the orchestra, in revealing her thoughts, softly recalls Scarpia's 'Lust' (Ex. 42) and Cavaradossi's 'Love' (Ex. 45). The act closes on the 'Scarpia' motive (Ex. 40a), which steals in imperceptibly, now ending in the minor and suggesting in its peculiar scoring a spectre rising above the stage. And how well calculated is Puccini's last touch—another drum-roll in the distance as a portent of the tragedy that is still to come! Altogether, this last scene is a classical instance of his ability to extract a maximum of effect from a minimum of means.

Act III, which is about a quarter of the length of the whole opera, consists of three main sections: Cavaradossi's solo scene culminating in his lament, his love scene with Tosca, and the execution followed by Tosca's suicide. The first and second acts had been all action. Puccini now feels the need for a respite in the tension and also for touching in an atmosphere strongly contrasted with the prevailing sombreness of the drama. Hence the orchestral piece which introduces Act III by evoking the utter peace of early dawn in the Eternal City. But hints of the imminent tragedy are not absent. One is the anticipation of the triumphant hymn which the lovers will sing in their last deceptive moments of blissful hope, here thundered out by four horns in unison before the curtain rises. The other hint, suggesting that Scarpia will still exercise an evil power beyond his death, is to be found in the menacing motto that punctuates this Aubade, an airy and most fragrant piece of orchestral music though it is not without a touch of mannerism in the frequent repetitions of a motive in parallel triads, the 'Morning'. An archaic element is added in the Shepherd's wistful folk-song 'Io de'sospiri', in its Lydian fourth (A♯ in E major), an interval which also colours the Aubade.

As dawn grows brighter, bells begin to toll from the surrounding churches, Puccini employing bells of different pitches to re-create the authentic atmosphere of Roman morning.

Of Cavaradossi's solo scene we have already spoken. In the following scene, the last meeting of the two lovers, Puccini, strangely enough, fails to rise to the occasion. In the dramatic context this love duet is too long and diffuse and lacks true inspiration, suggesting that the composer had exhausted himself by the time he came to compose this scene. Evidence for this is also found in the fact that the finest portion, Cavaradossi's caressing 'Amaro sol per te', was lifted bodily from the fourth act of the original version of *Edgar*. Ricordi's poor opinion of this duet was not far off the mark.* Nor can we suppress the feeling that the lovers' heroic hymn, 'Trionfal di nova speme', coming as it does after the prevailing sentimental mood of the pre-

* See his letter on p. 110.

vious section, sounds somewhat rhetorical and dragged in, just as does the 'revolutionary' trio of Act II.★

It is, very significantly, the Execution which sparks off Puccini's imagination, inspiring him to a kind of 'March to the Scaffold', than which there is little operatic music more suggestive of the inexorable tread of doom:

Ex. 54

Largo con gravità

It is difficult to put one's finger on how exactly this march achieves its impact. A combination of several factors: the insistent *ostinato* bass, the searing chromaticism of the inner parts in the continuation of Ex. 54,† and the frequent shifts to unrelated keys; there is also the manner in which the composer deploys the march over this whole grisly scene, gradually increasing the dynamic volume until, after the shooting of Cavaradossi, the full orchestra is engaged, with the horn quartet in unison blazing out Ex. 54 and with the two trumpets cutting into it with a brief chromatic figure like a knife.

This harrowing scene over, Puccini is, like Sardou, anxious to bring the drama to a rapid close. Tosca's realization of her deception by Scarpia would, one imagines, have inspired Verdi to one of his great monologues‡— Puccini, regrettably, dispatches this scene with mere 'situation' music, and in a rather perfunctory manner, for that matter. Faithful to the verists' customary method, he resorts for his peroration to the 'best' tune of the act—'E lucevan le stelle'—now thundered out in unison by virtually the whole orchestra, *con tutta forza e con grande slancio, fff!* The parallel with the close of *Bohème* need not be stressed. But what does need stressing is the dramatic irrelevance

---

★ The Hymn originated in the so-called Latin Hymn in praise of Rome, which Puccini found wholly unsuitable for the final climax of the love duet. He hoped, as he wrote to Ricordi, 'to do away with that last triumphal effusion [*trionfalata*]', and to finish with words which would make 'a passionate close'. He quotes the lines 'e mille ti dirò . . .', which, slightly altered and transposed, are indeed those of the present duet ending. Yet a last reminder of that chilling Latin Hymn is still to be found in some lines of the libretto (not in the text of the score). In these the lovers assure each other that wherever they might escape after their fearful ordeal, they would find a fatherland and the Latin spirit of ancient Rome. In the autograph score the lines of the present Hymn are missing, which suggests that even after completing Act III Puccini and his librettists had not yet been able to solve the textual problem of a 'passionate close' to the love duet.

† The similarity in texture with the 'Transformation Music' of *Parsifal* is noteworthy here.
‡ See p. 101.

and, indeed, illogicality of Puccini's quoting Cavaradossi's lament. The peroration in the previous opera repeated Mimi's 'Sono andati?', addressed to Rodolfo and may therefore be readily accepted as the expression of his disconsolate grief at his realization that the girl is dead. In *Tosca*, however, the hero's lament was, for one thing, *not* heard by the heroine, and for another, it conveys *his* anguish at having to depart for this world. Its quotation is hence devoid of any dramatic significance for the death of Tosca: either the 'Love' theme or the 'Execution' march or—perhaps most apposite —the 'Scarpia' motive as a last ironic salute from the grave would have been the logical conclusion of the opera. But for Puccini 'E lucevan le stelle' was the more effective piece to draw upon for his peroration and he thus blithely sacrificed the musical dramatist in him to the man of the theatre.

The act closes in E♭ minor, having begun in bright E major, which appears to suggest the same dramatic symbolism as the semitonal shift, from C major to C♯ minor, in the last act of *Bohème*.

XXX

Madama Butterfly

Principal Characters

Madama Butterfly (Cio-Cio-San)	Soprano
Suzuki, her servant	Mezzo-soprano
F. B. Pinkerton, Lieutenant in the United States Navy.. ..	Tenor
Goro, a marriage-broker	Tenor
Sharpless, Consul of the United States in Nagasaki	Baritone
Prince Yamadori	Tenor

Nagasaki—Time: The Present

I

PUCCINI'S LITTLE GEISHA has both an operatic and a literary ancestry. The first, somewhat older, is to be traced back to two heroines of French romantic opera: Selica in Meyerbeer's posthumous *L'Africaine* (1865) and Lakmé, the Indian protagonist of Delibes's alluring opera of that name (1883). Like Cio-Cio-San, both these characters belong to non-European races; like her, both fall in love with a white man, thus offending against a sacred custom of their people, and both commit suicide when their lovers desert them to return to their native lands. It is the clash of two cultures, the incompatibility of East and West and, by implication, the white man's superiority that form the underlying theme of these and other similar operatic subjects. Such stories were no doubt based on real incidents which must have often occurred during that part of the nineteenth century when countries once considered far off and legendary were being gradually brought into contact with European civilization through commerce and colonial expansion.* The Near East, lying in geographical proximity to Europe, had seen its operatic exploration at an earlier date, in the so-called 'Turkish operas' of the eighteenth century. With the countries of the Far East, notably Japan, it was a different matter. For it was not until about the 1860s, after a seclusion of about two and a half centuries, that Japan began to lower her barriers to the West. Foreign navies were permitted to call at her ports and it was reserved for a French naval officer to write what was probably the first novel about the land of the cherry-blossom, chrysanthemums, geishas and the *samurai*. This was Pierre Loti with his celebrated romance, *Madame Chrysanthème*, which with its appearance in 1887 set the fashion for the use of Japanese subjects in Western literature and opera. There were the novels

* Thus the subject of *Lakmé* is based on Pierre Loti's autobiographical *Le Mariage de Loti*, relating to his experiences in India.

of Lafcadio Hearn, and there were a number of 'Japanese' operas and operettas culminating in Puccini's *Madam Butterfly*.★ The Far East had now taken possession of the operatic stage just as had the Near East a century or so before.

Loti's heroine is the literary ancestress of Puccini's Cio-Cio-San. As this French novel has a direct as well as an indirect bearing on the Italian libretto, it will be interesting to consider it in some detail. It is an autobiographical novel and its treatment suggests a modern *Sentimental Journey*. Loti (1850–1923) had himself served as a captain in the French Navy and seen service in the Far East just when Japan had begun to undergo Westernization. The first literary fruit of these experiences was *Madame Chrysanthème*, in which Loti describes one of the less edifying aspects of this process, namely the curious custom according to which officers of foreign navies were permitted to enter into temporary marriages with geishas, which convenient arrangements would be terminated by the expiration of the 'husbands'' leave. As Loti dryly remarks, officers of the French, British and American navies availed themselves of this privilege with alacrity. His novel takes the form of a diary kept by Pierre (the author), a naval officer on the *Triomphante*, during his stay at Nagasaki from July to September 1885. To while away his time Pierre 'marries' a refined geisha girl. Knowing that their association will be shortlived, both parties enter it in the spirit of *carpe diem*. There is no tragedy when after three months Pierre joins his ship again. In fact, any feeling of regret or remorse Pierre might have felt at leaving his 'wife' is completely dispelled when, in bidding her farewell, he finds her counting the coins he had given her as a parting present, and testing them with a hammer 'with the competence and dexterity of an old moneylender'. On the face of it, this geisha would seem to have little in common with the heroine of the opera; yet it is in Loti's description of the girl, during the months of his love idyll, that we recognize features characteristic of Puccini's Cio-Cio-San. Chrysanthème is childlike, affectionate, tender, gay and playful by turns, 'a little creature made to laugh yet easily saddened', and '*mièvre de formes et de pensée*'. Like Pinkerton, Pierre considers her 'a quaint toy' ('*un jouet bizarre*'), yet there are moments when her '*petits yeux bridés ouverts semblent révéler quelque chose comme une âme, sous cettes enveloppes de marionette*'. Loti's exquisite poetic touches are seen, not only in his portrayal of the geisha herself but also in the atmosphere that surrounds her, in the delicacy and the loving care with which he describes the fragility of her world with all its tiny objects†—all of which comes to life again in Puccini's opera. Only a French writer could have written such a novel, which has no plot to speak of, but excels in poetic moods, atmospheric impressions and minutely observed

★ Sullivan's *The Mikado* (1885), Messager's *Madame Chrysanthème* (1893), Jones's *The Geisha* (1896) and *San Toy* (1899), and Mascagni's *Iris* (1898). The credit for being the first in this field goes, however, to Saint-Saëns's obscure but engaging one-act *opéra-comique, La Princesse Jaune*, written as early as 1872. It has but two characters, and the exotic atmosphere is largely evoked by means of pentatonic melodies.

† As Loti's European eyes see it, 'in describing this land one is tempted to use the word "tiny" six times in a line'.

details. In fact, the reader is frequently reminded of Mürger's impressionist treatment in the *Scènes de la Bohème*, even as Puccini's musical characterization of Cio-Cio-San recalls that of Mimì. In addition to the general atmosphere, there are, as we shall see presently, a number of other, more tangible scenic and dramatic features which Puccini took over from Loti, either directly or through Messager's *Madame Chrysanthème*, which is based on the French novel. But his chief material was Belasco's play.

2

In 1898 Long brought out his sensational magazine story *Madam Butterfly*, which Belasco, in collaboration with the author, adapted for the stage. This story, as mentioned already, is said to have been based on an authentic incident and this was later confirmed to Puccini by the wife of the Japanese Ambassador. Whether or no, Long patently derived many details from Loti but modified them to suit his purposes. If *Madame Chrysanthème* recorded a sensitive poet's impressions and experiences of a strange country, Long's *Madam Butterfly* was a crude realistic sketch intended to show a slice of Japanese life. Loti's heroine is a gentle and delightfully amusing geisha, Long's is a silly lovesick girl who tries to 'go all American', insisting that 'no one shall speak anythin' but those United States languages in these Lef-ten-ant Pik-ker-ton's house', and assuring all and sundry that her marriage to the American officer 'make me mos' bes' happy female woman in Japan—mebby in that whole worl'—w'at you thing?'

The Japanese name of Loti's heroine is Ki-Hou-San, meaning 'Chrysanthemum', which Long changed to Cho-Cho-San, then incongruously englished it into Madam Butterfly, from a line of Pinkerton's dialogue in which he compares his fragile acquisition to this delicate insect.* Again, Loti's French captain, the charmingly frivolous, witty and refined Pierre, changes to Long's callous, fatuous Benjamin Franklin Pinkerton of the American Navy, who is a practical joker and fancies himself in the role of a modern Pygmalion; 'it was exactly in his line to take this dainty, vivid, eager and formless material [Cho-Cho-San] and mould it to his most wantonly whimsical wish', reflects Long's American Consul, adding wryly that 'it was perhaps fortunate for Butterfly that his country had need of him so soon after his marriage'. Loti's Pierre, it is true, also feels himself the lord and master of his geisha, yet he hurts neither her nor her people in his playfully ironic attitude. The Pinkerton of Long (and Belasco), however, is so conceived as to become positively offensive in his arrogance.

As for the other characters which Long took over from Loti there is Kan-goo-rou, a rare combination of 'interpreter, laundryman and discreet agent for the crossing of races', who is transformed into the grotesque and greedy *Nakodo*, Goro; there is Chrysanthème's young friend Oyouki who becomes Butterfly's servant Suzuki; and there is the geisha's little brother who in Long turns into her child Trouble. (Loti has a delightful scene in

* Compare the description Pinkerton gives of her to Sharpless in Act I of the opera.

which the sister humours her little brother and carries him home pick-a-back.) To these, Long added three more characters which were either of his own invention or derived from persons involved in the authentic episode. There is, first, the American Consul Sharpless who cannot help acknowledging Butterfly's 'protean fascination'. A little grave and pompous, a little boring and colourless, yet good-natured and gentle, Long's Sharpless is the same character as we meet in Puccini.* Secondly, there is Yamadori, 'one of those modern pensioned Princes in Japan, a matrimonial article and preternaturally fascinating'. In the magazine story he speaks fluent English, has his permanent residence in New York and undertakes occasional pleasure trips to Japan. Finally, there is Kate Pinkerton who plays a more prominent part in Long than she does in either Belasco or Puccini. Where Long differed completely from Loti was in the semi-tragic twist he gave his story: after being told by the Consul of Pinkerton's desertion, the geisha's first resolve is to commit *hara-kiri*; she has already wounded herself when the thought of the child makes her change her mind. When at the end of the story Kate arrives at the geisha's house to take the child away she finds the rooms deserted, the implication being that Butterfly had returned to her former profession. Puccini's Butterfly considers this alternative in her aria 'Che tua madre' of Act II.

Long's story is admittedly too drawn out for its simple plot. It has no less than three introductory chapters showing Pinkerton and the geisha already married for several months and living in New York. Yet it must be said in favour of Long's treatment that he succeeded in rendering his characters credible in their particular setting, and once the tale gets properly under way a number of situations are introduced which are truly moving. There is, for example, the episode of Butterfly's visit to the American Consulate, where, accompanied by her child and Suzuki, she tries to ascertain from Sharpless the date of Pinkerton's expected return. While she is there a blonde American woman arrives—Kate Pinkerton—and wishes to send a telegram to her husband at Kobe. She dictates the contents of her cable within Butterfly's earshot, which runs: 'Just saw the baby and nurse. Can't we have him at once? He is lovely. Shall see the mother about it tomorrow. Was not at home when I was there today.' Kate then notices the geisha without realizing who she is and before leaving addresses her with the condescending words: 'The little Japanese, you pretty pretty plaything!' Butterfly, having guessed Kate's identity and realized the terrible truth contained in the words of the cable, thinks of ending her life. This was the episode on which Puccini based his original Act II, the so-called 'Consulate act', which he subsequently threw out because he wanted the action to move to its close 'without interruption, rapid, effective, terrible'.

* Illica's own description of the Consul is worth quoting: 'open-hearted, jovial, good and owing to his life in different countries, full of philosophy; disdainful of all customs and habits and appreciating only the good people be they English or Boers, American or Japanese . . . just like that great statesman who used to say: "all ideas are essentially good ones, it's only the men who corrupt them"' (To Ricordi. March 1901, *C.P.Let.*249).

The most poignant episode of the novel and, certainly, a unique one is Butterfly's vigil, which Long describes as follows:

> Not for a night, but for days and nights, eating little, sleeping little—less and less of these. Finally, Cho-Cho-San could no longer hold the glass with which she was scanning the harbour for Pinkerton's ship. She lay on the mats with the baby while the youthful handmaid watched. Every day the faded flowers were replaced by purchased ones—cheaper and cheaper ones. And there one day by accident Cho-Cho-San sees Pinkerton on deck with a blonde woman on his arm, and on the following morning the warship had disappeared.

3

This, then, was the story which Belasco, with his eye for an effective melodrama, adapted into a one-act play.* His most important modification of Long's plot was his wholly tragic ending; to heighten its pathos he brought Pinkerton back in the closing scene, whereas in the novel he never sets eyes again on Butterfly after his desertion. By a skilful elimination and compression of Long's episodes, Belasco achieved unity of time, place and action, the drama playing within twenty-four hours in the house of Butterfly. He retained, on the other hand, a great deal of Long's original dialogue, but far from attempting to tone down its crudities, he added some of his own—for example, Butterfly's last words to Pinkerton: 'Too bad those robins didn' nes' again.' Famous last words indeed! Compared with the play, Puccini's libretto almost assumes the stature of a poetic verse-drama. Many of Belasco's verbal realisms were either eliminated or mollified, Pinkerton's notorious 'milk punch or whisky' being one of the few specimens left in. Under the composer's and his librettists' hands the heroine reverts again to the gentle and affectionate girl she is in Loti's romance, and even Pinkerton—how could it be otherwise with a Puccinian tenor?—takes on softer and warmer colours and behaves in a markedly less brash fashion than in the novel and the play.†

Puccini's original intention had been to follow the design of Belasco's play and write a one-act opera with a prologue based on the introductory chapters of Long's story. This plan was soon discarded in favour of a full-length opera, which was a far more advantageous proposition since it allowed scope for dramatic development and fell in with the Italian public's preference for a substantial work. The original prologue was replaced by the present Act I, which serves several purposes, the most important being to show Butterfly in her shortlived happiness so as to render the subsequent drama

* Puccini considered the play far superior to Long's story which, incidentally, Giacosa published in *La Lettura* of February 1904 to coincide with the first-night of the opera.

† In his transplantation from play to opera, this egregious character was re-baptized several times. In an early draft he was called 'Sir Pinkerton', then he became 'B. F. Pinkerton', initials which lent themselves to a somewhat ambiguous interpretation in Anglo-Saxon countries, so that they were reversed to 'F. B.'. In the German version, he is called 'F. B. Linkerton', the reason for this change being the fact that 'Pinkerton' happened to be the name of a famous American detective agency, also of the hero of a series of German detective thrillers which in the 1900s enjoyed great popularity in Central Europe.

the more poignant. This in turn necessitated making of Pinkerton a far more important figure than he is in Belasco, where, in fact, he does not appear until the very end of the play. Moreover, what Puccini opera could do without an extended love scene? Last but not least, this introductory act furnished the composer the opportunity he always needed for a leisurely setting of the atmosphere. Furthermore, for certain details the librettists went to Loti's romance and Messager's opera. Thus the model for the drunkard Yakusidé (in the Milan version of the opera he has a whole scene to himself)* is to be found amongst Loti's *bonzes*, whom Pierre visits one day in their monastery to find that 'fat, chubby and shorn, they trouble about nothing in the world and are all too fond of our French liqueurs—Benedictine or Chartreuse!'. To Puccini's *bonze*, however, it is whisky that most appeals. As for the episodes derived from Messager's *Madame Chrysanthème*, they consist of the lovers' first meeting, the wedding ceremony with the crowd of congratulatory relations and the concluding love scene. On the other hand, the motive of the curse uttered by Puccini's Uncle Bonze against the geisha was evidently elaborated from a hint in Long's story, where the geisha, having adopted her husband's religion, was ostracized by her family.

4

Madam Butterfly stands apart from the rest of Puccini's operas for reasons dramatic and musical. Though couched in terms of a melodrama it contains an element of true tragedy. The catastrophe is the inevitable corollary of the geisha's character; because she is what she is, she cannot act otherwise than she does. Faced by three alternatives—marriage to Prince Yamadori or resumption of her former profession or death—she makes the most courageous choice. Caught in a *moral* conflict she solves it by self-annihilation and thus grows to a heroine in the true sense of the word. The second distinguishing feature of the opera is that Butterfly is Puccini's only heroine who is shown as a character developing in a continuous and consistent line—from the child-bride of Act I to the tragic woman at the end of the opera. Thirdly, the intrinsic action is psychological and is concentrated in the geisha, who is the centre of the whole drama. Butterfly has no real antagonists: Pinkerton is no more than a catalyst to set the tragedy in motion, and the remaining characters are satellites revolving round Butterfly's planet—lay figures who serve only to intensify the tense, quivering humanity of the little heroine; though the Consul and Suzuki act in something like the role of a Greek chorus. Lastly, because the geisha and her fate struck deepest into Puccini's unconscious images, he was able to probe her psyche more thoroughly than those of his other heroines, and to bend his whole resources to a minute musico-dramatic analysis of her shifting emotions and thoughts. *Butterfly* is his only opera to which the designation 'psychological music-drama' may be applied almost without reservation.

In genre it belongs, of course, to *opéra-comique* returning to the miniature,

* See p. 398.

the careful observation of details and the conversational style of *Bohème* but on a higher technical level. Apart from the heightened expressiveness and refinement of the purely lyrical style, we observe a new plasticity in melody, harmony and orchestral colours, and a more subtle use of leit-motives in the service of psychological delineation; Puccini's mosaic of little squares is now invested with the dramatic function of characterizing a world of diminutive people and things. There is, finally, a completely new aspect to Puccini's style: the exotic aroma which spreads over the greater part of the opera. Just as the heroine is inseparable from her peculiar ambience, so is the musical exoticism from the score. It is not an adventitious element —no mere *japonaiserie*. Atmosphere was a potent creative stimulus for Puccini and its fruitful results are seen in this opera in the perfect assimilation of features from Japanese music into his own style. For all the extensive use he made of authentic tunes, the pentatonic scale and certain instrumental exoticisms, the score contains not a bar that does not bear the Puccinian stamp.

5

In this process of assimilation Puccini resorts to two methods, the first of which is the simple one of quoting a Japanese tune either whole or in parts and embedding it in impressionist harmony. I have been able to identify seven such tunes.

Ex. 55

Japanese National Anthem

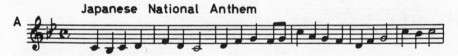

Ex. A announces the arrival of the Imperial Commissioner and the Marriage Registrar (Act I [59]).

Cherry-Blossom Song

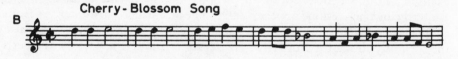

Ex. B is introduced at the point where Butterfly shows Pinkerton her various knick-knacks (Act I, 4 bars after [75]).

Japanese Song, "The Nihon Bashi"

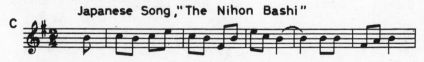

Ex. C, with its swaying line, accompanies the repeated bows with which Butterfly's friends offer their congratulations (Act I [87]).

385

Japanese Song, "My Prince"

Ex. D represents Prince Yamadori, its title having no doubt suggested this association. Its first occurrence, however, is in a different dramatic context (Act II, Part 1, 6 bars after [20]).

Japanese Folk Song

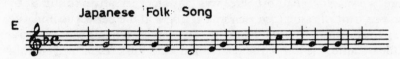

Ex. E is Suzuki's prayer melody (Act II, Part 1 [3]).

Japanese Folk Song

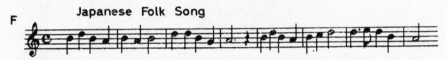

This is first heard at Butterfly's arrival on the scene (Act I [41]).

Japanese Classical Music

Ex. G is associated with the sad history of Butterfly's family (Act I [37] and [44]).*

Puccini's second and more pervasive method consists in inventing melodies in the Japanese manner and often working into them authentic motives, for example, in the delicious tune of woodwind, harp and bells to which Butterfly and her retinue appear on the scene and which partly derives from a Spring Song (Ex. F). To such half 'imaginary' folk-tunes belong also the sprightly music for Butterfly's chattering relatives (Ex. 62), the 'Father's Suicide' or 'The Sword' theme (Ex. 59a). Similarly, the abundance of short melodic-rhythmic patterns in lively two/four time serves to evoke the tripping character which Japanese music has for Western ears.

At the time, Puccini considered *Butterfly* his most modern work, which it certainly was, notably in its harmonic and orchestral style. As later in *Fanciulla* and *Turandot*, the exotic milieu appears to have inspired in him

* I identified Exx. A, B, D and F from *Sammlung von Japanischen Volksliedern* by Isawa Shuji, with piano arrangements by Georg Capellen. Leipzig, 1904. Exx. C, E and G are included in *Nippon Gakufu, Two series of Japanese Folk Songs*, ed. by Diettrich (Leipzig, 1894). Exx. B and E had also been used by Messager in *Madame Chrysanthème*.

a remarkable desire for experimentation and freedom in the manipulation of the devices he had been developing since *Manon Lescaut*. A few instances may serve as illustrations. Thus he telescopes the pentatonic scale A–B–D–E–G into chords, harmonizes the 'Yamadori' theme in a different 'exotic' manner on each of its six occurrences, writes bitonal-sounding passages (actually suspension chords):

Ex. 56

and makes telling dramatic use of the whole-tone scale and the tritone, and of sustained pedals and *ostinati*, the last features being prominent in Far Eastern music as well as in the composer's personal style. Even such a worn-out coin as the added sixth is made to take on a freshly minted look, as witness the very close of the opera where the addition of the note G to the B minor chord creates the effect of cataclysm.

Puccini's melodic and harmonic *trouvailles* are enhanced by the subtlest and most variegated orchestral hues; they often conjure up the thin, glassy, high-pitched sound of those kinds of Japanese music in which characteristic use is made of woodwind instruments and a large variety of bells and gongs. These light and gay colours predominate in Act I, whereas in the later part of the drama the composer resorts more frequently to the strings, low-lying clarinets, cor anglais and muted horns and trumpets. The final pages of the opera in which the pentatonic 'Geisha' theme is thundered out by the whole orchestra in unison, with the brass adding a quite peculiar harshness, is an almost exact reproduction of the timbre of Japanese temple-music.

6

But for all the pervasive exotic colouring, Puccini clearly contrasts the West with the East; in the music for Pinkerton and Sharpless he returns to his 'normal' style. And never completely consistent in his characterization, he allows Butterfly to cast off her Japanese musical garments and wear European dress, usually at moments of lyrical effusion. Even her two principal themes are free from any marked exotic flavour and might have equally suited Manon or Mimi, especially the sensuous, melting:

Ex. 57 Largo

Not the least magical effect of Ex. 57a resides in its instrumental and vocal texture: three solo strings, harp, muted horns and choral arpeggios in augmented triads envelop the solo voice in a delicate yet warm colour. The two themes are so conceived as to suggest both the loving bride and the wide expanse of sea and earth and the spring breeze of which Butterfly and her friends sing as they climb the hill—an exquisite example of how Puccini can hit off character as well as atmosphere in one and the same idea. Ex. 57a undergoes transformation according to psychological changes in the drama, as in Act II, Part 1:

Ex. 58

the first example illustrating the pathetic futility of Butterfly's love, the second her exuberance as mother of Pinkerton's child.

Of more than a dozen motives introduced in Act I, two assume great importance in the later course of the opera: 'The Father's Suicide' or 'The Sword':

Ex. 59

The Bonze's 'Curse' stands for Butterfly's ostracism and loneliness (Ex. b).

In Act II, Part 1, which plays three years later, Butterfly has grown to full maturity, and this is shown, above all, in the two arias which portray her in extremes of mood: fervent hope in 'Un bel dì' and tragic despair in 'Che tua madre'. The first, being sung on the concert platform in and out of season, has become so hackneyed a piece that its exquisite music and fine dramatic characterization is taken for granted. Butterfly's unfolding emotions —her trance-like state at the beginning as she visualizes the arrival of Pinkerton's ship, her growing agitation and final ecstasy as she pictures herself waiting on the hill and seeing him at last climb up and embrace her— all this is caught with perfect mastery. There is the opening with her dream-like, floating phrase, possibly inspired by the verbal image 'a thread of smoke' and an admirable example of Puccini's art of evolving a sustained line from tiny particles. There is the tender solo violin 'as if from a distance' and the muted violas 'like a distant murmur' enhancing the visionary quality of Butterfly's melody. There is, later, the gentle *arioso*, 'Mi metto là', blossoming out into the yearning whole-tone phrase of which the composer will make such poignant use shortly before the end of the opera:

Ex. 60

s'av-via per la col--li--na

And there is the final climax with the return of the opening melody now *con molta passione*, after which an orchestral epilogue sums up Butterfly's passionate longing as she embraces Suzuki.

Her second aria, 'Che tua madre', coming after the Consul's hint at Pinkerton's faithless desertion, is addressed to her child. It is one of Puccini's most noble inventions. Cast in the rare key of Ab minor its mood is that of unrelieved sadness, which possibly explains why this aria is never heard out-side the opera house, though it is more dramatic than 'Un bel dì', witness, for instance, the poignant octave leaps at 'morta' toward the end. 'Che tua madre' has the character of both a funeral march and a dance-song, with heavy, sarabande-like accents on the second beat of the bar and an ominous *col legno* passage at the line 'orribile destino, danzerà per te', a passage which at its *tutti* repeat before the close of the opera achieves a shattering effect.*

Finally, there is Butterfly's last farewell. Like the foregoing aria, this is addressed to her child and for this reason possibly inspired the composer to the most heartrending music of his whole work. It begins with a free *arioso*, 'Tu, tu piccolo Iddio!', and culminates in the cavatina 'O a me' (Ex. 4c), Puccini no doubt feeling that at this juncture another full-length aria would be out of place. This farewell has all the characteristics of the Puccinian lament and is, incidentally, in the same key as Cavaradossi's 'E lucevan le stelle' (B minor).

The musical characterization of the remaining figures will not detain us long. To depict Pinkerton as the repellent character he is manifestly went against the grain, for into the tenor Puccini unconsciously projected his own love for the little heroine. Thus he could not help endowing it with warm

---

* In the original version, the aria was longer and textually slightly different.

and, in the love duet, ardently impassioned music. Moreover, the Pinkerton of Act I had to be shown in the light of a romantic lover if Butterfly's devotion to him was to be made credible and if the necessary emotional equilibrium between the two roles was to be achieved. After all, Pinkerton *was* in love with the little geisha. Even toward the end of the opera when this character has been revealed in his callousness and cowardice, Puccini is at pains to mitigate our aversion in the tenor's brief *arioso* 'Addio fiorito asil', expressing his remorse—an afterthought added in the second version, though the shrewd Giacosa had vainly tried to insist on its being included in the first version.*

In a letter to Ricordi (23 April 1902) Puccini wrote that he was doing his best 'to make Mr. F. B. Pinkerton sing like an American'. The truth is that Pinkerton has all the characteristic attributes of a Puccinian tenor, with just a thin 'American' veneer spread over him, best noted in his only aria 'Dovunque al mondo' in which he expounds to the Consul his philosophy of easy hedonism. To characterize the Yankee, Puccini quotes the opening strain of *The Star-Spangled Banner* scored in military-band fashion (wood-wind and brass) and, in addition, lends this aria a certain breeziness and nonchalance by introducing more leaps in the vocal line than is usual in his tenor arias and, last but not least, by a sudden lapse into trivial verbal realism—the notorious line 'milk punch or whisky?'. The fact that even in the only aria he is given, Pinkerton is interrupted several times by the Consul who sings also the very last line, well demonstrates his lack of full tenor stature.

Of the subsidiary figures the Consul is the most articulate. Good-natured and compassionate he is mostly given lyrical music. His theme is suggestive of his honest, open-hearted nature:

Ex. 61

Goro, with his servile bowings and scrapings, is graphically caught in the harmonic motive (Ex. 61b) which Puccini also associates with Nagasaki and Japanese things in general. It vaguely recalls Benoit's figure in *Bohème*. The little that is to be said about Yamadori and Suzuki will be added in the following discussion of the musico-dramatic structure of the two acts.

* See his letters, pp. 136–138.

Faithful to his method, Puccini divides Act I into two halves. The first, serving the exposition of the drama and the establishment of atmosphere, is marked by swift, airy, light-fingered music of a strong exotic flavour; while the second half, the love scene, is inevitably static, purely lyrical and more 'Western' in style. An orchestral introduction at once plunges into the peculiar ambience of the opera. The nimble theme with its minute motives, 'snaps' and the subsequent four-part *fugato* to which it is subjected (all of which calls to mind the overture to Smetana's *Bartered Bride*) conjures up the patter of tiny, tripping feet and that 'quaint', fussy, doll-like world into which Pinkerton is presently to marry. The 'Goro' theme (Ex. 61b) provides a ready transition to the opening scene between him and the naval lieutenant. Of the diverse ideas thrown up in its lively course we note the quick-march with its woodwind syncopations, standing for Butterfly's relations, who are expected to arrive shortly.

Ex. 62

In the following scene with the Consul—like Butterfly, he announces his arrival offstage—the music gradually changes to a more solid 'Western' manner. Pinkerton's 'Non so' is a charming evocation of the graceful flutter of the butterfly to which he likens his bride, but to which Sharpless, recalling her visits to the Consulate, replies in grave, expansive phrases. The real stage-action begins with the arrival of Butterfly and her friends and the wedding ceremony, an extended scene in which Puccini introduces the majority of his authentic as well as 'home-made' Japanese melodies, and which provides a superb example of his handling of soloists and crowd who mix and separate with the casualness such a scene might show in real life.

It is designed to form three choral episodes with two intervening solo episodes. The first chorus, heard offstage, flows along in a broad melodic stream (Exx. 57a, b) and a telling detail lies in the fact that the choral climax is made to coincide precisely with Butterfly's and her friends' appearance on the stage in the flesh. This crowd scene slowly dissolves into the scene of the heroine's presentation to the Consul and her subsequent dialogue with Pinkerton during which the composer deftly drops the first hints of Butterfly's later tragedy by means of the 'Poverty' and 'Suicide' themes (Exx. G & 59a). We have learned all we need to know about herself and her family by the time this scene is terminated, at the right psychological moment, by the arrival of the Imperial Commissioner, the Official Registrar and the relatives.

The ensuing choral and solo ensemble, based on the 'Relation' theme (Ex. 62), engenders an atmosphere of fussy excitement, the simultaneous chatter of several groups, with a strict canon (at the unison) between sopranos and basses rendering the text unintelligible—a shrewd device to heighten the impression of noisy cross-talk. There follows a short lyrical episode between Pinkerton and the Consul, punctuated by a chuckling pentatonic motive to which Butterfly's relations and friends make critical comments on the bridegroom. Puccini both opposes and unites in the music the disparate worlds of West and East. The second solo scene, in which Butterfly shows Pinkerton her little knick-knacks, is an exquisite 'conversation piece' in the composer's characteristic *stile misto* (*arioso* and *parlando*). With a swift transition we turn to the actual wedding ceremony, which most composers might have inflated into a spectacular scene but which Puccini dispatches almost in a trice, the Imperial Commissioner reading the marriage contract in the perfunctory manner of a true official. Follows the toast to the bride, the gentle 'O Kami', which is rudely interrupted by Uncle Bonze's infuriated offstage cries 'Cio-Cio-San, abbominazione' to the discordant 'Curse' motive (Ex. 59b), which, combined with howling choral *portamenti*, strikes down upon the happy scene like a thunderbolt from the blue.

Having exposed the drama, established the atmosphere and delineated the characters in swift-moving scenes—a supreme example, this, of his musico-dramatic technique—Puccini now settles down to the lyrical half of Act I, the love duet, into which he poured half a dozen new ideas. This duet must rank as the finest he ever penned, so far as subtlety and pliancy of vocal line are concerned, and as his most analytical in the suggestion of the fluctuating emotions of the two characters. In no other love duet of Puccini's do we find the orchestra enhancing the voices to the same effect as here, both by its commentary and its variety of hues.* Almost for the first time in this act the strings take full command of the situation, with a solo violin to accompany Butterfly's gentle 'Vogliatemi bene', and there is a profusion of special markings to ensure a variety of sound effects (*dolce, cantando, sfumato, sfiorando, con sordina, sul tasto*). With passions waxing on the stage, the rest of the orchestra gradually enters, horns and trumpets raising their bells (rare in Puccini) at the ecstatic climax 'è notte serena'. What with a pervasive *tempo rubato* and an infinite diversity of rhythmic and dynamic nuances, this love duet demands an unceasing flexibility of style from singers and conductor alike.

In formal design it is also the most complex and ambitious of Puccini's duets. In the theatre we may well receive the impression of an almost improvisatory ebb and flow of ideas, yet on closer analysis the structure reveals a singularly coherent pattern. After an introduction, there follow four main sections, the first two of which are ternary and the third in a free *Bogen* or arch form—the only instance in Puccini of the use of this intellectual design. The last section represents the climactic epilogue repeating the music

* Illica thought that this duet was even more poetic than the one between Mimi and Rodolfo at the end of Act I of *La Bohème*. (Ricordi, March 1901. *C.P.*Let.249).

of Butterfly's arrival on the stage earlier in the act. The duet is anchored in A major but closes in F (the submediant of the home-key), and as the curtain falls the orchestra softly comes to rest on an added-sixth that sounds like a question-mark.*

8

The first part of Act II, in which Butterfly rapidly passes through a gamut of contradictory emotions, represents, perhaps, Puccini's highest achievement in psychological portraiture and musico-dramatic unity.

Three great scenes can be discerned. In the first scene the heroine is depicted in her despair at her isolation and poverty but also in her unshakable hope for Pinkerton's return. It is three years since he left her, yet her love has remained as ardent as on the first day of their encounter. Her mind is incapable of conceiving that he might, after all, have deserted her but her soul is oppressed. Puccini's opening of the act speaks a telltale language. The orchestral introduction in G minor—like that to Act I in form of a *fugato* but free, short and in three parts only—gives itself a light-hearted air (*allegretto mosso*) but its intrinsic effect is sadness. The curtain rises on Bonze's 'Curse' (Ex. 59b) to indicate Butterfly's desertion by her family, and Suzuki's ensuing Japanese prayer clinches this mood of desolation. The first unambiguous hint at the impending tragedy is given in the insistent repeats of an extended version of the 'Father's Suicide' motive:

Ex. 63   Allegro moderato

But gradually Butterfly's spirits rise and the scene culminates in her visionary aria 'Un bel dì'.

The second and longest scene is built up of three episodes of marked emotional contrast. The first episode takes in Sharpless's arrival, the ceremonial of his reception and Butterfly's constant digressions, thus preventing

---

* For the reader wishing to examine the form in detail I here give the following outline:

Introduction, [111]—1 bar before [116], an *arioso* based on reminiscences, and modulating to the dominant of A;

Section I, [116]—2 bars after [120]; ternary, new material, Key: A;

Section II, 3 bars after [120]—1 bar before [123]; ternary; new material; Key: A;

Section III, [123]—1 bar before [134], arch form; new material:

A; Pinkerton: 'Stolta paura'—A major

B; Butterfly: 'Adesso voi'—D major

C; Butterfly: 'Siete alto'—modulating

D; Butterfly: 'Vogliatemi bene'—Eb major

B; Butterfly: 'Dicon che oltre'—Bb major

A; Pinkerton: 'Via dall'anima'—A major

The music progresses from A to D, the 'keystone' of the arch, and, omitting C, retraces its step back to A.

The Epilogue, in which the voices unite, begins at [134].

393

the good Consul from explaining the real purpose of his visit. All this is treated in the lightest conversational style. The ensuing entry of Prince Yamadori, the second episode, represents a deft dramatic twist to draw out the suspense of the preceding conversation. Strangely enough, Yamadori's theme (Ex. D) is introduced in a previous context which by the widest stretch of imagination cannot be linked with that character.* Still more puzzling is the broad yearning melody, Tristanesque in flavour, with which Butterfly receives the Prince, who, according to Puccini's stage directions, is to her merely a figure of fun and tiresome in his marriage proposal:

Ex. 64

What is the explanation of this discrepancy? I venture to suggest that the appearance of Ex. 64 at this juncture only makes psychological sense if we assume that the composer wished Butterfly to simulate Yamadori's feelings for *her*, at the same time expressing her contempt for him in the drawn-out phrase to which she sings his name. The assumption that this theme is to be associated with Yamadori finds confirmation at the end of the episode, where, as the Prince departs with a deep sigh, the orchestra repeats Ex. 64. One thing is certain: Puccini's *musical* characterization of Yamadori fails to suggest the ridiculous and even grotesque figure that the latter cuts both in Long's magazine story and Belasco's play. In passing it may be noted that the *Valse lente* which accompanies the tea-party is the first instance of the kind of pretty-pretty drawing-room music which Puccini was to write in his operetta *La Rondine*.

The third episode leading up to the first great moment in the gradual unfolding of the tragedy begins with Sharpless's reading of Pinkerton's letter which Butterfly does not allow him to finish. The entrancing music for the 'Letter' scene recurs again in the scene of Butterfly's night vigil, so here I merely draw attention to the gossamer lightness of the texture whereby the spectator is enabled to follow every one of the Consul's and Butterfly's words.

Her reaction to his final question—the cutting of a Gordian knot— what she would do if Pinkerton were never to return, is treated in the music in a manner which combines a minimum of means with a maximum of effect. A single unison note (A) is struck, *ff*, by the drum and the strings 'dryly', then a pause, and before us stands Butterfly completely trans-

* Butterfly's conversation with the Consul, at the point at which she gaily draws his attention to the 'azure-blue sky' (5 bars after [20]).

formed—'as though struck by death'. Her answer 'Due cose potrei far' is set to one of those processional marches which haunt the imagination: the bassoon and the two low-lying clarinets intone a hocket-like *ostinato* (an *appoggiatura* motive interspersed with rests), which is like the halting beats of a wounded heart; and on Sharpless's entry Puccini adds a bass pedal D on the harp, with the effect of a distant death-knell. With the abruptness characteristic of realistic opera, we are now launched into the jubilant scene in which Butterfly introduces her child to the Consul, the opening motive representing a triumphant version of her love theme (Ex. 58b). After another dramatic change of mood in the sombre aria 'Che tua madre' Sharpless takes his leave, but not before being entrusted by Butterfly, now in a state of boundless exaltation, with a message to Pinkerton from the child that his name is still Trouble but on its father's return it shall be changed to Joy, the first pair of horns now thundering out the rapturous 'Un bel dì' figure.

The third and last scene again juxtaposes situations of strong emotional contrast: Butterfly's blinding fury at Goro's spiteful insinuations about the child's legitimacy, her repentance at her outburst, her tender thoughts for the child and her limitless joy at hearing the cannon-shot announcing the arrival of Pinkerton's ship in the harbour of Nagasaki—all dealt with in Puccini's 'logical reminiscences'. With the ensuing Flower Duet we arrive at another of those vignettes which release in the composer the full springs of tender lyrical music, music breathing the very sweetness of the blossoms with which the two women adorn the house. As in the love duet of Act I, Puccini casts this scene into a musically more complex mould: an introductory solo for the heroine in Gb, 'Scuoti quella fronda', followed by a rondo-like duet in Ab, with the *ritornello*

Ex. 65

which after an expansive climax, 'Gettiamo a mani piene', brings the whole piece to its poetic close.

The next scene, in which Butterfly makes her various preparations before settling down to her night vigil with the child and the nurse, is remarkable for Puccini's masterly combination of 'situation' music with psychological comment.* Even if we ignored her words, the eloquence of the orchestra is such that Butterfly's innermost thoughts are revealed;† and as she stares

* A charming realistic touch occurs at Butterfly's line 'We'll punch three little holes in the *shosi* to look out and we'll be quiet like little mice', at which point the solo flute plays a tiny figure of three staccato notes.

† In the first version of the opera this scene was both longer and musically richer. See p. 399.

through the holes of the *shosi* out into the night, a silent, rigid figure, the instruments break into a phrase of unbearable poignancy which peters out in the 'Curse' (Ex. 59b), once more indicating to the spectator the pathetic futility of her hopes and her utter isolation.

In Belasco, Butterfly's night vigil caught the imagination of all spectators; Puccini's music has rendered it one of the most poetic in all opera. This nocturne is as inspired a piece as ever sprang from the composer's head and I venture to suggest that it was sparked off, not by the 'Letter' scene where we first meet it, but by this final scene. Even a lullaby can be read into it—possibly suggested to Puccini by the gradual falling asleep of the child and the nurse—witness the gently rocking *ostinato*, *ppp*, on the flutes and the muted strings *pizz*. and the lulling wordless melody hummed by a chorus offstage, a melody instinct with the simplicity of a folk-song. (Puccini's doubling of it with a viola d'amore was done for the practical purpose of ensuring accurate intonation for the chorus and not to add an instrumental colour to the choral line. The viola d'amore should not be heard in the auditorium.) Puccini, no doubt, also associated this music with Butterfly's innocence and her unwavering faith in Pinkerton's love and hence made use of it in the previous 'Letter' scene where these character traits are stressed.

9

The second part of Act II, the shortest portion of the opera, shows some falling-off in lyrical invention. As in the final act of *Tosca*, here too the composer appears to have exhausted his fund of the memorable ideas he had scattered in such profusion over the previous scenes.

Again he opens with an orchestral introduction whose significance will be more clearly grasped if the spectator realizes that in the original version this piece was played before the open scene, when it expressed the warring emotions in Butterfly's troubled mind *during* the long hours of her solitary vigil, visions of the past, present and future mingling in her fantasies as in a dream. This prelude, which represents Puccini's most ambitious essay in symphonic writing in his operas, falls into two parts. The first part mirrors Butterfly's state of mind by means of deftly connected reminiscences and introduces a fresh idea in a broad undulating theme in twelve/eight time, as though Butterfly visualized Pinkerton's homecoming across the ocean. Into this interpretation fit the rousing brass fanfares, which, incidentally, recall the heroine's leading motive in Charpentier's *Louise*. The sailors' distant calls (whole-tone)—shortly before the curtain has risen—form the transition to the second part of the prelude—a mood-picture of the rising dawn, in contrast to the previous music diatonic and of simple texture, with some *stretto* passages to lend it a feeling of urgency. The opening scene in which Butterfly picks up the sleeping child and takes it into another room forms the close of the vigil.

The proper action begins with the arrival of Sharpless and Pinkerton. This gives rise to a threnody in G major, with grave processional steps in the bass—one of the few ideas of real distinction in this final act. On its subsequent repeat a semitone lower (G♭), it is turned into a trio for the two men and Suzuki who here grows into a musically more articulate figure than she has been so far, Puccini also making characterizing distinctions in the vocal parts. This trio represents a concession on the part of the dramatist to the musician, for the dramatic situation hardly warrants it, to say nothing of the fact that the climax, with Pinkerton emitting a high B♭, *ff*, is calculated to wake Butterfly and bring her on the scene forthwith! A striking instance, this, of how old operatic conventions still intrude upon what is perhaps Puccini's most realistic opera. The same holds true of Sharpless's solo 'Vel dissi?' and Pinkerton's brief *arioso* 'Addio fiorito asil', inserted for the Brescia production to render the tenor part somewhat more conspicuous in this scene.

The following scene is another splendid example of Puccini's conversational style and of the psychological use he makes of pauses and rests, witness the tense moment when Butterfly notices Kate Pinkerton in the garden or the little scene in which Suzuki replies, on the low A, *pp*, with a fateful 'sì' to Butterfly's question whether Pinkerton is alive.

With Kate's departure, the drama hastens to its tragic close, though not without a few retarding moments to heighten suspense, as when Suzuki sends the child into the room just as Butterfly is about to end her life so that her heart-aching Farewell is made to rise logically from the situation. As always in extreme situations, Puccini invents most fitting music to accompany the scene of the suicide: a syncopated march-rhythm on the low solo trumpet, *pp* and *tristemente*, punctuating a tortuous chromatic melody on cor anglais and violas. And as Butterfly, concealed behind a screen, is about to do away with herself, the orchestra quotes from her Farewell, thus telling the spectator that the mother's last thoughts are with her child. This is one of the subtlest psychological touches in an opera that abounds in them. Similarly, the choice of reminiscences for the very last scene, unlike that for the close of *Tosca*, is dramatically relevant and true. Thus, when we hear Pinkerton's anxious calls 'Butterfly! Butterfly!', trumpets and trombones reply in unison, *ff*, with that whole-tone phrase (Ex. 60) from her first aria in which she had visualized his happy homecoming. The effect of this quotation is one of ineffable poignancy.

10

In taking leave of *Butterfly*, it will be opportune to cast a brief critical glance at its first version. We recall that it suffered a sensational fiasco at La Scala on that rowdy evening of 17 February 1904, and that the composer, after withdrawing the work, subjected it to revision. In the biographical part of this book, the suggestion was made that this fiasco was in the first place occasioned by the machinations of an anti-Puccini clique which, whatever the true merits of the work, was bent on wrecking the performance at all costs. But Puccini's first version had its defects—on no account as grave as to warrant wholesale rejection by the audience, but certainly serious enough to call forth strictures from Italy's most responsible critics. To begin with,

there was the disequilibrium between the respective lengths of the two acts—
the first playing for nearly an hour and the second for an hour and a half.
This severely taxed the stamina of the Milan public and was especially singled
out for adverse comment at the time. But it is a criticism which we need
no longer accept. It is my conviction that present-day audiences, who
take the first act of *Die Götterdämmerung* and Strauss's two long one-act
operas in their strides, would not emerge exhausted from their seats after
hearing the second act of *Butterfly* as its author originally conceived it—
undivided. I for one have always felt the interval between first and second
part of that act as a disconcerting break in the continuity of the action to
achieve which was precisely Puccini's aim when he allowed Butterfly's
night vigil to merge, without interruption, into the scene of the rising
dawn, the whole accompanied by a continuous orchestral intermezzo. I
therefore agree with Mr. Ernest Newman in thinking that from an artistic
and dramatic point of view Puccini was right in his original conception
and that we should remain in our seats and, in listening to the intermezzo
before the open stage, live with Butterfly in imagination through her long
weary hours of waiting.[7]

On the other hand, it cannot be denied that many of the alterations made
by Puccini after the first production were improvements. Most of them
occur in Act I. Apparently over-anxious, in his first exotic opera, to reproduce an atmosphere of almost ethnographic authenticity, Puccini crammed
this act with scenic and musical details. This is notably the case in its first half,
especially in the scenes dealing with the arrival and introduction of Butterfly's
relations and friends to Pinkerton. Not only did all these amusing little
episodes retard the action, they were also irrelevant to it. Thus Butterfly's
uncle, Yakusidè, had an entire scene to himself, with a musical theme of his
own, designed to show him as an incorrigible drunkard and so to heighten
the comedy of the wedding party. Again, Butterfly's cousin is accompanied
by her little boy, who behaves as most little boys of all countries would
behave at a wedding party—but two children in the same opera was too
much and so out went the cousin's little horror in the second version,
leaving the field to Butterfly's Trouble. One set of cuts in Act I was apparently
made, not for the purpose of tightening up the dramatic structure, but
because tact dictated it. These cuts were of episodes and lines in the text
intended to illustrate certain national idiosyncrasies in the American and
Japanese peoples but in such dubious taste that they would have offended
the susceptibilities of both nations. Thus, Pinkerton mocks the culinary
peculiarities of the Japanese, referring to their 'nauseating gluttony' for
food and drink and their predilection for 'candied frogs and flies'. Similarly,
he assures Goro, he will not call Butterfly's servants by their proper names
but simply, 'Mug One—Mug Two—Mug Three'. Altogether the Pinkerton
of the original version—he is called 'Excellency' there—behaves with the
overbearing arrogance too often ascribed to the White Man in the age of
colonization. (Did not Ricordi call him a 'clyster'!) This has been greatly
toned down in the present version but apparently not enough to avoid a

Marxist interpretation.* In the light of Pinkerton's conduct in the original, we can appreciate Butterfly's reference to him as 'Un Americano, un barbaro!', words which, as she later tells him (in the love duet), were her retort to Goro when the latter suggested Pinkerton to her as an eligible candidate for marriage. These words, containing in a nutshell the larger theme of the opera and, in fact, giving the ultimate cause of Butterfly's tragedy—the incompatibility of East and West—were, regrettably, cut in the present version. Cut, too, were all those little episodes which illustrated the greed with which Butterfly's relatives fling themselves on the refreshments at the wedding party.

The alterations made in Act II are far fewer, amounting to a mere handful of pages here and there. The Flower Duet was shortened in one place and effectively enlarged in another, and Pinkerton was given the arietta 'Addio, fiorito asil!', which he would have had already in the first version if Puccini had followed Giacosa's advice. It is a pity, however, that he thought it necessary to make excisions in the entrancing scene where Suzuki attends Butterfly and her child, making them beautiful for the night vigil; the omitted episodes illustrated most vividly the childlike nature of the little geisha who passes like quicksilver from gaiety to a serious mood and back again. She also had an alluring Japanese nursery song to sing in that scene. The most important modification to Act II is, however, of a psychological kind and concerns Kate Pinkerton, from whom, incidentally, we learn that at this particular stage of the action she had been married to the naval lieutenant for only a year. In the first version it was she who appeals to Butterfly to hand over the child and, worse still, she makes this request at the very moment when the geisha realizes Pinkerton's betrayal. This was a piece of calculated mental cruelty and of utter tastelessness, withal, which Puccini was the first to recognize, and asked Giacosa to change. In the present version Sharpless takes over most of Kate's original part while Kate herself makes only a brief appearance on the scene, having no more than a few lines to sing. Excised *in toto* was a humiliating episode in which Sharpless, acting on Pinkerton's instruction, offers Butterfly a sum of money as a 'consolation prize' which she refuses with dignity.

---

* Communism has in fact seized on *Butterfly* as propaganda against 'colonial imperialism'. As reported in *The Times* of 14 October 1957, in a production given in Bucharest's new opera house, Pinkerton appeared complete with pipe and white flannel trousers suggesting a sort of composite Anglo-American colonial type, for whom it was difficult not to feel intense dislike. In addition, in order to impress the supposed Marxist moral of the plot on the audience, the programme book explained that the naval lieutenant's attitude was 'repulsive because it is the result of an odious conception of morals'. The morals were those of *bourgeois* society, that is, of the 'ruling class of the United States'. According to the writer of the programme book, 'Puccini had been a realist belonging to a movement which mirrored the hard life of the people, though, like other members of the movement, he was unable to understand the laws of class struggle in the resolution of social conflicts'. This is on a par with the fact that, when in the early years of the Soviet régime, the libretto of *Tosca* was rewritten, Cavaradossi painting his Attavanti-Magdalene was replaced by Delécluze painting a picture of the Triumph of the Commune.

These, then, were the most notable emendations for the second production of the opera at Brescia. Their total amounts to thirty-odd pages of vocal score (Italian edition)—certainly a small fraction for an opera which originally counted nearly 400 pages and whose present playing-time still is about two hours. Very little of intrinsic musical value was thus sacrificed and most of the music jettisoned consists of material heard elsewhere in the present version. On paper the difference between the two versions may not seem striking, yet on the stage, with its imponderable laws of weight, balance, timing and spacing of scenes, these alterations unquestionably served to heighten the overall effect of the opera. Nevertheless, one question remains to which there is no clear-cut answer: was it Puccini's revisions or a change of heart in his public that was ultimately responsible for the enthusiastic reception which *Butterfly* was accorded at Brescia only three months after its resounding failure in Milan?

XXXI

La Fanciulla del West

Principal Characters

Minnie ..	Soprano
Jack Rance, Sheriff	Baritone
Dick Johnson (Ramerrez)	Tenor
Billy Jackrabbit, an Indian Redskin	Bass
Wowkle, Billy's Squaw	Mezzo-soprano
Jake Wallace, A Travelling Camp Minstrel	Baritone

At the foot of the Cloudy Mountains in California. A Mining Camp in the days of the Gold Fever, 1849–50.

I

THREE REASONS PROMPTED PUCCINI to his excursion into Belasco's Wild West: the desire to conquer the lucrative American market with an 'American' opera; the opportunities the subject afforded for musical exoticism; and, most fundamentally, a desire to abandon the world of frail heroines and fragile little things. He had had enough, as he wrote to Ricordi,* 'of *Bohème, Butterfly & Co.* Even I am sick of them'. We remarked on this curious swing of his emotional pendulum. Just as after *Bohème* he turned to *Tosca*, so now, in reaction to *Butterfly*, he wished to tackle a subject with a tense, powerful plot, with virile robust characters and with a setting both unusual and spectacular—in brief, a subject of which something approaching a modern grand opera could be made. Belasco's *The Girl of the Golden West*—'a drama of love . . . against a dark and vast background of primitive characters and untrammelled nature' (Belasco)—promised to fulfil those desiderata. In a sense, it was Sardou's *Tosca* transplanted from Rome to the Cloudy Mountains of California. Like the French play, it was stark melodrama, even grimmer in general atmosphere, and its central situation bore so striking a resemblance to the older play that to assume a mere coincidence in this would be doing injustice to Belasco's skill as a borrower of other men's ideas. As in *Tosca*, the plot of *The Girl* centres on a triangular contest between two men and a woman in which the stakes are the woman's honour and her lover's life, and in which the villain of the piece is a Scarpia-like character occupying a position similar to that of the Roman Chief of Police—the Sheriff Rance. Like his Roman cousin, Rance is cheated of his prize; but here the parallels (or plagiarisms) end—there is no murder and no suicide, though there is no lack of spine-chilling situations,

* See p. 146.

e.g. the poker game, the man-hunt and Johnson's hairbreadth escape from the gallows. All ends happily in the victory of virtue over vice, of true and pure love over lust, the play thus conforming to the code of that naïve morality that still survives in a certain kind of transatlantic film.

If Belasco's plot was effective 'theatre', not the least contributory factor was its setting. The picturesquely romantic atmosphere of a gold-mining camp during the Californian Gold Rush, with its primitive passions and lawlessness, was bound to exercise a strong fascination on popular imagination, the more so as this chapter of American history was recent enough for it to be within the living memory of the older generation of American theatre-goers. Belasco's father, who died in 1911, had in his early years himself joined a gold-mining camp; the very scene in his son's play which strikes us as most contrived and improbable—Johnson's blood dripping from the loft and the subsequent poker game with his life as the stake (Act II)—follows an authentic incident said to have occurred in that camp. Similarly Jake Wallace, the camp minstrel, was drawn after an historic minstrel of that name who in the days of the Gold Rush had been a popular visitor to the various camps, singing the old '49 songs and accompanying himself on the banjo, just as he does in the play and the opera. Belasco, it should be added, knew a great deal about this milieu at first hand, having as a young actor toured in the 1860s the smaller towns of California and Nevada where the memory of the gold fever was still much alive. Admittedly, when the play was first produced voices were heard contesting the plausibility of its chief characters and the accuracy of certain local details. Belasco was, unquestionably, guilty of exaggerations and distortions for the sake of sensation, yet this was his right as a writer of melodrama and disciple of Sardou.

2

Let us now take a glance at his protagonists. He wrote the play chiefly to provide the famous actress Blanche Bates, a kind of American Sarah Bernhardt, with a 'bully' part, as he put it. And just because this part was conceived with both eyes on what this actress could do, Minnie turned out a wholly stagey creation, histrionically effective but psychologically impossible, and so she remains in Puccini's opera, too. In the preface to his play, Belasco describes her thus:

> Her utter frankness takes away all suggestions of vice—showing her to be unsmirched, happy, careless, untouched by the life about her. Yet she has a thorough knowledge of what the men of her generally want. She is used to flattery—knows exactly how to deal with men—is very shrewd—but quite capable of being a good friend to the camp boys.

This rare compound of hoyden, glorified barmaid and pure angel handles the revolver as easily as she pours out whisky, keeps a whole gang of miners under her thumb yet takes offence at the slightest impropriety, thinks nothing of cheating yet aspires to higher things and talks of moral redemption through the agency of pure love; and, though she has no more than 'thirty dollars' worth of education', reads a book 'about a couple, he was a classic an' his name was Dant', and thinks 'love's a tickling sensation at the heart that you can't scratch'. So much for fair Minnie. Johnson the noble bandit, a kind of Wild West Robin Hood, is no less contrived—'smooth-faced, tall, his clothing is bought in fashionable Sacramento. He is the one man in the place who has the air of a gentleman'. He drinks his whisky mixed with water, a sacrilege at Minnie's *Polka Saloon* where they drink it neat. 'At first acquaintance he bears himself easily but modestly. Yet at certain moments there is a devil-may-care recklessness about him. He is, however, the last man one would suspect of being the road-agent Ramerrez.'

Slightly more credible is the Sheriff—'a cool, waxen, deliberate gambler' and a dissolute rascal who, like Ramerrez, became what he is because of an unhappy home-life in his youth; Belasco thus anticipated modern findings about the psychology of criminals. Yet, strange to relate, unlike his more refined and more cunning Roman colleague in *Tosca*, Sheriff Rance is a man of honour. He loves Minnie with a mad passion, wants to marry her, and in the play makes no attempt to do violence to her. He is a good loser, withdrawing after his lost poker game if not with grace yet with some dignity, and he keeps his word by Minnie that Ramerrez should go scot free. It is Ashby, the agent of the Wells Fargo Company, who, assisted by the gold-miners, hunts down Ramerrez and compels Rance to discharge his duty by having the robber hanged.

These three characters are surrounded by a motley crowd of gold-miners, riff-raff representing diverse types of crude humanity as easy to move to sentimental tears as to hanging a man on the nearest tree. To complete this picture, there is the pair of Red Indians introduced to show the demoralizing effect which, despite Minnie's presence, camp life has had on the natives: Billy Jackrabbit steals cigars and whisky and is drunk most of the time; his squaw Wowkle has a child by him, but whenever Billy suggests making an honest woman of her, her reply is: 'Me don't know—p'haps me not stay marry with you for long time.' All this could be accepted as part of Belasco's crude realism, but what cannot be accepted is the play's intolerably false sentiment, that is, its underlying idea of moral redemption: the salvation of the souls of such evil men as Rance and some of the miners through the devotion of a pure woman. It is the idealistic Wagnerian motive transferred to the brutal realism of a Wild West drama.

But to Puccini such incongruities were no obstacle, and it is indeed doubtful whether he was aware of them. The fact was that the play possessed the qualities essential to him: a straightforward, self-evident plot, striking situations, characters caught in the white heat of passion and an unusual background entirely new to him. Yet to suit the play to the operatic stage, it needed alteration and we know from his librettist Zangarini* that the majority of changes were suggested by Puccini himself, some of them being most illuminating for his psychology as a dramatist. Thus it was he who from

* See p. 162 *n.*

a mere hint in Belasco conceived the Man-Hunt in the Californian Forest and invented the scene in which like a *dea ex machina* Minnie arrives on horseback—a Valkyrie of the Wild West—to save Johnson from the noose in the nick of time.* The moving scene of Minnie's farewell to the miners was also Puccini's invention. With these and other additions he managed to impart to his Act III appreciably more tension and to provide a closing scene far more effective and impressive as a stage picture than it is in Belasco. In the play, which has four acts, Johnson's trial takes place in the third act, laid in the *Polka Saloon*, while the fourth act, entitled *The Wilderness*, represents a mere tableau showing the two lovers alone on their way to freedom and a new life. Puccini originally intended to telescope Belasco's last two acts into one until he hit upon the idea of the man-hunt and transferred the lynching scene to the Californian Forest.

As for his treatment of the chief characters, Puccini remains faithful to his old principle of whitewashing the lovers and blackening the villain. Thus, in the so-called 'Academy' scene of the play, Minnie's 'school manual' is a book entitled *Old Joe Miller's Jokes*, while in the corresponding scene of the opera she teaches the Scriptures. That she had chosen the Fifty-first Psalm of David as the text for her lesson was Puccini's wish, because he considered it especially relevant to that scene in Act III in which Minnie appeals to the miners' hearts by reminding them of 'the best and highest teaching of Love'. Puccini's Johnson, too, evinces a nobility of character to which he can scarcely lay claim in Belasco. Even the roughnecks of miners are shown in Act I of the opera as less brutal and more deeply afflicted by homesickness than they are in the play; and as for the Puccinian pair of redskins, under Minnie's purifying influence they are firmly resolved to seek a Church blessing for their union. The Rance of the opera, however, is more savage and sinister than he is in Belasco; so as not to fall too far behind Scarpia, he too makes an attempt at rape on the open stage, to which he is never tempted in the play.

3

In setting this subject, Puccini was from the first contending against heavy odds; he described his work on it as 'most difficult'. It was as though he considered it a challenge to his prowess, a supreme test to prove his powers of translating into music a drama so unpromising. The problems he was faced with in *La Fanciulla* were of the same nature as those of *Tosca* but multiplied and intensified. Again he was confronted with incidents which at a first blush appeared to defy operatic treatment such as those in the first half of Act I, *the scène à faire* of Act II, the man-hunt and the projected lynching of Act III. As in *Tosca*, he was compelled to cope with cinematic changes of scenes still more rapid and abrupt than in the 'Roman' opera. The libretto thus afforded little scope for character development and lyrical scenes to check

* American critics later objected to the fact that Puccini made Billy Jackrabbit the would-be executioner of Johnson, their argument being that even in the Wildest West it was unheard-of for white men to allow a redskin to hang one of their fellows.

the rapidity of the action and provide a counterweight to the dramatic scenes. Moreover, all the characters without exception strike us as primitive and coarse; even Minnie and Johnson fail to enlist that degree of sympathy which we feel for Tosca and Cavaradossi. Indeed the entire subject appears altogether far less suitable than that of Puccini's first veristic essay and this, combined with a flagging melodic invention—the typical Puccini *cantilena* here flows only in thin trickles—explains why *Fanciulla* has consistently failed to establish itself in the normal repertory.

Yet any musician who has studied this score with care and has had the opportunity of seeing it in a good production, with a cast capable of singing *and* acting their parts as the composer conceived them, will be loth to dismiss the opera as an irretrievable failure and be obliged to acknowledge its stupendous craftsmanship.* In that respect *Fanciulla* is no less a masterpiece than *Tosca* and all that was said on the dramatic technique of that earlier opera holds true also of the later work, notably in the relevant use made of leitmotives and the close interpenetration of action and music. In point of style it was Puccini's reply to the 'eternal reproach that I repeated myself in my previous operas'; it represents his most complex and daring opera before *Turandot* and almost reads like a preliminary study for the latter, if we consider such features as the musical suggestion of an atmosphere of un-relieved savagery and the active role played by the chorus. The casting of the voices, moreover, emphasizes the masculine atmosphere of the setting. Of the eighteen singing characters, sixteen are male, and of these, significantly, ten are basses and baritones. The chorus is purely male and is throughout treated in unison and octaves to convey the primitiveness of the gold-miners.

Fanciulla was Puccini's second opera to have an exotic setting, and for characterization he resorted to the same two methods as in *Butterfly*: the use of authentic tunes and the invention of new material (melodic and rhythmic) in a quasi-authentic vein. To the first group belongs a small number of American folk-songs popular in the Californian Wild West in the 1850s which all make their appearance in Act I. The melody employed most frequently—one which in fact assumes the role of a theme-song—is the nostalgic *The Old Dog Tray*, also known as *Echoes from Home:*

Ex. 66

It stands for the homesickness by which that motley crowd of gold-diggers is as much plagued as it is by greed for the precious metal. First sung offstage by the camp minstrel at the beginning of the opening scene, Ex. 66 provides

* I was fortunate to see a Vienna production in the early 1920s, with Marie Jeritza in the name part, as well as an open-air production in the Roman Arena at Verona, after the second world war. Both served to drive home to me the intense, almost breathtaking dramatic nature of the music, the Verona production in particular bringing out its magnificent effect as a stage spectacle. Puccini himself considered the opera well suited for open-air performances.

a haunting round-off to the very close of the opera. Like the 'Yamadori' theme of *Butterfly*, it is set, almost on each one of its numerous appearances, in a different harmonic and rhythmic texture—most evocative, perhaps, in the barcarole-like version, in which it is first heard from the minstrel's lips and in the humming choruses of Acts I and III.* Two other original tunes are *Dear Old House* and the lively *Dooda Day*.† In addition, there are snatches of a ragtime, a cake-walk and a Spanish bolero, the latter to characterize Ramerrez and his Mexican greasers. The squaw rocking her baby sings a Red Indian lullaby to a text supposed to be based on original words (just as some of the American tunes retain their authentic words):

Ex. 67

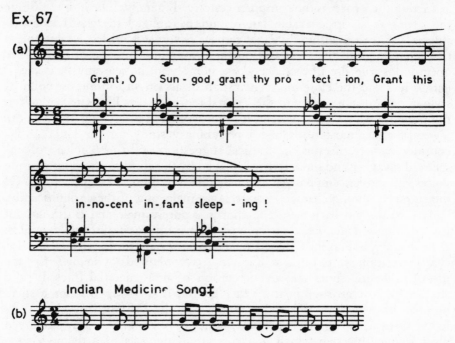

The characteristic features common to the majority of these melodies, including Puccini's self-invented folk-tunes, are the pentatonic steps, yet any similarity to the exotic style of *Butterfly* is obviated by their different rhythms, chiefly syncopated ones.

More frequent than pentatonic themes are themes based on the whole-tone scale. Puccini uses this scale as a kind of maid-of-all-work in this opera, but, as in *Tosca*, mostly in association with something brutal and terrifying, e.g. Rance's leitmotives (Ex. 75a, b), the music accompanying the fight

* For other interesting versions, see Act I [20] and four bars after [26] where the tune is enriched by a cello counterpoint.

† The first will be found 5 bars before [24], and the second 2 bars after [6], of Act I.

‡ I was unable to trace the original melody of this four-note lullaby but came across Ex. 67b, which bears a close resemblance to it, in *The Indian's Song Book*, by Natalie Curtis (New York, 1917).

between Rance and Sonora in Act I (the opening is almost identical with a passage near the close of *Butterfly*), and the man-hunt of Act III. Whole-tone, again, are the motives associated with the two Red Indians, the inarticulate, drunken Billy Jackrabbit of Act I being caught in these curious flickering figures:

Ex. 68

Lastly, following no doubt the Debussy of *Pelléas et Mélisande*, Puccini employs the whole-tone scale to more poetic effect, as in the yearning love-theme (Ex. 74) and Minnie's prayer of Act II with its strange parallels of sixths and tritones. In fact, as in *Tosca*, the tritone becomes an almost ubiquitous interval—most sinister in effect in the slow, march-like tune which accompanies the painful attempt of the wounded Johnson to climb to the loft of Minnie's log cabin in Act II:

Ex. 69*

Haunting in a different sense are the tritones in the opening scene of Act III, in which Rance awaits the result of the man-hunt on a bleak winter's dawn in the Californian Forest: a low pedal A–E♭, sounding like funeral bells, and, above it, the chords of F and B, shifting to and fro like heavy mist.

Another parallel with *Tosca* lies in the prevalence of discords, employed in the later work on a larger scale and far more daringly. Not until *Turandot* shall we again encounter such fierce clashes, which originate in a cunning use of *appoggiature*, passing and changing notes, seconds and, above all, unresolved dissonances. Minnie's theme (Ex. 72), for instance, is permeated by secondary sevenths and ninths taking the place of common chords, and Act I closes on an unresolved discord (B and D in a C major triad). In addition, we note the frequency of chromatic steps and rapid harmonic shifts which often lead to a complete obfuscation of tonality; a passage like the following has an almost dodecaphonic flavour:

* Significantly, the funeral march to which the Persian Prince in *Turandot* walks to his execution has the same tonality and the same tritone shift from E♭ to A in the bass.

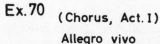

(Chorus, Act.I)

Allegro vivo

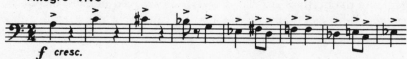

The advanced harmonic idiom of *Fanciulla* owes a debt to Debussy and the Strauss of *Salome*, yet without thus losing its individuality. The reaction to this on the part of certain admirers of the composer—a reaction also shared by not a few conservative critics—may be seen from what the composer wrote to his friend, Alberto Crecchi on 8 January 1911:

> So the harmonic idiom of *Fanciulla* has surprised you? No fear. On the orchestra everything is softened and smoothed out. The clashes scored for various instruments sound different from what they sound on the piano. (*C.P.Let.574*).

Equally suggestive of the atmosphere of the drama are certain rhythmic and dynamic features and diverse tempo markings. Apart from the dance rhythms already mentioned, we encounter brief figures in syncopated and dotted rhythms* whose ferocity is heightened by the composer's predilection for stereotyped repetitions. Some of these rhythmic ideas, derived from early rag-time music, acquire almost the status of a leitmotive:

Ex.71

No other score of Puccini's, not even that of *Turandot*, is studded with so many markings for excessive dynamics and a 'barbaric' manner of playing as that of his 'Wild West' opera: e.g. *allegro incisivo, allegro brutale, allegro feroce, come gridi* (like shouts), *con strazio* (tearing), *robusto, strepitoso,*

---

* Sketches I have seen show Puccini experimenting with such patterns.

staccatissimo, martellato, marcatissimo, vibratissimo e ben ritmato. Equally significant is the size of the orchestra, which includes quadruple woodwind, two harps, a vibraphone, a wind machine and a whistle. The general texture recalls that of *Tosca* in the massive scoring of the many *tutti*, with the brass as the hard core of it, but against such passages stand many others tinged with the most delicate hues. And, as always, Puccini resorts to uncommon or *outré* effects only very sparingly: the vibraphone at the end of Act I, the wind machine in the blizzard music of Act II and *col legno* here and there.

4

In the musical delineation of the three chief characters, Minnie demonstrably presented a difficult problem. Although the librettist painted her in a softer, more romantic light than she appears in Belasco's play, she still remains a hybrid—an odd cross-breed between the self-willed Tosca, with a touch or two of Brünnhilde, and the childlike Mimi and Butterfly. True, Puccini tried his best to present this artificial, unconvincing character in these various facets and the result is never less than adequate. As the young girl, dreaming of the blisses of pure, innocent love, she is well caught in her expansive, lyrical theme:

Ex. 72

But, when it comes to presenting a more elaborate portrait within the framework of an aria, Puccini fails to produce memorable music owing to his inability to identify himself entirely with this heroine. But he does succeed in writing, at any rate, characteristic music, as in Minnie's first aria 'Laggiù nel Soledad' (Act I) which shows her, first, as the little *ingénue*, gaily chattering away about her mother's home in passages marked by appropriate 'American' syncopations, and then as the impassioned young heroine who, like her mother, will give herself only to the man she loves (this aria is addressed to Rance):

Ex. 73

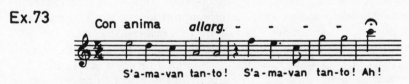

S'a-ma-van tan-to! S'a-ma-van tan-to! Ah!

Ex. 73 stands for many other passages similarly marked by wide, upward leaps and a high *tessitura*, demonstrating the close affinity of Minnie's part to that of Tosca and of Turandot. Her compass reaches from middle C♯ up to C *in alt.*, i.e. all but two octaves. Minnie's second aria, however ('Oh, se sapeste', Act II), with its un-Puccinian heartiness in gambolling coloratura, is a mediocre piece; to portray her as a Valkyrie of the Wild

West galloping on her pony through the mountain valleys was, strangely enough, beyond the powers of a composer who was himself a passionate lover of wild nature.

It is Johnson, the man on the run, who claimed the composer's deepest sympathy, inspiring him to the best lyrical music of the opera; yet significantly, such pages are not to be found until the scene in which the hero stands on the threshold of death. As Ramerrez the robber, he is introduced by a phrase in a violent rhythm (Ex. 71c), while the passionate lover of Minnie expresses himself in a swaying, yearning theme:

Ex. 74

Though Ex. 74 can scarcely be regarded as a theme of distinction it seems to have enjoyed Puccini's special favour, to judge from its unduly frequent occurrences; and with characteristic inconsistency he associated it with several other dramatic motives: the love between hero and heroine, moral redemption and homesickness. The paramount importance he attached to it is seen already from the orchestral introduction to Act I which is dominated by it.

Johnson has, surprisingly, only one full-length aria and this not until the scene of the last act in which he finds himself in a similar situation to Cavaradossi's at the beginning of Act III: he is to be executed and his last thoughts turn to his love. The *arioso* 'Risparmiate lo scherno' expresses the typical Puccinian despair by means of a drooping vocal line and a funereal *ostinato* in the harmony; the whole texture recalls that of Manon's famous 'Adieux, notre petite table' in Massenet's opera.* This *arioso*, interrupted by the miners' impatient shouts, forms a moving introduction to Johnson's aria. 'Ch'ella mi creda' admittedly has not the poignancy of Cavaradossi's 'E lucevan le stelle', yet in its emotional restraint and its broad, well-balanced melody (marked by a few 'American' pentatonic turns) it is a noble piece of music and happens to be the only aria from this opera to have found its way into the concert hall.†

The musical portrait of Rance will not detain us long. The Sheriff plays

---

* See Ex. 5a, b, on p. 292.

† Its popularity is further attested by the fact that during the first world war it became for the Italian Army on the Macedonian Front something like the equivalent of the British Army's *Tipperary* (see Vincent Seligman, op. cit.).

a far less conspicuous role in the drama than does Scarpia in *Tosca*; significant of this is the fact that the opening of *Fanciulla* makes, unlike that of *Tosca*, no allusion to this sinister character. Altogether Puccini treats him as musically a less articulate figure than his Roman colleague. True, the 'Rance' motives are characteristic enough in their jagged line and the whole-tone progressions of the bass, but are less striking than the 'Scarpia' figure:

Ex. 75

Rance's only set-piece, 'Minnie! Dalla mia casa' (Act I), is more in the vein of a declamatory *arioso* than a lyrical aria, which is in tune with this sullen, brutal character, and Puccini's reiteration of a curiously twisting five-bar theme well conveys the Sheriff's brooding mood. Like Scarpia, Rance is best characterized when in full action, with snatches of agitated recitative and short explosive figures in the orchestra.

5

Although *Fanciulla* is tense melodrama like *Tosca*, Puccini does not plunge into the action as in that earlier opera, but follows the method of *Bohème* and *Butterfly* in devoting considerable space to carefully establishing the atmosphere. The first half of Act I, *The Interior of the 'Polka'*, contains several dramatic incidents, but they do not bear directly on the action (which, indeed, does not commence until the arrival of Johnson) but serve to illustrate life in a gold-mining camp. If Puccini could refer, as he did in several letters, to *Fanciulla* as being 'a second *Bohème*', the reason is to be seen in the flexible treatment of the crowd scenes—the only common feature of these two operas otherwise poles apart from each other. Thus the opening half of the '*Polka*' act displays a kaleidoscopic change of situation in which, as in the *Latin Quarter* act of the earlier opera, the protagonists are adroitly dovetailed into the collective group of miners.* It is here that the American folk-songs are introduced. The emotional curve of these crowd scenes shows a lively zigzag, from the nostalgia of the *Old Dog Tray* song and Larkens's despairing homesickness to the brutality of the card-cheating incident and the murderous quarrel between Rance and Sonora. If violence has so far been the prevalent atmosphere, this changes at a stroke with Minnie's entry, to Ex. 72. Puccini then proceeds to paint a charming idyll in the Scripture Class, and the arrival of the Post-Boy, accompanied by what is probably one of the composer's 'imaginary' folk-tunes, affords another opportunity to show the camp ruffians in more appealing colours.

Having given the crowd its due, Puccini now turns his attention to the soloists. The scene between Minnie and Rance, containing his aforementioned aria, is presently followed by the sudden entry of Johnson, to the 'Robber' motive (Ex. 71c), and this generates the first real tension in the drama, soon to be relaxed in the ensuing waltz scene, an amusing realistic detail here being the barrel-organ orchestration of the accompaniment while the waltz tune is sung by the miners in unison. This homely mood is presently destroyed by the ferocious music accompanying the capture of Castro, which marks the end of the act's first half. From both the musical and dramatic point of view the exposition is faultless—the atmosphere is fully established, all the chief characters are introduced and their relation to one another firmly fixed.

Puccini can now settle down to the love scene and to more sustained music, yet the lyrical glow which marks the love scenes of his previous operas is all but absent. The duet is very nearly as long as that of *Butterfly* but few new ideas are introduced, the earlier waltz, though varied in texture, providing the main material. It is not until Minnie's lament-like *arioso* 'Quanti son', in which she describes to Johnson the sad lot of the gold-miners, that something like true inspiration seizes the composer. Poetic too is the dreamlike close of the act on the repeated 'Minnie' theme, growing softer and softer but bursting once more into flame at the very end, after which it dies away on an unresolved chord. This is like a question to which the answer is to be given in the next act.

Act II, *Minnie's Dwelling*, opens with a domestic idyll showing the two Red Indians with their baby, a scene given musical interest by the Indian lullaby (Ex. 67) and the impressionist colours of the orchestra. The ensuing love duet between Minnie and Johnson is more elaborate and richer in invention than its pendant of Act I; and although Minnie's aria lacks the true Puccinian stamp it introduces an exhilarating note into the otherwise languid

---

* Puccini was evidently anxious to achieve a group effect here. He wrote to Civinini, after receiving from him the libretto for these scenes: 'They seem good to me but they need a modification . . . there are too many soli for the men of the chorus, I should like to have groups of seven to eight men, who burst in, wild with rage.' From a letter, dated 23 June 1908; reproduced in *Autografi di Musicisti*, by Leonardo Lapiccirella (Florence, 1956).

feeling of this scene. The suggestion of falling snow outside the log cabin—parallel fifths, fourths and whiffs of thirds on the woodwind—is perhaps more graphic in effect than the similar picture at the opening of Act III of *Bohème*, and a fine orchestral storm, based on the 'Love' theme (Ex. 74), is let loose at the moment at which the lovers fall into an ecstatic embrace, the door suddenly flying open. We are here reminded of the scene between Sieglinde and Siegmund in Hunding's Hut in Act I of *Walküre*.

The ensuing scene—the arrival of the Sheriff and his investigating party—is briefly disposed of in recitative so as to arrive swiftly at the first great climax of the action. None the less, it would seem a pity that Puccini did not elaborate the episode in which Rance, as Scarpia does with Tosca, cunningly plays on Minnie's jealousy. What follows is a close juxtaposition of two *scènes à faire*, modelled, no doubt, on the corresponding act of *Tosca* where the sequel to Cavaradossi's torture comes in the great scene between the heroine and Scarpia. In *Fanciulla* the first of the two scenes takes place between the lovers alone. Johnson reveals to Minnie his true identity, namely that he is the robber Ramerrez pursued by the Sheriff, and this sends the girl into such moral indignation as to make her force Johnson to leave, disregarding the mortal danger that awaits him outside. He is shot at and Minnie, taking pity on him, brings him back again and conceals him in the loft. The second scene opens with the entry of Rance, who discovers the fugitive's presence through a tell-tale drop of blood dripping from the loft on his hand. Johnson is now brought down and the famous poker game for his life follows.

For these two scenes, notably the second, Puccini rolls out the whole arsenal of veristic devices to achieve a maximum of terror: rhythmic *ostinati*, grinding discords, *tremolo*, *martellato*, ferocious brass passages and and like.* Admittedly, this is all done with a technical cunning that far surpasses anything of this kind in the corresponding *Tosca* scenes, and the suggestion of characters in an almost pathological state of frenzy is complete; it is here, too, that the Strauss of *Salome* made his chief contribution to Puccini's score. Yet the sheer quality of musical as distinct from technical invention is mediocre. The *Andante triste* in F♯ minor, in the card-game episode, is but the palest reflection of that haunting theme in the same key deployed in the scene preceding Scarpia's murder by Tosca (Ex. 53).

Act III, *In the Californian Forest*, has no orchestral prelude, as has the corresponding act of *Tosca*, to break the stark atmosphere by a contrasting mood-picture. It opens almost at once with a recitative between Rance and Nick, the bleak melancholy dawn vaguely suggested by the orchestra. This act consists of three big scenes. The first—the man-hunt of Johnson, with the pursuing miners now heard offstage, now visible onstage—belongs more properly to the screen than the theatre,† and hence constitutes a

---

* Special points in the scoring are worth mentioning; e.g. the spine-chilling harp arpeggios in a quasi-bitonal texture, in illustration of the dripping blood, and the dull hypnotic throb of the double basses, in the scene of the card game.

† It was for this scene that Puccini demanded eight to ten horses.

difficult problem for the producer if it is to be shown as the composer visualized it. The second scene centres on Johnson's moving Farewell, already discussed, after which the preparations for his hanging proceed to a march of admittedly sinister ring but far less haunting than the 'March to the Scaffold' for the Execution in *Tosca*. And so we arrive at the big final scene, which is ushered in spectacularly by Minnie's unexpected arrival on horseback, with her hair dishevelled and a pistol between her teeth—gangster's moll, Fury and Valkyrie rolled into one. Her subsequent sermon to the miners, in which she reminds them of 'the highest teaching of love my brothers, that the very worst of sinners may be redeemed and shall find the way to Paradise' (on B *in alt.*!), finds no responsive echo in Puccini's music and could not find it if we recall what has been said on his psychological make-up. The entire scene is dealt with by means of his labour-saving 'logical reminiscences' in which the Camp Minstrel's nostalgic song of Act I takes the lion's share. For the rest, the composer relies on the visual effect of the stage-picture to carry the drama, and to that extent the close of the opera is unquestionably impressive: the lovers, now united, gradually disappear into the snowclad forest while the miners intone in subdued voices a last fragment of *Old Dog Tray*.

XXXII

La Rondine

Principal Characters

Magda de Civry	Soprano
Lisette, her maid	Soprano
Ruggero, a young man from Montauban	Tenor
Prunier, a poet	Tenor

Paris: The Second Empire.

I

WE DO NOT KNOW the nature of the original 'Viennese' libretto of *La Rondine* which Puccini was expected to set, beyond the fact that, according to him, it was 'the usual operetta clumsily made and banal, with the usual contrast between East and West; festive balls and dances, with no characters shown in depth, without any originality and interest (its most serious defect)'. (To Baron von Eisner, 14 December 1913.*C.P.*Let.638). No wonder he rejected it out of hand. The Parisian setting, as we now have it in the opera, may well have been the composer's own idea—it certainly suited his taste for a French atmosphere. On the other hand, two features bear an unmistakable Viennese stamp and were manifestly borrowed from *Fledermaus*. One is Magda's maid Lisette, a wench as saucy and quickwitted as Adele in the Johann Strauss operetta, and the other is the motive of the maid dressing up in her mistress's evening clothes and both going—unknown to one another—to the same ball where Magda recognizes Lisette but remains unrecognized by her, as in the case of Rosalinde and Adele.* The essential plot, however, bears so striking a resemblance to that of *Traviata* that we must find it positively odd that no mention whatever is made of this in Puccini's published correspondence. He was, after all, never slow in sniffing out even the faintest similarity in his libretti to those of other composers.

Imagine Verdi's opera without its tragic dénouement and with light relief in the addition of a pair of comic lovers and you have, broadly, the plot of *La Rondine*. Magda is a courtesan like Violetta, and at the beginning of the opera we meet her as the mistress of the wealthy banker Rambaldo, who recalls Violetta's Baron Douphol. Magda too yearns for true love, which comes to her in the shape of the young and romantic Ruggero, who, like Violetta's Alfredo, hails from the French countryside. But while Alfredo knows of Violetta's past already before he declares his love to her, Ruggero is presented as so innocent in mind that it is not until near the end of the

---

* This motive derived, undoubtedly, from the original Viennese libretto.

opera, and then only through her confession, that he is made aware of Magda's being 'no early violet', as Puccini put it somewhat cynically.. This tends to lend their scene of separation a forced note. Magda's decision to renounce her love for him and leave him is, as in the case of Verdi's heroine, brought about by parental intervention, a letter of Ruggero's mother playing the same decisive part as the visit Germont *père* pays to his son's mistress. Other parallels with Verdi's libretto are the party at Magda's elegant home at which Ruggero is introduced to her; Prunier's hand-reading scene which recalls the episode of the fortune-telling guests disguised as gipsies at Flora's party; and the retreat of the lovers to the country, where they are threatened by privation. Small wonder then that uncharitable tongues dubbed *La Rondine* 'the poor man's *Traviata*'.

Adami's libretto has variety and liveliness but is flawed by a fundamental weakness in the treatment of the two lovers and in fact of the whole plot. It falls between two stools, being neither light enough for a sentimental comedy, as which the work was intended, nor serious enough for a tragedy. This sitting on the fence, as it were, prevented Adami from clinching the matter either way. That Puccini was capable of composing a comic opera he later proved in *Gianni Schicchi*, but this was *pure* comic opera. In *La Rondine* the comic element, represented by the poet Prunier and the parlourmaid Lisette, is not far enough developed to provide a proper foil to the sentimental lovers. It is conceivable that Adami thought of repeating the happy blend of gaiety and pathos of *Bohème*. If so, he overlooked that Puccini needed a wholly tragic dénouement to bring out the best in him. It was, undoubtedly, this hybrid character of the libretto that made it impossible for the composer to identify himself with its characters as intimately as he did with the two contrasting pairs in *La Bohème*. He himself felt that, though it was 'light as a spider's web', it suffered from an ambiguity caused by the curious origin of the work.

2

La Rondine lacks the vital melodic spark and shows fatigue in lyrical invention, though it is by no means devoid of inspiration. Specht's dictum that it is 'feeble from beginning to end' and that 'hardly ever has Puccini been less inspired' is the pronouncement of a critic who can have given the work no more than a cursory glance. The composer was certainly not guilty of immodesty when he wrote to Adami that he thought 'the music has some value' (22 August 1915, *E*). With the exception of the final act, the action flows along in vivid musical scenes often reminiscent of *Bohème*. Particularly noteworthy is the remarkable fluency of the crowd scenes and the light conversational style adopted for certain episodes, with their effortless oscillation between *parlando* and more sustained lyrical passages. And though the mosaic still remains Puccini's chief method of melodic construction, he now resorts to it less frequently and often writes long-limbed, well-balanced phrases, notably in the love music of Magda and

Ruggero. Some of the set-pieces—Prunier's romanza, Magda's aria, Lisette's duet with the poet, and the waltzes—date from the time when Puccini had penned a few of the eight to ten separate numbers which he had been required to write for the Viennese publishers; and they are adroitly fitted into the 'action' music he composed later, with no seams showing. The seriousness with which he approached the composition of his *commedia lirica* is seen in the following features: some characters have their recurring representative themes (see below), there are a number of extended solo ensembles (duets, trios and quartets) and the orchestral texture is often elaborate; in one of the big choral ensembles of Act II the two chief waltz tunes are contrapuntally combined.

Waltzes are Puccini's chief means of characterizing the period of the Second Empire; two of these represent the theme song of the work:

Ex. 76

In this the composer follows the tradition of the classical Viennese operetta in which the waltz is the most characteristic feature; but to match the setting of *La Rondine*, his waltzes tend, in pace and melodic shape, to the French variety of the *valse lente*. Only once, in Act II, when the revelry *chez Bullier* reaches its height, do exuberant leaps and a sprightly rhythm recall Vienna and its waltz king. What strikes the critical ear, however, as incongruous, in view of the fact that the action takes place during the period of the Second Empire, are strong echoes from modern ballroom dances.* Thus Prunier's theme is in tango rhythm, Magda's duet with Ruggero, 'Perchè mai cercate' (Act II)—the only banality in the work—is a slow-foxtrot, and Ruggero's narration of his innocent escapades at Montauban proceeds in a one-step. Equally strange is it to find pentatonic melodies, as in Lisette's part in Act I, while the marionette-like music for the hand-reading scene in the same act

* In the same sort of way Richard Strauss in *Rosenkavalier* introduces nineteenth-century Viennese waltzes into an eighteenth-century setting.

strikingly anticipates the music for the Trio of the Three Masks in Act II of *Turandot*. The harmonic idiom continues the advanced style of *Fanciulla* with unresolved discords, abrupt shifts of key, pungent seconds, and an intense chromaticism, at times obscuring tonality. Prophetic of *Turandot* are progressions in rising fourths and more remarkable still are the bi-tonal passages in Lisette's music:

Ex. 77 Allegro vivo

What with this and the orchestration, sophisticated and exquisitely subtle, *La Rondine* surpasses any operetta known to me in craftsmanship and attention to detail. In brief, the work may be said to be as accomplished in its technique as any of Puccini's operas.

Where in fact it aspires to opera is in the music of the two sentimental lovers and in the choruses. Puccini was demonstrably more interested in his heroine than in her innocent rustic of a lover, who can boast but a single aria, 'Dimmi che vuoi' (Act III). Magda, on the other hand, is not only given a leitmotive in this yearning phrase:

Ex. 78 Sostenuto

but also the lion's share of the love music. That Magda belongs to the sphere of opera, and not operetta, is also seen from her exacting vocal part, studded with high notes, including several dramatic C's *in alt.*, and encompassing two octaves. The two sides of her character—sentimentality and lighthearted frivolity—are well portrayed in her aria 'Denaro! Niente altro che denaro' (Act I), which begins in a languid mood (Ex. 78) and presently veers round to a charming waltz. Act II contains the most inspired music for the two lovers. Their introductory duet, for example, includes, in 'Nella dolce carezza', a piece of genuine poetic feeling whose gentle, undulating line in euphonious thirds calls to mind the 'Flower' music of *Butterfly*; and it is an exquisite touch when presently the chorus echoes this melody in waltz rhythm, *molto piano e dolce.** A fine example of Puccini's *morbidezza* is the second duet

* This continuation of the duet into the waltz and the waltz itself is one of the many instances in which Puccini composed ahead of the actual libretto, subsequently asking Adami to provide him with a scene of corresponding 'unrestrained gaiety' (11 November 1914. *E*).

of this act, 'Bevo al tuo fresco sorriso', subsequently developed into a choral ensemble of truly operatic character.

The last act, however, where the drama turns to pathos and where we should have expected the composer to achieve his inspired best, proves on the whole disappointing. He launches into phrases of intense passion but the real afflatus is lacking—possibly because Magda's renunciation carries with it no hint of catastrophe. It is, incidentally, illuminating of the psychology of Puccini's creative processes that in the brief scene in which Magda soliloquizes on her dilemma, a scene somewhat similar to Butterfly's in Act II where she considers the two alternatives of becoming a geisha again or ending her life, the composer writes music of a similar puppet-like character:

Ex. 79

Allegro agitato

The ensuing 'Letter' scene is musically rather thin, nor does the subsequent *scène à faire*, in which Magda shatters Ruggero by her decision to leave him, rise to a memorable level, for all the dramatic support provided by the orchestra. On the other hand, the final farewell duet 'Ma come puoi', with its broad flowing melody, the soft harp arpeggios, the distant sound of low bells and Magda's closing phrase on a high A♭, *pianissimo*, succeeds well in conveying the mood of a final parting, though it lacks the dramatic poignancy of the characteristic Puccinian farewell. The composer felt this himself but argued with Adami that this was in keeping with the general mood of the last act. Perhaps he was right from the drama's point of view to have taken out 'all that dramatic stuff' and to have approached the end 'quietly and delicately, without any orchestral blaring or screaming'; yet this should have been no obstacle to his inventing music of more significance.

La Rondine would doubtless have gained in appeal had the comic pair been allowed more scope in the action and thus been given more music. The poet Prunier, a kind of drawing-room philosopher, is not vivacious and comic enough as a foil to the sentimental Ruggero from whom in fact he usurps, in Act I, the role of *primo tenore*. Like Magda, Prunier has a characteristic theme and the very first aria of the work, 'Che il bel sogno', is given to him, recalling Des Grieux's charming 'Tra voi belle'.★

★ Prunier's part contains a sly reference to Strauss's *Salome*. When the poet is requested by the ladies to name the ideal woman, that is, the woman who would most appeal to his artistic sensibility, he enumerates Galatea, Berenice, Francesca da Rimini and Salome, at which point Puccini quotes, on the clarinet (as in Strauss), the flickering motive of the Judaean Princess.

Owing to Puccini's vacillations Prunier started his operatic life as a baritone, then became a tenor, to change again to his original voice, and finally ended at a tenor.

Lisette is a more sprightly character, as seen from her lilting leitmotive:

Ex. 80

In temperament, she is a younger cousin of Musetta and it seems a pity that she was not permitted to express her frivolous charm in an aria of her own, comparable to Musetta's waltz. In compensation, Lisette and her poet have, in Act I, an extended and most alluring duet, 'T'amo! Menti!', that might have stepped out of *Bohème*. For some unknown reason, however, Puccini's musical interest in this pair abates in the subsequent two acts.

XXXIII

Il Trittico

PUCCINI HIMSELF WAS DOUBTFUL about the aptness of the generic title *Trittico*. Unlike the three panels of a triptych, his three operas form no narrative sequence nor is there any conceivable relationship between their subjects. Yet some faint and latent coherence does seem to exist. We recall the composer's initial plan of drawing the three episodes, respectively, from Dante's *Inferno—Purgatorio—Paradiso*, though in the event only *Schicchi* was so derived. Yet if we consider the characteristic atmosphere of each opera, it cannot be denied that each reflects, in a very general fashion, of course, the corresponding image in Dante's three concepts—*Tabarro*, with its oppressive and hopeless story, relates to the *Inferno*; *Suor Angelica*, a tale of mortal sin and salvation through Divine Grace, to the *Purgatorio*; and *Schicchi*, in its liberating and life-enhancing atmosphere, to the *Paradiso*. In this reading, the three episodes of the *Trittico* suggest the idea of a gradual rise from darkness to light, and therein lies, to my mind, an element—ideological rather than real—of cohesion. It is, of course, conceivable that the composer himself—though there is no reference to this in his published correspondence—saw his triple bill in that light and for that reason objected to its being 'so brutally torn to pieces' by opera houses later.* One more thing is in favour of giving the *Trittico* whole, as the composer intended it. The few complete productions I have seen proved that the *contrasts* between the three works act in and by themselves as a powerful dramatic agent, reinforcing retrospectively for the listener the impact of each individual opera. In addition, the cumulative effect of the whole *Trittico* far surpasses the effect created by separate productions of, say, *Tabarro* or *Schicchi*—an obvious observation, it is true, but one we are inclined to forget. There is an appreciable aesthetic gain in giving the three operas on one evening, which is wholly lost if they are produced separately.

(1) IL TABARRO

Principal characters

Michele, *Skipper*	..	..	50 years
Luigi, *a stevedore*	..	..	20 years
'Tinca', *a stevedore*	..	..	35 years
'Talpa', *a stevedore*	..	..	55 years
Giorgetta, *wife of Michele*	..	..	25 years
Frugola, *wife of Talpa*	..	..	50 years

Paris: Modern times.

* See p. 216.

I

Didier Gold's one-act play *La Houppelande—The Cloak*—belongs to the species of literature known in France as *pièce noire*.* Unrelieved in gloom, set in Parisian 'low life' and grimly realistic, it culminates in two simultaneous crimes of passion. Unlike the opera, the play contains a sub-plot running parallel to the main action. Like the skipper Michel, the stevedore Goujon has an unfaithful wife; worse still, she is a strumpet, and at the end of the play—no Cloak without Dagger—he stabs her to death in a quayside tavern, whence he emerges, brandishing a bloodstained knife, at the moment at which Michel presses his wife's face against that of her strangled lover. Puccini, for all his 'Neronic instinct', was wise enough to suppress the sub-plot and content himself with a single murder.†

All the same, the reader would be wrong in surmising that *La Houppelande* was unadulterated *Grand Guignol*. Though written as late as 1910, it strongly echoes the sombre realism of Zola, notably the Zola of *L'Assommoir* and *Le Ventre de Paris*, and deals by implication with a larger theme, which is, that vice—adultery, violence and crime—is the product of wretched social conditions, such as indeed prevailed in the lower Parisian working classes at that period. Gold, however, refrains from stating this theme in so many words; he merely describes, without putting any comment into the mouths of his characters. His method is to present his theme in terms of a melodrama, actuated by that time-honoured and effective device: the human triangle. What lends the play its *cachet* is the peculiar blend of realism with romantic and symbolic features, enhanced by the unusual setting. No wonder the play ran for several years in Paris and fascinated Puccini from the moment he saw it.

It will be interesting to consider it in greater detail to appreciate the alterations made for the operatic version. To reproduce an authentic proletarian atmosphere, Gold gave three of his characters such nicknames as might be common among Parisian bargemen and beggars. Thus, the first stevedore is called Goujon: 'Gudgeon'—Puccini's 'Tinca': 'Tench' (which is not an accurate translation of the French name); the second stevedore is named La Taupe: 'The Mole'—the 'Talpa' of the opera; and his wife's name is La Furette: 'The Rag-picker'—Puccini's La Frugola. She is a weird representative of the Parisian *Lumpenproletariat*, a kind of gutter philosopher, who might have stepped out of Charpentier's *Louise* and, indeed, have been modelled on the female rag-picker there who mysteriously reflects on the objects she collects from overturned rubbish-bins. All characters of the play speak Parisian argot and, with the sole exception of Georgette, use vulgar language; but all this is felt to be in complete *rapport* with the author's realistic, lifesize portrayal of them. Even their respective ages are given, which Puccini retained;‡ and, barring the double murder, the action remains well

---

* Some novels by Georges Simenon are more recent examples.
† The libretto merely hints at Goujon's domestic tragedy.
‡ See cast list.

within the bounds of verisimilitude. Thus the motivation for the adulterous love affair between Georgette and Louis resides in the eternal 'Youth belongs to Youth', and can almost be inferred from the ages given in the cast list: Michel is fifty, his wife half his age, and the stevedore twenty. Moreover, the lovers were born and bred in the same Parisian suburb and in them both, unlike the Skipper, pulses the life-breath of the big city which exercises such a fascination on them.* Hence Georgette's hatred of the nomad life she is compelled to lead on her husband's barge, here today and gone tomorrow. In the play it is she who seduces the young stevedore, who confesses to a profound feeling of moral guilt at the love affair. Puccini, on the other hand, prompted by his urge to whitewash his heroines, suppressed both these details.

Gold solved the dramatic problems inherent in a one-act play to perfection. The characters are established with a few well-aimed strokes, the exposition of the drama is neatly done, with the whole action compressed into two hours—from sunset to complete darkness, which is an effective though obvious touch of scenic symbolism. Long before the spectator arrives at a full realization of the triangular relationship and guesses at its tragic outcome, he is gradually being prepared by a succession of unobtrusive details. Thus, the young lover makes his first entry at the moment when the husband tries to kiss his wife on the lips, but she turns her cheek to him, at the same time staring with a fixed and intense glance at the young stevedore. A particularly subtle detail occurs after the rise of the curtain, when we perceive Michel with a pipe hanging from one corner of his mouth, *unlit*; his lighting it toward the end of the drama will lead the stevedore into his death-trap. Again, during the long duologue with Georgette (the husband-wife duet of the opera), Michel refers to Goujon's wife as a whore whom her husband, so the Skipper argues, would have killed long ago, had he not found consolation for his sorrows in drink. At this point the woman is seen passing with two men on her way to the quayside tavern, at the sight of which Georgette is deeply agitated. Lastly, the cloak of the title, the symbol of male protection for the female, will be used as a means to a grimly ironic end. In brief, all this gradual build-up of tension and suspense by the insertion of seemingly adventitious details is part of the machinery of French melodrama at its best—we encountered this already in Sardou's *Tosca*—and fully accorded with Puccini's own stage technique. Needless to say, he retained most of Gold's details.

The changes made in the libretto—and almost invariably at Puccini's instigation—are, largely, those which any adaptation of a spoken drama for operatic purposes would, inevitably, entail. The only radical alteration was the excision of the sub-plot, which in fact is irrelevant to the main action, as the composer visualized it. His characters bear essentially the same features as those of the play, except that they are painted in more romantic, emotionally richer colours. Thus, Luigi is presented as a more ardent lover than the

---

* The same motive, it will be recalled, drives the heroine in *Louise* to desert her parents' home.

rather matter-of-fact Louis. If Luigi intends to abandon Giorgetta at Rouen, it is because he cannot bear any longer to have to share her with her husband; if Louis is prompted to the same step, it is on account of his moral scruples. Puccini's change of motive is revealing. Most striking, however, is the following modification: while Gold's young stevedore has brought himself to a meek acceptance of his lot as a poor bargee, Puccini, whom we have so far not known as a political animal stirred by any social conscience, puts words into Luigi's mouth which read like those of a fanatical Marxist.* The remaining alterations include the deletion of all vulgarisms, the versification of Gold's prose text, new verses being added for the sake of lyrical expansion, such as those for the stevedores' offstage song and Frugola's little air about her beloved tabby-cat Corporal.† New also are the lines for her second song, expressing her longing for a little country cottage where she, her 'old man' and the cat will peacefully await death—'the remedy for all ills'. In this, Puccini seems to give vent to his own feelings about the country, even as he does again in the Trio for the Masks in Act II of *Turandot*. The insertion of such diverting little episodes sprang from his feeling for contrast and variety, qualities urgently needed to relieve the play's almost consistent mood of oppressive gloom. To the same end, he enlarged the scene of the Street-Song Vendor—a true Parisian touch—and introduced the brief episode of the pair of young lovers who pass by on the quay, singing a little ditty immediately preceding Michele's sombre monologue.

2

The one-act structure of *Tabarro* presented Puccini with a new set of musico-dramatic problems.‡ The core of it was to achieve in one act the completeness of a full-length opera—more precisely, to lend the characters, the action and the atmosphere such balanced treatment that the work should seem to possess a beginning, middle and end, and the same dramatic 'weight' as a full-length opera. Now *Tabarro*—and the same is true of the rest of the *Trittico*—meets these demands admirably, showing Puccini at the height of his powers as musical dramatist. Indeed he achieved here a degree of compression and terseness, as well as a close correspondence between means and ends, such as we encounter in no previous opera of his. *Tabarro* marks the full

---

* The lines in question occur in Luigi's *arioso* 'Hai ben ragione', i.e. 'bending your neck and bowing your head unshrinking . . . what good is life to us, poor toiling wretches . . . don't dare to raise your eyes, the whip is waiting . . . what time have we for love or other pleasures? . . . 'Tis better not to think!'

† In the play, the rag-picker peevishly refers to a dead old cat who used to make '*ses petites ordures où il ne fallait pas*'. Incidentally, Puccini's realistic detail of the motor-horn which is heard in the orchestral introduction and also later was manifestly suggested by some lines spoken by the rag-picker in the French drama: '*à vos maisons, c'est jamais que de la pierre noire! et vos automobiles, c'est jamais que de la féraille et du pétrole!*'

‡ Even the first, one-act version of *Le Villi* was in two parts, containing a change of scene.

beginning of his 'classical' style.* This may be observed in a number of features.

The structure of the melodies is more balanced and symmetrical and shows a longer arch than before. And while Puccini's mosaic has not disappeared, it now displays more organic coherence and there is a marked preference for using a few characteristic themes in their entirety, instead of a multiplicity of brief figures, e.g. the 'River' and 'Love' themes (Exx. 81 and 85). In the harmonic idiom we note a tendency away from viscous chord-clusters toward simpler harmonies, such as common chords and secondary sevenths; chromaticism and the whole-tone scale recede before diatonic writing and modality. Noteworthy too is the high degree of harmonic acerbity achieved, manifestly, under the influence of Stravinsky, by the use of 'naked' discords (major sevenths, tritones and seconds), and of bitonality. Puccini's recourse to these devices originated, we recall, in his desire to keep abreast of contemporary developments, yet their application in *Tabarro* is free from creating an impression of *voulu*; they are employed to lend point to the characterization. Even his series of parallel fourths and fifths, decorative and often mannered in his earlier style, now serve a strictly dramatic purpose, as for example, in the ominous progressions in the latter part of the duet between Michele and Giorgetta. Similarly, the scoring displays greater simplicity and directness. The orchestral lines are often drawn as though with pen, instead of brush, and stand out with a new sharpness. Puccini takes account of the peculiar atmosphere of the drama by selecting a palette of preponderantly subdued and sombre colours, ranging from the pale and shadowy to an impenetrable dark. Characteristic too is the frequent use of muted instruments (strings, horns and trumpets), of cellos and double basses for the 'River' music and Michele's part, and of voices offstage which produce an eerie, almost spectral effect. With the exception of a few passages, the style is that of orchestral chamber-music, despite the fact that Puccini employs a large orchestra: triple woodwind with cor anglais and bass clarinet (but only two bassoons), four horns, three trumpets, four trombones, timpani, various percussion including a low bell, two harps, of which the second is used on the stage, and for special realistic effects a cornet, a siren and a motor horn.

The fascination of *Tabarro* lies, above all, in the musical evocation of a tenebrous atmosphere, which largely emanates from the river. In the play this atmosphere remains a background only; in the opera it seems, by dint of the music, to invade the whole stage, like an evil mist through which the characters move. And while Gold merely hints at the poetic symbolism possessed by the eternal sluggish flow of the waters, Puccini brings it out to haunting effect. The river, reflecting the weariness and soul-destroying monotony that oppresses the life of the bargemen, is caught in the memorably graphic theme with which the opera opens and by which its first half is dominated:

* See p. 281.

Ex. 81

Andante moderato calmo

There is, undeniably, a *Cathédrale engloutie* air about this, but the Puccinian stamp is clearly seen in the languidly swaying top-line, making several attempts to rise until it finally sinks down through two octaves. What seems greatly to add to its suggestive effect is the tonal ambiguity. Fluctuating between G major and its myxolydian mode,* it is only in the eighth and last bar that the real key (G major) is established. This feeling of 'watery' oscillation is enhanced by the movement of bare parallel fifths and fourths in the treble—in themselves an expression of an emotional void—which create, with the bass, the impression of bitonality.† It is more than likely that Ex. 81 was inspired by the prefatory verses to the play, beginning: '*Lumineux, à grand traits, comme un immense flague, Le fleuve s'assoupit à l'ombre d'un bateau*'. In addition to the 'River' theme, the opera contains other suggestions of flowing waters, e.g. the slow and pervasive barcarole-like rhythms (six/eight, nine/eight, twelve/eight), drawn-out undulating melodies, gurgling triplet-figures, and low-lying basses (16 ft. and 32 ft.) which engender a feeling of fathomless depths. There emanates from all this 'water-music' an air of sadness and enervating languor.

3

What of the musical characters? Like the atmosphere that envelops them, they are weary, pathetic creatures and it is thus sometimes impossible to divorce Puccini's delineation of character from his atmosphere painting. Yet a wild, murderous passion smoulders in them, notably in Luigi and Michele.

* G major with F♮.
† In reality, the upper chords represent suspensions which are sounded together with their resolutions in the bass.

Let us consider the Skipper first. He does not come into his own until the second half of the opera—for the first time in his duet with Giorgetta. His despairing longing for the lost love of his unfaithful wife is expressed thus:

Ex. 82

The three-time repeat of the chromatic tail-end (Ex. b) seems to hint at the jealousy that continues to torment the Skipper's mind. That the image of Scarpia must have been in Puccini's unconscious thoughts when limning Michele is plainly suggested by the striking resemblance of the latter's phrase 'Resto vicina a me!' to the former's 'Ho più forte', in his first aria (*Tosca*, Act II). The explanation of this may well be that both characters find themselves in a similar situation at this juncture of the drama—Scarpia dreaming of his *future* conquest, and Michele of his *past* love. Puccini could not have been aware of what amounts to a virtual self-quotation, any more than he was of another *Tosca* phrase in the music of the Street-Song Vendor*— for, with his susceptibility to such unwitting 'reminiscences', he would assuredly have erased them.

The most impressive part of Michele's music is his monologue 'Nulla! Silenzio!', a piece almost worthy to rank with some of Verdi's great baritone and bass arias. At once powerful and sinister, it conjures the terrifying picture of the Skipper as he lies, like a beast of prey, in ambush for his victim, brooding in the dark night on his wife's infidelity and gradually working himself into a paroxysm of murderous jealousy.† The monologue is based on the

---

* At [19].

† It is at this point, in the play, that his stevedore Goujon passes by on his way to the *Belle Musette* where he will kill his wife.

'Cloak' theme, first heard in the preceding duet with Giorgetta, but also standing for the saturnine Michele himself:

Ex. 83 Andante grave e misterioso

Ex. a belongs to those characteristic themes which Puccini frequently associates with a situation preparatory to the final catastrophe—a funereal march in minor, 'sighing' *appoggiature* and double basses in a dull *pizz*.* A sinisterly mysterious effect lies in the chorale-like ending of the march, 'Chi? chi? Forse il *mio* sono!' In the repeat of the first part of this monologue —it is in ternary form—Michele's insensate rage and desire to drown himself together with his wife's lover are impressively caught in the rolling waves of the combined strings, savagely lashing against Ex. 83a, on the woodwind and brass. Similarly, the poignancy of Michele's final outcry, 'La pace è nella morte', is rendered almost intolerably painful by the searing seconds Puccini now adds to the chorale Ex. 83b:

Ex. 84

A subtle dramatic point in the music occurs ·in the middle section of the monologue, 'Chi l'ha trasformata?'. In it, Michele begins by wondering which of his three stevedores might be the lover of his wife. Talpa? Too old. Tinca? No, he drinks. But just before he comes to utter Luigi's name, Puccini inserts a brief pause, thus indicating Michele's momentary hesitation about

* Cf. the 'Execution' (Ex. 54) of *Tosca*, and the 'Suicide' theme of *Butterfly* (Act II, Part 2, 8 bars before [56]).

the young stevedore. Had the latter not told him the same evening that he wanted to disembark at Rouen never to return? No, it cannot be Luigi! But, like a Greek chorus, the orchestra, in quoting the lovers' theme (Ex. 85), reveals the truth still hidden to the character on the stage.

It is illuminating to cast a brief glance at the original version of Michele's monologue, which the composer modified in 1922.* In a letter to Adami, he stated that he found it 'too academic and altogether wrecking the drama', requesting the librettist to replace the text by 'something direct and telling, emotional, original and not long', and adding significantly: 'I want it to finish with a *muoio disperato*.'† This first version, beginning with 'Scorri, fiume eterno!', was based on the monologue delivered by the Michel of the play, which portrayed him in quite a different mood from that which informs the operatic character, as we have him now. In Gold, the Skipper began by wishing to end his life in the river, and then continued with meditations on the river's symbolism and on the motives that drove so many to commit suicide by drowning themselves in the Seine. During his long life he had fished many bodies out of its dark waters. His special compassion is reserved for those '*pauvres petites de seize ans avec des yeux comme des violettes*', for whom '*sans l'amour la vie n'est rien*'.‡ Michel has no thought of taking revenge on his wife's lover—in fact he makes no mention at all of the cause of his unhappiness—and he closes with an apostrophe to the river as the symbol of a peaceful haven from the miseries of life. This is also the Michele of Puccini's original version, but the composer rightly felt that such general meditations on life and death were out of key with the character as he, later, came to see him in the dramatic context of his opera. What he needed was a Michele more directly concerned with his personal tragedy, tortured by the question of who was his wife's lover and of how to revenge himself on him, if he could catch him. The Michele of the present version is thus deprived of that noble compassion he evinces in the first version, but, on the other hand, he has now grown to a far more powerful and frightening figure—from the dramatic point of view a demonstrable gain. The music of the original monologue was also different, in that the lugubrious march-theme (Ex. 83a) extended over the whole length of the piece, resulting in an inevitable monotony. The new verses provided by Adami afforded the composer scope for more variety and movement in the musical treatment, as may be seen in the insertion of the contrasting middle section, and thus rendered the present monologue far more telling than it was in the original.

4

Turning now to the lovers, we find that Luigi is the more fully characterized of the two; this represents a noteworthy departure from the composer's

* It can still be heard in an early recording. There are, in addition, a number of minor alterations both in *Il Tabarro* and the other two operas of the *Trittico*, most of which were made after the Rome première in 1919.

† November 1921 (*E*).

‡ This is the line from which Puccini evolved the Street-Song Vendor's 'Who lived for love, died for love'.

customary method of endowing his heroine with richer musical traits. The young stevedore is first introduced in the mood of an artificial vinous hilarity, in the drinking-song 'Eccola la passata!' Yet this forms no part of his true nature. For Puccini sees him as a despondent character weighed down by his miserable life, and as such he portrays him in the *arioso* 'Hai ben ragione!', a lament in the composer's typical vein yet more forceful and virile in expression than in any of his previous operas.★

Strangely enough, Giorgetta has no solo aria allotted to her but is delineated in her duets with Luigi and Michele. Her first duet with the stevedore, 'E ben altro', is the only occasion in the opera on which the star-crossed lovers are shown in a youthful and carefree mood. Both are children of Paris, to which they now address a paean of praise. With its short-winded phrases and capricious rhythmic changes it provides an example of Puccini's *ballabile* style applied to lyrical music; indeed Giorgetta's 'Alla sera', in which she sings of her little outings to the Bois de Boulogne, has the air of a tango —with a cuckoo call on the horns to remind us of the composer's love of tiny realistic details. Yet for all its light charm and the ecstatic climax at the close, this duet fails to achieve the lyrical glow of the true Puccinian love scene. On the other hand, the lovers' second duet, 'O Luigi!', is an inspired piece and masterly in its simultaneous suggestion of their guilty feelings and their longing for a brief hour of happiness. The slightly Verdian *ostinato* in the bass, the incessant repeat of the same vocal phrase, the minor key and the subdued colours of the orchestra (muted strings, *misterioso*), combine to characterize this situation admirably:

Ex. 85

★ The Massenet of Manon's 'Adieu, petite table!' still echoes in the texture of Luigi's more sustained 'Il pane lo guadagni', as witness the monotonous progressions of orchestral chords underpinning the tenor's sad strain.

The *Bohème* phrase at 'Va rubata' is another of those unconscious reminiscences characteristic of *Tabarro*.

Soon after the opening, the clarinets and the low flutes play a triplet-passage marked *come un tremito* (*like a shudder*), and there is an ominous ring about the sustained piccolo note and the roll of the bass-drum in the passage where Giorgetta describes how her hand always trembles before she lights the match to give Luigi the signal for their clandestine meetings. The climax of the duet is reached in Luigi's impassioned 'Non tremo', where the 'Love' theme (Ex. 85) is thundered out on the full orchestra against the tenor's frenzied cries, recalling the Des Grieux passage at the end of Act III of *Manon Lescaut*. Luigi's repeated notes on the high G♯ and the rapid mordent adds a ferocious touch to the phrase.★

Of the secondary characters, it is only La Frugola who receives special musical attention. Puccini seemed so fascinated by this grotesque figure that he treated her more generously than his heroine Giorgetta. Not only has the Rag-picker her own theme which recaptures her as she comes hobbling along, with a sack full of old things on her shoulder:

Ex. 86

but she is also given two songs. Both 'Se tu sapessi' and 'Ho sognato' share a bizarre, puppet-like element as well as a deliberate primitiveness of harmony and texture, all of which foreshadows the music of the Three Masks of *Turandot*—like La Frugola, somewhat unreal, fantastic characters. Both her songs are in the Dorian mode. The first is marked by sharp dynamic contrasts, prolonged *pizzicato* and *col legno* passages, and raucous-sounding grace-notes in the bass; and in one place the Rag-picker's cat is heard miaowing on the oboes and muted violas! Her second song is a mechanical patter, to a march-like *ostinato* on the orchestra, again with *col legno* strings, comic punctuations on the muted horn and grotesque bleatings on the oboe.†

In turning to the musico-dramatic structure, we note that *Tabarro* (and also *Suor Angelica*) is built in exactly the same way as the first acts of Puccini's full-length operas: two almost equal halves, of which the first serves to establish the atmosphere and introduce the characters while the second

★ The autograph score shows that the duet was originally in the key of C minor and was later transposed a semitone up, to impart more brilliance to the singers' high notes and also introduce tonal contrast with the final scene in C minor.

† We find again that similarity in character leads Puccini to the invention of similar motives: La Frugola's cadential phrase (bars 11 to 13) recalls Colline's closing phrase of his farewell to his old coat.

deals with the essential action. The first half, closing with the exit of all subsidiary characters, is remarkably varied in mood though always with a strong undercurrent of sombreness. The curtain is, as Puccini demands, to be raised *before* the beginning of the music so that the spectator's first impression is a purely visual one—a striking example of the importance the composer attached to a scenic picture. The opening scene begins in dumb-show— Giorgetta busying herself with trivial little doings, the stevedores unloading the barge, Michele standing immobile by the helm and watching the setting sun. During this scene the orchestra paints the atmosphere by means of the 'River' theme and two other ideas associated with the drab life of the barge- men. After the brief recitative between Michele and Giorgetta, the stevedores are given their musical due in what might be called a 'work-song', sung below deck. This is a melancholy air in the minor, the key rising step-wise in each of its three verses (A minor–B minor–C minor), and with a heavy, halting gait in nine/eight suggesting heaving and pushing (the basses are to play *ruvido*—roughly). Having established the basic atmosphere, the composer is now intent on introducing various diversions so that the gloom of the second half will be the more telling. There is, first, Luigi's drinking- song, on which a momentary shadow falls by Puccini's hint at the sad 'Love' theme (Ex. 85). Then the organ-grinder arrives and plays a waltz— partly Offenbachian, partly Chopinesque in flavour—on an old out-of-tune hurdy-gurdy. Following Stravinsky's example in the *Waltz* of *Petrushka*, Puccini suggests this, amusingly, in 'wrong' harmonies, i.e. major sevenths instead of octaves, scored for woodwind.* Yet during this diversionary scene, he continues with the exposition of the actual drama, setting against the waltz music a brief dialogue between Michele and his wife, the husband expressing his compassion for the penurious Luigi; this serves to render the Skipper a still more pathetic figure. Into this dialogue there sounds suddenly the voice of a Street-Song Vendor, offstage, and presently another touch of local colour is added in the Vendor's wistful little ditty 'Primavera'. It con- tains the line 'Chi ha vissuto per amore, per amore si morì'—'Who lived for love, for love will die', epitomizing the fundamental theme of Puccini's operas. The refrain of the three verses is 'È la storia di Mimì', in which Puccini, like Mozart in *Don Giovanni* and Wagner in *Die Meistersinger*, quotes from a previous opera of his, i.e. the 'Mimì' motive from *Bohème*. During this second diversion, the recitative between husband and wife still continues, hinting at their conflict of temperaments and the tension in their relationship. The arrival of La Frugola adds another grotesque element to the atmosphere and is the signal for Puccini to turn now to more self-contained lyrical music. This scene is masterly in its contrasts. The Rag-picker's two weird songs are separated by Luigi's poignant *arioso* and this in turn is set off by the lovers' ecstatic duet in praise of Paris. Having lit his bright lights,

---

* In the opera, Luigi addresses the organ-grinder with the ironic 'Professore!' In the play he describes him with '*Il a une gueule de singe mais il joue comme un ange!*' The pieces, incidentally, the organ-grinder plays there are two well-known Parisian ditties of the time (*Georgette* and *La Petite Tonkinoise*).

the composer now extinguishes them with dramatic suddenness in the subsequent scene: La Frugola and her old Talpa shuffle off into the dark night, softly murmuring a fantastic, ghost-like version of the previous 'Ho sognato'. After this follows the 'River' theme now sung *pp* offstage, by a *sopranino* answered by a distant *tenorino*, and the music then dies away into a prolonged siren-sound emitted by a far-off tug. Thus the first half of the opera is beautifully rounded off, closing on the music and in the mood of the beginning. In point of style, it affords an impressive example of Puccini's skill in blending romantic, impressionist and realistic elements in the service of the drama on the stage.

The contrast presented by the second half could not be stronger. Puccini now takes up action station, as it were. We are alone with the three chief characters, and just as night descends on the stage so do increasingly dark shadows descend on the music. Significant among other things is the prevalence of minor keys—a parallel to the last two acts of *Manon Lescaut*. The love duet between Luigi and Giorgetta is almost unvaryingly in C♯ minor; this may have been intentional but the result is a slight feeling of tonal monotony. Instead of the brief, vivid vignettes of before, we now have extended and slow-moving musical scenes, in which Puccini returns to the more stylized, formal design of his early operas, both the lovers' duet and Michele's monologue being in a clear ternary form, with the former also rounded off by a strictly thematic coda—Luigi's dramatic 'Vorrei tenerti!'.

The duet between Michele and Giorgetta, on the other hand, is loosely constructed, consisting of a succession of five different sections in which Michele's 'Love' and 'Cloak' themes (Exx. 82 & 83) make their first appearance. The sections, however, are held together by flowing, barcarole-like figures and rhythms and their central mood is sad reminiscences, Michele recalling the happiness of former days and pleading for the lost love of his wife, who, guilt-stricken, replies evasively. It is a fine psychological point that Puccini here gives Michele considerably more to sing than Giorgetta, who, apart from a few brief interjections, joins in with only two poignant phrases.* The close of the duet, into which a distant church bell strikes the hour of nine, is another of those masterly strokes in the evocation of the sinister so characteristic of this opera, e.g. the gurgle of the triplet figures in parallel fourths (violas), the 'fathom-deep' pedals of bare fifths (double basses), and the murmured words of the characters; and after Giorgetta has descended to her cabin, Puccini clinches the whole scene with the curt 'Squaldrina—harlot!' which Michele mutters between his teeth into an orchestral pause.

Remarkable for another reason is the brief episode which Puccini interpolates between this last duet and Michele's monologue when the shadows of two lovers are seen passing by, singing a gay little love song, 'Bocca di rosa fresca'. This is like a last evanescent ray of light before complete,

* In the original version Giorgetta sang even less, so that the duet virtually constituted a solo for Michele. Puccini, anxious however, to avoid monotony, requested Adami to enlarge Giorgetta's text, although he rightly felt that it was psychologically wrong to make the guilty woman speak at length in this particular situation.

all-engulfing darkness closes in on the scene, a short breathing-space in the mounting tension. The charming modal tune, which the composer may conceivably have derived from an old French folk-song, is sung by the lovers in antiphony, thus producing a delightful echo effect. And what with the piquancy of the polytonal harmonies, the airy scoring (harp and celesta) and the sound of a bugle call from a distant barracks, in the key of B♭ major, rubbing gently against the A minor in the orchestra, this little vignette is a masterly instance of Puccini's light touch in sketching a passing atmosphere.*

With a sudden shift to C minor, Puccini abruptly steps out of the deceptive calm of this nocturnal idyll and into the last stage of the drama. After Michele's monologue, the dénouement unfolds with the utmost rapidity. The incessant reiteration in the scene of Luigi's murder of the 'Cloak' theme in a fast tempo represents the only weak musical spot in this opera, recalling the same crudely veristic trick in the final pages of *Tosca*. Superb, however, is the following scene between husband and wife. Giorgetta emerges from the cabin to the 'Death' chorale from Michele's monologue (Ex. 83b) and while she feigns remorse, the anguished fear in her heart for the fate of Luigi is betrayed by the orchestra in the ominous *ostinato* from the 'Love' duet (Ex. 85). For the final *coup de théâtre* Puccini resorts to his favourite device of repeating the 'best' theme of the act—the shortened 'Cloak' followed by the chorale, now played *tutta forza* and *selvaggio*—'savagely'.

(2) SUOR ANGELICA

Principal Characters

Suor Angelica	..	Soprano
La Zia Principessa (*Angelica's Aunt*) ..	..	Contralto
Suor Genovieffa	..	Soprano

The Action takes place in a Convent at the end of the Seventeenth Century.

I

Suor Angelica shares with *Tabarro* both an uncommon subject and an uncommon setting: the suicide of a nun in the precincts of a convent. The essential plot appears to have been of Forzano's own invention, but there is little doubt that for certain features he drew on Massenet's enchanting *Le Jongleur de Notre-Dame* (1902). In Massenet the action takes place in a French monastery some time during the fourteenth century and all the

---

* The polytonality just referred to lies in the fact that the vocal melody fluctuates between Aeolian and Dorian while the orchestral accompaniment is in C major, the whole floating above a sustained pedal in A minor. An interesting rhythmic feature: while the song and its accompaniment moves in *allegretto* tempo, the pedal remains in *lento*, a crotchet of the former corresponding to a quaver of the latter; in other words, the song proceeds at twice the speed of the orchestral pedal.

characters are men; in Puccini the setting is an Italian convent at the end of the seventeenth century and all the characters are women. Both operas close with a miracle in which the sinner is granted pardon by the Holy Virgin appearing in a beatific light. Again, in both works a subsidiary character is allowed to stand out from a group—in the French work the delightful cook, Boniface, from among the monks, in the Italian the gentle and childlike Sister Genovieffa, from among the nuns. But this does not exhaust the list of parallels displayed by *Suor Angelica* with yet another opera, *Butterfly*, with which it shares several similar and even identical features. Both centre on a single character who is a woman. In both the chief motive for the heroine's suicide is the cruel frustration of a mother's love of her child. Both contain a scene subjecting the heroine to extreme mental torture, i.e. the visit of Sharpless, in which he informs the geisha of Pinkerton's desertion, is matched by the Aunt's visit in which she informs her niece of the death of her young son. And, lastly, Butterfly's farewell to her child just before committing suicide is paralleled by Angelica's lament addressed to the image of her dead child before she takes poison. Such striking similarities to Puccini's favourite opera clearly point to the active part he played in the fashioning of the libretto of *Angelica*.

His hand is also felt in its general dramatic structure, which, given the peculiar nature of the subject, is a first-rate piece of stagecraft. Characters, action and atmosphere are closely integrated and the seemingly casual insertion in the exposition of the drama of various important details concerning the heroine cannot but be attributed to the composer. The opera begins with a normal day in the life of a convent, yet everything done or said by Angelica or said about her during these preliminary scenes has a direct bearing on her character and her final tragedy. Equally noteworthy, it is only by successive stages that she emerges from the collective group of nuns as an individual character. Yet, despite its careful build-up, the drama suffers from an irremediable weakness. This is the sense of quietism and passivity inseparable from a cloistral atmosphere and therefore intrinsically undramatic.* The spectre of monotony hovers perilously over the stage and though, thanks to the composer's musical treatment, it never actually descends, its soporific presence is felt—at any rate, during the first half of the opera. Puccini was fascinated by the subject or, more precisely, its setting and either ignored this peril or, equally likely, considered it a challenge to his dramatic powers. That he met this challenge brilliantly cannot be denied, and if he was to remain true to the drama as he visualized it, it is difficult to see how he could have treated it in a different musical manner without falsification. Still, it has to be admitted that the absence from the story of the first of the two elements most essential in kindling his imagination—erotic love and intense suffering springing from it—does tell in the music. Its most inspired passages are associated with the great scene between the Aunt and Angelica and the latter's lament. Moreover, the score bears signs

* The same is true of Massenet's *Thaïs* (1894) and Poulenc's *Les Dialogues des Carmélites* (1957), though in both these operas the essential action is more varied than it is in Puccini's.

of creative fatigue and sameness of tone, with melodic invention halting and often thin. Small wonder, then, that *Angelica* has remained the Cinderella among the three sister-works comprising the *Trittico*. None the less, it is an opera of impeccable craftsmanship and capable of achieving an impact, if carefully staged and if the heroine's part is taken by a singer-actress of warmth and sincerity, like the great Lotte Lehmann.* The work, therefore, deserves more detailed examination than it has so far been accorded by Puccini's commentators.

2

As in *Tabarro*, the peculiar atmosphere of the setting pervades the whole drama and envelops its characters, who in a sense are emanations of it. The religious colouring of the music, though not all-pervasive, represents, hence, one of its most conspicuous features. For the quondam church-composer and organist of Lucca Cathedral the subject must have provided a welcome opportunity to exercise his old skill in writing liturgical music, and he may well have resorted to a few labour-saving 'loans' from his unpublished juvenilia, refurbishing them for his present purpose. The opening Prayer and the closing Miracle hymn are, not unexpectedly, the most ready examples of his theatrical church style, though it is strange to observe that he never attempts real polyphony there.† The score is, further, marked by pentatonic steps in the melody reminiscent of plainsong, modal turns, litany-like passages built round a few notes and *organum*-like progressions. The latter form part of Puccini's normal style but here they are applied to a strictly authentic purpose. In addition, the nuns' choruses are occasionally treated *a cappella.*

Seeing the particular atmosphere of this opera, the degree of pungency in its harmonic idiom must be considered remarkably high. The composer experiments, for example, with new dissonances, as when he telescopes major and minor thirds, e.g. the stabbing chords in the Aunt's part (Ex. 87a), or when he combines diatonic with whole-tone progressions as in one of the 'Nun' themes (Ex. b):

Ex. 87

The prevailing tempo of the opera is slow and measured. Puccini's orchestral

* See p. 216 *n.*

† Massenet, in his *Jongleur*, proved more enterprising in that respect, essaying a brilliant pastiche of a medieval motet, in the scene of The Rehearsal.

palette makes a major contribution to evolving the atmosphere in colours of the softest pastel and of a silvery, diaphanous sheen; the scoring, with its emphasis on wind instruments, often conjures up the various registers of an organ. The orchestral forces employed are large: triple woodwind (but only two bassoons), four horns, three trumpets, four trombones, a harp, timpani, triangle, celesta and glockenspiel. The score includes a separate orchestra offstage consisting of an organ, a piccolo, three trombones, bronze and steel bells, cymbals and two pianos, all of which are brought into action in the Miracle. Yet despite the presence of such forces, the orchestral style of *Suor Angelica* is for the greater part pure chamber-music, the vocal melodies being often accompanied by strings alone or a pair of woodwind instruments. Much use is made of *con sordino*, *pizzicato*, soft *tremolo*, and the string parts are occasionally marked '*vellutato*'—'velvety'. Some instruments are associated with a specific character or situation—Suor Angelica's part has, mostly, strings but often with the addition of a cor anglais, and in her great aria a solo violin plays in high positions on the A string; for the Aunt, on the other hand, it is the cellos and double basses of Scarpia, Rance and Michele that Puccini calls upon.

Under the head of scoring comes also Puccini's choice of voices. One reason for the monotonous effect of this opera is said to be the absence of male voices, but actual productions have proved to me the fallacy of this view. For Puccini's treatment of the female voices is remarkably flexible and individual. The preponderance of lower voices (twelve out of a total of fifteen) is noteworthy.

3

As in *Tosca*, the villain of the piece in *Angelica* inevitably engages our chief attention. The Aunt belongs to Puccini's most successful essays in psychological portraiture, and hers is the only significant role he wrote for a low female voice.* This cold, cruel bigot, his first production of the hateful Mother-Cum-Wife image, is caught in an idea that almost conjures up a reptile slowly rearing its head for its deadly thrust:

Ex. 88

Andante sostenuto

* The part of Tigrana in *Edgar*, rich though it be, is too conventional and Suzuki's in *Butterfly* is vocally all but negligible. On the other hand, the contralto part Puccini intended for the female revolutionary in the abortive *Maria Antionietta* would have evidently been an important one (see p. 100).

What with the chromatic wrenching of keys (from C♯ to C and D minor) and the dull chord on the muted horns which decapitates the string phrase, Ex. a provides a splendid example of Puccini's art of tense, epigrammatic characterization. Noteworthy too is the fact that with it he attempts, for the first time in his operas, something like a psychological development in the manner of the true leitmotive. During the brief scene in which the Abbess informs Sister Angelica of her Aunt's arrival, the rising fourth of Ex. 88a (figure *x*) is successively stretched to a fifth and sixth, while in the subsequent duet, the 'Aunt' theme, it is transformed into a sinister, march-like *ostinato* in the bass, with a creeping, chromatic phrase above it (Ex. 88b). We know this kind of motive from *Tosca*, and in point of fact the scene between the Aunt and Angelica compares with the 'Torture' scene of that opera, the difference being that now mere words represent the instruments of torture, the Aunt's mental cruelty taking the place of Scarpia's physical cruelty. Puccini here rises to his full dramatic height, characterizing with a pointedness and economy that surpasses anything he had written previously in that vein. Already the entry of the Aunt, which is in dumb-show, spreads an atmosphere of icy chill and impending disaster—caught musically in the march of Ex. 88b (derived from the 'Aunt' theme), and scenically in the whole appearance of this character, for which the most detailed stage directions are given.★ The Aunt begins and ends this crucial scene in a dull, expressionless monotone, the inhumanity of which is most marked at the point at which she shatters Sister Angelica with the news of the death of her young son. In between, she sings in a style half recitative, half *arioso*, which is Puccini's favourite method of imparting essential information. A study in itself is his subtly calculated placing of psychological rests, of pauses and of important words—musical

★ The Aunt is to be imagined as a severe autocratic figure, clad in black, completely self-controlled and deporting herself with aristocratic dignity. She walks with a measured step, supporting herself on an ebony stick. When Sister Angelica, full of emotion, moves toward her, the Aunt merely stretches out her left hand as if to indicate that she will only tolerate a submissive hand-kiss; and ostentatiously she stares straight ahead when her niece kneels before her and keeps imploring eyes on her face. The Aunt's exit, also in dumb-show, is described with similar elaboration.

speech, in short, which follows the verbal inflections and the mind of the speaker with admirable plasticity; yet it remains melodic and expressive.★ Only once does the Aunt lose her self-control, in 'Che dite!', marked by spiteful chromatic turns in the voice and angry, *stretto*-like passages in the orchestra. In slowly ascending fourths, underpinned by minor chords on muted horns and trombones, she subsequently tells of her mystic communion with the spirit of Angelica's dead mother—music of a hieratic, mysterious character entirely new in Puccini's language:

Ex. 89

Altogether, the Aunt represents a most original creation in the restricted gallery of Puccini's female characters.

In the portrayal of his heroine the composer is seen to make a distinction between Angelica, the member of a group of nuns, and Angelica, the individual suffering woman. In virtually all the scenes in which she appears with her companions, her characterization is 'collective', her music being identical with or only slightly different from theirs. Equally noteworthy is the symbolic touch, occurring in the Miracle, where Angelica, on the threshold of death and already more spirit than body, merges her voice with those of the angels. The sole jarring note here lies in her realistic cries of

★ See, for example, the Aunt's narrative which opens the scene.

439

joyous ecstasy, e.g. the downward *portamento* at the moment at which the Virgin motions the child to advance to its mother—a telltale sign—as is, likewise, the howl of agony in the scene with the Aunt—that *verismo* still exercised a certain hold on the composer.

The tragic Angelica first reveals herself in her brief aria of self-abnegation, 'I desiderii', notably in the impassioned climax of an orchestral phrase expressive of her longing for death.

While in the great scene with the Aunt, to be discussed presently, other traits are added, it is in the extended aria, 'Senza mamma', that we are presented with a coherent picture of the mother Angelica in her mortal grief. The changes in her state of mind are suggestively reflected in three successive stages: her anguish—her ecstatic vision of the child as an angel —her desire to die and join the child in heaven. Thus, the opening section is a true Puccinian lament in a minor key. The middle section, in the major and based on a hymn-like, long-limbed melody, represents perhaps the finest idea of the entire opera and one of the composer's noblest inspirations:

Ex. 90 Lento grave

The third section, turning to the A minor key of the opening, contains a yearningly expressive phrase of great beauty and is followed by the funereal rhythm of the 'Death' motive (foreshadowed in *Otello*, Act I, 3):

Ex. 91

Compared with the other arias which Puccini gave his heroines to sing at the point where tragedy is imminent, 'Senza mamma' displays a degree of pure feeling, a nobility of expression and an emotional restraint (the ending is on the high A *pp*!—rarely observed by singers) which may be said to set it apart.* The only serious flaw here is the lack of emotional and musical contrast in so extended an aria; Puccini further reduces its effect as the melodic climax of the opera by anticipating its music in one of the preceding scenes;† and he resorts to it yet a third time for the 'Suicide' scene—unquestionably a sign of temporary fatigue in his creative powers at that period that

* In the original version there was a second aria for Sister Angelica (*aria dei fiori*: 'Amici fiori') which was eighty bars long and which was heard in some early performances of the opera, until Puccini decided to cut it, evidently because it prolonged the scene of her suicide. This cut is seen in the printed score where rehearsal number 69 is followed by number 75, 70–74 belonging to the omitted piece. See Fedele D'Amico, 'Una ignorata pagina "malipieri-ana" di *Suor Angelica*', in *Rassegna musicale Curci*, March 1966, p. 7.

† The announcement that a visitor has arrived at the convent which set the nuns agog.

can scarcely be explained away by reference to his method of 'logical reminiscences'.

The crucial transformation of Angelica from nun to mother is effected in her scene with the Aunt, in which, not unlike the Butterfly of her second-act scene with Sharpless, she grows from a meek, submissive girl to a woman of almost tragic stature. Angelica reaches the dramatic apex of her role in 'Figlio mio!', which expresses her grief to the point of frenzied obsession with the image of her dead child, an obsession suggested by Puccini's reiteration, no less than eighteen times, though in changing keys and dynamics, of this *ostinato* figure:

Ex.92

Allegro moderato ma agitato

This derives, significantly, from the march-like 'Aunt' motive Ex. 88b. Noteworthy too is Angelica's subsequent 'Un altro istante' with its grating seconds, in which, almost out of her mind with agony, she threatens her Aunt with the curse of damnation unless she be told the truth about her child. This whole scene stands unique in Puccini's operas, not least for the skill with which the emotional contrast between the two women is brought out in the music.

4

The customary dichotomy observed in Puccini's first-act structure is here marked by the arrival of the Aunt, which sets the essential action going. Up to that point the music, in establishing the general ambience, fluctuates between the liturgical, the conversational and the lyrical. Most of it is *musiquette*—tiny supple phrases, now playful and sprightly, now slow and tinged with gentle sadness. As in *Butterfly*, the mosaic structure here serves the purpose of dramatic characterization. Here and there descriptive details are touched in, such as the 'Wasps' music of the Nursing Sister (usually cut) and the 'bleating' trills in Sister Genovieffa's air about the little lamb. The composer makes adroit use of the nuns' chorus for charming group effects but at the same time he draws thumbnail sketches of individual Sisters—the sternly reproving Monitor, the Two Novices in their childish chatter, the obstinate Sister Osmina, the fussy Nursing Sister and so forth. From this group picture the gentle yet lively Sister Genovieffa emerges in richer musical colours. She has more solo passages than the rest, and her wistful song, 'Soave Signor Mio!', in Eb minor, conveying the longing of this erstwhile shepherdess for her beloved lambs, provides an entrancing example of the composer's love of '*cose piccole*'. Moreover, following as it does almost immediately after Angelica's despairing 'I desiderii', it establishes a neat balance of mood.*

In the second half of the opera, with the action now properly getting under way, the musical characterization acquires more substance and more afflatus. As in *Tabarro*, the melodic phrases become more sustained, the musical scenes more extended, and up to a point minor tonalities prevail. After the aforementioned scene between the Aunt and Angelica and the latter's preparations for her suicide in dumb-show, the nun's farewell to her companions, 'Addio, buone sorelle!', introduces another of those tender, fragile passages so characteristic of this opera. Light as gossamer, it is irradiated by a subtle poignancy, a feeling that might be described as wistfulness transfigured.

The closing Miracle, however, occurs only on the stage. Despite the chorus of invisible angels with the 'celestial' orchestra offstage, the Hymn to the Mother of Mothers or *Marcia Reale* remains an expression of pasteboard religiosity. To convey mystic ecstasy and the cathartic power of Divine Love lay beyond the composer's powers. He merely saw the Miracle in terms of a telling stage spectacle, which it assuredly is, and composed music, neither stirring nor exalting, but theatrically effective—no more, no less.

(3) GIANNI SCHICCHI

Principal Characters

Gianni Schicchi	..	Baritone, 50 years
Lauretta, his daughter	..	Soprano, 21 years
La Zita, an old maid and cousin of Buoso Donati	..	Mezzo-soprano, 60 years
Rinuccio, her nephew	..	Tenor, 24 years
Simone, a cousin of Buoso Donati	.. ..	Bass, 70 years

The Action takes place in Florence in 1299.

I

Forzano (or Puccini?), in selecting from Dante's *Inferno* the episode dealing with Gianni Schicchi, chose a subject whose success on the stage, if deftly handled, was a foregone conclusion. *Schadenfreude* or malicious joy, psychologists assure us, represents the keenest of human joys—hence our unmitigated delight at comedies which treat of the hopes and fears of scheming heirs who, for all their clever stratagems, end by becoming the dupes of a wealthy or supposedly wealthy testator. This formed one of the favourite themes of the *commedia dell'arte* whence it entered *opera buffa*; it found one of its most brilliant illustrations in Ben Jonson's mordant *Volpone* and, to cite modern instances, there is Zola's little-known but sprightly comedy *Les Héritiers Rabourdin* and Lord Berners's sardonic *Funeral March for a Rich Aunt* for piano. Puccini's *Gianni Schicchi* has so far

* For Genovieffa's music Puccini used sketches from his abortive *Due Zoccoletti* (see p. 200).

remained the most successful exploitation of this theme on the operatic stage.*

The episode from which the plot was developed is found in Canto XXX of the *Inferno* where Dante and his guide Virgil descend to the Eighth Circle peopled by the Falsifiers of Words, Persons and Coins. There they meet 'two shades, naked, pale, possessed, who ran like a rutting hog that has made escape from the sty, biting and savaging all the rest'. The first shade is that of Myrrha, the daughter of the King of Cyprus, who, conceiving an incestuous passion for her father, achieved her aim disguised and under a false name; her punishment was to be changed into a myrtle tree. The second shade 'fell on Capocchio, catching his nape in its teeth and dragging him prostrate, so that it made his belly on the rough rock-bottom scour and scrape'. Virgil explains to Dante:

Quel folletto è Gianni Schicchi, e va rabbioso altrui così conciando.

That's Gianni Schicchi, that hell-hound there; He's rabid, he bites whatever he sees.

Schicchi's crime was that

per guadagnar la donna della torma, falsificare in se Buoso Donati, testando e dando al testamento norma.

to win the prize 'Queen of the Stable', lent his own false frame To Buoso de' Donati, and made a will In legal form, and forged it in his name.

Gianni Schicchi was an historical person who actually committed the crime for which Dante placed him in his *Inferno*, thus making him immortal. The story goes that when the wealthy Buoso Donati died, his son Simone was haunted by the fear that his father might have left some of the property he had dishonestly acquired to the Church, in order to atone for his crime. (One of Dante's commentators suggests that Simone was later accused of having caused his father's death.) Before making his father's death known, Simone consulted one Gianni Schicchi, a Florentine of the Cavalcanti family, who was known as a clever mimic and counterfeiter. Schicchi offered to impersonate Buoso as dying and dictate a will according to Simone's wishes, for which he was rewarded with a beautiful mare—Dante's 'Donna della torma'. Another version has it that Schicchi bequeathed to himself the mare and a very handsome legacy into the bargain. This is the version adopted by Puccini.

In relegating Gianni Schicchi to the Souls of the Damned and thus meting out to him a posthumous punishment for his misdeeds, the poet is said to have been prompted by personal animus. Dante's wife Gemma was a Donati, the family on which the rogue had played his trick. Moreover, Schicchi belonged to the peasant class, a class despised by Dante, who was a descendant of a Guelph family which prided itself on its pure Florentine blood. Indeed,

---

* It is noteworthy that Scottish balladry treats of the very same subject. Thus, *Tales of the Border* by John Wilson includes the story. *The Abbot of Drimock*, which, except for details, is the double of the Puccinian anecdote. This suggests that fraudulent impersonations of this kind must have occurred in real life in olden times and in a variety of countries.

in several places of the *Divina Commedia* the poet gives vent to his contempt of the *contadini* and the new breed of people who were invading aristocratic Florence from the surrounding country. Thus in Canto XVI of the *Inferno* he meets the shades of three noble Florentines who ask him for news about their native city. The poet replies:

> A glut of self-made men and quick-got gain
> Have bred excess in thee and pride, forsooth,
> O Florence! till e'en now thou criest for pain.

In his libretto Forzano has made amusing use of this class antagonism by making the patrician Donatis turn up their noses at the peasant upstart Schicchi, yet the sympathies of both the librettist and the composer lay wholly with the 'democratic party', represented by Schicchi and the young Rinuccio, who, although a Donati himself, belongs to the new generation and favours liberal ideas and social progress. It is, significantly, Rinuccio who sings the song in praise of Florence and of its 'new race and Gianni Schicchi'. True, Schicchi is a rogue but a lovable rogue whose claim on our sympathies is that he makes us laugh like his more famous northern cousin, Till Eulenspiegel, of whom he forcibly reminds us. In the opera Dante the humourless puritan receives a sly rebuke when Schicchi, in his final address to the audience, is made to say: 'For this little trick of mine I've been condemned to Hell. So be it! But if, by permission of the great Dante [con licenza del grande padre Dante], you have enjoyed yourself this evening, you will grant me extenuating circumstances!' Forzano also made an allusion to a chapter of Florentine political history. In the scene in which Schicchi warns Donati's heirs of the dire punishment that awaits the forger of wills and his abettors, he sings 'vo randagio come un Ghibellino'—'I'll go a-begging like a Ghibelline'. This is a reference to the lengthy warfare between the parties of the Guelphs and the Ghibellines which rent asunder virtually the whole of medieval Italy and which, so far as Florence was concerned, ended in 1267 with the expulsion of the Ghibellines.*

Admittedly, ignorance of the plot's social and historical background is no obstacle to our full enjoyment of the opera but knowledge of it renders us aware how faithfully the libretto reflects the spirit of medieval Florence and seems to lend the comedy a new dimension. In all this *Gianni Schicchi* reminds us of *Die Meistersinger*, another opera in which its composer conjures up the spirit of a famous old city of his native land and in which he sings her praises through the mouth of one of the protagonists. In parentheses, is not Wagner's *Prügel* scene and the ensuing calm, with the full moon stealing over old Nuremberg's streets, paralleled by the scene of the turmoil created by the expulsion of Donati's relatives from his house, followed by the serene tranquillity of the scene in which the towers of ancient Florence are seen in the background, bathed in the midday sun? If Wagner's comic opera may be said to be his most German in spirit, Puccini's is his most

---

* Since for English audiences the historical significance of this line is likely to remain obscure, the translator has aptly rendered it into 'My fate is now to beg from farm to farm'

Italian and one deserving the epithet 'national'. Not only because its real hero is medieval Florence but also because plot, characters and music spring from pure native soil: *commedia dell'arte* and *opera buffa*, the two great branches on the tree of Italian humour.

2

That the theme of which *Gianni Schicchi* treats was a favourite one with the ancient Comedy of Masks has already been mentioned. As for its characters, most of them represent stock figures of the *commedia* in disguise.* Gianni Schicchi at once recalls Harlequin, the astute and roguish servant. Then there is Puccini's pair of young lovers whose marriage is opposed by elderly relatives—a motive frequently employed in the old Italian comedy and comic opera; Lauretta clearly echoes Columbine, the vexatious daughter of an old father. There are Donati's relatives, with Simone reminiscent of Pantaloon, usually an old crusty bachelor, and Betto di Signa recalling a Zany, the clumsy valet who was also a buffoon; and there are the inevitable Doctor from Bologna speaking in Bolognese dialect, and the pompous Notary. Two other stock figures, the Spanish Captain and his Moor, are mentioned in the scene of the death-knell which sends Donati's relatives into a mortal panic. We now appreciate the closeness of Puccini's modern comedy to an ancient tradition.

Before elaborating this point further, let us in passing devote a few lines to the striking parallels which Puccini's plot displays with Ben Jonson's *Volpone* (1605). The thought cannot be altogether dismissed that Forzano borrowed from Jonson or used a common source from which he derived additional material for his libretto. In Jonson's play, whose plot and characters breathe the pungent air of *commedia dell'arte*, we have a group of greedy legacy-hunters offering bribes to Volpone's servant Mosca to achieve their ends; but they are eventually duped as are Donati's relatives. Both the sly fox Volpone, who pretends to be at death's door, and his roguish servant act very much like Schicchi, and like him they take a sadistic delight in playing on the avarice of their dupes. And when at the close of the play Volpone addresses the audience, inviting them to censure or praise the spectacle, this is matched by Schicchi's final apostrophe—though, admittedly, this was a stock device of the ancient Italian theatre, applied both to plays and operas.† But Jonson's Venetian Magnifico, more an abstraction than a real character, has an intellectual contempt for the ruck of humanity and, altogether, the English play is a mordant satire on human weaknesses. Puccini's hero, on the other hand, is a creature of flesh and blood and a practical joker, and the opera represents a comedy of situations, a farce in which the motives of greed and punishment for it serve to generate amusing incidents. Forzano and Puccini never attempted a satire from which a moral lesson was to be

---

* The fixed characters of *commedia dell'arte* rarely appeared in comic opera of the eighteenth century under their traditional names and masks.

† Known as *licenza*, it is still employed in the final ensembles of *Don Giovanni, Così fan tutte* and *Falstaff*.

445

drawn. *Gianni Schicchi* is uproarious fun; but in watching it we are made to forget, or very nearly so, that it contains truly gruesome elements: the presence, during the whole action, of a corpse on and later off the stage, the dishonest use that is made of it, then Schicchi's slipping into the bed in which Donati had died only a couple of hours before, and, finally, the threat of public mutilation—the severance of one hand, a motive whose Freudian symbolism is patent. Even in a comedy Puccini had to be provided with scope for the satisfaction of his macabre instinct.

Forzano's dramatic treatment could not be bettered. The action is built up by stroke after well-timed stroke, playing alternately on the hopes and fears of Donati's heirs; and as we approach the dénouement suspense is enhanced by the adroit insertion of retarding incidents. As for Puccini, this was a libretto entirely different from anything he had set before. That he possessed a comic vein he had proved in his tragic operas; but there the comic element was either incidental, inserted for the purpose of providing momentary relief (*Tosca*, *La Fanciulla de West*), or, where it was more extended, of balancing the element of pathos (*La Bohème*, *Butterfly* and *La Rondine*). Forzano's libretto, on the other hand, presented him with pure comedy from beginning to end, albeit with some sadistic touches. It is the only libretto in which the erotic element is not only of secondary importance but is treated in a lighthearted manner, though Puccini could not resist the temptation of some sentimentality in the music of the two lovers. In *Gianni Schicchi* he succeeded for once in freeing himself almost entirely from the grip of his unconscious fixations and the result was an astonishing extension of his creative range. Enjoyment of this new freedom is written on every page of his masterpiece. In its earthy humour there seems to flow the peasant blood that flowed in his own veins, inherited from that distant ancestor of his who came down to Lucca from the heights of the Apuan mountains more than two centuries before.

Gianni Schicchi has often been compared with *Falstaff*. Their common denominator is indeed high but not as high as to blind us to the lesser stature of Puccini's work. True, both are the creations of composers whose natural inclination was for tragedy and who after a lifetime devoted to that genre suddenly turned their hands to comedy.★ Both are masterpieces whose success was unexpected because contemporary audiences had been given no cause to suspect in their composers such potent *vis comica*. Both works resuscitate the spirit of *commedia dell'arte* and *opera buffa* in their robust gaiety and vigour, their wit, vivacity and general loquacity—features that remained unchanged from Pergolesi and Rossini to Verdi and Puccini. In both operas the comic hero is a baritone, which is as much part of the tradition of eighteenth-century comic opera as are the soprano-tenor pairs of young lovers, Nannetta and Fenton in *Falstaff* and Lauretta and Rinuccio in *Schicchi*, who represent the *donna seria* and *uomo serio* in a world of utterly comic and grotesque figures. But there the parallel ends.

Verdi's work is character comedy, for all the horseplay and practical jokes

★ Verdi's early essay in comic opera, *Un Giorno di Regno* (1840) was a complete failure.

in certain scenes; Puccini's is farce, in which the fun lies more in the action than in the musical characterization, which more often than not accompanies and underlines the comic situations rather than transmutes them. Nor is Puccini's invention as rich or varied as Verdi's; but, on the other hand, allowance must be made for the difference in plot and, equally important, for the fact that Verdi's is a full-length opera while the one-act form of Puccini's comedy demanded compression and brevity, which he achieved to brilliant effect. Then, too, there is that lightest imaginable 'specific gravity' possessed by Verdi's comedy: a chuckling, goodnatured, humane humour, qualities not to be found in Puccini's work. His brand of humour is dry, brittle, cutting and even has something cruel about it. *Gianni Schicchi* is not so much a release of good spirits as the utterance of a harsh cynicism; its laughter is loud but scornful. The fact that *Gianni Schicchi* was followed by a work such as *Turandot* makes us indeed wonder whether Puccini would have ever attained—had he lived to Verdi's age—that serenity of spirit, that gay, liberating philosophy, enshrined in the line 'Tutto nel mondo è burla', which informs the swansong of the older master.

3

The paramount stylistic feature of *Gianni Schicchi* is the evidence it provides of Puccini's capacity to adapt his general manner, moulded and hammered out in his tragic operas, to the spirit of sheer comedy. Though the music could not have come from any other pen but his, in its inflections and specific tang it differs astoundingly from the rest of his scores—perhaps the most immediately striking illustration of his ability to create, in each opera, a work with a musical personality of its own. The first thing to be noted in this respect is the prevalent rapid movement of the music and the dynamic thrust of its straightforward incisive rhythms, mostly in two/four and four/four. With the exception of the music for the two young lovers, themes and motives display an admirable brevity and clear-cut edge. The melodic style is predominantly diatonic, marked by wide leaps and off-beat phrases in the vocal parts. Some portions of it are popular and even folk-song in flavour, as witness Rinuccio's aria in praise of Florence and Schicchi's 'Warning' song (Ex. 95). Novel too is the predilection for fanfares, brass flourishes and signals. Again, the harmonic idiom, almost free from chromaticism, displays a quality, *sec*, gritty and percussive; and pungently comic effects are obtained from the use of grating dissonances, as in Schicchi's furious cries 'Niente, niente!' and the diverse 'Rage' ensembles of Donati's relatives. Major keys are all but ubiquitous and they belong mostly to the 'flat' region; the opera begins in Bb major and closes on Gb major. When Puccini does turn to the minor, it is to suggest the hypocrisy in the relatives' lament for the dead Buoso or to underline their fuming rage at Schicchi's monstrous deception.

Similarly, the orchestra shines in a hard, metallic coruscation. *Gianni Schicchi* might almost be termed a 'woodwind' opera, on account of the prominent part played in the score by these instruments, but the expressive strings remain the leaders in the music of the two lovers. If transparency and light touch have always formed one of the hall-marks of Puccini's orchestral style, here it often takes on an eighteenth-century aspect:

Ex. 93

Barring the robust and massive *tutti* in the ensemble scenes, passages abound
in which Puccini writes delightfully comic chamber-music. But, as
customary, the orchestral complement is large: triple woodwind, including
piccolo, cor anglais and bass clarinet (but only two bassoons), four horns,

449

three trumpets, four trombones, harp, celesta, a funeral bell, timpani and several percussion instruments from which some grotesque effects are obtained.

The comic spirit of the opera is incarnated in the title-role—hence the pervasive use Puccini makes of the 'Schicchi' motives. There are altogether three, all short, incisive, sprightly and fanfare-like:

Ex. 94

To judge from the context in which Ex. a usually occurs, Puccini appears to associate it with Schicchi the clever impersonator; and it is a subtle dramatic point that he first introduces it long before his hero's arrival on the scene—in the relatives' 'Whisper' scene and the scene of the reading of the will, thus hinting at the savage prank that Schicchi is to play on them. This is a typical illustration of the composer's peculiar method of revealing the true significance of a leitmotive *a posteriori*. Ex. 94a will undergo some amusing transformations, e.g. the orchestral march to which Schicchi paces up and down the room reading Donati's will, and the scene in which he raises a trembling hand to the Notary. Ex. 94b, first heard at Rinuccio's mention of the rogue, was obviously inspired by the name 'Gianni Schicchi', of which the second word recalls the English 'giggle'; it sounds like an onomatopoeic suggestion of a high-pitched chuckle. The fanfare, Ex. 94c, first introduced in Rinuccio's aria, appears to symbolize Schicchi's superiority, his vitality and zest as a member of the 'new race' of Florentines. It is on this motive that the opera closes.

Schicchi has two arias. Both are pointedly characteristic pieces, but perhaps not particularly memorable in sheer melodic invention. The first aria, 'Si corre dal notaio', illustrates the two aspects of Schicchi's nature: his volubility and drive in the opening D major Allegro into which Puccini deftly works the 'Notary' and the 'Warning' motives (Exx. 100 & 95), while his macabre humour is caught in the ensuing Andante in C minor, in which he unfolds his plan for the impersonation of the dead Donati. This section with its automaton-like progression of desiccated chords recalls La Frugola's weird song in *Tabarro*, but far more interesting is its essential similarity of style to Michele's monologue; both have the quality of a spectral march, both are based on a processional idea in C minor, in both the voice leaps suddenly up a fifth at the climax, from C to G, where it is punctuated by harsh orchestral discords. The emotional effect achieved by those two arias could not be more dissimilar, it is true, yet it is pertinent to ask here: what does this striking similarity of style imply? The implication is the same as lies in the family likeness which we observe between the musical portrayals of Verdi's Iago and Falstaff, namely a fundamental unity of language that marks even the most opposed utterances of composers of genius. It is almost as though Verdi and Puccini, in their own fashion, sought to parody their tragic manner by applying it to the portraiture of a comic character.

Schicchi's second aria or, rather, song, 'Prima un avvertimento', in which he warns Donati's relatives of the dire punishment awaiting the forger of wills, is an equally delicious essay in comic irony. Starting in a mood of sham mystery, Schicchi turns in 'Addio, Firenze' to address them with a lachrymose farewell, during which he menacingly raises a handless arm:

Ex. 95

This un-Puccinian theme, partly modal and with a characteristic *melisma* (x), breathes the flavour of Tuscan folk-songs, in which melodic turns, like figure x, are frequent.[9] Excruciatingly comic is the use made of this theme in the later scene where Schicchi dictates his will to the Notary: alternately sung and half spoken and with the melismatic figure now amusingly extended, like a magic formula it holds the fuming relatives in complete check. What with *falsetto* and a breathless delivery in other parts of his music, the interpreter of Schicchi must command a nimble gift of vocal characterization, let alone histrionic agility.

4

Of the remaining characters it is only the two lovers who receive a more individual attention. They are limned in this yearning idea, typically Puccinian with its short-winded figures and sentimental suspensions on the first beat of every bar—a theme, though, standing worlds apart from the limpid purity of Fenton's and Nanetta's 'Bocca baciata' in Verdi's *Falstaff*:

Ex. 96

Ex. 96 will be beautifully expanded in the love duet at the close of the opera, creating there the effect of an apotheosis, with the lovers happily embracing each other after their tribulations, while in the background the towers of Florence shine in the light of a glorious midday sun. Rinuccio and Lauretta have an aria each. 'Avete torto' is the longest of Puccini's mature tenor arias, the reason for this being, evidently, his intention to make it serve several purposes. In the opening section Rinuccio gives a brief characterization of Schicchi (Exx. 94b, c), then follows the longest part, 'Firenze è come un albero', its soaring line and strong, fresh rhythm expressing Rinuccio's youth and fervour; at the same time, it is a paean on the ancient glories of Florence and on the new spirit represented by Gianni Schicchi. Puccini inscribed this piece with 'in the manner of a Tuscan *stornello*', a reference applying not so much to the music as to the verses which are hendecasyllabic, eleven being the favourite number of syllables of popular songs not only in Tuscany but also other regions. The character of the music is that of a festive march with rousing signals and flourishes. The fact that, unlike the typical Puccinian tenor aria, it eschews lyrical *cantilena* in the traditional sense is probably responsible for having kept this splendid piece out of the concert hall.*

In the middle of Rinuccio's hymn occurs this broad, flowing phrase, associated with ancient Florence and the River Arno:

Ex. 97

Yet with his customary laxity in the strict use of characterizing themes, Puccini evidently considered Ex. 97 equally suggestive of the sweet Lauretta. For in the subsequent scene of her arrival with her father, the orchestra announces it in contrapuntal combination with the 'Schicchi' motive (Ex. 94b). It also provides the material for Lauretta's famous aria, 'O mio babbino caro', in which she threatens to throw herself into the River Arno unless allowed to go to Porta Rossa and buy herself a wedding ring. It is charming music in a flowing *siciliano* rhythm (six/eight), and in its melodic and harmonic simplicity (it never leaves the key of A♭), wholly in character with the childlike Lauretta.† Puccini's marking is *andantino ingenuo*! Unlike Rinuccio's *stornello*, which gives the impression of being somewhat dragged in, Lauretta's song arises naturally from the situation. Yet, though it introduces a needed point of repose after the agitation of the preceding scene, its sentimental and slightly lachrymose expression seems slightly out of character with this dry, crackling score; being in the composer's true lyrical vein was, probably, the very reason why, unlike the tenor's aria, it has found its way into the concert hall.

The relatives receive all too summary treatment. This is a pity, for

* The original version was in A major; the subsequent transposition to B♭ was made in order to add more brilliance to the vocal part.

† The composer wanted for this role 'an *ingénue* small of figure, fresh of voice, and without any dramatic allure.' (To Clausetti, 8 April 1918. C.P.Let.718).

Simone and La Zita might well have called for a more individual characterization, such as, for example, Verdi gave to his secondary figures in *Falstaff*. Puccini sees Donati's relatives as a group; they are less characters to him than vehicles for certain basic emotions. There is, first, their feigned grief at Buoso's demise, graphically caught in the mourning motive which also stands for Donati's death:

Ex. 98

Again, we note an element of self-parody, in that Ex. a shows features characteristic of Puccini's music for his tragic death-scenes: an *ostinato* figure with bare lugubrious fifths in the bass and a drooping melody, punctuated by woeful *appoggiature* which conjure up the movement of drooping heads. Amusing too is Puccini's placing of the *appoggiature* which, contrary to the normal practice, fall on the weak beat of the bar so that at first our ears are deceived into accepting the up-beat as the strong beat. Equally comic is the alternation between major and minor and also the abrupt change from slow to fast in later scenes. Ex. 98a is the most important single idea in the relatives' music, dominating the opening scenes and undergoing some striking transformations (Ex. b). The rest of the 'Relatives' themes serve to express their various degrees of sound and fury, some being redolent of Rossini:

Ex. 99

With one or two exceptions, *Gianni Schicchi* contains no extended ensembles of an elaborate order, the action proceeding too rapidly for this. The concerted music, which springs directly from the situation, is mostly in the nature of violent explosions—hence its simple, almost primitive texture, and hence the strictly syllabic setting of the words—all in the tradition of the old *opera buffa*. However, in the 'Quarrel' scene, which follows La Zita's refusal to allow her nephew to marry Lauretta, Puccini permits himself a more individual treatment of the voices, viz. the furious Allegro in C minor which the lovers interrupt, to most comic effect, with their plaintive 'Addio, speranza bella' (Ex. 96). The only self-contained ensemble comes in the trio of La Vecchia, La Ciesca and Nella, in which these three flowers of Florentine womanhood express their admiration for Schicchi's roguery in lyrical form, as they busy themselves with dressing him in one of Buoso's nightgowns. This trio, written chiefly no doubt to provide the subsidiary characters with some musical interest of their own, is a delightful piece, again in *siciliano* character, varied in its part-writing and amusingly punctuated by Schicchi's 'Impersonation' motive (Ex. 94a). It reaches its grand climax in the deliciously parodistic phrase, 'O Gianni Schicchi, nostro salvatore!'.

For the Medico and the Notary Puccini invents a collective theme which also serves to symbolize Donati's will. Pompous, solemn and sounding like a scholastic formula it recalls similar ideas in *Die Meistersinger*:

Ex. 100

Allegro moderato, ma un poco sostenuto

One of the most delightful uses to which it is put occurs in the scene of the dictation of the will where it accompanies the Notary's perfunctory and rapid mumbling of the Latin preamble, in four-part counterpoint. The learned lawyer could not have been better suggested than by Puccini's scholastic device.*

There is little profit in discussing the musico-dramatic structure of *Gianni Schicchi* in detail. The scenes succeed each other with such rapidity and the changes of mood are so numerous and mercurial that any verbal analysis would be inadequate. All we need is to add a few general remarks. With the brief orchestral prelude in which the 'Mourning' figure (Ex. 98a) is first heard, we are incontinently catapulted into the action. There is no leisurely setting of local atmosphere, nor do we find Puccini's customary division of his acts into two halves. True, Schicchi's arrival might be considered the beginning of a second half, yet it actually heightens the comedy that has been set in motion already with the very first bar. *Parlando*, *arioso*, solo pieces and dramatic ensembles alternate as if by sleight-of-hand, Puccini coping with the succession of scenes in so elastic and fluent a manner that the ear is often unable to follow. All these are qualities the work shares with Verdi's masterpiece. Small wonder that *Gianni Schicchi* has so far remained the last supreme example of Italian operatic humour.

* Sullivan, in *Iolanthe* (1882), prefaces the Lord Chancellor's song, 'The Law is the true embodiment', with a three-part *fugato*.

XXXIV

Turandot

Principal Characters

The Princess Turandot	..	..	.. '	..	Soprano
The Unknown Prince (Calaf)	..	..	..	Tenor
Liù, a young slave-girl	..	..	..	..	Soprano
Ping, Grand Chancellor	..	..	..	..	Baritone
Pang, General Purveyor		..	..	..	Tenor
Pong, Chief Cook	..	..	..	..	Tenor

Peking: in Legendary Times.

I

Turandot STANDS APART from the rest of Puccini's operas on account of its subject—an uncommon blend of tragedy with grotesque comedy and the fantastications of a fairy-tale. How much of this sprang from the composer's imagination and how much from the play on which the libretto is based? To answer this question it will be necessary to touch briefly on an obscure but lively and entertaining chapter of Italian theatrical history during the second half of the eighteenth century.

Gozzi's *Turandotte*, a tragi-comedy in five acts, was the fourth in a series of ten so-called *fiabe drammatiche* or dramatic fables, written by the Venetian playwright between 1761–1765 and initially occasioned by a heated literary dispute between him and his rival Goldoni. The bone of contention was the *commedia dell'arte*, adored by Gozzi and despised by Goldoni. Count Carlo Gozzi (1720–1806), scion of an impoverished family of Venetian nobles, perceived in this ancient genre the most vital expression of the comic spirit in Italian drama and, in particular, regarded the Venetian *commedia** as the living link with the period of glory and splendour which his native city had enjoyed in the past. But around the middle of the eighteenth century a new taste began to assert itself, born of a more realistic and more natural treatment of comedy in both France and Italy and threatening to undermine the foundations on which *commedia dell'arte* had rested for some two hundred years. The spearhead of this 'modern' movement and its most successful exponent in Italy was Carlo Goldoni (1707–93), a lawyer by profession and member of the Venetian middle class. He saw in the time-honoured Comedy of Masks no more than an artificial and moribund art form—which indeed it had become by the time the quarrel with Gozzi started. He attacked it on

* There was also a Neapolitan Comedy of Mask, which had little connection with its Venetian counterpart.

several counts: the monotony and poverty of its stereotyped subjects, the admixture of trivial intrigues and crude farce in the plot, its rigid and inhuman characters and the inanity of the dialogue, which was improvised almost in its entirety and in which the actors sought to shine in brilliant impromptus, to the complete neglect of any literary polish and graces. Goldoni's aim was to create genuine comedy, a comedy with characters drawn from real life, human beings with natural emotions and behaving in a natural way, instead of the caricature and horseplay indulged in by the stock figures of the *commedia*. Apart from his realism, Goldoni sought to substitute literary drama for low-class entertainment. His plays—some of which can still delight a modern audience, while others have provided material for innumerable opera libretti, in which Goldoni himself proved an expert practitioner—eventually dealt the old comic genre its *coup de grâce*. Yet, before its demise, it was once more revived, though for only a brief spell, by the blood transfusion given it by Gozzi. Endowed with caustic wit, Gozzi began in the 1750s to arraign Goldoni, in polemical pamphlets and highly satirical poems, for the triviality of *his* plays, notably for the introduction of types from the low Venetian classes—gondoliers, washerwomen and fisherfolk. When Goldoni good-humouredly pointed to the big crowds that were filling the theatre for his 'realistic low comedies' Gozzi's retort was that 'any novelty, even Truffaldino and a dancing bear', was good enough to attract the large public.[10] If Goldoni set out to depict human nature as found in real life—very well, he (Gozzi) would give the public something that was *not* natural—'I shall stage a fairy-tale, one of those stories with which grandfathers and wet-nurses entertain the children on a winter's evening by the fireside, and the Venetians will applaud me more than Goldoni'. His challenge took the form of a dramatized fairy-tale, entitled *L'Amore delle tre melarance—The Love for the Three Oranges,** known to modern audiences through Prokofiev's delightful opera. Availing himself of the presence in Venice of Antonio Sacchi's famous strolling company, which specialized in *commedia dell'arte*, he got them to produce this play in 1761. In it he established the model for all his subsequent *fiabe*. The subject was an oriental tale, decked out for the entertainment of the groundlings with spectacular stage effects, such as speaking monsters, rocks and trees and tempests with thunder and lightning. His heroes and heroines were all of princely blood, endowed with great moral fortitude and valour, getting involved in a series of fantastic adventures and love intrigues from which they always emerge triumphant at the close of the play. Yet Gozzi's most striking and wholly novel feature was the incongruous presence in this oriental setting of the stock figures from the Venetian Masks—an idea that may have been suggested to him by the prolonged sojourn in China of his celebrated compatriot Marco Polo in the thirteenth century. More incongruous still, these Masks, who improvise their dialogue, speak in broad Venetian dialect. Their absurd impromptus were based, however, on

---

* It was based on a story from Basile's *Pentameron* (1600), a famous book of fairy-tales in Neapolitan dialect.

written cues, and this furnished Gozzi with the opportunity to make the Masks the mouthpiece for all kinds of satirical allusions to persons, customs and institutions in contemporary Venice—in *Turandotte*, for example, to the inferior status of women, and in *The Love for the Three Oranges* to Goldoni and his other rival Chiari, caricatured in two of the comic characters, while Prince Tartaglia represented the Venetian public. Gozzi had never written a play before the *Three Oranges* nor did he intend to write any more thereafter, but its success was such that in the event he produced nine more in that vein. They displayed a more careful dramatic construction, notably *Turandotte*; and while in his initial essay almost the entire dialogue was improvised,* in the later fables it was written out for the serious characters and even the part of the Masks was so fully epitomized that there was no difficulty in turning it into direct speech.

Despite the great acclaim with which these *fiabe* were received, their vogue was shortlived. By the end of the eighteenth century they were eclipsed by Goldoni's plays and the Italian romantics scorned them for being mere 'farce', devoid of any human and literary interest. Moreover, given the fact that the large Italian public, realists and sceptics by temperament, have always evinced an aversion to the introduction of the fantastic and supernatural on the stage,† inevitably Gozzi became a mere name in the history of the Italian theatre; yet it is noteworthy that a new and scholarly edition of his plays was instigated by no less a personage than Carducci.

Significantly enough, the country in which Gozzi fared far better was Germany, where it was precisely the fantastic element that attracted the German romantics to his plays, the first of which was translated as early as 1777. Goethe, Schiller, Schlegel, Tieck and E. T. A. Hoffmann were filled with admiration for Gozzi, who was indeed declared to be the 'Father of Romanticism'. *Turandotte* in particular caught their imagination, and when in 1790 Goethe and Schiller conceived the plan of a German National Theatre at Weimar, the repertory of which was to consist of the best native and foreign plays, Gozzi's drama was included in their choice. It was produced there in 1804, in a German adaptation by Schiller on which Puccini drew for his libretto.‡ It was for the Schiller version that Carl Maria von Weber wrote in 1809 his *Turandot* overture and incidental music, in which he anticipated Puccini's exoticism by incorporating a Chinese melody.§

---

* The text of *Three Oranges* exists only in synoptic form.

† See also p. 306.

‡ Goethe, who in 1786 had himself seen productions of some Gozzi plays in Venice, confessed in later years to a special fascination for *Turandotte*. He described its essence as '*das Abenteuerliche verschlungener menschlicher Schicksale*'—'human destinies fantastically interwoven'. He also alluded to the play in his poem *Der Festzug*. The choice of it for the Weimar theatre was probably his, and when he directed its production in 1804, he is said to have demonstrated to his company the manner in which the Masks ought to be acted so entertainingly that the whole cast was convulsed with laughter.

§ Weber is supposed to have taken it from the theoretical writings of Athanasius Kircher or Rousseau's *Dictionnaire de Musique* (1768). Motives of it recur in the music of Puccini's Masks.

Gozzi's influence on the German stage is best seen in those absurdly fantastic and spectacular scenes which began to find their way into the Viennese *Stegreifkomödie*, a local pendant to the Italian Comedy of Masks—low-class farces with a largely improvised dialogue. A Gozzian echo is clearly heard in *Die Zauberflöte*, as witness the fantastic plot in an oriental setting, the spectacular stage effects, and the two comic characters, Papageno and Monostatos—Viennese cousins of Truffaldino and the Moor of the Italian Masks. Gozzi has even coloured the vernacular comedies of the Austrian playwrights Raimund and Nestroy.

Equally noteworthy is the fact that it was German romantic opera which first discovered Gozzi as source-material for operatic subjects, with Wagner's youthful *Die Feen* as the best-known instance.* *Turandotte*, however, figures as the favourite subject, having been set at least six times, with Puccini's and Busoni's operas as the most outstanding examples. In addition, the contemporary Austrian composer Gottfried von Einem based a ballet on it; of the five musicians who wrote incidental music for the play, Weber was the first and Ernst Toch, so far, the last. There are altogether some two dozen musical works associated with Gozzi's plays.

2

Gozzi appears to have derived the subject of *Turandotte* either from a collection of Persian tales which in a French translation entitled *Le Cabinet des Fées* became known in Europe toward the end of the seventeenth century; or, more likely, from *The Arabian Nights*, first introduced to the West, again in a French translation by Antoine Galland, at the beginning of the eighteenth century. The origin of the legend seems Persian; this is at any rate suggested by the name of the heroine which derives from the word *Turan*, the Persian name for *Turkestan*. It possibly arose from some remote historical event but its larger theme is the perennial one of the war of the sexes—the male relentless in pursuit of the female, who both desires and resists her conquest. In the legend this theme is illustrated in the character of the virgin Chinese princess who erects the most fearful obstacles against her final surrender. The ambivalence of love-hate, which exercised so strong a fascination on Puccini, is clearly symbolized in Turandot: at first cruel to the point of sadism and then yielding and loving, she is actuated by contradictory yet complementary impulses, even as Calaf and the rest of the suitors are motivated by the Eros-Thanatos ambivalence, an equally potent psychological motive in Puccini's dramatic concepts. The latent sexual symbolism of the legend is further attested by such features as the *three* riddles of Turandot (the three wishes of other fairy-tales) and the decapitation of the suitors. It is not surprising that a theme of such elemental and universal

* After *La Donna Serpente*. The first German composer to turn to Gozzi was one Friedrich Himmel of Berlin, in his singspiel *Sylphen* (1806), after the same play on which Wagner based his opera. In more recent times there has been Casella's *Donna Serpente* (1931) and *King Stag* (1956) after *Il Re Cervo*, by Hans Werner Henze. Brahms once toyed with the idea of an opera on this subject.

significance is seen to underlie, in manifold variants, a number of myths, legends and fairy-tales, and that certain characteristic motives of it recur on the dramatic stage. Molière's *La Princesse d'Élide*, for instance, is an almost faithful reproduction of the Turandot legend; and Portia's three caskets in *The Merchant of Venice* play a similar role to the Chinese princess's three riddles. The legend is also known in Central Europe. Thus, the German fairy tale *Das Rätsel—The Riddle*—included in the famous Grimm collection, represents the Turandot situation in reverse. Here it is the suitors who by the princess's decree are compelled to put riddles to *her*, which she, a miraculously omniscient maiden, always solves and thus sends her unfortunate suitors to the scaffold. Equally striking, and pointing perhaps to a common origin, is the resemblance of the Turandot story to the myth of the Amazons. One of its many versions* tells of Queen Tanais, whose peaceful country by the Euxine was invaded by the Ethiopian King Vexoris, whose army plundered and burned the land, killing all men and raping the women, while the King forced Tanais to marry him. But he was stabbed by her on the wedding night, and this gave the signal for a holocaust of the victorious army, after which the Amazons decided to establish a women's state, with a queen at its head, who would yield only to the man who could conquer her in battle. Now the most noteworthy parallel between the two legends lies in the fact that both Turandot and the new Amazon queen are inspired by an atavistic hatred of the male, originating in the violence suffered by an ancestress at the hands of a foreign barbarian king. It is highly significant that this motive, absent from Gozzi's play, was introduced by Puccini into his opera—the rape and murder of Turandot's ancestress Lo-u-ling by a foreign invader-king—and introduced for the purpose of providing a motive for her man-hating impulses and her cruel decree. Similarly the Amazon queen's vow to yield only to the man who proves superior to her in a physical battle is matched by Turandot's vow to marry only the suitor who vanquishes her in a battle of wits. From all this it would appear that Puccini and his librettists drew on material additional to Gozzi's play.

Now *The Arabian Nights*, to which the Venetian playwright had recourse for several of his *fiabe*, contains a tale with the suggestive title *Wisdom under the Severed Heads*[11]—which is, however, one of the dullest stories with which Scheherezade regales her Sultan. Little wonder, then, that, after she had finished her narration, the Sultan longed to hear 'a short and delightful anecdote'. The 'Wisdom' of the title is possessed by the son of the King of Rūm who is not only the handsomest but the brightest lad of his age—'the marvel of the earth'. In the course of his adventures he arrives at a great city ruled by a princess, 'the wisest and most beautiful of damsels of all ages', who, however, treats her suitors with the same tender mercies as does Puccini's Turandot! (In the Persian tale, the prince and the princess have no names.) The trial begins, yet it is not merely a question of three riddles but of as many as can be accommodated between the morning and the evening

---

* It is the version on which Heinrich von Kleist based his verse-play *Penthesilea*, which in turn inspired Hugo Wolf's symphonic poem of that name.

prayers. Needless to say, the Prince solves them all and in doing so seizes the opportunity to shine in his miraculous wisdom, the whole long scene recalling that of a medieval disputation or a modern debating society. The gallant prince even grows concerned lest this lengthy battle of wits should fatigue the princess's 'glorious voice', and so he interrupts her in her barrage of questions and now asks *her* a riddle, which is complex and entirely different from Calaf's in Gozzi and Puccini. But she is unable to solve it and the tale ends in the happy union of the exalted pair.

This then was the material from which Gozzi appears to have fashioned *Turandotte*, enriching the original in several respects in the process. In addition, he enlarged the plot and introduced a number of new characters such as Adelma, Turandot's confidante and rival, and several subsidiary figures, of which the most conspicuous are the four Masks from the *commedia dell'arte*: Pantalone, Brighella, Tartaglia and Truffáldino, who in Puccini become the three Chinese courtiers.

3

Turandotte, given by the Sacchi Company in Venice at the Teatro San Salvadore on 22 January 1762, is by common consent Gozzi's outstanding play. The suggestion has been made that he desired to prove his ability to write a drama, serious in import, human in appeal and stripped of those fantastications and sensational scenic stunts for which he had been so mercilessly attacked by Goldoni and other writers. His intention was to illustrate a moral theme—the all-conquering power of true love—and to exalt the ancient virtues of courage, loyalty, fortitude in suffering, gratitude and self-sacrifice. These virtues are embodied in Calaf, his father Timur and his tutor Barak; to the first two Puccini was to add his Liù as a character of like traits. Gozzi's Turandot is, like Puccini's, torn between hatred and love for the Unknown, yet in the play she is represented as far less cold, cruel and hieratic than in the opera. Her antagonism to the male sex springs, not from an atavistic impulse (as in Puccini), but from a rational and moral reason: she deeply resents the oriental's attitude to women, who are considered inferior beings, at once slaves and the means for the satisfaction of man's sensual pleasure. Gozzi's Turandot argues her point in a long monologue before the assembled Divan (its counterpart in the opera is the heroine's great aria of Act II), in which she expresses her conviction of her own moral righteousness; though the method by which she tries to remedy this state of affairs—the chopping-off of male heads—appears somewhat drastic.* In her final scene, having been transformed by Calaf's undaunted love from a kind of suffragette to a woman of natural feelings, she comes to realize that it was her own sex—she and Adelma—who behaved with treachery and cruelty, while the men evinced the highest degree of moral courage and generosity of heart—Calaf, by his offer to release her from her pledge of marriage

---

* Gozzi is said to have implied in Turandot's monologue a plea for a more egalitarian treatment of women in his own Venice.

though he *had* solved her enigmas; Timur and Barak, by their readiness to sacrifice their lives to save the Prince's. The play closes with her admission that she had been sadly mistaken in her man-hating attitude; stepping forward for the customary *licenza*, she addresses the audience with the affable lines:

Sappia, questo gentil popol dei maschi
Ch'io gli amo tutti!*

Gozzi's play was in five acts, containing a great many scenes and characters, with a plot far less straightforward than we know it from Puccini's opera. Thus, the intrigue set in motion by Turandot to obtain the secret of the Unknown's name is highly involved, occupying four long scenes, which in Puccini were compressed into the brief 'Temptation' of the final act. It would take us too far to discuss in detail the simplifications, condensations, modifications, excisions and invention of new episodes to which the play was subjected in order to suit the composer's purposes. Suffice it to point out only the most significant differences.

In comparing the play with the opera the reader is most forcibly struck by the contrast in general tone and temper. Gozzi conceals the ferocious sex-war behind a treatment which transforms the story into a charmingly innocent, naïve and essentially comic fairy-tale; he merely skirts tragedy and in some scenes the Masks occupy the centre of the action, almost to the point of overshadowing its more serious aspect. In Puccini, the prevalent atmosphere is one of sombre grandeur, cruel and barbaric. Touch after touch is added from the start to emphasize this: the Mandarin's reading of Turandot's inhuman edict, the ferocious crowds yelling for the Executioner, the ghoulish appearance of Pu-tin-tao in person, the sharpening of the axe, the procession of the Persian Prince to the scaffold, the cruel threats of the Masks to Calaf, the torture of Liù. New too are the spectral voices of Turandot's executed suitors as well as the mysterious offstage choruses of the last act, all investing the opera with an eerie, supernatural air. Puccini thus completes the full cycle begun with *Le Villi*, with its ghost-maidens made of paste-board.

The character in which the barbarous spirit of legendary China finds its chief personification is the heroine. Quite unlike Gozzi's Turandot, Puccini's remains an inhuman and impersonal figure until the penultimate scene, an inaccessible Goddess of Destruction and a projection of the composer's Mother-cum-Wife image far more terrifying than the old Princess of *Suor Angelica*. On her first brief appearance in Act I she suggests, not a creature of flesh and blood, but an idol, a hieratic symbol, an apparition—'come una visione', says the stage direction—who, with a curt imperious gesture, sends the Persian Prince to his death. In the opening act she utters not a single note—a superb psychological touch and not, as has been suggested, an offence against what is presumed to be a cardinal rule of opera, namely to introduce the leading character as a *singing* character. Just because

* Harken! These kind people of our comedy, I love them all!

Turandot is made to preserve an icy silence she achieves Puccini's intended effect of casting a petrifying, hypnotic spell on the turbulent crowds in front of the palace. It is not until challenged in her womanhood in Act II that she betrays anything like human feelings, when she is made to sing; which strikes then with the redoubled force of delayed action. Equally appropriate to her is the nature of her three riddles to which the solutions are 'Hope—Blood—Turandot', three concepts which in the context of the drama become invested with an almost primeval force. This feeling of something purely instinctive and elemental stands in marked contrast to the abstract, intellectual enigmas put into Turandot's mouth by other authors, of which the solutions are:

Gozzi	Schiller	Busoni
Sun	Year	The Human Mind
Year	Eye	Custom
The Lion of the Adria*	Plough	Art

Similarly, compared with Gozzi's treatment of the ambivalent hate-love motive, Puccini's brings it out with far more directness, as when Turandot, in the great love duet of Act III, sings:

> Yes, for thine eye was shining
> With the radiance of victory,
> And for that I did hate thee,
> And for that I did love thee,
> Torn hither and thither by two conflicting terrors:
> Conquer thee or be conquered.

Again, the contrast between Calaf's insensate passion and the inhuman coldness of Turandot is shown in the opera in the keenest light, and both protagonists are portrayed as heroic superhumans, compared with whom Gozzi's two characters appear Lilliputian. It is not improbable that Puccini modelled his two protagonists along lines suggested by Schiller's adaptation, where they are indeed portrayed in more heroic and poetic colours than they are in Gozzi.† Again, the play contains no love scene so called; the opera, on the other hand, has a great love-duet which, we recall, constituted for Puccini one of the central scenes of the whole drama. Some significant changes of dramatic details, all made to enhance the romantic aspect of the drama, are also worth noting. Thus, in Gozzi it is Adelma who by a treacherous ruse obtains the secret of the Unknown's name; in Puccini it is the Prince himself who of his own will discloses his identity to the Princess. Again, while in the play it is Calaf's attempted suicide that softens Turandot's heart, in the opera this is brought about by a less drastic and more romantic twist which was Puccini's idea: Calaf's kiss, which acts on

* The heraldic sign of Venice.

† On the other hand, Schiller tended to intellectualize his version. Also, with the rather stilted verses and the prim jokes he put into the mouths of the Masks, it seems to reflect the austere and humourless Weimar of Prince August rather than the gay, frivolous Venice of Gozzi and Goldoni.

her like a magic spell. Equally poetic is the touch that occurs in the final 'Jubilation' before the Divan where Turandot, instead of announcing Calaf's name, sings 'Il suo nome è . . . Amore!'. But the most significant single modification introduced into Gozzi's plot was the creation of the character of Liù, who is first mentioned in a Puccini letter of August 1920 when the libretto was still in an inchoate state.

How and why did Liù enter into Puccini's dramatic scheme? Already Gozzi, in enlarging the original tale from *The Arabian Nights*, felt the need to heighten its tension by the creation of a rival to Turandot, who is Adelma. The resulting triangular situation is not dissimilar to that obtaining between Aida, Amneris and Radamès in Verdi's opera. Adelma is a Tartar princess who, after the conquest of her country and the murder of her family by the army of the Emperor Altoum, was brought to Peking as a slave for Turandot and in time became her confidante. In the days of happiness at her father Ceicobad's court, she had noticed a young and handsome gardener to whom, unknown to him, she felt much attracted. This youth was none other than the fugitive Unknown whom she now recognizes at Turandot's trial at the Divan. She falls in love with him and becomes madly jealous of Turandot, resorting to various stratagems to persuade him to flee with her—which he refuses. In revenge Adelma obtains the secret of his origin and name from his own lips, partly by a ruse, partly by accident, and discloses it to Turandot. In the last scene but one, her treachery is brought to light and she tries to stab herself but is hindered by Calaf. Turandot forgives her and Adelma is given back her lost kingdom, to which she returns forthwith.

From this it becomes plain that Gozzi's Tartar princess provided a part-model for Puccini's little slave-girl. Like Adelma, Liù had met Calaf in the past and secretly loved him ever since; like Adelma, she becomes Turandot's rival for the Prince's love and like her—albeit with a tragic result—she lays hands on herself. There the parallel ceases. The motive for Adelma's attempted suicide was despair at the failure of her intrigue to gain the Unknown for herself. The motive for Liù's self-immolation is her unbounded love for him, prompting her to die with the secret of his name undisclosed so as to enable him to win Turandot's heart. Hers is an act of pure self-sacrifice, moving and heroic. Through it she becomes a tragic figure who, not unlike Butterfly, atones for her 'guilt' of having loved a man entirely out of her own sphere—wherein lies, to my mind, the ultimate significance of her self-chosen death. But from a dramatic point of view this episode is wholly adventitious, having no influence whatever on the further course of the action, namely the psychological transformation of Turandot into a loving woman. It will be recalled that at one period during the gestation of the libretto, Puccini did consider providing an inner link between Liù's suicide and Turandot's subsequent change of heart—'it could help', he wrote to Adami, 'to soften the heart of the Princess'.* The absence of this link in the ultimate version of the opera constitutes a serious psychological weakness

* See letter on p. 232.

and one of the strangest puzzles in the composer's dramatic thinking. He may conceivably have argued that leaving Turandot wholly unaffected by Liù's death would serve to emphasize all the more strongly the Princess's inhumanity, so that her subsequent 'humanization' under the magic spell of Calaf's kiss would strike with redoubled force. What of Calaf's reaction? The fact that he too remains unmoved by Liù's death has been interpreted as the sign of an utter callousness, alienating our sympathies. Yet a moment's consideration proves the fallacy of this view. Calaf was never in love with the slave-girl, he did not desert her for Turandot and it is even possible to interpret Liù's suicide as the act of a lovesick little girl whose balance of mind had been upset by the threat of torture. Moreover, from the moment Calaf sets his eyes on Turandot, he is under a hypnotic spell, acting almost throughout as though in a trance and all but oblivious of the happenings around him. This spell does not cease until he has conquered Turandot's heart. Hence, his behaviour after Liù's death remains wholly consistent with his general conduct since the opening of the drama.

To return to Liù. Though her function in the context of Puccini's drama is similar to that of Adelma's in Gozzi's, as a character she stands poles apart from her. Turandot's confidante is ambitious, vengeful and imperious—after all, she is a king's daughter. Liù is of humble origin, a slave-girl, gentle and dedicated in her love—a true Puccinian heroine. Yet though she is essentially the composer's brain-child, Gozzi provided him with some sort of sketch for her in Turandot's slave-girl Zuleima. Like Liù, she is a gentle and affectionate creature, who in fact encourages the Princess to yield to her growing love for Calaf. And, as we suggested in the biographical part of this book, it is probable that the character and the ultimate fate of the unfortunate Doria Manfredi* also contributed some traits to the portrayal of the operatic character. Liù is thus a composite figure, and though she does not advance the essential drama by one iota, it must be conceded that her presence serves to enlarge both the emotional and musical range of the opera appreciably, and that she remains the only character who touches our heart. Puccini needed the poignant element embodied in Liù to kindle his fundamentally 'tragic' imagination. In addition, her death serves to reduce the curiously hybrid nature of Gozzi's tragi-comedy, though, admittedly, not to the extent of removing this unsatisfactory feature altogether. In a sense, the happy ending of the opera comes as a perilous anticlimax after Liù's final scene.

4

Let us now turn to Puccini's three Masks. In them he was confronted with a type of character he had never dealt with before and whose treatment raised a number of difficult dramatic problems. In the play the Masks form a wholly incongruous element, which was of course intentional and part of Gozzi's concept. There we have four such figures: Pantalone, the Emperor's Prime Minister; Tartaglia, his Grand Chancellor; Brighella,

* See Chapter XIV.

the Master of the Pages; and Truffaldino, who is Turandot's Chief Eunuch and at once recalls the blustering Osmin of Mozart's *Entführung*. We learn that the reason which brought them to China many years before was that each had been involved in some disreputable business in their native Venice. Unlike Puccini's courtiers, they take no direct part in the action and play the role of a Greek chorus. Speaking in Venetian dialect, their prosaic comments reflect the famous horse-sense of the Venetians. They often indulge in cheerful cynicism and are not above making obscene remarks and using vulgar language when among themselves. Thus, they refer to the Princess Turandot as 'quella porchetta'—'that little pig'—and 'questa cagna'—'that bitch'.*
Small wonder that Puccini felt uncertain for some time about the right treatment of these clowns, and even thought of eliminating them altogether. If they were to be retained, then not too much, he admonished his librettist, should be made of them—they are to be philosophers and clowns, here and there throwing in a comic remark or an opinion, but they must never obtrude; as in Gozzi, they should represent 'an Italian element in the midst of so much Chinese mannerisms . . . with a keen observation of Pantalone and Co. bringing us back to the reality of our lives'.† He remembered Shakespeare's treatment in *The Tempest* of Trinculo, Stephano and Caliban, who 'drink, use bad language and speak ill of the king', and urged his librettist to do something in the same vein. Yet in the same breath he expresses his fears lest the Masks should spoil the opera, and wonders whether it might not be possible to enrich them with and attune them to the Chinese element. This in the event proved the right solution. Thus Gozzi's Pantalone, Tartaglia, Brighella and Truffaldino were transformed into Ping the Grand Chancellor, Pang the General Purveyor and Pong the Chief Cook. But it must be admitted that the *chinoiserie* of these new names is not altogether happy, on account of the association with a popular Western ball game. Even their words, Puccini demanded, should occasionally breathe a Chinese flavour, and to give Adami some idea of what he had in mind he sent him dummy verses, with assonances on the vowels *a* and *ia*.‡

Yet far more important than these changes in names and national costumes is the inner transformation which Gozzi's Masks undergo in Puccini. They now become grotesquely sinister figures, with a sadistic streak in them and indulging in macabre humour. In other words, they are turned into

---

* Puccini's text echoes such remarks, as when in Act I his three courtiers attempt to rob Calaf of all illusion about Turandot: 'And what is she after all? Nothing but a woman with a crown on her head and a bordered mantle! But let her unrobe, and nothing remains but human flesh! Raw flesh! Not even good to eat!'

† See letter on pp. 212–3.

‡
Puccini	*Adami*
Canticchiamo pian piano sommessi	Nei giardini sussurran le rose
nell'uscir siam prudenti in giardin.	e tintinnan campanule d'or,
Se inciampiamo nei sassi sconnessi	si sospiran parole amorose
disturbiamo il felice Calaf!	di rugiada s'imperlano i fior! (Trio, Act II).

See letter of 22 January 1924 (E).

Turandot's creatures, worlds apart from the essentially good-natured and almost genial originals of the play. Yet from time to time Ping, Pang and Pong show themselves stirred by more humane feelings, as in the scene of Liù's death; and in their nostalgia for the serenity of country life they are capable of a poetic mood wholly unknown to Gozzi's prosaic Masks.

As for the few remaining characters in the play, Calaf's father and his tutor Barak, both of some importance there, are in the opera telescoped into Timur, a pathetic and musically almost negligible father, while Gozzi's Altoum, an active and energetic Emperor, is reduced in Puccini to a senile dotard singing in a thin weary voice.*

The dramatic structure of the libretto, which was as much Puccini's work as that of his two librettists, is all but impeccable—the qualification referring to the last two scenes, to be discussed in their musical context. As in *Tosca*, the strict observance of the three classical unities greatly adds to the spectator's impression of concentration and compactness in the action, which takes place within twenty-four hours. As in *Tosca*, the drama is set in motion with the rise of the curtain, and the essential plot is rapidly deployed.† The chief characters are neatly introduced, one after the other, with Turandot appearing last. Puccini the musician is given his head, yet without thus affecting the essential drama. In addition, Gozzi's quasi-historical allusions are all excised, the libretto concentrating on the pure fairy-tale. This not only enhances the atmosphere of remoteness and timelessness but also emphasizes the universal significance of the larger underlying theme—a feature not encountered before in Puccini's operas. This alone would account for the unique position which *Turandot* occupies in his *œuvre*. Yet what renders it his greatest and richest masterpiece is the remarkable fusion he achieved of the four separate elements so distinctive of his general style: the lyric-sentimental (Liù)—the heroic-grandiose (Calaf and Turandot)—the comic-grotesque (the Masks)—the exotic. It is this synthesis that is responsible for the far wider orbit which *Turandot* shows in comparison with that of his previous operas. Puccini's swansong thus represents the consummation of his whole creative career.

5

In discussing the music it is convenient to start with the last of those four elements—the exotic. Unlike *Butterfly*, where the plot entailed a division into an 'Eastern' and a 'Western' manner, *Turandot* is saturated from the first

* Strangely enough, the librettists lose sight of Timur after the scene of Liù's death forgetting that in Gozzi he shares, as is logical, in his son's final triumph. No doubt, but for his death Puccini would have tied up this loose end in the dramatic knot.

† Thus the opera begins with the Mandarin's reading of the cruel edict so that we are at once acquainted with the situation from which the whole action springs, whereas in the play that scene does not occur until the second act. Gozzi opens with a leisurely 'recognition' scene between Calaf and his tutor Barak, who in true oriental fashion takes his time over informing the Prince about Turandot and her whims.

page to the last in exoticism, though with notable exceptions to be mentioned anon. Puccini's method in re-creating the atmosphere is his customary one: use of authentic and self-invented Chinese melodies which he invests with 'primitive' harmonies, 'barbaric' rhythms and orchestral colours that often recall those of a *fauve* painting. His initial misgiving, that the style of his 'Chinese' opera might be too reminiscent of that of his 'Japanese' work, arose possibly from the fact that in both the pentatonic element is very strong; yet he avoided all similarity on that score by an entirely different treatment of the vocal, rhythmic and instrumental textures.

Of the authentic themes incorporated in the score I have been able to identify eight:

Ex. 101

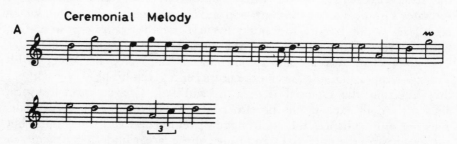

This is a ceremonial tune played on court occasions and also occurs in Chinese chamber music. It is first heard in Act II, at the point at which the Emperor's standards are carried through the cloud of incense, in preparation for the Divan. It stands for the idea of legendary China, incarnated in the Emperor, and it is intoned in all the scenes of ceremonial pomp.

This tune, entitled *Moo-Lee-Wha*, became first known in Europe at the end of the eighteenth century and is quoted in an English travel-book as well as in a German volume on musical history. In the opera it is chiefly used to denote the 'official' Turandot, the Daughter of the Emperor. Its first appearance is in Act I, in the Boys' Chorus, which heralds the procession of the Persian Prince. Next to Ex. A, it is the most frequently employed in the opera. Both are likely to have been those melodies that Puccini heard on the ancient Chinese musical-box owned by his friend, Baron Fassini (see p. 226).

Temple Music: "Guiding March"

C

This is a so-called 'Guiding March' characteristic of Chinese temple music and intoned at the entry of the Emperor into the Temple. In the opera it is associated with the idea of the Wedding and is first heard in Act II, in the 'Pavilion' scene of the Masks, at the point at which they refer to the preparations for the nuptial chamber.

Temple Music

D

This again is a temple melody used in connection with sacrificial rites. It first occurs in the music of the Masks (Act I, 37).

Hymn of Confucius

E

Puccini never uses this hymn in its entirety but only fragments of it on which he plays variations.

National Anthem

F

This is the modern Imperial Hymn, composed in 1912. In the opera the Masks make their first entry with it (Act I, 28).

Folksong

G

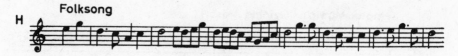

H Folksong

Both these tunes derive from Chinese folk-songs, which is possibly the reason why Puccini used them exclusively in the music for the Masks.*

In addition, *Turandot* contains a number of characteristic pentatonic motives either genuine or invented by the composer. The favourite keys in which Puccini presents his exotic material are G♭ major and E♭ minor, evidently because the black keys on the piano present the pentatonic notes and lie well under the hand. (Puccini, we recall, composed at the piano.) There are also whole-tone melodies and themes with the step of the augmented second, a characteristic of Near-Eastern music and aptly introduced in the march accompanying the procession of the Persian Prince and in the brief dance of the Odalisques, in the 'Temptation' scene of Act III.

The exoticism of *Turandot* is not all-pervasive. At times the composer steps out of it and into his 'Western' idiom, chiefly in situations which demand music of a broad, lyrical character. Nor is the plangent melody associated with Liù (Ex. 4d, p. 275) recognizably Eastern. But with this sole exception, Liù is the only one of the three protagonists who, like the Masks, is dressed in national musical costume throughout, though this costume may bear the trademark 'Made in Italy'—Puccini's Italy, to be precise. It is interesting to observe how he characterizes by the particular *build* of a melody. For the diminutive Liù and the Masks he mostly resorts to his aphoristic mosaic, whereas Turandot, Calaf and the solemn choruses of Acts II and III are given broad, slow and long-arched themes of more or less symmetrical structure (2 + 2 and 4 + 4 bars). So much for the general melodic aspect.

As to the exotic ingredients of the harmonic idiom, they comprise all those we met in *Butterfly* and *Fanciulla* (parallel fourths and fifths, pedals, tritones, etc.) to which Puccini now adds new spices, culled from the field of the new music of his time. The atmosphere of *Turandot* indeed invited a harmonic style invested with a high degree of dissonance, and this, in combination with certain new rhythmic and orchestral devices, renders this opera Puccini's most advanced work. There is bitonality, as for example in the music to which the Mandarin reads Turandot's decree at the beginning of Act I, or the opening of the grotesque Trio of the Masks in Act II (a combination of the two modes of the whole-tone scale):

* Ex. A is quoted from *Harvard Dictionary of Music*, by Willi Apel (Harvard, 1944). Ex. B is reproduced in *Travels in China*, by John Barrow (London, 1806) and *Geschichte der Musik*, by A. W. Ambros (Leipzig, 1883). Exx. C, E, G and H are quoted from *Chinese Music*, by J. A. Aalst (Shanghai, 1884. New ed. 1933); Ex. D from *Encyclopédie de la Musique*, by Alfred Lavignac (Paris, 1939), and Ex. F from article, 'National Anthems', in *Grove's Dictionary* etc. (op. cit.).

Ex. 102

Ex. b derives from the 'Turandot' theme, Ex. 107a. There is successive polytonality in those violent transitions from one key to another, e.g. the frenzied choruses of Act I. There are passages which suggest that Puccini sought to imitate the strange effects of heterophony, a primitive kind of polyphony in Eastern music in which the same melody is repeated simultaneously in various instruments with slight variations:

Ex. 103 *

(a)   Siamese "score"

* Ex. 103a is quoted from Carl Stumpf, *Sammelbände für vergleichende Musikwissenschaft*, Vol. I (Berlin, 1922).

(b)   Turandot, Act III

(The Shrove-tide Fair in Stravinsky's *Petrushka* displays a similar texture, even as in his opera *La Rossignol* (1917) the highly dissonant music in the scene at the Chinese Emperor's Court anticipates that for similar scenes in *Turandot*.) Lastly, there are harmonies of extraordinary pungency created by the clashes of adjacent notes (Ex. 104a, b).

Ex. b, with its strange six-and-seven-note chords and the pallid, disembodied hues of the orchestration, belongs to the music of the ghost voices and appears to owe something to Schoenberg's *Pierrot Lunaire* (1912), that remarkable masterpiece of nightmare suggestion. (We recall that Puccini made a special journey to Florence to attend a performance of it under the composer's direction.) In this connection I venture to suggest that something of the macabre quality of Giraud's verses also coloured the lines which Puccini's chorus addresses to the moon in Act I.★

★ Cf. the lines beginning: 'Perchè tarda la luna', with No. 4 (*Eine blasse Wäscherin*) and No. 7 (*Der kranke Mond*) of *Pierrot Lunaire*.

Ex. 104

As in *Fanciulla*, yet far more pervasively, Puccini resorts to savage percussive rhythms (mostly in simple two/four and three/four) and rhythmic *ostinati* which in the frenzied choruses of Act I generate the physiological excitement characteristic of certain oriental music, while its polyrhythmic patterns are reflected in passages such as:

Ex. 105

A whole chapter could be devoted to a study of the orchestral score—Puccini's most complex and richest essay in instrumental exoticism. The orchestra was the largest he ever employed. There are in fact two orchestras, the second of which plays offstage. The main body comprises strings, treble woodwind, four horns, three trumpets, four trombones, harp, celesta, timpani and an array of percussion, including diverse drums, cymbals, triangle, glockenspiel, xylophone, bass xylophone, Chinese gongs and tubular bells. The stage orchestra, again, consists of brass, two saxophones, percussion and organ; it is chiefly confined to the Court scenes of Acts II and III, but also comes into action once or twice in the opening act, as in the mysterious boys' chorus, with its doubling by two nostalgic saxophones.

In none of the composer's previous operas is the orchestra given such an active part as in *Turandot*—not only in the painting of the atmosphere but in underlining dramatic and psychological moments. Yet, for all its importance, it never usurps the hegemony from the singers, who remain the musical core of the whole complex texture. The chief characters and certain recurring situations are associated with particular instruments—the Court with the heavy brass, Turandot with the combined wind and strings and Calaf with the strings. For Liù, on the other hand, are reserved the most delicate tints, with some exquisite touches brushed in by a solo instrument—flute, oboe or violin. The Masks, again, disport themselves to the dry crackle of woodwind, frequently punctuated by *pizzicato* and harmonics on the string, glassy celesta chords and rattling strokes on the xylophone, to which are occasionally added the grotesque sounds of a squeaking piccolo and high-pitched muted trumpets.

One of the great features of *Turandot* is Puccini's handling of the chorus, which (as in *Fanciulla*), serves him as a most powerful means of engendering atmosphere, notably in Act I where the crowd takes a direct part in the action. The savage populace is characterized by a theme that, significantly, stands also for Pu-tin-tao, the Executioner:

Ex.106

Melody, key and rhythm at once recall Mussorgsky's celebrated song *Gopak*, even as the general treatment of the *Turandot* choruses calls to mind the dramatic crowd scenes of *Boris Godunov*. Yet the Puccinian stamp is unmistakable in the way in which the choral lines are broken up by brief fragmentary interjections—the mere sight of the score suggests a wildly excited and milling crowd—while the orchestra sustains the melody. As might be expected, the choral writing is of the simplest homophony, yet from time to time Puccini seems to remember his early contrapuntal training as, for example, in the dramatic four-part *stretto* of Act I, 'Dolce amanti, avanti!' and the 'Gloria' choruses of Act II. In the last two acts, however, the chorus no longer represents so dynamic a factor but is largely used as a musical-scenic *décor* for the Court ceremonials, with 'primitive' block harmonies, solemn and chorale-like, and with the parts occasionally widely spaced so as to create a rich sonority.* Most exquisite are, in Act I, some impressionist choruses such as the crowd's subdued apostrophe to the rising moon, with its wisps of melody delicately floating up in the air, and the wistful boys' chorus already mentioned; nor has Puccini ever before used a chorus to such haunting effect as in the scene in Act III following Liù's death, in which the basses descend to E and E♭ below the stave.

6

So much for the musical setting of the atmosphere. Let us now consider the characterization of the three protagonists. Of these Turandot is the most variously portrayed. To begin with, she has two distinct themes. One is the *Moo-Lee-Wha* tune (Ex. 101B), which, as mentioned before, represents the 'official' Turandot, daughter of the Emperor. Apart from changes of tempo and note values, it remains unaltered throughout the opera. The second leading theme stands for Turandot as the embodiment of an evil power:

Ex.107

(a) "Turandot"

Andante sostenuto

(b) "Otello", Iago's Credo
Allegro sostenuto

Transformations of "Turandot" theme

(c)

(d)

(e)

Co - sa u - ma - na non so - no

* See, for example, the Prayer 'Diecimila anni al nostro Imperatore!', Act II.

While not as pervasive as the first, Ex. 107a undergoes a number of metamorphoses of a kind Puccini had never attempted before (Ex. c, d and e). Most noteworthy is its resemblance, in melodic and rhythmic shape as well as in orchestration (brass), with the grandiose theme from Iago's 'Credo' in Verdi's *Otello* (Ex. 107b); I have little doubt that Puccini, consciously or otherwise, modelled his 'Turandot' theme on it. We are also reminded of the 'Scarpia' motive, in that Ex. 107a is partly based on the 'evil' whole-tone scale, has the same graphic terseness in its suggestion of something ferocious, and prefaces the opera like a motto.

If Ex. 107a conveys the essence of Turandot's nature before her miraculous transformation in Act III, a full portrait of her as the haughty, cruel Princess is painted in her great aria of Act II, 'In questa Reggia', which may be said to be, on the whole, more striking in its powerful dramatic characterization than in melodic invention. Its length is in itself a point in the characterization of that imperious figure. It falls into two sections through which shows the old form of recitative and aria: the narration of the story of her murdered ancestress, the Princess Lo-u-ling, with which Turandot motivates her vow, and the reaffirmation of this vow. The aria is not a pure solo piece; Puccini punctuates it to dramatic effect by interjections of the chorus and, later, of Calaf. The narration is appropriately treated in a declamatory style, opening in a heroic manner but subsequently growing chant-like and vision-ary, an effect greatly enhanced by the hushed choral refrain 'fu grande il Re'. Yet, when Turandot arrives in her story at the point at which she refers to the many princes on whom she has avenged the death of her ancestress, her agitation grows visibly and culminates in the splendidly dramatic phrase 'quel grido e quella morte!'. This phrase leads to the second part of the aria which is in Puccini's favourite 'lyrical' key G♭ and introduces one of the great themes in this opera, an idea of magnificent sweep and range:

Ex. 108

Gli e - nig - mi so - no tre, la mor - te è u - na

Repeating her oath never to yield to a man, Turandot rises to menacing grandeur in the emphatic 'the enigmas are three, death is one!' (Ex. b).*

* A sketch dating from as late as February 1924, shows that Puccini originally tried to develop a theme or, more accurately, a tentative version of it, into a period of eight bars in F major which was to be balanced by a repeat in A major. In the ultimate version he made use of the incisive 'enigmi' motive *only* treating it in a rising sequence—E flat major—F sharp major—A flat major. This conveys the mounting tension to a climax between Turandot and Calaf in a far more concentrated and dramatically more telling manner than did Puccini's original idea.

(This phrase, incidentally, is cast in the same hendecasyllabic pattern as Rinuccio's 'Florentine' song.) Immediately after, Ex. b is repeated—transposed a fourth up—by her and Calaf in unison, the orchestra doubling it in several octaves—an effect that must count as the most powerful in all Puccini. 'In questa Reggia' is a gruelling test for the singer of Turandot, on account of the wide, leaping intervals, of a *tessitura* lying around the awkward voice-break between the middle and high registers (E-F), and of the many high notes with which this aria is studded (several As, Bs and C *in alt.*). Here as elsewhere in the part of Turandot, the influence of the Strauss of *Elektra* is manifest.

By contrast, Turandot's second aria 'Del primo pianto', which she sings in her love duet with Calaf in Act III, portrays her as a woman now conquered by the power of true love. Admittedly this is not as inspired a piece as 'In questa Reggia' but it succeeds in suggesting something of the psychological change in Turandot by its tender lyricism, witness the flowing and expansive 'C'era negli occhi tuoi'. Although a more heroic expression asserts itself in the latter part of this aria, the vocal line here is far less exacting than in Turandot's great monologue, rising no higher than A *in alt.*

Of the three chief characters, Calaf is the only one who appears in all three acts and who is hence allotted more music than either Turandot or Liù. Yet, unlike the heroine, the hero has no leading theme as pervasive as hers, nor does he make his first bow with it. It is, in fact, not until the 'Enigma' scene of Act II, at the point where he poses *his* riddle, that Calaf becomes associated with a melody of his own—the 'Name' or 'Love' theme, Puccini's use of it suggesting that these two concepts were interchangeable in his mind:

Ex. 109

This ardent theme dominates Calaf's aria in Act III and serves also for the apotheosis of the final scene. Like Turandot, Calaf is conceived in a heroic vein but being a far more human character, his music is at once warmer, more expressive and suppler in vocal line. It displays, however, a virile fibre missing from Puccini's other tenor-heroes, with the possible exception of Johnson in *Fanciulla* and Luigi in *Tabarro*; nor does the composer allow him to break out into the hysteria characteristic of Cavaradossi.

When we first meet Calaf, in Act I, he is an impetuous young prince obsessed by his resolve to win Turandot, yet he is also capable of sympathy for the little slave-girl, a feeling to which he gives moving expression in his first aria 'Non piangere, Liù!'. It is, however, significant that this situation prompted Puccini to an aria in which the Prince, although exhorting Liù not to weep, himself expresses his sentiments in terms of the composer's characteristic lament. Calaf here stands nearer to the emotional world of

Liù than that of Turandot, a fact also reflected in certain similarities which his aria shows to Liù's 'Farewell' of Act III.* Again, Puccini fetters Calaf's aria to the action by means of the sad interjections on the part of Liù and Timur and by the smooth, imperceptible way in which it is made to flow into the next scene; in fact it is out of Calaf's last phrase that grows the magnificent theme of the final ensemble.

In an entirely different vein is his third-act *romanza* 'Nessun dorma'. Calaf, having emerged triumphant from the cruel test of the enigmas, now allows his mind to dream of his final victory over Turandot. Softly and meditatively, he takes up the heralds' distant cry which sounds through the still night, Puccini evoking the nocturnal atmosphere with exquisitely delicate harmonies and orchestral timbres. As the Prince's ardour grows, he intones the 'Love' theme (Ex. 109), violas and cellos lending a lovely mellowness to the vocal line; and a signally poetic touch is the distant female chorus echoing that theme to the words 'Pena la morte!', while Calaf continues it in impassioned tones. 'Nessun dorma' has indeed a nobility and beauty which singles it out from the composer's other tenor arias. And we are compelled to admire his sense of psychological transition when with perfect naturalness he leads the chorus of the heralds into the aria, and again from its ecstatic close into the grotesque music of the Masks who suddenly burst upon the tranquil scene.

And now to Liù. She is the only character in the opera who touches the heart, a Mimi or a Butterfly transported from realistic surroundings to the fantastic world of legendary China. Whatever Liù sings bears the imprint of true inspiration, yet it is strange that the composer should not have honoured her with a leading theme, possibly because she is after all an episodic figure. There is, however, a theme which, to judge from the context in which it occurs, Puccini appears to have associated with Liù and the pitiful Timur whose companion she is (Ex. 4d).† This plangent strain, a typical *'povera faccia'* melody, is heard soon after the opening of the opera, in the scene in which the ruthless guards push back the frightened crowd, many getting trampled under in the ensuing panic. The music does not fit this brutal scene at all and will only make sense if we relate it to Liù expressing her anxiety for Timur's life. This interpretation finds additional support in the fact that Puccini's second and last use of this theme occurs in the scene of Act III where Liù and Timur are dragged before Turandot, to be made to reveal the name of the Unknown Prince. Ex. 4d displays, incidentally, a strong family likeness to the sombre melody accompanying Tosca's last scene with Scarpia;‡ and, like it, seems to date from a much earlier period, possibly the period of *Manon Lescaut*.

* E.g. the same key (E♭ minor), the same dirge-like opening with monotonously repeated chords and the drooping tendency of the vocal melody. One or two reminiscences from Butterfly's 'Farewell' to her child—a situation which is psychologically somewhat akin to that obtaining between Calaf and Liù in Act I—can also be spotted in the tenor's aria.

† See p. 292.

‡ Ex. 53a, p. 375; viz. the similar melodic and rhythmic pattern, the same scoring (strings in octaves) and the same key (F♯ minor).

Puccini's musical bias for Liù is seen in the fact that he allotted her three arias as against two each for Turandot and Calaf. True, the first two arias are in the nature of a cavatina or song, as befits this diminutive character. 'Signore, ascolta!', which is in the 'black piano-keys' key of Gb, introduces her as a gentle, affectionate and warm-hearted creature whose musical portrait recalls the limpidity and delicacy of a Chinese pen-drawing. The swaying vocal line is formed by a succession of tiny pentatonic motives, supported by solo woodwind and muted violins, while the despairing passion that burns for the Prince in her little heart finds poignant expression in her closing phrase 'Liù non regge più', marked by a sudden upward leap of an octave and pungent harmonies. Of much the same character is the first of Liù's two third-act arias, 'Tanto amore segreto', in which she openly declares before Turandot her love for the Unknown Prince whose name she knows, but will not reveal even under torture.

It is, however, for Liù's farewell, 'Tu che di gel sei cinta', that Puccini reserved his finest invention. We recall that, as with Cavaradossi's 'Muoio disperato', the music for this aria was one of the first things that leapt into his mind before he was in possession of the proper text, and that, when, two years later, he finally requested Adami to provide two quatrains in a seven-syllable metre to fit the music, it was his own dummy verses that were adopted as they stood.* Liù's aria displays all the characteristic features of the Puccinian lament, rendered more exquisite by the exotic colouring. Liù's emotional crescendo, reaching its climax in the heartrending phrase 'per non vederlo più!' after which she stabs herself, is beautifully mirrored in Puccini's scoring, which represents a gradually rising terrace of sound.† It was an inspiration to continue with Liù's music into the subsequent scene of general remorse and pity at her horrible end. Calaf and Timur now add their sad voices to the dirge, the superstitious crowd sings in hushed tones a prayer for forgiveness to be granted them by Liù's shade, and even the Masks are moved to compassion. Add the close, with the procession carrying the little body out into the darkness of night and the choral voices dying away into nothingness, and the result is a scene which musically no less than visually constitutes one of the most moving in all opera.

7

There remain the Three Masks. They form a kind of miniature chorus, Puccini treating them not so much as individual characters but as a group singing the same music—rather like the relatives in *Gianni Schicchi*. The chief contrast lies in their voices, Ping being a baritone and his two companions tenors, as lightly calibrated as the *tenori di grazia* of the old comic opera.

* Cf. Letter of 12 November 1923 (E).

† Solo oboe and bassoon—cor anglais—strings—full orchestra. Nor should we overlook a rhythmic subtlety here: the true phrasing of Liù's aria would be a regular six/four pattern but by harnessing the melody on to an alternating two/four and four/four beat the feeling of an asymmetrical rhythm is created and thus the deadening effect of a regular accentuation obviated.

They often fall into an almost conversational style which distinguishes them most sharply from the rest of the characters. They are given no leitmotives but are instead limned by a multiplicity of short pentatonic figures,* which succeed each other in kaleidoscopic fashion. Equally characteristic is the *ballabile* style of their music, e.g. the dance-like scherzo, 'Fermo! Che fai?', with which the Masks fling themselves across Calaf's path, in order to prevent him from striking the gong (Act I). This, conjoined to skipping intervals in the vocal parts, jerky rhythms and a *sec*, brittle orchestration, conjures up graphically the image of puppet-like creatures at once comically grotesque and malevolent. The Masks are given extended scenes in all three acts and altogether help to lend the opera its unique character. Which brings us to a noteworthy feature of Puccini's treatment of the comic element in this opera.

I have referred before to the remarkable fusion he achieved in *Turandot* of the four distinctive features of his general style. This can best be studied in the admirable way in which the Masks are merged with the prevalent serious atmosphere of the drama. They are not superimposed on it but are, in contrast to Gozzi's treatment, an organic part of it. In this Puccini proved far more successful than Strauss in *Ariadne auf Naxos*, where a similar attempt is made to merge the stock types of *commedia dell'arte* with a serious drama. But Strauss and Hofmannsthal by-pass the problem of intrinsic fusion, allowing the comic element merely to alternate with the serious, instead of uniting them, dramatically and contrapuntally, as was the sudden whim of Monsieur Jourdain when he asked his singers to give a *simultaneous* performance of *opera seria* and *opera buffa*. Nor do Strauss's Masks impinge on the essential action as they do in Puccini's opera where, while always remaining grotesque drolls, they take an active part in the drama, *vide* the latter scenes of Act I and the 'Temptation' of Act III.

In this connection brief mention may be made of Busoni's *Turandot*, in which there is a similar synthesis of comic and serious. Puccini is unlikely ever to have seen this opera,† but he may well have had occasion to peruse the vocal score. Busoni kept far closer to the spirit of Gozzi's play than did Puccini, emphasizing the comedy in the 'tragi-comedy'; hence the problem of merging the Masks with the essential drama presented less difficulty than to Puccini. In fact, Busoni intended his *Turandot* (and its companion-piece, *Arlecchino*, given with it in a double bill) as an example of 'the new *commedia dell'arte*' in which the Masks are treated in the traditional manner. Thus Tartaglia stammers,‡ and Pantalone delivers himself of sarcastic remarks on topical issues of the time, as when he says to the Emperor Altoum: 'With us in Italy everyone loves to see blood and thunder on the stage'—

* Several derive from Exx. 101 D, F, G, & H, pp. 469–70.

† After its first production at Zürich in 1917 it was, to my knowledge, never given again within Puccini's lifetime.

‡ The name of this stock figure derives from *tartagliare*—'to stammer'. It was Gozzi who first introduced this character into the Venetian Mask, importing him from the Neapolitan *commedia dell'arte*.

a shaft aimed by Busoni at veristic opera, which he held in contempt. It is significant of his approach to Gozzi's subject that of the serious characters none engaged the composer's sympathies more than the Emperor, whom he conceived in the image of Mozart's Sarastro. Though intellectually stimulating and in its spirit more contemporary than Puccini's work, Busoni's opera suffers from a strange hotchpotch of styles (which may have been intentional) containing, of all things, a waltz and the old English folksong *Greensleeves*. Altogether, no two works dealing with the same subject and written within five or six years of each other could be more dissimilar in dramatic concept and aesthetic aim than the *Turandots* of the two Tuscan composers, Busoni and Puccini.

Let us now cast a glance over the musico-dramatic structure of *Turandot*. Of the three acts, the first must in this respect be reckoned the best and indeed the outstanding among all Puccini's opening acts. The most striking feature here is a large-scale design such as he had never attempted before, a design broadly resembling that of a symphony in four continuous movements held together by a central mood. Borrowing from the symphonic terminology, we may describe the opening scene, the Reading of Turandot's Edict, as the 'slow introduction'. The 'Allegro' is a mainly choral movement extending to the close of the chorus, 'Ungi, arrota!'; its general character is one of ferocity, its basic tempo fast, and its main key F♯ minor. The ensuing 'Andante' opens with the choral apostrophe to the moon and closes with the march of the Persian Prince; the music is partly evocative, partly dramatic in a sombre way, generally slow, its chief tonalities being D major and E♭ minor. So far the musical scenes have been dominated by the chorus—now it is the soloists who take the lead. A brief transition, formed by the exchanges between Calaf and his father Timur, leads to the 'Scherzo' of the Masks; light and capricious in mood, its basic rhythm is three/four and major keys predominate. The first part of this movement is an almost self-contained piece in ternary form firmly anchored in A♭. Even two contrasting 'trios' may be discerned—the first in the chorus of Turandot's maids bidding the Masks be silent (an Andante lento in C♯ minor), and the second in the eerie chorus of the dead suitors (a Lento resting on a long sustained pedal on the note A). After the 'Scherzo' another transition—Timur's appeal to his son to desist from his reckless venture—leads to the Finale, the crowning movement of Puccini's 'symphony'. This comprises the arias of Liù and Calaf and culminates in the great ensemble 'Ah! per ultima volta!'. The emotional curve described by this Finale—it begins in G♭ major and ends on the relative minor, E♭—rises from the plangent lyricism of the arias to the wild agitation of the last ensemble; the tempo is slow throughout. Such a large-scale design—four distinct sections, each with its own thematic material, its own rhythmic patterns and tonalities, and each different in emotional character, yet the whole act springing from a central dramatic mood—can scarcely be regarded as a matter of accident. On the contrary, it argues a deliberate and calculated plan and testifies to the consummate power of organization which Puccini achieved in his last period.

Before we leave this great act, a word or two must be said on its final ensemble, easily Puccini's most impressive essay in the handling of concerted solo and choral voices, and recalling the 'Embarkation' of *Manon Lescaut*, with which indeed it displays a strong stylistic affinity.* And like that early ensemble, it springs directly from the action, Liù, Timur, the Masks and the chorus joining in a last desperate effort to prevent the Prince from striking the fateful gong.† Observe how the constant to-ing and fro-ing on the stage is graphically mirrored in this rolling, heaving theme:

Ex. 110

Observe, too, how dramatic suspense is built up by the masterly treatment of the voices. Opening with broken-up phrases, fragments of Ex. 110 are tossed from one soloist to the other, until at the repeat (at [47]) the texture begins to grow fuller and more sustained. At the psychological moment enter an invisible chorus and a brass orchestra adding a new element to the mounting tension, which finally reaches explosion point in Calaf's thrice-repeated cry 'Turandot', dramatically answered by the choral 'La Morte!' And how overwhelming is the following section when, after Calaf's three gong-strokes, the stately 'Turandot' theme (Ex. 101B) is solemnly intoned in the glorious radiance of D major; after so much sombre Eb minor, the sudden semitonal shift in this context produces a stupendous dramatic effect. Even the Verdi of *Otello* could not have penned a greater Finale than this.

8

If Act I confronted us with dynamic action and ferocious crowd scenes, Act II is largely static and introduces us to the exalted ceremonious atmosphere of the Emperor's Court. This contrast is as finely calculated as is the contrast within Act II itself, which is divided into a comic first half and a serious second half. Puccini felt, evidently, so attracted by the Masks that he decided to allot them an entire scene to themselves—the delightful 'Pavilion' scene preceding the great Divan. This comic interlude, in the form of a Trio, is comparable in idea to the scene in *Ariadne* in which Zerbinetta addresses the heroine with her aria. Like Strauss's long solo piece, Puccini's extended trio may at first sight seem to represent a superfluous

* Both are also in the same key, Eb minor.

† The details of this scene were sketched out by Puccini and with a few minor alterations retained in the final version of the libretto. (Puccini to Adami, 26 December 1921. (*C.P.*Let. 821).

addition to the essential drama and in fact retard the action. It may indeed be likened to the ballet divertissement of the old-style grand opera, merely thrown in for the spectator's delectation. Yet it does serve two essential purposes—one psychological, the other aesthetic. It is in this trio that something like human emotions first surge up in the desiccated hearts of the three Chinese courtiers, thus rousing our sympathies for them. Secondly, it provides a most welcome relief in the sombre drama which will not brighten until the last two scenes. In this light, the Masks' solo scene appears fully justified and proves once again the sure instinct Puccini possessed for dramatic and emotional variety.

Nor would we wish to miss this Trio. It represents a most entrancing piece of musical *chinoiserie*, for all that the composer laboured over it. We almost hear his own chuckle in it, half ironic and half delighted with his puppets. The effect of whimsical humour springs partly from his deft manipulation of snatches of Chinese and Chinese-sounding tunes, partly from innumerable pointed touches in the orchestration, and partly from the swift changes introduced into the vocal expression. Thus, the Masks are made to sing: now mysterious and serious, now gay and with 'comic desolation', now staccato and now legato, now with *falsetto* and closed mouths, now again with natural voices, now loud and now *mezza voce*. Puccini, by his minute markings of their parts, leaves nothing to chance to achieve a droll and grotesque effect. One of the most alluring sections of this Trio is the Andante mosso in which the Masks, so to speak, drop their masks entirely and, now human beings, dream their nostalgic dreams of pastoral bliss and tranquillity, far away from the cruel Court of Turandot—Ping of his 'house in Honan by a lake of blue, all surrounded by bamboo', Pang of his 'forest near Tsiang, nothing fairer could there be', and Pong of his 'garden near to Kiù . . . which my eyes no more shall view!'. Puccini responded to this longing for rural solitude, so dear to his own heart, in the most exquisite music. Here is his image of the gentle ripples on Ping's beloved 'laghetto blu tutto cinto di bambù':

Ex. 111

suo la - ghet - to blù

No less delicious is the Allegretto in three/eight, 'Non ricordate', with its orchestral tintinnabulation like the sound of the most fragile of glass,* into which suddenly bursts the savage offstage chorus with 'Ungi, arrota' (Ex. 106). Exotic *jeu d'esprit* has rarely been played with nimbler and more loving fingers than in this intermezzo.

The second and dramatically crucial half of Act II, linked to the preceding scene by transformation-music in a ceremonial Chinese style, centres on the scene of the Enigmas—the first of the two great *peripeteiae* of the drama. This scene is beautifully framed in solemn choruses, the Emperor's Hymn (Ex. 101A) introducing and closing (in the same key, F. major) the decisive contest between Turandot and Calaf. Puccini plays out his trumps with careful deliberation and an admirable sense of timing. There is, first, the aged Emperor's vain attempt, in a weary blanched voice, to dissuade the Prince from his reckless resolve. This is followed by the Mandarin's formal reading of the edict and finally comes Turandot's great monologue—all by way of an exordium to the 'Enigma' scene and generating a mounting tension.

Specht, in his biography (op. cit.) criticizes the fact that both Turandot's Three Riddles and Calaf's answers are set to the same music; and he wonders why Puccini, with his inborn sense of the theatre, did not give pictorial expression to the different subjects of the Riddles and their solutions ('Hope'—'Blood'—'Turandot'), which would have heightened suspense and at the same time achieved a musical crescendo, instead of the 'stately monotony which ends by exasperating our nerves'. This is a point worth making. Puccini must unquestionably have considered some such solution to the problem as Specht suggested, a solution which in the particular circumstances would have appeared the most obvious one. Why then did he eschew it? Specht sees in that a 'fourth riddle', added to Turandot's three. But there seems to me a possible answer to it: Turandot's posing of the riddles is in the nature of a ritual, a rigidly fixed ceremony which had been performed in the past with each of her unfortunate suitors, and from Gozzi we learn that there had been ninety-nine before Calaf. Now it is a characteristic of a primitive

* Piccolo, celesta, harp, glockenspiel and xylophone.

ritual that its hieratic rigidity and sameness engenders an effect hypnotic in its monotony and it is precisely this effect, I suggest, which Puccini sought to achieve when he set the three stages of the 'Enigma' scene to the same music. Moreover, he appears to have taken the cue for this treatment from *Aida*, where in the 'Judgment' scene of Act IV the Priests address Radamès three times and where Verdi creates tension through cumulative monotony, i.e. through his thrice-repeated statement of the same music. The only difference is that while Verdi moves a semitone up with each repeat, Puccini does so only in Turandot's third riddle.★

It must be admitted, however, that the music for the 'Enigma' scene is 'functional' rather than inspired though it fits the dramatic situation like a glove. For the riddles Puccini resorts to a formula which is evidently derived from the main 'Turandot' motive:

Ex. 112

Andante sostenuto

Both Turandot's and Calaf's parts are declamatory, only sparsely underlined in the orchestra so that the crucial words may be heard with the greatest clarity throughout. At the same time, however, there are a number of subtle instrumental touches to add point to the words, to wit: the muted horns and trumpets for the stabbing chords of Ex. 112, the 'sighing' *appoggiature* ('come un lamento'), the nervous flicker of arpeggios at Turandot's words 'Gelo che ti dà fuoco!', the cold glassy sound of the combined glockenspiel, celesta and harp when she sings of 'the vivid flash of sunset', and the like. Observe, too, such symbolic details as Turandot's gradual descent of the majestic staircase down to the bottom, after each of Calaf's correct answers to her riddles (not in Gozzi); or that Calaf poses *his* riddle, not to the formula Ex. 112, but to the noble melody of the 'Love' theme, Ex. 109. With the background of pomp and circumstance before which the two protagonists measure their strength against each other—the Emperor seated on a high throne at the top of the staircase like an idol, the courtiers in their multicoloured ceremonial costumes, the agitated populace, the waving of flags and banners—the 'Enigma' scene bears eloquent testimony to Puccini's ear and eye for a tremendous stage spectacle.

★ Another minor parallel with Verdi is that Puccini separates the three identical Riddle episodes by making the Eight Wise Men confirm each of Calaf's three correct answers, just as Amneris prays for Radamès's salvation after each of the Priests' three questions. Also, Verdi's trumpet calls are matched by Puccini's signal at the opening of the 'Enigma' scene.

9

Like Act II, the closing act consists of two parts, linked by transformation music—the scene in the garden of the palace and the one in the interior of the palace. The opening scene, by far the longer of the two, shows a similar structure to that of the first act. Again we discern four sections of strong emotional contrast and with their own musical material; but instead of a design resembling a four-movement symphony, we are here put in mind of a suite with the looser cohesion that goes with it. The opening section, with the Heralds' distant voices and Calaf's aria, has the character of a nocturne. After this static 'night music', the sudden irruption of the Three Masks, at the head of a crowd of dim figures, brings an abrupt change of mood, and with it a resumption of the essential action. Like the scenes of the Masks in the previous two acts, the present one is in the vein of a scherzo-cum-rondo: the tempo is fast, two/four is the main time signature and the prevailing key is a pentatonic D major; the sprightly Chinese folk-tune (Ex. 101H) recurs in the manner of a rondo ritornello. One of the 'episodes' introduces a more serious note when the Masks—after their unsuccessful attempt to extract the name from the lips of the great Unknown Prince by promises and blandishments—turn in despair to threats to achieve their end. For this little scene Puccini invents a broad, expansive melody with a marked Chinese flavour ('Straniero, tu non sai'). Again an abrupt change of situation and mood: Timur and Liù, having been discovered by the guards, are now dragged before Turandot to be made to reveal the name of the Unknown. This episode forms the brief transition to the third scene of the act, which, opening with the hieratic 'Turandot' theme (Ex. 101B), comprises the sad 'Liù-Timur' melody from Act I (Ex. 4d), Liù's two arias and, following her suicide, the chorus of the funeral procession. The whole represents an 'Adagio mesto', draped in sombre orchestral colours and cast in minor keys.

Liù's death and the funeral cortège constitute, dramatically and musically, a scene of such finality that the opera might well have closed with it—an impossible thought from the point of Puccini's whole conception of the drama; but the very fact that it suggests itself indicates the extent of the psychological error which he is felt to have committed with this scene. For the sense of finality it evokes, allied to our subsequent realization of how useless Liù's self-sacrifice was to affect the further course of the action, makes the ensuing love scene appear superimposed and also out of key with the emotional drift of the preceding scenes. Puccini's fundamental miscalculation here lies in the fact that, having roused all our sympathies for the little slave-girl, he asks us, in almost the same breath, to transfer them to the Princess whom, up to that point in the drama, he had done his Puccinian best to portray as an inhuman monster. This cannot be done—not at any rate in the manner in which it is actually presented to us. A possible solution of the dilemma might have been to let the curtain come down after the funeral procession, insert a symphonic interlude describing the warring emotions in Turandot's heart and thus preparing the audience for what is to happen in the ensuing scene.* It is arguable that such a procedure would have resulted in rendering the spectator at once more sympathetic to Turandot's capitulation as a cruel Princess and more responsive to the transformation her whole being undergoes in the love scene. It is not beyond the bounds of possibility that, had Puccini lived to complete the opera, he might have considered some such changes, possibly after seeing the first production —as was the case with *Butterfly*.

I approach a discussion of the last two scenes with considerable diffidence. How is one to judge them? They are Puccini's, and yet they are not. The sketches he left for them were sufficiently detailed for Alfano to elaborate into a complete and viable shape. (In fact Alfano omitted to make full use of them, as some sketches were tautological.) Alfano was a composer of no marked individuality and his style had been formed under Puccini's influence— two facts that rendered him especially suitable for his task. Toscanini's choice of him was certainly the best that could have been made. Alfano may indeed be said to have played the Süssmayr to Puccini's Mozart. Yet a break in style remains, and very perceptibly so. It shows in the bare, harsh texture of the orchestration and the rigidity of line in the vocal parts—features which must strike the student of Puccini's style as uncharacteristic, as does also the startling brevity of the final 'Jubilation'.

There are, roughly, three main sets of sketches: (a) a copy of the complete text of the love duet, with some music jotted down in the margin; (b) a number of detached leaves of music manuscript paper on which Puccini elaborated various ideas; and (c) thirty-six pages in short score which contain a complete and continuous outline of the last two scenes. This was the set on which Alfano based his completion, which begins two bars after 36. After the first production Alfano revised his completion and cut out more than a hundred bars.†

Admittedly the love scene, which introduces the second and most decisive turning-point of the drama, is conceived on an imposing scale and in a vein of heroic lyricism. There are no less than eight fresh themes in it—evidence of the surpassing importance the composer attached to it. Yet we miss the white heat of inspiration, the incandescent glow that burns in the majority of his love duets. We sense the mental labour and fatigue that accompanied its birth. Certainly, the insidious advance of Puccini's mortal malady played its part in this. Yet there is also the incontrovertible fact that the music for this duet was conceived at least two years, if not more, before the first

---

* In the Intermezzo of *Butterfly*, Puccini deftly achieved the kind of psychological transition by symphonic means such as I have in mind for the last act of *Turandot*.

† See, Cecil Hopkinson (*op. cit.*), p. 52. In 1926 Ricordi brought out both versions in vocal score, one with Alfano's 'complete' completion, the other in the shortened version.

For details about the whole question of the *Turandot* sketches, see Teodoro Celli's two articles, 'Scoprire la melodia' and 'L'ultimo canto', in *La Scala*, April and May 1951. Celli provides a highly instructive description of the sketches several of which he reproduces, including those for the 'enigmi' motive and Liù's last aria. Moreover, he offers interesting suggestions on the meaning of Puccini's enigmatic entries, 'nel villaggio' (sketch on a detached page) and 'poi Tristano' (p. 27 of the complete sketches).

symptoms of the illness appeared. We further recall the immense toil expended on the dramatic and musical shaping of it and the moods of suicidal despair by which he was seized during his work on it. No other scene in either this or any other of his operas had caused him such trouble. Are we then far wrong in interpreting all this as a sign of the inner difficulty he experienced in identifying himself with the spiritual kernel of this scene? In *Turandot* Puccini desired with all his heart and mind to glorify love as an all-conquering, cathartic and exalting power, and this idea was to find its apotheosis in the spiritual transformation of the heroine. Yet the very scene in which this takes place remains profoundly disappointing—intrinsically it must be reckoned both a dramatic and musical failure. It was Puccini's tragedy that, for all his wonderful gifts, his flashes of true genius, something in the deepest layer of his psyche prevented him from soaring to the empyrean, as he attempted in his last opera. What bitter irony of fate that he died over this attempt!

APPENDIX A: GENEALOGICAL TREE OF THE PUCCINI FAMILY

Giacomo (1712–81)
|
Antonio Benedetto Maria (1747–1832),
   married to Caterina Tesei.
|
Domenico Vincenzo (1771–1815),
   married to Angela Cerù.
|
Michele (1813–64),
   married to Albina Magi.
|
Giacomo Antonio Domenico Michele Secondo Maria (1858–1924),
  married to Elvira Bonturi-Gemignani (1860–1930).

LE VILLI

A Village in the Black Forest.

Act I. It is a day in spring. The villagers are celebrating the betrothal of Anna (soprano) to Roberto (tenor). But Anna's heart is heavy (aria: 'Se come voi'), for Roberto is to set out the same evening on a journey to Mainz where he is to claim a rich fortune left him by his aunt. In a duet Roberto tries to cheer Anna, saying that he will be away only a short while, but he fails to dispel her forebodings. The crowd now surges forward to speed Roberto on his journey.

Act II. At Mainz Roberto has succumbed to the lures of an adventuress and forgotten Anna, who after months of waiting for his return has died of a broken heart. Her soul has joined the Villi, the ghosts of betrothed maidens who have died as the result of desertion by their lovers. At night they waylay the faithless ones to dance them to death.

The curtain rises on the same scene as in Act I, but it is now midnight in winter. The Villi appear to perform their spectral dance (ballet). Anna's father, Guglielmo (baritone) comes out of the house. He curses Roberto and calls on Anna's ghost to take revenge on her lover (aria: 'No! possibile non è'). Roberto, driven by remorse, has returned to his native village and is now seen making his way to Anna's house. A cold shudder seizes him as he is about to knock at the door. In a monologue ('Ecco la casa') he expresses his passionate longing for Anna. She appears with the Villi but Roberto still thinks her to be the real Anna and embraces her. He is drawn into a whirling dance and falls dead at Anna's feet. The Villi disappear and a distant chorus sings *Hosanna.*

EDGAR

Flanders, in 1302.

Act I. A Village. A morning in spring. Edgar (tenor) is torn between his pure love for Fidelia (soprano) and his sensual passion for Tigrana (mezzo-soprano), who was abandoned as a young child by wandering Moors and brought up by Fidelia's father. Fidelia's brother, Frank (baritone), loves Tigrana but is scorned by her. As the villagers leave the church after Sunday Mass, they encounter Tigrana, who taunts them with a frivolous song. The crowd threatens her, when Edgar appears and protects her. In his rage he sets his house on fire and decides to leave his native village with Tigrana. Frank intervenes and a fight ensues with his rival in which Frank is wounded. Edgar and Tigrana make their escape, cursed by the villagers.

Act II. The Terrace of a Palace. It is night. Edgar, sated with Tigrana's charms and filled with remorse at his desertion of

Fidelia, joins a group of passing soldiers. In their captain he recognizes Frank, with whom he makes his peace. Tigrana swears revenge on her faithless lover.

Act III. The Bastion of a Fortress near Courtrai. A Requiem Mass is being sung for Edgar, supposed to have fallen in battle. A monk suddenly steps forward and reveals to the horrified crowd the crimes which, he alleges, Edgar committed during his life. The soldiers fling themselves on the catafalque intending to throw Edgar's body to the ravens but all that remains in their hands are pieces of armour. Terror now strikes the crowd. The monk tears off his habit: he is none other than Edgar. Fidelia rushes into his arms, when she is stabbed by Tigrana. The murderess is led away to be executed while Edgar throws himself on Fidelia's body.

MANON LESCAUT
Time: Second Half of the Eighteenth Century.

Act I. At Amiens. Manon (soprano), a young girl of good family, is about to enter a convent. Accompanied by her brother Lescaut (baritone), she breaks her journey at an inn at Amiens where she encounters the young student Des Grieux (tenor). It is love at first sight between them (aria: 'Donna non vidi'). One of Manon's travelling companions on the coach was the elderly Treasurer-General Geronte de Ravoir (bass), who desires her and who now arranges with the host of the inn to abduct her in a carriage. They are overheard by the student Edmondo (tenor), who apprises Des Grieux of Geronte's plan. The Chevalier persuades Manon to elope with him to Paris. The greedy Lescaut, knowing his sister's pleasure-loving nature, offers Geronte his services to induce her to desert her poor young lover for the wealthy old libertine.

Act II. In Paris. Lescaut's plan has been successful. Manon has become the mistress of Geronte, living in a palace but already weary of its cold splendour and luxury. Her thoughts turn to Des Grieux and her short-lived happiness with him (aria: 'In quelle trine morbide'). Lescaut, interpreting Manon's mood correctly, goes to fetch Des Grieux, who since her treacherous desertion has been living on his wits. He arrives and an impassioned love scene develops which is disturbed by the unexpected entry of Geronte. The latter withdraws presently, after uttering an ominous threat. Lescaut urges the two lovers to make their immediate escape, but Manon will not leave until she has collected all the jewels Geronte had given her. The delay is fatal: the Royal Guards arrive, led by Geronte, to arrest Manon as a common thief and loose woman.

Act III. Le Havre. Manon is to be deported to a prison colony at New Orleans. It is dawn. Des Grieux, assisted by Lescaut, makes an abortive raid on the prison in which Manon, together with eleven other girls of easy virtue, is awaiting her embarkation. An agitated crowd of townspeople gather and watch, with lively comments, the roll-call of the prostitutes. Des Grieux, in his despair at losing Manon, entreats the ship's captain to permit him to accompany her (aria: 'Vi pigliate!'). The captain consents.

Act IV. In America. A duel, in which Des Grieux believes he has killed his opponent, has forced him and Manon to escape from New Orleans. As they try to make their way to an English settlement across a vast desert, Manon dies of thirst and exhaustion.

LA BOHÈME
Paris, about 1830

Act I. The Garret. It is Christmas Eve. Marcello (baritone) is seen at work on a painting while the poet Rodolfo (tenor) pensively stares out of the window over the snow-clad roofs of Paris (aria: 'Nei cieli bigi'). It is freezingly cold and the poet lights the stove with the manuscript of his great tragic drama. Presently enter Colline, a philosopher and bookworm (bass), followed by Schaunard, a musician (baritone), who, thanks to the munificence of a patron, has been enabled to purchase food and drink with which to celebrate Christmas Eve. The hilarity is suddenly brought to an end by the unexpected entry of the landlord Benoit (bass), who importunes the four Bohemians with his demand for rent over-due. Some wine loosens his tongue and he boasts of his easy conquest of women. Feigning indignation at his extra-marital escapades, the four friends eject him from the room. They now decide to continue their celebration at the Café Momus in the Latin Quarter, where Rodolfo will join them after finishing an article for his paper, *The Beaver*. The poet is left alone.

A knock on the door is heard: it is Mimi (soprano), a neighbour, who begs a light for her candle. Seized by an ominous cough, she swoons and Rodolfo sprinkles water on her face to revive her. As she lights her candle by his, a draught of air blows out both candles and in the dark Mimi drops her key. They search for it on the floor;

Rodolfo finds it and conceals it in his pocket. He touches her cold hand, takes it into his and begins to tell her of his dreams and fancies as a poet (aria: 'Che gelida manina'). It is now Mimi's turn to give an account of herself (aria: 'Mi chiamano Mimi'). From the courtyard the voices of the three Bohemians are heard urging Rodolfo to join them. He takes Mimi in his arms (duet) and slowly walks with her out of the room.

Act II. The Latin Quarter. A lively Christmas Eve crowd fills the street in front of the Café Momus. Rodolfo and Mimi stop at a milliner's to buy her a hat, Colline acquires a shabby greatcoat from a clothes dealer, while Schaunard is haggling with a tinsmith over the price of a horn. A commotion in the crowd indicates the arrival of Musetta (soprano), accompanied by her elderly beau, Alcindoro (bass). She was Marcello's friend, but after one of their customary quarrels parted company with him. Yet she still loves him, and in order to make him aware of her feelings, she addresses her waltz-song ('Quando me'n vo') to him, without arousing Alcindoro's suspicions. To get her old gallant out of the way, she now pretends that her shoe is hurting her, and removing it from her foot sends Alcindoro to a cobbler with it. Musetta and Marcello embrace. A military tattoo presently passes by; the crowd and the four Bohemians with their two women friends join in and disappear. When Alcindoro returns with a brand-new pair of shoes, he finds his precious lovebird flown away. He is left to pay a large bill for what the Bohemians have consumed at the café.

Act III. The Barrière d'Enfer. It is the dawn of a February morning and snow covers the ground. The jealous Rodolfo has had a quarrel with Mimi, whom he left a few hours ago to come to stay at an inn where Marcello is employed to paint the signboard. Mimi appears and tells Marcello that her lover has decided to leave her for good. She hides behind a tree, as Rodolfo comes out of the inn, and overhears his conversation with Marcello, in which the poet informs his friend that Mimi's coquettish nature has been the cause of their quarrels and that he has resolved to part from her. Her cough betrays her presence. The two lovers embrace and decide to separate in springtime, while Musetta is once again at loggerheads with Marcello, and they part with vociferous mutual vituperations.

Act IV. The Garret. Rodolfo and Marcello are in nostalgic mood, recalling their days of happiness with Mimi and Musetta. Colline and Schaunard enter and the four Bohemians now seek to drown their sorrows and forget their poverty in revelry, singing a toast, dancing a quadrille and fighting a mock duel. At the height of their frolics Musetta bursts into the room with the tidings that Mimi is standing outside the door, mortally ill. The girl is brought in and placed on Rodolfo's bed. In order to buy cordials and medicine for Mimi, Musetta now bids Marcello go out and sell her earrings. Colline does the same with his old coat (aria: 'Vecchia zimarra') and Musetta rushes off to get her muff to warm Mimi's cold hands. Left alone, the two lovers are overcome by memories of their first transports of love (duet: 'Sono andati?'). The Bohemians return. While Rodolfo goes to the window to obscure the light so as to help Mimi to sleep, Schaunard notices a curious stillness on her face. Mimi is not asleep but dead. Rodolfo, reading the tragic truth from his friends' faces, rushes to the bed and falls sobbing over Mimi's body.

TOSCA

Rome, in 1800.

Act I. The Interior of the Church of Sant'Andrea della Valle. Angelotti (bass), formerly consul of the Parthenopean Republic of Naples, had been arrested by the Royalists and imprisoned in the Castel Sant'Angelo in Rome where the Chief of Police is the dreaded Scarpia (baritone). Through the aid of his sister, the Marchesa Attavanti, Angelotti has been able to make his escape from the fortress and take refuge at the church where his sister has left him clothes in the Attavanti Chapel with which to disguise himself. Mario Cavaradossi (tenor), a painter, enters and resumes work on a painting of Maria Madgalena, in which the Sacristan (bass) recognizes the features of a strange lady who has lately been paying the church frequent visits — the Marchesa Attavanti. Cavaradossi meditates on the curious likeness displayed by his portrait to both the mysterious worshipper and to the woman he loves, the famous diva, Floria Tosca (soprano). Angelotti, who thinks the church empty, emerges from his hiding-place in the chapel and recognizes in the painter an old friend of his. He tells his unfortunate story and Cavaradossi promises to help him to safety, when Tosca's impatient call 'Mario, Mario!' is heard from outside. Angelotti conceals himself and Tosca now enters filled with suspicion, her jealousy having been aroused by the whispers she had heard. Cavaradossi pacifies her and the lovers exchange ardent sentiments (love duet). They arrange to meet the same evening and Tosca leaves. Angelotti now discusses with the painter a plan which will enable him to escape from Rome when a cannon shot startles them. It is the signal that Angelotti's escape from the Castel Sant'Angelo has been discovered. There is no time to lose and Cavaradossi decides to take Angelotti to his villa outside the city and hide him there.

No sooner have the two friends left than the Sacristan returns to give Cavaradossi the great news of Napoleon's defeat, but is surprised to find the painter vanished. Acolytes and choristers now crowd upon the scene in preparation for the solemn *Te Deum* to be sung in celebration of the Royalist victory. Enter Scarpia, whose appearance brings the excited bustle to a sudden halt. The discovery of a fan bearing the coat of arms of the Attavanti family is evidence that Angelotti had been in hiding in the church. Similarly, the Sacristan's testimony that Cavaradossi's food-basket had been full only a little while ago and is now completely empty, suggests to Scarpia that the painter must be implicated in the fugitive's escape. Tosca returns unexpectedly to inform Cavaradossi that she will be singing in the festive cantata to be given at the Palazzo Farnese by Queen Caroline in celebration of the victory, and this will prevent her from meeting her lover in the evening. Not finding him in the church, her jealous suspicion is aroused again. Scarpia plays on this weakness of hers by showing

her the Marchesa Attavanti's fan. The ruse works. Tosca leaves in agitation for Cavaradossi's villa, where she is certain to surprise the painter with her supposed rival. She is secretly followed by Scarpia's agent Spoletta (tenor). The *Te Deum* begins. As Scarpia kneels down, there flashes through his mind the diabolical plan of sending Cavaradossi to the gallows and making Tosca yield to his desires.

Act II. Scarpia's Room in the Palazzo Farnese. The Chief of Police is seen seated at table for supper and reflecting on his sinister stratagem (aria: 'Ha più forte sapore'). The sounds of a gavotte are heard from another part of the Palace to indicate that the Queen's celebration is in full progress. Cavaradossi is brought in for interrogation but disclaims any knowledge of Angelotti's whereabouts. This scene proceeds while the cantata, with Tosca's voice, is heard from a distance until Scarpia, enraged at the painter's obstinacy, closes the window to shut out the sound of the music. Presently Tosca arrives, alarmed at the contents of a note Scarpia had sent her previously. Her lover is now led into an adjoining room where he is subjected to third-degree torture to make him betray Angelotti's hide-out. Tosca, unable to suffer any longer his cries of pain and agony heard through the open door, reveals Angelotti's secret, whereupon Scarpia gives the order to release Cavaradossi from his torture. The news is now brought in of Napoleon's victory at Marengo, prompting Cavaradossi to a rousing expression of joy. With this he signs his death-warrant and he is now taken away to be executed. Tosca entreats Scarpia to show mercy (aria: 'Vissi d'arte'), when Spoletta enters with the tidings that Angelotti has killed himself at the moment of his arrest. Scarpia, playing his last and strongest trump, tells Tosca that her lover will be the next to die, but suggests that his life could be saved in exchange for Tosca's favours. Tosca agrees to the infamous bargain, and Scarpia, pretending to alter his original scheme, commands that Cavaradossi be mock-executed but secretly countermands this order. After signing a safe-conduct for Tosca and Cavaradossi he tries to embrace her when with a swift stroke of a knife, snatched from his supper-table, she stabs him to death.

Act III. The Platform of the Castel Sant' Angelo.
It is the hour before dawn and from the
distance the song of a shepherd is heard.
Cavaradossi is brought up from his cell. His
last thoughts turn to Tosca (aria: 'E lucevan
le stelle'). She arrives presently to tell him
of how Scarpia found his deserved end, and
instructs him how to simulate death after
the mock-shooting. They exchange tender
sentiments and dream of their future
happiness and freedom (duet: 'Dolci mani

mansuete'). The execution takes place·
After the firing-party has marched off'
Tosca calls to Cavaradossi to rise, but dis-
quieted at his silence she raises the cloth the
soldiers had laid over his body, to find
a corpse. She realizes the fiendish trick
Scarpia has played on her. His murder has
meanwhile been discovered. Spoletta and
the soldiers come rushing to the platform to
arrest Tosca, but she climbs on to the parapet
and hurls herself down to her death.

MADAMA BUTTERFLY
Nagasaki. Time: The Present.

*Act I. The Exterior of a little house on a hill
overlooking the harbour of Nagasaki.* It is the
house which F. B. Pinkerton, Lieutenant in
the U.S. Navy (tenor), will occupy with
Cio-Cio-San (soprano) a geisha with
whom he has contracted a 'Japanese
marriage'. The wedding ceremony is to
take place presently. As the curtain rises,
Goro, a marriage-broker (tenor), is showing Pinkerton over the house when
Sharpless, the American Consul at Nagasaki
(baritone), arrives. The levity with which
Pinkerton regards his marriage—a mere
pastime to be broken off when convenient
(aria: 'Dovunque al mondo')—prompts the
Consul to utter a grave warning. Butterfly,
accompanied by her mother, relatives and
friends, arrives and the wedding takes place.
Into the midst of the ensuing merriment
bursts the curse of Butterfly's uncle, the
Bonze, denouncing her for having renounced her faith. Pinkerton, enraged at this
crude interruption, commands the geisha's
relatives and friends to depart. Left alone, the
geisha weeps bitterly but is comforted by
Pinkerton's tender words. Night descends
and the act closes with an extended love duet.

*Act II. Part 1. The Interior of Butterfly's
House.* Three years have elapsed since
Pinkerton left his 'wife', promising to return
'when the robins nest'. In her childlike
devotion the geisha has been awaiting his
return ever since (aria: 'Un bel di'). Presently Sharpless calls with a letter from
Pinkerton instructing him to inform
Butterfly of his new marriage to an American
woman. As the Consul proceeds to read out
the letter he is interrupted by the arrival of
Prince Yamadori (tenor), a wealthy suitor

brought by Goro. But despite her dwindling
resources and the threat of poverty, Butterfly
turns a deaf ear to his marriage proposal;
she protests that she is married already and
is awaiting her husband's return. After
Yamadori's departure, Sharpless bluntly
asks Butterfly what she would do if Pinkerton
were never to return again. Her answer
is: either resume her former life as geisha or
kill herself. She fetches her child, arguing
with the Consul that its father would hasten
back if he knew what a splendid son she
had borne him. She now addresses her child
(aria: 'Che tua madre'). Sharpless, knowing
that a tragedy is inevitable, leaves, profoundly disturbed. A cannon salute
announces the arrival in harbour of a man-
of-war. Butterfly, seizing a telescope,
recognizes Pinkerton's ship, the *Abraham
Lincoln*. The Consul was wrong after all—
Pinkerton *has* come back to her, as she always
believed. She and Suzuki (mezzo-soprano),
the child's nurse, now proceed to adorn the
room with flowers (duet: 'Scuoti quella
fronda') and Butterfly dons her wedding
dress. Night descends. Butterfly settles down
to her vigil with her child and Suzuki,
having pierced three holes into the *shosi*
through which they peer out into the dark
in expectation of Pinkerton's arrival.

Act II. Part 2. The scene as before. Dawn has
arrived and Butterfly, weary of her futile
vigil, is urged by Suzuki to retire for rest
to another room. Pinkerton presently calls,
accompanied by his wife Kate (soprano)
and the Consul. They have come to persuade
Butterfly to hand the child over to their care.
Pinkerton, overcome by remorse, decides
to leave without seeing Butterfly, which he

does after addressing a brief farewell to the house full of poignant memories (aria: 'Addio, fiorito asil!'). Butterfly, having heard voices, rushes into the room expecting to find Pinkerton, but on seeing a strange woman with the Consul she realizes the awful truth that this is Pinkerton's wife and that the object of her visit is to take the child away from its mother. Butterfly receives the blow with utter humility, declaring that she will hand it over to its father if he calls in half an hour. Kate and the Consul leave to give Pinkerton this

message. Butterfly now prepares to commit *hara-kiri*, but is momentarily restrained by the child, which Suzuki has sent into the room. After a moving farewell (aria: 'Tu, piccolo Iddio!'), she withdraws behind a screen with her father's sword on which are inscribed the words 'To die in honour when one can live no longer in honour!' Pinkerton returns calling 'Butterfly' from outside. Mortally wounded, the geisha staggers from behind the screen toward the door as though wanting to open it, but collapses and dies.

LA FANCIULLA DEL WEST

A Mining Camp in the Cloudy Mountains of California during the Gold-Fever, 1849–50.

Act I. The Interior of the 'Polka' Saloon. The curtain rises to the distant strain of a camp minstrel's song. Gold-miners are seen gambling, drinking and quarrelling; among the crowd is Sheriff Rance (baritone). Ashby, an agent of the Wells Fargo Transport Company, enters to inform the Sheriff that he is on the trail of the notorious highway robber and outlaw Ramerrez, who, with his men, has for some time been making the region unsafe. Presently Minnie (soprano) arrives. She is the proprietor of the 'Polka' and the guardian angel of the miners' spiritual and material welfare. She proceeds to hold her Bible class. Rance, who has been pursuing her, tries again to force his attention upon her (aria: 'Minnie, dalla mia casa'), but she refuses his advances. A stranger enters—Dick Johnson (tenor) alias Ramerrez, who recognizes in Minnie the girl whom he once met at Sacramento and to whom he felt attracted. Rance observes the two with a mixture of suspicion and jealousy. The capture of one of Ramerrez's Mexican greasers is announced: he is brought in, recognizes his chief and pretending that he will lead them to the robbers' hiding-place, departs with the Sheriff and the miners. Minnie and Johnson engage in a conversation during which she refers to the gold which the miners are in the habit of leaving in her trust; this, she says, she will protect with her life. Johnson, by now in love with Minnie, renounces his plan to steal the gold. Minnie invites him to continue their friendly talk at her log cabin, where they will be undisturbed.

Act II. The Interior of Minnie's Log Cabin. After a brief scene between the two Red Indians, Billy Jackrabbit and his squaw, who is employed in Minnie's service, Minnie enters and begins to make preparations for Johnson's visit; he arrives presently. Minnie explains to him the reasons that brought her to the mining camp, describing the thrills of her life in the Sierra Mountains (aria: 'O, se sapeste'). They declare their love for each other. A knock at the door is heard; Minnie, not wanting to be found alone with Johnson, urges him to hide. The visitors are the Sheriff and his posse who have come to warn Minnie of the bandit whose trail brought them to the log cabin. She sends them away pretending to be alone. Johnson attempts to explain the circumstances that had forced him to become a highway robber; but Minnie, incensed at his deception of her, bids him leave, although a blizzard is raging outside and the Sheriff is keeping a close watch on the log cabin. No sooner has Johnson stepped outside than he is shot. Minnie, overcome by pity and love, drags him back and conceals him in the loft. Hard on his heels enters the Sheriff, certain of finding his prey; but he is persuaded by Minnie that the fugitive made his escape. At that moment a drop of blood falls from the loft, betraying Johnson's presence. In her desperation Minnie proposes a bargain to the Sheriff: they are to play a game of poker in which the stakes are herself and her lover's life. If the Sheriff wins, she will be his and Johnson will be brought to justice; if she wins, then the Sheriff must give up his pursuit.

He agrees and Minnie, by an act of brazen cheating, wins the game and Johnson's life.

Act III. Dawn in the Great Californian Forest. Johnson, who, recovered from his wound under Minnie's care, has left her and has been captured by the miners who resolve to apply lynch law to him. But before being strung up on the branch of a huge tree, he prays that Minnie may never learn of his ignominious end and that she be led to believe that he left her to start a new life (aria: 'Ch'ella mi creda libero!'). At the crucial moment Minnie arrives on horseback, gun in hand. Recalling to the miners the greatest teaching of love—that the worst sinner may be redeemed—she pleads with them to spare Johnson's life. Despite angry protests on the part of the jealous Rance, Johnson is freed and, after bidding their farewell to the crowd, he and Minnie leave to begin a new life together.

LA RONDINE
Paris, during the Second Empire.

Act I. An elegant drawing-room in the house of Magda de Civry (soprano), the mistress of the wealthy banker Rambaldo (baritone). As the curtain rises, a party is in progress. The poet Prunier (tenor) declares with cynical amusement that romantic love, having become the fashion again, has seized Parisian society like an epidemic. This leads Magda to recall to her friends a brief encounter she had had in the past, at *Le Bal Bullier*, with a young student who awakened first love in her (aria: 'Ore dolci e divine'). The poet, an adept at palmistry, predicts that, like a swallow, Magda will fly to the sea, but on her further questioning, refuses to complete his prophecy. Meanwhile a new visitor has arrived—Ruggero Lastouc (tenor), a young man from the provinces and the son of a friend of Rambaldo's who had asked him to meet him at Magda's *salon*. It is Ruggero's first visit to Paris, and at the suggestion of Lisette (soprano), Magda's pert chambermaid, he decides to spend his first evening *Chez Bullier*. The mention of this place suggests to Magda the idea of visiting it too.

Act II. A large ballroom at Bullier's. Students with their *grisettes* are seen waltzing. Presently Magda arrives, wearing her maid's dress so as to remain unrecognized. Some students importune her with requests for a dance. To evade them, she pretends that she has an assignation, and seeing a young stranger seated alone by his table, goes up to him and asks to be allowed to sit down. He is none other than Ruggero, whom she scarcely noticed when he came to her house. She introduces herself as Paulette. They feel attracted to each other and finally declare their mutual love. Magda's dream of a romance has come true.

Act III. A terrace in front of a little villa, on a height overlooking the Mediterranean. Magda and Ruggero have been living here in undisturbed bliss for some months. He wishes to marry her and has written to his mother for permission. His mother's letter arrives and he reads it out to Magda. This moves Magda to declare that her past is such that it renders her unworthy of becoming his wife. She leaves him to return to Rambaldo.

IL TRITTICO
(I) IL TABARRO
Paris, at the beginning of the present century.

A barge moored in the River Seine. In the background are seen the outlines of Notre Dame illuminated by the rays of the setting sun. Luigi (tenor), a steward, is the secret lover of Giorgetta (soprano), the young wife of the skipper Michele (baritone). Weary of his miserable life and no longer able to bear the torment of his clandestine love affair, Luigi tells Michele that he will abandon the barge as soon as they arrive at Rouen. Michele descends below deck, and the two lovers, left alone, give expression to their unhappiness (duet: 'Dimmi, perchè gli hai chiesto?'), arranging to meet in an hour's time. Giorgetta will give Luigi the usual signal: the lighting of a match. After the steward has left, Michele reappears and recalls to his wife the bliss of their early love when he used to shelter her under his big cloak. Giorgetta remains cold and, feigning fatigue, retires to her cabin. It has grown dark. Michele broods on his misery and is determined to discover the identity of his wife's lover. His mind turns to his three stewards, but none, he feels, is likely to be the culprit—least of all Luigi: had Luigi not asked him only this evening for permission to leave at Rouen for good? (monologue: 'Nulla! Silenzio!'). Michele lights his pipe. Luigi, who had been waiting on the quay hidden in the darkness, mistakes this for the arranged signal and rushes on board. Michele seizes him, forces him to confess and strangles him, concealing the body under his cloak. Giorgetta, alarmed by the noises she had heard, comes on deck but feels assured when finding Michele alone. To allay his suspicion, she pretends to repent her coolness toward him and asks to be taken under his cloak, as in former years. Michele opens the cloak and presses his wife's face against her dead lover.

(II) Suor Angelica

An Italian Convent, toward the end of the Seventeenth Century.

The cloister of a convent. Sister Angelica (soprano), the daughter of a noble family, has brought shame and disgrace on their name by an illicit passion, the fruit of which was a child. In expiation of her sin, she has taken the veil, but cannot forget her son. She forfeited her share of the patrimony, and presently her Aunt (contralto) arrives to demand of her the formal signing away of all her claims. In the course of this scene the Aunt informs Sister Angelica, with harsh, cruel words, that her son had died two years before. She departs, leaving the nun in mortal despair (aria: 'Senza mamma!'). Angelica ends her life by a poison she has distilled from herbs, but in her last agony she is overcome by a tormenting sense of the sin she committed by her act of self-destruction. She prays to the Virgin Mary for salvation from damnation. Her prayer is answered by a Miracle: a celestial choir intones a solemn hymn, the adjoining chapel becomes suffused with radiant light, the gates of the chapel open and on the threshold stands the Virgin, gently motioning a young child toward the dying Angelica.

(III) Gianni Schicchi

Florence. Time: 1299

The large bedroom in the house of the wealthy Buoso Donati, who has died a few hours ago. His body, covered by drapery, is seen lying in a fourposter bed. His relations have gathered to lament his demise, but their greedy minds are troubled by the rumour that Buoso has left his entire fortune to the monks of Signa, in expiation for the malpractices by which he had acquired it. The relatives, headed by old Simone (bass) and La Zita (mezzo-soprano), an old cousin of the deceased, ransack every nook and cranny of the house in search of the will. Rinuccio (tenor), the young nephew of La Zita, finally lights on the precious document, but before handing it over to his aunt exacts from her the promise that he will be allowed to marry Lauretta (soprano), the daughter of the upstart Gianni Schicchi (baritone). If all receive their inheritance, the aunt tells him, then he may marry whomever he will—even the daughter of a beggar. They begin to read the will and discover to their mortification that the rumour was true after all: Buoso has left everything to a monastery. Rinuccio now suggests calling in Schicchi, known for his shrewdness and the only person to help them in their predicament. But the family refuses to have anything to do with such a rogue and upstart until Rinuccio convinces them of the unreasonableness of their prejudice (rec. and aria: 'Avete torto!'). He has secretly sent for Schicchi, who presently arrives with his daughter. A quarrel ensues in which La Zita tells Schicchi that she will not permit her nephew to marry a girl without a dowry. The enraged Schicchi is about to depart when Lauretta, threatening to throw herself into the River Arno unless she be allowed to marry Rinuccio, pleads with her father to stay and help her lover's family (aria: 'O mio babbino caro!'). Schicchi relents. On being told that the contents of the will had not yet been made public, he lights on a ruse: he will impersonate Buoso in his deathbed and dictate to the Notary a new will bequeathing the estate to the dead man's relatives. They are overjoyed at his cleverness and each attempts, surreptitiously, to bribe him into making over to him or her the most valuable items of Buoso's fortune. Schicchi blandly consents. He is dressed in the dead man's clothes—the body having meanwhile been carried to another room— and is placed in the bed. The Notary is sent for and presently arrives, to whom Buoso Donati, alias Gianni Schicchi, dictates his will making everything over to himself. The mortified relations have to remain silent, for they are implicated in a fraud the

punishment for which, according to ancient Florentine law, is the severance of a hand, as Schicchi had previously reminded them (aria: 'Prima un avvertimento!'). The Notary leaves, whereupon the fuming relatives fall on Schicchi with curses and abuse, but are chased by him out of the house whose new proprietor he has become. While Rinuccio and Lauretta embrace, Schicchi turns to the audience asking them whether they could imagine a better use made of Buoso's fortune than helping the young lovers. For this little trick of his, he remarks, he had been condemned to the Inferno; but by permission of the 'Great Father Dante', who had placed him there, he invites the public to grant him extenuating circumstances if they have enjoyed the evening's entertainment.

TURANDOT

Peking, in Legendary Times.

The Princess Turandot, daughter of the Emperor Altoum, has sworn a sacred vow that she will marry only a suitor of noble birth who is able to solve her three enigmas; if he fails, he will forfeit his life.

Act I. A square in front of the Imperial Palace. It is sunset. At the rise of the curtain, a large crowd is assembled to hear a Mandarin pronounce the death sentence on a Persian Prince who has lost his battle of wits against Turandot. Among the crowd is Timur (bass), the deposed King of Tartary, and his faithful companion, the slave-girl Liù (soprano), who had fled from their country after its invasion by the Chinese Emperor. Among the dense crowd they presently discover Calaf (tenor), the son of Timur, whom they had thought killed in battle. But they have to suppress their joy at meeting him because no one in Peking is to know the name and origin of the young Prince, an enemy fugitive. Darkness falls and a sad procession passes by, leading the Persian Prince to the scaffold. Moved by this sight, the crowd clamours for mercy and Calaf curses Turandot for her cruelty. The Princess appears on the balcony for a brief moment and with a silent, imperious gesture sends the Persian suitor to his death by execution. Calaf is spellbound by her beauty and resolves to win her heart.

Suddenly there appear three Courtiers— Ping (baritone), Pang (tenor) and Pong (tenor)—attempting to dissuade him from his foolhardy venture. Presently Timur and Liù add their entreaties, the slave-girl reminding the Prince of the fate that would befall his old father if Calaf failed (aria: 'Signore, ascolta!'). The Prince consoles her (aria: 'Non piangere, Liù'), but his mind is set on winning Turandot or losing his head in the venture. He strikes the fatal gong, thus announcing his decision to submit to the trial of the three riddles.

Act II. Scene 1. A pavilion in the Palace. The three Courtiers bemoan the present state of China where heads roll and peace has vanished—all on account of Turandot's cruel caprice. Nostalgically they dream of their idyllic retreats in the country, far away from Peking and the Princess. They pray that at last she may desist from her cruel game and find true love (Trio of the Three Masks).

Act II. Scene 2. A square inside the Palace. A monumental staircase leads up to the throne on which the Emperor is seated surrounded by the whole court, assembled for the crucial enigma scene. Turandot begins by explaining the reason for her vow: many thousand years ago her ancestress, Lo-u-ling, was carried off by a barbarian king and died; it is to avenge this crime that she has imposed this cruel trial on her suitors. Once more she counsels Calaf to withdraw (aria: 'In questa Reggia'). But the Prince remains adamant and the trial begins. One by one, he gives the correct answers to Turandot's three riddles ('Hope'—'Blood'—'Turandot'). The Princess, mortified by her defeat, entreats the Emperor not to permit her to become the slave of a foreign man, but Altoum reminds her of her sacred vow, which must now be fulfilled. Calaf now makes the generous offer to release her from her pledge, on condition that she discovers his name and origin by dawn; if she succeeds, then he is ready to die.

Act III. Scene 1. A garden in the Palace. Through the stillness of night, the voices of heralds are heard announcing Turandot's decree that no one in the city must sleep until the name of the Unknown is discovered. Calaf, certain of his triumph, muses on Turandot whose love he will awaken by a kiss (aria: 'Nessun dorma!'). The three Courtiers suddenly burst upon the scene and attempt, first by blandishments and promises and then by threats, to compel Calaf to reveal his name; but in vain. Timur and Liù, who had been seen in the company of the Prince (Act I), are now dragged by the guards before Turandot. Liù, fearing that Timur will be subjected to torture, steps forth and declares that she alone knows the Prince's name; but rather than betray it under torture she stabs herself to death. Her body is carried away in a funeral procession. Calaf and Turandot are alone. He upbraids her for her cruelty and taunts her for her supposedly cold heart. Boldly taking her in his arms, he presses a kiss on her lips which, like a magic spell, transforms the Princess. She now realizes that she had loved the Prince from the first moment she had set eyes on him and that Calaf's love was such that he was prepared to risk his life in releasing her from her vow. He reveals his name to her.

Act III. Scene 2. The Emperor's Divan, as in Act II. Turandot addresses the assembly, declaring that she has learned the name of the Unknown, it is—love. The opera closes in general jubilation.

APPENDIX C: CATALOGUE OF WORKS

OPERAS

TITLE	LIBRETTO	FIRST PRODUCTION
Le Villi (1 act)	Fontana	Milan, Teatro dal Verme; 31 May 1884
(Revised Version in 2 acts)		Turin, Teatro Regio; 26 December 1884
Edgar (4 acts)	Fontana (based on Musset's *La Coupe et les Lèvres*)	Milan, Teatro alla Scala; 21 April 1889
(Revised Version in 3 acts)		Ferrara; 28 February 1892
Manon Lescaut	Leoncavallo, Praga, Oliva, Illica and Giacosa (based on Prévost's novel)	Turin, Teatro Regio; 1 February 1893
La Bohème	Giacosa and Illica (based on Mürger's novel)	Turin, Teatro Regio; 1 February 1896
La Tosca	Giacosa and Illica (based on Sardou's drama)	Rome, Teatro Costanzi; 14 January 1900
Madama Butterfly	Giacosa and Illica (based on Belasco's dramatized version of a story by J. L. Long)	Milan, Teatro alla Scala; 17 February 1904
(Revised Version)		Brescia; 28 May 1904
La Fanciulla del West	Civinini and Zangarini (based on Belasco's drama)	New York, Metropolitan Opera House; 10 December 1910
La Rondine	Adami (based on a German libretto by Willner and Reichert)	Monte Carlo; 27 March 1917
Il Trittico:		New York, Metropolitan Opera House; 14 December 1918
Il Tabarro	Adami (based on Gold's *La Houppelande*)	
Suor Angelica	Forzano	
Gianni Schicchi	Forzano (based on an episode in Dante's *Inferno*)	
Turandot	Adami and Simoni (based on Gozzi's play)	Milan, Teatro alla Scala; 25 April 1926

CHURCH MUSIC

Vexilla Regis prodeunt, for two-part men's chorus and organ (1878)	Lucca; 1878
Motet and Credo in Honour of San Paolino	Lucca; 1878
Mass for four voices and orchestra (incorporating the above two pieces)	Lucca; 1880 (pub. 1951)
Salve del ciel regina, for soprano and harmonium (before 1880)	
Requiem for mixed voices and organ or harmonium (1905)	

CHORAL MUSIC

Cantata: *I Figli d'Italia bella* (1877)
Cantata a Giove (1897)
Inno a Diana (Salvatori), for chorus and piano (pub. 1899)
Avanti, Urania! (Fucini), for chorus and piano (pub. 1899)
Orchestral version known as *Inno di Roma* (pub. 1919) Rome; June 1920

ORCHESTRAL WORKS

Preludio Sinfonico (1876)
Capriccio Sinfonico (piano duet version, pub. 1884)

Milan, Conservatoire; 14 July 1883

March, *Scossa elettrica* (1896)

CHAMBER MUSIC

Scherzo for string quartet (between 1880 and 1883)
String Quartet in D (between 1880 and 1883)
Fugues for string quartet (1882–3)
La Sconsolata, for violin and piano (1883)
Three Minuets for string quartet (pub. 1890)
Crisantemi, for string quartet (pub. 1890)
Fragment of a Piano Trio (?)

ORGAN AND PIANO

Several early pieces for organ (before 1880)
Two pieces for piano (1910?, pub. 1942): *Foglio d'Album*
Piccolo Tango

SONGS WITH PIANO

Melanconia (Ghislanzoni) (1881)
Allor ch'io sarò morto (Ghislanzoni) (1881)
Noi leggeramo (Ghislanzoni) (1882)
Spirto gentil (Ghislanzoni) (1882)
Storiella d'amore (Puccini) (1883)
Romanza, *Menti all' avviso* (Romani) (1883)
Solfeggi (1888)
Sole e amore (1888)
E l'uccellino (Fucini) (1899)
Terra e mare (Panzacchi) (1902)
Morire? (Adami) (1917)

APPENDIX D: REFERENCES

FIRST PART: THE MAN

(1) For a detailed account of this period, see *Giacomo Puccini e i suoi antenati*, by Alfredo Bonaccorsi (Milan, 1950), and the same author's *Spettacoli musicali lucchesi: Le Tasche* (Lucca, 1935). Also, *Storia della musica in Lucca*, by Luigi Nerici, in *Memorie e documenti per servire alla storia di Lucca*. Vol. XII (Lucca, 1880).

    The three examples quoted from the music of Puccini's ancestors have been taken from Bonaccorsi's first-named book.

(2) These letters form part of the correspondence of Padre Martini, preserved at the Library of the Bologna Conservatoire and largely unpublished. Some of Puccini's letters are reproduced in Bonaccorsi, op. cit.

(3) The full text of this submission is reproduced in Bonaccorsi, op. cit.

(4) *Discorso in morte di Michele Puccini*, by Giovanni Pacini (Lucca, 1865).

(5) The facsimile of this lengthy decree is reproduced in *Epistolario di Giacomo Puccini*. A cura di Giuseppe Adami (Milan, 1928).

(6) *Il 'Pretino' di Giacomo Puccini racconta*, by Pietro Panichelli. 3rd ed. (Pisa, 1949).

(7) Quoted from the full text reproduced in *Immortal Bohemian. An Intimate Memoir of Giacomo Puccini*, by Dante del Fiorentino (London, 1952).

(8) Its full text is reproduced in del Fiorentino's book, op. cit.

(9) *Ibid.*

(10) Facsimile letter reproduced in *Puccini nelle imagini*, ed. Leopoldo Marchetti (Milan, 1949).

(11) *Toscanini*, by Howard Taubmann (London, 1951).

(12) *Lettere di Alfredo Catalani a Giuseppe Depanis*, ed. Carlo Gatti (Milan, 1946). See also, *Catalani. La Vita e le Opera*, by Carlo Gatti (Milan, 1953).

(13) Reproduced in *I concerti popolari ed il Teatro Regio di Torino*, by Giuseppe Depanis (Turin, 1914).

(14) Vol. IV of *Carteggi Verdiani*, ed. by A. Luzio (Rome, 1947), in which these letters are reproduced.

(15) This and the following excerpts are from a letter addressed to Tito Ricordi which is partially reproduced in *Giulio Ricordi: L'amico dei musicisti italiani*, by Giuseppe Adami (Milan, 1945).

(16) *Puccini*, by Giuseppe Adami (Milan, 1935).

(17) Reproduced in *La Vita di Arrigo Boito*, by Piero Nardi. 2nd ed. (Milan, 1944), on which I have drawn for details on Boito's relationship with Puccini.

(18) *Ibid.*

(19) *Giulio Ricordi* etc., by Adami, op. cit.

(20) *I copialettere di Giuseppe Verdi*, ed. by G. Cesari and A. Luzio (Milan, 1913).

(21) *Puccini*, by Adami, op. cit.

(22) Letter in the Verdi Archives at Sant'Agata; copied by Frank Walker by whose kind permission it is here reproduced.

(23) From a letter, reproduced in *Clara Novello. 1818–1908*, by Averil Mackenzie-Grieve (London, 1955).

(24) *Immortal Bohemian* etc., by del Fiorentino, op. cit.

(25) *Giacomo Puccini Intimo*, by Guido Marotti and Ferrucio Pagni (Florence, 1926).

(26) This and the following excerpts from Puccini's letters to the singer are quoted from *Tamagno. Il Più Grande Fenomeno Canoro dell'Ottocento*, by Mario Corsi (Milan, 1937).

(27) *Franco Faccio e Verdi*, by Raffaele de Rensis (Milan, 1934).
(28) Reproduced in full in *Puccini. A Biography*, by George R. Marek (London, 1952).
(29) *Tamagno*, by Corsi, op. cit.
(30) Marotti and Pagni, op. cit.
(31) Reproduced in *Immortal Bohemian*, by del Fiorentino; without date, op. cit.
(32) *La Vita di Giacomo Puccini*, by Arnaldo Fraccaroli (Milan, 1925).
(33) del Fiorentino, op. cit.
(34) Adami, op. cit.
(35) del Fiorentino, op. cit.
(36) The full text of these letters is reproduced in Marek's book, op. cit.
(37) Fraccaroli, op. cit.
(38) *Giacomo Puccini. The Man, His Life, His Work*, by Richard Specht (London, 1933).
(39) Marotti and Pagni, op. cit.
(40) *Vita e Tempo di Giuseppe Giacosa*, by Piero Nardi (Milan, 1949), which contains hitherto unpublished correspondence between Giacosa, Ricordi and Puccini from which this and all the following excerpts have been quoted.
(41) *Catalani* etc., op. cit.
(42) 13 October 1781. *The Letters of Mozart*, etc., op. cit.
(43) Op. cit.
(44) Op. cit.
(45) *La Vita di Giacomo Puccini*, op. cit.
(46) *Ibid.*
(47) From a letter to Ippolito Valetta; quoted in a footnote in *Itinerari Verdiani*, by Giovanni Cenzato (Parma, 1949).
(48) Quoted in *Giulio Ricordi* etc., by Adami, op. cit.
(49) Fraccaroli, op. cit.
(50) *The Golden Age of Opera*, by Herman Klein (London, 1933).
(51) Fraccaroli, op. cit.
(52) Quoted in *Epistolario*, op. cit.
(53) *La Vita di Giacomo Puccini*, op. cit.
(54) *Giacomo Puccini et la sua opera*, by Gino Monaldi (Rome, n.d.).
(55) Fraccaroli, op. cit.
(56) I have culled these sentences from several letters reproduced in del Fiorentino's book, op. cit.
(57) *Vite dei musicisti italiani*, by Lucio d'Ambra (Milan, n.d.).
(58) *Puccini Among Friends*, by Seligman, op. cit.
(59) *Toscanini*, by Taubman, op. cit.
(60) Undated letter to his sister Dide (*E*).
(61) *Ibid.*
(62) Said to Fraccaroli, op. cit.
(63) *Sogni di Giacomo Puccini*, by Mario Morini, in the periodical, *La Scala*, February 1957.
(64) *The Life of David Belasco*, by William Winter (New York, 1918).
(65) *The Theatre through its Stage Door*, by David Belasco (New York, 1928).
(66) Article on David Belasco, in *Dictionary of American Biography* (New York, 1937).
(67) Letter to Ricordi, 20 November 1900 (*E*).
(68) Letter to Ricordi, 18 September (?) 1902 (*E*).
(69) *The Times*, 12 September 1957.
(70) A short collection of Puccini's letters to Vandini, which contains, however, little information of substantial interest, was published in *Puccini: In un gruppo di lettere inedite a un amico*, by Carlo Gatti (Milan, 1944). Most of the letters are reproduced without date.
(71) Letter to Sybil, 31 October 1906 (*S*).
(72) Reproduced in *Immortal Bohemian* etc., op. cit.
(73) Letter to Ricordi, 23 February 1905 (*E*).

(74) *Ibid.*
(75) Letter to Ricordi, 21 March 1905 (*E*).
(76) *Puccini Among Friends*, op. cit.
(77) Letter to Sybil, 2 January 1906 (*S*).
(78) *Libri Segreti.* CVIII.
(79) Quoted in *Giulio Ricordi*, etc., by Adami, op. cit. This letter is not included in either the *Copialettere* nor the *Carteggi Verdiani* (opp. cit.).
(80) To Sybil, 15 April 1907 (*S*).
(81) Letter to Ricordi, 15 November 1906 (*E*).
(82) Undated letter to Sybil (*S*).
(83) To Ricordi on 14 November 1906 (*E*).
(84) *Puccini. Lettere inedite*, etc., by Carlo Gatti, op. cit.
(85) Undated letter to Sybil (*S*).
(86) Milan, 22 February 1921 (*S*).
(87) Marotti and Pagni, op. cit.
(88) Letter in possession of Mr. Jacques Samuel of London, who kindly placed it at my disposal.
(89) Letter to Sybil, October 1907 (*S*).
(90) Letter to Sybil, 21 September 1908 (*S*).
(91) Reproduced by Pietro Panichelli in his *Il 'Pretino' di Giacomo Puccini racconta* . . . , op. cit.
(92) Information given me by Mrs. Violet Schiff.
(93) Op. cit.
(94) Letter to Adami, 10 November 1920 (*E*).
(95) Reproduced in Fraccaroli, op. cit.
(96) Marotti and Pagni, op. cit.
(97) *The Magic Baton. Toscanini's Life for Music*, by Filippo Sacchi (London, 1957).
(98) Facsimile letter reproduced in *Puccini nelle imagini*, op. cit.
(99) Torre, 16 April 1909 (*S*).
(100) Marotti and Pagni, op. cit.
(101) Undated letter to Tito Ricordi, Paris (*E*).
(102) Marotti and Pagni, op. cit.
(103) *Ibid.*
(104) Undated letter written around 1903 (*M*).
(105) *Puccini Among Friends*, op. cit.
(106) Letter from Torre, 6 March 1909 (*S*).
(107) I quote from the deposition which Doria's family later laid before the court, a transcription of which is reproduced in Marek, op. cit.
(108) To Sybil, Torre, 6 March 1909 (*S*).
(109) Letter to Tonio, 24 May 1909 (*M*).
(110) Letter from Milan, 12 June 1909 (*M*).
(111) To Sybil, March 1909 (*S*).
(112) 28 June 1923 (*E*).
(113) *The Life of David Belasco*, op. cit.
(114) Letter to Ricordi, Torre, 4 April 1907 (*E*).
(115) Letter to Sybil, Torre, 27 January 1913 (*S*).
(116) *Puccini*, by Adami, op. cit.
(117) The respective dates of the three letters to Sybil, from which I have culled these excerpts, are: Milan, 27 January 1913; Torre, 1 May 1914; Milan, 14 May 1914 (*S*).
(118) *Puccini*, by Adami, op. cit.
(119) *Ibid.*
(120) *Ibid.*
(121) *Ibid.*
(122) Letter to Adami, Torre, 19 November 1914 (*E*).
(123) *Puccini*, op. cit.
(124) 15 October 1915 (*S*).

(125) Letter to Sybil, Torre, 31 August 1919 (S).
(126) Seligman, op. cit.
(127) Torre, 5 November 1921 (S).
(128) *The Magic Baton. Toscanini's Life for Music*, op. cit.
(129) Cf. Letters to Sybil of 11 February and 23 and 24 March 1915 (S).
(130) 22 February 1916 (S).
(131) Il 'Pretino', etc., op. cit.
(132) Both this and the following doggerel are reproduced in Fraccaroli, op. cit.
(133) *Giacomo Puccini Intimo*, op. cit.
(134) *The Magic Baton* etc., op. cit.
(135) Letter from Torre, 15 July 1920 (S).
(136) Letter to Sybil, Bagni di Lucca, 27 July 1920 (S).
(137) Viareggio, undated (E).
(138) To Adami, undated (E).
(139) Facsimile letter reproduced in *Puccini nelle imagini*, op. cit.
(140) A verbal account of this audience is reproduced in Marotti and Pagni, op. cit.
(141) Letters of 12 November 1923 and 22 January 1924, respectively (E).
(142) Fraccaroli, op. cit.
(143) *The Magic Baton* etc., op. cit.

SECOND PART: THE ARTIST

(1) Foreword to his *Madrigali guerreri ed amorosi* (Venice, 1638).
(2) Mozart to his father, Vienna, 26 September 1781. *The Letters of Mozart and His Family*, op. cit.
(3) *French Music. From the Death of Berlioz to the Death of Fauré* (London, 1951).
(4) Quoted, in *Émile Zola*, by Hemmings, op. cit.
(5) From a letter (2 November 1919) quoted in *Musica e Verismo*, by Mario Rinaldi (Rome, 1932).
(6) Letter to Maestro Tebaldini, quoted in *Pietro Mascagni nella vita e nell'arte*, by E. Pompei (Rome, 1912), from which all subsequent quotations are taken.
(7) Quoted in the article 'Mascagni' in *Encyclopaedia of the Opera*, by David Ewen (London, 1956).
(8) The critic Guido Maffiotti in *Il Biellese* of 1 October 1929.
(9) *Musicisti Contemporanei. Saggi critici* (Milan, 1914). See also, *Ildebrando Pizzetti*, by Guido M. Gatti (Eng. ed. London, 1951).
(10) *Puccini*, by Adami, op. cit.
(11) *Ibid.*
(12) *New Introductory Lectures on Psychoanalysis* (London, 1933).
(13) *Mozart's Operas. A Critical Study*, by E. J. Dent. Rev. ed. (London, 1947).
(14) *Verdi*. Master Musician Series. Ed. Eric Blom (London, 1940).
(15) *The Magic Baton*, etc., by Sacchi, op. cit.

THIRD PART: THE WORK

(1) *Per la musica italiana*, by Alfredo Copotelli (Orvieto, 1919).
(2) The translation used here is by L. W. Tancock. See, *Abbé Prévost. Manon Lescaut*. Penguin Books (London, 1949).
(3) *The Legend of the Latin Quarter*, by Arthur Moss and Evalyn Marvre (London, 1947), on which I have drawn for certain details of Mürger's life.
(4) English edition, translated by Norman Cameron (London, 1949).
(5) Debussy is reported as having said this to Falla. See, *Manuel de Falla*, by Jaime Pahissa (London, 1954).

(6) *Sardou and the Sardou Plays,* by J. A. Mart (London, 1913).
Le Vie Prodigieuse de V. Sardou, by G. Mouly (Paris, 1931).
Quarante Ans de Théâtre, Vol. VI, by Fr. Sarcey (Paris, 1901).

(7) *More Opera Nights,* by Ernest Newman (London, 1954).

(8) The translation used here is by Dorothy L. Sayers. See, *The Comedy of Dante Alighieri, The Florentine.* Cantica I; *Hell.* Penguin Books (London, 1949).

(9) *Le Arti e le tradizioni popolari d'Italia,* by F. Balilla Pratella (Udine, 1941), which contains musical examples.
Fiorita di canti tradizionali del popolo italiano, ed. by E. Levi (Milan, n.d.).

(10) *I Tempi, La Vita e Gli Scritti di Carlo Gozzi,* by Giov. Battista Magrini (Benvenuto, 1883).
Studies in Modern Italian Literature, by Ernesto Grillo (Glasgow, 1930).

(11) *The Book of the Thousand Nights and One Night.* Rendered into English from the literal and complete French translation of Dr. J. C. M. Mardrus. By Powys Mathers (London, 1949).

BIBLIOGRAPHY

Adami, G. *Puccini* (Milan, 1935).
   Il romanzo della vita di Giacomo Puccini (Milan and Rome, 1944).
   Le opere che Puccini non scrisse, 'La Lettura', 1921.
Bianchi, R. *La Bohème* (Rome, 1923).
Billeci, A. *La Bohème di Giacomo Puccini. Studio critico* (Palermo, 1931).
Bonaccorsi, A. *Giacomo Puccini e i suoi antenati musicali* (Milan, 1950).
   Le musiche sacre dei Puccini, in 'Bollettino Storico Lucchese', Vol. VI, 1934.
Bonaventura, A. *Giacomo Puccini. L'uomo—l'artista* (Livorno, 1924).
Carner, M. *In Defence of Puccini*.
   The First Version of 'Madam Butterfly'.
   The Two 'Manons'.
   Puccini's Early Operas.
   Puccini's Symphonic Venture: the Capriccio Sinfonico.
   A Puccini Operetta: 'La Rondine'.
   The Exotic Element in Puccini, all in 'Of Men and Music' (3rd ed., London, 1945).
Chop, M. *Die Bohème* (Leipzig, n.d.).
   Madame Butterfly (Leipzig, n.d.).
   Die Tosca (Leipzig, 1924).
Cœuroy, A. *La Tosca de Puccini. Étude historique et critique* (Paris, 1923).
Coppotelli. A. *Per la musica d'Italia. Puccini nella critica del Torrefranca* (Orvieto, 1919).
Csáth, G. *Ueber Puccini. Eine Studie*. Translated from the Hungarian by H. Horvath (Budapest, 1912).
Dean, W. *Giacomo Puccini*, in 'The Heritage of Music', Vol. III (London, 1951).
Del Fiorentino, D. *Immortal Bohemian. An Intimate Memoir of Giacomo Puccini* (London, 1952).
Dry, W. *Giacomo Puccini* (London, 1906).
Fellerer, K. G. *Giacomo Puccini* (Potsdam, 1937).
Fontana, F. *Puccini visto dal suo primo librettista*, in 'Musica d'oggi', 1933.
Fraccaroli, A. *La vita di Giacomo Puccini* (Milan, 1925).
Gatti, C. *Puccini: In un gruppo di lettere inedite a un amico* (Milan, 1944).
Gatti, G. M. *Rileggendo le opere di G. Puccini*, in 'Il Pianoforte', August 1927.
Gerigk, H. *Puccini* (Potsdam, 1937).
Greenfield, E. *Puccini: Keeper of the Seal* (London, 1958).
Gui, V. *Giacomo Puccini*, in 'Il Pianoforte', February 1922.
Hopkinson, C. *A Bibliography of the Works of Giacomo Puccini 1858-1924* (New York, 1968).
Hughes, S. *Famous Puccini Operas* (London, 1959).
Knosp, G. *G. Puccini* (Brussels, 1937).
Korngold, J. *Tosca—Madame Butterfly—Manon Lescaut—Das Mädchen aus dem goldenen Westen—Der Mantel—Schwester Angelica—Gianni Schicchi*, in 'Die romanische Oper der Gegenwart' (Vienna, 1922).
Maisch, W. *Puccinis musikalische Formgebung, untersucht an der Oper 'La Bohème'* (Neustadt a.d. Aisch, 1934).
Marchetti, L. *Puccini nelle immagini* (Milan, 1949).
Marek, G. R. *Puccini. A Biography* (New York, 1951; London, 1952).
Mariani, R. *L'ultimo Puccini*, in 'Rassegna musicale', Vol. IX, 1936.
Marini, R. B. *La 'Turandot' di Giacomo Puccini* (Florence, 1942).

Marotti, G. and Pagni, F. *Giacomo Puccini intimo* (Florence, 1926).

Marotti, G. *Giacomo Puccini* (Florence, 1949).

Monaldi, G. *Giacomo Puccini e la sua opera* (Rome, n.d.).

Neisser, A. *Giacomo Puccini. Sein Leben und sein Werk* (Leipzig, 1928).

Newman, E. *La Bohème—Tosca—Madam Butterfly*, in 'More Opera Nights' (London, 1954). *Turandot—Gianni Schicchi*, in 'Opera Nights' (London, 1943).

Panichelli, P. *Il 'Pretino' di Giacomo Puccini racconta* (3rd ed. Pisa, 1949).

Petrocchi, G. *L'opera di Giacomo Puccini nel giudizio della critica*, in 'Rivista Musicale', 1941.

Pizzetti, I. *Giacomo Puccini*, in 'Musicisti contemporanei' (Milan, 1914).

Puccini, G. *Carteggi pucciniani*, ed. Eugenio Gara (Milan, 1958).

Puccini, G. *Epistolario*, ed. by Giuseppe Adami (Milan, 1928). English Edition, by Ena Makin (London, 1931).

Giacomo Puccini. A Symposium, ed. Claudio Sartori (Milan, 1959).

Ricci, L. *Puccini interprete di se stesso* (Milan, 1954).

Rinaldi, M. *La Fanciulla del West* (Milan, 1940).

Roux, O. *Memorie giovanili autobiografiche* (Florence, n.d.).

Salerno, F. *Le donne pucciniane* (Palermo, 1928).

Sartori, C. *Puccini* (Milan, 1958).

Seligman, V. *Puccini Among Friends* (London, 1938).

Setaccioli, G. *Il contenuto musicale del Gianni Schicchi* (Rome, 1920).

Specht, R. *Giacomo Puccini. Das Leben—Der Mensch—Das Werk* (Berlin, 1931). English Translation by C. A. Phillips (London, 1933).

Thiess, F. *Puccini. Versuch einer Psychologie seiner Musik* (Vienna, 1947).

Torchi, L. *La Tosca*, in 'Rivista musicale', 1900.

Torrefranca, F. *Giacomo Puccini e l'opera internazionale* (Turin, 1912).

Weissmann, A. *Giacomo Puccini* (Munich, 1922).

(Note: Only a few of the most important periodical references have been listed. A large number of other books and periodicals have been consulted some of which are mentioned in footnotes and others in Appendix D.)

INDEX OF NAMES

INDEX OF MUSICAL ILLUSTRATIONS